For Kevin Rich

You are one of the good guys! I am grateful to have the privilege to know you. Thank you for your service to our country and your continued service in law enforcement! Stay true to yourself and the people in your life.

Jack Shipman

YELLOW FOOTPRINTS

1969 MARINE CORPS BOOT CAMP

JACK SHIPMAN

iUniverse, Inc.
Bloomington

Yellow Footprints
1969 Marine Corps Boot Camp

Copyright © 2011 by Jack Shipman

All rights reserved. No part of this book may be used or reproduced by any means, graphic, electronic, or mechanical, including photocopying, recording, taping or by any information storage retrieval system without the written permission of the publisher except in the case of brief quotations embodied in critical articles and reviews.

Neither the United States Marine Corps, nor any other component of the Department of Defense, has approved, endorsed, or authorized this book.

The Eagle, Globe and Anchor is a trademark of the
U.S. Marine Corps, used with permission.

iUniverse books may be ordered through booksellers or by contacting:

iUniverse
1663 Liberty Drive
Bloomington, IN 47403
www.iuniverse.com
1-800-Authors (1-800-288-4677)

Because of the dynamic nature of the Internet, any Web addresses or links contained in this book may have changed since publication and may no longer be valid. The views expressed in this work are solely those of the author and do not necessarily reflect the views of the publisher, and the publisher hereby disclaims any responsibility for them.

All photographs for "Yellow Footprints 1969" were edited and/or created courtesy of "Vintage Portraits, LLC."

ISBN: 978-1-4502-8373-1 (sc)
ISBN: 978-1-4502-8374-8 (dj)
ISBN: 978-1-4502-8375-5 (ebook)

Printed in the United States of America

iUniverse rev. date: 04/28/2011

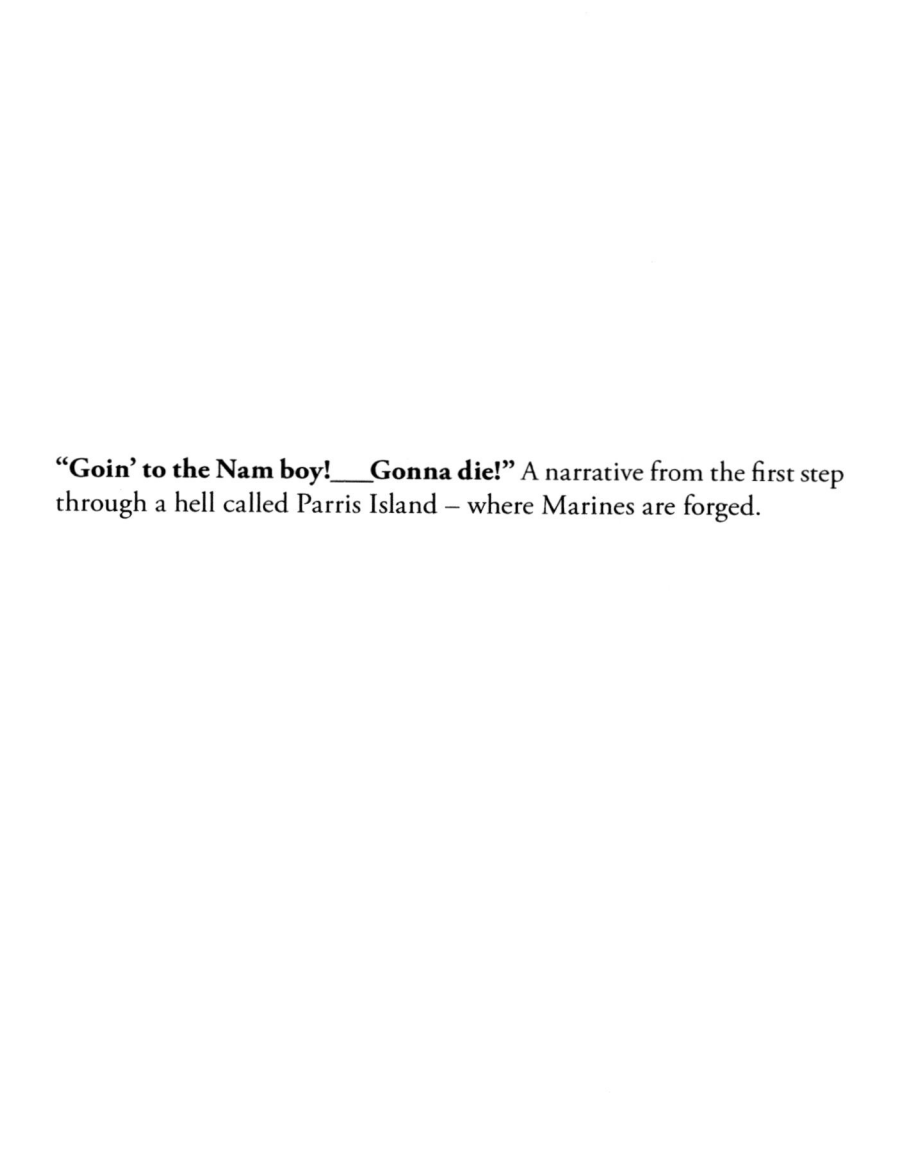

"Goin' to the Nam boy!___Gonna die!" A narrative from the first step through a hell called Parris Island – where Marines are forged.

BOOK NOTE: The capitalizing of the word **Island**, other than when used in conversations, throughout this book, was to emphasize the magnitude of this overwhelming place that we recruits could not escape from. The use of (___) between conversations, is important for the reader to experience the normal pauses and the taking of a breath by the speaker, during a conversation, or to properly space the tempo, while drill instructors order a military function.

CONTENTS

PROLOGUE 1
CHAPTER 1: THE RECEPTION 12
CHAPTER 2: GEARING UP 38
CHAPTER 3: THE MENTORS 65
CHAPTER 4: IT'S NOT A DREAM 90
CHAPTER 5: LEGACIES 115
CHAPTER 6: DROPPED 153
CHAPTER 7: RETREAD 213
CHAPTER 8: RIFLE RANGE 252
CHAPTER 9: QUALIFYING 285
CHAPTER 10: MESS AND MAINTENANCE 327
CHAPTER 11: ENDURANCE 358
CHAPTER 12: REWARDS 390
CHAPTER 13: COURT-MARTIAL 426
EPILOGUE 484
AFTERWORD 490
ACKNOWLEDGMENTS 497
APPENDIX: FAMILY HISTORY 499
USMC RANK STRUCTURE 558
WORD GLOSSARY 560
BIBLIOGRAPHY 567

PROLOGUE

The terrible dust of World War II had barely begun to settle during August of 1945 after the only two atomic bombs ever unleashed on mankind had visited horrific death and destruction on the Imperial Japanese homeland. The Second World War had finally ended.

In Indochina, during the middle of that same month, Ho Chi Minh (He Who Enlightens), leader of the Viet Nam Doc Lap Dong Minh Hoi, (League for Vietnamese Independence) better known as the Vietminh forces, invaded Hanoi without encountering resistance.

By 2 September of that year, the day Imperial Japan formally surrendered to General Douglas MacArthur on board the battleship U.S.S. Missouri, Ho Chi Minh proclaimed the Democratic Republic of Vietnam. In an attempt to punctuate his proclamation, he even chose words from the U.S. Declaration of Independence.

At the end of World War II, British troops were sent into Annam and Cochin China (South Vietnam) and Nationalist Chinese troops were sent into Tonkin (North Vietnam) to accept the Japanese surrender in those areas. However, this created setbacks for the Vietnamese independence movement. The British freed the French troops held captive by the Japanese and armed them. In addition, also allowing the Japanese to remain armed in order to assist the French, the British thereby helped the Colonist drive the Vietminh out of Saigon. Feeling alienated by the brutal Vietminh tactics, the southern Vietnamese had become supportive of the French.

In Tonkin, 150,000 Nationalist Chinese were looting and disrupting the North Vietnamese. Ho Chi Minh protested, while the

Nationalist Chinese threatened to stay indefinitely. Finding no other solution to this dilemma, Ho Chi Minh approached the French and requested their assistance in sending troops into Tonkin, for a short time only, to move the interlopers out. Assistance was offered, including a formal recognition of the state of Tonkin, whereupon the Nationalist Chinese left.

On 6 March 1946, the French Government signed the Franco-Vietnamese Accords. These accords were engaged due to the mounting pressure from the Vietnamese movement for independence, as well as the anti-imperialist sentiment in France since World War II ended. An agreement was signed by representatives from France, Annam and Tonkin, recognizing the independence of Annam and Tonkin and admitting them into the French Union, however French troops remained in the those colonies. To measure public opinion about the unification of Cochin China with Annam and Tonkin, France scheduled elections.

This was followed on 1 June 1946, as the French government maneuvering the return of their former Indochina colonies and reestablish their imperial apparatus, convened the Fontainebleau Conference in France. A conservative French government, under Georges Bidault, wishing subserviency, favored a French Union tightly connecting the former colonies to France politically.

Preferring a much more open arrangement, similar to the British Commonwealth of Nations, Ho Chi Minh desired to create an independent Vietnam with Cochin China, Annam, and Tonkin united under one flag, and thus opposed the French plan. After long weeks of debate, Ho Chi Minh initialed an agreement accepting a temporary modus vivendi, which he was to resent for the rest of his life. He left France that September.

When the French returned to Vietnam in 1946, with troops, Ho Chi Minh's plans, presented at the Fontainebleau Conference, were not to materialize. On 19 December 1946, due to the breakdown of the Conference, the Vietminh attacked the French Army in Tonkin, formally beginning the First Indochina War, which would last until 1954.

In 1950, Ho Chi Minh formed the Democratic Republic of Vietnam and was quickly recognized by most Soviet-bloc countries. Meanwhile, the French had named Boa Dai head of state of Vietnam on 5 June 1948. Prior to that, on 8 March of that year, French president Vincent Auriol and his puppet Emperor Bao Dai signed the Elysee Agreement, in Paris.

Although the Elysee Agreement declared that Vietnam was recognized as an independent nation, France still held authority over financial, diplomatic and defensive matters there. Furthermore, the agreement promised to incorporate Cochin China into a unified Vietnamese nation. This did absolutely nothing to promote real independence and Boa Dai fully realized this. Ho Chi Minh and the Vietnamese communists, knowing this to be a sellout, concluded there could never be any peaceful approach toward securing independence from the French.

President Harry S. Truman preferred to let the European powers resume their imperial positions as a means of fighting communist expansion in the world. He distrusted Ho Chi Minh, refusing to accept him as a legitimate nationalist, instead perceived him to be a hard corps communist, especially because of his strong ties with Moscow.

During the late 1940s and early 1950s the United States chose a pro-French neutrality posture regarding the war in Indochina. However, colonial ventures in Indochina were financed by hundreds of millions of diverted American dollars of Red Flint Plan assistance.

During the months of June and August 1950, President Harry S. Truman announced increased U.S. military assistance to Vietnam and created the United States Military Assistance and Advisory Group (MAAG), which was sent to Saigon, in Cochin China. MAAG, consisting of approximately sixty men, was sent to process, monitor and evaluate American military aid to the French forces fighting in Southeast Asia. At first, the American mission did not provide for the training or advising of the Vietnamese National Army (VNA).

By the end of 1953 the U.S. was financing 80% of the war in Indo China with annual assistance exceeding one billion dollars a year.

After the French defeat at Dien Bien Phu on 7 May 1954, the role of MAAG was to change. In 1955 and 1956 MAAG began the training and organization of the VNA left behind by the French. At that time, these troops were being trained by the U.S. in conventional warfare tactics, with little or no attention given to guerrilla warfare tactics. This mistake was to be corrected as the strength of the Communist insurgency in South Vietnam, during the early 1960s, prompted a change in military doctrine.

On 8 May 1954, the Geneva Conference met to determine the political future of Indochina, specifically drafting a number of political arrangements for Vietnam. On 21 July 1954, France finally reached an agreement and signed a cease-fire ending hostilities in Indochina and which, starting on 1 August 1954, prompted the first of over one million refugees from North Vietnam to spill into South Vietnam, before the deadline after 300 days, to freely decide in which zone they wished to live. Propaganda, disinformation and American PsyOps (Psychological Operations) efforts in Tonkin had assisted in turning North Vietnamese minds against a safe or prosperous future in the north. Furthermore, the Geneva accords required that Vietnam be divided at the seventeenth parallel, creating the Republic of Vietnam in the south and the Democratic Republic of Vietnam in the north. A cease-fire was provided for the peaceful withdrawal of French forces in North Vietnam and Vietminh forces from South Vietnam. New foreign troop placements were prohibited throughout Vietnam. All troops were also ordered to be withdrawn from Cambodia and Laos.

Finally, crucial to Vietnamese people's future, provisions were made for free elections in both North and South Vietnam to be held in 1956, with a goal for reunification and the removal of the artificial barrier at the seventeenth parallel.

The South Vietnamese representatives neglected to sign the peace accord, as was also the case of the United States. The United States however, did agree with them and did promise to avoid the use of military force in the area and to support the principle of self-determination in Indochina. Appearing supportive by not signing the agreement, the United States held the advantage of not being bound by its provisions. The United States scuttled the free elections set for 1956, because it was becoming evident that Ho Chi Minh's followers had rallied the majority of support in both North and South Vietnam. Once the U.S. had made the decision to scuttle the provisions of the accord, they threw all their support, both economic and military, behind the South Vietnamese government, led by its puppet Ngo Dinh Diem, the new president of South Vietnam. On 6 July 1955, Diem openly repudiated the Geneva Agreements and refused to plan for open elections throughout the country. He then proclaimed the Republic of Vietnam on 26 October 1955, with himself as president.

The Geneva Convention set limits on the number of foreign troops allowed in Vietnam. Using assorted legal pretexts, to avoid open violations of the Geneva accords, the size of the U.S. advisor force reached almost 700 personnel toward the end of the 1950s. The inherited VNA were at first poorly led, trained, or equipped, under the French, creating an almost insurmountable problem for MAAG, Vietnam. American advisors, like the French colonists, were viewed as intruders, or interlopers, and were largely distrusted by the Vietnamese.

The United States had adopted an open support policy towards the French involvement in Indochina when Harry S. Truman left the White House in 1953. Since Senator Joe McCarthy started rummaging America's closets for Commies, the fear of communism became the central interest, demanding total vigilance and prompt eradication, and thus superseding past opposition to imperialism, that paranoia manifested as America's official Third World policy.

The domino theory, first proposed by Harry S. Truman in 1946, prophesied the fall of countries, one after the other, to the communist armies, envisioned as a fire burning across dry grassland. This theory prompted treaties such as the Southeast Asia Treaty Organization (SEATO), created as part of the Manila Pact, a regional defense scheme for the South Pacific, which was overwhelmingly supported by Congress and signed by president Dwight D. Eisenhower. It would later be used by President Lyndon B. Johnson to justify the American commitment in Vietnam. Ironically, President Richard M. Nixon denied that SEATO membership guaranteed the commitment of U.S. troops in Asian conflicts. Nevertheless, that membership in SEATO greatly increased U.S. involvement in Asian politics.

The first two American advisors were killed on 8 July 1959, at Bien Hoa, by a Vietcong rocket attack. The only American killed prior to this was Peter Dewey, who was the head of the OSS mission (Office of Strategic Services) in Saigon and was killed by Vietminh on 26 September 1946.

The Vietcong (South Vietnamese Communists) were formally organized on 20 December 1960, by Ho Chi Minh, as the National Liberation Front (NLF), with Nguyen Huu Tho serving as chairman. The original members were Vietminh who came from the south and rallied to support Ho Chi Minh during the war with the French. In compliance with the Geneva Convention, Ho Chi Minh ordered his forces to return back to North Vietnam. Since to some, South Vietnam was their home, they decided to stay there. They were few, and remained under Hanoi's restraint.

After the national elections were scuttled and South Vietnam's new leader, President Diem, had ensured military dominance over the south, Ho Chi Minh decided to participate in the revolutionary movement of the southern communists. He reactivated the former Vietminh from the south and ordered the active recruitment of new supporters, to be trained in guerrilla tactics, with the mission of disrupting the South Vietnamese regime. This was accomplished through terrorist attacks on government installations and pro Diem villages, with brutal assassinations of village officials, teachers or citizens who resisted. The purpose of these actions was to create a climate for a general uprising, which would unite the south with the north.

American involvement in Vietnam at first gradually and later rapidly escalated from 1960 to 1965. By the end of 1960, approximately 900 U.S. military personnel were in country.

In 1961, President John F. Kennedy approved a counterinsurgency plan and South Vietnamese President Ngo Dinh Diem asked for U.S. military advisors to train the South Vietnamese Army and requested a bilateral defense treaty. By the end of 1961, the U.S. troop strength in Vietnam reached 3,205.

In 1962, the Military Assistance Command Vietnam (MACV) was established in Saigon, replacing MAAG. President Kennedy authorized U.S. military advisors to return fire, if fired upon. 5,000 U.S. Marines and 50 jet fighters were sent to Thailand to counter communist aggression in Laos. By the end of 1962, the total U.S. troop strength in Vietnam reached 11,300.

In 1963, President Ngo Dinh Diem and his brother Ngo Dinh Nhu were assassinated a day after a military coup overthrew Diem's government. By the end of 1963, the total U.S. troop strength in Vietnam reached 16,300.

In 1964, Viet Cong attacked the Bien Hoa Air Base killing five U.S. military personnel. Viet Cong attacked the Brinks Hotel in Saigon killing two U.S. military personnel. The Gulf of Tonkin incident, where two U.S. war ships were attacked, provided a blank check for increased U.S. involvement and authorized U.S. military personnel in Vietnam to return fire. By the end of 1964, the U.S. troop strength in Vietnam reached 23,300.

In 1965, the Viet Cong launched widespread attacks on U.S. military installations throughout South Vietnam. On 8 March 1965, the first American combat troops were ordered to Vietnam by President Lyndon B. Johnson. The Third Marine Regiment landed on the beaches of South Vietnam to defend Da Nang, a port city in Annam. President Johnson authorized the use of U.S. troops in direct combat if the South Vietnamese Army requested such assistance.

And so it started. Those countries who rallied to the plight of South Vietnam, sending troops, were the United States of America, Australia, South Korea, Philippines, Spain, Taiwan, New Zealand and Thailand. In all, forty countries, termed Free World Military Forces, provided assistance to the Republic of Vietnam.

By the end of 1965 there were 184,300 U.S. military personnel in Vietnam with 636 killed in action. In addition, allied troops sent to Vietnam totaled 22,420.

As the conflict in Vietnam escalated, American commitment ultimately required the drafting of many thousands of American citizens and a recruiting effort for volunteers not seen since World War II.

The U.S. troop strength rose to 536,000, with 30,610 Americans killed in action by the end of 1968 and 65,600 Allied troops in country. (In country: A term meaning actually serving in Vietnam, as opposed to outside Vietnam era military support).

The U.S. Marine Corps had, by the end of 1968, required 85,520 troops in country, almost one third of their total strength of 317,400 at that time. The war in Vietnam was still very intense at the beginning of 1969 and showing no signs of hostilities ending. By mid 1969 there were almost 544,000 troops in Vietnam.

By the end of the Vietnam War in 1975, over 450,000 Marines had served at least part of the standard thirteen month tour in country, of 730,000 Marines who served during the Vietnam era. In comparison 600,000 Marines served during the war against Japan. There were 20,000 U.S. Marines killed in action, and 70,000 wounded in action, while fighting against Imperial Japan, compared to almost 15,000 killed in action and 89,000 wounded in action fighting against North

Vietnam. The U. S. Marine Corps suffered a total of 90,709 casulties during World War II compared to a total of 103,453 casulties during the Vietnam War.

During the Vietnam War, while assigned mainly to I Corps (the northern most of the four Corps area sectors designated across South Vietnam), along with U.S. Marines assigned to the other three Corps areas, the U.S. Marine Corps accounted for 28.4 percent of the total U.S. war casualties and 33.5 percent of the total U.S. wounded.

The U.S. Marine Corps, made up of three active divisions, deployed two divisions to Vietnam, the 1st and 3rd, under command of III MAF (Marine Amphibious Force). They were reinforced by two Regimental Landing Teams, a reinforced Air Wing, several Battalion Landing Teams (BLTs) attached to the 7th Fleet, who were on imminent call. Smaller units were attached to the U.S. Army, the South Vietnamese Marine Corps and a detachment of Marines to protect the U.S. Embassy, Consulate and U.S. Naval installations in the Saigon and Danang area. Combined Action Platoons (CAP) were assigned with Regional and Popular Forces for defense of villages. The breakdown of such a large force included 24 infantry regiments, 4 combined action battalions, 2 force reconnaissance companies, 2 reconnaissance battalions, 2 antitank battalions, 26 aircraft squadrons, 4 armored battalions, over 10 artillery battalions, 5 engineering battalions, 5 motor transportation battalions, 2 medical battalions along with hundreds of U.S. Navy doctors, corpsmen and nurses. (Sources: *The Marines in Vietnam, 1954-1973*; Shelby L. Stanton, *Vietnam Order of Battle*, 1981; Robert Moskin, *The U.S. Marine Corps Story*, 1982. Dudley Acker, *Dictionary of the Vietnam War*). This includes the 26th and 27th Infantry Regiments of the 5th Marine Division, along with their support elements, and the 1st Marine Aircraft Wing (MAG), which was comprised of MAG 11,12,13,15,16 and the 36th were reactivated during 1966.

With the demand to field combat troops of such a magnitude, which had also to meet the stringent demands of America's shock troops, the pressure was felt by the two Marine Corps Recruit Depots, MCRD Parris Island and MCRD San Diego.

During the seven years the U.S. Marine Corps served in Vietnam, before its units were withdrawn in the spring of 1971, there were between 85,000 and 120,000 men and women either enlisted or drafted into or discharged from the Corps in each of those years. There were Marines still serving throughout the length and breadth of the Republic of Vietnam from 1 July 1971 through 30 April 1975. These Marines included advisors, communicators, U.S. Embassy, Consulate and Mission security, along with supporting arms specialists.

This demand was felt directly and personally by the drill instructors, a small group of exceptional Marine non commissioned officers, who were not only tasked with training recruits to carry on the rich and valiant customs and traditions of the U.S. Marine Corps and literally passing the baton to the future stewards of that Corps, but to instill those Corps values and train them to the caliber expected in a shorter training period than during peacetime.

The venerable history of the U.S. Marine Corps, as being the fiercest branch of the American Armed Forces, which unlike the Army, Navy, or Air Force, required the successful completion of boot camp, where they became trainees prior to the start of their basic Marine training at either of the two Infantry Training Regiments (ITR), where they would be trained to become combat-ready infantrymen, put an expectation on the drill instructors to consistently grind out the perfect private.

This method of receiving groups of recruits for 'boot camp' training dates back to 1911, at the Marine Barracks, located in South Carolina and established as part of the Port Royal Naval Station. The Marine Coprs Recruit Depot in San Diego, California was established in 1923.

After several months, recruit training was moved to Virginia and conducted at the Norfolk Naval Station until 1915 when they returned to the Marine Barracks at Port Royal. In 1919, the name of the Marine Corps recruit training depot at the Marine Barracks, became Marine Corps Recruit Depot (MCRD), Parris Island. Recruit training became institutionalized during the late 1920s, into much the same form of training as we have today. Once institutionalized, a unity began, a pride amongst Marines for where they went through recruit training. Whether undergoing recruit training at San Diego or Parris Island, there was the same reverence one would find between college alumni or athletic teams.

Parris Island, a sweltering hot and humid chunk of real estate, located amid salt water marshes and swarming with sand fleas, is accessed by a causeway connecting it with the mainland at Beaufort, South Carolina.

The winters there are mild, enabling virtually uninterrupted training all through the year.

The ability of the recruit to meet the harsh regimen of prescribed Marine Corps training was a burden placed on the drill instructors, who would meet the challenge by developing a tough, hard, determined presence, to display this dogma to the recruit and convey the doctrine for the success of the Corp's future.

The shock treatment, which was the fundamental element of Marine recruit training involved abruptly and stressfully changing the recruit's world from civilian to military life. The immediate removal of the recruit's personal identity and civilian status, by shearing off all of his hair and replacing his civilian clothing with a new wrinkled green uniform, placed each recruit on an equal starting point with his peers.

In this new and unfamiliar surrounding, all normal civilian habits, such as doing whatever one wants at that moment, were strictly forbidden. That, combined with an exhausting hectic schedule and seemingly perpetually irate drill instructors constantly screaming, cursing and violating each recruit's personal space with face-to face and nose-to-nose harangues, served to achieve the recruit's total disorientation.

As with any group, there are those drill instructors who, consistently performed above expectations, those who consistently achieved requirements, and then there are some who started off achieving that goal, and later deviated into failure or into their own regimen of training preference. With no other role models, the ideal training expectation is for the recruits to identify with their drill instructors, to imitate them to become Marines just like them.

This book is based on actual events during the training of Platoon 3074 in 1969. The venerable traditions of the U.S. Marine Corps, up to and well past the period of the completion of Platoon 3074 training during the year 1969, would still involve the same aggressive nature and approach the Corps is famous for.

The purpose for the telling of this incident is not to discredit the U.S. Marine Corps, but to share with other Marines the trails and tribulations of our odyssey through the gauntlet of boot camp training.

Without the necessity of researching any facts, knowing full well that it happened in its own form, it can be stated here that all Marine recruits who passed through this gauntlet received a hearty welcome from their drill instructors and were required to follow the same regimen towards completion of training during the Vietnam War years.

The lives of those recruits who trained in Platoon 3074 would forever be changed as a result of the singular events told in this book. I believe these events also caused the disqualification of some recruits who otherwise may have succeeded in meeting the standard training regimen.

This tale recounts the actions of a Marine Corps sergeant, who was assigned to a position where he was able to act like a demigod, ignoring the principles and expectations of the Marine Corps training program and invoking his own iniquitous prescription for making Marines out of civilians.

During the training period 1 July through 31 December 1969, a total of 23,809 recruits were received at Parris Island. Of this total, 1,834 were discharged as unsuited, 17 were given undesirable discharges (UD), 9 were minority (under aged) discharges, 3 were granted hardship discharges, and 715 were medical survey discharges.

During 1969 the Marine Corps was training recruits full bore for Vietnam. The death toll in Vietnam was staggering, which led to a natural anxiety that all of those who ventured to those shores could perish, if not properly hardened and trained.

That perception was so real that the Marine Corps placed plaques over the doors of training barracks, which proclaimed:

Let's be damn sure that no man's ghost will ever say,...

**"If your training program
had only done it's job!"**

CHAPTER 1
THE RECEPTION

ONE

The airplane's tires touched the runway several times with short yelps screaming their protest, which echoed through the Charleston South Carolina night, as though the airplane was gingerly feeling it out before deciding to let gravity take over and go all the way.

The aircraft shot forward down the runway, rapidly at first, followed by a loud roar as the pilot reversed thrust, causing the flaps to raise and the air to rush noisily over the wings. This allowed the airplane to reduce speed from 140 knots to 100 knots and soon, with steady speed reduction, they were rolling along smoothly towards the end of the runway.

The DC-8 was a direct Delta flight out of Baltimore's Friendship International Airport. Among its passengers were some that were going on through, to connect with the next leg of their journey, while many were arriving home from business elsewhere. There were students and families coming back from vacations or a weekend break away from school, some were at funerals, and a few had finally visited those relatives put off for so long.

Most exhibited faces resembling solemn masks, signifying how tired they were from the trip. Doubtless, they were all glad to be home, or at least this far along on their journey, and able to disembark and stretch for awhile.

In addition, there was a large group of young men, who would not be flying out on a connecting flight, but instead would be continuing their journey away from Charleston on another mode of transportation. This group was collected from the greater Baltimore area in Maryland, where they had been inducted into the U.S. military at Fort Holybird.

Fort Holybird, located in Baltimore, Maryland, was an Armed Forces Entrance Examination Station (AFEES), one of many located throughout the United States.

The aircraft began its taxi toward the main terminal building of the Charleston International Airport, to link up with the jet-way. Upon reaching the jet-way, the aircraft nuzzled up to the accordion-like frame surrounding the end portion.

Once this accordion framed platform was properly secured around the door of the aircraft, the door was opened by a stewardess. The passengers, by now, were already standing in the isle or crouched with bent knees or bodies curved in varied contortions in front of their seats, some ducking the low overhead storage compartments, while they impatiently waited to finally get off the aircraft.

The group of young men had been seated dispersed throughout the aircraft. Then, once the passengers heard the door being opened, as if the cork had just popped from a bottle of champagne, they poured out and spilled into the terminal.

Inside the terminal, waiting at the end of the access tunnel, were two men in military uniform. They collected the young men as they disembarked the aircraft and motioned for them to form up at one corner of the waiting room.

One of the inductees had a large manila envelope, which had been entrusted to him at AFEES by a man wearing an Army uniform. The inductee was now ordered by one of these uniformed men to hand over that envelope. The envelope contained AFEES medical and other initial military personnel records for each of these young men.

After all of the young men had been collected, one of the uniformed men ordered the group to follow him. The young men followed, looking more like a ragged mob of long-haired, bell-bottomed, tie-dyed, medallion-bedecked, slouchy kids, compared to these neat, short-haired, well-tailored, starched, ribbon-bedecked, stiff-backed, military men.

These young men entered into a lower floor area of the terminal, where other groups of young men had already been assembled, some of which were sitting, while others stood around. There were several uniformed men off to the side, obviously keeping an eye on the group.

The main group waited quietly for several more hours as more groups, pairs or individuals periodically joined their growing ranks, each time accompanied by the same two uniformed men who had collected the young men from Baltimore.

Although the main group had grown considerably large by now, the young men could hardly be heard talking amongst themselves. Their speech was hushed and clipped, sort of nervous sounding to anyone passing by. Most conversation was smothered by the Airport's stereo system, which was at that moment playing Jefferson Airplane's *Somebody To Love*. As new additions arrived, there would be exchanges between them asking each group were they were from. Some said Cincinnati, Philadelphia, New York City, and others Atlanta, Tampa, Montgomery, Detroit and places in between only those who were from there had ever known existed.

While the group milled around or sat, the terminal life was seemingly becoming a separate world. People walking by were curiously looking over at the large group of young men who had been just sitting or standing there for such a long time, separated from the terminal population by a group of uniformed men. The ages of these young men ranged between seventeen and twenty years old, with a few as old as twenty-four.

Most observers just gawked as they walked on by, however some were opined to state something. Those who were displaying an irresistible desire to say something were dressed much the same as the young men in the group, but due to the uniformed boundary, the inductees were no longer related to the heckler's society.

Passing youngsters shouted obscenities and accusations, and in return were largely ignored or were rewarded with disingenuous smiles from the uniformed men. It all seemed old hat, as if rehearsed, leaving the individual persons uninvolved, as if all were jaded by the repetition of this monologue.

The group from Baltimore had now been waiting in the terminal for four and one half hours, many even longer, and it was now nearly midnight. Over the Airport stereo system Norman Greenbaum's *Spirit In The Sky* played to nobody and everybody, as it mixed with the cacophony of terminal noises.

The men in uniform started shouting orders to the group to assemble outside the main terminal and to line up by the Greyhound bus by the curb.

TWO

The young men filed out of the airport terminal and stepped up into the waiting Greyhound bus. They sat in the plush cushioned seats with a grateful sigh of relief, after having had to endure those uncomfortable plastic shell seats provided in the airport lobby or from standing for that long period of time.

It was impossible to ignore the vile smelling mixture of diesel, vomit, sweat, booze, hair oil, urine, and baby powder, and other unmentionable foul human residue. All of the odors came from the accumulation of thousands of previous passengers.

As the procession of boarders kept coming down the bus aisle, looking left to right, right to left, for any face that would not offer offense or at best, a non-threatening personality to sit next to, the seats filled. Some were content to find a sleeper, so they would be left alone or could also catch some sleep. Others were looking for their own color, in response to preference, fear, shyness or just plain habit.

There was a mixture of Hispanics, Blacks, Whites, Indians, and Asians. Some in the group were clean-cut Ivy Leaguers and some were dressed neat with stylish long hair, while others had loose tie-dyed shirts, bell bottom pants and sandals. These wild dressers also sported very long unkempt hair. There were afros and greased-down hair styles as well.

There were also a few young country boys in the group, wearing plaid shirts, blue jeans with big buckles and cowboy boots. They preferred crew cuts or plain short hair cuts, a carry over from way back in the 1940s. A man in uniform handed the piles of yellow envelopes to the bus driver and once they finished ensuring the head count to be correct, disembarked the bus. There was a passenger capacity of forty eight, and the bus was full.

Swoosh! The hydraulic door sealed shut, followed by metal hitting metal, as the locking mechanism engaged. There came a discordant sound of the air brakes being released. A low mumbling hum of the diesel engine vibrated throughout the bus as the driver moved through the gears in sequence with the acceleration of the bus.

The sound within the bus could be distinguished as the gears grinded downward from cruise through the sequence to stop each time, as the driver navigated his way out of the airport and along the smaller roads heading toward the major highway.

Finally, the bus had settled into a hardly discernible hum as it cruised southeast along Highway 52 towards Route 7, the Rittenberg Boulevard, which then headed south towards Highway 17, called the Savannah Highway. From there the highway headed somewhat westward towards Jacksonville, South Carolina where it would then head south toward Highway 21 at Gardens Corner. That highway would head east toward Beaufort, South Carolina.

This round about route was necessary to bypass the rivers and marshes, which are numerous in this part of South Carolina, where they joined with Saint Helena Sound, off the Atlantic Coast.

As the bus passed through the night, many of the young men began engaging in small talk, as is seemingly inevitable when people sit side by side for a length of time. Still there were those who simply preferred sleeping.

The overhead lights provided personal beams of illumination in spaced islands throughout the blackness in the bus. Many were still turned on as the journey started, because the passengers were starting to open up and share personal background information between their little groups or with their seat partners.

Somewhere a transistor radio played James Brown's *Night Train*. They were as excited about what was about to happen, as they were nervous and unsure.

Many of these young men had never traveled far from home and this was the first time they were to be separated from their families. Some were escaping bad homes, bad neighborhoods, or trouble they had either started or fell into. This was the first time a few had ever held an interracial conversation or for many to really share personal stories about their girlfriends and family members.

There, amongst these young men, were the odd tough guys who habitually interjected put-downs, whenever possible, toward those who openly discussed their lives, personalities, opinions and preferences about issues, people or things. Still there were some who slept the entire trip. However, as the time started wearing on and the miles passed, others followed the example of those who slept and the lights winked off here and there. Soon, the bus was quietly passing through the night in darkness, with only the sound of the hum of the diesel engine.

Occasionally, the distinct metallic *click* of a Zippo lighter being opened, struck and shut, a cough or rustle of snack wrappers invaded the darkness.

The miles passed and the young men sat silently in the darkness, staring out of the bus windows at the passing signs warning of road conditions, or of connecting roads to places no one knew existed, places like Ashepoo, Waterloo, Ritter, Sheldon, Coosawatchie, Pocotaligo, Gardens Corner, Lobeco, and onward toward Beaufort.

THREE

The bus ended the 75 mile trip and entered the Beaufort city limits. In response to the lower speed limits of the town, the bus driver started down shifting and the louder roar of the diesel engine straining, started vibrating through the bus again. Some of the young men, startled by the sounds, opened their eyes, yawned and sleepily looked out of the bus windows at the dark forms of the downtown buildings and at the blinking red and yellow traffic lights.

The city of Beaufort was quiet at 2:30 a.m., nothing moved except the Greyhound bus they were in, as it negotiated the corners of streets and worked its way toward the causeway, which accessed the gate leading into Parris Island.

At the end of the causeway there was a gate, which had two rectanglar red brick pillars, located at both ends. These supported both ends of a huge red sign, which appeared to be approximately twenty or twenty five feet across and six feet high. There was a scroll under a bible, inscribed with unreadable words as the bus passed. The pillar held the inscription: "Here stood Charles Fort, built 1562 by Jean Ribault for Admiral Chenault, a refuge for Huguenots and to the glory of France".

To each side of the pillar were two huge emblems of the earth with North and South America displayed over the globe. The globes were pierced by an anchor and the American Bald Eagle, with wings proudly outstretched, perched atop each globe. This was the venerable symbol of the U.S. Marine Corps. In huge gold letters, across the entire red sign, was announced:

U.S. MARINE CORPS RECRUIT DEPOT
PARRIS ISLAND SOUTH CAROLINA

Several Military Policemen motioned the bus to stop and approached the driver, by the port window where the driver sat, spoke to the driver, then stepped back and motioned the bus through the gate into Parris Island.

Somebody's transistor radio came alive with The Maverick's *Blue Moon*. More and more, the young men were waking up and some had begun talking excitedly, nervously lighting cigarettes or popping chewing gum, as the bus pulled onto Boulevard de France and ever closer to their final destination.

There was a group of white barracks with one displaying a sign stating RECEIVING BARRACKS. The bus turned right onto Panama Street and stopped, with the sound of air breaks loudly hissing air in short yelps.

The door opened with a loud *woosh* and the combined sounds of metal unlocking amidst the hydraulic hiss. A new smell immediately drifted into the rank smelling bus. This fetid smell was of moss, decaying vegetation and humidity, a smell none of the young men would ever forget.

A very large black man bounded up the steps of the bus. He wore a well tailored uniform, with three rows of multi-colored ribbons on the left side of his chest, a prominent silver rectangle belt buckle secured a wide black leather belt, which separated dark green dress trousers from a sharply creased khaki shirt, complemented by a khaki tie, fastened at midpoint with a golden tie clasp, decorated by a small Marine Corps emblem.

On each sleeve of his shirt were chevrons in green, five stripes in all, three inverted vees over two loops, with two crossed rifles centered between the stripes and the loops, referred to as rockers.

He wore spit-shined black dress shoes and a campaign hat resembling a Smokey-the-Bear hat. This campaign hat was adorned with a large Marine Corps emblem in black, which prominently displayed the eagle, globe and anchor. He wore the campaign hat at the prescribed angle, titled more downward in the front, which created a very sinister profile, while still appearing military and professional.

The Marine started walking toward the rear of the bus. He towered above the seated men, nearly touching the roof of the bus. He had a small waist, which supported a massive chest and shoulders that spread his mass over the heads of the men who sat in both sides of the aisle seats. He had very dark ebony skin and his features were richly defined. Due to his dark complexion, his eyes were like two snowballs, with a chunk of black coal centered in them. His ivory teeth complemented the whites of his eyes and illustrated a triangular effect on a square black background. His nose was smashed into his face with wide flaring nostrils, set over heavy red lips. His fierce presence resembled a leather-lunged gorilla and he definitely scared the hell out of all those aboard the bus. He then walked back to the steps by the door of the bus and turned full bodied toward the recruits.

"Welcome to Marine Corps Recruit Depot, Parris Island, South Carolina", he screamed in a southern drawl and without a break continued, "my name is Gunnery Sergeant Carver.____Spit out yer gum, put out yer cigarettes and git yer fuckin' maggotty asses offa my bus!____You have exactly five seconds to line up on those yellow footprints," he said pointing toward the front of the receiving barracks, "and three of em are already gone!____Now move the fuck out!____Move it!____Move it!" Carver screamed even louder then before and stepped off the bus.

The young men, bumping into each other, jumped off that bus so fast they appeared to fly out of the windows. They ran hard to line up on the yellow footprints, which were painted on the asphalt at forty five degree angles, facing the open barracks doors. There were forty eight young men in all, evenly spaced, due to the pre-spaced yellow footprints.

In a comic sense, to an observer, this would appear from a distance as if an instant and precise military formation had been achieved by untrained civilians. For rabble to achieve such precision on their first attempt was unheard of and still is. However, with hearts still pounding hard and beads of sweat forming across their foreheads, these Marine Corps recruits were not now thinking comic. They had just exercised compliance to their first order in the Marine Corps.

They waited for the next barrage of obscenities to be hurled at them between screamed orders. The shock of Gunnery Sergeant Carver's explosion into the bus was only seconds old. The recruits were standing on those yellow footprints, frozen numb, not at attention, rather more like stiff with fear.

Who was this gorilla, they wondered? So far, he was the first Marine they had seen dressed this way. The campaign hat and black belt were not part of the Marine Corps uniform the Marines at Charleston Airport were wearing, nor their Marine Corps Recruiters. The Marines at Charleston Airport had worn a full khaki dress uniform. They had worn a creased khaki hat, which they folded flat and neatly tucked about an inch of it up under their belt at their side, when they were not wearing it.

Now this Gunnery Sergeant Carver clearly came across as hostile, while all the other Marines, up to this point, had been either polite or ambivalent, as they did not speak much at all to the group, or even to each other. This Carver was an anomaly, compared to all the others.

Gunnery Sergeant Carver suddenly shouted through the darkness from somewhere to the rear or side of the formation of young men waiting on the yellow footprints.

"Did I tell eny ah you shit-birds ta drop yer gear on da deck?____ Pick it up!" Carver growled. When Carver said I it sounded like Ah.

"Don't look at me, numb-nuts!" Gunnery Sergeant Carver berated somebody else in the formation. "Listen up, ladies," he went on, "until I specifically tell ya ta do enythang, don't!____If ya feel ya need ta do enythang other than to jus' stand there and wait till I say to do somethin',____don't even think it!" There was a moment of silence in the crisp night air as the recruits digested his deep southern drawl or mused over words like anything, which really sounded like enythang.

"From this moment on____," he continued his instructions, "you are not authorized ta speak at eny time, unless you are spokin' to.____You will answer eny direct question to eny one of you,____if affirmative,____ with a 'Sir, yes Sir' and if negative, with a 'Sir, no Sir!'.____If the whole group is addressed with a question, then you answer simply 'Sir, yes or no, Sir!'.____You will respond to all orders with 'Sir, aye-aye Sir!'.____ Simply put, every time ya open yer holes yer first word will be 'Sir!' and yer last word will be 'Sir!'.____You will stand straight with yer fuckin' eyeballs fixed straight ahead at all times and you will double time every thing ya do or place ya go!" Carver then boomed. "Do you unnerstan' me?"

There was no answer from the group of recruits.

"I asked if you ignorant pieces ah shit unnerstan' me?"

Here and there a few recruits, in various pitches, responded with a "Sir, yes Sir!"

"I can't hear you!" Carver yelled again.

"Sir, yes Sir!" This time the group shouted in more unison, but not yet loud enough.

At this response, Carver snarled, "I still can't hear you pukes!___ And the proper response is,___Sir, yes Sir!"

And in response to his anger, the group screamed a somewhat unified "Sir, yes Sir!"

Since Carver did not pursue any further desire for unity and pitch, the group felt they had learned the desired response, however Carver knew there was little more to expect at this stage.

The Receiving Barrack door opened suddenly, sending a wide bright V of light over the group. Several more Marines stood in the doorway, dressed much the same as Carver however, they each wore a green cartridge belt. The cartridge belt is normally used in the field to carry canteens, pistol, magazine pouches and other such equipment. The brass eyelets, spaced evenly in vertical rows of three along its length, were painted black. The Marines scrubbed the cartridge belts so they appeared whitish green in color and the black eyelets complimented that color.

Each Marine wore a large brass belt buckle, the size of a billfold, adorned with a large brass Marine Corps emblem. On their shirt sleeves, they each wore three stripes, inverted vees, with crossed rifles underneath the stripes, without any rockers.

They stood on the threshold of the door with hard faces and silently stared down at the group of recruits. A large red painted wooden sign hung above the door that was surrounded by a wide yellow boarder with large yellow letters boldly stating:

THROUGH THIS PORTAL PASS
PROSPECTS FOR THE WORLDS
FINEST FIGHTING FORCE
UNITED STATES MARINE CORPS

Then one of them nodded toward Gunnery Sergeant Carver, which prompted him to shout.

"Listen up!___You will file through that door and into the barrack where there are two rows of tables, there you will proceed to the far end of the room and fall in behind the tables on the outboard side of the tables only.___Do not stand between the rows.___When the first row has been completely filled, proceed to the second row.___Do you understand me?" Carver had pronounced the words precisely, without the southern drawl.

"Sir, yes Sir!" the disorganized, yet loud response was attempted. Several recruits moved a step forward. Immediately, Carver rebuked them.

"Did I tell ya to move, shit-birds?"

The recruits shuffled backwards to reclaim the safety of the yellow footprints. Again Carver spoke and gave the order to move out.

"Okay girls, file inta the barrack startin' with the left column an' each column ta follow after it, do ya unnerstan'?"

"Sir, yes Sir!" the loud, yet disconcerted response sputtered into the dank night air.

"Move out, turds!" Carver clipped.

The young men surged forward, line after line, onward towards their destiny.

FOUR

The recruits filed quickly, one behind the other as ordered, into the room before them. The Marines observed their actions to ensure compliance with the order and were shouting close it up to the recruits as they stopped in front of the tables.

The long tables were the type one often sees in churches or schools. They were designed with legs that could be folded up underneath the table top, which makes it easier to stack and store them out of the way.

There were two rows of these tables, as Carver had stated, which were joined end to end, creating a long working surface, interrupted occasionally by wooden support posts which ran the length of the room on both sides.

The recruits were now facing each other across the room. There was a wide walking space between the two rows. In this walking area were large galvanized garbage cans, spaced evenly, every six feet. Carver and the other two Marines moved to the far end of the room, in the space between the tables. At intervals of one Marine to a table, they started working their way down the line.

"Put yer bags and all other pers'nal property on the table in front of you," Gunnery Sergeant Carver bellowed, "and take absolutely every article or item you have out of yer pockets or attached to yer body," a few recruits placed their bags on the table or started digging into their pockets.

"Jesus fuckin' Christ!" Carver exploded in disbelief, "Can't you fuck-heads remember enythin' I said to ya?___I tol' ya not ta do a damn thang 'less'n I tol' ya ta do it first!" Carver drawled on in an ever deepening southern accent.

The recruits who had committed the act were now very confused. A few started to move again to retrieve their stuff. As they fidgeted, sticking the items back in their pockets, Carver simply watched them, while shaking his head slowly. They stared back at Carver in total fear and confusion now, wondering what he would do now. They got their answer immediately.

Carver and the other two Marines ran up and down the tables, grabbing up the items and throwing them at their owner's chests.

Those few, who moved the second time, Carver shoved backwards with a strong arm.

"Last warning, cocksuckers!" he bellowed with genuine loathing while he shoved recruits. "You stay a step behind these other hogs 'till I say move!___Got that morons?"

The recruits just stood there like statues.

"Good,___yer learnin'.___Now step back!" Carver said while smiling. Five recruits, after saying "Sir, yes Sir!" took a step back and now stood silently behind the rest.

With the tables bare once again, Carver ordered, "all of you proceed to place all of yer pers'nal property on the table",___he paused, looking around,___"Do it!"

All of the recruits started digging through their pockets, throwing their contents on the table. They placed bags, jackets, hats and all other such items on the table as well.

The Marines methodically started unzipping bags, rummaging

their contents, sifting through the individual articles on the table, prying wallets, checking pockets of jackets and ordered all trouser pockets turned inside out.

The Marines then moved down the line, pitching various items into the garbage cans, which they had discerned to be unnecessary for completion of Marine Corps boot camp.

Articles discarded included playing cards, plastic Pez dispensers, chewing gum, eight-track cassette tapes, hair combs, Black Power hair picks, with the clenched fist handle, chocolates, candies, assorted junk foods, and numerous other civilian survival necessities.

The property purge continued, rating right up there with General Sherman's march through the south. Carver, along with his assistants, methodically dissected the recruit's personal belongings, when he suddenly stood erect, throwing the recruit in front of him a repugnant glare, and thrust something he held in his hand towards the recruit's face.

"What the hell is this?" he asked in a high pitched voice, infused with a strange excitement, as he held a switchblade knife, letting a wicked, six inch long blade fly out, sweeping not less than an inch from the recruit's insipid face. His ease of the knife's use, indicating personal familiarity, was very evident.

The knifes owner, a light brown haired boy with long curly sideburns jutting out from under his very greasy hair, which oozed down to the shoulders, starred straight ahead in shock. He wore a black leather jacket decorated with silver buckles and silver fasteners, faded bell-bottomed blue jeans, held up by a psychedelic patterned belt with a big silver buckle emblazoned with a peace-symbol. His chin appeared stuck to his chest as his eyes peered up, trying to see through his upper eye sockets at Gunnery Sergeant Carver. He started to answer, when Carver slammed the switchblade knife on the table, making such a loud sound, it totally unnerved the youth.

"Shut the fuck up, scum bag, did I say you could talk?" Carter exploded so loud the boy reeled back a step.

"Did I say you could move, ya cocksucka?" Carter reached out across the table and grabbed the grease-ball by his jacket collar, first pulling him forward and then shoving him away.

"We got us a real dangerous one here.___A real city punk.___ Brought his own arsenal,___didn't trust we'd provide him a weapon here.___Right,___tough guy?" Carver, with loathing, spewed the words at the recruit.

"Sa-Sir, no Sir!" the greaseball's reply was shaky.

"I wonder if ya ever used this pig sticka on enyone?___Well, have ya,___shit-head?" Carver asked unkindly, and continued his harsh inquisition.

"Na-no Sir!" The greaseball's next stammered reply was equally shaky.

"I thought so.___A real tough chicken-shit,____ain't cha maggot?"

"Sir, no Sir!"

"What's yer name, asshole?"

"Mike..er, Michael Kerr."

The Marine glared at him with tight lips and asked, "where does a greasy piece ah shit like you come from,____huh?"

"Sir, Philadelphia, Sir!"

"Why doesn't that sa'prise me, scuz-bucket.___I never met enyone ah quality from that fuckin' no 'count Yankee sewer hole.___Folks from Philadelphia is all chicken-shit, back stabbers, an' ain't never ta' be trusted!" he spit out the words with obvious bile in his comment. His pronunciation now purposely sounding deep trashy southern, as though he was ensured further distancing from this Yankee cocksucker from Philadelphia.

"Do ya suck cocks, faggot?" he asked, egging him further.

"No!"

"Don't ya know how ta say Suh,___cocksucka?" he questioned, while pushing him back a little.

"No Sir!" Kerr answered with a growing red hue on his face.

"What cha say?___Isn't that sappose' ta be a Suh, yes, Suh,___from you,__ puke?"

"No Sir!" Kerr's eyes were now wide and his mouth drawn down.

"No Suh what?"___"No, Suh, you do suck cocks!" or "No Suh,___ you don't hafta say Suh, yes Suh ta this Marine?"

Kerr just stood there, a dazed look on his now beet red face.

"Well, ya wanna-be-Marine cocksucka,___ya won't make it here, and ya won't be needin' this where yer a goin'." he growled and tossed the knife into one of the garbage cans, among the other useless items.

"Sergeant, get this piece ah shit outta my sight!" Carver called to one of his assistants.

The sergeant led Kerr off through a door at the back end of the barrack. After a few minutes the sergeant returned alone and continued the job of sorting through the piles on the tables.

There were loud exchanges here and there along the tables as the Marines discovered items proscribed by the Marine Corps or that were too humorous to let pass without a personal hassle session.

"Hey boy, you certainly came prepared. Didn't you?" one of the sergeants queried a recruit who resembled an Ivy-Leaguer, as he held up a condom.

"Sir, yes Sir!" the boy shouted, a cocky grin materializing on his face, obviously thinking that this was something bonding between men, while he looked directly at the Marine.

The Marine sergeant stared at the fair-featured young recruit, while his own features underwent a metamorphic shift from hard to devious.

"Get your fairy eyes off of me, faggot. Who do you plan to fuck here, you ugly piece of shit? Your bunky? Or me? Are you a queer?"

"Sir, no Sir!" the youth, his smile replaced by a facial contortion resembling a diarrhea attack, responded.

"What's your name, sweetheart?" the sergeant inquired.

"Gordon, George A.!" he replied in a whinny tone.

"With the initials G.A.G., you gotta be a cock sucker!" the Marine said as he tore open the condom package, extracting the rubbery device and threw it into the recruits face. It bounced off his face and fell onto the table. "An' I did not ask for your fucking first name asshole!"

"Pick it up, asshole! I want you to blow it up, so I can see how good you can blow." The Sergeant smirked at the recruit. "Do it!"

"Sir, yes Sir!" the recruit answered while picking up the condom and moved it to his lips.

"Ready, blow!" the Marine ordered.

The recruit started puffing and blowing air into the condom.

"That's enough sweet-pea!" The sergeant said, grabbing a trash can and swinging it upward towards the recruit. "Throw that disgusting thing in the can, shit-for-brains!"

"Sir, yes Sir!" the recruit replied, and tossed the condom into the trash can.

The sergeant gave him a hard look and moved on to the next recruit.

A whistle pierced the room, followed by an exaggerated deep voice from the other Marine assisting Carver.

"Figured you'd be lonely down here sweetpea?___What's your name?"

"Howard Rosenberg, Sir!" he said, raising his voice only slightly, sounding oily and whiney.

The Marine was holding a girlie magazine with the word *Swank* printed boldly on the cover.

"Jerk-off material for lonely nights, eh?___No wonder your face looks the way it does." The sergeant scrunched his face and shook it side to side at the same time. He was referring to Rosenberg's many blackheads and pimples.

"Don't you know jerkin' off causes your face to break out,___stupid!"

"Sir, na...no Sir!" Rosenberg was answering, when the sergeant suddenly noticed that the recruit was clenching something tight in his left fist.

"What the fucks in your left hand?___Stick out your hand and open it this fuckin' second!

Rosenberg, with tears spilling down his cheeks looked like he had thin-shit running down his legs, as he opened his fist, revealing two joints.

"*Nooo!*___I don't believe it!___What's this, a going away present from your hippy friends asshole?___Where ya think you'd smoke those around here,___numb-nuts?" the sergeant asked in disgust.

Rosenberg remained silent, staring straight ahead with vacant eyes, obviously starting to register the gravity of his error.

"Gunnery Sergeant Carver!" the assistant DI called out, not moving his eyes from the recruit. "Could you come over here for a moment?"

Carver walked over, taking in the situation immediately.

"Well, well!___Got a pot habit, boy?___Don't cha worry none, 'cause where yer goin', they'll definitely cure ya!___Yer goin' to the brig!___That's a jail to civilian dope-heads like you." Suddenly Carver's face grew hostile, as he moved it to within a few inches from Rosenbergs' face and screamed with spittle spraying forth, "we got no place for dope-heads in this Marine Corps!"

Carver had continued tempestuously screaming other loathsome words at Rosenberg as he simultaneously slammed his fists down on the wooden table top, so hard that the items laying about the table jumped up several inches.

Rosenberg flinched at the combined assault of booming voice and slamming fists and tears formed in his eyes.

"Don't cha even open yer filthy mouth!___Yer outta here,___ya pusillanimous piece ah shit!" Carver clipped petulantly between clenched teeth.

The assistant, now holding the marijuana, walked around the tables and up to Rosenberg. He then grabbed him from the back of his shirt collar, twisting his hand full of material in such a way it balled in a knot.

The Marine extracted the felon from the line of recruits and maneuvered him towards the same door Kerr had been taken through several minutes earlier.

"Wait a minute!" Carver called to the Marine holding Rosenberg by the collar. "Put the evidence in a marked envelope and___(he walked over to the trash can which held the switchblade knife, stooped, retrieved it, then turned to hand it to the sergeant) take this evidence as well and turn it all over to the Duty Officer,___I'll write statements up after I've finished processing this herd.___Call the MPs and have them haul away this garbage!" he ordered, and his southern accent was hardly discernible now. The sergeant nodded affirmatively and then proceeded through the door as Carver's voice enveloped the barrack.

"Those dumb shits ain't gittin' inta my M'rine Corps.___Real losers dey is,___*uh huh*,___any more of ya fergit where yew was ah goin' an bring yer git-inta-jail-free card?" he asked. His southern drawl back even more now then before.

"Sir, no Sir!" A shaky response, loud enough for the drill instructor, indicated the recruits now knew for certain that this was not some kind of summer camp.

The other assistant DI and Carver continued their work, going through wallets, guffawing at pictures of really ugly girlfriends, or at the recruits who brought pictures of their parents, or worse, a picture of their mother, alone. They mocked everything, it seemed to the recruits. The pictures were nevertheless left on the tables. However, toilet articles, books, magazines, candies and many other such nonessential articles were tossed into the garbage cans.

In the end, all that remained in the personal possession of the recruits were wallets, money, family photos, identification cards or other such cards normally found in American society and carried in the back pockets of it's male citizens.

Although these items were allowed to be kept, they would not be utilized while the recruits were on the Island. Even pictures of mothers would be shunned, as the recruit would soon come to blame her for bringing him into this hostile world, where escape was hopeless.

All the garbage cans were near full with the discarded items by the time the Marines had finished their search. By the end of the shakedown, almost every recruit had been either verbally challenged or chastised for possession of some unauthorized item, or for speaking to another recruit without permission, or incorrectly addressing a Marine, such as failing to state sir, or answer fast or loud enough. The one thing that was most evident was the facial expressions on each recruit. They had masks of fear and uncertainty and their movements became hesitant, due to the new certainty of sudden punishment.

The clock on the wall displayed 4:30 a.m., or rather 0430.

FIVE

"Listen up___ladies.___It's 0430.___We got a lot ta do.___Move it___ sweet-peas!" Gunnery Sergeant Carver boomed as he addressed the entire room. "You will start filin' into the room adjoining the starboard bulkhead.___The right wall, to you dip-shits.___You will wait for an empty barber's chair and upon discov'ry of such a vacancy,___you will immediately occupy it.___Do you unnerstan' me?"

There followed a dissonant "Sir, yes Sir!"

"Move it!"

The recruits started darting fast to form a single file toward the door Carver had indicated. There was a row of barber chairs, each attended by an elderly man. They each wore white short-sleeved barber smocks, snapped up the right side all the way up to the neck, holding the priest-like collar firmly around their necks.

The recruits occupied the first chairs, while the rest stood in a line reaching from the door and continued along the wall of the outer room, awaiting their turn.

Each barber picked up their electric shears and started testing them.

Bbeezz, bop-baabez, bbezzz, the shears resonated across the room and then the barbers dove them into their waiting recruits' hair, driving the clippers up from the back of their head first, then up over the top towards the front making *bbeeezz, bburrr* sounds as the shears purchased hair. The recruits started out with a very visible and ridiculous swath plowed over the center of their heads. Within thirty seconds they were completely bald.

The effect of this first passage of the shears on straight-haired recruits resembled water splashing off to each side like one sees when a water skier cuts a trough. A humorous observation, lost immediately as the barber attacked the sides of their head.

The heavy clumps of hair fell to the floor, cascading off the recruit's ears, shoulders and chest, collecting in their laps or on the growing mountains of hair surrounding the barber chairs. The barber's shoes were soon hidden under the harvest.

As each recruit donated his hair, the piles developed into a motley mixture of red, black, yellow, brown, platinum and orange, in curly, straight and wavy shards.

To a well read observer or an actual death camp survivor, this act would have reminded them of the 'Final Solution', when Nazi Germany processed the Jews and other political prisoners through Auschwitz, Treblinka, Bergen-Belsen, Dachau and other such concentration camps during World War II.

Those camps were mostly located in Poland and Germany, and there the Nazis received the Jews and other political prisoners for sonder behandlung (special treatment). It was at those places that the Nazis ordered the prisoner's heads shaved to obtain a usable product. Of course, this act not only provided a usable product and controlled lice, but also acted to injure through humiliation and denied the Jew's sense of individuality. Here at Parris Island it served to strip the recruits of their individuality and to create uniformity.

They were ordered to strip by the Schutzstaffel (SS) and were processed through that regime's system. It was a system where ambivalent soldiers routinely removed the prisoner's identities in stages, while enjoying screaming obscenities at them during their passage through that ordeal. Since they no longer held any individual identity, it was easier to deal with them collectively.

The paradox being that the majority of those who entered the Nazi camps, ended their ordeal unsuccessfully, either shot, starved or gassed, then buried or burned to ashes.

Those who successfully completed the ordeal of Marine Corps boot camp, ended their ordeal with honor, in excellent shape, earning a magnificent uniform to display that success. However, in order to earn these things, the Marine Corps first burned their asses.

Those prisoners who were processed through the death camps lost their dignity, fellowship and pride of past accomplishments in life. The Marine recruit who graduates boot camp aspires to dignity, joins a fellowship and experiences a lifelong pride from that accomplishment.

Therefore, though the venerated toughness of the training regimen of Marine Corps boot camp and processing can be juxtaposed with Nazi concentration camps, the tragedy of one cannot here be paralleled.

The Nazis were the malefactors in the end, and the Marine Corps is certainly not in that category. Therefore, Marine Corps recruits become obsequious, without greater reservation, beyond an awareness that this adventure, this training ordeal, although designed to be very difficult for them, should in the process, not threaten their health, nor endanger their lives, for the most part.

A barber shouted over to one of the Marines and beckoned him to come over and have a look at the recruit he was shearing. The Marine obliged him and walked over to the barber's chair and looked at the head before him. Huge swatches of dark brown hair still clung to the side of his incompletely shorn head. With the back and top now bare, the Marine sergeant could see what the barber was concerned about.

There were splotches covering his head, which appeared oozy. They were dark brown and looking like chewing tobacco had been spit onto his head, resulting in a splat effect, spaying out in all directions. His head was covered with them and they presented a very unhealthy visage.

"*Ugh!*" The Marine grimaced, turning up his top lip on the right side of his face.

The barber looked at the sergeant with agreement registered on his face.

"*Gawd!*___What the hell you been doing?" he finally asked the recruit, while still holding up his lip, at the same time throwing his upper body back, so as not to get too near.

"What's your name, you filthy piece of shit?"

The recruit simply sat there, eyes staring straight ahead, saying nothing, apparently too embarrassed to reply.

"Scuzz-ball!" the sergeant raised his voice. "I asked you what your fuckin' name is?___How about this fucking century!"

"Shawn O'Brian!" the recruit answered, saying his name very fast, as one word and almost unintelligible.

"Christ!___Can't say his name properly,___can't bathe properly,___can't be sane either.___Are you crazy boy?" the sergeant inquired, expecting this to be the only rational answer.

O'Brian just sat there silently.

"Where the hell does a filthy dirt-bag like you come from anyway?" the Marine inquired further.

"Boston!" the recruit's whispered reply irritated the DI even more.

"No Sir?" the sergeant asked.

"Yes, I am so from Boston!" the recruit stated quietly and matter-of-factly.

"I asked if you wouldn't mind stating Sir, as required,___shit-for-brains,___I'm not holding a fuckin' conversation with you!" The Marine growled as he was now growing livid.

"Finish cutting this bums hair", he said to the barber, "and then you report to Gunnery Sergeant Carver, dirt-bag!" he instructed the recruit. "Understand?"

"Sir, yes Sir!" O'Brian's halfhearted and half whispered reply dribbled out of his slack-jawed mouth.

The Marine was not in the mood to harass the recruit while the barbers were working, as this would only slow the process. The entire exchange with the recruit lasted under a minute. The Marine already knew Carver would chew the ass off this dirt bag later, anyway.

"Once I finish this cut, I'll have to sterilize the clippers!" the barber complained to the Marine moodily, but probably really more for the benefit of the other recruits.

The barber's shears droned on as they dutifully continued shearing the recruits. The long line was swiftly getting shorter. After all, there was no need to wait for personalized haircuts here.

The recruits, once sheared, were ushered out of another door by a Marine and sent upstairs into a squad bay. The squad bay was a large room in the barrack, where lined up along each side were metal bunk beds. The bunk beds each had a bare mattress, folded in half, revealing the single layer of interlocked metal loop configurations, which held up a mattress, but in no way was a bed spring in the conventional sense.

There were already many other recruits in the squad bay who arrived earlier and had their hair shorn off and shaved their faces. They were sitting on the edge of the bare bunks or standing between them, some using the top bunk as a place to lean their folded arms to support their heads while they were waiting. The room was absolutely silent with both parties of recruits staring at each other with dazed eyes as though they were looking at themselves in a mirror.

A large bathroom was located at one end of the squad bay. The bathroom had long rows of sinks with mirrors mounted on the wall above each one of them. There were rows of toilets, with black U shaped toilet seats and no divider walls for privacy. There would be no privacy on the Island.

The toilets were installed along the wall on two sides of the room. A shorter wall was centered in the room, with sinks and mirrors attached to both sides of that wall in a parallel manner across from the toilets. One could thus walk completely around the room, either way, to access the facilities. At the far side wall was a large rectangle opening, without doors, which led into a shower room, which was a cavernous area with shower nozzles and faucets running along all the walls.

Unlike civilian public bathroom areas, there were no disgusting shit and snot smears between obscenities written by mindless idiots on the walls of this bathroom, this was a brightly lit, spotlessly clean functional room. One could hardly go anywhere in public without encountering the residue of disgusting perverts or the wall scrawling authored by social deviates.

The Marine downstairs had told each recruit to go upstairs into the squad bay and to shave all remaining unauthorized hair on their heads. Shaving gear was provided and waiting on the sinks.

The recruits arrived upstairs with an outrageous array of appearances.

Some of them had mustaches and side burns, others only sideburns, big, long or bushy, and still others had beards, side burns and mustaches. With their shaved heads, this appeared as a last cruel joke, it seemed, for the entertainment of the Marines and the barbers.

The recruits were now busy shaving their side burns, mustaches and beards off, as ordered. A Marine sergeant was patrolling behind the recruits as they hacked away at their facial hair.

Suddenly, a shout rang out through the bathroom as the Marine started chewing out several recruits at once.

"You hear me tell you to do that?" he snapped and continued, "You see anyone else in here doing that?"

There, for all to witness, was a recruit, shaving cream on his head, razor in hand, with obvious razor swaths across his cream laden head.

The other recruit, standing there, arm extended downward and away from his side, his hand stupidly dangling the razor with which he had just shaved off one eye brow. His other eyebrow was still lathered with shaving cream.

"Jesus Christ!" the Marine screamed, sounding truly surprised.

"You two are, without a doubt, the most fucked-up, stupid, without reservation, bottom-of-the-barrel, slimy, dumb-shit, scrotum-headed, ignorant fucks, I've ever seen!" he screamed the torrent of profanities in one breath.

"Is this what we're getting for recruits these days?__No way!" he went on now screaming ever louder.

"Get your dumb asses downstairs this second,___as you are,___ don't wipe off anything!" he ordered menacingly.

He followed them downstairs to display them to Gunnery Sergeant Carver whos voice exploded so loudly, it could be heard upstairs as well.

He could be overheard ordering the two recruits to the same room the other three idiots, Kerr, O'Brian and Rosenberg had been sent to earlier.

The recruits were now finished shaving their faces of unauthorized hair. They stood around or sat on the bare bunks in the squad bay and waited for their next orders. Unaccustomed to not having hair, many recruits were constantly rubbing the short hard bristles on their heads.

They were already learning not to just do what they wanted,

even though a few were sitting down now, without specifically being authorized to do so. The fact that the Marine patrolling the area did not say anything about their sitting, did not indicate approval. The majority were too weary to take a chance.

The clock in the squad bay displayed 0500. Outside, coming through the open windows, was the sound of a bugle playing reveille. The Island was awake now and in full operation. Several minutes later platoons started falling out into formation and the sounds of cadence and other activities could be heard shouted all over the Island as the new day began.

"Platoon!____Ahh____ten____hut!"
"One, two, three, four, United States Marine Corps!"
"Yer lo,___hi,___leh,___hi,___de___lo!"
"Sir, aye-aye Sir!"
"Ahhoorraah!"

Gunnery Sergeant Carver had entered the squad bay a few seconds after reveille had been sounded.

SIX

"Alright you shit-birds, fall out on the yellow footprints___and face in the opposite direction!___Move out!" Gunnery Sergeant Carver shouted as he entered the squad bay.

The recruits ran down the stairs and out the door onto the pavement.

That's when I made a mistake. I was in such a hurry to be first in the line that I had managed to get to the head of the formation, in the far left column.

I was full of energy, young and sure of myself. I was seventeen years old.

It was the early morning of October 16, 1969 as I stood in formation waiting for Gunnery Sergeant Carver to give the next order.

The morning air was cool, damp, and had a distinct odor of decaying vegetation. My breath fogged out with each exhalation. It was still dark outside, but the dim light provided by the moon and the nearby lighting was grey and offered a grainy vision of all the discernable area.

I stood there on my yellow footprints, wearing light tan colored

Levi jeans, scuffed tennis shoes and a well worn short-sleeved, button down collar, paisley-print shirt. I weighed about 140 pounds and I was nearsighted.

I had not yet fully developed. My hair was a reddish-blond. My face was lightly sprinkled with brown freckles. As faces go, mine was on the thin side, however with the ability to grow into a rounder face with age, as was evidenced in my older family members and relatives, whos pictures indicated they had started out with about the same weight.

My hazel eyes were hard looking, even at my young age. This look could also be compared to how an animal, or person, looks when angered or when they have been hurt. My nose was somewhat straight and narrow, pointing to average sized lips. This montage of facial elements was set between two parenthetic ears.

My reason for joining the Marine Corps, was in direct response to years of excessive hardships at home. Home, *ha*! It was only another four letter word to me, since I could hardly call my fragmented upbringing a childhood with a loving and stable set of parents. The last male in my life was no father figure, not by a long shot. My mother could definately pick them and he sure was a prime whiskey-swilling, child-intimidating, womanizing, life-draining, hateful predator. In fact, he was also a pedophile, who just a few days ago had his cover blown.

His name was Charlie Huston and he had been raping my fourteen year old sister for some time and with that whiskey breath had whispered, into her ear, his threats to murder our entire family, if she ever talked. He kept me and my brother Lucious out of the way by repeatedly talking our mother into exiling us to relatives, who grudgingly accepted us.

Life at home, or with relatives, had lost its appeal, and since, up until my enlistment, events, if judged by the card deck of life, had dealt me thus far, an unusable hand. I had made the decision to strike out onto a path in life of my own choosing. I had planned to make an independent life now that I was seventeen years old. What the hell, whatever was out there could only be as hard as I was already used to, the only difference was that I chose the stage setting, instead of my parents or relatives choosing one for me.

I had joined the Marine Corps through Fort Holybird, in Baltimore, Maryland. My life would now be moving into new and uncharted waters.

"Platoon!___Ah___ten___hut!___Foart___huah!" Gunnery Sergeant Carver growled and we engaged our first footstep off those yellow footprints into the unknown gauntlet of Marine Corps training in this sub-basement of hell called Parris Island. The Island.

CHAPTER 2
GEARING UP

ONE

Gunnery Sergeant Carver walked swiftly to the middle point, off to the side of our motley formation of recruits, and observed our movements as we stepped off of the yellow footprints.

At the command *huah*, which meant to march, for those with greater interpretive skills, we had all stepped off with either foot, indifferent to whether it was militarily correct. Of course those who chose their left foot involuntarily, to be sure, were accidentally militarily correct.

The formation moved forward inelegantly down Panama Street.

"Route-step,____march!" Carver ordered, in a clear, normal tone, as though tired or indifferent. Although, he was basically wasting his breath, since that was already how we were marching and we knew absolutely nothing about a route-step.

This meant to walk in formation, with no need to keep in step. We moved on, towards a group of white wooden two story barracks. There was a series of large-diameter silver pipes running above ground, paralleling the road. These pipes ran approximately nine feet above ground, and where a road was to be crossed, suddenly shot up, over and down again, at ninety-degree angles. They appeared high enough for military trucks to safely drive under.

We were nearing the first recruit training barracks, when suddenly, sounding as though an explosion had just occurred, the doors of many barracks simultaneously crashed open. Instant platoon formations were created from the hundreds of recruits, wearing tennis shoes and exercise clothing, who had spilled out onto the side of the road. It was now approximately quarter past 5 a.m. as we were nearing these platoons.

They were bathed in lights, which were mounted on the telephone poles running along the road. Their formations were dark masses except for their ghostly faces, which were reflecting the lights, producing a singular glowing effect. Their breaths, produced steam, which expelled forward and wrapped around their faces, adding further to their eerie visage.

We walked past their formation now and could see the red guidon flags of each platoon. These were 2nd Battalion recruits, which could be discerned by the series numbers displayed in yellow on red backgrounds. Some discernible numbers revealed 2058 and 2059 while others were wrapped about their poles revealing only bits of the series numbers. This was the Twilight Zone as 2nd Battalion was referred to. This bit of history however, was totally unknown to our raggedy mob at this time.

Their sergeants were not yet outside with them, allowing opportunity for several bold recruits to snipe at us with hushed comments and hoots as we passed by.

"You'll be soorryy!"___"Look at the Girl Scouts!"___"There's no turning back now, sweet-peas!"___"You're all fucked!"___"Cannon fodder!"____"Look at the fuckin' new guys!"___"Yo, FNGs."

Carver may have heard them from where he walked, but said nothing, perhaps allowing this hoary exchange as part of Marine Corps tradition.

There was more truth in their remarks, than perhaps some of the others thought, or maybe all of us felt the same about this whole ordeal. Anyway, we weren't given the opportunity to discuss it amongst ourselves. This silence on our part was equally strange. We had not been specifically told to shut-up when the Sergeant wasn't around, though we nevertheless did keep silent. However, it could be that our being tired, shocked, and unsure of our new surroundings, caused silence. We were not indoctrinated in all things on the Island yet and the twenty four hour a day silence, unless speaking to your instructor, was one mandatory part of training as we would soon learn.

Onward we walked, straight ahead, until the road was intersected by another road. Carver was on the left side of our group.

"Callum____let,____huah!" he barked suddenly.

We kept going straight and by the time we were half way into the intersection, Carver started screaming.

"Goddamn it, stop!____I said stop,____ya miserable fuck-ups!"

We stopped and I was about to look around to see what he was so upset about.

At the exact moment we had stopped, I was suddenly flying into the air, landing to my left, in that area of gravel and sand between the road and the grass, which paralleled the road. There I lay shocked, my face blushing bright red with fear, while I was looking up at Gunnery Sergeant Carver. He was staring back at me, his body bent at his waist, with hands on his knees, teeth clenched in a mean grimace. Then he bawled a barrage of loathsome obscenities at me.

"Cain't you unnerstan' a simple orda', ya stewpid fuck-head?____I said collum leht, asshole, not straight ahead.____You are a total fuckin' worthless puke!____Here I was thinkin' this miserable bunch o' civilians was not goin' ta give me eny problems and then ya sabotage the whole thang!____I swear,____you are not worth shit, ya stupid scumbag.____Now git yer ass back to the end o' the callum.____Move it!" he growled.

I scrambled to my feet and ran to the end of the formation. My pride hurt more than my ass, where Carver had planted his huge combat boot. What Carver had done was grab me by the collar from behind and as he jerked me backwards and off to the left, he simultaneously kicked me forward.

Carver had scarred me, affecting me more personally now, than my feelings registered fear toward anything I had heard him scream at others, since we arrived.

I was going to be dead meat now that he had discovered my existence. I thought glumly.

We turned left and continued our journey up the street to the next intersection, where we were able to achieve the left turn at Carver's clear and slowly pronounced command of *column____left,____march.*

Carver finally gave orders to halt in front of a gray metal building to our right side. "Startin' with the left column,____move into the building. Head to yer right an' run all the way 'round the tables inside an' stop!____Fill in that side first an' repeat on t'other side.____Move it!" Carver shouted in his loud gravelly southern voice.

Off we ran, column after column, into the building, a warehouse really, and filled in the area until each of us stood before a wooden bin about two feet by two feet. There was a long row of these bins, with the same thing on the other side. Waist high was a wooden retainer board to contain the contents of each bin, which contained such necessities as shoe polish, cotton swabs, shoe strings and dozens of other items. In the center, running the entire length of these bins was a raised walkway approximately a foot wide.

On top of this walkway stood a Marine in a green work uniform, wearing a web belt with a shiny brass buckle and a campaign hat. He had two assistants, standing on each side of the room, who were similarly dressed. They appeared agitated and impatient to get underway with their tasks.

TWO

"Listen up!" shouted the Marine on the walking platform, and while walking back and forth, continued. "My name is Sergeant Aikens."

He was about six feet tall, with large shoulders and a significantly smaller waist. This displayed a pronounced vee shape. His facial expression was set in stone, displaying unsmiling eyes, long straight narrow nose and a straight gash, where his mouth should be. His lips were almost nonexistent. The overall affect of his facial components were intensified by slight cheekbones and a square jaw with a cleft chin.

When he spoke, it was a deep commanding voice. More clear to the ear than Carver's thickly coated southern drawl pronunciations.

Perhaps it would be easier to march to this man's orders.____Anything would be an improvement over getting your ass kicked just because you can't understand cotton-mouthed grunts. I mused.

"Before each of you is a bin", he continued sonorously, "inside of which is part of your initial issue of essential articles required for your training while here at Parris Island.____When I hold up an item,____I will describe it,____and if any of you do not have the item called out,____you will continue to hold your hand in the air after everyone else drops theirs.____You will wait for one of my assistants to provide you with that item.____Do you understand me?" he spoke in a machine-like cadence and ended in a harsch bark.

"Sir, yes Sir!" we mumbled our disconcerted response.

"Do you understand me?" Sergeant Aikens again shouted.

"Sir, yes Sir!" we responded again, however more together and louder this time.

Apparently, Aikens let this response go and continued with the first item in his hand. He held up some kind of white cloth, which one of his assistants had just handed up to him from a bin filled exactly like ours. As Aikens called the item, the second assistant checked off that item on a clipboard resting over his left forearm.

"Bag, linin, cotton,____one each!" he said, and we all held up our linen bags.

Aikens then instructed us to place each following item into the linen bag, as we went along.

"Toothpaste,____tube,____one each!" he said, holding up a tube of *Crest* toothpaste.

"Toothbrush,____two each!"

"Razor,____one each." he called out holding up a *Gillette* razor and then the blades.

"Blades,____razor,____one issue each!"

"Cream,____shaving,____one can!" he said, shaking the can of *Barbasol* shaving cream.

"Clippers,____nail, with chain,____one each!" he continued.

"Soap,____bar,____three each!" The stacked *Safeguard* soap boxes rose up high over his head.

"Kerchief,____hand,____one issue!" He swung the plastic bag, which contained several linen handkerchiefs up and down by bending his wrist rapidly.

"Powder,____foot,____one each!" Aikens waived a plastic dispenser of *Mixana* foot powder.

"Stick,____styptic,____one each!"

"Kit,____sewing,____one each!" Up went a flat green pouch, about two and one half by six inches.

"Pad,____stamp,____one each!" He held a metal container advertising the name *Carter's*.

"Polish,____shoe,____black,____one can each!" Up came a can of *Cavalier*.

"Brush,___scrub,___one each!" Waived a wooden brush, from side to side, above Aiken's head.

"Brass,___cleaner,___can,___one each!" he said, displaying a can of cotton soaked brass cleaner.

"Brush,___shoe,___one each!"

"Pin,___clothes,___wood,___one package each!"

"Padlock,___combination,___two each!" Aiken held up two *Masters* pad-locks.

"Flashlight,___battery powered,___plastic.___One each!"

"Battery,___D-type,___two each!" He held two *Ray-o-Vac* batteries up.

"Book,___Guide,___U.S. Marine Corps,___one each!" he exclaimed, holding a book over his head.

"Brush,___paint,___one each!" A wooden handled black bristled brush painted the air as he flicked his wrist.

"Plug,___ear,___two each!"

"Balm,___lip,___one each!"

"Lace,___boot,___two each!"

"Kit,___button,___one each!" A black vinyl packet, approximately three by four inches, was scanned around the room, held between both of his hands.

"Cleaner,___pipe,___one package each!"

"Swabs,___ear,___one box each!"

"Soap,___bar,___clothing,___two bars each!"

"Stamp kit,___Letterpoint,___one each!" Aikens swung the kit for stamping names, through the air.

"Shoes,___shower,___one pair each!"

"Shoes,___athletic,___one pair each!" He displayed sneakers.

"Supporter,___athletic,___one each!" Made by *Florico*, Aikens deemed it necessary to inform us.

"Kit,___letter writing,___one each!" Up came a handsome green letter sized folder with a gold Marine Corps emblem embossed upon it.

This continued for wash cloths, towels, combination cotton shorts for swimming and physical exercises, plastic toilet kit bag with zipper, sweat shirt, and other items deemed necessary by the U.S. Marine Corps for survival on the Island. All the while Aikens strode back and forth on the walking platform, tossing each item called out back to his assistant and extended his hand to accept the next item. Surprising us all was the carton of cigarettes being issued to each of us.

"Place one of your towels around your neck!" Aikens ordered. We all drapped a white cotton towel around our necks, however we had no idea why.

Our linen bags were now bulging and the drawstring barely closed over the bag, when we were ordered to secure our gear by tying the bag up for hand transport. This entire equipment issue went smoothly for approximately forty five minutes. Occasionally, a recruit would not have the item described or, had two when only one was prescribed. The other Marines quickly corrected these glitches.

"Pick up yer gear an' fall outside into the same formation you were in before.___Move it!" Gunnery Sergeant Carver commanded in a deep voice.

We ran quickly outside, as much as the size of the door and the now added bulk of these overstuffed white cotton bags allowed us. Getting reformed in ranks was more difficult now than as before, we soon discovered. The cookie-cutter yellow footprints were no longer there to form us up neatly and since nobody advised us, we failed to familiarize ourselves with the freshly cut cue ball previously in front of us. I for one made sure I was in the rear. Those previously in front or immediately behind the first recruits in the four columns, as were the other three in the rear, were also able to reform as before, with no sweat. The rest looked about perplexed for that recently held spot, which was no longer discernable.

THREE

"Aah___ten___huat!___Foart____huah!" Carver croaked loudly. Off we moved down the road. "Callum,___ret,___huah!" his next order followed, however we kept going straight.

"Stop___you shit-heads,___stop!" Carver screamed. The poor recruit in the first position of the right column was now being summarily chastised.

"Ya stupid fuck!" Carver's voice erupted over our formation. He gave this recruit as much attention toward retraining, as I had received. So I no longer felt privileged. Our procession was now given a new right column guide. It was simple, the fired recruit was moved to the rear of his column and this bumped up the man previously behind him. That poor guy was probably thinking, "What the hell was that? Cam ret huh?___Or was it Comretah?___*Jeez!*"

As the chastised recruit was arranging himself into his spot, he shot me a quick nervous glance, offering a facial message of "*Ouch!* I now know how you felt, brother!"

Carver got us moving. "Forward,___march!___Column right,___ march!" he shouted in a slow, very clear, very simple voice. His voice however, evidently conveyed that he was treating us as though we were simple-minded children on a Sunday school outing.

I could have understood that. I thought, and wondered why he didn't just speak plainly to begin with.

He managed to get the horde going to the right now, and with a second order to the right, we moved down the street a short distance past the intersection we had last turned onto Panama street from, before receiving our initial issue.

We were halted before another building, to our right, just a little way down and across the street from where we had just come from. We filed into this building and Gunnery Sergeant Carver informed us that we were to strip out of our clothing, wrap the towel we had drapped over our necks around our waists and bundle up our civvies. Each of us was given a box and a card to fill out with our home address. After we were issued our new clothing, we would pack our personal property in that box and that would end our last feelings of civilian individuality.

We were then told to form into lines in front of various tables, chairs or shelves where several Marines stood.

Once again there came that eerie parallel with Nazi death camps, where the prisoners were told to strip. After which, they were assured their personal belongings would be returned to them later. And finally they were ordered to fall into lines, which would either result in receiving an issue of work uniforms or an order to head toward the lethal gas showers. We at least felt confident there were no lethal gas chambers here.

The Marines working inside this building did not wear the campaign hats, nor the cartridge belt with large brass buckle and Marine Corps Emblem. They wore the green Marine Corps work uniform, referred to as utilities. These Marines were part of Headquarters and Supply Company (H&S Co.) on the Island.

The first line was for our skivvies issue.

Thank God we don't have to stand around in our birthday suits any longer. I thought with relief. Even though we were able to wrap a cotton towel around our waist, the feeling was sort of like awaiting a new beginning, like being born.

We were issued boxer type underwear, crew neck undershirts and green socks. The green socks were for wear with field boots. They felt very comfortable and were thick with an even thicker padded toe-and-heel section. The fresh new skivvies were also very comfortable. Looking down the rows of recruits, I noted that it was the first time we were all truly alike, with our shaved heads and uniform appearance in the white skivvies and green socks.

We got up on a table that had two foot scales for measuring our feet before issuing our boots.

"Size 9R." The Marine measuring foot sizes stated. Another Marine behind him threw a pair of boots at me, which were tied at the laces. I caught them, draped them across my neck as the others did and moved on to the next line.

Soon, I was measured for waist and head size and received three sets of utility trousers, with shirts and several green utility caps. The Marines issuing the utilities were calling out the various nomenclatures.

"Shirt,__ man's,__cotton."

"Trousers,__man's,__cotton."

"Cap,__utility,__cotton."

The uniforms were shiny in the light, severely wrinkled from box storage and they smelled of mothballs. The cap, referred to as a cover was all smashed and wrinkled as well. The visors of these covers were bent in all sorts of shapes, providing a real comical appearance of non-uniformity, however in a short time they would undergo a metamorphosis definitely creating uniformity.

I glanced at the white tag of the cover I was issued and read the combinations of words, letters and numbers.

CAP,UTILITY;COTTON
SATEEN, OG-107
DSA 100-73-C-0651
8405-285-2070
PROPPER INTERNATIONAL, INC.

Running up and down the five lines on the right side of the label was the word SMALL. On the front of the cover, centered, was a Marine Corps emblem stamped in black.

The Marines threw the utilities to the passing recruits with shouts of, "30,___34,___32,___you'll lean to wear them,___36,___go on,___ it'll fit you, you'll see fat-body!___Move on,___32."

Then we received khaki belts and brass buckles. We were told how to fasten them on to the belts, which were now much too long however, we were ordered to wear them as is. The result was a long section dangling off to the side, due to the uncut length of about ten or more inches extending from the buckle. We dressed as we went through the lines.

Next they issued us utility coats, called field jackets, but properly referred to as COAT, MAN'S, FIELD, OLIVE GREEN 107, M 1951, which were fifty percent cotton and fifty percent nylon. These field jackets were faded in many shades of green, due to their age, numerous washing and exposure to the elements. These were reissued to each incoming series of recruits.

As I laced up my new field boots and stood in line with these stiff boots, smooth, without the creases of wear, my thought was that it made us all look like the mannequins in a store. We were told to leave our trouser legs loose, hanging over our boots, button our top shirt buttons and to put on our field jackets and zip them all the way up.

To ensure we were properly attired, we were ordered up onto a two tiered bench, which held six recruits on each section. There was a step which led to the higher of the two bench platforms and the line of recruits were waiting their turn to step up. A Marine was pushing his thumb into the toe area of each recruit's boot to ensure a proper fit. He told us that improperly fitted boots could cause a recruit to sustain injuries during the rigorous training guaranteed at PI.

He then checked the utilities to ensure all excess lengths were properly rolled up, the belts were properly fastened, the shirts were buttoned all the way up and the sleeves and pockets were buttoned as well. Once the six recruits on the lower tier were checked, they would step off and the six on the upper tier would step down and their vacancy promptly filled by six more waiting in the long line.

We definitely looked different from the Marines in the room with us. They wore stiffly starched utilities, which were faded from numerous washings, giving them that salty look. They had their boots broken in and spit shined. Their utility trousers were bloused over their boots with an elastic device, which produced a bagged appearance. Their white crew neck undershirts looked like scarves behind the open collars of their utility shirts and their covers were starched with a dip or saddle fashioned from the front to the rear.

Compared to them, one learned where the term Joe-Shit-the-Rag-Man originated. We were him! We had finished stuffing the articles of clothing into a canvas sea bag and were starting to wonder what was next. Our curiosity was almost immediately answered.

"Form up outside!" Carver boomed, and herded us over to another part of the complex. However, this time with the weight of our newly issued gear stuffed into the sea bags along with the additional weight of the bulging white cotton bags, also stuffed into the sea bags. Carver had not allowed a minute of unused time, since he had jumped on that bus hours before.

We were walking along in route step, a sea of wrinkled green creatures forming odd curves to the left or right as our bodies protested in response to this new manner of walking while carrying a heavy sea bag. Our sense of balance was being challenged for the first time. We jerked and bobbed and staggered into the feet of the recruits in front of us. Walking in these very stiff field boots proved difficult as it was, as they also played their roll in making us appear awkward and clumsy.

FOUR

We were heading back to Panama Street and towards a large building, which was sensed before it was seen. The smell of eggs and bacon mixed with other hearty meal-time odors wafted its way into our nostrils.

You mean there is to be food for us, they really feed you here! I mused with a bit of criticism.

It was now nearly 0700 as we were soon to learn how to refer to the time. So far, with all the efforts by the Marine Corps to properly supply us our initial issue, the time up until now was forgotten. The method of issue was so smooth and so well organized, we had hardly any incident. That the shear size of our platoon required so little time to complete was amazing and a true tribute to organization.

As I recall, so far since leaving the Receiving Barracks, no recruit caused an outburst of anger or an explosive response from Carver. Even the two times we screwed-up on the turns, he had only barked. It seems we were either doing everything according to their wishes or Carver just figured he would have lost valuable time needed to get us through the issue phase and on to the mess hall for chow. We were also to learn that a cafeteria was referred to as a mess hall and food was referred to as chow. Thus chow time meant going to the mess hall to chow down. Our changing vocabulary was learned very quickly.

Carver ordered us to halt and then directed us to drop our gear in the grass, remember our exact spots in the formation, and to line up to the doors of the mess hall asshole-to-belly-button, take off our covers once we passed through the hatch, pick up a metal tray, place it in front of our face dropping it only at the beginning of the serving line and proceed down the serving line and on over to the tables, where Carver informed us he would be standing, waiting to seat us.

"Fall out!" Carver ordered. After a sloppy "Sir, yes Sir" was regretfully accepted by Carver, we proceeded up to the door of the mess hall, stood in line stuck together like a green snake and in turn picked up trays and side stepped down the serving line, much like we would have walked down a serving line in school. Only here we moved with stiff precison.

The food servers appeared amused as we walked by with trays extended. They mechanically dumped heaping ladles of food onto our trays as long as we held it out to them. They did not smile, nor speak, nor did they look at us directly. If we held our tray out over all the food available, we got all the food available. In other words, your tray would end up heaped to a considerable sloppy height. These servers were recruits who were serving their Mess and Maintenance duty week, which was part of the PI training criteria.

We went over to the tables Carver had pointed out. They were long tables joined together at their ends and there were long benches to sit on. There were hundreds more of these tables crammed with recruits in the cavernous building. They were the recruits already in training. With the exception of the sounds of eating utensils hitting the metal trays, the room was silent.

There were instructors, and other enlisted administrative Marines in work or dress uniforms sitting in a corner area of the mess hall. Their muted conversations were personal and further drowned out by the larger dissonant noises of the recruits chowing down.

A strange thing started to happen at this time. We came into the mess hall famished after the long trip and equally long sleepless night and through the goings-on of the initial issue. However, here we sat, with a pile of food in front of us, which it appeared we were all just picking at.

I glanced down the tables we sat at and could see the faces of the group I was with. They had transformed now into unrecognizable droids, with their hairless faces and heads. I had a hard time recognizing them from how they looked before. What a drastic change we had undergone in only a few hours. We had absolutely no way of knowing what a drastic change we all were to undergo by the time boot camp was over.

As I was looking at the recruits at my table, my eyes shot beyond them and focused on the tables of other recruits who were from various platoons in various stages of training. Some had a swath of short hair growing on the top part of their heads, while still sporting the shaved sides and back of their heads. These recruits, we would soon learn, were in their third phase of training, their final phase before graduating. They sat ramrod straight and put food from their plates to their mouths, instead of leaning sloppily over their plates and scooping the food a short distance to the mouth as our motley mob displayed.

Gunnery Sergeant Carver had told us to, "eat what you got!" So we sat perplexed now as we contemplated methods to dispose of our uneaten chow. The simpler way to deal with this problem was to just eat it. But no, that was the last possible desire. Drop it on the floor, as though it had fallen by accident. Yes, that was a possibility! No, not really, actually a very bad idea, because Carver would undoubtedly want us to get down and eat it off the floor.

Glancing up and down the tables, I could see no candidate to offer my food to, that is, there was no chow hound, as the Corps referred to a big eater, amongst those at our tables. No, that was not an option. But before I could think of another option Carver's voice boomed over the clatter of the mess hall.

"Fall out in the rear,___ladies!" Carver growled sounding re-energized and we were caught now with a big dilemma. What to do with our mountains of chow. There were scrambled eggs, along with toast, butter, grits, hash-brown potatoes, biscuits, sausage, grapefruit, and small cereal boxes to finish. Carver starred at us, but said only, "I said fall out in the rear,___scum-bags!"

As sure as he had been countless times before, when dealing with a fresh bunch of recruits, Carver was now aware of things we were not, and we proved no different. He knew we had no idea how to get the proper amount of food we needed for ourselves, onto our trays, without getting more than we could possibly eat. He knew the recruits on mess duty would automatically dispense more and more food the longer you lingered over their serving station. He even knew that the tradition of mess duty recruits was to pile it on to those first-day-arrivees. Why? They had already been there and knew the routines, which caused great anxiety for the FNGs. He was aware that the shock of this sudden change in the young men's routine resulted in initial loss of appetite, among other bodily changes.

Should an instructor wish to utilize this situation for shits and grins, he could have a field day on the recruits. Making recruits eat their chow directly off their tray like pigs eating slop was an Island favorite. Even so, Carver did not choose to, he had other apparent priorities. That meant we were excused to dump the food in the big garbage cans at the rear wall where we were to stack our trays and fall out back and regroup in our formation. However, we did not know this and did not presume we could nor dare to.

As I walked down the isles between the vast rows of tables, I heard several recruits make noises. *Pssst!* That sound caused me to glance at a recruit on the end of the table who looked up to me with his empty tray in both hands, which he held up over the table, about six inches. His head slightly jerked several times toward his tray, while his eyebrows arched. He whispered through clenched teeth, without moving his lips.

"Dump it here or switch trays!"

I was momentarily startled. But, glancing ahead, I had noticed other recruits were engaged in similar exchanges all the way up the isle.

I quickly shoved my food laden tray toward him with one hand and snatched up his empty tray with the other hand, all in one motion.

By the time we got to the rear of the mess hall, many of us had empty trays to drop into the rectangle opening in the wall, where a mess duty recruit was receiving the dirty trays. Those other recruits busily wolfed down the chow we traded off, as starving men would when relief arrived.

We did not know yet, that a recruit could not simply get up, walk back over to the serving line and refill his tray. We would also quickly learn, once our training started, that our appetites would equal those of the recruits who had waylaid our food before it hit the dumpster. Without knowing it, this exchange and chow grabbing episode was our first practical application of adapt, overcome and improvise, a valuable ingredient in a Marine. Carver and other drill instructors may have witnessed this slight of hand, but because this was a very important ingredient in making us into Marines, it was apparently accepted.

FIVE

Once again, we were formed into ranks at the rear of the mess hall. Gunnery Sergeant Carver hustled us over to where we had previously stowed our gear before entering the mess hall.

"Pick up yer gear!" Carver bellowed out and then followed with, "Aah____ten____huat!____Foart,____huah!" he grunted, sounding out the *huah* from deep inside his gut, and off we surged, in a great disorganized wave of wrinkled green.

Our field jacket collars each sprouted individualistic designs, since we were required to zip and button them all the way up. Due to their wrinkly condition, from being tightly crammed in storage boxes, the collars appeared very unmilitary as they twisted around the back of the neck or the tips of the collars alternately curled upward or downward. The appearance of our apparel was made more comical by the even more wrinkled utilities, especially the utility covers, which were so new and bent and wrinkled that they literally topped off the effect.

We were marched, if one could have called it that, down Boulevard de France, toward another group of white painted two story barrack style buildings, which were on our right. I could see a sign in front of these buildings identifying them as Medical and Dental facilities and beyond those were the regimental headquarters buildings. Upon nearing an exterior stair section of the medical building, which accessed the second floor, we were ordered to halt.

"Drop yer gear in place and fall out in a single file headin' up those stairs!" Carver ordered, while pointing towards the stairs, "As before, in columns starting with the left,___move out!"

At the top, the door was already propped open. A man stood there, wearing a white smock type shirt over khaki uniform trousers, which rested on top of shiny black dress shoes. This man started giving us orders now. He had a short military hair cut, with a small flip in the front. His hair was almost black on top, with the sides appearing as salt and pepper, with thick framed black eye glasses separating his hair from his cleanly shaven, however, obviously heavy bearded face. His mouth, scarce lipped, was pulled down at the edges and was enclosed by deep parenthesis shaped creases, about one inch from the corners. His nose was straight, with a sharp point.

He looks like Mr. Mitchell___Dennis the Menaces' father, in the comics. I thought. Overall, though, he appeared professional and no-nonsense.

"Alright!____Listen to me!" he said with a calm but authoritative voice. "My name is Commander Walsh.____You will fall into the adjoining room,___strip down to your skivvies and wait for instructions as to where you will go next!" He simply pointed and our long file darted up the stairs and forward into the designated room.

We were then told by a Navy corpsman to carry our uniforms with us to each station we go through. There were many sailors in the area. They wore heavy looking dark blue uniforms with pullover shirts with open vee shaped necks over white crew neck undershirts. These pullover shirts, with their traditional flaps draped over their backs, hung loose over bell-bottom trousers, which sprouted rows of buttons up each side of the front. The bells were so large, they only allowed the toes of the corpsman's shiny black dress shoes to be exposed.

The pants looked to be a bitch to wear when you had to take a leak in a hurry. I chuckled to myself.

On their left sleeves they wore their rating, over which was the medical symbol, the caduceus. A black name tag with white lettering was pinned high over their right breast. All medical and dental requirements were provided by the Navy, as there are no such personnel in the Marine Corps.

One of the corpsman, a short heavy built chief petty officer, started writing numbers on each of our chests and the back of our right hand with a marker pen. Once again, there was that parallelism with Nazi death camp processing procedures. Again, the feeling of loss of self, due to this despotic series of events we were all undergoing. We were only numbers to these men in uniform.

Little did we think at the time of our processing, that it was a ritual all personnel had to undergo when they had transitioned from civilian life to military life. The corpsman scrawled the number twenty-seven on my scrawny chest and then pointed to the line ahead, indicating I must go there to start my physical examination.

As I stood in line waiting for my blood pressure to be taken, I noticed, for what seemed to be the first time, that the majority of these boys were also skinny, with shoulder blades jutting out, ribs visible and underdeveloped pectoral muscles. White, Black, Hispanic, Indian, it didn't matter, because with few exceptions, they all appeared to look alike. There were a few jock types, boys who had a head start on body development. As with any gathering of many human beings, there will surely be the occasional fat person, and we had a few here. There was one in particular, with the number fifty-seven dancing in and out of the fatty folds of a very flabby chest.

Hell, that boy has tits! I chuckled inwardly.

Fifty-seven was orange haired and very fat, with so many cellulite dimples, it appeared one was looking across the surface of the moon. His skin was as white as snow, with red rashes scattered about.

Within the many ranges of rashes, there were scabs and purple scab scars, from the past, where he had obviously habitually scratched those nasty looking red bumps. Fifty-seven was so out of shape that his huge, over six foot high body, spilled downward over its frame in ripples and folds of grotesque red dotted ivory fat. His huge gut hung low over his skivvies offering no evidence of a naval, his knees buckled inward, always rubbing each other. The legs were hideous shapeless logs. His splay-footed posture noticeably caused the corpsman, doctors and recruits alike to display trepidation, as if fifty-seven were contagious. His recruiter was either responding to an ass chewing for not making his required quota or he was pissed off for not getting an expected promotion and laughed his ass off when he sent this great white pear to PI.

This trepidation was most evident when the recruits immediately in front and behind fifty-seven were forced to touch him when Carver suddenly ordered everyone to close up the line asshole-to-belly-button, while we were proceeding through the physical examination. Because Carver was momentarily displeased with something he had reacted with that request. The result of that order is that all bodies are meshed together so tightly that ones chin rested on top of or up against the head in front of him.

The physical examination was very thorough.

These doctors were acting as though they were distrustful of the AFEES examination results. I thought.

However, these examinations not only catch any new developments since our AFEES exams, they also ensured each of us was fit for the rigid training we were to undergo here on the Island. As we went through each station, a corpsman or doctor wrote something in the folder we each carried with us. The chief who had started us off into these lines had provided each of us with a manila folder. These folders ended up filled with considerably more medical information records about each of us at the end of our physicals, than AFEES had initially compiled.

A doctor listened to our hearts and lungs with a stethoscope, checked our blood pressure, then poked, prodded, tapped, peered, pinched and otherwise scrutinized every inch of our bodies. Judging from the variety of facial expressions the doctor made, one would think he found a rare disease, a nasty fungus, a questionable ailment or was just plain unhappy that he could not find a reason to classify anyone unfit for military service.

Two corpsmen were stationed opposite one another, with just enough space for the width of a recruit's shoulders to fit. Each corpsman held a gun-like device in his right hand. The gun was designed to hold a serum vial, upside down, stuck onto the center of the top of the device. Attached to the bottom of the gun butt were two black hoses. These were pneumatic guns, for the rapid dispensing of a series of inoculations.

We were to receive influenza, polio virus, typhoid, plague, tetanus toxoid, small-pox, cholera, yellow feaver and tuburculin PPD vaccines at the Immunization Section.

As we waited, still crammed asshole-to-bellybutton in this line, my turn came. Up to this point, I had scarcely heard the pneumatic *tsch-poof, tsch-poof* of the injection guns. When I stood between the two corpsman, I heard Carver screaming at someone at first and then at everybody in one long exclamation.

"Shut the fuck up!___Lock your lips____and tighten up those lines!"

Now that order created another problem. When the recruits behind me tightened, with Carver's forceful hand shoving them, it happened.

"*Ouch!*" I silently hissed out between clenched teeth. The line had been jostled forward and into my back, as a result of Carver's shoving. At that precise moment I heard *tsch-poof* simultaneously, causing a neat half inch slice across both sides of my upper arms. The corpsmen simply passed me on and injected the next recruit.

Blood started to ooze down both of my arms. Not a lot, but enough to make it sloppy. It started to bead out of the slits and than slowly slid down my arms a couple of inches and there was a burning, stinging sensation.

Apparently, another corpsman noticed it, and came over to observe it a little more closely. He departed and returned shortly with a couple of cotton swabs, soaked with alcohol, wiped the areas and placed a bandage over each cut.

Damned nice of him! I thought, because I did not expect anyone to care. I said absolutely nothing.

As the physical continued, we eventually entered a large room. It was apparently an empty barrack, designed like the other barrack rooms we had been in since arriving. However, the others were furnished with tables, work stations and other equipment, making the rooms appear smaller. This barrack was empty, and opened into what seemed to be a cavernous area, when anyone first walked into it. We were ordered to line up in two rows of approximately forty five recruits to a row.

A very sturdy looking woman, about five feet tall, walked into the room. She wore a long white medical coat over which a stethoscope was dangling. The stethoscope was clamped around her stumpy neck. She had short, wire bristle, grey hair, a double chin propping up a small pouting mouth which was surrounded by fat sausage-like lips. Above which sat an acne scarred bulbous nose that divided two equally acne scarred puffy cheeks. The wide spaced eyes were washed out grey blue and bugged out with thick folds of skin surrounding and restraining each orb, clearly attempting to prevent them from popping out.

She is one butt-ugly woman! I winced and laughed inwardly.

Yellow Footprints

She was also the doctor in charge. When she had walked toward the center of the double file of recruits, she stopped, looked at us for what seemed a long time, as if she wanted us to absorb her ugliness. Watching her, I was suddenly aware that she may be ugly, but she also looked professional, really military. Those waxy, pock marked cheeks started to move up and down as she addressed us.

"My name is Captain Hellick!" she said in a raspy voice, "You in the back row will take six steps backwards and turn around!"

"Move it!" Carver's ever present voice sounded. The row behind me could be heard stepping backwards now, in a series of footsteps. There was to be no success at military uniformity by our herd this day.

There were several corpsmen standing with Captain Hellick. They each held items, which Hellick would require to perform this phase of our physical. One held a large jar of Vaseline, while the other carried a box of rubber gloves and a small trash can.

"Okay girls,___drop yer skivvies,___bend over, an' spread yer cheeks wide.____Ya heah?" Carver's voice came across with a staccato that ended in a low 'ya' and a higher long drawn 'heah', of course meaning 'you hear'? Carver left the room after that.

Snap...snap! The sound of Hellick's rubber gloves cracked through the stale barrack air. I waited for what I thought was an eternity for her little inspection group to reach number twenty-seven and also wished it would take them longer to get to me, when they arrived. Then I felt Hellick's lubricated finger slide up my rectum. Her finger moved around as if searching, for what I did not know, nor care. I prayed for her leave me immediately and go to the next recruit.

Gawd! How humiliating! My mind acted out the body shake of disgust that my physical body dared not do here and I thought not unlike the others, I'm sure. *Hellick was no Ear, Nose and Throat doctor, that's for damn sure.* On went the sound of *snap...snap!*

"Stand up straight for now!" One of the pair of corpsman told each of us as she finished. It was a long wait before we heard Hellick suddenly speak out.

"Listen up!___You will once again drop your skivvies and wait for your Gamma-Globulin shot!"

She must live for these recruit physicals. I decided.

Again, we waited for the arrival of her unwelcome visit to our rear. As time passed, I received my awaited visit. Hellick shoved the syringe into my left buttock muscle and it felt as though she had also whacked it as it hung there, deeply embedded into the muscle.

Uggaahh! My mind sounded the sensation slowly, as if the mental comment would ease the strange pain. Then the syringe was withdrawn with a sting to remember the needle by. However, the sting was a welcome memory compared to the deep aching, throbbing this hideous injection created almost immediately in the muscle.

Her next act required us to drop shorts once again as she cupped our balls and had us turn our head to the side and cough, as she checked for hernias.

When Hellick had finished one of the corpsman left the room, apparently to inform Carver.

Gunnery Sergeant Carver entered the room again. He went over to the captain and spoke silently to her. She responded back to him and he nodded his head once. Carver appeared to have actually stood at attention when he spoke to the Navy doctor. He made an about face, as smooth as a well oiled door hinge, and walked toward our two files.

Maybe he's afraid she'll do the same thing to him she did to us. I observed wryly.

"You in the rear file,____turn around and face me.____Now!" he barked, than loudly shouted, "Aah___ten___huat!"

There we stood, for what seemed to be more than fifteen minutes. Carver had gone away again, apparently finishing business somewhere. He returned at length and I for one hoped he would order at ease! However, no such luck, and we were definitely unaccustomed to standing still for such a period of time.

Suddenly, there was a sound, a heavy thud, which sounded like a large slab of meat being thrown down. I glanced a little to my far right just in time to see orange hair. It was fifty-seven, the fat slob.

"Alright, get yer eyes to the front!" Carver shouted with intense aggravation and stormed over to where fifty-seven lay motionless.

"Git on yer feet this fuckin' second,___you miserable,___ugly,___ fat piece ah whale shit!___Git up, I said!____Ya fell the wrong way,___ if yer tryin' to fake passin' out!" Carver's voice exploded louder than ever before. As if fifty-seven were poked with a hot iron in that fat ass of his, he jerked himself off the floor and stood all the way up.

"God!___Look at chu.____How did you ever get this far,___you fat slime-body?___I bet you sucked your recruiter's dick!___Didn't you?" Carver spit the words out like poison darts, "Get yer ugly fat-assed carcas out of my sight this fuckin' second, numb-nuts,____move it!"

Fifty-seven started running along the barrack wall, with absolutely no idea where he was supposed to go. He was bounding blindly as Carver went after him screaming.

"Get the fuck outta my Marine Corps!___What are you anyway,___a fuckin' draftee cock-sucker____huh?"

Fifty-seven took clumsy large strides, which caused his body to jiggle like jello. His face wore a mask of sheer fright. He moved along the walls in abject fear, appearing oblivious to us all, except for Carver.

A corpsman came into the room. He was the Vaseline dispenser from before. Carver called him over, not unkindly, and in the same moment shouted toward fifty-seven.

"Get yer sloshy ass over here maggot, and go with this corpsman!___ Wait a fuckin' minute asshole,___what's yer fuckin' name?" Carver demanded causing spittle to fly from his mouth.

"Bu-bullock, Jeffrey!" fifty-seven stammered.

Carver just glared at him and walked away saying, "The corpsman knows what to do with disgusting fat bodies like you!___Get out of my sight Heinz fifty-seven!"

The corpsman escorted fifty-seven through the door and as Carver had requested, away from here.

He never returned to our platoon.

"Alright, you listen up now!" Carver's voice came across as if nothing had just happened.

"Get dressed, make a head call, then fall out to where yer gear was stowed!____Got it girls?"

A few seconds ticked by and Carver blew up again. "I did not hear an affirmative to my last order,____sweet-peas!____What are ya s'posed ta say when I give an order?"

"Sir, yes Sir!" our pitiful mob chorused a sporadic response loudly.

We dressed quickly, took a quick piss and in groups of fives, sixes or more, ran to the exit, only to scrunch ourselves in the doorjamb in our frantic attempt to expeditiously do what Carver had ordered.

We were starting to pick up on the subtle decrease in Carver's acceptance of our unmilitary behavior and his definite increase in swift corrective action.

SIX

Gunnery Sergeant Carver walked out of a lower level door of the barracks we had just been in. He stopped a few yards from the door and surveyed our formation. Shaking his head slowly from right to left several times, Carver continued walking toward us. This time he had a hard faced appearance. As he came up to the center of the third column, which faced the barracks, he snapped.____Did any of you hear me tell you to pick up yer gear?"

From my vantage point at the rear of the first column, I could see what Carver was pissed at. A large number of recruits had picked up their sea bags and I was luckily not one of them.

Carver shouted over our heads, while he simultaneously moved his head side to side. "Ah will let you in on a bit of advice.____Ah have already told you once this morning.____In this Marine Corps you don't do a goddamn thang during training lessin' ya hear it from ah s'perior first.____Got that?"

"Sir, yes Sir!" we all responded loudly but out of kilter. Although our ability to sound off as one was still sorely inadequate, he let it ride. It would take much more than one day to achieve what requires an intuitive timing capability.

Hell, no doubt they'll expect us to sound-off perfectly by tomorrow. I was thinking.

"Now, those of you who are holding yer gear, drop it!" Carver continued loudly. Those who held sea bags dropped them on the ground by their feet.

"That's better.____Now pick up yer gear!" he bawled as soon as those recruits who had just that second straightened out. They resembled trees being whipped by a strong wind as we screamed out our affirmative response in between their actions.

"Aah____ten____huat!" Carver bellowed.

"Foart,____huah!" The next order came deep from the gut. And once again we surged forward, no less sloppy than as before and headed down Boulevard de France. We hadn't gone more than ten yards when Carver sounded off with, "Callam____let,____huah!"

Yellow Footprints

We actually reacted to that order with a fairly uniform response.

"Callum___ret,___huah!" Carver barked again and the same process as a moment before was acted out. We were now headed back up Boulevard de France toward Panama Street. There was one sea bag, which had remained on the grass.

"Ah declare, you hogs are pickin' up the drill," Carver said, with genuine surprise.

"Most times___arrivees spend the first couple a days like a mess ah spaghetti,___gettin' their legs all tangled up."

It would appear that the Marine Corps prefers a snappy response and demands an immediate obedience, offering no delay, as if one would be foolish enough to doubt or hesitate. Like a mess of spaghetti, hell, that's not a bad analogy of how we must appear to him. I thought. So, he actually said we had done something right.

I kept up with the cue ball, sticking out from under the wrinkled green cover, in front of me and tried to stay aligned as best I could. Carver, up ahead, was counting cadence.

"Let,___let,___yer let, hiat, let." The sonorous chant repeated over and over.

As we approached Panama Street, Carver ordered a turn.

"Callum___ret,___huah!" Our columns made the turn even better than the last execution. We were learning, but only a little.

Gunnery Sergeant Carver maneuvered us near the mess hall and called us to a halt.

"Drop yer gear in place and in columns, starting from the right, fall into the mess hall.___Move it!" he shouted in a tired sounding voice.

We formed up in line asshole-to-belly-button and proceeded into the building, grabbed metal trays, eating utensils and side-stepped down the chow line.

The Marine Corps refers to food as chow, so time to eat is chow time and therefore, to sit down to eat is to chow down. My mind rehearsed.

Once again, we were loaded up, as though we were at a smorgasbord, although still involuntarily. We had yet to learn the tactics of chow time. As we were led by Carver to the area we were to be seated, we once again passed recruits in various phases of their training. They were scarfing-up their chow the way puppies tear into their food, fearing that to delay may result in the loss of that food. Of course we were no more capable of eating now than earlier that morning.

As soon as we were finished trying to eat, we fell into formation
Gunnery Sergeant Carver came out and called us to attention and then ordered us to pick up our gear. This time nobody had screwed-up by picking up their sea bags before being ordered to do so by Carver.

"Callum___let,___huah!" Carver maneuvered our mothball-smelling raggedy mob left toward the road, then right and down the road toward Boulevard de France. He then ordered a column left and we were pointed toward the main parade field, the meat grinder. As we approached the parade field, I saw the large bronze monument of five Marines raising the U.S. flag over Mount Suribachi on Iwo Jima, which was positioned in the grassy area between the boulevard and the parade deck.

I could see white two story barracks at the far side of the parade field. They appeared very far away. These barracks were identical to the barracks we had passed while marching through 2nd battalion earlier that morning. Behind these barracks was marsh and further out I could only see water.

A group of drill instructors, in dress uniform, were standing near the monument as we marched up to their location. Carver ordered us to halt. All of a sudden the other drill instructors converged on our platoon shouting.

"Move it out!___Move it!___Double time across the parade field!___Get your asses in gear!___Now shit-heads!" Their commands were all jumbled, loud and urgent. However, one thing was clear and that was they were seriously intent on getting us across the meat grinder.

What the hell?___I thought Carver was in charge of us.___Who the hell are these guys? My mind questioned, as surely every one of us did at that moment.

Carver was also shouting now, leaving no hope that he would object to the others telling us what to do. We were literally assaulted by these drill instructors. They ran straight into our ranks shouting orders, while pushing and shoving recruits and pointing in the direction of the old white barracks across the meat grinder. They herded us recruits like cowboys herding cattle while whistling, prodding, pushing, kicking and tripping recruits into a panic-run.

We ran hard in the general direction of those old white barracks. Which one of them was ours, was still a mystery to us. Recruits slammed hard into the rough surface of the meat grinder as they tripped over others who had fallen in front or to the side of them. Brand new boots were suddenly deeply scuffed, while wrinkly new utility trousers and shirts were rent with rips and tears.

We wobbled unsteadily as we ran with the weight of the sea bags, which yanked us down when we tripped, as though an anchor was tied around our neck and had been cast overboard.

The drill instructors purposefully kept us in a tight group. This had added to the difficulty for us to run, while keeping our gear on our shoulders and of course delighted the DIs. While the slower recruits tripped most of us up, the DIs tripped the rest, making sure none of us escaped falling down during this first gauntlet. Two recruits on each side of me crashed forward, one fell on top of his sea bag and the other fell under his.

The meat grinder was an immense surface. It took a long time to run across in general and under these circumstances it felt like an eternity. I ran hard, straining under the awkward weight of the bulky sea bag, first dropping to my right knee as my outstretched arm met the wall of resistance of the mass of recruits in front as they buckled and fell over those in front of them. And then I fell over several recruits who veered into my forward momentum. There was no possibility to escape the inevitable, because the pressing recruits to our rear crashed into us.

The DIs screamed curses at us while we slammed into each other, or the deck, all the way across the meat grinder. I caught glimpses of recruits who fell and lay there in shock as two and sometimes three DIs bent over them screaming "Get up cock-sucker!___C'mon wimp!___ Move yer ass!___*Aahooorrraahh!*"

I had fallen, only to get up and fall again. I slammed my face into the rough texture of somebody's sea bag and than I tripped over a recruit and slammed into several others as they in turn rolled over obstacles to their front. My shoulder slid down the wall of recruits to my right and before I hit the deck others surged into my right, lifting me and throwing me to my left. I was desperately clutching my sea bag in fear that should I drop it, they would tear me a new asshole.

Madness!___How can they do this to American citizens? My mind exploded the thought, while I tried not to fall and be trampled or get beaten by these maniacs. I recalled our lesson during my stay at the Children's Home. *Soren Kierkegaard held that truth is subjectivity, therefore, man's relationship to God requires suffering.* These Drill Instructors appeared to be devoutly intent on carrying out Kierkegaard's beliefs!

This was every recruits unfortunate dilemma however, it was even worse for those who gave up or fell under the trampling feet of the stampeding herd and were singled out for special treatment by the DIs.

"Pick it up! Pick up your fucking gear numb-nuts. Ya don't ever drop your gear in this Marine Corps. Ah said pick it the fuck up!" one of the DIs bellowed at a recruit somewhere to our rear. It was during this insane stampede that my mind started to question my decision to be here.

What the hell have I done, this was a big mistake, why the hell did I join the Marine Corps? How can anybody make it through this madness? I must have died and gone to hell! My mind was stuck in replay and this thought played over and over.

We were finally in front of a building, herded toward one of the barrack doors and injected into the first floor. The DIs screamed instructions that we were to line up two to a rack. The racks, or bunk beds, were lined up in two rows of about fifty sets on each side of the large room. With our asses dragging, our bodies aching and our breath long lost on the meat grinder we sought out a bunk and each of us stood dripping sweat on the painted line we were ordered to stand on. There was a line painted on each side of the squad bay, which ran from end to end in front of our bunk beds.

Some of the DIs, who had herded us across the parade field, departed the barracks along with Gunnery Sergeant Carver, without saying another word.

CHAPTER 3
THE MENTORS

ONE

There were three of them. They slowly walked down the length of the barrack squad bay, their bodies ramrod straight, their campaign hats tilted forward at a sharp angle, which rested just above their eyes. They wore full dress uniforms with neat razor sharp creases. Their blouses adorned with rows of campaign ribbons and firearms qualification medallions over their left breast pockets. The one in front, a gunnery sergeant, was the senior drill instructor. As he walked, he was trailed by the two assistant drill instructor sergeants (ADI). The gunnery sergeant and one of the ADIs wore scowls on their faces. As they passed, they eyed each recruit. We were lined up, facing inward along both sides of the squad bay. When they had reached the end of the squad bay they all pivoted, as if on silent command, and started their return walk.

Our barracks were white painted wooden two floor constructions. We were on the first floor. They were old, obviously built during World War II. The squad bay was lighted by rows of windows and florescent lights hanging from the ceiling. The floor was wood, worn white from thousands of recruits scrubbing it over the years. There were wood support posts at intervals running along both sides of the room, leaving a walkway down the length of the squad bay approximately ten feet wide. Between the inside walls and each row of support posts were metal bunk beds, with two wooden footlockers underneath the lower bunk of each set. Four bladed fans, spaced approximately every ten feet along the length of the barrack were suspended from the ceiling.

Slowly rotating their propeller-like blades, they only served to circulate the fetid, stagnant, suffocating, hot humid air of the Island.

Our sweating bodies were shakily standing at attention, even with the rows of wooden posts on each side, with sea bags slung, by their straps, from our right shoulders, while our minds were banging at the hatches to get the hell out of this place.

"My name is Gunnery Sergeant Bishop,__I am the senior drill instructor of Platoon 3063,__this platoon,__your Platoon,____I am your senior drill instructor,__you will refer to me as Sir,__I do not want to hear you filthy sewers refer to me as sarge,____gunny,____Sergeant Bishop,____or in any other way except Sir._____Do I make myself clear?" he lectured us with very loud, sharp, stern and precisely sounded words.

"Sir, yes Sir!" we chorused raggedly.

"As of this moment,____if you maggots don't start sounding off like you got a set of balls,___you will definitely regret the error.____Do you understand my meaning?" Bishop bawled the threat menacingly.

"Sir, yes Sir!" we managed a much improved response.

"This is Staff Sergeant Rogers, one of my assistant drill instructors", Bishop motioned with a sweep of his open hand to the right, while his elbow and upper arm were held vertically along his side, "and this is Sergeant Kranz, my other assistant drill instructor." Bishop moved the same hand back to the left, indicating Kranz. Neither assistant drill instructor made any indication acknowledging the introduction.

Bishop was a muscular black man, in his early thirties, standing approximately five foot ten, with a shiny mahogany skin tone, sienna irises suspended in very white eyeballs sunk deep underneath prominent eyebrows, muscular cheeks exhibiting ridges, full dark lips surrounding straight white teeth, which revealled a diastema, a space between the front teeth, above that was a wide flat nose with wide flared nostrils and below the mouth was a rounded chin centering a muscular jaw.

Sergeant Kranz was white, slightly shorter than Bishop, hazel-eyed with puffy cheeks, which were pulled down and wrapped together in a cleft chin. There were deep lines originating from the side of his bulbous nose at the nostrils, which connected with the corners of an upper lip, which had no more definition then a piece of modeling clay rolled to the size of a pencil and curved with a close copy for the lower lip.

Staff Sergeant Rogers was also white, about six feet tall, with a finely featured, slightly thin, face enclosing sad eyes, which pulled downward on each side of his face. His appearance was more like a high school quarterback with his straight narrow nose and a mouth, which was a combination of a slightly thin upper lip with a pronounced U shape in the center and a medium sized lower lip over a jutting square jaw.

Bishop continued his introduction speech. "During your training here at Parris Island, my assistants and I will be your mother, your father, your guardian and your only concern in life will be to ensure you meet your training expectations___and that during this training you do not piss us off,___because achieving that will ensure all of you will be punished for any one recruit's mistake.___You do not have an identity here,___you are all equally whale shit, the lowest form of scum on the bottom of the ocean.___Training on the island will be the hardest test of your lives.___There are several ways to leave this island.___In disgrace as an undesirable fuck-up, medically unfit, or as a Marine.___When you are addressed by a drill instructor, you will keep your faggotty eyes six inches over their heads or centered on their chest___and under no circumstances will you dare look directly at a drill instructor.___When you are reporting to the drill instructors shack, you will stand at attention with your left shoulder to the left side of the hatch and swing your arm,___with right palm open,___over your head and slap the bulkhead three times, loudly.___Under no circumstances will you ever use the words I or you,___because___here you will always refer to yourselves in the third person as the recruit.___ Do you understand me?"

"Sir, yes Sir!" we chorused loudly.

"This morning you were all issued a combination lock,___which I want you to retrieve from your sea bag.___Drop your sea bag and start digging now.___Move it!" Bishop barked.

"Sir, yes Sir!" we bellowed somewhat uniformly and immediately dug into our sea bags trying to find the elusive device.

"Any day girls!" Bishop snapped impatiently. Sergeants Rogers and Kranz were moving along the squad bay goading individual recruits to move faster.

Within about a minute all of us were standing on line, hopefully with our combination lock in hand.

"You girls are already pissing me off.___You move like you got rocks in your pockets.___Now hold out your combination locks in your right hand!" Bishop snarled. The DIs checked down the line to verify that each recruit not only found their combination lock, but also held it in their right hand.

There was a combined barrage of attacks as each DI discovered a non-compliant recruit.

"Where's yer lock shit-fer-brains?____Find it asshole!___Now!"

"Don't cha know your left hand from your right?____Gawd!____ What are you holding your fucking hand out for,___air-head,___if you don't have anything in it?"

"What the fuck do you have your arm raised in the air for,___you stupid fuck?____You think you're in school here?" Gunnery Sergeant Bishop bawled at a white recruit I'd noticed earlier and thought was a football jock. The recruit was tall and muscular.

"Sir, I just wanted to know if I could do some push-ups and just sort of loosen up a little... ."

"Shut your holy mother-fucking mouth you ignorant fucking piece of shit!____I can't believe you could be so goddamned stupid!____You think I'm your coach or something.____You know where you are___ brainless?____And what the hell are you referring to yourself as I for,___dick-head?____Drop your sorry ass down on the deck this damn second and start counting push-ups.____Do it!"

The recruit dropped to the deck and started cranking out push-ups. While he was in the process Bishop asked, "What's your name stupid?"

The recruit shouted back between puffs, "Recruit Tillman Sir!" after he had already done about fifteen push-ups.

"Don't you know you're supposed to stand at attention when you address a drill instructor asshole?" Bishop continued his attack.

Tillman stopped doing push-ups and stood up.

"Did I tell you to stop doing push-ups,___idiot?" Bishop snapped. "Get your ass back down on the deck!"

Tillman responded and continued doing push-ups.

"Don't you know the proper response to an order is aye-aye Sir,___ slime-ball?"

This time Tillman stayed down and continued doing push-ups.

"I'm talking to you asshole!" Bishop growled.

Tillman was as confused as ever at this point, as he was not told to stop and get up, yet he was also unable to get up to properly respond to Bishop.

"I can't hear you counting fuck-head!___Start over at one!" By now Tillman had already done approximately forty push-ups.

"One__two__three." Tillman counted off.

"That's one, Sir,__two, Sir,__got it shit-head?" Bishop attacked once again.

This time Bishop placed his foot on Tillman's back and ordered him to start counting.

Tillman could no longer move, except for his head and a little of his upper chest. He strained and grunted deeply while the veins in his neck and head throbbed and stood out nearly bursting. He was crimson red and soaked with sweat.

Bishop moved his foot off and said, "Continue from one___sweet-pea!____Let this be a lesson to you not to kiss ass and try to impress me that you think you are already fit and don't need my Marine Corps training,___because one thing I can promise all of you is that you never dreamed how much you will be required to achieve during boot camp training and until this day what you pussies thought was hard wasn't shit to me!___Do you understand me maggots?"

"Sir, yes Sir!" we screamed in shocked terror.

"Get up Tillman!" Bishop ordered.

"Sir, aye-aye Sir!" Tillman shouted and gladly stood up. He was woozy, light headed, red-faced and sweat poured down his face.

By now the ADIs had ensured that every recruit had a combination lock in their hand.

"Alright ladies,___I want you to read your combinations,___which are attached to your locks and memorize the combination, you have twenty seconds.___Start memorizing!"

We stood there staring at the combination cards and as sure as I was feeling that if any one of us was wrong, hell would break out for all of us, and I hoped all of us were thinking the same.

"Times up!" Bishop barked loudly. "Place your combination cards on your racks and take your locks and attach them to the foot lockers under your racks.__That's bunk beds to you__girls!___Do it!"

"Sir, aye-aye Sir!" we responded and scrambled back between our racks, and creating a cacophony of sounds, attached our locks. No sooner had we succeeded in attaching the locks, Bishop ordered us back on line in front of our racks.

"You will have thirty seconds to retrieve your locks and hold them in your right hand.___Move it!"

Again we broke from our positions on line and with much banging and scraping we attacked our locks.

"Get your asses back on line!" Bishop demanded.

We rushed to the line, while at the same moment, Staff Sergeant Rogers and Sergeant Kranz came down the line grabbing any recruit who had either failed to obtain his lock or had sloppily left his footlocker askew between the racks. Any recruit who was grabbed was also yanked forward into the center of the squad bay. There were about seventeen recruits who were caught in the round-up and luckily I was not among them.

Each recruit was taken on by whichever DI had finished with a recruit they had chewed out before them. They were screamed at with demands to get their combination cards and hand them to whichever DI had issued the order. They were then required to recite their combination numbers and then run and open their lockers, of course this time properly placing the locker back under the rack. We went through this drill four more times until Gunnery Sergeant Bishop felt we were able to do it without incident for the remaining training period. He collected all the combination cards and threw them in the trash. He then decided we needed a reward for our achievement.

"You are the slowest bunch of hogs I have ever put through training.___Because it took you so damn long to learn the simple task of memorizing your combination lock numbers I have decided to treat you to something guaranteed to help you remember.___Grab your foot lockers and place them on end to your right side, locks facing outboard.___Move it!"

"Sir, aye-aye Sir!" we blurted and scrapped and scuffed, grabbing our footlockers from their niche under our bunk beds and rebounded onto the white line.

"Ah___ten___huat!" bawled Gunnery Sergeant Bishop.

We snapped our bodies straight however, we were still unable to do it as one perfect unit.

"When I say port arms,___you will bring your footlocker up and hold it in front of your chest at an angle approximately forty five degrees.____That is from the right hip to the left shoulder and support the upper part of the footlocker with the left hand.____Do you understand me?"

"Sir, yes Sir!" we chorused sloppily.

"When I order left shoulder arms,____you will push your footlocker leftwards with your right hand, while maneuvering it up onto your shoulder with your left hand, smartly dropping your right hand to the seam of your trouser leg,____and repeat this movement in reverse for right shoulder arms!" we raggedly stammered our affirmative.

"Port,____harms!" Gunnery Sergeant Bishop ordered loudly.

There was a real cluster-fuck of footlockers crashing onto the floor and recruits bending sideways under the clumsy and awkward size of these boxes, which were about three feet long by one and a half feet wide and one and a half feet deep. Other recruits were bending forward to either catch their elusive boxes or to attempt picking them up quickly before a DI saw their accident. Whatever we thought we were attempting, we were not impressing Gunnery Sergeant Bishop.

"Stop!____Stop!____Get your footlocker and your clumsy asses back on the line now!" Gunnery Sergeant Bishop bellowed and we obliged.

"One more time.____Ah____ten____huat,____port harms!" he ordered.

Once again there were gyrations by many recruits, however many other accomplished a smoother movement. This time there were only three boxes crashing to the deck.

"If I hear one more footlocker hit the deck, you will be doing push-ups from now till hell freezes.____Do you get my drift girls!" Gunnery Sergeant Bishop said in a monotone of disgust. "And, for those who don't know what a deck is, it's what you're standing on. Before you ever leave this island you will have fallen on, marched on, crawled on, sweat on, bled on, slept on, puked on, hugged and cleaned the deck a hundred thousand times."

"Let's try it again and this time, do not even think about dropping your footlocker.____Ready girls?" he inquired, while looking up and down the squad bay, talking as he walked and again boomed. "Ah____ten____huat!____Poart,____harms!"

Not one footlocker fell to the deck and fewer recruits gyrated during the execution.

"Right shoulder,___harms!___Left shoulder,___harms!___Port,___harms!" We continued this 'manual-of-boxes', instead of 'manual-of-arms', for twenty minutes until Gunnery Sergeant Bishop suddenly ordered us to place them back under our bunks and grab our sea bags.

"For your sloppy handling of the footlocker and your overall lack of coordination, I will impress upon you that you will only achieve uniformity through constant effort.___Civilians would say through trail and error.___However, here on the island you will not be allowed to make any errors.___I know that civilians say to 'err is human and to forgive is divine', but neither is Marine Corps policy.___Do you numb-nuts understand me?"

"Sir, yes Sir!" we screamed.

At this point the senior DI ordered a series of manual-of-arms with the sea bag and added a few additional maneuvers of his own, which included pumping the bag up and over our head, lowering it behind our head and then up again, to drop it down in front of our face. Our sea bags currently weighed between 30 to 40 pounds, because it was not yet packed with dress uniforms and other gear, which would normally average between 70 to 80 pounds for a regular Marines sea bag. However, for what we were doing right now, it felt like it weighed a ton.

The sea bags were starting to weigh down on us and we arched our backs, while waiting for his order to do any thing other then the thing we were doing at this moment.

"Get those backs straight girls!____No slouching!" Gunnery Sergeant Bishop urged and then started his exercise program in earnest.

"Down in front!___Up!___Down in back!___Up!___Down!___Up...!" he went on and on for what seemed like an hour.

Recruits were opening their mouths to aid in getting enough oxygen to crank out the next lift. Some had one arm cocked or bent no longer able to straighten it out fully. Many faces were twisted masks of anguish, fear and strain. The weaker recruits were starting to show signs of tears however, with the DIs prowling the ranks, even they persevered, knowing instinctively that an even more painful punishment would result.

On and on, this first day ritual continued, until nearly all the platoon had been unable to lift their sea bag one more time. We heard Gunnery Sergeant Bishop demanding another lift, but it didn't happen. The sea bags were resting atop our heads or on bent necks. Only two or three were demonstrating enough reserve strength to lift the bag over their head one more time. I was not among those.

"Look at the Girl Scouts!" Gunnery Sergeant Bishop said exasperated. "Do you girls think this is too much?___Do you want to go home?____ This is the United States Marine Corps, not equaled anywhere else in the world.____You have no idea how tough the training you have before you will be.___But let me give you a heads up ladies.___Before you get half way through boot camp you'll look back at this little session of sea bag tossing as an easy warm-up exercise.___You have yet to learn what real PT is.___Do you understand me?"

"Sir, yes Sir!" we replied in agony.

"Port__harms!___Order__harms!" He watched our hesitation. "That means put the goddamed bag on the deck along your right side." He made us repeat the maneuver.

We were all showing relief that this simple little warm up exercise was at least over for now. It was 1500 Hours, and we still had the remainder of the afternoon and the entire evening ahead of us and it was only the first day.

Maybe what Mack told me is true, when he told me recruits never sleep on the island. They'll PT us all night for sure. I thought with a wave of apprehension and recalled that my friend Mack had never played down what his experience in boot camp was like.

"Listen up!" Sergeant Kranz bellowed suddenly. "Grab your red book!_____The Guide For Marines.___Stick them in your left hip pocket and use your right hip pocket for your utility cover and always have them on you.____Stowe your sea bags by your bunks and prepare to fall out and form up in front of the barracks!"

"Sir, aye-aye Sir!" we responded with a domino-effect sound.

"Move!" was his only response.

We grabbed our red books, stowed our sea bags and started to stampede toward the door when Sergeant Kranz ordered us back in front of our racks and explained, in a harsh tone, that from this moment on, when ordered to fall out, the row nearest the hatch will always move out first and then followed by the other side.

In this barrack port side was nearest the hatch and starboard was on the other side.

TWO

Once outside, I was amazed at how hot and sticky it had become. We waited in formation as instructed until Sergeant Kranz came out. There was a black Marine with him who must have been a DI as well, because he also wore a cartridge belt. Sergeant Kranz addressed us.

"This is Sergeant Jordan, he will instruct you in the proper procedure of making up your bunk in the Marine Corps." A rack was already placed by a tree to the right of the barrack hatchway. There were sheets, a mattress cover, a pillow with a cover and a blanket, all laying neatly on top of the mattress.

Sergeant Kranz departed and made his way toward Gunnery Sergeant Bishop and Staff Sergeant Rogers, who were already headed in the direction of the barracks next door.

"Platoon, at ease!" Sergeant Jordan commanded. He saw the looks on our faces that clearly expressed our confusion as to what to do next.

"Oh hell,___that means get your asses in a looser posture than you were already in,___but don't move from your left foot's current placement.___Got it?" We proceeded to melt from our frozen position of attention, but only to the slightest degree.

Sergeant Jordan, noticing our ever-so-slight move went further to reduce our deep freeze by ordering us to completely circle around the rack to our side.

"Sir, aye-aye Sir!" we answered and moved to comply.

Sergeant Jordan was a small built man with very distinctive muscle tones in his face. He was endowed with bright eyes which, if he were not a DI, would make a stranger feel comfortable to talk with him. He had a small sharp nose and small lips topping a pointed chin. He had very white eyes dotted with near black irises. His voice was mid-range and sounded like the clipped staccato of a machine gun when he addressed us. In other words, he spoke very fast, very clear and even a little jocular. He was a retreat from Gunnery Sergeant Bishop, whom we had only known for several hours.

This DI was wearing utilities so starched, they appeared as shiny plywood molded over his body. Nevertheless, he knelt down on one knee, clearly wrinkling the crease, and started his lesson.

"Listen up!___This being your first day here on the island and so on,___I feel it is my duty to inform you that some weird shit lies just behind these barracks.____Hell, it lies all around this entire island.____ What I'm trying to tell you is that there are all kinds of snakes,___ poisonous ones,___sharks and big bad-ass alligators too.____It's a long swim between the island and the main continent.____The only way there safely, is over the causeway, the bridge to Beaufort."

"You don't want to fuck-up on this island.___No siree,___you sure don't.___If you try to swim for it, some slimy snake's gonna put a bite on you and if not, some alligator or shark will definitely take a giant chunk outta your ass." Then, in an after-thought, Sergeant Jordan added. "Hell, maybe you'll get bit by both.____Even if they don't get you, the sea weeds will tangle around your silly ass and the tidal waters will suck you under and drown you."

Sergeant Jordan, wearing a no-bull-shit expression, looked around at each of our faces. He suddenly grinned and said, "Besides,___once I instruct you on how to properly prepare your bunks, you'll be so happy to be tucked in all safe and sound, you won't ever be afraid of the big bad swamp critters.____Right?"

"Sir, yes Sir!" our response betrayed the wide range of trepidation he had fostered in our minds.

"I'd advise you to think long and hard before trying to leave this island before completing boot camp.___There are only two ways to leave this island.____As a Marine___or in a pine box!" He did not ask us if we understood him this time. He did leave a chill down my spine as I'm sure he had affected the others similarly. We were ripe to believe anything else he said this day, as we were in utter shock since arriving here and had yet to recover. I did not even remember that Gunnery Sergeant Bishop had earlier said there were several ways to leave, but a pine box wasn't one of his options.

Sergeant Jordan went on as if he hadn't spoken to us up to this point.

"I will attempt to teach you the procedure required by the Marine Corps to properly make up your bunk and pass the inspections you will undergo daily."

Once again, not awaiting any response from us, he just went right on and pointed out two recruits. He instructed them to move the bedding from the rack and begin pulling a cover over the mattress. The cover had three strings, spaced along each open edge, which the recruits were told to tie.

"This here mattress cover is referred to in the Corps as a fart sack.____One sheet will cover the mattress and over that you will place the second sheet followed by the blanket."

Sergeant Jordan placed a sheet over the mattress cover, allowing equal lengths to hang from all four sides. He then tucked the four sides tightly under the mattress starting first at the head and foot and then each side. This created neatly creased folds at each corner, which he referred to as squaring. He then repeated the process with the other sheet and blanket. These were tucked in at the foot first. He demonstrated the proper number of folds of the upper sheet and blanket to be turned back from the head of the rack, leaving a twelve-inch area as wide as the pillow. The fold was six inches wide. Then he tucked the sides in repeating the sharp overlap folds at the foot. The pillow was stuffed into the case was then placed on the rack. The end result was a bunk made up so tight and uniform it appeared as though it were built from wood and painted to look like one. It looked very military. Sergeant Jordan stood up and stepped behind the bunk to face the platoon.

"I hope you all paid attention to the demonstration.____You will each prepare this bunk in turn,____with fifteen seconds to complete the task.____Line up!"

"Sir, aye-aye Sir!" we moved to line up.

The first recruit stood in front of the rack and waited for the DI to tear it apart. Only the fart sack remained over the mattress.

"Ready,____start!" Sergeant Jordan held a stop watch and clicked the timer as he spoke.

Surprisingly, the first recruit was actually good at it and no sooner had he finished he was ordered to tear it apart. The second recruit was not very successful at it. He tore it apart and was ordered to the back of our line to try it again. Many were placed in another line as they met Sergeant Jordan's expectations. I was moderately successful, thanks to the sisters of Kinderheim St. Joseph.

Sergeant Jordan, evidently pressed for time, did not yell at anyone of us, but he did make frequent instructive comments. When all of us had completed our turn and the first of those recruits who had been sent back into the line once again stood before the rack, Sergeant Jordan started riding them.

"You're going to have to move faster.___Fold it under.___Don't just jab, lift and tuck.___That's it,___tighten it,___pull it tight.___Yeh, that's it.___Make sure the sheet and blanket hang over evenly.___Hurry up.___Get those creases out.___Do both sheet and blanket at the same time.___Yeh, that's the way.___Next."

Sergeant Jordan had some recruits make the bunk up several more times until all had finally passed.

Staff Sergeant Rogers walked up to our group. Sergeant Jordan yelled, "Platoon,___fall in!" They spoke to each other quietly for a moment and then Sergeant Jordan walked away.

Staff Sergeant Rogers ordered us to follow him in a single file towards the back of the barrack. There were rows of concrete wash basins. The troughs were just over waist high with plumbing running across the length of the top. There were spigots attached along the pipes at intervals of about two feet. The concrete troughs were long enough for the entire platoon. There were many of these constructions, enough for every platoon in the barracks. A short distance beyond the wash basins was the swamp, the snakes and the alligators. Staff Sergeant Rogers explained that the purpose of the wash rack was for scrubbing our laundry and as the smoking area.

We marched off to receive our bedding and returned to the barrack to make-up our bunks. Gunnery Sergeant Bishop and Sergeant Kranz were already in the squad bay waiting. Gunnery Sergeant Bishop ordered us on the line with our bedding held directly in front of us by both arms.

"Okay girls,___listen up!___Now that you have completed your home economics class on making a military bunk, let's see what you learned.___You have ten seconds to get your fart sack over your mattress.___Move it, turds!"

"Sir, aye-aye Sir!" we bellowed wasting at least two seconds doing so and bumped into each other trying to get between our racks to attempt the impossible in less than ten seconds. There was a problem here. Bishop knew it, expected it and waited for us to realize it. However, since we were scared and under orders to complete the task, we engaged the project, right or wrong.

The first problem was a placement issue. We did not know what to do with the pillows, blankets and sheets while we worked on the mattresses, as Bishop did not tell us to drop them on the deck or place them anywhere else. The second problem was a space issue. Since there were two recruits between each rack in a very narrow area at the same time trying to wrestle two fairly large mattresses, we did little more then frustrate each others efforts. The third problem was a time issue. We had ten seconds to totally fuck-up, nothing more could have been accomplished. Sure as shit, we anticipated Bishop's displeasure with us.

"Get your silly asses back on line!" he snapped as he walked down the squad bay shaking his head side to side. "Did you learn anything, sweet-peas?___The one thing you did do right was to not get anything accomplished___You can't in a cluster-fuck.___No team work and all that."

Bishop continued. "This time try it in teams of two.___Place all the bedding on one bunk.__After removing a mattress,___in teams,____slide the fart sack over the mattress___in teams,__prepare each bunk.___Just move the bedding back and forth as you go___and make sure only two between the racks.___Facing the rack,___the top bunk recruit to port and the lower to starboard.___Top racks place pillow inboard and lower racks outboard___got it girls.___Now move it!"

"Sir, aye-aye Sir!" we retorted and moved to the task. Sure as he said it, we managed to get the bunks made up in what appeared to be seconds.

"Come on, come on!" Bishop clipped impatiently. "Get it done!____ Get on the line!"

Those who were slower were finally slipping into the vacant slots on the line. Sergeant Kranz and Staff Sergeant Rogers were busy inspecting the bunks and of course busily tearing bunks apart, which had even the smallest deviation from what the Marine Corps expected.

"Okay you turds.___Apparently you were sleeping while Sergeant Jordon was instructing you, maybe you need some encouragement.___ Those who fucked-up their bunks have twenty seconds to get them un-fucked and those who are not working on their bunks will pay for your mistakes.___At my command those who have bunks to make,___get at 'em___and those who are not,___drop to push-up position.___Do it!___Now!" Bishop was loud and showing his impatience.

"Sir, aye-aye Sir!" we responded as some jumped to their bunks, while I and the remaining recruits fell to the deck.

"Count off!" Bishop demanded.

"Sir, aye-aye Sir!" we responded miraculously in unison and glad that there was no failure to do that correctly, which would surely have added more push-ups.

"One_____two_____three_____four..." we stammered, while the other recruits were being challenged by the three DIs to make their bunks correctly. It was now 1600 hours and we felt like the day so far had been a week and we had no idea how long they would keep us going like this.

"Platoon,___ah___ten___huat!" Gunnery Sergeant Bishop bellowed. We sprang to our feet and moved into position along the white line, as did those making their bunks. We were sweating hard, while those who were making bunks were pale with fear, because some were still not getting with the program.

"What's the matter,__slime buckets?___You look like you have worked hard.___Like you think you have had a lot of PT.___Like you couldn't do another push-up.___Right girls?" Gunnery Sergeant Bishop belittled us. "Well sweet-peas, you are going to find that you can do more___and you will,___before you are finished with the island!___Do you understand me?" he growled.

"Sir, yes Sir!" we screamed back.

It was 1730 hours when Staff Sergeant Rogers announced, "Chow time!___Fall out for chow!___Do you hear me?" he barked and then realizing we hadn't made a head call for some time, added that as our first order.

"Sir, aye-aye Sir!" we answered.

"When you are ordered to fall out,___at any time,___you will wait in port and starboard side formation along the white line until the drill instructor announces which side goes first.___Then that side repeats their order first.___Clear?" Staff Sergeant Rogers stated.

"Sir, yes Sir!" we retorted.

"Port side make a head call and fall outside when you have finished.___You have fifteen seconds.___Move it!"

"Sir, port side make a head call and fall out for chow!___aye-aye

Sir!" we shouted out our very sloppy and totally non-rehearsed response. Some left out the first or second part and it sounded ragged indeed.

"You turds don't deserve it,___but get out now!" Sergeant Kranz had ordered loudly.

Starboard side had done the same and was now arranging itself into platoon formation outside the barrack.

THREE

"Plaatoon,___aah___ten__huat!" Sergeant Kranz sounded the order in a drawn out pronunciation. We did not exactly snap to attention in the prescribed manner, but it was not challenged.

"Foart,___huah!" he continued, sounding the 'huah' from his stomach.

Off we stepped and tried to maintain proper distances and correct foot forward, even though we were not properly instructed yet. Onward we marched across the main parade deck, the meat grinder, where we had, only a few hours ago, been herded like cattle.

A whole lot had happened since that time, we had learned how to use our foot lockers for things other than their intended purpose, we were proficient in combination lock and unlock requirements, we learned how to do more than one thing at a time, such as when part of the platoon was learning how to make their bunks properly, the other recruits were doing PT. However, we did have our first lesson in team work when we made up our bunks.

It was still a lot more learning experience in a short time than we were accustomed to. Between all the PT and general DI attacks, we had to learn how to properly place our gear in the footlocker and footlocker tray. The foot locker tray was a neat invention. It was an insert device about four inches deep with a divider wall in the center, which would accommodate all of our essentials, such as a shaving kit, shoe polish, Brasso, towels (rolled) and writing gear, plus much more. The larger lower area was for our sea bag, uniforms (utilities) undergarments and all other clothing issues. The tray sat on top of the larger lower portion, on an inner lip or retaining shelf, which allowed the lid to close over it. We were given instruction on what items go into our dite (pronounced ditty) bag and where it was to be placed for proper display and usage. Staff Sergeant Rogers even gave us a bit of history about that. He had explained that the word ditty had its origins from the Anglo-Saxon word dite, which meant neat. Sailors used the dite bag for carrying small tools or personal gear. We were instructed to hang the ditty bag from each side of the top bunks rear rack posts facing the bulkhead.

We had finally reached the far side of the parade deck and could see the Iwo Jima monument to our right. It was situated along Boulevard de France and the grinder. The march across the grinder was no small walk as this was indeed a large drill field.

"Road guards out!" Sergeant Kranz bellowed. "No, no!___You two at the end of the two outer squads run out and stand at parade rest facing each lane of oncoming traffic." he explained rapidly, while we approached the Boulevard. Sergeant Kranz did not squawk about it as he knew that we were absolutely unfamiliar with this maneuver.

The two recruits ran from the rear as told and not yet knowing what parade rest was, just stood in the middle of the road with arms dangling at their sides.

The traffic stopped anyway and we surged across the street, made a left column turn, then a right column turn and moved up through the 2nd Battalion barracks to Panama Street, where we made another left turn. Sergeant Kranz had called for road guards and the two recruits repeated their unmilitary drill. Sergeant Kranz took note to instruct the proper procedures of the maneuver as soon as possible.

We marched down Panama Street to the mess hall and were moved into an area to the side of the mess hall, where Sergeant Kranz commenced some lessons.

"When I call road guards out, the two rear port and starboard recruits will run out into the oncoming traffic lanes and stand at parade rest facing the traffic." he explained and demonstrated parade rest. "After the platoon has passed,___the drill instructor will call road guards in, and you will return to the platoon column from which you left.___Is that clear?"

"Sir, yes Sir!" we responded.

"When I say fall out, you will run up to the mess hall hatch starting with the port side, one squad after the other, and close it up once there___Is that clear?"

"Sir, yes Sir!" we responded louder then the last time.

"Fall out for chow!" Sergeant Kranz ordered.

"Sir, aye-aye Sir!" we bellowed and rushed in files toward the entrance with surprising alacrity.

"Close it up!___Asshole-to-belly-button!" Sergeant Kranz shouted. Sergeant Kranz was shoving the rear of the column into the front of the column leaving us with our chin or lips stuck to the recruits head in front of us with our bodies locked into the guy in front and in back of each of us. We were not accustomed to having people inside of our personnel space like this.

"When you go inside you will each grab a food tray and place it in front of your face and side step along the food line. When you reach the serving area you will drop your tray to receive chow. Once you receive chow you will obtain your drink at the dispensers and move to the tables where I will be standing.___Do you understand me?" Sergeant Kranz barked with clarity.

"Sir, yes Sir!" we replied impatiently, wanting to untangle ourselves, eat and drink something and knock off the talking. The sounds of metal clinking against metal of hundreds of recruits in a feeding-frenzy beckoned to us through the entrance.

"Move out!" Sergeant Kranz ordered and we surged forward into the mess hall entrance grabbing trays and resembling robots, moved sideways along the line to the serving area where, with eyes staring straight ahead, we dropped our trays to receive chow from the serving line.

Thud, splat, and *dribble* were the sounds of serving along the line, while we were loaded up to the gunnels again, just as this morning, with mountains of food. We had a mountain of mashed potatoes with gravy flowing off of it like lava, which in turn mixed with the corn, which had a milk-like liquid. This mixed in with the mashed potatoes and gravy and was sopped up by the corn bread or overflowed and mixed with the Salisbury steak. We moved to the dispensers where we obtained scuffed plastic glasses and by pushing a lever upward received icy cold milk, which was probably most desired over all the served food. Sergeant Kranz was standing next to a series of connected folding tables with benches. He motioned the first recruits to move to the far end of the tables. When we were all there, standing between the tables and benches, and after a few recruits were yelled at for placing their trays down on the table before having heard the command, we waited for the proper command.

"Ready,___seat!" Sergeant Kranz ordered.

"Sir, aye-aye Sir!" we complied and promptly sat.

"Work on the seating response meat-heads." Sergeant Kranz offered in response to our sorry seating skills and then he continued. "When you finish chow, you will drop your trays into that rack." he said, pointing to metal racks on wheels with slots running up their sides to shelf the trays. "You will fall outside in platoon formation and wait for the drill instructor.___While you wait,___at attention,___you will extend you red book at arms length and start reading.___Do you understand me?"

"Sir, yes Sir!" we screamed impatient to start eating the food, which now resembled slop.

"Ready,___eat!" Sergeant Kranz ordered.

"Sir, aye-aye Sir!" we commenced to chow down.

As we were eating a wave of events and observations were to present themselves.

First, the GG shot or formally known as the Gamma Globulin shot we received in the left gluteus maximus earlier this morning, was starting to hurt like hell. These GG shots were of blood plasma, containing antibodies effective against certain micro organisms, such as those found in measles, infectious hepatitis and poliomyelitis. The pressure of sitting down was extremely uncomfortable and we had been standing or exercising all day, so we did not feel it as much before.

Second, we were eating or pecking as if we were at home, some leaning over their trays, while others put elbows on top of the table and sort of scooped the food up, dropping most back onto the tray, or worse, onto their lap.

Third, we were catching glimpses of the mess hall environment, seeing the DIs eating in their own area and other platoons were eating all around us. Some of the recruits were wearing brand new uniforms, like us, and some of those were equally disorganized at eating, like us. Others wore wash-faded utilities. They were suntanned, sitting straight, bringing their food up to their mouths. They looked like a well disciplined, finely trained unit. I wondered if we would or even could ever look that good.

Fourth, while we dribbled, drooled, slouched and whispered, there came a loud crash and scrapping of benches as Sergeant Kranz jumped on top of the table and stomped along its length kicking trays aside screaming a scintillating torrent of abusive language. Sergeant Kranz had, since this morning, seemed inimical toward us recruits, and was now tempestuously berating our newly formed mob.

"Where the hell do you skinny fucks think you are,___in the high school cafeteria?___At home slouching around the television?___You will get your sorry faggotty asses in gear.___Do you get my drift?___Ass-holes!" he bellowed at the top of his lungs, while running back and forth across the table sending food trays askew. "You do not speak,___ever,___unless you are told to speak!___You will keep your backs straight and place your fork into your mouth by bringing it up!" He stood there on top of the table with legs spread wide and upper body bent low as he wore a scowl and demonstrated the motion as he veered around to let us all see. "You will eat all of your chow!___Don't waste it!___You all will be dying for more by this time tomorrow.___I fucking guarantee it!___Do you understand me you sorry pieces of shit?" he stated with utter exasperation.

When Sergeant Kranz finished and was about to jump off of the table, one of the recruits on my side of the table suddenly fell backwards off of the bench and was experiencing what appeared to be an epileptic seizure. Sergeant Kranz jumped down next to the recruit as two other DIs, whom we did not recognize, also ran up to the recruit. I heard Sergeant Kranz say, "Get me a butter knife and I'll cut him a nice big breathing-hole in his throat!" As one of the other DIs grabbed one off of our table the recruit suddenly jumped up. "Thought so!" Sneered Sergeant Kranz, as he pushed the recruit away from him towards the mess hall doors.

Sergeant Kranz came back inside the mess hall, jumped back on the table and gave us a lecture on trying to fake anything while going through training. He finished with the following shocking statement. "Remember, that fat red-headed fuck Gunnery Sergeant Carver got rid of?___Called him Heinz fifty-seven,___right?____Do you know what happened to him?____Huh? _Well you're eating him, shit-heads,____ that's what happened to his fat ass."

A real meal killer! I thought with distaste.

We were forming up outside as Sergeant Kranz ordered us to do. We had tried to shove our randomly eaten mess trays into the rolling storage shelf only to find Sergeant Kranz staring at the offenders whom he had shoved toward the bulkhead and forced to finish their tray. I was one of those.

We were outside dutifully reading our Guide Book known as the 'Little Red Monster', awaiting the last of the dietetic recruits to fall into formation.

I was reading, 'To walk my post in a military manner, keeping always on the alert and observing everything that takes place within sight or hearing', as Sergeant Kranz called us to attention. I had been advised by my recruiter to have all of the eleven General Orders totally memorized before going to Parris Island and I had done so.

We were marched over to an area that had a series of posts supporting a roof. There were no walls. Under the roof were a few long rows of troughs with water spigots. We were ordered to line up along these troughs and a Navy corpsman issued us each a toothbrush. He then moved along our platoon and squeezed a small amount of Prophy Laxis Paste, referred to as 'Prophy', on the bristles of our brushes. Upon finishing, he moved to the center of the enclosure and began shouting instructions.

"Listen up recruits!___You will place the brush in your mouth and brush vigorously in a vertical motion inside and outside of your teeth for one minute. You will experience a granular texture.___That is pumice,___which while sealing the teeth also allows the fluoride to penetrate.___Start brushing now!" he ordered, measured the time on his watch and shouted, "Alright,___stop brushing!"

We ceased brushing, looking forward to spitting the sandy textured paste out of our mouths. Instead, we were told to keep the toothbrushes and ordered to file out to form up in platoon formation. As we marched, we were swallowing the vile pumice and paste combination running our tongues all through our mouths and lips to remove the last vestiges of the gritty event. We marched back to the barracks, made a head call and continued training. It was 1830 hours.

We had unpacked our sea bags earlier and following the DIs instruction, learned how each article of clothing or equipment was to be placed in our footlocker or the tray. We had each been issued a rubber name stamping set with ink pad which Bishop now had us set up with our name to stamp each article of our uniform issue. During this exercise there were many disciplinary interruptions with a variety of push-ups, bends and thrusts and sit-ups. The sea bag, which belonged to that recruit who had faked the epileptic seizure was repacked and carried into the DI shack by the recently selected House Mouse.

Apparently the faker isn't coming back. I surmised with little personal care and then refocused my attention on the show starting in our squad bay.

Gunnery Sergeant Bishop ordered us to remove all of our brass and a towel from our gear and then taught us how to polish our brass. He instructed us to place a towel over our footlocker and take out our Brasso and a washcloth.

"Okay girls, listen up!___You have two belts with brass tips and two brass belt buckles.___These items have a protective coating on them, which you will first remove in order to properly shine your brass in accordance with Marine Corps standards.___You will use the washcloth as your permanent cleaning cloth and you will not get any Brasso on your belt fabric.___The tooth brush you used today to seal your teeth will now be used for cleaning your fabric and cartridge belts.___I will not accept any sloppy cleaning of your gear,___that means there will be no residual protective coating on your brass and there will be no Brasso stains on your belts.___Now commence cleaning your gear!" Gunnery Sergeant Bishop barked.

We started scrubbing and immediately found the protective coating extremely difficult to remove, but under the constant patrolling glare of the DIs we eventually succeeded. Even Sergeant Kranz pitched in with regular intervals of the foulest profanity he could muster.

At 1930 hours we were inspected by all three drill instructors and learned the meaning of true disaster.

"You call this shined?___Shit-for-brains!"

"Are you blind?___Can't you see all the crud you left in the corners of the buckles?___Dip shit!"

"You used too much Brasso.___It's all over you, the towel, your belt and obviously you could not see the protective coating because of all the Brasso,___you blind fuck!___You got five minutes to pass inspection.___Do it!"

By 2000 hours we were either acceptable or behind schedule, whichever, as it was now time for other fun and games.

"Secure your cleaning gear!___Move it!" Gunnery Sergeant Bishop bellowed.

"Sir, aye-aye Sir!" we responded to the order while still seated, cleaning gear askew on our footlockers, between our knees or in our hands.

"Get on your fucking feet maggots!" Sergeant Kranz and Gunnery Sergeant Bishop ordered incredulously and simultaneously.

"I can't believe you shit-heads just sat there and spoke!___Gawd,___ what a bunch of whale shit I got here!" Gunnery Sergeant Bishop exclaimed exasperated.

"Get on your feet!___Now!" he screamed.

We jumped to our feet and he ordered us to drop for bends and thrusts, which in the Corps are referred to as 'bends and mother-fuckers'. We poured sweat for most of the next hour as we were introduced to a variety of exercises, some of which we were familiar with from sport activities in school, but there were many new ones here.

"Get on your feet!___Secure your cleaning gear.___Strip and wrap your towels around your waists, grab your toothbrush, paste and soap and prepare for showers!" Gunnery Sergeant Bishop ordered.

"Sir, aye-aye Sir!" we screamed so loud we even shocked ourselves. After a couple of minutes had passed and we had all scampered about following Gunnery Sergeant Bishop's orders, we stood on line with wrapped towel around our mid-section, holding our new soap, new toothbrush and paste in our hands.

Gunnery Sergeant Bishop walked down the middle of the squad bay eyeing each of us hard. As he walked, he told us to hang our utilities on a prescribed portion of our bunk beds head section, to place our daily dirty laundry in our ditty bags until we were able to scrub them outside on the wash racks and to ensure our foot lockers were placed under our racks, centered and locked, upon completion of our shower.

"Port side,___prepare to make a head call and shower!" Gunnery Sergeant Bishop ordered.

"Sir, port side make a head call and shower,___aye-aye Sir!" port side bellowed, thanking God they did not forget what side was left in Marine jargon and equally thankful no numb-nuts on starboard side were confused enough to shout with us and get us all PTing.

"Move out!" Gunnery Sergeant Bishop continued and we made a smart left turn and ran in single file towards the head to quickly piss, brush and shower and return as fast as possible to our racks.

"Starboard side,___make a head call and shower!" Sergeant Kranz yelled.

Starboard side answered and ran into the head. Shortly they too stood in their skivvies along the line and waited for the next ordeal. Instead Gunnery Sergeant Bishop surprised us by ordering us to hit the racks and explained the procedures for that maneuver.

"Prepare to mount!" Gunnery Sergeant Bishop barked and we ran to the mid portion of our racks and waited for the second part of the order. "Mount!" he continued and we jumped onto our bunks with alternating heads on each rack so no head was across from the neighboring rack. Bishop was not impressed. "Get back you slow maggots and do it over.___Prepare to mount.___Mount!"

This time we sprang like Gazelles, only to find several recruits were more akin to Sloths.

"Damn you turds!___I can keep this up all night,___so it's up to you." he snarled and then ordered us to try once more. "Prepare to mount.____Mount!"

This time the whole herd did it smoothly and fast enough to receive the blessing to stay put and at last earn rest for our weary feet.

Staff Sergeant Rogers went by the racks and picked out recruits who he said were to be the Fire Watch for the night. I heard him explain that each man had a one hour Fire Watch and was responsible for waking each man in his turn and to wake the duty DI at 0430 hours or if anything happens. The first Fire Watch was tossed over a chrome-painted helmet, a list of those chosen for the nights watch and told that all shifts will wear the helmet.

"Good night ladies!" Gunnery Sergeant Bishop shouted and waited.

"Sir, good night Sir!" we responded, amazed that we instinctively answered properly.

"Hit the lights!" Gunnery Sergeant Bishop ordered the first shift Fire Watch.

"*Wwheuu!*" Was the silent expulsion in every mind on this night. We were finally resting. It had been a terribly long day on top of the flight and bus ride. We were still pissing beer and soda from civilian life, yet we felt we had already been here forever and it had only been the first day.

My God! What will tomorrow be like? I shuddered with the exclamation.

We were numb in the mind, in a state of shock, aching in every muscle and joint. Many were thinking the same thoughts tonight and some were more afraid than others, because they had already been punished for some infraction during the long day. Others, because of what those who were slapped, punched or kicked had endured, were fearful of the following days ahead and their own fate!

Was it possible? Was this the true Marine Corps, the one we saw in the proud movies, on the recruiting posters or even the occasional real one we saw in our neighborhoods? My God! How can anyone survive this? We recruits were only here for one day and we were shaking with fear and uncertainty. My mind was racing with these fearful thoughts and I had loath of a rising sun.

We were individuals yesterday and today we are door mats, scum, maggots and as Gunnery Sergeant Bishop stated, we are whale shit, the lowest form of scum in the universe. Many were afraid to sleep, for fear Bishop or Kranz would catch them at it and rip them apart. What happened to all those guys who came with us, who were systematically extracted from our group?

Poor ol' Heinz fifty-seven, we hardly knew ya! I thought. But the abject fear on Heinz fifty-seven's eyes was still visible in the minds-eye of all of us recruits. As many recruits worn from the day's ordeal drifted into the blackness of sleep, their last though had to be,_____can I make it? I even heard some stifled sobs.

I had my mind so full of these thoughts I almost forgot about my mother and the girls and that son-of-a-bitch Hueston. *Was he still going over to her house to bother them? What could I do for them if he did? My decision to join the Marine Corps was not such a great idea after all. I am so sore, I can't even think I'll make it through all this?*_____*Four years!*_____ *Damn!* I drifted into the blackness of sleep hoping for salvation and fearing that there will be a tomorrow and the DIs. Or will I wake up and find it was all only a bad dream?

CHAPTER 4
IT'S NOT A DREAM

ONE

An explosion shook me out of a deep sleep and literally jarred all of us out of our bunks. The explosion was caused by all three DIs throwing the large galvanized steel trash cans across the deck, creating loud hollow metallic sounds. Each barrack had three of these trash cans, referred to as shit-cans, positioned at equal distances along the center of the squad bays.

The combined sounds of the obscenities screamed by the DIs and the crashing shit-cans overwhelmed all of us. Terror struck, we ejected from our bunks and hit the white line, while the DIs dashed about grabbing slower recruits from between their racks. The DIs kicked them in the ass, cuffed them behind the heads or pulled them toward the white line.

"Get the fuck out of your bunks.__Move it!__Mooove it shit-heads!__Hit the line!____Count off!" chorused all three DIs over and over, establishing the urgency of time. We were to learn that there was little dead time during our training since the DIs were already required to do in eight weeks what was done in twelve weeks before the war in Vietnam demanded a more rapid fielding of warm bodies. Even basic training, which followed boot camp, called ITR, was intensified by adding, on top of an already brutal training load, the training missed in boot camp without lengthening or shortening the regimen. Simply put, all usual training is provided, however in a more compressed time period.

It was 0500 hours and our first real day of training was starting. Not allowed to stretch, yawn, scratch our ass and shuffle around as we did at home, this wake-up shocked ninety-nine percent of us immediately into awareness and preparedness, as we proved by immediately counting off.

"You better wake up maggot!" one our DIs shouted from somewhere down the squad bay, followed by the sound of a rack falling over and spilling its top occupant.

We were lined up along the white line, staring at our fellow recruits across from us. I could literally see the fear in their wide eyed faces as they stared back at their mirrors in our faces. We stood at attention, wearing our new issue of white tee-shirts and baggy white boxer shorts. Many recruits had erections, which did not escape the ever observant DIs.

"When you're told to stand at attention,___that means in a military manner___and some of you are not doing what the others are doing.____Get on the deck!___Get the fuck on your faces!" Sergeant Kranz shouted with exasperation.

We replied in the affirmative and fell to our faces. Sergeant Kranz then ordered thirty push-ups, which many of us couldn't yet give him. Of course this was met by all three DIs hazing those who were unable to do proper push-ups. When we were ordered to stand on the line again, there were more attacks at those who did not have their shower shoes on. That was most of us, and from this day on – none of us. We immediately learned how to dive from our bunks directly into our shower shoes.

"There's nothing here to fuck except the deck.____So don't stand around with hard-ons in my Marine Corps!" Gunnery Sergeant Bishop boomed down the squad bay. "Or I'll have you fucking the deck twenty times a day!" He insinuated by moving his balled fist and forearm up and down toward the deck.

"Sir, yes Sir!" we replied, while wondering how to stop a normal reaction. There were rumors back home that they put saltpeter (potassium nitrate) in our chow, which suppresses sexual urges. After a few days the irregular positions of attention were to become regular and therefore military. Perhaps there was truth in the rumor.

All of this haranguing and physical activity had lasted about five minutes.

"You have five minutes to shit, shower and shave girls!___Drop your skivvies at your racks.____First, wrap yourselves in a towel and grab your gear.____Starboard side make a head call,___Move it!" Gunnery Sergeant Bishop barked.

"Sir,___starboard side make a head call,____aye-aye Sir!" the starboard side replied and then at Bishop's "Do it!" turned to their bunks, stripped, grabbed their towels and head kits and ran for the head.

"Port side, make your bunks and ready yourselves for a head call!" Bishop ordered next.

We responded and executed our orders. I returned to the line with a towel wrapped around my waist, holding my wash cloth and head kit. The head kit was a small zippered bag, which contained shaving cream, razor, soap, styptic stick, toothbrush and paste.

Within five minutes starboard side was back on line. It was not because they were that efficient. While they were in the head, we portsiders could hear the DIs constant harassing to get them through in the allotted time with unrelenting goading and threats.

"Port side___make a head call!" Sergeant Kranz's harsh shout arrived as on time as one of Mussolini's trains.

We responded and ran into the head knowing all the while that we would get the same treatment as the others. We were not disappointed. Once in the head we grabbed the first crapper we came to. I don't think anyone took a crap or could have. I know I couldn't. So after a morning piss I ran to a sink and applied shaving cream to a face that didn't yet need a shave, dutifully scrapped it off, brushed my teeth, and then ran into the showers to soap up. I rinsed off, grabbed my towel and dried myself on the run. I retrieved my gear from a wooden bench and hauled ass to stow my gear and get back on line.

"*Whew!*" I thought while standing on line. "*I made it through without getting my butt kicked.___Great!*" That is, I didn't get singled out, but I did run the gauntlet of constant shouts to move it as I ran past the DIs. As I thought about it more, I decided that it was unnerving to take a crap while being subjected to the stares and shouting of a group of drill instructors, even if I had to shit.

"You have three minutes to get into your utilities!" Staff Sergeant Rogers stated.

"Sir, aye-aye Sir!"

"Move!"

Surprisingly, we almost did it on time. Slow pokes exist in all groups of people. Although I didn't think about it at the time, those same recruits would be the same ones that were to cause the rest of us plenty of extra punishment. Until they either got with the program after harsh discipline or were dropped, we could not become a crack team. Naturally, there followed abusive language, shoving and hazing against the slackers specifically and the rest of us generally.

"You, you and you grab brooms!____You six,____mops and buckets!__You,____you little shit,____since you're the house mouse, you will be permanently responsible for the DI shack!____You six empty the shit-cans!_____Do it after you get dressed!" Gunnery Sergeant Bishop barked at whatever recruits were in his view at that moment. The only exception was the shortest guy in the platoon who, from this day on, would have his own chores.

The house mouse, traditionally the smallest recruit, was always given that billet. Bishop had pegged our mouse the first day. He was Recruit Wiley, who was about five foot five, but looked solidly built. A house mouse performed a wide assortment of duties from cleaning the DI shack, making the bunk and the coffee, to running errands around the battalion area.

"Sir, aye-aye Sir!" we chorused back with apparent adequacy, as no rebuttal was offered.

"Move!" he followed-up.

We pulled on our utilities and boots as though we had a fire under our asses, and after what seemed like only a minute, were back on line. Apparently, what we thought of as a minute and a quick response was longer then a minute and a lousy response by Bishop's reckoning. We repeated it four more times, along with some push-ups, before he resumed the normal routine The recruits ordered to police the squad bay were busily completing their tasks mopping out the head, sweeping down the squad bay and dumping the trash outside in the dumpster and then returned to their position on line.

All three DIs walked down the squad bay and eyed each of us.

"Button your top shirt button!__Do it!____You,__re-tie your

boots!___You call that shirt tucked in?" They repeated these corrections and a variety of others as they inspected us.

"Listen up.___You will keep your top buttons buttoned, your trouser legs un-bloused and your covers pulled down tightly over your skulls at all times, because you are all fucking worthless maggots.___ Don't ever let me catch a shirt unbuttoned, a button missing or a flap unbuttoned,___or I promise___I'll rip that button off and if it is an unbuttoned flap I'll rip that off as well.___However!" he shouted louder, "If I catch any of you with your dick-skinners in your pocket,___I'll fill your pocket with sand before you sew it shut___to make sure you never forget!" Gunnery Sergeant Bishop had finished his lecture with a clipped 'never forget' and then gave a command. "Take two steps forward!"

"Sir, aye-aye Sir!" our nervous reply echoed in the squad bay.

"Ready,___step!"

They walked back down the squad bay, this time behind us. As they walked by several recruits who had failed to catch their errors, buttons were ripped from their utility trouser pockets. They were ordered to stick out their tongues where upon the DI dropped the button. This procedure was to serve as a reminder not to forget to secure their pockets in the future and they were further reminded that they had until before morning chow to sew the button back on. Luckily this time no infractions required sand, as sand would absorb body sweat and the area of skin underneath would be rubbed raw.

"What is your major malfunction?___Why are you eye-balling me maggot?" Sergeant Kranz barked at a recruit.

"Sir, this recruit was't looking at you___*uh*___Sir!" the recruit stated confidently.

"Holy Christ!___I can't belive you just called me a female sheep___ ass-hole!"

'Sir, this recruit doesn't understand the drill instructor's meaning___ Sir!"

"Well hell___shit-for-brains!___I'll explain it so that even a cave-dweller like you can understand what you did wrong!" Kranz spat verbally. "A ewe is a female sheep!___Do I look wooly to you?___Do I have an udder?"

"Sir, no Sir!" the recruit shouted with a noticeable fear in his voice.

"You calling me a liar sweet-pea?" Kranz asked coldly. "Do you like me sweet-pea?"

"Sir, no Sir!" the recruit shouted with increased fear due to the on-going attention, or wrath, he had suddenly had befall him.

"What!___I can't believe what you just said!" Sergeant Kranz backed up a step and shouted down the squad bay. "Did you all hear what this twinkle-toed communist shit-bird just said?___He said he dosen't like me!___Well I'm going to give you another chance shit-head!___Do you like your drill instructor__*thump?*" Krance demanded as he landed a short jab of his knuckle into the recruit's solar plexus.

Sir, yes Sir!___This recruit likes his drill instructor Sir!" he screamed with abject fear in his voice now.

Sergeant Kranz shouted in surprise again, while he backed up with shaky-knee exaggeration.

"Goddamn boy!__I just can't understand you.___First you hate me__and then you like me!___Well___let me tell you something___boy!___Liking leads to lovin'___and lovin' leads to fuckin'!___Are you trying to fuck me faggot?" Kranz drove home his verbal sword and just as suddenly walked away from the shattered recruit to finish inspecting unbuttoned pockets.

A few more minutes passed as those who needed to sew got busy while the rest of us were ordered to watch television. As a reminder punishment for the platoon regarding button infractions we who were not violators of this treasonable act were spread over the squad bay deck on toes and elbows with our bodies off the deck and our hands on both cheeks. Once in a while a DI would order us to change channels. We would then be on three points with our right arm fully extended and our wrist twisting thin air. We had been up for fifteen minutes and already so much had happened. Finally, the last numb-nut got his button on and his gear secured and we were allowed to stand up and get back on line.

"Fall out for chow!___Move!" Gunnery Sergeant Bishop ordered.

We replied raggedly and exited with port side going first, as earlier instructed, while Gunnery Sergeant Bishop was heard behind us, promising we had one last chance to sound off like a bunch of civilian shit-heads before he found a reminder for us to get it right by. It was dark and foggy outside and the fetid stench of decaying vegetation assailed our nostrils as we marched off to the mess hall. There were muffled sounds, which sounded like they had to tear through the pea soup fog to reach our ears. Even our boots fell dully onto the pavement. The drill instructor's drill calls were almost lost, as if caught in the fabric-like air.

TWO

After we had endured chow, we continued our new day by heading to a large galvanized metal building. The morning sun was illuminating the Island with a bright golden glow. As we halted for another platoon of recruits to pass by, I noticed the recruits were deeply tanned. They wore stiffly starched utility covers, which sat angled downward on top of their heads, projecting a slightly curved visor. This visor covered their entire forehead and eyebrows. The effect of wearing the cover that way appeared to make their body straighter than it already was. Their utilities were faded into a light green and their trouser bottoms were bloused neatly over spit shined boots. Their top shirt buttons were undone, revealing the white of tee-shirts. They looked absolutely splendid as they marched by with rifles slung over their right shoulders, making the heavy sound of one foot-fall at a time. Even their DI exhibited a confident pride as he quietly sounded "lep,__lep,__lep,rye__doe__lep!"

These recruits were in their last few days of training. They were returning their 7-82 gear and their buckets. They were going into the building we were waiting to enter, so that we could be issued our 7-82 gear. They held their buckets, which were neatly filled with their gear, with both hands, against their stomachs. Even with their awkward burden, they achieved a perfect military appearance and precision march.

"Look at those recruits!__Look hard!__They are about to graduate and become Marines.__Do you think you will ever amount to that,__maggots?" Sergeant Kranz asked.

"Sir, yes Sir!" we screamed in what was our first truly uniform response. We now felt more depressed, because we were not Marines yet. However, seeing those senior boots march by with such confidence, we felt motivated by envy to meet the challenge. I never forgot that platoon marching by. It was very impressive.

We entered the building and immediately started passing rows and rows of two-by-four posts supporting four-level plywood shelves. Each shelf contained galvanized buckets capped with a canvas shelter-half and three tent pegs poking out. Each bucket also contained a variety of other gear, which we would soon be issued.

"Keep moving, keep moving!" Sergeant Kranz goaded us along into another area where there were wooden racks built to hold M-14 rifles.

I had never seen so many rifles in my life. There was row after row of rifle butts with about an inch of space between them. The rows were about ten feet across and held five rifles stacked top to bottom on the racks. I couldn't attempt to count how many rows per rack or how many racks were in the room. Each of us was provided a ten by six inch card and ordered to line up and receive our rifles. A sergeant handed each of us a rifle as we filed by. A corporal issued pencils and showed us where to find the serial number and how to fill out the card. We provided our name, the date, rifle serial number and our platoon number. After the corporal verified the serial number and other information we filed out and formed up next to Staff Sergeant Rogers. We were told to hang on to the pencils.

Staff Sergeant Rogers moved us back to the 7-82 gear storage room and with rifle slung over our shoulder, we filed by another Marine who handed each of us a another card and told us to retrieve a bucket from a shelf as we went by and to form up outside.

We fell out in a grassy area surrounded by those silver above-ground steam pipes, which seemed to run endlessly about the Island. When all of us were formed up, Staff Sergeant Rogers, Sergeant Kranz and the Marine who issued us our buckets came outside. The Marine, a corporal, brought a bucket out with him and stopped about ten feet in front of our platoon formation.

Sergeant Kranz ordered us to attention and opened ranks. We were ordered to place our buckets on the ground in front of us. The corporal emptied his bucket on the ground and Kranz ordered us to do the same.

"Listen up!" Staff Sergeant Rogers shouted. "As each item of equipment is held up, you will hold that same item up and acknowledge it in unison.____If you do not have that article of equipment, you will keep your hand raised after the others have dropped theirs.____Do you understand me?"

"Sir, yes Sir!"

We went through the entire inventory and when finished were

told to check off each item on our card and fill it out with the other identifying information. This done, we were now the custodian of the following gear:

BELT, CARTRIDGE	1 EACH
CANTEEN, W/CUP AND COVER	1 EACH
MAGAZINE, RIFLE/M-14	2 EACH
COVER, MAGAZINE/M-14	2 EACH
PEG, SHELTER-HALF	5 EACH
POLE, SECTION, SHELTER-HALF	3 EACH
BAYONET, W/SCABBARD	1 EACH
SACK, HAVER	1 EACH
PACK, FIELD	1 EACH
STRAP, SUSPENDER	1 PAIR
PONCHO, RAIN	1 EACH
SHELTER-HALF	1 EACH
KIT, FIRST AID	1 EACH
CORD, SHELTER-HALF	1 EACH
KIT, MESS, W/KNIFE/FORK/SPOON	1 EACH
STRAPS, W/BUCKLES	3 EACH

There was more military gear crammed into those buckets than any of us would have believed possible.

"Okay!__Pack it back into the bucket.__The way it was__and get ready to move out!" Staff Sergeant Rogers ordered. We had clumsily held onto our rifles throughout the 7-82 gear inventory and now again found ourselves tugging, pulling and pinning the damned thing with our right forearm to keep it from falling as we micro sized our gear to fit into the small bucket. Since the corporal told us to just dump our buckets it was more difficult to cram so much gear into the bucket then one would have believed. We finally achieved this difficulty with a few re-dumps.

"*Damn this rifle sure is heavy!*" I thought as we marched back to our barrack. We held our buckets into our stomachs with both arms as we marched sloppily along, looking absolutely nothing like the platoon of graduates we had observed earlier.

"Get your sorry asses in the barn,____hogs!" Sergeant Kranz bellowed.

Once inside we immediately began to prepare our new gear for utilization. First we fitted our cartridge belt for waist size and placed the first aid pouch on the back, centered, the canteen to the right of the first-aid kit and the magazine pouches on each side of the front. Instead of dealing with the rest of our gear an order to stop was heard.

"Okay girls__fun time is about to begin!" Sergeant Kranz said in a very sinister voice. "Get on you PT gear, sneakers, jock straps, and sweatshirts and fall out!" We scrambled about getting changed and I feared that we were somehow not doing something correctly, such as where to put our boots and utilities. As if reading our minds, Staff Sergeant Rogers solved our dilemma and told us to hang our utilities on the rear top corners of our racks and place our boots to the right side of our foot lockers. With that done, we filed out and formed up in front of the impatiently waiting Sergeant Kranz.

THREE

"First, let's start learning how to fall into proper formation.__Forty and thirty all around girls.__That's forty inches from shoulder to shoulder and thirty inches from chest to chest__ Let's get it done right the first time around!" he barked and then continued, "When I say dress right dress, each recruit will extend a rigid right arm up in a horizontal position and with finger tips touch the shoulder to your right,___and when I say dress it up,___you will move closer together or further apart to achieve the proper distance and hold the position until I give the command,___ready,___to!"

"Plaatooon!__Aah__ten__huat!__Dress___riat___dress!___ Cover!___Ready,___huah!___Forward,___huah!" The sequence of drill orders came in a froggy croak.

We had managed about ten paces when he suddenly shouted, "Quick step,__huah!" Which he had then immediately changed to, "Double time,____huah!____Keep it tight, stay in step and keep the pace." he said as he observed every one of us to ensure we understood the need to keep tight control and not just scatter and dash about like high school kids on a jog around a football field.

"Keep in step damn it!" Sergeant Kranz barked repeatedly.

We ran across the meat grinder and made a right turn onto Boulevard de France, continued on until we made a left turn onto Yorktown Road and then headed straight toward the Circuit Course.

The Circuit Course was a large grassy training field a short distance from the 3rd Battalion barrack complex. The barrack complex was on the right side of Yorktown Road and on the left was the Circuit Course. The Confidence and Obstacle Courses were across the street from the Circuit Course. Still further up the road was a right turn onto Wake Boulevard, which ran past the Weapons Training Battalion area, with the Rifle Range located on the right side and the barracks, mess hall, swimming pool, Weapons Training Battalion offices, Medical and Physical Conditioning Platoons on the left side. Drown Proofing training took place there and recruits were placed into the range barracks for two weeks, while undergoing pistol and rifle range training. When recruits suffered injuries or had psychological problems they were transferred there as well. Overweight, extremely skinny or weak recruits are sent to the Physical Conditioning Platoon, also referred to as Fat Body or Pork Chop Platoon. However, we were to learn about the location of these facilities off Wake Boulevard at a later date during our training.

As we ran past the old red brick barracks to our right, my eye caught a large red sign with yellow lettering announcing 3rd RECRUIT TRAINING BATTALION. Our platoon belonged to Hotel Company, 3rd Battalion however, for the next week we would remain temporarily billeted in the old 1st Battalion barracks. 1st Battalion had recently relocated to brand new modern brick barracks located near Regimental Headquarters. Their new buildings were huge compared to our old wooden World War II barracks.

We moved off the main road toward the left and entered a dirt and gravel track, which encircled the entire Circuit Course. Inside the circle was a field of grass with randomly placed wooden platforms standing approximately four feet off the ground.

On several of these platforms stood a Marine Physical Training Instructor demonstrating a variety of exercises to groups of recruits surrounding their platform. Their individual platoon guidon poles were planted in the ground with their flag fluttering in the breeze. Some guidons had multiple colored streamers whipping randomly from the tops of the poles. We entered this pow-wow with no guidon to proudly announce our arrival. We did not rate any identification at this point in our training.

There were many hundreds of recruits on the field screaming, swinging limbs executing training maneuvers, singing running songs and counting off numbers. We entered the field and were immediately swallowed up in the sweaty melee.

"Okay ladies,__let's get with the program!" Sergeant Kranz said while grinning at us with malice in his eyes. He knew that we were already feeling strain from our fairly long jaunt from the 1st Battalion area and were nowhere near the required physical condition to be expected of us before completing boot camp.

Sergeant Kranz ordered us to a halt and kept us at attention while he talked to one of the Physical Training Instructors. I listened to the sounds around me. There were many commands being called by the DIs, shouts of physical exercise counts repeated over and over and mixed with the same calls from other training groups. What I heard sounded more like: four, one, three, four, one, two, three, four, two, three, all mixed up at different sound levels depending on the distances. Those sounds were invaded with platoon running songs. The field was very alive and vibrant with activity.

Sergeant Kranz returned and moved us over to the running track at a run. As our sneakers purchased gravel, Sergeant Kranz started our first running song.

> "Birdie, birdie in the sky,
> dropped a little white spot in my eye,
> even though I won't cry,
> I'm just glad that cows can't fly!"

"Repeat the song,__one verse at a time,__after me!" Sergeant Kranz shouted.

"Sir, aye-aye Sir!" we responded, sounding each word with each step. I thought that was the best and most coordinated response we had made since arriving yesterday. I felt good about that and stuck out my chest to display the Marine Corps emblem printed boldly over its front.

"Birdie, birdie in the sky." Sergeant Kranz started.

"Birdie, birdie in the sky." our echo sounded each word or word part with each foot fall.

"Dropped a little white spot in my eye." he continued and we replied.

"Dropped a little white spot in my eye."

"So I coaxed him in with a piece of bread,

then I smashed his fucking head."

This method seemed to help us establish a rhythm, which would also aid us in learning marching skills. Other platoons had passed us coming from the opposite direction. Fragments of their songs could be heard.

"...if that chute don't open round,

I'll be the first mother on the ground!"

"When I call count off,__you will call one through four between three silent steps,__then again with each number between two steps__ then with one step between numbers,__finishing with one through four with no breaks,__followed with United States Marine Corps.____Got it?" he yelled loudly.

"*Oh hell!*" I thought mortified. *"Nobody will get that load of information right and we'll be running forever for the screw-up."* To my surprise, we did it with only a few odd numbers shouted during what should have been silent steps.

"Do it again, shit-heads!" was his rebuke. "Count off!"

"Sir, aye-aye Sir!__*Puff, puff,* one, *step, step, step,* two, *step, step, step,* three, *step, step, step,* four, *step, step, step,* one, *step, step,* two, *step, step,* three, *step, step,* four, *step, step,* one, *step,* two, *step,* three, *step,* four, *step,* one, two, three, four, United States Marine Corps, *puff, puff.*"

Onward we ran, passing other oncoming platoons engaged in singing the Parris Island Top Ten songs.

"...Little baby sucking mama's tit,
Now chemicals don't give a shit,
Napalm sticks to kids.
One mile, no good,
two miles, no good,"
As they pass us, we hear trailing off...
"three miles, no good,

four miles, no good,
five miles, um good
gimme some PT, um good."

All across the field we could hear the non-ending sounds of training as our platoon continued rounding the circuit. I was feeling woozy from the heat, the pace and the lack of experience running this long and I had a stitch in my side. We were all showing the signs and more then a few fell out. I didn't see them, but Gunnery Sergeant Bishop and Staff Sergeant Rogers were on the field mopping up the stragglers. It was not pretty for those guys. They wanted to see what their new batch-of-hogs were capable of and determine who would be culled from the heard and sent to PCP.

"Keep it tight girls!___This ain't shit!___Wait until we really start running." Kranz said effortlessly and continued grinning at us menacingly from a sweat free face. He had definitely perfected a cruel-grin capability.

We ran for an additional period of what seemed like twenty minutes when Sergeant Kranz suddenly called us to a halt and continued the order to have us marching at a regular pace. He directed us to one of the wooden platforms, upon which stood a Physical Training Instructor with arms folded, glaring down at us.

"Plaatooon,___halt!____Right,___huah!___Second squad back step five paces.___Third squad back step ten paces.___Fourth squad back fifteen paces.____Ready,____huah!" We executed the unfamiliar maneuver without creating a major disaster.

Now we were set up for the Physical Training Instructor to take charge of us.

"My name is Staff Sergeant Behrens.___I am your PT Instructor.___You will follow my examples for each exercise!" he shouted, "Do you understand me?"

"Sir, yes Sir!" our screamed reply sounded like a wet duck fart in a wind storm.

"You'd better,__or you'll only suffer more!" he finished his speech and immediately continued with position instructions and movement demonstrations.

"Side-straddle-hops!__Assume the position."

"Sir, aye-aye Sir!"

"Just get into the correct positions and continue the program without the responses from this point on!" he stated bluntly.

We worked hard following his regimen. He had us complete side-straddle-hops, four-count, ten repetitions or reps; push-ups, four-count, fifteen reps; rowing exercises, four-count, fifteen reps; body-twists, fifteen reps; elbow-rest-leg-lifts, four-count, fifteen reps; bent-knee-sit-ups and mountain-climbers for one minute each exercise and then repeated. There was also a session of bends and thrusts, which were called bends and mother-fuckers.

Even though the temperature was only seventy-seven degrees, we were sweating and dizzy from the heat and aching severely from this unusual ordeal, we finally left Staff Sergeant Behrens' yard-of-sadism and were run over to the pull-up bars. The pull-up bars were constructed between a long series of posts enabling many recruits to perform the exercise at the same time. We were lined up by squads and in turn, under the watchful eyes of the DIs, proceeded to jump up, with palms facing outward, and try to do as many as we could. Twenty was the required amount.

Gunnery Sergeant Bishop and the other DIs only watched us this first day and made many mental notes on their observation of our capabilities. We would soon be notified of our individual weaknesses.

When my turn came to do pull-ups, I was shattered with the embarrassment that I could only pump out eight. Gunnery Sergeant Bishop responded. "If you want to become a Marine, you had better be able to do better than that sweet-pea!"

Upon completion of the pull-ups we were run back to the barrack with Sergeant Kranz while he continued to perfect our running songs. The distance back felt like it was twice as far as it was on our run to the Circuit Course. Once in the barrack our tired bodies hoped for a rest in order to recover our strength from what was to us a hard ordeal so far. However, Gunnery Sergeant Bishop was not impressed. He had torn up quite a few of our bunks before heading out to the Circuit Course. It was 1030 hours.

Gunnery Sergeant Bishop announced that since some of us were unable to properly make up a bunk, a PT session for those who did properly make their bunks was in order, while those who were sloppy remade their bunks. Naturally we instantly hated those who caused us further pain. I assumed that some of the fuck-ups were the same recruits who were slow getting out of their bunks, messed up on their combination locks, slow to complete head calls, fell out during the run and now couldn't make up their bunks. I could remember some of their voices and others could as well. It was difficult to look directly at anyone or thing whenever any of us wanted to look, so it was difficult for all of us to witness the foul-up recruits. After only two days we were settling into several distinct groups.

After about fifteen minutes of punishment PT, Gunnery Sergeant Bishop ordered us to get our rifles. He commenced instruction from proper sling adjustments, for various marching styles and tri-stacking to placement of the rifle on our racks. He made us learn the manual of arms with breaks of pain and punishment interspersed between the instruction period. Except for the small group of fuck-ups, we would not forget what he taught us.

This was followed with instruction on the nomenclature of the M-14 rifle.

"The M-14 rifle weighs eight point five pounds and has three main groups,____the trigger housing group or firing mechanism assembly,____ the barrel and receiver group____and the stock group." Bishop explained in a froggy voice and continued. "You will be provided classroom instruction in the assembly and disassembly of your weapon.____As Marine recruits you will learn how to properly clean and care for your rifle, how to field-strip and reassemble your weapon under normal and combat conditions.____You will be so familiar with your rifle that you will be capable of disassembling and assembling your piece blindfolded.____Do you understand me?" Bishop boomed suddenly.

"Sir, yes Sir!" we sounded off in ever-improving unity.

"A Marine and his rifle are one.____A Marine becomes his rifle.____God has blessed the Marine Corps and we offer him a creed with a prayer for his favoritism toward us.____You will memorize the Rifleman's Creed.____Repeat after me." Gunnery Sergeant Bishop said and rendered the solemn words.

"This is my rifle.
There are many like it,
but this one is mine.
My rifle is my best friend.
It is my life.

My rifle without me is useless.
Without my rifle, I am useless.
I must fire my rifle true.
I must shoot straighter than my enemy,
who is trying to kill me.
I must shoot him before he shoots me,
I will."

After repeating the creed, Gunnery Sergeant Bishop informed us that the words are in our red handbook and promised harsh punishment for failure to memorize the words.

I thought we weren't allowed to use the first person on the island, yet this prayer allows us to be individuals.___Then again, to say the recruit must fire his rifle true and the recruit must shoot straighter then his enemy,__the recruit must shoot him before he shoots the recruit,__the recruit will.___ Wow!___That sounds a little fucked-up___What the hell,__do what they say. I mused.

FOUR

It was 1130 hours when he ordered us to fall out for chow.

We returned from chow, which was another disaster for us, since we were still unsettled, unused to the routine and unable to eat the mountain of food they insisted we required at each meal. Once again, outside of the mess hall, there was the ever present hazing with harsh threats, promises of punishment for not eating all of our chow. Beyond that, several skulls of dilatory recruits were cuffed. No surprise that they were the same turds, who have lagged behind since we arrived on the Island.

"Try my patience shit-birds!" Sergeant Kranz screamed at the turds, "I goddamn guarantee you'll be sent to the Motivation Platoon tomorrow!"

Inside our barrack we received the promised punishment. Using our rifle as a barbell we raised then up over our heads then lowered them behind our heads, up again and then down in front of our chins, straight out from our chests, back into the chin. This exercise was repeated over and over until Gunnery Sergeant Bishop returned from chow and organized our next lesson for the day.

"Listen up girls.___You have a red Guide Book For Marines,___ which you are required to have out and in front of your faces at all times when at attention awaiting your drill instructor.___Inside your guide book you will find the section titled Interior Guard, which lists eleven General Orders.___For the next thirty minutes you will memorize these General Orders and then we'll see what you have learned.___Do it!" Bishop ordered and then turned and went into the DI shack.

"Sir, aye-aye Sir!" our response boomed after him.

For half an hour we stood with arms stretched out in front of us and branded the subject in our brains.

Thanks Master Sergeant Herbert! I thought remembering back several weeks ago when he gave me a copy of the General Orders at the recruiting office and stated that, if nothing else, I should memorize them before I went to boot camp. I did memorize them and wondered how many of the other recruits here had recruiters who had urged them to do the same or who had the chance, but who were just plain lazy.

As promised, Gunnery Sergeant Bishop came down the squad bay and stopped randomly in front of recruits.

"What's your seventh General Order?"

"To talk to no one,___except in the line of duty!" the recruit responded with pride, as he knew he was correct.

"Get on your face and assume the position numb-nuts!" Bishop responded icily, "The proper reply starts with Sir!___Twenty,___ready,___start!"

The other DIs also randomly picked recruits as well. Staff Sergeant Rogers came up to me. "Name?"

"Sir, Recruit Shipman Sir!" I sounded off loudly, while staring straight ahead.

"What's your eleventh General Order?"

"Sir, the recruit's eleventh General Order is,___to be especially watchful at night and, during the time for challenging,___to challenge all persons on or near my post, and to allow no one to pass without proper authority,___Sir!"

He moved on to another recruit who I heard reciting the third General Order.

"Sir, recruit Hopkins, Sir!___the recruit's third General Order is,___to report all violations of orders I am instructed to enforce,___Sir!"

"You had better understand something dirt bags.___Tomorrow I will ask you again and if any of you are unable to reply correctly with the General Order I ask for, you will all enjoy the punishment, while the idiots suffer watching you.___Got it?" Bishop rasped in that froggy voice again.

"Sir, yes Sir!" we replied sounding ever more in unison.

"You are to remember at all times who is who in the Marine Corps___therefore, the following names of Marines will become as personal to you as your family.___The Commandant of the Marine Corps is General Leonard F. Chapman___the Commanding General of Marine Corps Recruit Depot Parris Island is Major General Oscar F. Peatross,___the Commanding Officer of Recruit Training Regiment is Colonel Robert J. Perrich,___the 3rd Battalion Commander is Lieutenant Colonel P. M. Johnson,___your Company Commander is First Lieutenant Gains,___your Series Officer is First Lieutenant Lindseay,___your Chief Drill Instructor is Master Sergeant Rite and your Series Gunnery Sergeant is Gunnery Sergeant Neal."

Gunnery Sergeant Bishop and his assistants spent the next half hour ensuring that we remembered. It is true that some things are painful to remember.

We were marched in the direction of the Regimental Headquarters where we were yesterday when we received our physicals. This time we entered a building marked Optometrist and were processed through as orderly as we had been during our physical examination. I was issued the type of eye glasses that I would never have purchased in civilian life. These were black thick-framed devices with a cord to secure them to our heads. I was amazed to see how many of our platoon required eye-wear.

Then we were ushered to the dental facilities for our checkup. Those of us requiring additional work were scheduled through the DIs who would insure we made the appointment on the date and time specified.

It was 1700 hours when we returned to the barrack, Sergeant Kranz ordered us to make a head-call, grab our cartridge belts and rifles and fall back out for close order drill.

Once we were in formation, we were reorganized based on our heights, with the exception of the squad leaders and the guide. Apparently, there had been a decision formed by the DIs as to who rated these responsibilities.

"Southworth, get up here!" Sergeant Kranz barked.

The recruit ran up to Sergeant Kranz and shouted. "Sir,____Recruit Southworth reporting as ordered Sir!"

"You had drill experience in a military school?" he queried.

"Sir, the Virginia Military Institute, Sir!" he replied proudly.

"Go all the way at VMI?" Sergeant Kranz asked bluntly.

"Sir, no Sir!" Southworth replied with somewhat less pride.

"Why not?__Were you a shit-bird?" Sergeant Kranz goaded him.

"Sir, lack of family funds, Sir!" he spit out with obvious embarrassment.

"Well, if you have some experience in drill you'll be the platoon guide,__for now.__So don't fuck-up and maybe you will remain the guide." Sergeant Kranz stated dryly and then suddenly shouted for the House Mouse.

"Sir, yes Sir!" Recruit Wiley responded.

"Grab the guidon!" he ordered. The Mouse barked in the affirmative and scurried into the barrack and nearly tripped on his way back out of the hatchway.

With guidon in hand, Sergeant Kranz walked up to Recruit Southworth. "Since your name has the word south in it and you went to a Southern school, your name is Rebel now.___Got it?" Sergeant Kranz stated and then ordered him to fall into position with the platoon.

"Sir, yes Sir!" Rebel screamed with pure pride and proved his prior drill experience by executing precise military maneuvers as he withdrew and positioned himself at the head of the first squad. There he stood proudly holding our platoon flag, which fluttered in the breeze displaying the number 3063 in red on a yellow field.

Sergeant Kranz called out the Squad Leaders next. "Hadley, Ortega___Griffin and Wheaton get up here!" They responded smartly.

Hadley was white, big boned and had bulging blue eyes. Ortega was Hispanic with a dark complexion and heavy shadow of beard, which along with the similarly appearing stubble of his head left a non-hairy area around his eyes resembling a mask. Griffin had a pointed nose, practically non-blinking eyes, that flitted quickly from one place to another like a reptile. Wheaton, who looked much older then the majority of us, stood over six feet tall and had a skin color almost as black as his boots.

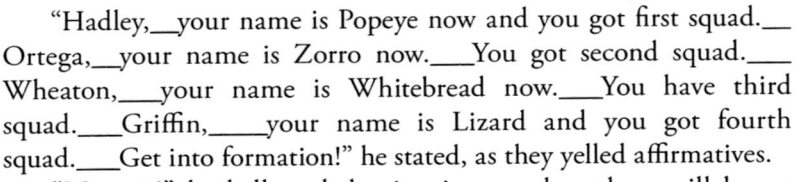

"Hadley,__your name is Popeye now and you got first squad.__ Ortega,__your name is Zorro now.___You got second squad.___ Wheaton,___your name is Whitebread now.___You have third squad.___Griffin,____your name is Lizard and you got fourth squad.___Get into formation!" he stated, as they yelled affirmatives.

"Move it!" he bellowed, leaving it very clear there will be no rebuttal.

"Ah___ten___huat!____Port,__harms!____Raet shoulder____huat!____Raet____hace!___Foart,__huah!" We stepped off with the unfamiliar burden of the M-14 rifle resting on our shoulder.

"Callum let,__huah!" he commanded next and we complied sloppily.

"Shit!" he shouted suddenly, "Lock your elbows in on your sides and listen to my commands.___When I give the command you will execute the order on your next foot fall.___Got it?"

"Sir, yes Sir!"

"Callum raet,__huah!"

The platoon pivoted to the right without any major screw-ups and although we were shabby, Sergeant Kranz was concentrating on trying to keep us on the move so he could see how bad we were in certain executions and which recruits were responsible for foul-ups.

Sergeant Kranz jumped in through our ranks repeatedly correcting a recruits' posture, position of rifle angle or elbow. He slammed elbows into the offending recruits' side, screamed orders to straighten up their slouching posture or grabbed their arm and rifle at the same time pulling both up and the back down into the proper position.

"Stop ditty-bopping girls!" he barked at us, after he finally got the platoon marching with proper posture. However, we had been bouncing up and down with each step. "Move your body from your hips and legs.___No bouncing.___Keep your upper body still.___No swaying of your shoulders.___Understand?"

"Sir, yes Sir!" we answered clearly. As we moved along on the huge parade field I noticed Gunnery Sergeant Bishop and Staff Sergeant Rogers were watching our progress from the barrack lawn. They were taking notes as well. We drilled on for what felt like hours with many mistakes. One such error caused a recruit to receive the flat hand of Sergeant Kranz across the back of his head. This caused his cover to fly off and land on the deck.

"Hippity hop mob stop!" Sergeant Kranz shouted angrily. "What are you doing in my Marine Corps formation without your cover on___shit-head?"

The recruit tried to bend down to pick it up without acknowledging the question verbally. He received a knee to his side for that ill-advised maneuver. This harassment kept up for a few more minuits only because Kranz already knew why, would not accept any answers as correct anyway and needed to get on with the drill. The only possible solution to the recruit's dilemma other then saying 'You knocked it off!' and commiting verbal suicide, was to simply place his hand over his head. That would have served as a cover until a real one was furnished. It would also have demonstrated 'adapt, overcome and improvise' capabilities that a DI is watching for in recruits. It is the proven reason why Marines are so successful in combat.

"I asked you a question numb-nuts!___Why are you not wearing your cover in my Marine Corps formation___sweet-pea?"

The recruit, unable to answer, was ordered to run around the marching platoon with his rifle pumping up and down in front and in back of his head with each pump.

At 1750 hours Sergeant Kranz returned us to the barrack to secure our gear and then marched us to chow. Once in line outside the mess hall he shoved us into asshole-to-belly-button formation obviously letting us know he didn't think much of our earlier drill capabilities as we did a lousy job marching to chow and thus demonstrating we had learned absolutely nothing.

FIVE

The chow was becoming ever-more threatening. We were unable to shit. All of us felt stressed, disoriented and now faced another ordeal of receiving what we dreaded to eat. The meal was meatloaf, mashed potatoes, gravy, corn and two slices of bread, a heavy meal. Once again, I observed other recruits wolfing down their meals and amazed at what I saw. I wondered how they could be so content to eat what we loathed to receive. The sadistic mess duty recruits piled the chow on our trays, as usual, as we side stepped, like robots, along the serving line.

We arrived at the designated tables and stood at attention between the seats and the tables awaiting Sergeant Kranz.

"Ready!" he snapped.

"Sir, yes Sir!" we responded.

"Seat!" he barked and reminded us that we had better eat every bit of the chow we received.

"Sir, aye-aye Sir!"

As we sat in silence, with backs erect, bringing the fork up to our mouths without slouching, I was amazed at how we were already starting to transform and resemble the recruits we observed returning their 7-82 gear and even now mirrored the veteran recruits seated in the mess hall. Then again I thought only as remotely as a fish compared to a shark.

I was initially poking at my mountain of chow and mentally reaching inside myself to find the nerve to start eating when, after a few mouth full bites, I found myself actually chewing faster and faster, anticipating the next full fork.

What the hell is happening? I wondered as I began competing with time to eat as much and as fast as I could. I was ravenous and even shot glances at other recruits to see if I could snatch additional food from them. What I saw was the other recruits stuffing themselves as fast as I was.

We were all very hungry from the ordeal we had been through since yesterday, yet the memory of our lack of appetite was still with us when we came in to eat, but we did not connect mentally that all the physical activity we had undergone had taken a lot out of our system leaving our bodies craving nutrition.

When I was finished with my tray, I was sorry there was no more food to eat, and also surprised that I had accomplished cleaning my tray. When I headed towards the back exit to drop my tray Sergeant Kranz was there, sure as hell, examining our trays. I was surprised to see some of our platoon still had problems eating every thing on their trays. There were six or seven recruits standing against the wall with trays in hand using their fingers to shove chow into their mouths.

Damn those guys, they're the same ass-holes who have been messing up every time! I grumbled to myself as I ran outside to get into formation and begin reading my little red monster. *This handbook covers a hell of a lot of information for its size.* I considered, as I tried to focus on the subject I was staring at.

Once back in the barrack, Gunnery Sergeant Bishop put us to

work polishing our brass again. We were far from meeting his and more specifically Marine Corps standards for polished brass. The new brass had a protective layer of a shellac or varnish that was extreamly hard to totally rub off.

Sergeant Kranz ordered barrack police call and I found myself on head detail. I did not find this job unusual, since I had plenty of experience mopping the floors at Wagon Wheel Diners and the Drug Store.

When we had finished policing the barrack, it was 2030 hours. We retrieved our M-14 rifles and Gunnery Sergeant Bishop and Sergeant Kranz filled in the time by conducting manual-of-arms.

"Port,___harms!" The first command came, followed by instruction on right and left shoulder arms, parade rest, present arms, interspersed with physical training, such as utilizing the M-14 in up and arm shoulders. We held the rifle in a horizontal position straight out in front of our chests, then pulled it in to the neck, then lifted it straight up over our head and then dropped it behind our neck. That was only one repetition.

We did that for many dozens of repetitions. This exercise was only broken up by moments holding the rifle straight out for a minute at a time. The M-14 rifle begins to weigh fifty pounds after doing this exercise for any length of time, and holding it straight out for even one minute will break many young men. I was also failing at it after a time. When any recruit dropped his arms we all received more punishment. Thank God no asshole dropped his rifle, because we would have surely been driven mad with more punishment.

At 2045 hours Gunnery Sergeant Bishop ordered us to the showers. There was the expected hazing, and as during last evening, no recruit could take a shit yet. After showers we were ordered to sweep down the deck fore and aft, using only our small scrub brushes. This procedure required either hurting our backs by bending the entire time, while we pushed the small brush in short forward sweeps, or equally painful was to kneel and walk forward on our knees as we swept. Our DI didn't much care which pain we preferred.

Once we were allowed to hit the rack, Gunnery Sergeant Bishop had us recite the Rifleman's Creed. The only reason we didn't have more punishment PT was due to the method Bishop used to recite the Creed. He began each verse for us to repeat, so we got it right.

"Lights out!____Sleep tight turds!" he stated in a staccato voice.

"Sir, aye-aye Sir,___good night Sir!" we bellowed back, not at all worthy of compliment.

The lights went out and although I didn't exactly hear the expulsion of breath, I was sure every one in the platoon did as I did and let it out. It was only the second day and it was already apparent that the only time for peace and escape was after lights out, or was it. My mind reviewed the day's events and calculated that I faired well considering the odds. I was ashamed that I did so poorly on the pull-up bars and vowed to do better, hell, to be the best. At the same instant I feared where I was and, for the best, drifted off to sleep before I found other detrimental thoughts.

CHAPTER 5
LEGACIES

ONE

Crash! We hit the deck with surprising speed, considering we had only been on the Island for three days. I think we were even feeling cocky about our ability to exercise our movements on command with so little experience.

"Hit the fucking deck sweet-peas!" Gunnery Sergeant Bishop bellowed at the exact second the lights went on, "You are slow and you disappoint me very much.___Since it is such a beautiful morning I want you to invigorate your bodies and at the same time make you remember where you are___and it isn't at home where you were used to crawling out of the rack at your leisure.___Push-ups, four-count, ready,___begin!"

I was wrong. We didn't impress him at all. I thought, as I flung myself onto the deck.

"Sir, aye-aye Sir!" was our raspy first words of the day response and down onto the deck we went slapping our hands on the wooden planks. From the prone position we counted off with hoarse shouts. After twenty repetitions we were herded into the head and quickly out of the barrack for chow. Apparently, the senior DI was not really pissed-off at us, but it was an unusual way to start a morning for us. I certainly felt that we, as a whole, were not accustomed to this change in habits. It was demanding and we never knew when a PT session was going to happen nor how much or how long it would last.

After our hearty breakfast, we ran to the Confidence Course and repeated the regimen of exercises we had been required to achieve the day before. The only difference occurred when we arrived at the pull-up bars station.

It was apparent, from Gunnery Sergeant Bishop's demeanor, that what we accomplished yesterday with only a comment from the senior DI would not cut it this time.

Gunnery Sergeant Bishop chewed ass this morning. Any recruit not meeting his expectations was scorned and retried.

"You call that a pull-up?___Strain!___You can do it if you try!___Damn,___show some guts!___Do it!___*Arrgh!*___Get out of my face,___wimpy!" his admonishments were heard over and over.

When my turn came I got embarrassed over my dismal attempt. I was only able to crank out seven pull-ups with the palm facing outward. In school we had done pull-ups with the palm facing inward and I had only been average doing them that way. This technique obviously utilized different muscle groups. Now we were using different and undeveloped muscle groups. Some of the recruits were able to accomplish many more than I had, perhaps due to prior experience with this technique, but many more of us did not display any aptitude. Gunnery Sergeant Bishop and Staff Sergeant Rogers were scribbling comments on a clip board, obviously next to each of our names since we had to scream out our names before we jumped up to grab a pull-up bar.

"Recruit Shipman do you really think you belong here?___You get your skinny ass back in line and do it over again." Bishop growled at me.

"Sir, aye-aye Sir!" I shouted and with a crimson face ran to the back of the line.

I will do more this time or die trying, damn I feel like shit not being able to keep up. I thought with self-disgust while waiting in line before materializing in front of the DI again.

"Seven___eh-eight___naa-nine___*arrgh*, te-ten___*umph*, e-e-eleven!" I screamed out each count and locked my elbows in a half chocked position as I strained for number twelve. But number twelve was too elusive. Hell, it was never to be this day.

"Better!" Was Bishop's only comment to my miraculous comeback. At least I was not ridiculed and sent back to do it again as was the fate of several others.

After we departed the Circuit Course, Staff Sergeant Rogers ran us back to the barrack to change out of PT gear and into utilities along with instructions to fall right back out. We were so sweat soaked, that it was not easy to pull on dry cloths over sticky bodies.

Staff Sergeant Rogers called cadence in a low voice and headed us toward some buildings we had not been to before. As we neared the group of buildings he ordered us to halt in front of a hatch very much like any of the rest of the hatches in front of the other buildings. Other then a number painted on the hatch, there was no sign advertising the purpose of any of these buildings.

We entered the building and stood with the backs of our knees touching the benches behind rows of tables and waited for the next thing to happen. Up to this point we were not told very much if anything in advance about what we were to do until it was the moment we did it. Why then should they tell us why we were now standing here in this room.

A staff sergeant walked into the room from a door located behind the instructors desk and greeted us. Our lips were locked.

"Sound off with the appropriate greeting when you see a Marine!" Staff Sergeant Rogers barked with obvious indignation. "Whenever you see a Marine approaching,___you shout out the appropriate greeting.___Even if he hasn't said a word.___Do you understand?" he finished.

"Sir, yes Sir!____Sir, good morning Sir!" we shouted loudly.

"Good morning recruits.____My name is Staff Sergeant Dunnigan and I am your instructor in Marine Corps history.___Pay very close attention, because you will be required to know this subject___and I know you will remember what you learn here,___because next to the bible it will be the best story you will have ever heard before this day.___Seat!"

"Sir, aye-aye Sir!" we responded loudly and sat with anticipation evident on our faces.

Staff Sergeant Dunnigan was medium in build and height and had an oval intelligent looking face. His hair was thick with rusty colored wiry curls and his dress uniform was crisp with razor sharp creases. His chest displayed four rows of ribbons.

"Those of you, who pass your trial here on Parris Island and become Marines, will carry on the magnificent traditions of devotion to duty, self sacrifice, versatility and dependability.___You will learn the traditions of loyalty to country and to the Corps.___These traditions include uniform, insignia and equipment. Ever since the Corps was formed by an act of the Continental Congress during the American Revolution, Marines have maintained and preserved these traditions."

Staff Sergeant Dunnigan paused and looked around the room to see if he had our rapt attention. Apparently feeling we were giving it, he continued.

"These traditions are as much a part of a Marine's equipment as his rifle, pack or ammunition.___Therefore,___pride of person___is instilled in every Marine.___Although looking smart in uniform,___ performing outstanding drill and achieving a high state of discipline is the goal of a Marine,___it is not as important as learning to know how to use his equipment so that he is ready to meet any emergency that comes his way and be able to report___'The Marines have landed and the situation is well in hand!' "

"The Marine Corps emblem was not worn by the Revolution era Marines, in fact it was not adopted until 1868.___The spread eagle, which is the symbol of our nation, holds in it's beak a streamer bearing our famed motto Semper Fidelis,___which is a Latin word meaning Always Faithful, and the globe and anchor signifies our function and sea traditions as part of the Naval service worldwide."

"How many of you recruits have ever heard the term Leatherneck used when referring to the Marines?___Raise your hands if you have." A score of hands went into the air, not including mine. My father was in the Air Force and the years in England and Germany really limited my chance to see any Marines and during the few years I had lived in the States never touched on the word, nor even after I finally did meet one. Mack never used the term around me.

I guess Mack either never mentioned it, or we were always too shit-faced to remember if he had. I decided with a mental shrug.

"From 1798 to 1872 Marines wore a 3.5 inch high stiff black leather stock around their necks. This collar was worn to protect the neck, specifically the jugular vein, from the slash of a saber or cutlass,___ according to legend.___However, official records have not fully corroborated this as factual,___that is that it was to protect them. The device was considered torturous by Marines and although dropped as part of the uniform, the term Leatherneck derived from this period."

"From the halls of Montezuma to the shores of Tripoli," Staff Sergeant Dunnigan suddenly sang the beginning verse of the Marine Corps hymn. "Tripoli,___a seaport located on the North African shore at a place known today as the capital of Libya,___where in 1805 Marine Lieutenant Presley N. O'Bannon and his Marines climaxed the fight on those shores by raising the American flag for the first time in the old world.___The former Pasha of Tripoli presented Lieutenant O'Bannon a sword with a Mameluke hilt for his services.___In 1826, the Mameluke sword was adopted and became the symbol of authority of Marine Corps officers to the present, the longest continual service of a weapon in the American Armed Forces."

"The origins of Marines goes back approximately five centuries before Christianity, to the ancient days of Greeks and Phoenicians.___ All of the maritime states of Greece and the Phoenicians placed fighting men aboard their vessels.___These fighting men had tactical missions to fight off boarding parties of the enemy and to serve as boarding parties on combatant vessels.___Furthermore,___they protected the harbors in unfriendly terrain from land approaches of enemy troops, while their fleets were in port and served to strike or raid inland against enemy installations."

"The British continued the custom of using fighting men aboard ships.___The first permanent placement of such troops under the Naval service or more specifically under the authority of the British Admiralty, occurred during the reign of Charles II.___On 28 October 1664,___an Order in Council directed the organization of 'The Admiral's Maritime Regiment' at the request of the Duke of York and Albany.___The Duke was Lord High Admiral of England and apparently saw the value of having a Marine fighting force at his disposal.___Soon after their creation, they were renamed the 'Regiment of Marines' and whenever hostilities against England were declared, they were the first to embark with the fleet for tactical service."

"During 1740,___three regiments of American Colonial Marines were raised from the colonies for service with the British fleet on operations in the West Indies along with the reestablishment of the British Marines.___Under the command of Admiral Edward Vernon of the Royal Navy, the Colonial Marines were considered better fitted for service in that climate than were the Europeans.___Even their uniforms, different from those of the English, were better suited for the climate and duties.___The Colonial Marines wore camlet coats, which were plush, waterproof and very durable. They also wore brown linen waistcoats and canvas trousers."

"The Colonial Marines were commanded by Alexander Spotswood, former Governor of the Colony of Virginia.___The King of England commissioned him a Colonel on 2 April 1740.___He died 7 June 1740 and was replaced by Colonel William Gooch of the Colony of Virginia.___At this time the three regiments were reformed into a single regiment of four battalions and ranked under the British Army as the 43 Regiment and they were referred to as 'Gooch's Marines'.___Lawrence Washington, who was George Washington's half brother, served as one of the officers in Gooch's Marines.___The use of the colors gold and red commemorates the reestablishment of the British Marines and the creation of the Colonial Marines and their joint service in the Caribbean campaigns."

"On 10 November 1775,___by an Act of the Continental Congress,___an organization of Marines, as part of the regular branches of the Continental service, was created.___This date, 10 November, is now observed throughout the world as the Marine Corps birthday.___The Marines served with distinction during the American Revolution making several expeditions with the Navy to the Bahamas and on the Great Lakes.___They served with John Paul Jones on Lake Champlain operations.___During the Revolution individual States had their own navies, but they did not have their own Marines.___They requested the Colonial Marines.___George Washington utilized their services during the battles of Princeton and Assanpink Creek.___At the end of the revolution the Navy and Marine Corps were disbanded."

That's not smart. I thought. *They'll need them before the ink has dried.*

"Now the Marine Corps you recruits are endeavoring to become a part of was formed by the Act of 11 July 1798,___when the Naval War with France started, and they saw service between 1798 and 1801 and continued service in the war with the Barbary corsairs from 1801 to 1805.___Remember Lieutenant Presley N. O'Bannon's actions in Tripoli?___After a short period of peace the Marines were put into action once again during the War of 1812 against the British.___They served on practically every American ship of war that had engaged the enemy.___Marines saw action with the American Army at Bladensburg and fought the British with Andrew Jackson at the Battle of New Orleans."

"When pirates where operating out of Cuba in 1824, Marines were organized as a landing force to put a stop to their enterprises.___In 1832 another threat of pirates required the services of a combined Navy and Marine landing force from the U.S. frigate Potomac to punish the Malay pirates at Quallah Battoo island of Sumatra,___after they had captured and plundered the USS Friendship."

"Never a dull moment for the Marines,___they were sent to Georgia and Florida to help the Army fight the Siminole and Creek Indians from 1836 to 1837.___The Marines were led by the Commandant,___Colonel Archibald Henderson.___The Marines considered Seminole Chief Osceola the toughest enemy commander they had fought up to that time."

"Keep those eyes open sweet-peas!___No nodding off!___Remember,__you will be tested on this subject.___Do you hear me?" Staff Sergeant Rogers suddenly snapped in a froggy voice, which served to rattle the platoon into instant alertness.

"Sir, aye-aye Sir!" we jumped to our feet at the same time shouting our reply.

"Ready,___seat!" Staff Sergeant Rogers followed.

This little episode served to get us all alert again. At least I know it did for me.

Staff Sergeant Dunnigan was apparently used to sudden attacks by drill instructors during his classes. It is also apparent that a large part of the human population has an interest level for history that can be described as little to none. I did not fall into that class of people and literally ate this stuff up. However, with so many recruits and others in this room the temperature rose very high. That is, we got very sleepy.

"The Mexican War is of particular interest,__because it resulted in many of the traditions we adopted and still carry as part of the Corps traditions.___That war was fought on both the Pacific and Atlantic coasts of the continent in which the Marines played an integral part.___The war resulted in the conquest of California.___Marines assisted in the capture of Monterey, Maltazan, Yerba Buena, Vera Cruz,

Tobasco and Tampico.___In case you aren't familiar with the name Yerba Beuna, it is now called San Francisco."

In a civilian classroom the audience would generally comment on this information with some crack like San Francisco being an easier word to remember or some such observation. However, we recruits just sat there and absorbed information like a sponge.

"As you recruits continue your training, you will become more aware of the significance of these events and how your uniforms reflect that heritage and history.___For now, I will cover the beginnings of that subject and you will attend other classes on Uniforms and Traditions of the Corps that will elaborate on their purpose and adoption as symbols of the legacy of the Corps."

Since I knew nothing about the Corps and its history, I couldn't wait for him to continue his lecture.

"General Scott led a battalion of Marines to Mexico City,____ and participated in the attack on the Castle of Chapultepec and then marched to the National Palace,___which were the Halls of the Montezumas.___During the battle of Chapultepec more Marine non-commissioned and commissioned officers were killed then enlisted men.___Today___Marines above the rank of Lance Corporal___ wear a red stripe down both legs of their Dress Blue trouser legs to commemorate the loss of their blood on that battle field,___as you will again cover in your Uniforms and Traditions class."

"In 1859,___under the command of Army Major Robert E. Lee,___Marines took part in the capture of John Brown at Harpers Ferry, Virginia.___During the Civil War___Union Marines served in the battle of Bull Run, at Manassas, Virginia.___They served afloat and ashore and took part in all of the most important naval operations.___ Marines attacked Confederate Atlantic seaboard coastal defenses, on the Gulf of Mexico and up into the Mississippi Valley.___They also participated in the capture of New Orleans.___The capture of Fort Fisher was the last great amphibious operation of the war and___you guessed it recruits,___the Marines were also in on that battle."

I doubt we guessed any of that, unless he means that Marines are in on every conflict. I decided

"Class,___aah___ten___huat!" Staff Sergeant Dunnigan shouted suddenly. "You apparently find my class boring!___Don't you?" he queried very loudly.

Stunned by his sudden outburst, we were suddenly standing ramrod straight.

"Sir, no Sir!" we answered sloppily, due to his sudden outburst.

"Where did Lieutenant O'Bannon raise the American flag in 1805?" he asked while pointing to the first recruit his finger found.

"Sir, in Tripoli Sir!" the recruit responded confidently, while the rest of us praised him silently for saving our asses.

"Alright!___You're paying attention___and it's you're asses if you're not.___Ready, seat!" he commanded and then continued his lecture, "The war with Spain in 1898,___where the Marines were the first to storm the shores at Quantanamo Bay, Cuba and fought at Santiago de Cuba in a Naval engagement.___They also participated in the battles at Manila Bay and Cavite in the Philippines___and fought in Puerto Rico."

So that's how those places got to be involved with America. I tought, and recalled seeing their locations on the globe.

"The Boxer Rebellion in China from 1900 to 1901 was engaged by a Regiment of Marines, which was part of a relief force at Peking from Taku and other Marines from the Asiatic Fleet.___There was desperate fighting at the walls of Tientsin, where five other countries Marine Corps fought along side the U.S. Marine Corps.___The Royal Welsh Marines and the U.S. Marines came to each others assistance on numerous occasions, which created such a mutual admiration between the two___that on every Saint David's Day,___the first day of March,___greetings are cabled between each organization,___with the ancient Welsh password 'And Saint David!' "

Staff Sergeant Dunnigan continued his lecture covering Marine involvements during the period from 1903 to 1908 in Santo, Domingo, Korea, Abyssinia, Panama and Nicaragua.

"Your next lesson will cover Marine Corps involvement from World War I to the Korean War. I suggest you read up on the subjects we discussed today.___You will find them in your guidebook."

"Class,___aah___ten___huat!" Staff Sergeant Rogers barked.

Our platoon shot upright with lightning speed.

"Fall out and form up!"

"Sir, aye-aye Sir!" we responded and upon his grunt to execute, scrambled outside and formed up in line formation. Line formation was one of several new terms we learned from Sergeant Kranz during our first close order drill exercise. It was the forming up of the platoon with the four squads facing a building or road and the drill instructor faces us from the opposite side centered on our platoon.

The classroom hatch burst open and Staff Sergeant Rogers barked orders to dress right as he headed towards us. That maneuver enabled us recruits to achieve a forty inch distance between each other, for normal or equal intervals. We stretched our right arms out straight to touch the shoulder of the recruit next to us. For close intervals we would place our hand or arm on hip and bend our elbow out to touch the recruit next to us to achieve a four-inch distance. When the drill instructor desires us to begin marching, he would then order a right or left facing movement and this would become a platoon in columns. We were learning.

TWO

I was still as shaken-up as I was on the first day we arrived and was sure, by no means, any less so than the rest of the platoon. I could sense the slow, hard and expected transition from civilian to Marine. We were noticeably becoming a team and we had the first bit of Marine Corps History in our minds. There was already a perceptible change in how we formed up and marched away from the history class room. We were prouder for what we learned about this Marine Corps, with its vast usage, its trusted ability to accomplish difficult missions and its culture. Even though I did not yet understand all of this at this moment, I started to notice a distinct difference in these Marines, our teachers. It was a pride, a loyalty, a unity very detached from civilian life and habits.

We recruits were like stones and these drill instructors were like stone-knappers. If we proved to be the type of stone suitable to be shaped, then we will become the new members of this fraternity of elite warriors. As we marched to chow, I found myself thinking about the next class on Marine Corps history and anticipated more great stories. Staff Sergeant Dunnigan was an excellent story teller.

"Road guards out!" Staff Sergeant Rogers ordered, and the sound of his voice snapped me out of my daydream. I was once again totally focused on my position in the world of Parris Island. The outside sounds crashed back into focus with the froggy croaks, the patois of yelling drill instructors and sweaty recruit platoons marching or double-timing all around us to their commands. The soup of sounds was a mixture of boot heels hitting the pavement, rifles being slapped by recruit hands, metal clanging in repetitious rhythms and a convertible GTO, that had stopped for us to cross the street, was blaring *Sugar Sugar* by the Archies.

I stood in line at the mess hall with my mouth pressed hard against the back of the head of the recruit in front of me, my body crushed tightly between the recruits in front and in back of me. I could feel the recruit in back of me clenching and unclenching his jaw muscles obviously undergoing the same sense of strangeness in this invasion of our civilian personal space-bubbles.

The line moved forward with precision and soon I was holding my mess tray flat in front of my face, only revealing my eyes, while robotically moving down the chow line, until the serving started, whereupon I dropped the tray to my waist level and stared straight ahead. The food, as always, was heaped on the tray forming Alpine peaks and I pondered, without a hint of joy, the constipation ordeal awaiting me as I mechanically side-stepped down the line. I still had not taken a shit since leaving Maryland and wondered where this pile of food would be crammed inside my body.

Drill, drill and more drill was what followed chow. At least we were working off our full stomachs and sweating off the extra weight that soft civilian life had draped around our bodies.

It became obvious that Staff Sergeant Rogers was not prone to scream at us while we drilled. He would have the offenders of drill maneuvers drop out and run laps around the platoon, with their rifles held high over their heads as we marched on. Sergeant Kranz, on the other hand, spent the entire drill period jerking offenders out of the ranks, while screaming obscenities at them and the entire platoon, at the same time, pushing, kicking and slapping the slow, the stupid, the deaf and the diddle-boppers. Diddle-bopping was an observable characteristic in some people, while they walked or marched in that their head and body bobbed up and down. It sounded more like 'diddy-bopping' was actually being said. The only proper method was to move from the hips down, keeping the upper body from moving at all when performing the manual-of-arms or just plain marching. Today Staff Sergeant Rogers was teaching us how to march to the oblique, to the flank and to the rear. We struggled on the hot meat grinder and attempted over and over to get each drill maneuver perfected.

"Let___let, yer let, raet, let,___column raet,___huah!___Let,___ let, yer let, raet, let,___raet oblige,___huah!" Staff Sergeant Rogers commanded.

Our left foot pivoted to turn our bodies on a forty-five degree angle and we stepped off. That is, some of us stepped off and more joined the track team. In a matter of a half hour at least fifteen recruits were huffing and puffing around our platoon. With so much activity distracting us, it became increasingly more difficult for us to concentrate on our own marching. Staff Sergeant Rogers ordered the platoon to a halt, brought the track team in and lectured us on proper marching procedures.

"OK girls, let's try it again.___Platoon,___aah___ten___huat!___ Foart huah!" The platoon was showing improvement, but when Staff Sergeant Rogers ordered to the rear march, we had a train wreck. Since this was our first try at it, half of the recruits kept going straight ahead while the other half were effecting the turn. What was even more chaotic was that the recruits who failed to turn were interspersed throughout the platoon. What Staff Sergeant Rogers saw was the total disintegration of the formation. A real train wreck. He took off his campaign hat and slapped it along his leg as he shouted for us to reform.

"Goddamn it!___If you want to act like disorganized rabble, then what you need is some discipline.___Open ranks!___First squad take six steps forward.___Second squad take four steps forward,___third squad take two steps forward,___fourth squad stay in place!___Move it!" We complied and awaited his wrath. "Drop to push-up position.___ Ready count!___One, two, three, four.... ." We counted off to twenty, which was really forty. "Bends and thrusts!___Ready begin!" Sweat dripped in rivulets off our faces as we slammed into the hot asphalt of the meat grinder. The heat formed blisters on our hands and Rogers did not show any sympathy. But an end did come, more due to time constraints rather than mercy.

"Okay,___stop!" he clipped, and then got us back into formation and tried the maneuver again. This time only three recruits failed to get it right and lucky for us were extracted and placed back on the rifle track team. The big problem with these guys was that they were noticeable always amongst those the drill instructors called the ten percent shit-birds and now they were off running instead of participating and learning with the rest of us. This meant they would screw-up again the next time and we would all be doing PT forever with this system.

We drilled for another hour, at least, before Staff Sergeant Rogers ceased the drill and double timed the platoon back to the old 1st Battalion barracks. When we arrived, we were drenched in sweat and had only five minutes to get into PT training gear.

I think these guys are crazy. I decided, and wondered if, in the old Marine Corps, they had to put up with all this insanity. And then I thought. *Yes they did, and they probably bitched just as much.___This is the Corps, and why should they lighten up just for us.* I continued my comical day dream. While I was in the depths of misery and felt no more could possible add to our despair, Sergeant Kranz came out to take us to the Circuit Course.

Oh Shit, It's Sergeant Kranz.___Now we are really in for it. I really dreaded his presence and breathed in lots of fresh air to ready myself for a really hard afternoon.

"You people have pissed off Staff Sergeant Rogers." he began. "You people should know what I think of your slovenliness and your disrespect for Staff Sergeant Rogers.___Platoon,___ah___ten___huat!___Foart huah!" he croaked in that same froggy voice we were hearing all over the 3rd Battalion area, when we went there.

"Since you are not showing the Corps you are interested in doing your best,___perhaps I should encourage you with some special treatment.___Any one drops out of this PT goes to Motivation Platoon tomorrow!___Got it girls?"

"Sir, yes Sir!" we shouted back with trepidation in our voices.

"Double time,___huah!" We were running hell-bent not to piss off Sergeant Kranz. In quicker time then before, we passed the 3rd Battalion area and entered the Circuit Course. The same noises heard the day before greeted us again. It was almost tribal, that sound. It was like the primitive tribes we saw in the movies preparing for war. Sergeant Kranz ran us around the track before he delivered us to our physical training instructor for rounds two through ten of his sadistic specialties.

We went through our side-straddle-hops, push-ups, rowing-exercises, body-twists, elbow-rests, leg-lifts, bent-knee-sit-ups and mountain-climbers. The fact that we were already limbered up from all the earlier punishment exercises made this round less stressful on our muscles, however, we were running low on energy. The big meal we ate was now totally depleted and hunger started to rumble in my stomach. I started to develop a bad headache and stomach cramps.

No shit!___Yep that's it.___No shit, yet, and probably, no shit again today.___That is why my head and stomach hurts.___The drill instructors took their shit today and they don't give a shit for us who can't take a shit.___Ooh shit,___now I gotta shit! I let my mind play with the concept humorously and it helped distract me from the strain of the PT and natures call tearing at my guts. I created all kinds of nonsense in my mind as we continued our ordeal to keep a comical outlook, while hoping to make my mind think about other things, as I groveled on the dry, dusty sand flea infested ground and flinched at the ever hungry sand flea bite we could not scratch.

Sergeant Kranz had us back on the running track as soon as we completed the exercises and pushed us harder today than he had yesterday. "You maggots have been slackin'___haven't you?___Right!___Well ol' Sergeant Kranz will try very hard to get you motivated again.___Don't you worry none." Suddenly, he broke into a running song.

"I Love working for Uncle Sam."
We repeated after each verse.
"Let's me know just who I am,
one_two_three_four,
United States Marine Corps.
One_two_three_four,
I love the Marine Corps,
My Corps. *step, step*
Your Corps. *step, step*
Our Corps. *step, step*
Marine Corps."

We repeated the song twice and puffed through several more miles of Parris Island dust and heat while dreaming of the showers, sleep and let's not forget that head-call. Sergeant Kranz finally headed us toward our barrack, still running and singing more songs, while flashing us his evil sadistic shit-eating grin all the way back.

"Okay hogs,___hit the showers!___Port side goes first.___Do it!"

Sergeant Kranz bellowed down the squad bay. Miracles upon miracles, within twenty minutes we were again formed up outside and began marching.

"Let's see what you learned today ladies.___To the rear march." We obliged and sure as all hell, the same three recruits fucked-up again. Sergeant Kranz surged through the ranks and slapped one across the back of his head, while he grabbed that offender by the back of his collar and pulling him along, he kicked the others out of formation with his boot. "Get out of my platoon formation you dead-beats!___Walk ten feet behind the formation and do not try to march.___You can't anyhow!" he croaked menacingly.

The three recruits, shamed and wearing red faces, walked along behind the platoon. They were sure to feel lost and no longer part of the team, our team. They would hopefully see that it is better to work hard to remain part of the team, than to be thrown out, as failures. It was reminiscent of that sick feeling of rejection a boy feels when all the other boys are picked to form up a baseball or football team, while they sit unchosen to play at all.

"You're not gung ho!____For you dick-wads who don't know what that means,___it means to strive to work together." he yelled back to the three, but loudly for our education as well.

Sergeant Kranz got the platoon together again and marched us over to a building we had not visited before. He got us into a single file and moved the line inside the building. There was a large screen with a camera and lighting in front of it. There were tables with stacks of garrison covers stretched over with the white cloth for dress blues. Next to the covers were stacks of dress blue uniforms, however these were for funerals. They were drapped over the shoulders and clipped from behind. They only reached to the middle of our stomachs. The photograper then snapped each of our pictures, where the bottom of each shot was slightly above the bottom of the cut-off dress blue drape. This entire process lasted well under an hour and we were once again marching off to a new event.

Our boots pounded the tar in more cohesive sounding steps, creating a plausible promise that we would be perfect in the next weeks. Our destination was another class room. Once inside, we stood behind more of the same type of long tables with the backs of our knees touching long benches and waited for the next order. A gunnery sergeant walked in to the classroom, went up to the front and turned to face us. He just stood there and held a straight face. Suddenly he said "Well?"

"Sir, good afternoon Sir!" our irregular greeting came out far too late.

"That the best this platoon can do?" he chided with a disgusted frown. We repeated our greeting, this time with a uniform and sure-voiced clarity.

"Better.___Why can't you just do it like that from the beginning and not have to repeat yourselves wasting everyone's time?" he continued, "My name is Gunnery Sergeant Joe Lasik and I am here to discuss the Uniform Code of Military Justice,___in short, referred to as the UCMJ.___The purpose of the UCMJ or Military Law is to establish good order and discipline within the Armed Forces.___A military community cannot survive if everyone acts as an individual who responds to their own desires.___When a member of the military violates good order and discipline or commits a crime,___the UCMJ serves the same as criminal status in the civilian community.___Each of you is personally responsible for total obedience to military law."

Gunnery Sergeant Lasik was starting his lecture with sternness. His voice, bearing and delivery were professional, no-nonsense and each sentence was spoken with short staccato bursts much like a machine gun burst. He was a tall slim man with pale skin. His face was oval with high cheek bones, sharp pointed nose and his eyes were hard and piercing, like those of a hawk. His hair was a short cropped swath of grayish brown resting on top of his head and shaven around the sides. He had a serious scar and dent on the side of his forehead. He almost looked like an Indian except for the pale skin color. His ribbons reflected Vietnam along with a purple-heart ribbon. He continued his lecture.

"Without discipline you are worthless.___Nothing.___In the Marine Corps we are a small group of professionals.___Our success is literally based on discipline.___Fire-discipline,___marching-discipline,___water-discipline and your personal-discipline, encompasses the sole factor in team, unit, battalion and Corps-discipline."

We sat transfixed, listening to this new awareness, this trust thrust upon us to carry the badge of the Corps for our Country. Next, we became aware that discipline was a state of order expected of each of us through the exact execution of orders resulting from an intelligent, willing obedience.

"While you recruits undergo training in rifle-drill, close-order-drill and bayonet-drill,___you are literally undergoing the metamorphosis from disorganized civilian slime-balls to organized Marine Corps professionals.___Punishment is sometimes necessary to correct and reform those whose performance is deemed unfit to be on the team.___ To learn discipline on the battlefield would be too late, and if you wait to appreciate discipline at that time, should you be alive to see it, you probably cost the lives of many of your fellow Marines by then."

We sat there absorbing this wisdom when I suddenly realized at that moment that he was telling us that we can overcome any difficult situation as a disciplined team, regardless of our personal fears, because fear is the enemy of discipline. If we can't work as a team and panic, we have lost.

"If you learn to work as a team you will find that when well equipped, well trained and well led,___you can defeat the enemies of our Country." Gunnery Sergeant Lasik said and continued his motivating lecture.

"In the old Corps days the UCMJ was referred to as 'Rocks and Shoals'___The UCMJ includes the Constitution of the United States and international law, which includes the Law of War.___Enacted by Congress and signed into Law by the President on 31 May 1951, it has been known from that day on as the Uniform Code of Military Justice." Gunnery Sergeant Lasik went on to explain that the UCMJ requires that important articles of the code be thoroughly explained to every enlisted person at the time of entrance into the active military, or within six days. Thereafter, it is to be explained upon six months of service and upon re-enlistment. He explained about the agencies through which military jurisdiction is exercised. These agencies include military commissions, provost courts and courts-martial for the trial of offenders against Military Law. In the case of general courts-martial, there is a trial of persons who by laws of war are subject to trial by military tribunals, commanding officers and officers in charge of non-judicial punishment in accordance with Article 15 of the UCMJ. He informed us that among these agencies the one with which the members of the Armed Forces are most familiar are those relating to commanding officers, non-judicial punishment, which in the Marine Corps is known as 'Office Hours' and courts-martial, which in the order of ascendancy in power and jurisdiction are the summary court-martial, the lowest court-martial, the special court-martial, which is an intermediate court of limited jurisdiction and the general court-martial, the highest trial court in the military.

The class continued with specific procedures for each of the courts-martial, courts procedures and the rights of the accused. When Lasik finished my head ached trying hard to remember all that was said and I feared forgetting any of it, should I be asked by one of our drill instructors for the particulars.

I'd hate to ever be involved in one of these courts-martial proceedings. I thought with conviction.

"Remember recruits,___you will be able to review and learn these courts-martial procedures in your Guidebooks." Gunnery Sergeant Lasik said suddenly, and just as suddenly, I was able to relax and the headache started to subside.

"Aahh__ten__huat!" Sergeant Kranz bellowed as Gunnery Sergeant Lasik started to leave.

"Fall out!" he croaked and we responsed crisply and exited the classroom to march over to the mess hall. I was definitely hungry. After we got through the line at the mess hall, I marveled at the mountain of food on my tray. We had fried chicken, mashed potatoes, corn, cornbread with butter and a cool cup of milk. There were newly arrived recruits coming in behind our platoon. Sneaking a glance at them, I thought of our first meal on the Island. They walked by with bug-eyed fear on their faces and trays so over loaded they dripped. Seeing those massive piles of chow actually caused my mouth to salivate and I mentally chuckled, as I remembered those recruits who willingly tried to scarf-up our uneaten trays of food. Now I was glancing around, without moving my head of course, trying like a radar, to locate more chow. But, alas, I was too far away from any first day recruits to catch a free meal.

There were more drill exercises on our march back to the barracks. The drill instructors never left a moment free from some form of training. It was always double-time or strict attention required when not at double-time. Each evening was now becoming routine, with bouts of punishment PT, threats to individuals who did not meet performance expectations to be designated for the next mornings

Motivation Platoon, polishing boots and brass and eternally cleaning our rifles. In between those events we stood at attention along the white line with our red books held straight out in front of our faces at arms length and studied Marine Corps history, regulations, customs, guard duty and many other subjects.

THREE

Sleep was definitely our reward for a day of sacrifice on Parris Island. The nights were totally silent and dreams were our only escape from the hellish day time activities. However, sleep was not long underway when the crash of shit-cans came echoing down the squad bay accompanied by the foul cursing of one or more drill instructors, causing us to spring out of our racks and on to the white lines.

"Count off!" Was the duty drill instructors' first order each day and our Pavlovian response of, "One Sir, two Sir, three Sir, four Sir, five Sir…, and on up to eighty-nine, went the sounds of recruits trying their utmost to shake off the fog of sleep and sound bright and eager. And so it started again this morning.

"Port side, make a head call." Staff Sergeant Rogers shouted.

We responded appropriately and double-timed to the head. Then it happened, it hit me like gravity sucking at my guts. I had to take a shit, that shit, the elusive one that neatly doubled me over yesterday. So it was not only just had to, it was to be my first since we had arrived on the Island. I was so happy to finally have to go that I hopped on the first black lidded shitter I came to without bashfulness and *splash*…, bombs away, all came out, or did I in my excitement only think it. No, I definitely dropped something and then as I stood up to flush I was amazed to see only a dark black sliver of digested matter. My headache was gone suddenly and I figured the headaches I was suffering were directly related to the constipation. Where was all the food I had eaten? Was it all used up as energy leaving only a few fibers? No matter, I felt great and quickly brushed my teeth, shaved my peach fuzzed face and ran into the shower. I now felt revitalized.

Breakfast was eagerly consumed and the morning was starting out great, since no recruits had fouled up the drill orders this morning. We marched and then double-timed back to the barrack to change into PT gear. Staff Sergeant Rogers took us to the Circuit Course this time. It was his first time to take us alone. He did run us at normal double-time to the track, however he did not run us around the entire track first before delivering us to the PT Instructor's platform.

Our physical training regimen was the same as on the other days, however I felt that I was more able to achieve the required posture and stamina than on the previous days. The only requirements that still caused me severe strain and effort were the pull-up bar and rope climbing. I celebrated a small amount of progress, because I was able to crank out twelve pull-ups this morning and climb the rope to the top several seconds faster than before.

Staff Sergeant Rogers urged us on instead of slinging constant foul accusations, occasional slaps upside our heads or shoves, as Sergeant Kranz enjoyed doing. The rope was straight, that is, there were no knots tied every several feet. It took effort to learn how to swiftly get your foot wrapped around the rope using the other foot as a breaker and grab hand over hand to sprint up the damn slippery thing. We were told that later on we would be expected to climb up with hands only, so try to achieve it now to get the gist. Staff Sergeant Rogers even had a different style of running then that of Sergeant Kranz. Rogers started us off at a pace more like double-time and steadily increased our pace until we were running like hell, but still maintaining a tight platoon formation. Sergeant Kranz started us off fast, kept us fast and before we were half way, we started losing platoon integrity. This only resulted in more yelling, cursing and the cuffing of recruits. The cuffings were not severe, as they were more like a father cuffing a wayward child. Nevertheless, it was humiliating to catch an open hand, as I knew from the hands of nuns at the Children's Home in Germany. Perhaps this was what caused the restrained sobs I heard at night. So far, I had yet to shed a tear on the Island.

We started singing a running song. This song was called *Amen* and we stretched the word Amen over several foot falls, which sounded out more like A-a-ah-men, several times and followed it with a series of short sentences with words like "let me hear ya now", 'all together now', and the like. Later in training, one recruit, usually a black recruit, would voice out lines to this song that sounded like verses from a Baptist church service. The song Amen was the most flexible song we would sing on the Island. Hot, dusty, sweaty and again hungry, we double timed back down the Boulevard de France and then across the meat grinder to our barrack. We usually beat the other three platoons in our series and today left them back in China for all the distance we were ahead of them. As we entered our barrack, I stole a glance back to Boulevard de France and saw the other three platoons, over two hundred seventy recruits, looking like the whole Marine Corps in their mass.

A quick run under the showers, then back into utilities, we charged outside again and conducted close-order-drill for about an hour. Staff Sergeant Rogers was so pleased when he ordered "to the rear march" and everyone did it correctly, that he stopped the platoon and asked jokingly. "Did you guys swap the shit-birds for new recruits,____or did you kill them to reduce your mistakes,____or did you feel sorry for ol' Staff Sergeant Rogers and decide to act as a team?"

That's the ticket. It should appease him and we were proud of our accomplishment. But, on this Island one should never assume a DI would leave us alone for our effort.

"Well guess what!____I am still angry for the foul-ups from yesterday!____So drop to push-up position!____A*ahoorrah!*" he ordered with a smile and barked the Marine growl. Our first germinating accomplishment was smashed and dropping to the blistering asphalt somehow felt the natural direction to go. In our mental state fifty push-ups was expected, but we only pumped out twenty push-ups, when suddenly and to our surprise, he ordered us back up. Still grinning, he had us resume marching.

"Don't let your successes go to your heads girls," he said in a jocular tone, while continuing his grinning, "there are sixty-two basic movements in drill____and you Cub Scouts have not yet learned a dozen."

Our marching skills were definitely improving. When we passed other platoons from our series and the angle offered an ability to observe them, I noticed they each had more serious problems to overcome compared to our platoon. I suppose Staff Sergeant Rogers knew this and was smacking his lips anticipating our platoon getting the Drill Competition streamer. The Drill Competition, we had already been informed, was one of the intra-series challenges, due after the Series Physical Fitness Test. The best platoon gets a colored ribbon, called a streamer, to affix to their guidon. I started to hear our platoon stomp with the sound of one foot-fall hitting the deck at the same time. This was pure music to our ears and I hoped we could keep this ability up for the Drill Competition or was today just a fluke where all of us were lucky to be in form.

He directed our platoon off the meat grinder and over to the Regimental Headquarters area. Staff Sergeant Rogers halted us in front of the barber shop and ordered us into single file. I hadn't really noticed it, but our hair had already begun to grow out quite a bit and now what we gained we were to lose again. *Beez--ba bop--buzz*, that familiar sound resonated in our ears again reminding us old salts of the far away first day when we heard the same sounds.

Yeh sure, salts, shit, what a laugh, we were still pissing civilian Kool Aid and have a fucking mountain to climb before we could wear the Eagle, Globe and Anchor. I reminded myself.

Our heads shorn once again and our stomp growing ever more confident, Rogers marched us straight back to our barrack for a DI-instructed class on military rank. The lesson taught us what the equivalent ranks for each branch of service looked like, for instant recognition.

Staff Sergeant Rogers got a little perturbed when he got to the Navy rear admiral rank. He explained that naval officers promoted from captain to rear admiral are equivalent to brigadier generals, a one-star general. However, the Navy has rear admiral lower half and the next promotion is rear admiral upper half. The rear admiral lower half wears a shoulder board with one star and the rear admiral upper half has two stars. This is fine when you see them coming, he said, but the problem is the rank title rear admiral when a phone call alerts ones arrival. They simple say rear admiral and a Marine, Army, or Air Force major general gets nervous that they may be junior, not to mention what a senior brigadier general thinks when the admiral arrives and is actually out-ranked by that visited brigadier general.

"In other words, the Navy simply finds it clumsy to announce their rank as lower or upper half and instead just say rear admiral.___This is also a habit in other ranks such as saying sergeant for E-5 through E-9 ranks instead of the proper rank title.___Lieutenant-colonel and colonels also do this very often and it is considered acceptable," he explained, "for instance, if a lieutenant-colonel calls from somewhere, he may say this is colonel so and so.___Got it?"

"Sir, yes Sir!" we chorused back.

"The Navy says lieutenant for the rank, which is referred to by the other branches of the military, of a captain.___The second lieutenant in the other branches equals an ensign in the Navy.___A first lieutenant in these other branches is a lieutenant jg.,___or junior grade, in the Navy." he glanced around with a wry smile to gauge our bewilderment and confusion.

"Now my favorite is the term captain,___as it has more meanings than the other ranks.___To make my point,___let's say a Navy captain boards a naval vessel to meet the ship's captain and brings along a Marine captain and they use a small civilian boat to get out to the ship." he said, then stopped abruptly, and smiled.

I guess he's anticipating the punch line will be so funny it will make the platoon laugh and then get us punishment PT for laughing. I assumed, because every thing else around here has proven to be designed to inflict doubt, pain and general misery through any number of punishments. But, I was wrong here.

"The small boat operator could be a chief petty officer, but he is the captain of his craft. The Navy captain is equal to a colonel and the Navy ship captain could be an ensign, lieutenant jg., or lieutenant, all the way up to a commander, and the Marine captain could out rank the ships captain if he winds up being an ensign or lieutenant jg., and he would be equal to a Navy lieutenant and could be senior to him based on their date of rank," he grinned and looked all around for our laughter.

We just looked straight ahead and held our dumbfounded stare. I don't think anyone of us figured on a drill instructor joking anyhow. It was time for chow and he got us headed that direction in a strangely quiet manner. The meal was heavy, consisting of meat-loaf, mashed potatoes, peas, bread slices and a welcome cold cup of milk. I devoured the entire pile in seconds, even at the angle of approach we were taught to assume while eating. That is, fork to mouth and no leaning over our trays. This at first caused quite a few recruits to eat awkwardly. However, the lessons of Children Home St. Joseph were ingrained in me and I was very much at ease eating this way.

Staff Sergeant Rogers told us to hurry up so we could get over to the Marine Corps History classroom for part two of our lessons. I was happy to hear we were going to part two of Marine Corps History after chow and anticipated the new stories, as I really did not know anything about this branch of the military. Hell, I knew very little about any of the others as well, even though my father was career Air Force. We never saw him as it was. How does a kid learn? I knew more about the Romans, Visigoths, Ostrogoths, Vikings, Luft Waffe, Wehrmacht and Waffen SS, because that had been my environment.

"Platoon,___aah-ten-huat!___Foart,___huah!" Staff Sergeant Rogers shouted loudly. We stepped off with a loud left foot echoing across the mess hall parking lot and then Rogers ordered in a croaky voice. "Count cadence,___delayed cadence,___count cadence,___count!"

"One *step, step, step,* two, *step, step, step,* three, *step, step, step,* four, *step, step, step,* one, *step, step,* two, *step, step,* three, *step, step,* four, *step, step,* one, *step,* two, *step,* three, *step,* four, *step,* one, two, three, four, United States Marine Corps!" we sounded off proudly.

"My Corps!" he continued.

"My Corps!" we responded back.

"Your Corps!" he went on.

"Your Corps!" we answered.

"Our Corps!" he finished.

"Our Corps!" we responded louder than before.

The order was given to enter and our eagerness to continue learning about our Corps could be seen by our impatience to enter that class room, but was really fear of the DI. Staff Sergeant Dunnigan was standing by the lectern waiting. After we had filed in, we promptly shouted. "Sir, good afternoon Sir!"

"Good afternoon recruits!" he returned snappily.

"Today we will continue the History of the Marine Corps from World War I, World War II through Korea, Dominican Republic and up to Vietnam." Once seated our breathing ceased to make noise as our minds awaited the continuation of the great stories of the Marine Corps expeditions, which were to become the pinnacle of their successes and achievements to date."

"Soissons,___St. Mihiel,__Blanc Mount Ridge,___Belleau Wood____and the Argonne.____These battles were fought by the 5th and 6th Marine Regiments supported by the 6th Machine Gun Battalion, who were one of the infantry brigades of the 2nd American Division in France.___Up to that time, the engagements these Marines fought were the heaviest and hardest.___In June 1918, at Belleau Wood, Marines of the 4th Brigade fought with such ferocity that the Germans referred to them as 'teufel-hunden' or 'devil dogs' in their official reports.____

Devil Dogs is a name for Marines, which has increased in popularity over time. Other Marine units involved during that war included the 5th Marine Brigade, composed of the 11th and 13th Regiments and the 5th Brigade Machine Gun Battalion, took part performing mostly guard duty." He continued his lecture explaining how the first Marine Aviation Units under Major Alfred A. Cunningham rendered day duty or Day Wing for the Northern Bombing Group in Northern France and Belgium.

"Some areas and dates where Marines were most actively involved, were Haiti from 1915 to 1934, where two wars were fought with the Cacos.___In the Dominican Republic, Marines had fought for six years to suppress banditry."

"One of our most famous Marines was Chesty Puller.___He was to become our most decorated Marine for heroism. Although, Gunnery Sergeant Lou Diamond was acclaimed by many as the perfect Marine, many more would choose Chesty Puller for that distinction.___Chesty Puller was awarded five Navy crosses and the Army's Distinguished Service Cross, the Silver Star and many more awards for valor in combat.____He wore a total of fifty-three decorations when he retired," he said and actually looked sad as he said the last.

"Chesty Puller was promoted to Lieutenant General in 1955, after having begun his career as a private here at Parris Island in 1918____ where, in those days,____they slept in tents.___He served in Haiti in 1919 as a second Lieutenant and in Nicaragua in 1926.____In 1939 he served on board the USS Augusta in China____and in 1940,___as a Major with the 4th Marine Regiment in Shanghai, China.___He commanded the 1st Battalion of the 7th Marine Regiment on Guadalcanal and commanded the 1st Marine Regiment in Korea," he stated and then showed us a picture of Chesty Puller.

This guy Chesty Puller looks like a squat bulldog. I thought.

Our instructor continued with stories of the Marine Corps through the first three decades of the twentieth century. And as he was covering the beginning of 1929, and how the Marines, by then referred to as the 3rd Marine Brigade, had improved the situation in China." he concluded, looked up and scanned the room for survivors. Seeing no drowning recruits, he continued.

Facts, facts and more facts! I thought and felt many in our platoon could not digest this avalanche of Marine history and lore. *It's a good thing the Corps isn't four hundred years old. These history haters would be climbing the bulkheads by now.* I laughed inwardly.

"Prior to the beginning of World War II, the Marine Corps was relatively small in number of personnel.___It was not unusual for many Marines to know the names of each other regardless of where the others were stationed as they may have been in training together, served together at duty stations or heard stories about others,___to the point they felt they knew those individuals.___It was a tight group of professionals in the pre-war days.___There were some two thousand Marines stationed in the Pacific and Asian Continent during 1941.___The 4th Marine Regiment in Shanghai, China had several detachments stationed in North China at Peiping and Tientsin and in the Philippines at Cavite and Hongapo.___Several thousand more were stationed on the Island of Hawaii, Wake, Guam, American Samoa, in the Panama Canal Zone and on Cuba.___The 2nd Marine Division was stationed at San Diego in those days and is now operating out of Camp Lejeune, North Carolina.___During the prewar years there were provisional Marine Brigades taken from the 2nd Marine Division and sent to Caribbean Islands, Iceland and other islands in the Atlantic Ocean," he said and then stopped for a moment, while glancing at some papers.

"On 7 December 1941, the Japanese attacked Pearl Harbor Hawaii.___The 4th Marines had relocated to the Philippines just prior to the attack, leaving some detachments to remain in Tientsin and Peiping China.___The 4th Marines participated in the defense of Bataan and Corregidor until over-powered by the larger forces of the Japanese," he coughed, and with a serious face, went on, "The goddamned U.S. Army was in command and their general organized a parley with the Japs to surrender.___This move forced the Marines to surrender their colors, but the Marines said 'fuck-you' and burned them before submitting, since the 'other Americans" gave up and the bulk of the fighting force was no longer in the field to fight."

"The beginning of the United States offensive operation against the Japanese Empire began on 7 August 1942 when General Alexander A.Vandergrift was ordered to assault the Japanese on Guadalcanal from New Zealand bases.

"Guadalcanal was hard won,___after four more months of savage combat.___Their memorable battles took place at Bloody Ridge, Tenaru

River and Matanikau River, while the Marine and Army Airmen fought and performed legendary feats to fend off Japanese air attacks.___The Solomons campaigns were finished-up by the 3rd Marine Division, which fought at Koromokina Lagoon and Piva Fork."

"Get on your feet maggots!" Staff Sergeant Rogers suddenly yelled. We jumped up and stood at attention, snapped out of our world of history.___I was totally engrossed and hungered for more.___However, there were a few of our platoon who apparently found this boring and subsequently went dopey.___The drill instructor, seeing this, decided we were not interested in his Marine Corps history and decided to snap us back into reality and reinvigorate our lagging interest."

"Get your asses outside on the double!" he barked. Tired from the hot room, we ran drunkenly outside and formed up. He ordered push-ups and bends and thrusts. After doing what seemed like an hours worth, but was really only about fifteen minutes, we were ordered back into the classroom. With our hearts pounding, while sweat dripped off our faces and down our backs, we sat attentive for the continuation of the History lesson. Staff Sergeant Dunnigan was not at all perturbed about Staff Sergeant Roger's interruption. Perhaps he also needed a break and figured we needed stimulation to get our minds refreshed and alert.

Once back inside the classroom, feeling very alert we were surprised to see a projector set up for a film showing. The film displayed actual footage of Marines fighting in the Pacific islands campaigns during World War II. The film ended with footage of the Korean War.

"The allied offensive against Japan intensified after the defeat of Japanese forces on Bouganville.___Tarawa,___recruits!___It was an island the Japanese had bragged it would take one million Americans, one hundred years, to take their triangular defenses consisting of Makin, Betio and Tarawa.___Well, it took the 2nd Marines seventy-six hours.___How could this feat possibly have been accomplished?___Those Marines,___like you recruits,___were taught that we Marines are invincible,___that we can achieve anything against all odds___and most importantly our Espirit de Corps makes it a mission for Marines never to let a fellow Marine down and therefore let down the legend the Marines have achieved.___There were 4836 Japanese Marines and some Korean Laborers on Tarawa, of which, only 146, mostly laborers were taken prisoner."

"During 76 hours of combat 1085 Marines lost their lives and 2233 Marines were wounded.___I feel that the battle of Tarawa defines the true soul of a Marine Corps, in that Marines are always willing to fight against any greater enemy strength and viciously kick ass!"

"Saipan was then assaulted by the 2nd and 4th Marine Divisions with the 27th Army Division in reserve.___They landed abreast on the western side and fought three separate stages for the conquest of the island," he said, and held up three fingers.

"The Japanese were fighting on their homeland here and savagely fought back on the beachhead, then the fight for Mount Topotchau line,___and finally the seizure of the northern part of the island, where a desperate Bonzai attack occurred.___The key terrain feature on the island was Mount Topochau, where Marines had to blast the enemy out of the many caves.___Hundreds of Japanese civilians and military personnel, fearing capture, and due to propaganda, which led them to believe the Americans would eat them, jumped off the cliffs into the ocean," he stated, as his right hand flew downward.

"Guam and Tinian islands were secured during this campaign and air fields were constructed to support B-29 bombers for the first raids on Mainland Japan since General Dolittle's daring carrier-based raid with sixteen B-25s at the beginning of the war."

Our ability to remain alert and attentive was being worn thin in the hot stifling room as the Marine Corps' history lecture went on and on in glorious detail. But the room temperature overcame our ability to concentrate.

"Stand up!___Stretch recruits!" Staff Sergeant Dunnigan quipped suddenly.

"Sir, aye-aye Sir!" we numbly responded and stood with sweat dripping off of our faces.

"I said move around and stretch!" he said, and we obeyed. While we stretched he spoke about the next segment of our Marine Corps History and told us that we were about to hear a part of the Marine Corps finest history, a place called Iwo Jima.

"Ready,___seat!" he snapped. Staff Sergeant Rogers just stood there against a wall and blankly stared at us. Apparently, the order given to us by another to stretch was not an order he would disagree with and maybe he was zoned-out with the heat as well. We sat and felt surprisingly more attentive. The history was not boring at all, however, sitting in a very warm room for long periods without being allowed to move at all can cause anybody to feel uncomfortable and tired. How Gunnery Sergeant Lasik endured, is anybody's guess.

"Iwo Jima,___Mount Suribachi,___these names were to become common usage in American society.____A bleak, black-sand volcanic island,___which prior to 23 February 1945___was totally unknown to the average person___and was to become as familiar as the Alamo or Gettysburg.____There were three airfields on the island which threatened American B-29 bombers based out of the Marianas.___The purpose for taking Iwo Jima was to stop that threat and also to place our fighters there to protect B-29 missions out of the Marianas flying towards Japan."

"The 4th and 5th Marine Divisions were to land on Iwo Jima with the 3rd Division in reserve.___Fierce fighting was required to tackle the many fortifications and fanatical spirit of the Japanese defending their home soil.___The famous flag raising over Mount Suribachi by five Marines and a Navy corpsman was to become the outstanding symbol of America's war effort.___The Japanese forces were defeated on 16 March 1945."

"Okay hogs,___fall out for some wake up PT!" Staff Sergeant Rogers barked suddenly.

The shock of the order had so totally taken us by such surprise that the PT would not be necessary, however he had other plans.

It seems none of us can keep an alert mind when we have to endure history in an oven. I surmised.

FOUR

After a brisk bout of push-ups and mountain-climbers, Staff Sergeant Rogers must have decided that we were sufficiently awake to hear about Korea and the rest. The order to get our lame-asses back into the classroom was given, and once again we sat with forced rapt attention, awaiting more of Staff Sergeant Dunnigan's tales of the Corps daring exploits.

"Okay,___let's start with 25 June 1950. That's when the Communist North Koreans invaded the Republic of South Korea.___Things happened so fast, that the first American troops available to resist the invasion were Army occupation forces stationed in Japan.___The

Marine Corps had been so severely reduced in size after World War II that it had to scrape up Marines from all active units and call in reservists to build a division.___Meanwhile, on the 7 July 1950, while the build-up was underway, the first Marines to enter the conflict were the 1st Provisional Marine Brigade, which were made up mostly of the 5th Marine Regiment, with reinforcements, and their air support group, MAG-33. By 2 August 1950, MAG-33 was engaged with the enemy in offensive operations and by 7 August 1950, the Brigade was engaging North Korean lines."

"Finally, on 15 September 1950, the X Corps Landing Force, with the 1st Marine Division, minus the 7th Marines, as the landing force, made a very difficult amphibious landing at Inchon.___The North Korean army was thus outflanked."

"The regiment engaged an entire Communist Chinese division and after four days of battle the 7th Marines had so badly busted the Chinese up, that division would never be able to participate in the Korean conflict again.___That did not mean the Chinese were out of the war.___Not by a long shot.___On 27 November, the 5th and 7th Marines who had advanced to Yudam-ni were attacked west of the Chosin Reservoir and the Chinese also cut the supply line.___Between 28 November and 2 December the 1st Marine Division held off ten Chinese divisions with two more Chinese divisions in reserve," he said and finished talking while looking around the room.

"Okay,___sounds bad,___huh?" Staff Sergeant Dunnigan asked in serious tone. "Damn right it was.___Hell, the Chinese had cut off part of the 1st Marine Division.___Those guys had to begin a fighting withdrawal in heavy snowstorms and sub-zero temperatures.___There were over seventy miles of dangerous roads through mountain passes and canyons,___saturated with Chinese soldiers.___These Marines battled onwards toward Hagaru-ri and had to protect the long convoy by clearing the sloops of each mountain, of Chinese troops.___The reverse slopes were attacked by the Marine air wing.___The situation was so desperate that all Marines, including the cooks, clerks, mechanics and other support personnel grabbed their rifles and fought as infantry.___ And you all know that all Marines are trained infantrymen for exactly that reason___right?___When Chesty Puller was asked by news agents about Marines withdrawing in combat,___his answer was simply 'Withdraw hell!___We're just attacking in a different direction!'___

And you can see why this would be the case,___based on the current situation I have described to you."

"Sir, yes Sir!" our platoon bellowed with pride in our tone.

"Well,___the bravery of those Marines allowed them to reunite with the division at Hagaru-ri.___After a resupply drop and using a makeshift air field to evacuate their wounded the column began its breakout through enemy forces on the 6 December 1950.___They headed for Koto-ri where the additional casualties were evacuated by air.___The 1st Marine Division reached Hamhung on 11 December and the main body was evacuated by Task Force 90 on the 15th to South Korea.___The 1st Marine Division brought back its vehicles, equipment, wounded and dead,___that were found,___through the gauntlet of that Chinese infested snow blizzard from hell." Staff Sergeant Dunnigan, wearing a solemn face, paused for a moment. He took a deep breath and then continued.

"The 1st Marine Division returned to Pusan and starting on 22 April there were several large scale Chinese attacks in the Hwachon Reservoir area, which were beaten back by the Marines at great loss to the enemy."

"Peace talks,___which began in July 1951, were to fail and the Marines used this time to experiment with using helicopters to fly troops and supplies over the hills of Korea.___On 27 July 1953 the truce was finally signed.___The 1st Marine Division would return to the United States in the Spring of 1955, after serving five years in Korea."

"Okay,___stand up and stretch.___Do it!" Staff Sergeant Rogers ordered.

"Sir, aye-aye Sir!" we gladly responded and eagerly complied.

"Ready,___seat!" he barked, after about thirty seconds.

"Congress and the President, seeing the value and necessity of a ready professional fighting force___and not wanting to wait again for long rebuilding and refitting, while our country demands more immediate action, as had happened in World War II and Korea,___ passed legislation to expand the size of the Marine Corps.___It was 1952, and this legislation authorized three active combat divisions along with three air wings with supporting troops.___The Marine Commandant would be a full General, instead of the previous highest rank of Lieutenant General and would have full status with the Joint Chiefs of Staff.___Up to that point, the Commandant was subordinate to the senior Navy Admiral in all matters concerning the Corps.___On 20 June 1951 the 3rd Marine Brigade was activated at Camp Pendleton, California and soon afterwards on 7 January 1952 it became the 3rd Marine Division and deployed to Japan the following year.___The 3rd Marine Division is composed of the 3rd ,4th, and 9th Regiments and the 12th Artillery Regiment and the divisions' separate battalions.___The 3rd Marine Aircraft Wing was activated at Miami, Florida and composed of MAG's 31, 32 and 45."

Christ! The Corps is a hell of a lot bigger then I would have ever guessed. I thought and eagerly wanted to hear much more. I even like the way Staff Sergeant Dunnigan's voice got strong and loud when attacks occurred or soft, caring and almost silent when danger or destruction visited the Marines. He sounded just like those narrators in the movie theaters who presented the World News just before the movie started.

"During the 1950s the Corps assisted countries in numerous ways.___The Marine Corps started developing a concept for rapid assault force from the sea as far back as 1948.___This concept integrated amphibious and heli-borne forces to rapidly attack from special designed ships.___The Navy designed the LPH,___a combat vessel capable of carrying an entire Marine battalion landing team.___The first ones were converted aircraft carriers left over from the war,___but the first one specifically built for this purpose was the Iwo Jima,___built in 1961.___The Iwo Jima has made around sixty amphibious landings in Vietnam so far, with Marine Special Landing Forces."

"During the early sixties Marine Battalion Landing Teams in the South China Sea provided assistance in standby readiness when the Communists invaded Laos and provided logistical helicopter support for the Laotian government.___The 3rd Marine Amphibious Unit was committed to Thailand due to boarder pressure from the Communists. HMM-362 of the 1st Marine Aircraft Wing was sent to the Mekong Delta of South Vietnam to fly combat support missions for the South Vietnamese armed forces in operations code named 'Shofly'___and they were later sent north to Da Nang in I Corps."

Okay!___Now we are getting Marine Corps history on the present and what we will be involved with if we go to Vietnam. I thought and perked up instantly.

"Meanwhile,___in the early sixties___on our side of the world,___ specifically during October 1962, there was the Cuban Missile Crisis. President Kennedy mobilized the American Armed Forces.___The Marine base in Quantanamo Bay, Cuba was reinforced.___Elements of the 2nd Marine Division and 2nd Marine Air Wing were deployed to forward positions for instant assault capability.___Soon after the 2nd Marine Division was on station an Expeditionary brigade of the 1st Marine Division arrived.___This show of American military resolve forced the Soviet Union into a decision to take out their missiles and go home."

"Not long after the Cuban Crisis, the war in Vietnam started escalating and on 8 March, 1965, the 9th Marine Expeditionary Brigade,___called a MEB,___landed in Da Nang to provide security to the air-base there against Communist air strikes.___And by 12 March, approximately 5000 Marines of the 3rd Marine Expeditionary Force out of Okinawa, had landed.___And,___as if things couldn't get worse,___the following April, Battalion Landing Team 3/6 and HMM-264 under command of Caribbean Task Group 44.9 was ordered to proceed to an off-shore station from the Dominican Republic."

Man,__the Marines were really gettin' into the shit then. I appreciated with awe.

"A coup was in progress and the Marines were to stand by for evacuation of American personnel and other foreign nationals.___Four days after the alert was given to proceed there, 500 Marines were landed.___The situation got more hostile and by the next day,___the 29th of April,___there were 1500 Marines ashore.___Think things were resolved by then?__No.__The Army sent in Airborne units.___ On 1 May, the 4th Marine Expeditionary Brigade,__under Brigadier General John G. Bouker, was activated.___The American forces on the island engaged rebel forces in fire fights and there was much sniper fire.___Brazilian Peace troops were sent in on 25 May 1965 by vote from the Organization of American States and the American forces began withdrawing the next day.___But it wasn't over yet___and soon Honduras, Costa Rica, Paraguay and Nicaragua sent in troops.___By 6 June 1965, when the last elements of the 4th MEB left,___there had been 8000 Marines involved."

"There were casualties in the Dominican Republic,___and by the end of the conflict 9 Marines had been killed and 30 wounded.___While this was going on Major General William R, Collins had arrived at Da

Nang on 3 May 1965 with an advance party of the 3rd Marine Division. The 9th MEB was deactivated and the 3rd Marine Expeditionary Force was established along with the 3rd Marine Division, Forward. At that time the ground elements had consisted mainly of the 3rd Marine Regiment and came under the command of MAG-16, along with all aviation units in country," he finished for a moment and checked our faces for attentiveness and decided to continue.

"By 11 May, the 1st MAG, Advance, had landed in Da Nang commanded by Major General Paul J. Fontana. He assumed operational control of all fixed wing and rotary aircraft in country. The South Vietnamese didn't like the term Expeditionary. Something to do with the ill fated French Expeditionary Forces who had used that term. So on 7 May, it was changed to III MAF for Marine Amphibious Force and Major General Collins was both the division and force commander."

"The 3rd MAB made an amphibious landing the same day of the change-over to III MAF, fifty five miles south of Da Nang, at a place called Chu Lai. An air field was constructed there by Seabees and Marine engineers. The 3rd Marine enclave was established there. Major General Lewis W. Walt took over command of III MAF and the 3rd Marine Division on 5 June 1965. He was in operational command of all U.S. forces in I Corps and I Corps fell under overall control, along with the II, III and IV Corps areas in Vietnam, by the Military Assistance Command Vietnam, or MACV. Army General William C. Westmoreland was given overall command in Vietnam."

"The 7th Marines arrived in Vietnam in August 1965 and General Walt started offensive operations in I Corps. Operation Starlite was the first major U.S. operation of the war. Over six hundred of the 1st Viet Cong Regiment were killed as the Marine maneuvered their forces toward the sea. An additional one hundred eighty nine were killed by the 7th Marines on 18 September. By the end of 1965 there were hundreds more enemy killed, and by then thirty-eight thousand Marines were in country," Staff Sergeant Dunnigan said, pausing to look up and away in thought for a moment as if remembering something.

"During January 1966 President Johnson ordered the entire 1st Marine Division to Vietnam, where they joined their advance units of the 7th Marines and two additional battalions.___By June, the 5th Marines joined their Division in country.___During 1966 operations Double Eagle, Utah and Texas resulted in killing over one thousand enemy troops and captured tons of their supplies.___Marine operations also helped the local population by protecting the villagers during rice harvest and taking census while helping villages with medical aid, food and entertainment.___While such assistance was given, the villages would be surrounded by Marines and South Vietnamese Forces to capture escaping VC.___These operations were called Golden Fleece and County Fair.___Both operations were the idea of the 9th Marines."

We took a wake-up break even though it appeared that nobody was caught nodding off during this section of history. When we came back into the classroom the projector had already been set up for us to view combat footage of Vietnam. After the projector was shut off our verbal history lesson continued.

That country is in a world of shit! I thought with apprehension.

"Combined Action Platoons were created by the 3rd Battalion of the 4th Marines where a fourteen man squad along with a Navy corpsman would literally stay with a village to provide security, train villagers and integrate into thirty five man Popular Force, or PF, teams,___as it was referred to.___The PF program was to defend the villages while keeping the VC from recruiting, taxing and obtaining supplies."

"At the beginning of July 1966 the 324th North Vietnamese Army moved south across the Demilitarized Zone,___commonly called the DMZ,___into Quang Tri Province.___The 324th NVA was trying to force the Marines to pull out of the village enclaves and engage them,___which would relieve the pressure from their guerrilla allies,___ the Viet Cong. Operation Hastings was the response the Corps gave the visitors.___There were eight thousand Marines and three thousand South Vietnamese soldiers in that operation,___against a division of NVA,___the 324th.___By the 3rd of August the battered remnants of the 324th NVA retreated back north over the DMZ,___leaving over one thousand of their division's dead in Quang Tri Province."

"By October 1966, the 3rd Marine Division moved north from Chu Lai to Phu Bai,___north of Da Nang,___in response to the threat from the north.____Dong Ha became their advance Command Post.___The 1st Marine Division moved north from Chu Lai to Da Nang and the

U.S. Army took over Chu Lai.___The Marines were now focused on the north and soon Operation Prairie was underway to keep pressure on the enemy."

"Early in 1967,___at a very remote outpost called Khe Sanh,___at the northwestern tip of South Vietnam,___by the DMZ,___the 325C NVA Division attacked.___This thrust by the NVA was answered by two battalions of the 3rd Marines,___along with heavy artillery fire and massive bombing.____The Marines successfully drove the NVA off the hills surrounding the base.___It took two weeks of hard uphill fighting and almost one thousand NVA were killed and cost the Marines one hundred twenty five dead.___The NVA were persistent in their attempt to invade the south,___because, by July of 1967, they again entered through the DMZ,___but farther east this time.___The 9th Marines,___in operation Buffalo,___successfully blocked that attempt,___but not without one Marine company being badly beaten up when five NVA battalions surrounded them.___Six Marine battalions, including the two Special Landing Forces, entered the fight and mauled the NVA.___The NVA retreated north leaving thirteen hundred dead behind," he said and looked pleased as he said this.

We were definitely caught up in his lecture and he was visably pleased that we were absorbing our generation's reality.

"The NVA were not happy with their heavy losses,___so they started sending rockets, artillery and mortar fire over the DMZ into a Marine base called Con Thien,___which was located near the DMZ.___Con Thien received fire all through the summer and fall of 1967,___but they didn't pack up and move.___South of Da Nang___the 1st Marine Division, U.S. Army units of Task Force Oregon, along with South Vietnamese units attacked the 2nd NVA Division and left it like a declawed cat,___no longer effective by the end of the year," he grinned with that.

Could we do that to the enemy if we go there?___Would we be just as capable? I mused in a combination of fear of the place, fear of maybe not having the same ability to perform as those already there had, and fear of failure.

"The Vietnamese Lunar New Year is called the TET holiday season___and on 31 January 1968 the monsoon weather was foul and the Communists assaulted the south with an all out massive attack.___The enemy infiltrated approximately sixty-eight thousand troops into cities, towns and other heavily populated areas.___They hoped to get mass desertion of South Vietnamese troops to join their cause___and topple the government.___Only due to the surprise and swiftness of their attack did they enjoy initial successes,___however Allied troops promptly drove them out of the populated areas,___except for Saigon and Hue.___The fighting in those two areas lasted for several more weeks and when the enemy was finally forced to retreat after the third week,___they had lost thirty two thousand soldiers killed throughout the south."

"Operation Hue City was the designated term for the struggle to pry a force of NVA close to divisional size from the city and the old imperial grounds of the Citadel.___South Vietnamese Army troops, U.S. Army troops and U.S. Marines were involved in the fight for the city.___Task Force X-Ray under command by Brigadier General Foster LaHue,___consisting of the 1st and 5th Marines, had the southern half of the city to clear.___To avoid heavy civilian loss of life, the heavy punch of supporting arms could not be used.___They fought street by street and lost blood for every yard in the first city fighting since Seoul, Korea during that war.___After the 1st and 5th Marines cleared the streets and buildings, they turned toward the walls of the Citadel.___The enemy's flag had flown over the Citadel for twenty four days, until 24 February, when it was ripped down, while the last pockets of resistance were being ferreted out.___The NVA lost five thousand killed," he stated, while opening his eyes wider and grinning broadly.

Jeez,___The Marines are in some heavy duty shit over there. I thought and was in total amazement of the history Staff Sergeant Dunnigan was rattling off and without looking at notes.

"Well if that was not enough,___the NVA had hit Khe Sanh again,___even before TET had started.___The 26th Marines were attacked by the 325C and 304th NVA Divisions on 21 January 1968.___General Cushman,___who had relieved General Walt in May 1967,___and General Westmoreland ordered the 1st Battalion 9th Marines and the 37th ARVN Ranger Battalion to reinforce Khe Sanh.___This became known as Operation Scotland and if not the most,___one of the most dramatic battles of the war.___The battle raged for two and a half months with daily barrages of artillery, mortars and rockets raining on the base.___The Army and Marine artillery batteries fired over one hundred fifty thousand shells and the air forces dropped over one hundred thousand tons of bombs.___A combined force, consisting of U. S. Marines, U.S. Army and an ARVN Task Force advanced along Route 9 from the east.___This combined action force,___called Operation Pegasus,___forced the enemy to withdraw.___There are estimates of up to twelve thousand enemy killed in both engagements.___However,___it is officially listed that only three thousand were counted during both operations."

"From May 1968 up until today in 1969, the 3rd Marine Division had been stopping numerous enemy attempts to secure a major victory over the south in Operations Scotland II,___Lancaster,___Kentucky,___Napoleon/Saline.___While during the same time south of Da Nang, the 1st Marine Division was involved in Operations Allen Brook,___Mameluke Thrust and Meade River.___The 101st Airborne and the 1st Air Calvalry Divisions moved north into I Corps and the 27th Marines arrived in country,___as part of III MAF under command of General Cushman.___He then commanded one hundred sixty three thousand American troops___more then any Marine general in the history of the Corps."

"The 3rd Marine Division is returning to Okinawa___and the 1st Marine Division and the 26th Marines are still in Vietnam today." This last was sobering news and was also the end of our history lesson. From this day on we would be the makers of further Marine Corps history. Staff Sergeant Rogers herded us back to our barn and I tried to recall as much of the history we had been provided as I could. However, the Guidebook For Marines covered it all and made reading it simpler, since we had heard it all already.

CHAPTER 6
DROPPED

ONE

Dazed would aptly describe the way I felt each morning when the lights were clicked on. It had become routine for the still of night to be violated by the crash and clang of a galvanized shit-can tumbling down the squad bay.

Damn, do they have to do that every morning? I thought, with irritation, as I stood stiffly on the white line. It seemed the lights being turned on created a Pavlovian response to hit the deck and stand rigidly at attention with a frozen stare that offered a locked-in peripheral view of the faces of about eight recruits across the squad bay.

Only the two recruits directly in front were clearly in my focus area, while the others were only fuzzy statues to each side. The faces I saw were mirrors of mine, with their bald heads and faces exhibiting the shock and fear of being here and anxiety of what this day would bring. I felt a little more tired than usual, because I had pulled fire watch duty from 0300 to 0400 hours.

We had been on the Island for eight days now and each day was harder than the last. As a platoon, we were starting to become more organized in our tasks and more confident in our approach to tackle those tasks.

The past week had been packed with a variety of training, including visits to class rooms and service buildings. Our second hair cut had been scheduled yesterday. As our platoon marched over to let the barbers clip off what little we grew over the past week, the drill instructor ordered us to vigorously brush our heads with both hands before we entered the barber shop. He had explained that it pisses off the barbers when recruits have sand in our hair. Sand definitely did stick to the sweat on our heads and a surprisingly large amount always fell to the deck when I rubbed the bristles on my head.

However, the trip to the dental facilities proved to be the worst day for me so far, as it must have also been for many others. When I sat in the dental chair the dentist literally attacked my mouth. He just about stuck his whole hand in my mouth, while he probed and fished for some work. X-rays were taken, which were followed by the statement that my incisor teeth had to go, because they were set out from the rest.

Hell, I was starting to look like a vampire. I chuckled mentally.

As he had stated, the incisor teeth had to go and he pulled them, as simple as that. I was not consulted, rather, I was casually informed of the deed and had to endure the act before the sound of his words had evaporated the statement.

My mouth numb, my head aching and my spirit low, I marched along. Sergeant Kranz, not giving a big shit that some of us were feeling crappy, just continued his routine. He slapped heads, pushed non-complying recruits, while following up these actions with harsh threats. He promised a hard day every day.

Each night contained repeated drill on field stripping our M-14 rifles and cleaning them. This was followed by rapid assembly and a guaranteed inspection. When not engaged in cleaning our rifles, we shined our brass and boots. The new brass was a dog to shine, due to the protective coating the factory sprayed on each piece. Until every speck of the coating was removed the brass always looked like shit.

We even started to receive mail now and discovered the drill instructors also had this event recorded in their book of games. This event offered them a limitless variety of methods to retrieve ones mail. Some had to duck-walk up to the drill instructor to retrieve the letter and return the same way. Others were ordered to drop and offer a requisite amount of push-ups and still others were asked to recite a General Order, part of the M-14's function or nomenclature. The most often asked question dealt with some aspect of Marine Corps history. They smelled the letters to detect perfume and ran the envelope between their thumb and forefinger to detect contraband items, such as chewing gum. I decided it was better not to receive any mail and thereby avoid being discovered and receiving special treatment. Sergeant Kranz had hung around when his afternoon to evening shift ended and was the prime initiator for mail call antics.

I started thinking about finally writing Mom a letter, for it had been a while since I left home and all she got was that quick card they had us fill out stating I was alive and here. Now, at least I could tell her a little more about my slow death since arriving.

I'll start a letter tomorrow. I promised myself. I had increasing thoughts about what was happening at home, and more pressing was the question if that bastard Hueston was bothering the family.

"Alright, those of you not remembered by your families can read something too!___Grab your red books and study.___The rest of you read your mail and then hit your red books.___Study,___because you will be tested." Staff Sergeant Rogers informed us, but not unkindly. This was becoming routine at mail call and it did relieve my apprehensive feelings several days earlier when I kept asking myself if I could figure out when I could find the time to study. Up until now we could only read for several minutes, while waiting for everyone to fall out from chow until the drill instructor arrived or when we stood on the white line in the barrack for the few minutes awaiting the drill instructor's next training assignment or punishment exercises. There was also the Guide Book for Marines and I had decided to keep to the sections we already had classes on, or which the drill instructor's had covered.

Perhaps I would feel confident enough in a few weeks to browse other sections for familiarity before those subjects are scheduled. I thought. Up to this point, we had been studying Marine Corps history, insignia and grade, drill, code of conduct, common military terms, the nomenclature of the M-14 rifle, courtesy and discipline. There was still so very much more to learn.

TWO

Gunnery Sergeant Bishop started us practicing hand and rifle salutes and explained when to salute civilians of high rank such as the President, when to or not to salute in situations such as working parties, while guarding prisoners, under battle-field conditions or when your hands are occupied with objects, or if you had a cigarette or cigar in your mouth. And so, the fact that we were given this information, apparently prompted Sergeant Kranz, who when later was drilling us, to suddenly yell out my name.

"Shipman!___When you are indoors and see an officer, what courtesy is rendered?"

"Sir, when the recruit is indoors and not wearing a cover, the recruit stands at attention and offers a formal greeting such as good evening Sir!___Sir!" I blasted out loudly.

"What if you are wearing a pistol or carrying your rifle?" he queried further.

"Sir, the recruit would render a hand salute while wearing a pistol or rifle salute if carrying a rifle,___Sir!" I continued and thanked God I had just read that a few hours earlier.

"Whitebread!" Sergeant Kranz shouted to Wheaton, the third squad leader.

"Sir, yes Sir!" he responded hoarsely.

"If a group of you maggots were walking past an officer,___what should you do?"

"Sir, the recruit would wait for the senior Marine in the group to initiate the order to attention and all would salute,___Sir!" he yelled his answer loudly.

"Well Whitebread___since I asked if a bunch of you maggots were together how would you know who was senior in a bunch of recruits?___When you're all lowly scum,___huh?"

"Sir, the uh,___the uh___recruit doesn't know Sir!" he stammered with deep embarrassment in his voice.

"You're fired!___You are no longer squad leader Whitebread, get your ass in back of third squad!" Sergeant Kranz barked in his froggy voice and halted the platoon. The dejected Wheaton fell out from the front of his squad and Kranz ordered the next man forward to take over. He asked that recruit if he should salute while working with a working party. The recruit answered affirmative that he'd drop his tools and salute. He too was promptly fired.

"Whitebread!" Sergeant Kranz called. "I'll give you another chance to regain your position.___What was the proper answer to my question to you?"

"Sir, the recruit is a squad leader and is therefore the senior recruit in the group of recruits and we would not stop at attention, but continue passing while the salute is being redered, Sir!" he screamed from the rear as load as he could.

"Go to the head of the class,___numb-nuts!" Sergeant Kranz bellowed back.

What if there were two or even three squad leaders in that imaginary group. What would the answer be then? Christ, Kranz was playing around with Whitebread's head and was actually giving him a break allowing him time to think out one of the scenarios. I thought and at the same time decided we had better know our lessons to survive these random quizzes. These quizzes were starting to become standard while we drilled or while we were on the white line. Over the past week several recruits were ordered to Motivation Platoon for failure to keep up on the daily runs, failure to shave properly or make up their bunks. So, it was off to that feared place after several ass chewing episodes failed to do it for any of them.

Motivation Platoon was described to us as a day in the sub-basement of Hell's sub-basement, where the recruits from all the other training platoons, who had screwed-up, were concentrated daily for non-stop exercise, including running or crawling through slimy mud, or crawling through the same shit under barbed wire. It was definitely not a pleasant place to go. We saw these subdued wretches late in the evenings as they tiredly reported to the duty Drill Instructor. They stood there, all scratched up, covered in mud and dripping water all over the deck. Only one of the four cronic shit-birds who had been sent this week was stupid enough to get sent again. Gunnery Sergeant Bishop also picked recruits at random, if any of the three DIs were pissed off and just wanted to crap on the recruit. They stated it was because there was a quota expected at Motivation Platoon.

"You, you and___you!" he would say as he looked at a face and then point at the recruit next to that recruit, or suddenly turn and point across from him. Over the past week I became nervous whenever a recruit was seen packing his sea bag and walking out of our squad bay. Our platoon members were decreasing. Those recruits were dropped from the platoon and sent to various places for further evaluation as prospective Marines or processed out through a Casual Platoon, with undesirable, for the good of the Corps or medical discharges.

It was a strange thing to be in a large group of people and yet never know any of them as individuals. There were many whose faces

I had yet to actually recognize. That is, none of us could ever look long enough to remember the face, the kid, the recruit in our platoon. Those dropped walked away wearing dejected faces. I did not remember having really seen most of them. Several were familiar, only because I saw them being reprimanded five or ten feet away from our formations, which put them in my field of vision. They were the repeat offenders, the Motivation Platoon warriors, referred to as the ten percent factor of misfits. Gunnery Sergeant Bishop had told us from the beginning that there was always a ten percent factor in any group. That this percentile was always going to exhibit inabilities in all common activities in which ninety percent function normally. They were the unreliable people no Marine would want next to them in combat.

As for me, I was trying my hardest to get through each event, each hour of the day. I was never content at mess as the heaping trays of food were now appearing too small for my increasingly ravenous appetite. The other recruits must have felt as I did, since they scarfed up their chow within seconds and stared at the trays of those recruits across from them, apparently hoping one would not want an item or two. We were still too green and too scared to chance grabbing a tray from the new arrives who passed by our tables. They appeared to be wearing shock masks on each of their faces, identical to ours over a week ago, as they filed past our tables.

Did we look that way? I wondered. We were not clear of the initial shock yet, but now exhibited similar faces to those platoons who had not been on the Island much longer. However, the third phase recruits who marched past us on the meat grinder were tanned, self confident looking men. Their jaws were set in a cocky 'can do' angle as they slipped past with one foot fall echoing out from under their many heels.

Gawd, they sound great! We are still screwing up and I can hear the difference between us and that other platoon like hearing the sound of one shot versus a machine gun, and that was us. I observed.

"You turds think you'll ever look that good?" Sergeant Kranz taunted us.

"Sir, yes Sir!" we eagerly responded.

"Then try harder girls!____You are far from that dream,____ but__I'll kick your asses until you do!" he countered in a very serious voice. Sergeant Kranz was definitely our hard-ass drill instructor, the heavy hat. He was prone to be very physical. Staff Sergeant Rogers was tough, but less physical. Gunnery Sergeant Bishop was just plain stern and, in general, on an even keel. Or at least it appeared so until now. However, none of them would let a moment pass where they could jump in our shit and make an example of the thing which had annoyed them and delight in punishing us to the point that any recruit with common sense would never forget to do it right, or say it correctly the next time.

Our eighth day had finally ended. We hit the racks, again grateful to rest and become delitescent under our sheets.

THREE

It was Friday, our ninth day, and it began the same as all the other days. We continued with the same regimen of studies, skills training and physical training. It was amazing how fast our daily pace was and how much we were absorbing. Our transformation was becoming noticeable as we had started to lose our nasty civilian habits and began to slowly evolve into the amphibious creatures the Marine Corps desired. If we had to become frogs to graduate, then we were now breaking out of our eggs, to become tadpoles. While we neared lights-out, I began my first letter home.

24 October 69

Dear Mom and Girls,
The training gets rougher day by day, but will-power gives the motivation and strength. Many have dropped out of our eighty-nine man platoon so far and the drill instructors can be pure mean, but they have their jobs to train us. We have eighty left. Hope everything is fine at home now. Have you received any more threats from that bastard? Well, I've got eight minutes left tonight, so I'll finish tomorrow. Good night.

I secured my writing gear and prepared to hit the rack. It had been a full day for me. Here on the Island one thing is an absolute and that one thing is that we would always keep busy. Our tenth day was filled with instructions of proper footlocker arrangements, inspections of the same and in some cases re-packing the contents after they had been dumped onto the deck by a disapproving drill instructor. There was also instruction on cutting our web belts to the proper lengths. At least this exercise also served to make us look more like Marines then before. Up to this point, the extra six to eight inches most of us had left over after tightening our belts just flopped over and downward from the belt loop and hung there very sloppily.

Some of our utility trousers had buttons to secure the fly and others had zippers, but regardless of the fly our brass buckle had to be aligned with the edge of that fly. We cut the web belts so they were about an inch past the first belt loop to the left, exposing the brass tip of the belt neatly along the belt behind it. We were also instructed to use a toothbrush and toothpaste to scrub our khaki colored belts. This removed the new look of the belt and resulted in changing them from the shiny dark khaki to a matte whitish look. They became softer and looked salty as well.

After a vigorous run and an ass-kicking regimen of PT, where we were lucky to come in first, Sergeant Kranz rushed us back to our barn. We put in a couple more hours standing inspections of our ditty bags, foot lockers and rifles. The inspections finally ceased after they checked our towel arrangements on our racks. Again, many items were tossed about, as the disagreeing drill instructors cut their path through the barrack. As this day finally neared its end, I had been cleaning my rifle and then attempted to finish my letter, but only had energy for one paragraph.

> *Well it's the next night. I'm tired from all the running and exercises etc... Our platoon came in first today at physical training, called PT(running etc...). I have to go to sleep now.*

This was not exactly true, but I was so damned beat and my muscles ached so much, that I felt no joy in writing or doing anything except to grab ahold of that sleep ring and let it whisk me away from this place for a few hours of repair and escape.

Ever since my arrival here, I had constant feelings of fear that harm would befall my mother and two little sisters. I made up my mind that I should talk to a drill instructor about this and Staff Sergeant Rogers had the duty now without the other two around. I felt that, of the three, I could more risk talking with him, over the other two. Since we were in the squad bay working on our rifles and other free time necessities, I had decided to make the attempt to talk with him. I got up from the deck, where I had been sitting behind my towel covered footlocker, while cleaning my rifle. During this type of activity we were apparently trusted to keep our mouths shut, eyes glued on our work and ensure that our personal activity was not to be cause for the entire platoon's punishment.

He was in the DI shack. I positioned myself along the left bulkhead near the DI shack hatch frame. Nervously inhaling very deeply, I raised my arm and slapped my open palm loudly on the bulkhead. This was accomplished by swinging my entire arm up and over my head without moving any other part of my body. Staff Sergeant Rogers responded immediately.

"Who's rapping on my chamber door?" A pause. "Enter sweet-pea!"

I took one step forward, executed a stiff left turn, entered with two steps forward and snapped to rigid attention.

"Sir, Recruit Shipman requests permission to speak to the drill instructor, Sir!" I stated with determination.

"What about recruit?" he asked flatly.

"Sir, a personal matter concerning the recruit's mother and sisters,__sir!" I sounded off matter-of-factly.

He looked at me for what seemed like ten seconds before he spoke.

"Let's hear it," he stated in an undecipherable voice.

"Sir, the recruit left home while a serious problem was going on, Sir!" I said and just as suddenly feared I was now on uncharted and dangerous waters.

"What problem?" he asked in the same tone.

I explained all about how Houston had raped my sister and threatened my mother's life if she proceeded with her charges against him. All of the pertinent problems and fears I perceived were explained. However, this was not the usual way one discusses such a subject. Here I was speaking in fast clipped sentences with my body locked at rigid attention, while staring straight over the head of Staff Sergeant Rogers.

Normally, a person would be seated and facing the other person, also seated, in order to look at that person to determine their interest or boredom.

"Do you really feel you should speak with your mother?" he asked, "Personal calls are not authorized as you well know."

"Sir, the recruit could perhaps warn or give advice to his mother, Sir!" I answered promptly and hoped he would understand my dilemma. Staff Sergeant Rogers was silent for what seemed like almost a full minute and then gave his answer.

"I'll try to arrange for you to call,___and this is not something for you to make a habit of.___Hell, I could wind up in the brig for this,___ but you have been keeping up, and therefore keeping out of my hair.___ So I'll try,___but I can't guarantee anything," he explained, speaking in what I considered as sort of a normal sounding voice. I would never have tried to see any drill instructor for any other situation, other than the one I had, and no other DI then him, for this situation.

"That it?" he asked plainly.

"Sir, yes Sir!" I replied with noticeable respect and relief.

"Get back to work," he said in a calm, low voice.

"Sir, aye-aye Sir!" I took two steps backwards, executed an about face, took two steps out into the hallway, make a right turn and hauled my already-melting ass back to my bunk. I spent the remaining time that night in terror for what I had done, feeling it was not authorized to have any personal unresolved burdens while here on the Island.

Staff Sergeant Rogers was relieved from his duty shift earlier than usual the next morning and so, I never did get to make that call, nor did he ever address the problem we spoke about. Maybe he had decided I'd officially hear of any problems about home by mail and therefore, risking a call was not worth it. I decided that, like it or not, that was the way of it.

Sunday, our eleventh morning, started out with religious services. I attended the Catholic Mass for my second time and found it to be a calming experience. I noticed that, as we recruits sang, our faces appeared less stressed. Even the drill instructors in church attendance appeared to exhibit normal un-contorted faces. That is, they did not look at us with threatening glances. They simply participated in the services as we did.

The rest of the day was used to square away all loose ends. We cleaned up the squad bay and heads and then practiced field stripping our rifles. Later we studied our red books, while standing on the white line, for what seemed several hours. There was absolutely no casual talking allowed on any day in recruit training, ever. Toward evening we had mail call and I was suddenly called to receive a letter.

"Shipman,___front and center!" Staff Sergeant Rogers barked.

"Sir, aye-aye Sir!" I bellowed back and before the last sounds left my mouth I had already covered ten feet towards the DI desk located at the far end of the squad bay to receive my letter.

"If you want this letter, tell me who the Commandant of the Marine Corps is!" he said in a clipped voice.

"Sir, the Commandant of the Marine Corps is General Leonard F. Chapman, Jr. Sir!" I shouted positively.

"Grab your mail and get!" he said.

"Sir, aye-aye Sir!" I answered and took two steps backwards and did a smart about face, which caused my shower shoes to tangle around my toes, and proceeded to run. The shower shoes stayed on my feet, however they were twisted to the side of my feet, resulting in my bare feet hitting the deck. Once back at my rack I was able to straighten them out.

We were in 'free time' period now and everyone was either, writing letters, shining boots or cleaning brass during this period, so I decided to open my letter and read it.

20 October 1969

Dear Jack,
*   I haf not yet heard from you and am now frightened that you are in trouble. Write me soon and tell me how you are. It is not endet, this thing with Hueston. As he has made trouble for me at my new apartment. I call the police to make complaint. He is a crazy man and I want nothing more to do with him. The girls are afrait of him and cry when der is trouble, but for a little time now he has been leaving us alone....*

She was writing the words as the English words sounded to her ear. She had trouble with spelling and she wrote as the Germans do, which is spell it like it sounded. I decided to finish my letter to her now and cheer her up and then I thought that afterward I should write my brother Ian while I was in a writing mood. I continued my letter to my mother.

> *Well it's Sunday night and I am glad you wrote me and things are good. Please send me the Red Flint Arkansas addresses, OK. I forgot most of them. The days are passing as long as I keep up and do my work right. I'll stay in this platoon and spend only seven more weeks here. It is possible for anyone to get in trouble here for the slightest mistakes and end up being put back in training. We have gotten used to our meals now and we are running off everything we eat and when toilet time comes little of what we eat comes out. So the rest seems to be used up by our bodies.*
>
> *The drill instructor asked for artists tonight. I volunteered with about seven or eight others. We will draw charts etc... . I was so worried about you that I spoke with one of my DIs and he offered to let me call you today. But he was relieved early this morning and I couldn't make the call, but now you wrote and I'm happy. Five minutes left now. Well I have to go as there are lots of recruits being yelled at right now.*
>
> *Please don't write any stuff on your letter envelopes or send anything except the paper you have written on, OK. Because they make fun of us recruits. The climate is hot and swampy here with lots of sand fleas and gnats and mosquitoes etc.... and there are cold ocean winds. Well, good night.*
>
> Love Always,
Jack

I hastily grabbed an envelope. The Iwo Jima Flag Raising Memorial was proudly displayed on the entire left side just under a gold Marine Corps emblem. It was my first proof to show my mother that I truly was here in training to become a Marine. After addressing the envelope, I quickly ran up to deposit the envelope in a box, sitting on the drill instructor's desk at the end of the squad bay.

FOUR

It had been nearly a week since I had sent my letter home. I still waited for the news, but there were no more letters since the first one. The painful training days became one big muddy puddle, wherein time and memory were lost.

Thursday morning was drizzly and cool with a soft thunder resonating across a dark grey sky. The circuit course was wet and muddy and, regardless of the weather, we continued our training. Recruits became creatures of the swamp. We had slimly mud cascading from our bodies. Our faces appeared ghoulish and our arms became tentacles whipping streams of mud in all directions creating a slow motion ballet of liquid ooze.

We grunted loudly during sit-ups and splashed geysers of mud with our backs. Side straddle hops caused recruits to spray mud into the faces of those recruits to each side and of course everyone received the same splattering. The drill instructors wore a clear plastic rain protector over their campaign hats, but their utility trousers had lost their starchy creases and bagged sloppily around their legs. They wore sweat shirts, as did we, during physical training and these absorbed copious amounts of water. They were miserable, I'm sure, but not as miserable as we were feeling, because we were the doers and they were the watchers. The run back was when the pain started. The mud had gotten inside my trousers, and as we ran, it acted like sand paper and rubbed between my legs creating such a rash that it burned like alcohol on a raw wound. Later, I saw evidence that most of us suffered the same rash. I put foot powder on it after showers that evening and it helped get rid of the rash, while it also immediately eased the itching.

Gunnery Sergeant Bishop watched several of us spread powder on our rashes and didn't say anything to us. Perhaps he agreed that we were taking care of ourselves as best as we could. Several more recruits had been dropped over the past week. They were dropped due to injuries. One had a swollen knee and the other a broken thumb.

The following day, Friday, 31 October, was our sixteenth day on the

Island and the day of our series physical fitness competition. Gunnery Sergeant Bishop had given us a motivational pep talk concerning our taking the field during the physical fitness training and being awarded our first platoon streamer. A streamer was about one and a half feet long, made of nylon and colored for each event during boot camp. Winning platoons hung these streamers from the tip of their platoon guidon.

With eagerness and desire to win, our platoon crashed through our barrack hatchway and, like a magnet had pulled us together, created an instant formation. Orders to march came just as instantly and we surged toward the Circuit Course, located just across the street from our new barrack.

We had relocated to our permanent 3rd Battalion barracks several days earlier. These barracks were red brick three story buildings, which were built during the 1950's, I figured. The 1st Battalion was relocated from our former World War II barracks to brand new modern barracks located next to the Regimental Headquarters. The 2nd Battalion barracks were between us, in the Twilight Zone, which were old two story World War II structures like our first barracks had been.

The barrack we now occupied was located on the second deck of a barracks extended out closest to the Circuit Course. Therefore, we had simply crossed the street from our fall out formation area.

As if a light switch had been flipped, the anguish of men in physical engagement exploded into our ears as soon as we crossed the street and injected our own cries of aggression as our platoon entered into the din of the Circuit Course. Once into the conflagration of body heat exuded by the hundreds of recruit bodies pushing to their limits of endurance the smell of their sweat was accompanied with the ear shattering shouts from every platoon on the field. Today the cacophony of sound was louder than we had heard before. *Ahoorrah,____aahoorrah,____ aahoorrah,* the shrill unintelligible screaming sounds blasted into my ears. No matter how hard I tried to discern some distinct clarity in the words, none held meaning. There was clearly excitement in all the voices on this day.

The regimen of competition consisted of relays, push-ups and sit-up bouts, followed by a tug-of-war event. Each event was hotly contested and I was amazed after each event at my ability to keep up and represent my platoon.

A coach announced the tug-of-war and Gunnery Sergeant Bishop started pointing at recruits to grab the rope. I was one of those selected to participate in this event. Our group lined up along the heavy rope and waited for the order to reach down and grab ahold of it. The order came and we all crashed to the ground and got a solid grip on the rope.

Cries and grunts erupted along the line of recruits on each side. I looked down at my hands to see why I felt a feeling of movement away from my grip. My hands squeezed harder to attempt to stop the slippage. It had no effect, so I only grunted, slid forward with our entire team and gritted my teeth, assuming that would assist in the resistance we offered in this attempt to win. The strain only hurt my mouth as we inched forward. With desperation, I dug my boot toes into the muddy earth extending my instep severely downward, while our team was inching forward. Again and again I drove my boots hard into the earth to anchor myself. The effort to stop the forward movement required forcing my toes into the mud and this was excruciatingly painful. Now, as we felt ourselves moving backwards our heels were needed. With heels slamming wedges into the soil and cries of straining, we clawed and pulled the rope from our opponents.

We were just pulling the center of the rope over to our side when I felt a sharp searing pain shoot through my left foot. The pain originated on top of my foot several inches up from my third toe and sent shock waves up my leg.

We won the streamer that day and our senior DI was in a great mood. He was so pleased, he didn't have all of us dropping to the deck for punishment PT when he caught several recruits eye-fucking the area. Sergeant Kranz simply bounced a flat hand off the backs of their heads and that was that.

The guide was proudly holding the platoon guidon straight up with its one streamer fluttering in the breeze. It was such a total rout this day that I decided to get that letter off to my brother Ian.

31 October 69

Dear Ian and Jutta,
I am beat, but willing to write you anyway. Today, we ran the (PFT) which means Physical

Fitness Test. It included our whole series (4 Platoons of about 80 to 100 recruits in each. We won today, that is, our platoon competed with the others and we topped them. I think I really hurt my foot bad though. The bone between my instep and the third toe really hurts. Maybe it will feel better tomorrow. I did it participating in a tug-of-war (a big one with a bunch of recruits). Training has been very hard and the DIs (drill instructors) give no mercy. I am still in shock, because we never know what is going to happen from minute to minute here. How is Jutta and your horse Chico doing? Say hi to them. Gotta go. Servus,

Jack

Three more days of hard marching, physical training and studying went by. Our PT was heavier now with five more repetitions added per exercise, making it a fifteen count now.

Twenty days had passed since we were last marched over to the Regimental Headquarters area. Today, Tuesday, the temperature was in the upper sixties, providing comfortable warmth. Once there, we were herded into a building full of classrooms. They found one that suited their needs, it would seem, because they pushed us in hard to find a seat and wait.

Minutes passed as we sat at attention and finally somebody entered. It was a female in a winter green Marine Corps uniform with sergeant strips on her sleeves. She informed us that we were going to take the General Classification Test or GCT. She further explained that this series of tests would be the basis for our Military Occupation Specialty or MOS as it was normally referred to.

True to her warnings about it being an experience, we plodded along and checked boxes, penciled in blocks and answered all other forms of questions the Marine Corps felt it should ask of us in the best way we felt the Marine Corps wanted to hear our answers. The test was intense, covering many subjects. I enjoyed the questions related to logistics the most, however, I came away feeling I did not know if I did well or not on any of the subjects.

Each day since the physical fitness test I had increased pain and swelling in my left foot. Regardless, I did not let on at all. However, the day after our MOS tests Staff Sergeant Rogers observed my boot was improperly laced.

He yelled at me to lace it up tightly and I attempted to follow his orders. While I went through the maneuvers to tighten it up he suddenly realized that I was pulling the laces tight without reducing the bulging of the lace.

"Take off your boot and sock recruit!" he ordered.

I took off the boot, then the sock as ordered.

"Holy shit!____What the hell have you done to that foot?" he inquired.

My foot was very red and twice the normal size around the ankle, with a hump over the top of my foot. He went to the DI shack and called sickbay for a corpsman to pick me up and take me to the infirmary. After he returned he ordered me to pull out my footlocker and sit down until the corpsman arrived.

There were two corpsmen, each wearing Marine Corps utilities with Navy rank insignia. They checked my foot and told staff sergeant Rogers that it would be necessary to transport me to the infirmary.

They told me to put my sock back on and slip my boot on unlaced. I was then assisted out of the squad bay and down the stairs.

Ain't this nice.____Why the concern now, when I have pounded up and down these stairs for the past four days now without any damned assistance. I thought defiantly.

A grey Navy ambulance was parked right next to the hatch of our barrack. They placed me in the back and told me to sit on what looked to me to be a stretcher or rolling bed device and drove me to the main hospital by the Regimental Headquarters. The ambulance came to a jolting stop and the back doors opened to each side. Once again, I was assisted off the vehicle and they escorted me into the building and seated me on a bench in a hallway.

There were doctors and corpsmen darting in and out of rooms or scurrying up and down the hallway. After a lengthy wait I was finally called by a corpsman to follow him.

"Chit!" he said in a flat voice. I had thought he had said 'shit' and ignored him.

"Chit!" he said again, this time holding out his hand.

Oh, I figured it out now. He wants that piece of paper Staff Sergeant

Rogers filled out for me to authorize my going to this place. I handed the paper over to him.

"Seat!" he said as we entered a small room.

He's not much of a conversationalist.___But then, who is around here. I decided, and sat where directed.___*And why aren't they helping me around now?* I questioned silently. After another ten minutes an officer or rather a Navy doctor entered the room. I couldn't discern his rank, because he wore a white smock. I assumed he was a doctor, because he was doing the exam and I also figured they were always officers, as I had observed since going through AFEES.

"Take off your boot and sock!" he said as an order. He was old looking, with grey hair cropped short. He had a wrinkly oval face and gold-rimmed eye glasses assisting two cold, dark smallish eyes.

"How did this happen?" he inquired curtly.

I replied by explaining the series competitions and the tug-of-war event.

"How long ago?" he asked just as curt and now sounding indifferent.

"Sir, four days ago Sir!" I replied in a low voice.

"Why didn't you come here earlier?" he asked and immediately added, "don't shout the answer."

"Sir, the recruit expected the swelling to go away in a short time Sir," I explained, while thinking. *What the hell do you think this is,___the boy scouts?___Any recruit who is here to become a Marine would try their damned best to keep from being dropped!*

"Only makes it worse.___Your delay," he stated, as though I was supposed to be knowledgeable enough in medicine to know this bit of diagnosis. He ordered a corpsman to x-ray the foot and left me to wait in the hallway for another lengthy time.

A corpsman told me to go back into the same room as before. This maneuver was also accomplished without their assistance. The doctor finally entered the room and was holding the x-ray.

"Stress fracture of a metatarsal, just up from the phalanges.___In other words you broke a bone in your foot."

I did not even understand what the proper medical terms he used for the bone were. So when he said simply that I had a broken bone, I immediately comprehended my dilemma.

Oh shit, they're gonna drop me for sure.____Damn, damn, damn!___ What next?__What's gonna happen to me, my training, my chances of

170

making it through this place to become a Marine and I can't go home in shame? I thought in rapid scenarios of panic.

"I'm sending you to the Medical Platoon, you'll pack your gear up at your barrack on the way!" he stated with total detachment and consistent with his demeanor, exited the room and forgot my existence in the same instant.

Emotionless fucking bastard. I fumed and my mind was suddenly numb with panic. I really was afraid I had failed to make the grade. The emotions were interspersed with memories of that asshole Hueston always calling me a failure. Now I had failed and felt weak with despair. The emotions of all that had happened up to this moment had gotten the best of me and without my ability to control them, tears welled up in my eyes, and a few trickled down my cheeks. Then, with shame and realization this was happening, knowing that I could not simply stop them, I tried to get my bearings and straightened myself out. But, before this could happen he had suddenly returned for no reason I could see.

"Cut the crying out!____Marines don't cry!" the doctor said coldly. Apparently, he must have read that somewhere.

Fuck you!____What do you know asshole.____I had not wanted to drop out and now you,____you stupid shit-head,____have arranged it.____And I ain't no Marine yet,____as you should know. I flared in my mind. I was mad as hell now with no ability to state my feelings or plead my case. In forced surrender, I received my medical instruction papers along with orders to the Medical Platoon and followed a Marine private-first-class out to a small grey bus. He drove me back to the barrack and told me to pack my trash and get back out to the bus pronto. I entered the empty squad bay and walked slowly and awkwardly down the isle to the DI's shack and slammed my palm three times.

"Enter!" Staff Sergeant Roger's voice boomed. Apparently he had stayed to do paperwork while Gunnery Sergeant Bishop had the platoon out for training.

I entered and announced myself properly.

"Let's see the paperwork!" he said, not unkindly, with one hand extended to receive it.

"Well shit!" he said and continued, "you have been dropped from platoon 3063 to go to the Medical Platoon.____But first you will stay in a recovery barrack before you will be able to get around enough to handle the Medical Platoon," he finished with a surprisingly calm voice. There was no hint of the frog sound, the aggravated responses we generally received from these DIs, nor the attitude that I was a fuck-up.

"Sir, aye-aye Sir!" I responded and he caught the hurt in my voice.

"Look Shipman,___you did not do this to get out of training.___I know.___But, you will recover and start at this point of training in another platoon.___You were doing your job here and I wish you luck.___Okay,___now, pack your trash and get back out to your ride.___Dismissed!" he said in positive and supportive sounding way.

As I packed my gear, I thought about Staff Sergeant Rogers' calm reassurance when I suddenly realized what that cold doctor meant about Marines not crying. They were both telling me not to fret and lose spirit, because the chances of my foot healing and my being placed back in training is a higher percentage than my foot not mending to the requirements of the physical standards of the Corps. I made up my mind all was not lost and that I would make it back to training.

The 7-82 gear now packed inside my sea bag made it considerably heavier. Nevertheless, I was able to lug the heavy bag down the stairwell and up to the bus stop.

The bus was still parked where I was dropped off and the PFC was as sarcastic as before. I was the only passenger on the bus and this created more anxiety, as it made me feel I was pulled from the collective, the team, the reassurance measured from the other recruits that I was keeping up with them. Now I was alone and suddenly felt weak.

The PFC cranked the engine and after many jerky movements, due to all of the stops he had to engage to get out of the back area of the 3rd Battalion, and then bounced down Wake Boulavard toward the Rifle Range. My thoughts locked on to *Na Na Hey Hey Kiss Him Goodbye*, by Steam, as the driver turned left across from the range and continued a few more blocks and finally stopped in front of a wooden building. I limped off the bus and entered the building.

Once inside, I had no other choice then to go over to a pudgy corpsman sitting at a desk, reading a paper, with his left elbow on the desk and curled fingers drumming under his chin.

"Paperwork!" he stated without looking at me and at the same time rotated his wrist to place his palm up. He read the paperwork and then got up slowly, looked at me for a split second, and made a face suggesting irritation that I had just ruined his comfortable position. He started walking, turned and motioned for me to follow him.

Do all of these corpsmen only speak in one-word comments? I mentally shook my head side to side.

We walked down a hall to a supply room where he grabbed one, out of many, prepared piles lined up on the shelves and handed me bedding and pajamas. The pajamas looked military compared to what civilians wore. I was then led to a room with two sets of bunk beds and told to find a bunk. That was a strange request, as there were already three recruits occupying the room. All I could do was grab the only vacant bunk.

Wow! He must have busted a blood vessel having said three words together. I figured.

I proceeded to square away my area and following recruit training policy kept my mouth shut and my eyes from wandering. The three recruits watched me in silence for about ten minutes. Suddenly they all started talking loudly and stated, "Look at that!___A real live Marine recruit.___He don't talk!___He don't look at us!" They all began laughing loudly. I felt I must now be in the wacko-closet of the sub-basement in hell.

FIVE

Within the first minutes I discovered there were few restrictions here. That is to say we could talk, read and go to the head, as we pleased. The other three recruits were misfits as far as I was concerned. So I mentally referred to them as Moe, Larry and Curly. Moe, formerly from the 1st Battalion, was a dark-haired, eighteen year old kid from Michigan. He had a pulled tendon in his right leg. He was also a wise guy who couldn't say three words without making a cut against another person. He was a pale-skinned, slim-faced, medium-built teenager with large teeth and sad black eyes.

Larry, formerly of 2nd Battalion, was a blond headed young man of twenty-one who had a round face sprinkled with freckles and spoke with a nasal voice. He had cheerful blue eyes, stood about six feet tall and wore a chronic smile. He was from Boston, Massachusetts. He was taciturn for the most part, however when Moe started in on him or on anybody, he would always counter-attack with a drill instructor's voice and capability. Usually the joke was on Moe. Stated in a humorous way, Larry explained how he had fallen from an obstacle on the course and injured his spine. I found out that the obstacle was called the 'Dirty Name'.

Curly, from my battalion, was a total cut-up. He was about five feet five and built very solid. His body was a virtual powerhouse of muscles. From his feet to his waist he appeared to have two oak tree trunks for legs, which supported a larger than usual upper body erupting from his waist to his shoulders in a wide vee. On top of this was a wood chopping block of squat muscles holding a bowling ball head. He had silver blond hair, appearing almost as though he was bald, due to the virtual invisibility of it. His eyes were always watery and were held in by exaggerated rolls of flesh for eyelids. He was capable of constant laughter, however chuckles would better describe it.

Curly, was eighteen and came from Portland Oregon originally, but had enlisted from Atlanta, Georgia. He was a logger before he enlisted. His personality was to crack a silly joke about anything and chuckle loudly at it, regardless of his audience's lack of appreciation for the punch line. Mostly, Curly made no sense when he spoke or joked. He was evidently not well educated and perhaps got through life trying to be funny to off-set people rather then show his slow wit in real conversation. He had fractured his left tibia and needed crutches to walk. I came to like Curly the most, perhaps because he was a genuine and truly kind hearted kid. The other two, although nice enough, had hidden problems and kept a part of themselves in reserve. Who was I to talk, as I had the most difficulty in all of those categories. I suppose they assessed me to be a snob, because I spoke differently. They would say, I used words they had never heard before or that I knew words that I should not know. Moe would often say, I was far too serious for a kid of seventeen.

While they were at each other hourly, harassing, haranguing or playing tricks on each other. I would lie in my upper bunk and look down observantly, but would not participate. This attitude I maintained was really due to my disappointment at being dropped. They all openly cherished their deliverance from training and thought I was going to be a lifer in the Corps with thoughts like mine.

After several days had passed I warmed to their attempts to include me in what seemed to be their favorite pass-time to kill the hours each day. That is to say, the chronic delinquent chatter about nothing important, but never-the-less, attempts at humor. In other words, 'the nonsensical ravings of a lunatic mind'. They did the same to the duty corpsmen who always had one word to comment back, 'sick'.

On my forth morning there, I woke to hear the other three engaged in yacketyyak about something or more likely nothing. Moe and Larry were taunting Curly in his upper bunk about beating his meat. My eyes were blurry from sleep, however when I looked over at Curley he was lying there with his sheet pulled down to his knees and appeared to be moving his hand up and down around his crotch holding what appeared to be his member.

"Got no class!" Moe shot out.

"Man, do you have to do it in front of us?" Larry complained trying to sound serious, and then in a drill instructor's voice yelled. "Drop yer cock an' grab your socks!___What's this___pee-wee?___You're enjoying my Corps too much!"

I could not really believe what I thought I was seeing, as I looked over at Curly.

"Hey!___What ya think Shipman?" Larry yelled up from under my bunk. "He's a fiend, isn't he?___A regular sex fiend,___huh?" he went on as I tried to grasp what was going on here. An instant later I suddenly blushed and said.

"Hey Curly!___You must not be eating any chow on this island,___ because they lace it with salt peter, ya know, and therefore what you're doing is impossible."

"Can't get me down," he said continuing his stroking actions.

The other two suddenly broke out with laughter. The kind that follows when one is holding back a laugh for a while. Then I saw how the gag was set up. Curly had taken the tan colored rubber pad from the top of one of his crutches and placed it between the folds of his skivvy shorts fly and, with his hand covering most of it, imitated masturbation.

"Ha-ha,___what a jack-off." Moe chided in.

It was the funniest stunt anyone had accomplished while I was there.

"Hell Shipman," Curly said suddenly, "ya gotta get a prosdedic to do this on this island.___Can't expect life to spring up in it no mo!"

he continued, obviously making fun of the word prosthetic, making it sound like pros-dead-dick.

After four more days had passed I was ordered over to the dispensary. It was across the street from my room. The building's interior walls painted in the ever present light green I had seen in every building on the Island. It was not a pleasant color when there are no other colors to offset its dreariness.

I sat pensively on a bench in a hallway and waited. I had heard that being in the military one must learn patience and endure long waiting periods. They always order you to hurry up getting some place and then you are guaranteed that long wait.

Finally, and much later than later, a corpsman walked by and without missing a forward moving step waved for me to follow him to the x-ray room. The corpsman wore Marine utilities and I noticed he was a petty officer second class. He told me to return to the bench and wait. His exact word was 'wait', so I figured he meant find a seat. The bench was the only option.

Later, perhaps a half hour had passed since the x-rays had been completed, I was summoned to a room across the hall by a doctor and shown my x-rays. He explained where a fracture had been and indicated an actual separation to some degree. Then he explained how I could be sent to the Medical Platoon for a while until the injury healed. He was a kindly man with graying temples and a ruddy complexion who apparently saw many recruits in the twilight zone of this Island, who would either be discharged medically or have a chance to heal and return to training. My face must have told him I wanted to be a Marine, because of what he said next.

"Do not engage in any exercise that could further injure your foot or that will exacerbate the healing process," he said with a rye smile, "and the drill instructors will be informed of your condition and exemptions once they read this form." he explained and handed me the sheet of paper outlining my injury.

"Report to the Medical Platoon today.___A corpsman will assist you in getting your gear and you over to the barrack," he finished and dismissed me. "Good luck!" he said at the last moment.

The entire time I was in front of him I stood at rigid attention and when I started to make the appropriate withdrawal movements he held up his first finger and moved it back and forth in the negative to indicate the movement was proscribed for the time being.

Once outside I almost shouted, "*Yes,___that's great news!*", but thought it would only draw critical attention to me, so I just continued on my way back to my room. On the way I saw something that really depressed me. As I stood waiting to cross the street, platoon 3063 marched passed me. Not one of them, including Sergeant Kranz, looked at me. I was no longer part of that team. Hell, even if they had looked, they would have only seen a bald headed blob in wrinkled utilities, looking no different then the thousands of other recruits.

They were in their second phase, for rifle range training and the series had moved into temporary barracks here at the Weapons Training Battalion for two weeks.

I packed my sea bag, put on my cartridge belt, shouldered my rifle and wished the three stooges luck in continuing their dodge from duty and left with a corpsman. He actually carried my sea bag for me. I felt that I could talk to him about where we were going and asked away. With no hint of annoyance, he told me to keep myself in the same frame of mind as I had in my platoon. That way the drill instructors would leave me alone. He also explained how some recruits think they were no longer in training, abuse the drill instructors attempts to keep order and wind up in Motivation Platoon after they heal-up, instead of going directly to a new platoon at the point they left off. This corpsman, looking like Jughead in the Archie comics, was probably only eighteen years old and I appreciated his candor.

We entered the Medical Platoon barrack and I was presented to the duty drill instructor. He was a staff sergeant with grey hair, hard brown eyes and a rough wrinkled face. On his dress green blouse were pinned four rows of ribbons. He had been around. His sleeve showed four hash marks signifying he had been in the Corps between sixteen and twenty years.

"Paperwork recruit!" he barked. The corpsman had already started to depart leaving me no chance to thank him. It was probably for the best, because this was a real DI in front of me, who wouldn't give a rat-fart about my feelings.

I handed him the sheet of paper the doctor had provided me.

"Grab a rack,___stow yer gear and start readin' yer red book.___ Move it gimpy!" he barked sourly. His name was Staff Sergeant

Marriner and the corpsman was correct when he described how it would be here. I moved down toward the end of the squad bay and found an empty bunk. It was on the port side and fourth rack from the back bulkhead.

The squad bay was packed with a static crew of recruits who sat with eyes staring blindly into their red books.

Christ, how many times can a guy read this stuff?___Just keep acting and the DI ignores you, I guess. I considered as I walked by them.

The only exception here was that they were allowed to be seated due to their injuries. They sat on their footlockers, but not on their bunks, I noticed. Once I had stowed my gear in the prescribed manner, I opened my red book and tried to read for a half hour when my unsuccessful attempt was terminated by the order to fall out for chow. The march over to the mess hall was not long. We entered asshole-to-belly button, which further indicated this was as close to a regular training platoon as they could make it. Staff Sergeant Marriner walked up to me and squinted his eyes at me making me feel he'd hit me next.

"Yer too skinny, maggot!___When you walk down the chow line you will call out 'skinny-body', he growled, "do you understand,___ gimpy?" he queried unnecessarily.

"Sir, yes Sir!" I responded loudly. He stopped by a few others who were ordered to state 'fat-body', because the drill instructor deemed them too fat for training. Several more were designated skinny-bodies and with the many others who had already been designated before today, it ended up sounding hilarious as we walked down the serving line. It sounded like a chorus, as we had to state it before each food server.

The day ended with several ass-chewings and a nut-case wanting me to stab him in the thigh. No sooner did that incident get settled with a firm question of 'are you fuckin'nuts man?', when another recruit cut his wrists.

Boy howdy-howdy this barrack was a looney bin. I thought with amazement.

The duty drill instructor ran down the squad bay, looked at the bleeding recruit and grabbed him roughly with one arm, jerking him upward from his footlocker. The drill instructor, a sergeant, had one arm in a cast. According to the ribbons on his chest, he had been to Vietnam. There were two and a half rows of ribbons accompanied by a deep sea diving helmet and gold wings. He was a recon Marine, but I didn't know that much about the Corps to recognize what such devices signified yet.

His name was Sergeant Rodriquez. He was about five feet nine inches tall, slim and tanned. His face was young, but his facial expression reflected a tired look, as though he had endured something overwhelming in his young life. I thought he looked like he didn't much give a shit about anything and didn't take prisoners. Sergeant Rodriquez had several recruits put towels around the bleeding recruit's wrist and ordered them to hold his arms up straight up.

He hurried to the DI shack and called for an ambulance. As if they were sitting in their vehicle waiting for any calls from the Medical Platoon, it seemed like only a few minutes had passed when there were two corpsmen running into the barrack and just as speedily rushed the recruit to a doctor. Their only comment was 'Yep!' "

That night I slept nervously, waking often and looking around in the darkness of our squad bay. I was not happy here. These recruits were not all here for physical injuries. It was apparent that some of them were pure nut-cases waiting for mental evaluation and hopefully a medical discharge. If Parris Island was a place in hell, then the Medical Platoon was Erebus, the dark place in Greek mythology where souls go before going on to Hades, or hell as we call it. In my case, I was already in hell and got a strange reprieve, or R&R, to land here before returning to hell's sub-basement, if I am deemed fit by the doctors. Parris Island is so upside-down from the outside world that a recruit would rather stay in the hell he was already in, then take a journey into the unknown of Erebus.

The next morning Sergeant Rodriquez and a corporal performed the ritual shit-can roll to get us up. The corporal was the other junior drill instructor. He was black and small in stature. He wore a mean scowl as he limped down the squad bay. He had severely sprained his ankle, I would learn later, and was sent here only two days earlier. Staff Sergeant Marriner had injured his lower back and was in the final stages of recovery. That is why he never showed any physical signs of injury, since I had seen him. Sergeant Rodriquez had introduced the corporal as Davis.

Corporal Davis reamed us during our morning preparations. He kept threatening no chow if we didn't move faster. However, we somehow got our entire compliment ejected from the barn and achieved an acceptable formation, gauging Davis' decision to start marching us toward the mess hall. Sergeant Rodriquez must have decided to let the young corporal do his thing and herd us to chow, as he silently marched along with or platoon as those of us with foot and leg problems spastically jerked about.

There was a heavy fog surrounding the area and it was very dark. We heard foot-falls from another platoon somewhere off in the soup. Evidently, they were also marching to chow, but we could not see them yet. A few minutes passed and then I observed them partially concealed in fog as they stomped heavily down the road in our direction. They were all very fat and all that was missing here was them singing *heh-oh-hey*, like giants on the prowl in a Walt Disney flick. I was surprised to see this. However, the skeletons following behind the balloon-boys surprised me more, due to the comical appearance of it all. They were far too skinny.

They could never be capable of meeting the demands of a regular platoon's training schedule. I exclaimed silently. However, being young and ignorant of the bigger picture of life, I could not realize that many of these young men not only lost weight or gained weight, but also made it through boot camp and some even achieved honors. My mind however, was made up. Specifically, that of course was why they were in that platoon, because they were fat pieces of pusillanimous shit or weak little girls according to the drill instructors on the Island, the Marine Corps training policy and we capable and achieving recruits.

I wonder if those skinny guys have to shout 'very skinny body' while they go through the chow line. I guffawed mentally. *Holy crap!___I can't believe it.* There, in the third squad, was ol' Heinz fifty-seven, appearing as pasty as I had first seen him. He passed by only a few feet from me. There was a sad, dissatisfied frown on his face.

"Listen up hogs!" Sergeant Rodriquez shouted. "Today is the one hundred and ninety fourth year of the Marine Corps.___It's the Marine Corps birthday.___This evening, there will be cake.___One of the few times you will ever receive sweet stuff on this island.___However, those fat-bodies will only be allowed to look at the cake,___while those skinny guys following them will get to eat the fat-bodies' cake as well as their own." he stated in a very matter-of-fact voice, while indicating the passing platoon.

It obviously figured he was totally disgusted with the fat-bodies. But, every day is a learning experience. I thought, with no real care myself.

"Do not think that I desire that those recruits do not get to participate in celebrating our beloved Corps' birthday.___Believe me,___when I say that this is what being a part of the Corps is all about and so,___I wish those poor bastards could.___You never know,___they might yet taste that cake another time girls," he concluded his heavy comment.

Energized with chow, our sick, lame, and lazy mob soon got its ass in gear with a heavy dose of medically approved PT. This was followed by our religious practice of rifle cleaning, manual-of-arms training and their holy doctrine that no day should go by without a formal rifle inspection. There was also the dogma that no recruit shall consume chow without paying a penance. Therefore, rain or shine, we broken recruits performed our parody of boot camp PT.

"You hogs aren't out of my Corps yet!" Corporal Davis, with his chest puffed out nearly popping his National Defense Ribbon from his chest, shouted at us in apparent disgust at our performance. Drop for push-ups!" he shouted angrily, and then moaned. "Exempted may not participate." he started his order in a high spirited voice, but the exemption order sounded more like a disgusted after thought.

If he had his way, we would all have to drop and start shouting counts. I thought with some malice. *From now on I'll think of him as Corporal Shiny-Balls.*

I had no restriction from push-ups and dropped as ordered. However, there was sudden pressure accompanied by a sharp stab in my foot, but the Corps knows what's best for me.

I wonder if any of the other guys feel pain while doing these exercises? I thought with much apprehension.

Bends and mother-fuckers followed, and again I was performing the ordered exercise. This was awkward for me, since I had to put all my weight and balance on my right foot. Each backward thrust of my legs created discomfort and a sharp pain so severe that I almost gave up. Regardless of how high I tried to keep my foot, I could not keep from banging my toes into the deck. Exhaustion and gravity caused this to happen. Yeah, it hurt!

Several long bouts of PT games had passed and a new pleasure appeared to our shiny-balls corporal. He wasn't very original, but he definitely followed Marine Corps values. Fearing a threat that heavy dust particles abounded in our squad bay, Corporal Davis marched up and down the squad bay snatching each of our rifles, peering desperately into each piece ensuring we dented-maggots did not allow one speck of dust to sneak into our bores during his watch.

He required that we present arms when he approached us. During his inspection, he would always ask each recruit a question regarding Marine Corps history, rifle components and capabilities, general orders or important names.

My big event for the day was to get x-rays of my foot. The doctor finally went over my results with me, after I had waited for what seemed like three hours.

We celebrated the Marine Corps birthday that evening in the mess hall. As Sergeant Rodriquez had promised, we got our cake. Each slice was about three inches by three inches and the slices were piled high on a tray. Some recruits had icing on both the top and the side of their slice, some had icing on the top only, while others had only the cake from deep inner slices.

My slice was normal. That is, it had icing, and I was content, since I had always felt a cake without icing was bull-shit. The meal was great, and of course, I had a large pile of it all. However, when I yelled skinny body to the cake server, he ignored me. After we had returned from chow, Sergeant Rodriquez stated we had the evening to ourselves.

Great! I decided to write my mother a letter. While I was engaged in assimilating her letter, mail-call was announced. My name was shouted, and in my eagerness to get news from family I surely broke a limping track record. I was so surprised to get a letter from my brother Ian in Germany that I forgot to sound-off to the DI and properly retreat from him. Apparently, Staff Sergeant Marriner sensed I was far too happy for him to piss on me tonight, because he let my foul-up go unpunished. However, he may be willing to wait for another time. These DIs are devious like that.

Ian was just letting me know about his horse and girl friend Jutta. He had no idea what my training consisted of, except that he presumed we marched a lot. Inside the envelope there was a small cartoon of a guy with his leg in a cast, apparently thinking marching can hurt your legs. He had no idea his joke was my reality.

I placed my brother's letter in my footlocker and continued the letter to my mother.

10 November 1969

Dear Mom and girls,
    How are things at home? I have been worried about you, since I have not yet received any more letters from you. Today was the Marine's 194th birthday and we had it a little easier and had a big dinner. I'll probably mail you a menu of it, if they made any. Also, we have more free time tonight. The drill instructor we have tonight is strict, never-the-less like every night.
    My former platoon is here at the rifle range and has been for three days out of the two weeks they will be here. The Medical Platoon is also at the Rifle Range. It made me sad to see them, because when they finish here, it marks one half of their training completed. And today I had another x-ray and it showed my foot bone broke, and actually was separared. It is worse by the looks of it, but healing just the same. The stress fracture never really heals and three in the same place means a medical discharge. A boy cut his wrists last night and another did the same, more seriously three or four days ago, I heard. They are the crazy ones. One nearby my bunk, a 17 year old and a real baby, keeps asking recruits to cut off his hands or his fingers or wants his legs bashed etc...,but it's all talk. Don't get me wrong, or get all shook up, they are sick-minded and want attention. So they get it and they don't die. We see films here on Vietnam alot now, along with other training films. That was during my old platoon training. Around here we never say 'I' or 'me' or 'he' or 'they'. It's always private or recruit this or that. There are quite a few 17 year olds here, and I and one other one I met here, are the only ones in this barrack who really care about doing things right. We have our 'shit together' as the drill instructors call it. This friend is already near graduating and has earned a sharp shooters badge. That's very good shooting. Here is a

drawing of what's wrong with my foot, or at least one drawn as good as I could.

I drew a foot outline at the bottom left side of the page with all the toe and foot bones inside of it as close to what the x-ray I saw today looked like.

But in eight days I report back for another check-up. So wish me luck. I realize you are really working hard, so if you write, do it only when you're not too tired, please get rest mom and pray. I go to church and communion every Sunday now. A real change, huh? Because here you can really use some help from above. Hey mail call was just sounded, ha ha. Guess what, I got a letter from Ian and Jutta. It is a card with a sick person with his leg in a cast. He wrote nice and mentioned something about a letter with Eddie's address he had sent, which I didn't get, but I'll write him quickly and sign off. I hope Lucious had a great birthday. 19 years old now, a real old fart, huh! Tell him hi from me.

Lots of Love,
Pvt. Jack

PS: Please send me stamps and mainly some for Germany, because, I'm running low on them and have none for Germany. Bye.

(Oh, you can send pictures, but good ones, not crazy ones, as the drill instructors open our mail and look inside, but don't read. They look for candy, gum or other crap. Hey, I hear a BAM singing the Halls of Montezuma and the Marine Corps Hymn right now, ha-ha, it's actually nice. Oh, I forgot to tell you before that a BAM means 'Broad-Assed-Marine'. They are women Marines.

The woman Marine was singing the Marine Corps hymn all over

the Island on the loud speaker system. It was solemn and sounded so extremely clear.

Man,___that was beautiful! I thought with mental recalls of the sounds. Then came the order to secure and hit the racks.

My night was a fitful one. I stared at the black ceiling illuminated ever so slightly by the low light of the head. I could hear the soft foot falls of the fire watch pass by my bunk every so often as I wondered what was to come next for me? Would I get sent back to training where I left off, or get shit-canned?

Try to study as much as possible while here, so I'd be more prepared then the other recruits in a new platoon. I figured in a fit of panic.

Seven more days passed and an extreme boredom had come over me. The only thing breaking our boring schedule was the weekly trip to the barber shop. We had of course, maintained our daily regimen of 'gimpy' PT. There were naturally many rifle drills and inspections. I had used this dead time to learn how to field-strip and reassemble my rifle, while blindfolded. I got it down to around a minute and a half to disassemble and a minute and a half to reassemble.

Three days earlier I had been sitting across from a recently damaged recruit during chow. It was breakfast time and we had the usual oatmeal mush splashed in our trays. The other selection, a rarity to even have a choice, was French toast with syrup. The reason I found this breakfast combo worthy of mention was how it played hell on that new boot. He was a strange fellow. He had a swarthy skin, very dark hair and eyes of coal. He was also the hairiest boy I ever laid eyes on.

His hair was growing out of just about every exposed part of his body. There was a mat of hair pouring up over his tee-shirt and it was cropped straight as a hedge just under his Adam's apple. What we would refer to as human arms, appeared more animal-like on him. They were so hairy there were tufts sticking out of his sleeves and continued over the backs of his hands and little tufts sprouted out of the fingers between the knuckle and each of the joints. Topping all of this off was such a thick, although shaven, shadow of beard that appeared to be growing as I looked at it.

This poor fellow had a serious disability about him. As he stiffly sat there in his battered utility jacket, zipped up to the neck like the rest of us, he would simply tilt severely to his right. His entire body would tilt to that side and every few minutes he literally adjusted his posture by grabbing the left side of the table and hauled his body to a straighter position. These were not slight tilts. They were very-very substantial tilts of about a foot.

Psst! I risked trying to talk to him. *He really looks scared, hell more like in shock. What the hell happened to him and how long has he been on the island?* I wondered. He looked directly at me with big, sad, watery dark eyes.

"Hey, what happen to get you sent here? How long ya been on board, huh?" I whispered. They did not allow any talking, even at the Medical Platoon, but everyone tried to get some news and there was always side-talk. Side-talk was when someone spoke, they looked straight ahead, but whispered out of the side of their mouth, or had their back to the drill instructors. Recruits have found a way to establish a network since the day after Tun Tavern. Some violators were caught and we all always suffered for the offense with a bout of PT.

"Got here yesterday," he whispered and his body shivered nervously trying to do just that much.

"Fell down when we was running across that big black-topped area. Some recruits boot kicked me in the back of my head.___Can't stand or sit straight anymore.___My equilibrium is all fucked-up, the doctor told me," he finished, his tone sounding confused.

Perhaps he felt as I did, that he won't become a Marine and would be shipped home with a medical discharge. As he sat there, eating little bites, his utility jacket sleeves would always hit the tray and became goopy with syrup and oatmeal.

He did not belong here, poor kid, he should be in a hospital. I thought. It turned out that way in the end. I never asked him his name, but he was sent to a hospital several days later and he was looking worse then when I met him. I thought of the skiing accident at the Children's Home in Germany when our class-mate Fritz Kastner died after hitting his head.

There were a few explosions during this week. They were not metallic in nature, but just as messy. On two occasions, recruits rebelled against Corporal Davis. Perhaps he had been too eager to accomplish total compliance to his orders. Both incidents resulted from his desire to make recruits complete exercises where the recruits refused to comply, due to medical problems.

The problem was not caused by Corporal Davis' ignoring their medical restriction sheets, rather because the exercises caused pain to these recruits regardless of what type of exercises and regardless of any doctor's diagnosis or consideration concerning the recruits injury or capability. In the end Staff Sergeant Marriner had to be notified. He talked with the recruits, that is, in his drill instructor voice. He really intimidated them into admitting they could have complied and extracted statements that they will comply in the future. Whether this was true or not was irrelevant.

This let Corporal Davis off the hook, it would appear. However, the recruits whispered the word around that they were hurting and Marriner just made it worse. They feared Marriner, as I did. He was not soft on anyone and he acted as though he could really care less about whining recruits.

Shiny-Balls, after Marriner's talk, had turned crimson yelling at the non-compliant recruits. The first incident resulted in the back of that recruit's head getting whacked. The second incident resulted in a boot kick to the prone non-complaint recruit's ass. There were threats that upon discharge from Medical Platoon they would go directly to Correctional Custody Platoon for that kind of shit.

In the Correctional Custody Platoon, called CC, all they would do is move a large sand pile from one end of a field to the other by holding out two sand filled buckets, at arms length, all the way, all day.

The days at the Medical Platoon also created anxieties in other ways. Each day was filled with the sounds of M-14 rifle fire across the road. The recruits here at the Rifle Range were now in Phase Two of their training. They appeared organized and industrious. When not on the range firing or snapping in they could be observed outside standing along some long wooden tables field-stripping their rifles and scrubbing them with bore cleaner. Others were scrubbing their uniforms and skivees on concrete wash racks. They would march by wearing green shooting jackets and a fingerless leather shooting glove on their shooting hand. Most were right handed, but there were even a few who wore them on their left hand. The Marine Corps doesn't care which hand the trigger finger is on as long as you can shot and kill the enemy.

The anxiety I felt when observing all of this was due to my yearning to be back in real training. After another full week had passed, since the Marine Corps Birthday, I was falling into a deeper funk. It was a real depression, which made me act more and more robotic. I had lost my willingness to do anything. The next day caused me to rebound again, when Sergeant Rodriquez told me to report to the dispensary for x-rays and a check-up. I double timed over to the dispensary. That is, I limped over like old grandpa McCoy on the television show *The Real McCoys*. The fact that I was limping had more to do with a habit I had developed then how my foot felt. In all fairness I would have said I felt fine until the doctor got ahold of my foot. Finally, after the x-rays had been taken, I was ordered to wait in the hall way. I sat on that same long hard bench in the dispensary, staring at the long ugly green painted walls.

"Well looks good.___You feeling any pain?" he inquired and ordered me to take off my left boot. As soon as I put my foot out for his inspection, he pressed the area just above the fracture. Damn, it hurt, sending a shearing pain through my foot.

"Still tenda right?" he queried in a very southern drawl.

"Sir, yes Sir!" I responded, wishing at that split second that I had said no.

"Well,___give it a while longah an' it'll feel bettah." he continued. I reported back to Sergeant Rodriquez and gave him my medical paperwork. He told me to go study my 'red monster' and informed me that we were going to have a question-session in awhile. He asks the questions and we answer. In the end, I did not fail to answer about five questions fired at me involving history, weapons, general orders and military courtesy.

The next day I had been reluctant to see Staff Sergeant Marriner about what I had on me. The day before, while returning from the dispensary, I spotted two shiny objects lying in the grass. I picked them up, and sure as shit, they were unexpended 7.62 MM, M-14 rounds. The date, 1960, was stamped on the brass base. I pocketed them and continued on to my barrack.

How in the hell am I going to do this? I wondered. *The drill instructor is going to chew my ass out, I know he will.___They don't give anybody the chance to just do something in a normal way.* I reasoned. *Well here goes nothing.* I got up and approached Staff Sergeant Marriner who sat at the desk at the end of the squad bay.

"Sir, the recruit requests permission to speak to the drill instructor Sir!" I sounded off.

"Speak numb-nuts," he answered glumly.

"Sir, the recruit found these rounds in the grass and requests permission to get rid of them Sir!"

"Holy mother of God!___Where the fuck did ya get your maggoty hands on these?" he exploded loudly.

The whole platoon was alert by the exchange now. They sat, stunned into numbness, because as often as Marriner yelled he never sounded this way. He was clearly angry and seemed at the same time confused as to what to do or how to deal with me.

Well shit sir, don't yell at me.___I only thought this shouldn't just lay around waiting for someone else to pick it up. I thought in defense. *Like somebody pissed off enough to shoot somebody,___like a DI.* I chuckled to myself and thought again. *They act as if we were all deranged hardened criminals here.*

Marriner took the two rounds, glanced up at me and simply said, "Beat it,___numb-nuts!" His concern was obviously that if a crazy recruit got ahold of these, he may have fired on drill instructors or other recruits. There was one of those in our barrack, the guy who was always asking someone to cut off his fingers or hands.

The subject of the rounds was never brought up again. But Marriner had warned everyone to report to him if any more rounds were found.

Five more days had passed when I was ordered to the dispensary for my follow-up. The doctor decided I was fit and prepared paperwork releasing me to continue training. I was excited about continuing my training and instantly shivered with renewed fear of the unknown training difficulties ahead. Now I can finish this ordeal and become a Marine, was my main thought. That thought motivated me to grab ahold of the imaginary ring of the marry-go-round called Parris Island Marine Corps Recruit Training and ride the big bad demon called training.

My paperwork was prepared by Staff Sergeant Marriner and he ordered me to report to Platoon 3074 in H Company, 3rd Battalion. I packed my trash and went to the designated area to await a bus that would take me to the 3rd Battalion Series Office to report in.

As I stood at the bus stop, I was joined by two guys wearing first phase haircuts, but who wore mismatched loose fitting wrinkled civilian clothes.

"What's up?" I inquired in a low voice. They informed me they were both being kicked out of the Corps with undesirable discharges, called UDs. One had shown me the stitches in his wrists and the other admitted to chronic bed wetting. The bed wetter even looked like a chronic cry baby. He had red swollen eyes and a pout on his mouth. The crazy one looked like a skinny punk, he wore a sneer on his mouth and stared with obvious defiance in his eyes.

What a pair of shit birds. I decided. *America is loaded with dreamers like these two shit-asses.___They are full of desire to become something, in this case Marines, but they don't pack the gear to get through the tough process required.___These guys will always fail at what-ever they undertake in life.___They had no goddamn stamina, no internal fortitude.___They definitely never read in the bible where God spoke to Job and said 'Gird up now thy Loins and act like a Man'.* I thought with disgust

The bus dropped me off at the 3rd Battalion bus stop. I got off and never looked at the two shit-birds who shared the ride with me. Having located H Company, I entered and reported to a gunnery sergeant whos desk name plate stated he was Neal.

He filed my paperwork, issued me a set of orders and told me where the barrack was for Platoon 3074. He finished by telling me who my drill instructors would be.

"Your DIs are Staff Sergeant Louis, who will be your senior DI and sergeants Black and Wyeth are his assistants."

Lugging my sea bag, I climbed the concrete steps to the second floor of my new barrack. I entered the barrack and found it empty. I walked down the squad bay, to the drill instructor shack, placed my sea bag by my left leg, rifle over my right shoulder, cover tucked into my left rear trouser pocket, and pounded three times on the bulkhead by the hatch.

My Opa (Grandfather) served in the Bavarian Cavalry during World War I in France. He is pictured here (on right) with his brother-in-law Josef. (1914-1915).

Schloss Paehl (Castle in Paehl, Bavaria Germany), where my mother was born in 1925. (Photo taken 2008).

Schloss Paehl courtyard. (Photos taken 2008).

My mother and Opa walking in Weilheim, (Bavaria) Germany. (Circa 1937).

My uncle Max, while he was serving in the German Luftwaffe during WWII. (Circa 1943).

My parents in Germany soon after they met. (Circa 1947).

Family photo taken in Ipswitch England, during Oma's (Grandmother's) visit. Ian (L), Lucious (R), Sarah held by mom. (Circa 1955)

Author, Garmisch-Partenkirchen, Bavarian Alps, Germany. (Circa 1961).

Manfred Jahn, our German family friend, nicknamed after "Bomber-Eddie" in the Walt Disney Scrooge McDuck comics, in Weilheim (Bavaria) Germany. (Circa 1962).

Kinderheim Sankt Josef (Children Home Saint Joseph). (Photo taken 2008).

Family photo taken on Easter Sunday. (L to R) Annie, Sarah, author and Lucious. (Circa 1963).

Church down the hill from the Kinderheim across from my 1962-1964 classroom window. (Photo taken 2008).

Family photo inside the Kinderheim courtyard, taken during a visit by my mother and Oma. (L to R) Sarah, mom, Annie, author, Lucious, Ian and Oma. (Circa 1964).

Main gate looking into courtyard at the Kinderheim. (Photo taken 2008).

Sister Maria Theresa inside the courtyard. (Top) and Sister Maria Theodolinda on the side of the Kinderheim near the bee hives. These were my first drill instructors. (1964).

This photo was taken right after Lewis B. "Chesty" Puller and his son L.B. Puller, Jr., in a wheel chair, had conducted a courtesy inspection of our battalion prior to our deployment overseas. (1970).

My friend Johnny Williams (left) and me during liberty. (1970).

Vietnam, minutes after a Viet Cong attack that had wounded a U.S. Marine and a South Vietnamese guard. Note the M26 fragmentation grenade shrapnel holes in the wall. (1971).

Vietnam. Thirsty at a Vietnamese 7-11. "No hot dogs?" (1971).

Vietnam. "I thought I saw a rabbit!" (1971).

Vietnam. On a gloomy monsoon day. (1971).

Vietnam. Outside Danang area. (1971).

Author, while a platoon sergeant with.3rd Battalion, 8th Marines in Panama. (1973).

Author revisiting the Children's home since leaving there in 1964. (2008).

Author at the Vietnam Memorial, Washington, D.C.. (2005).

CHAPTER 7
RETREAD

ONE

"Sound Off." A harsh froggy reply exploded out from the office door. I stepped inside the drill instructor's shack properly, while carrying my sea bag over my left shoulder rifle over the right shoulder, and while directing my gaze well over his head, reported.

"Sir, Recruit Shipman reporting in to Platoon 3074 as ordered Sir!" I bellowed loudly. The drill instructor sat for long seconds observing me and then asked for my paperwork.

"Been laying around hog?___Been taking it easy!___Huh?" he queried.

"Sir, no Sir!" I responded defensively.

"You challenging me puke?" he said nastily.

"Sir, no Sir!" my reflex response was automatic, and then I thought. *Welcome back to the nether-world of Marine Corps boot camp hell.*

"If you have an attitude shit-bird,____I'll tell you right now, I'll tear it out of you right here!" he growled again in that froggy voice.

I noticed he wore staff sergeant chevrons. *This must be Staff Sergeant Louis.* I thought with some apprehension. Not a big man, but more of a slight build with facial features consisting of hard strained eyes over a smallish nose pointing to a fairly straight mouth with the ends turned down a little pointing to his oval chin. His shirt bore five ribbons, which included two Vietnam service ribbons and a Combat Action Ribbon or CAR. He ordered me to follow him into the squad bay and showed me where my bunk would be.

"You will unpack your sea bag, square away your gear and stand on the line reading your red monster until the platoon returns from PT."

"The house mouse will draw bedding when he returns.____Got it?"

"Sir, aye-aye Sir!"

"Do it!" he growled as he walked back into the DI shack.

"Sir, by your leave Sir!" I shouted, as he entered the DI shack, and then did two steps backward and executed an about face to absolutely nobody.

It was 1100 hours when I started squaring away my gear. I finished by 1110 hours, and placed my toes on the white line and started reading my red book. I had already read the book twenty times front to back, but it never hurt to make appearances.

Clang! The hatch swung open, banging solidly against the bulkhead. The platoon, streaming sweat and wearing PT gear, spilled into the squad bay followed by a sergeant. He was a black Marine, tall and solid looking. He was a skinny man with a long narrow face, flat wide nose, full distinct lips rested over a round bulging chin, which protruded out of an angular jaw line. Under each eye were deep furrowed lines, which ran down his cheeks in drastic slants. His eyes were coal black and stern.

There were far more recruits here then in platoon 3063. I noticed immediately. I was to learn that this platoon had started with one hundred recruits.

"Move yer asses!____You hogs got one minute to prepare for showers!____Move it!" he shouted in a gravelly voice. The froggy sound was not so evident as was his own growl, which sounded deep and much like a stone crusher at work. He turned and zeroed in on me.

"Report!____Who the hell are you,____numb-nuts?" he inquired of me with a booming voice, accompanied by a steely eyed glare.

I sounded off and figured he'd start breaking me in. Instead, he called the house mouse over and ordered bedding. He turned suddenly and yelled. "Port side, make a head call and hit the showers!"

"Sir, port side make a head call and hit the showers,____aye-aye Sir!" we boomed in a long drawn out, but with good unison, voice.

"Hit it!" he ordered and now finished with the platoon focused on me. "You will make up yer bunk in the mean time,____hog!" he snapped and walked away.

Approximately twenty minutes later we marched to chow and were pushed into asshole-to-belly-button position by an aggravated Sergeant Black, as I learned the black drill instructor was called. Since I was no longer in Medical Platoon, I wondered if I should still state skinny-body while passing by the serving line.

What the hell.___I can try it and defend it if I get yelled at. I figured and proceeded to sound off skinny-body,__skinny-body!" I waited for the wrath of Sergeant Black, but there was no response. I *guess it is acceptable here as well.* I decided. The serving line recruits, however, were not clued into the meaning of what I was saying and simply served the usual amounts. *Oh well.* The recruits from my platoon, who could hear me and were also not clued in, must have shit themselves at what I had done and awaited my crucifixion.

While we were waiting to be seated Sergeant Black growled at me.

"Knock off the skinny-body shit,___maggot!___This ain't the Medical Platoon!___Got it?"

"Sir, yes Sir!" I answered, and that was that.

The remaining training for the day involved drill, rifle inspection and questions on military subject matter. While drilling, an unusual number of recruits were singled out for laps around the meat grinder with rifles held over their heads. Sergeant Black was strict and would chew ass at any opportunity. I was not yet sure who the meanest drill instructor was here, as Sergeant Wyeth had not yet reported for duty.

Sergeant Wyeth had the evening and night duty and soon made his presence known. He came down the squad bay with a scowl on his face. He shouted at recruits on his way and grabbed one by the front of the utility shirt and pulled him close to his own face. Others were cuffed over the head. He was a lean tall white Marine with sunken sullen gray eyes. His skin was ash colored and he had a slit for a mouth. The mouth was pulled down severely on one end which projected a sneer. He had a straight slim nose and a vee shaped chin. His jaw line was angled back to his ears in straight slanted lines. That his overall face was a composition of sharp angles would perhaps best describe him. He spotted me instantly and introduced himself to me. I swear he hissed like a snake as he tilted his head and then maneuvered his head and campaign hat around to the side of my head.

"Who the fuck er' you an' what the fuck er' you doin' breathing the air in my barn,___asshole?" he screamed right into my ear, as he was only as far from my ear as the brim of his campaign cover separated us. The campaign cover brim even tapped on my skull, as one would knock on a door. He sniffed me like a dog would, and exclaimed. "I don't smell enough hardship on you puke.___You cain't possibly be part a' my herd,___'cause they work hard!" he said, dragging out the word hard. I ended up doing thirty-five push-ups and not all of them pleased him, so I started them over on at least five occasions. His voice was deep southern and he pronounced each word slowly.

"Git yer sorry ass in gear,___fuck-head!___Yer soft as shit from layin' 'round in Medical Platoon," he finished, and finally walked up the squad bay and sat at the desk, apparently tired of playing with me.

It's obvious he thinks all we do in the Medical Platoon is lay-around in our racks and turn into marshmellows. I thought with a feeling of genuine hate towards him. Later that evening he had a ball with mail call. Seems he enjoyed punishment PT very much and let us perform it for him often. No recruit, who got mail, got away to read his letter without sacrificing sweat and dignity. I decided to crank out a quick letter home to let mom know I am back in training.

24 November 1969

Dear Mom and Girls,
Hi, I only have a few minutes. Today, I was released and put back in training. Also, I had no trouble like a lot of new pick-up recruits in platoons. Platoon 3063 was my old platoon, so now platoon 3074 is my new platoon. Okay, I may be new here, but so far I feel welcome. I have been on this island far longer then they have. So I'll write about it all later. I ran around the track and PT'ed in the barracks today and did alright with my foot. I started here around the same in their training as I had left-off in my old platoon.

NEW ADDRESS:
PLT. 3074 "H" Company
3rd Battalion
Parris Island, SC 29905

Love Always
Your Son,
Jack

PS: I have had my picture taken while in Platoon 3063, but you'll have to wait awhile before I would be able to send any to you.

I sealed the letter and thought of how this first night brought back the memory of the nights while in Platoon 3063. I was feeling that first week shock again and thankful for the upcoming reprieve the night offered for rest. There were also recruits in Platoon 3074 who had not yet adjusted to this hell, which was evidenced by their stifled sobs.

TWO

It is my first morning with Platoon 3074 and I ran the standard platoon training for the first time since being dropped. We ran two miles with rifles, packs, helmets and completed the full training regimen required on the Circuit Course.

Later that day we started bayonet training. We trained with a scabbard over our bayonet. Staff Sergeant Ebbitt was on a platform waiting to teach our platoon. We shouted a very loud formal greeting and Staff Sergeant Ebbitt started his course lecture without delay.

"This is the day you begin your lessons in the skills of bayonet training.___There is no room for sentimentality in the use of this weapon, while engaging your enemies.___You will learn how to cut your enemy's belly wide open and then stick his fuckin' guts into his fuckin' mouth.___Is that clear?"

"Sir, yes Sir!" we stammered lamely.

"I can't hear you!"

"Sir, yes Sir!" our unity and clarity improved.

"Louder goddammit!"

"Sir, yes Sir!" our lungs ached from the effort and our unity and pitch were dead-on. So he continued.

"You'll be able to cut a fuckin' tatoo into his silly ass with this weapon.___You will ram your bayonet into his body and when he is on the deck you will kick his fuckin' head as hard as you can to make damn sure you killed his fuckin' ass.___And never let the enemy fake you out by duckin' to the side___so you end up falling flat on your kisser.___You will learn to kill all types of people from all over the fuckin' world and they will know what you are capable of doing,___ because here you are trained in the art of war with only one goal.___To kill, kill, kill!___What will you do to the enemy?" he finished his death lecture.

"Sir, kill, kill, kill Sir!" we screamed as loud as a moment before and with dedication in our voices. He had psyched us up and motivated us to the task we were about to undertake.

I was hearing the most dedication by recruits I had heard so far on this Island and it only increased in fervor as we soon assaulted the bayonet obstacles. The madness of the guttural screams of recruits as they practiced each bayonet engagement pierced our ears.

"Assume the basic stance,___killers." Staff Sergeant Ebbitt stated and let out a fierce *ahoorraah!* "You will sound off like warriors with each maneuver.___Got it girls?"

"Sir, aye-aye Sir!" we chorused eagerly.

He then positioned the squads into distances which allowed for these movements without accidentally hitting another recruit. His first movement brought the rifle up pointing the barrel straight out thrusting the butt into his right armpit with his right arm forward resting along the rifle and his left hand just forward of his right. Then he started jabbing forward pulling the rifle out from his armpit, turning the blade flat to the deck, while rotating his body to the right. The butt was pulled up toward the armpit and this was followed by a strong thrust forward. He turned his body back to his basic stance at the same time and followed through with more.

"That is referred to as a jab.___It is useful at close quarter fighting, such as in trenches, fighting holes or while assaulting over obstacles.___Assume the stance!"

We assumed the stance and following his counts jabbed and jabbed, all the while screaming *ahoorraah!*

This was followed by slashes, butt strokes, blocks, smashes and parries. The momentum increased causing our cries and screams to elevate into barbaric mindlessness. I was exhausted but still slashing on while my face reddened into shades of crimson and purple. Other recruits were screaming hoarsely, having long since lost their voices.

Later, we were paired off and I exchanged parries with another recruit. Our rifles were much longer now with the bayonets and we developed confidence in the thought that we could keep an enemy that far away from us. But then I thought about how it would be in real combat and realized there would be total chaos with sharp metal jabbing and slashing while others were smashing or thrusting butt strokes. Hell, a man could be doing a great job with his opponent, while the enemy carved out his kidneys from behind. You lose anyway.

Just hope we kill all of them before they get to me and that we always out-number them. I hoped sourly.

Suddenly, the senior drill instructor started yelling at Ditz. This caused our momentum to come to a dead halt.

"What's your major malfunction___piss ant?" Staff Sergeant Louis growled at a cowering recruit. The sobbing recruit was lying on the ground in a fetal position.

"Sir, I'm scared!___*Sob, sniffle.*___I don't want to die.___*Sob, sniffle, sob.*___This is more than I can take.___*Sob, sniffle.*"

The recruit was totally out of control. Not only was he using the first person, but he let his rifle fall into the dust and was apparently incapable of supporting his weight at this point. Staff Sergeant Louis kicked the recruit hard somewhere near his ribs and followed this with a cuff to the back of his head.

"Get up and pick up your rifle, you dumb-ass coward!___You are really a masterpiece." Louis grabbed the recruit's collar and yanked him upwards. The recruit had barely grabbed his weapon when this happened. The force of Louis' yank caused the recruit to twist and fall backward, flat on his back, which sent his rifle into the air where it appeared to sail in slow motion and struck the ground, corking the bore with dirt.

"Get out of my sight maggot!___You disgust me!___You disgust the entire platoon!___Report to the barrack and pack your trash,___now!" Staff Sergeant Louis was madder than any drill instructor I had observed to date. That recruit apparently felt the same thing I did about the horror of hand to hand combat. But, I did not let it get to me and that was the difference. Perhaps all of us feared this type of combat equally. Only a fool would think it enjoyable. Our only hope was that if it did happen, we would be a team holding back our enemy and not individuals wondering if the other fellows were capable of defeating us.

"Listen up killers.___I want you to know something." Staff Sergeant Louis got our attention and began his story. "During the Korean War, a platoon of Marines was holed up behind large boulders, while engaged in a fire fight with Communist Chinese.___The Chinese suddenly stopped firing and their commanding officer yelled a challenge over to the Marine lieutenant.___He wanted to know if the famous Marines were as good at bayonet fighting as we say we are.___The Marine lieutenant yelled back, 'Hell yes, come on!'___So the Chinese advanced toward the Marines,___when suddenly,___the Marines opened up and shot every one of them.___The moral of this story is,___don't get into bayonet fighting unless you can't do otherwise."

We stank of sweat and were covered with dust that combined to make mud, which streaked down our bodies. No matter. Staff Sergeant Louis continued our morning with drill. We reattached our bayonets and scabbards to our cartridge belts, shouldered our weapons and then proceeded to dig our boot heels into the sand a million times. The drill continued for over an hour and our utilities displayed huge rings of salt around our arm pits, backs, chests and crotches.

Gunnery Sergeant Bishop would never have accepted some of these guys. I grumbled silently. *There are a lot more mistakes with drill maneuvers in this platoon.___Bunch of shit-birds!*

"Hit the deck!___Hit the deck!" Staff Sergeant Louis ordered. Aggravation was evident in his voice. "You can't march!___Maybe you need motivation.__Push-up positions!__Ready,___count!" he finished angrily.

Rifles dropped onto the dusty ground as we dived down and began our push-ups. The sun was hot and taxed our bodies for buckets of sweat. The senior drill instructor was also sweating from literally kicking any butts that had stuck up in the air too far or from kicking his boot toe up under stomachs sagging too low. The counts were four-count and we repeated the count from the beginning many times, due to the misfits in the platoon, who were forever fucking-up.

His anger appeased or the clock depriving him continuance, Staff Sergeant Louis called us to form up and double-timed our filthy, salt-stained, blistered, ass-dragging mob back to the barn. Once back in the barrack we started cleaning our rifles, stood inspection and finally hit the showers.

Ditz, having packed his sea bag, had been ordered to stand facing the bulkhead during the entire period we worked. He stood there forlornly, with the sea bag beside him, and it began to bother us, 'would that be one of us next?', was sure to be going through each of our minds. For Ditz it must have been pure horror, because his father was a serving DI in the 1st Battalion and yesterday had visited his son here and stated his lack of confidence in 'Junior's' prospects to endure boot camp. However, Staff Sergeant Louis barked at Ditz to rejoin the platoon and hit the showers with us. "Last chance Ditz.___Fuck-up one more time, or choke on your ability to act like a man, and your ass is history.___Got it?" he snarled meanly.

The showers were a relief, hell much more then that, they were a renewal of the body and a promise to the soul that we lived on, as the hot streams massaged our tortured bodies. Revitalized, and wearing fresh utilities, we were now ready for the second half of the day. My utilities had become so stiff with sweat, during these morning workouts, that the comfort of the soft clean change of utilities actually soothed my muscles now as we fell out for noon chow.

As always, I was starving after eating my food, which was heaped on as usual, but I was still unsatisfied. There were no picky recruits in this platoon. They all scarfed down their chow the same as I had, so there was no more to be had. After chow we got haircuts, and while on the way and back, Staff Sergeant Louis put us through every type of marching drill he could think of. All the while chewing our asses for being the sloppiest hogs he had ever been forced to train.

Our heads shorn and bristly, we marched toward a classroom for instruction on Burn and Wound treatments of every sort, from snake bites to bullet wounds. The class subject matter was surprisingly interesting despite the instructors' presentation. A corpsman provided the class instruction. He had two other corpsmen for assistance.

"You must first clear the air way.___Place the casualty on his back and kneel beside his head," the scrawny young corpsman droned on nasally in a monotone voice. "Clear the airway by removing any obstruction in his mouth.___Place your hand under the casualty's neck and put your other hand on the casualty's forehead,___like this," he said demonstrating on a volunteer, one he pointed at to get up and lay down in front of him. He informed us we could tell by looking, listening or feeling for breathing. In conclusion, he instructed us on mouth to mouth resuscitation.

Poor recruit. I chuckled to myself. *He seems to be scared shitless that the corpsman was going to put his mouth over his, hell so would I and I'm damn glad he didn't pick me, because like the song says Na Na Hey Hey Kiss Him Goodbye,'cause nobody here wants to really put their lips there, so it's definitely going to be goodbye for that guy.*

In the end the corpsman only indicated the maneuver by first placing his hand over the recruit's mouth before he put his own mouth on top of his own hand.

"Believe me, when I tell you recruits that in real combat, you will perform resuscitation without pause,___because you damn sure want your buddies to live!" the corpsman said with serious eyes on us. He apparently knew from experience.

The lesson went on endlessly covering sucking chest wounds, severed limbs, tourniquets, burns and broken bones. I thought about the recruit who had gone crazy on the bayonet course today. What does he think of this stuff? Probably wants to puke. I thought Staff Sergeant Louis kicked him out of the platoon, but, he was still here.

After classes had ended and we had marched back to the barrack, Staff Sergeant Louis ordered wash-time. With dirty laundry in hand, we formed up around the concrete wash racks. We scrubbed the caked sweat and mud of the days toil, from our utilities and tried to get our skivvies white again. Using our wooden handled scrub brushes, with soap to tackle the work, I thought of the thousands of recruits who had stood here before my time, and how they struggled to get their clothing clean. This also made me feel that our platoon was not alone in this ritual.

Sergeant Black had taken over for the night, and finished supervising our laundry detail, which meant we would have Sergeant Wyeth for tomorrow's training.

Wondering what was to come of the next day lasted for five seconds after the lights were finally flicked off and I fell into a deep dreamless sleep.

Our new day began with Sergeant Wyeth not forgetting his threat. He did not let us down one bit. He ran us through PT and through the Confidence Course. This Confidence Course involved negotiating a large number of obstacles. Our first obstacle had proved for many recruits, to be insurmountable. It was officially called the 'Low-Belly-Over' obstacle, but was really called the 'Dirty Name' by recruits. The obstacle was built by placing six huge tree trunks vertically set into the ground, with horizontal logs strapped-down over the top of these posts with wide metal bands. The first log was about two feet off the ground, the second horizontal log was about one and a half times a man's height and the higher back log was about two and a half times a man's height.

We ran up to it and jumped onto the lower log, jumped up to the middle log and mounted that log with our stomachs. The tree was so thick our arms only hung across the tops, but we scampered on top by clawing into the bark. Once on the middle log we pulled ourselves up to a standing position and then jumped up to the top log. From there we slid over, dropped and landing jarringly onto the ground with a grunt, while cussing the thing. For those recruits who failed to get over, they were ordered back to attempt it over and over, with Sergeant Wyeth ensuring a personal ass-chewing for each one.

The course continued with straight-rope climbing and then over logs traversing deep ditches. The scene on the obstacle course had transformed into an alien planet landscape, which was caused by the activities of the series platoons raising such a cloud of dust that we were only visible from the waist up. Recruits appeared dazed from the sweltering heat and punishment engaging the cruel obstacles. They ran with dry mouths agape in anguish. There were long jumps over wide ditches, which required grabbing ropes and swinging over water filled trenches, followed by jumping hurdles and into the trenches.

Seemingly endless, there were many more crafty obstacles meandering over the field. There was a huge flat wall built to defy many recruits. A reverse climb obstacle built of seven widely spaced logs required climbing up the front and then awkwardly down the inclined reverse side. The horizontal traversing obstacle was simply a long metal pipe, high up, which we had to cross hand over hand as we did at the horizontal ladder further down the course. The horizontal ladder was at least familiar from our school days. However, this was no small elementary school play ground construction. There was a long galvanized drain pipe, which was barely wide enough for a man to crawl through. The drill instructors stood on top of these as we crawled through and beat sticks over the metal, creating a claustrophobic environment.

After climbing a very large cargo net and crawling under low rails, we vaulted over a series of hurdles. These hurdles were hip high and made of logs running in a long paralleled series. Then there was the low barbed wire. This obstacle was very low to the ground and we had to crawl on our backs, while kicking our heels into the sand, to propel ourselves forward. This was all shadowed by a very high obstacle, which was really two very tall telephone poles with logs, smaller in diameter, bolted horizontally, creating a ladder with steps about three feet apart all the way to the top. We climbed this mammoth obstacle only to roll over the top and climb back down, hoping the recruits going up the other side did not smash our fingers with their boots, or we theirs. Our DI straddled the top log and screamed at each of us to move faster.

The last obstacle was truly the show piece of Parris Island. There was a tall tower that had a platform built on top from which ran three very long ropes downwards, over a body of swamp water where they were tied down securely on short posts.

Since the entire series was out here today, there were also many drill instructors. They all congregated along the bank of the pond at the midway point of the ropes. The recruits mounted the ropes with one instep of a boot stuck out backward resting on top of the rope, which served to balance the body, while it was on top of the rope, and the other leg dangled straight down freely. Both hands were positioned forward and overlapping. The order was given for the first three to start down. This procedure could be considered an invariable, since ninety percent of the recruits ended up slipping under the rope and climbing hand over hand, upside-down, to the center point, head first, with both legs crossed over the rope. At the midway point the order was given to reverse the body and swing both feet over the rope. We would now be hanging straight off the rope by both hands over the water. With attempts to swing our legs forward and upward we would catch the rope and work our way down the rest of the way, feet pointing downward on the rope. Those recruits who had flipped under the rope from the top to the midway point would also have to drop their legs, hang by both hands, and try to get their legs back over the rope with their feet pointing toward the far bank.

Quite a few recruits dropped into the water, either from their hands slipping off the sweaty ropes or because they simply could not swing enough to snare the rope and lost strength to hold on. The other way to fall was due to the fear of disobeying an order. The drill instructors were standing there watching us and often a recruits name would be called out. This usually occurred when a recruit was upside down with one leg over the rope and his second leg dangling down or he was hanging too long at the change-over point. Once a recruit heard his name called, he bellowed back,___"Sir, recruit so and so, Sir!" The recruit would naturally come to attention and then plunge far down into the muddy water below. This apparently delighted the drill instructors immensely, for it was their pay-back time. Every recruit who was on their shit-list was called out today. I was happy that I at least came out of it only wet with sweat.

The return run to our barn was a chaffing misery for those who fell into the muddy water. There was a distinct and different sound to our platoon with the wet rubbings of many utility trousers and the squish of water logged boots since our platoon now consisted of worn, torn, bruised and muddy recruits. Some limped, while others winced with pain and determination as they sloshed wetly along. Showers and a hot meal restored us.

After chow came more close order drill on the meat grinder with rifles, web belts and canteens. Sergeant Wyeth loved to call close-order-drill and enforce strict adherence to the manual-of-arms.

"Keep yer arms parallel to the deck when ya carry the rifles hogs!___Keep the angles off yer shoulders,___be uniform.___Listen to the others timing when executing the manual-of-arms.___That way ya git it rayt.___One click sound foah each movement!" he drawled in his hillbilly shit-kicker accent. His pronunciation of arms sounded more like *ahms*.

Before we were half way through drill at least twenty recruits were running around the meat grinder with their arms stretched out straight over their heads holding their rifles high.

"Doan none of ya'll thank yer eny betta at this yet jus' cause I ran those shit-birds outta the platoon.___Yer all nearly as bad!" he snarled out the reproof. Then, to the total surprise of the platoon we were marching over to the PX. Sergeant Wyeth told us we were allowed to spend forty dollars on Christmas gifts for our families. There was not a wide selection to choose from when one thinks of Christmas shopping in a mall, but I found a key chain, and two bracelets with the Marine Corps emblem proudly displayed on them. I wrote a short message on an envelope before I secured the box they provided for mailing them home. I quickly jotted down some words on the back of a legal sized plain white envelope:

> *26 Nov 69*
> *Mom, they let us have a $40.00 check to buy Xmas gifts with. So I spent $22.00 of it and I did my best to find something. Training is the same (hard). My foot is a constant worry to me. I hope you like the gifts. Sorry I couldn't wrap them, but they're all marked with names. January 12 is graduation day. I pray to God I graduate, as it's hard and trying here, a job for a man, but I try to keep up. Well, I have to get this box sealed now.*
> *Merry early Christmas!*
> Love,
Jack

Our time lost diddle-bopping around the PX was made up by a hard run back to the barn. After securing our rifles on our bunk racks we began training on field marching pack preparation. We practiced folding procedures and placement of equipment into our packs. Tent pegs and poles were neatly rolled into blankets sandwiched over our shelter-halves. The rolled shelter-half was secured around the pack with small canvas straps. The required length of the rolled shelter-half was determined by which type of pack arrangement we were using. For instance, a shorter roll was for a field marching pack, while a longer roll was used for a field transport pack. The object was to uniformly cover three sides of the pack design ordered, where the end of the roll is even with the bottom of the pack. A pack without the shelter half was called a light marching pack.

Staff Sergeant Louis was working on paperwork in the DI shack and Sergeant Black had come into the barrack earlier then usual. He had the night duty. Sergeant Wyeth was working with us to prepare for our Phase One test.

"Why in hell did ya evah come in ta mah Coar Ditz?" Sergeant Wyeth boomed suddenly with deadly malice in his tone. "Ya lil' chicken shit,___cain't even handle tha bayonet coase___an now yer unable ta make up a simple field marchin' pack.___Gawd!___Yer 'bout tha dummest,___most worthless piece ah shit Ah evah saw.___Hell that's what yer new fuckin' name is.___Shits!___Ditz Shits!" He was shaking both fists outwards from his sides with anger. "You got Motivation Platoon next trip Shits,___an' as a send-off all ya'll hit tha deck.___Now!___Bends an motha-fuckas,___foah count,___an Ah want ta heah Ditz befoah ya drop,___an Shits when ya hit!___Ovah an ovah!___Got it ass-holes?" He was livid with rage now and Staff Sergeant Louis and Sergeant Black came out to see what was happening. Apparently they were equally fed up with Ditz and joined in taunting him while we PT'd.

"Sir, yes Sir!" The barn exploded with our response and the subsequent screaming of the name Ditz___Shits over and over for nearly a half hour. While sweat poured off our bodies during push-ups, bends and thrusts, mountain-climbers, watching TV, duck-walking and other devious inventions from Sergeant Wyeth's book of pain, Ditz was forced to stand there and watch us suffer due to his incompetence and endure our non-stop screaming of his corrupted name.

Neither Sergeant Wyeth, nor the other two DIs ever touched him. All they had to do, besides making Ditz watch and hear us was to shout into his ear what a totally worthless coward he was and how he was getting dropped. Ditz went bonkers during this avalanche of abuse and broke into a berserk run toward the main hatchway.

"Stop that piece ah shit!" came a shouted order in a sharp tone and it was as though the heat and hatred we felt towards him smashed deep into the mind and spirit of the small weak body of Ditz.

Shit!___This platoon is nuts! I stood dripping sweat, breathing hard and stared numbly at the writhing body of one of our own platoon members. He was not to be the only injury from the crash of bodies. There was a recruit with a bloody nose and two others limping in circles as though trying to shake the pain off. Ditz, had blood dripping from his nose as he crawled slowly to his knees and, while sobbing uncontrollably in great shuttering spasms, gained his unsteady feet. He froze still, with abject fear glazing over his eyes and looked around for the next assault.

"Alright get back on line!" Sergeant Black ordered. Staff Sergeant Louis walked rapidly over to the terrified Ditz and escorted the sobbing, bleeding recruit to the DI shack, where he waited until corpsmen arrived to take him away. Sergeant Black tended to the bloody nose and limping recruits. Sergeant Wyeth, calm now, as though nothing had just happened, told us to get our packs on and stand on line.

Was it Sergeant Wyeth who yelled to stop Ditz? Yeah, it was him.___I wonder why Staff Sergeant Louis wasn't the one who would have yelled that order?___This is all really weird. I thought and it was starting to hurt my brain to logically accept what had just happened here. *It appeared we had just about mentally and physically disemboweled Ditz.* I decided after pondering something beyond my experiences in life and then my thoughts were jolted and I realized I was very aware of what had happened. *This was exactly what that veil son-of-a-bitch Hueston had been doing to me and Lucious all these years. Fuck-me!___What am I doing here with thousands of Huestons.* I was getting very nervous. *Will it be me next?* I feared. *Na Na Hey Hey... .*

After our first attempt at pack assembly, before the Ditz interuption, we formed along the white line on the deck and turned around to see how we did. Wyeth walked down the squad bay tugging, yanking and pulling packs, which failed his sense of military orderliness. Tent pegs loudly clattered to the deck and tent poles rattled woodenly. From the frequent sounds I assumed we failed the inspection miserably. Suddenly, I felt a yank on my back.

Oh Shit!____I fucked-up,____damn! I felt panicked, only to find out he had already pulled many others the same way, only to see how tight we had hitched the pack to our bodies.

We did the packs up again and stood several more inspections until Wyeth felt enough of us got it right. Sergeant Black helped in the pack inspection and then took over for the evening. He first ordered us to do our laundry and to shine boots, clean rifles and shine brass later.

Once finished, we showered and then stood on our foot lockers with our hands held out for review. Our upper arms were straight down our sides, locked in to our sides, with our elbows bent and forearms pointed forward with palms facing downward. Sergeant Black inspected our hands and feet for injuries and cleanliness. Afterwards, he ordered us to present our boots, brass and rifles. Finding few complaints, he ordered us to prepare to hit the rack.

"Tomorrow is Thanksgiving Day maggots.___Even though I don't think you've earned anything,__you will get a Thanksgiving Day meal." The lights finally went out and I felt I had kept up another day in this very serious adult world I had foolishly demanded to enter.

THREE

Crash, clang, bang, resounded through the barrack on Thanksgiving morning.

Why should today be any different? I complained mentally as I sprang from my bunk and hit the white line and fixed my thousand yard stare straight ahead. Sergeant Wyeth had the duty again today. Apparently, Staff Sergeant Louis had taken the holiday off and Wyeth was given the duty.

At least Sergeant Black could go home for this day as well. I observed wondering why the hell I even cared. *This day is not going to be any different from any other day, especially with Wyeth on duty.* I thought, feeling regret that we couldn't at least enjoy one day!

We were all still showing signs of fear. Fear of personal failure, fear of letting down the platoon and definitely, fear of the drill instructors. Just because this platoon had been on the Island for three and a half weeks of training, it was not enough time to create any feelings of relaxation. The contrary was the case. With each day we had replaced the initial shock and confusion with abject fear. My additional time in the Medical Platoon did not help me to relax one bit. In fact, that place was run exactly like a regular training platoon and there was no opportunity for anyone to get fat and happy. The only memorable period of escape was the few days I spent with the three stooges. In a way, I now missed those goof-balls.

"Ya got fave minits to git yer shit oan hogs!____Do it!" Sergeant Wyeth said in a slow froggy southern drawl as he walked down the squad bay always presenting a forward tilt of his body. He literally stood in a concave curve staring out from those cold grey sunken eyes. He barely moved his neck. When he looked to either side, it seemed he only shifted his eyes instead of his whole head. He got the morning underway in his typical style of terror.

Every time he says do it, I swear it sounds like doot. I laughed deep inside my mind in that place I prayed this crazy DI could never reach. I had a growing fear of this sergeant now, and I could not do anything about it.

We ran through the head and then outside to form up. The morning was chilly and there was a ground fog. A cold drizzling rain started as we stood waiting to march to chow and I felt like crap. The breakfast turned out to be perfect for the kind of weather we had. There was chipped beef and gravy this morning, along with sausage links, biscuits and fried potatoes. It was a real southern style breakfast. As we sat eating, there was only the sound of clatter made by metal on metal when suddenly, as if he had just materialized out of thin air, Sergeant Wyeth stood at the end of our table and started yelling. "You uncouth hogs!___That's it hogs,___just a slopping away at yer chow.___Damn!___Ya doan slouch over yer tray an' scoop it in,___ya sit straight an' bring yer fork up to yer mouth,___in a military fashion,___ya buncha numb-nuts!___Ya read me?" he chastised the platoon.

"Sir, yes Sir!" we screamed with mouths full of the last fork-full of chow.

I'm already doing what he is demanding of us, but I find it odd as hell for a hillbilly shit-kicker like him to be giving a lecture in eating etiquette. I thought while I mentally shook my head.

With Pavlovian reflex, everyone of us, including even other recruits from different platoons, who were within earshot, stiffened up and proceeded to lift their forks high. That good feeling we had going into the chow line had vanished. Sergeant Wyeth was sure to give us more hell outside for pissing him off during his chow time. He had apparently been watching us from the drill instructor's dining section. It was our fault, since we were told how to eat from the first day on the Island. We just got sloppy, that's all, we were slacking-off and we already knew how to do it the correct way.

It didn't help things between the recruits and our drill instructor, when a guide from another platoon ran into a Marine sergeant outside on the mess hall steps, as he was entering the mess hall, at the same time we were in line. The guide knocked the sergeant flat onto the deck and then proceeded to place his guidon pole into the slotted rack outside the mess hall hatch. He did not stop and say "Sir, by your leave Sir!" or "Sir, the recruit is responsible and requests the Sergeant's pardon Sir". No, not that recruit, because he was hell-bent on getting into line for chow. Several drill instructors saw the incident and a severe ass-chewing ensued. The recruit was told he was worthless and had shown such a lack of military courtesy that he no longer deserved to be a guide.

We could hear all the shouting, because we were standing in the hatchway in our usual asshole-to-belly button formation. The pissed off drill instructor of the guide's platoon finished the incident by ordering the platoon flag to be rolled up and secured with rubber bands. That recruit had done the unpardonable. Technically he had physically assaulted a Marine non-commissioned officer. They told us never to touch a Marine, and this incident, although an accident, was to them an assault. It appeared this incident did not warrant a formal written charge, because it was enough just to humiliate the recruit and take some of the platoon's pride away, by rolling up the colors.

Our next surprise for the day occurred after we did twenty minutes of punishment PT in our barracks for the sloppy eating incident. I knew he wouldn't forget us. Anyway, we got the morning off. There would be no training. The usual squad bay cleaning details were required, but after that we were allowed to work on our gear, write letters or read from our red book or Guide Book for Marines until noon. Many recruits also did their laundry. I polished my brass and boots and then took toothpaste and my spare toothbrush and scrubbed my web belt and cartridge belt until they acquired that salty look. The web belt always looked whiter and became softer with each cleaning. The cartridge belts took on a light whitish green color. They were originally a dark olive drab green. It was acceptable to use our EmNu, a black lacquer, which came in a very small jar with a brush attached to the cap to blacken the rows of eyelets and the buckle of the cartridge belt.

Finally, Thanksgiving dinner was in front of us. It did not in any way resemble a traditional layout like we had at home, where the turkey was usually in the center of the dining room table, along with all the extra dishes for the feast, rather, it only smelled familiar. The turkey on our trays was indeed real and smelled right, but cut in such a way that only smell could identify it. It looked like round slices with light and dark meats mixed together. Gravy smothered the mashed potatoes that soaked into the stuffing. This, plus a heaping pile of corn, all surrounded a hockey puck slice of jellied cranberry. In addition, we had cornbread, butter and a slice of pumpkin pie.

I remembered my fathers' insistence on the layout of the food on Thanksgiving Day and my mothers' eager attention to cook it in the American holiday style. I missed being home with them and reaching out for a turkey leg, he had ripped off the giant bird, just for me. The ability to scarf down two or three plates full was my custom, before I had considered myself to have properly celebrated this feasting day. Nevertheless, we had huge portions here and this filled us up nicely.

After chow we were once again surprised back at the barrack.

Sergeant Wyeth informed us that every opportunity to review and prepare ourselves to stand the Phase One test, which we were going to have to take next week, should be taken to qualify our platoon's readiness to move to Phase Two. He started by taking us through the manual-of-arms first, as a group. He then walked down the squad bay and barked rifle movement orders to individual recruits.

"Port,__huah!__Snappy hogs!__Make a snappy movement!___Let me heah one loud slap!" he flung each word out like a dog's bark, albeit a very southern hound.

Our response was on target, and the sounds of our hands slapping the wooden rifle stocks, was thunderous in the confines of our barrack.

"Raet shoulda,____huah!____Keep the rifle firm and angled prop'ly.____Present,____huah!" He checked for form and execution and then walked to the next recruit.___Me!

Lord I wish he would get a phone call or some other distraction.___ Hell, I bet I'm not the only one.___I'm sure we all think the same when a DI, especially this one, is in our face. I cringed with the thought and awaited his mood.

"Raet shoulda,___huah!___Present,__huah!__Rifle salute,___ huah!" he spat out the commands so fast I could barely meet his pace.

I did alright, since all of me was still standing. I chuckled nervously in my mind as he moved on. *No sweat!___Right!*

This inspection was not without pain for several recruits. They failed to get a procedure correctly executed and received a fist in the gut for their mistakes. Next was a demonstration of our confidence with the rifle and bayonet. Sergeant Wyeth proceeded to call us in order of our position in the line up to his duty desk. He sat there and called each of us to report in front of his desk. As each recruit reported, Wyeth barked out his desired execution of the rifle and bayonet maneuvers. When my turn came, and that same dread mixed with fear of failure and his punishment whim, filled my mind. I ran up the squad bay, stood at attention and waited for his commands.

"Slash!" he ordered.

I assumed the basic stance and pulled my rifle up to port arms and smoothly moved the rifle butt into my right armpit. My right arm now rested along the stock with my left arm fully extended grasping the rifle forward. I continued the maneuver by thrusting forward rotating my body to the right and brought the blade down towards the deck. Then I rotated back to the basic stance. He called for a butt stroke and high and low blocks. Finally he called for left and right parries and then dismissed me. I ran back to my bunk passing my bunk mate as he ran up to demonstrate his skills. I was feeling good about myself, right about now, because I made it solo in front of Sergeant Wyeth without any bites. Many recruits were able to get through this, however those who failed were busy in the hallway by the head or next to Wyeth's desk pumping out push-ups.

I just know those hogs are in pain doing push-ups with full stomachs. My movements also felt sluggish, because I was so stuffed with chow. They gave us all double portions today. Sergeant Wyeth continued with first aid procedures. He asked every sort of question for a specific type of wound. The platoon was marginal in this area and this resulted in a study time being ordered. Just as we started to pull out our Little Red Monsters, a shout was heard toward the end of the squad bay, near the DI house.

"I!___Is that what I heard yah say turd-brain?___"Are you the famous Private I?"

"Sir, no Sir!" the famous Private I retorted.

"Well Ah beg ta diffah!" Wyeth hissed. "Yah best staht lookin' fer yoah clue!___Up an' undah the entire bottow row a'racks numb-nuts!___Hand in front ah yer face!"___Git chir ass down till Ah say stop!___Do it!"

"Sir, aye-aye Sir!" the famous Private I shouted and started sliding under bunks and over the mattresses of the bottom bunks, while holding his hand in front of his face, as if holding a magnifying glass. With each movement he shouted, "My name is Private I and I am looking for a clue!" as Sergeant Wyeth had ordered.

"Foa tha next auah ya'll keep yer Little Red Monsters out an' study first aid.____Do it!" he drawled in an even deeper southern twang then usual. We studied first aid and I started to catch many procedures that I seemed to have missed during our classroom session. Perhaps the reason for missing some of the points for each procedure resulted from concentrating and mentally reviewing procedures demonstrated on the previous injury dressing as he had continued to the next wound. I could not just sit there and hear him talk in order to remember. He was really there to illustrate or demonstrate the various injuries and first aid procedures. We had to read and learn the meat of this subject ourselves. It was not enough for me to have read it several times while in the Medical Platoon, because the corpsmen demonstrated many things not written in the book. But now it was all falling in to place as I read and visualized the demonstrations of the corpsmen. Throughout this period the voice of the famous Private I could be heard over and over and with less strength with this passing of time. Obviously, he was not able to study. Sergeant Wyeth repeated his questioning after an hour had passed.

We did remarkably better this time. I was becoming increasingly aware that I was getting pissed off at this platoon. There seemed to be more fuck-ups here than in 3063 and I had to pay quite a lot more sweat here for their poor capabilities. Perhaps it was due to Sergeant Wyeth. These guys have been under him for almost a month and he is definitely the mean DI in this platoon. He pushes us harder than any other drill instructor I have seen on the Island to date and he beats us more than any others had as well. Without any doubt, the recruits are all afraid of him.

Hell!___I am afraid of him! I confirmed mentally.

Since my being attached to this platoon, at least six recruits had reported to sick bay with bad bruises on their shins, ribs, thighs, faces and feet. These injuries were a result of Sergeant Wyeth's personally smacking them or they slipped on an obstacle at one of the courses when he got aggravated with them and slammed them into the wooden structures. Some had big bumps on their heads. Then there was the Ditz-blitz, where several other recruits got busted up as well.

There was also still some night-time crying in this platoon. I hadn't heard any of that after the first week in 3063. I know I ached more since being here, but attributed that to plain training pains. The abundant platoon punishment PT and the motivation drills we ran were also toll-takers.

By evening chow we had burned off the big noon meal and were ravenously attacking our trays once more, but this time with backs erect and the forks coming up high to our mouths. After chow, we got Sergeant Black back. He relieved Sergeant Wyeth and gave us free time for the rest of the evening. I started a letter home.

27 November 1969

Dear Mom and Girls,
Hi, how are things working out back home in your present situation? Good I hope. Are you at least having a nice time now Mom? Your letters are nice and long, but I don't have time to write you long ones back. Today is Thanksgiving Day, we had a big meal and no hard training. Yesterday we went to the PX and bought presents, which are on their way to you now. So have an early Christmas. I am OK now and my new platoon is different from the other one. There are some dumb hogs here who can cause the whole platoon to be set back if they keep messing up. Today we had a simulation Phase One test getting ready for next weeks actual test. All but about twelve failed something. I and another private got the highest marks and we didn't have any punishment PT. I'm getting heavier now and stronger in the arms and body. The running worries me now and we will start three-mile runs soon, beginning at the rifle range next week. I always pray that I don't hurt my foot again. Yesterday we ran two miles with our rifles, helmets and packs and we always run in combat boots (no sneakers). We use M-14 rifles here and they can get very heavy. They weigh around 9 pounds. We also had bayonet training, which really wore out my arms. It's hard to understand the drill instructors, you never know if they like you, because they are always yelling at you. I hope nothing messes me up from here on. I really want to graduate and get out of this hell-hole. Please say hi to your new friend from me. Tell Sarah and Anna to be good and pray for their brother, I need it. We have six weeks left. There will be two weeks on the rifle range, a week of mess and maintenance, one for tests and the final one is preparation for graduation.

Love Always,
Jack

After depositing the letter in the box on the drill instructor's desk at the end of the squad bay, I decided to clean my rifle and practice assembling and disassembling it blind. I quickly pulled out a white towel and covered my footlocker. Then I placed my rifle along the width of the box. I watched the clock on the bulkhead over the duty desk and waited for the second hand to hit twelve. I shut my eyes and tore into my rifle. The parts disintegrated from the whole and were soon scattered about my footlocker. I opened my eyes as the last piece dropped and saw that it had taken me eighty seconds.

No damn good! I thought setting my mouth extending the lower lip in a pulled down manner illustrating how I felt. I arranged my rifle parts neatly over the towel and glanced back up at the clock. *Ready!___Go!* The parts were immediately familiar to the touch, but finding them on the towel required many hand pats. I opened my eyes and once again looked disgusted. Two minutes. Damn! I was not letting these times be my best. I began again and then again several more times stripping, laying the parts out and reassembling. My times were improving. I disassembled in fifty five seconds and reassembled in seventy five seconds. They were my fastest so far, but not as goon as in the Medical Platoon.

Hey what's this? I looked around, taken aback, and then did a mental *ahoorraah*. There were perhaps twenty recruits doing the same thing now. Having seen me look around Sergeant Black shouted down the squad bay.

"Damn Shipman,___see what you started here!___Hell don't stop,___keep at it.___I been wanting to start training the platoon on this in a few days.___Keep it up," he said it in a normal voice. Hearing this more and more recruits secured their gear and started field stripping their rifles. This had apparently become too interesting for Sergeant Black to ignore and he decided we were in the mood now. Why wait for a few days to do it. That time can surely be used for other important training.

"Listen up!" he said loudly, but not unkindly, "Since practically everyone of you are already practicing,___let's all get the rifles out and I'll time the platoon.___Get it ready."

"Sir, aye-aye Sir!" we shouted a hearty response. I had found this to be a fun exercise and felt the rest of the guys must enjoy it as well. We had a blast. Our timing was always improving. Only a few hogs were still floundering. The sport of this exercise caused many recruits to involuntarily sound out *Ah Shit!* or *Ahoorraah!*

Sergeant Black was apparently in a good mood, since he never corrected anybody for sloppy rifle assembly times or for speaking out.

"Overall average for disassembly is seventy seconds and reassembly is eighty seconds,___let's get it down hogs." Sergeant Black urged us. We kept at it until the times were 60/75. He informed us that we need to get it to 45/60, before we can call ourselves any good. This went on until it was time for lights out.

The night ended on a good note and sleep was welcome. We felt motivated, the day was full of lessons we had learned and we were still improving. The only part of the day that bothered me was the First Aid Training. The platoon had to do better, because so many failed today, Sergeant Wyeth threatened to put the whole platoon back if we kept messing around. These were my thoughts as I drifted off.

I dreamed that night and it was all about the Confidence Course. I was crawling through the galvanized tunnel and the yelling and pounding was exploding in my head as if a barrage of artillery shells were detonating. The obstacles appeared gigantic and I couldn't get over them. It did not occur to my subconscious state that I had already made it through and over all of them. The dream got longer and longer until I was in a dead-man march, shakily stumbling one foot in front of the other with fifty extremely large drill instructors mobbing around me all shouting, sneering and pointing their fingers at me. The loud roar of their froggy voices was totally nonsensical. I woke up and stared at the black overhead.

What the hell was that all about? I thought and felt at once scared. *What will it be like tomorrow?* It was my last thought as I sank back into a deep sleep.

FOUR

The new day was filled with platoon training, Confidence Course and drill. Staff Sergeant Louis apparently missed us over the holiday. Because, he missed us so much, he wanted to be with us all day participating in all sorts of fun and games. His style was different from Black's and Wyeth's. Staff Sergeant Louis did not strike us as much as Wyeth did. Sergeant Black never struck us. Staff Sergeant Louis was a repeater. He made us keep doing the same drill or exercise over and over until it was perfected. Sergeant Wyeth would make us repeat several times, beat the offenders and move onto the next thing. Sergeant Black would tell us what we did wrong and expect us to do it right the next time. The only time he had repeated a thing over and over was when we field stripped our rifles.

I had begun to recognize many of the recruits in the platoon. Until now, I only sensed the presence of recruits or heard them. Because we could only use peripheral vision, while standing at attention, or while performing our functions, it was near impossible to see anything or anybody long enough to get an identity fix. I could see the recruits' faces all day long during the training, but the snap-shot moments of visual awareness did not give me time to study who was who. If I saw a face, it did not project a familiarity of the recruit himself. As we trained, I started noticing who had screwed-up by his voice and after seeing him once, being punished, could mentally see his face when he screwed-up again. There were seventeen black recruits and six Hispanics out of the eighty recruits in our platoon. I heard there had been one-hundred recruits when they formed up. That means twenty have dropped out so far and there would surely be more before we graduated.

Our guide was sharp. He obviously had been to a military school before coming here. His name was Don Delahay. He was white, had serious eyes, small straight mouth, slim straight nose, slim build and ears with an inward curve at the middle and the upper fold projecting outwards. All of these features were fitted in a narrow long face, which sat on a thick muscular neck. He reminded me of a hawk. He obviously knew his shit, since I never heard a drill instructor jump on him yet. Don Delahay had a twin brother in the platoon. They were not identical, but there were very close physical similarities between them. His brother had about a dozen large scars all over his head in the hair area only. The scars must have been the result of having been beaten with a hammer. What else?

The similarities were facial only as their personalities were night and day. For every positive, military or procedural event we engaged that Don could breeze through, his brother failed miserably. There were countless times when his brother had fucked-up so bad we all got punishment PT. The drill instructors would always swear they came from different parents. They were Jekyll and Hyde, with Don being

Jekyll. His brother would fall asleep in classrooms, drop out of runs, fail to scale an obstacle, foul up a rifle drill movement, leaving his top blouse button undone and more. His last act of brilliance involved putting his trouser blousing bands on and then blousing his trousers. We were still stove-piping, as it was strictly prohibited to wear the blousing bands, as we had not yet earned the right. Because of this breach of platoon orderliness, we were informed we would not blouse our trousers at the normal phase of training as the rest of the series would.

The house mouse was not the shortest guy in our platoon. There were four recruits around the same height. But they picked Davids. He was a hard-boned white recruit who reminded me of the look I often observed in Arkansas and other southern states. There was a noticeable scar running from the mid point of his smallish nose about an inch and a half toward his left cheek. It was a quarter inch wide and slanted downward toward his left nostril. He had very sad blue eyes and a protruding Adams apple. His thin, hard, freckle face held a small mouth with a straight line for a smile. The straight line smile was the military look most often used by our drill instructors and officers as well, I had observed.

Davids was tireless and efficient in his many duties. He made the DIs coffee, made up their duty bunk, ran errands, picked up the mail and shined the boots and shoes for the drill instructors. On top of all of this, he carried himself through training with capabilities above the majority of the platoon.

We had three reservists, all white, in the platoon. One of them was Haught, who was also the platoon scribe. The other, Wilam, was a hard-charging athletic white recruit with a strong square jaw, hawk-like eyes set over a small beak-like nose and straight lips. Haught was one of the two oldest recruits in the platoon and looked to me to be about 28 years old. He was close to six feet tall with a strong chiseled face. His jaw was large and supported a larger than normal vaguely cleaved chin with the right side slightly longer than the left side. The sides of this rough hewn face were very vertical giving the appearance of a new paper bag standing straight, while something bulged heavily through the bottom. There were deep crease lines running from his nostrils to the corner of his parenthetic mouth. His blue eyes were observant and calm. He projected a feeling of confidence in himself and maturity.

Haught was responsible to the drill instructors for completion of paperwork. This paperwork covered daily rosters, memorandum postings, training schedules, sickbay requests, drops and a myriad of other such administrative issues. The other older recruit was Kirkland, also a reservist. He was already bald on the top of his head, leaving a hedge of hair around the sides and back. He looked like a lawyer to me, with his confident smile, the kind that curves downward at the side of the mouth and then like a Corsair's wing-tips, flared up. He had dark sunken introspective eyes with signs of bags forming under the eye sockets.

Our four squad leaders were Shannahan, Jackman, Wilam and Martinelli. Shannahan was white, tall and skinny. He wore glasses which perched on a long boney narrow nose. His small mouth was set firm with hardly an upper lip and this rested over a long angular cleaved jaw. His overall face was narrow and vee shaped. His calculating cool blue eyes left one wondering which side of his acceptance chart they were on.

Jackman was a solidly built dark-skinned black man of medium height. His round face held calm studious dark eyes, which he cast with a look of disdain. He had a short wide nose with flaring nostrils and large lips. His jaw was large and appeared to have muscle bulges accentuating it. His overall look was of a tough character. He was self-assured and carried himself well in training.

Wilam, the reservist, kept his squad squared away.

Martinelli, who appeared very Italian, was also of medium height. He had dark almond shaped eyes and a narrow nose pointing down to hard thin lips set between a squarish jaw. His lips had a slight downward curve. There were two slight indentations in his cheeks, which created a smile and giving one the assumption he was an easy going friendly guy. In reality, he was hard to figure out, because we couldn't talk and the squad leaders had to pantomime or demonstrate every thing, and he was not prone to show any emotions, while he fussed over his squad members.

Martinelli was my squad leader and he did a good job checking us all out to ensure we had our heads-and-asses wired together. He would pantomime by shaking his head back and forth if it was wrong, or nodding up and down for yes along with hand and arm jestures. While checking our gear, he would pull it, tug it, remove it, or show us what was to be done, by exhibiting his completed work. We naturally hoped that his gear was always correct. Here on the Island, except when told to do so, there was never an excuse for talking and even though our DIs considered the word GEAR meant Goddamn Excess Army Rejects, because it came from them in shitty condition, we had to deal with it in silence. Not even in the case where example discussions, explanations of procedures or to compliment or berate a fellow recruit was normally required, could a squad leader talk. The code was absolute silence, except when responding to our drill instructors was required.

The philosophy of the drill instructors regarding mandatory silence was perhaps that our screaming, shouting, and singing when we sounded off, was enough. So why allow a lot of extra chatter. This was also thought to be the route toward loss of discipline. We were showing signs of developing ourselves into the culture of the Corps now. Our newly acquired habits were reflected in how we ate, how we worked as a team and how we strived to beat the other platoons during competitive events. We had an ethos and took no shit from any other platoon.

It was evident that we were undergoing a transformation from our slovenly civilian lives. The punks were shocked to find they couldn't hack it here or were barely hacking it to stay. While the majority of those who had joined to see if they were the miserable loser their fathers or peers had branded in their minds, were rising to the challenge and stomping big holes into the sand flea infested sand of Parris Island to prove it. Our job was to keep hanging on against the cruel challenges the big bad green machine threw at us. It was the DIs job to keep throwing us back into that machine until we either assimilated or proved to be worthless pieces of amphibious shit and kick us the hell out of their beloved Corps.

Unless you wanted to think back to the day you could not hack boot camp and wonder why you gave up, there was only one answer. Suck it up and become a Marine.

FIVE

Phase One was coming to the end and we could sense the aggravation on the faces of our drill instructors and in their emphasis on the instructions they gave during each day of training that got us nearer to our testing day. Finally, the day had arrived and we were plenty motivated to do our finest. Staff Sergeant Louis gave us a pep talk before we marched over to a building on the side of 3rd Battalion's parade deck. There was anxiety in the air. Inside the building were about a dozen officers and staff NCOs waiting to begin the testing and see what phase of amphibious shit we had evolved into.

I had a chance to find a period of total peace in which to review for today. Last night I had begun my training in guard duty. It was a drizzly night with cold air breezing across the Island. Those of us who were assigned guard duty had reported to a brick building directly across the parade deck to the rear of our barrack. We wore our ponchos over our utility jackets and donned our cartridge belts with canteen, magazine pouches, with magazines for this work. Sergeant Wyeth had the evening duty and had instructed us to report to the Sergeant of the Guard. With rifles slung over our shoulders, in a formation of six, we stood at attention and one of the front two recruits reported in. The Sergeant of the Guard was not a drill instructor. He wore staff sergeant chevrons and was wearing dress greens. He had been in the Corps for over sixteen years according to his four hash marks. The only reason I figured he was not a drill instructor was that he did not wear the ADI cartridge belt with that huge brass buckle and Marine Corps emblem or the SDI black leather belt.

There was a Corporal of the Guard, who wore utilities and a utility jacket with a normal cartridge belt and pistol holster containing a M1911A1 .45 caliber pistol. He told us to fall out in formation and then began marching us to various areas around the battalion where guards were always posted. We would be ordered to come to a halt at each post and the corporal would walk toward the guard on duty. The guard on duty would call over and say, "Halt!_Who goes there?" The corporal would then call out, "Corporal of the Guard with relief detail". The guard would then call back and say "Advance", if in a well lighted area or "Advance and be recognized", if in a dark area and they would meet for the relief.

The Corporal called for me to take post number four. It was the Bayonet Course. He told me what the perimeter of my post would be by naming certain prominent features or structures we were all familiar with. He ordered me to recite the second General Order and without hesitation I barked the proper reply.

"Sir, the recruit's second General Order is:___To walk my post in a

Military manner, keeping always on the alert and observing everything that's taken place within sight or hearing,___Sir."

It was pitch black out there and I could not really see anything until I was right on top of it. It was still raining a fine drizzle and I heard the loudest concentrations of insect chatter I had ever experienced.

Damn bugs, must be some sort of a convention going on here. I said half aloud. As I walked along the edge of the water, I heard splashing. *What the hell is that?___Alligators?____Might be.____They said there were plenty of them on the island,____but this is not the Beaufort River nor Archers or Ribbon Creeks.___But, they can walk over to this place.* I concluded.

There was a large body of water, really a pond, across the street from Talase Street, which was slightly north-west of the back areas of 3rd Battalion when looking from Wake Boulivard. My post at the Bayonet Course was approximately fifteen hundred feet from that pond. West of the course, totally surrounding three sides of the back half of the course grounds was a hugh swamp. Edding Creek fatly wriggled directly into the vast part of that swamp, with Ribbon Creek south-west in the same swamp. There was a tremendous variety of racket coming from the reeds. Frogs, birds, snakes and other aquatic critters were jumping off the bank into the water as I passed by. At the back half I actually steered clear of the swamp edge due to the intensity of the chattering sounds.

During my tour of guard duty, in the dark and free of barrack stress, I felt the stress of the entire barrack pressure evaporate, leaving my mind at peace. This peace allowed me to think harder and thus more clearly and so I began to review what I had learned so far. I mentally pictured first-aid procedures and then since nobody could see me, went through the bayonet attack maneuvers with my rifle. In order not to make noise, I did not slap my rifle loudly while I practiced the Manual-of-Arms. With each maneuver I had a mental snap shot of the same movements I had practiced during the training course. This was practice time that was like winning a poker hand. Very few recruits would have found the opportunity to do this much extra practice training.

There I was, in a swamp in the middle of a pitch black night jabbing, slashing and butt stroking away. The best part was that if I screwed-up any moves it was free, because no DI was there to pounce. The time during my tour of guard duty passed far too swiftly, to my regret.

When the Corporal of the Guard came to relieve me, I had challenged him. Satisfied with his response, I stated, "Sir, Recruit Shipman reporting post number four all secure Sir." After we all reported to the guard shack and were accounted for, the duty NCO ordered us to return to our barrack.

I had enjoyed my first guard duty and felt relaxed when I had entered the barrack and hit the rack.

SIX

"What cha do fer yer buddy when e's gut shot boy?"
"What is your eighth General Order?"
"Horizontal butt stroke,___huah!"
"What do you do about superficial frostbite,___numb-nuts?"
"Recite your fifth General Order!"
"Block against a slash recruit!___Quick now!"

It was like an inquisition and had been going on at this rate since we arrived after chow this morning. Now I stood before the inspection team. I was nervous, not because of inability to meet each of their orders or questions, but in my reaction to the way they were hammering us for it. They required us to demonstrate bayonet attack skills, Manual-of-Arms or recite the General Orders, history, Code of Conduct and first aid procedures, without pauses between the queries.

We demonstrated dressing chest wounds, carrying wounded, administering mouth to mouth resuscitation and many other things.

"Recruit, what does Article 11 of the Code of Conduct state?" a lean, leathery lieutenant asked me.

"Sir, Article 11 of the Code of Conduct states:___I will never surrender my men, while they still have the means to resist, Sir!" I boomed out the answer.

"Your ninth General Order?"

"Sir, the recruit's ninth General Order is:___To call the Corporal of the Guard in any case not covered by instructions, Sir!"

He then ordered me to demonstrate placing a pressure dressing on an imaginary wound of another recruit. I was in my glory. The lieutenant was apparently content with only asking me questions. He moved on to the next recruit. This was not a quiet place with only one person asking the questions and one answer clearly resounding throughout the building. Each of the judges was going after the recruits with rapid fire questions. What I could hear from my platoon members, when I could make it out, were accurate replies to their questions. But the room was noisy. I was feeling proud right now.

Our senior drill instructor was as nervous as a first-time father in a waiting room. Sergeant Wyeth was also nervous and it was noticeable in how he got a meaner scowl on his face, which promised later reprisals such as slamming us on the deck, if somebody so much as farted during this test. But today we were all confident and motivated and it must have equally pissed him off that we gave him no extra reasons to slam us. Yes it was all going great until a gunnery sergeant started asking Shelton some questions.

Shelton was our current winner of the platoon fuck-up award. He was a white kid with a narrow face and the top of his head mushroomed outward. His ears were of the sort that hardly have any lobes. The lower three quarters of them curved up widely and shot up and in under the upper curve of the ear. It reminded me of two pieces of chain link with the lower half facing you and the upper half is showing the side. His eyes were light and very mischievous looking. To me he looked like a Chihuahua and with his nervous jerky movements he acted like one, because his cheek muscles bulged in a circular fashion joining a chin, which looked like a snout.

Shelton was grandly fucking-up right this second. The gunnery sergeant asked him to recite his first General Order and he responded nervously.

"Sir, the recruit's first General Order is to report all violations___ no, that's not it___uh_____Sir, the recruit's first General Order is to take charge of this post and all Government property in view,___Sir!"

An unsteady approach, but still a good landing. I chuckled to myself, because it would have been odder if Shelton answered correctly right off. He was asked to present arms and execute a jab to mid-section with his rifle and to parry right and left. His execution was smooth and correct. From the stumble on his first answer he had recovered and passed the remaining testing. I had a perfect view of Shelton from my position across from him. He was visibly relieved when the judge walked on to the next recruit.

Later, we were inspected on our field marching pack assembly and fit over our shoulders. Sure as shit, Shelton was called on his packs fit.

This miffed me. This guy will cause us to fail, was all I could think. It seemed to me that anybody could get such a simple thing as pulling straps tight done right. I wondered how many of the other recruits in 3074 screwed-up any of their questions.

In the end, I had worried for nothing. Staff Sergeant Louis walked down the squad bay and said nothing. When he reached the far end he stopped, turned and slowly walked back, while letting us know the results.

"Listen up sweet-peas.___You think you did well during testing don't you?___Well let me tell you how bad you did.___You sons of bitches won the streamer,___you came in first!___Keep it up recruits."

"Sir, aye-aye Sir!" our happy and thunderous reply exploded. Staff Sergeant Louis held up a white cloth streamer and called for Delahey to grab the platoon guidon and bring it to him. Delahey was quick and in seconds held the guidon out so Staff Sergeant Louis could affix it above the platoon flag.

"You people will also take the range streamer!___Won't you?" he inquired in a 'you better or else' voice.

"Sir, yes Sir!" our confident response boomed through the barn.

"To show my appreciation for this splendid work girls.___I will authorize a hog board on which you will display pictures of your girlfriends or whatever,___as long as they are good looking. If you don't have one,___write a letter and have one sent."

"Sir, aye-aye Sir!" we happily answered and went to work on our gear. Later that evening we were allowed to have one cigarette out by the wash basins. It was the first cigarette I had so far during boot camp, however it did not really matter to me that we rarely smoked, since I was not a smoker. So I took the prize. We stood around the concrete wash basins and shouted the requisite words.

"Sir, the smoking lamp is lit for one cigarette and one cigarette only Sir!"

"Light em up girls!" Staff Sergeant Louis groweled with a slight grin.

"Sir, aye-aye Sir!" we eagerly responded and lit our reward.

SEVEN

Signs that the platoon was moving on and slowly becoming Marines were becoming an achievable reality. One strong sign was what we were to receive when we had marched over to a metal building, a butler building, and carried our sea bags. Inside were piles of boxes and rows of tables stacked with uniforms. There were about twenty Marines inside who stood waiting behind the tables. We filed inside and were ordered to strip to our skivees and get in line. This done, we started down the building where we were first measured and given our individual measurements. As we encountered each table we were issued a part of a uniform in the size we stated. There were khaki trousers and short-sleeved shirts, tropical trousers, long-sleeved shirts and winter green sets followed. Dress shoes, leather garrison cap visors, brass winter green blouse belt buckles, Marine Corps insignia devices were also issued. Seeing these devices, but knowing that we still had to prove ourselves to earn them, was both aggravating and motivating at the same time.

With eager haste we put them on and stood on the wooden platforms built like steps. There were several civilians who waited at the platforms. They took pins and soap and marked or folded our uniforms securing them with pins where they needed to be hemmed in. I instantly felt more like a Marine when I put on my uniform. The whole process was pleasant, because it was relatively quiet in the building and there was no yelling from the drill instructors. The moment was solemn and I could see other recruits puffing out their chest just a tad more today.

For me, the coolest uniform item issued, was the overcoat. It was a long green woolen great coat. It reminded me of the coats I saw in pictures of World War I, from our class on history where it appeared the soldiers of all the armies wore similar looking great coats. We left all the items needing to be altered, gathered up and folded our remaining items, stuffed them inside our sea bags and fell outside to form up. Instead of marching back to the barn our next stop was to be our second visit to the PX.

It was an opportunity to buy more shoe polish, Brasso, EmNu, shaving cream, toothpaste, clothes pins or whatever items were needed for ensuring we squared ourselves away during training. Another sign of our moving on to that day of graduation was evidenced by our having been on the Island long enough to have used up much of our initial hygiene and other cleaning items.

Dropping the gear on the grass we entered the mess hall and ate a meal that, for the first time since Thanksgiving Day, was enjoyed after a lazy morning. That was to change after chow though. We went to the barrack and changed into PT gear and worked off the flab we acquired during the first half of the day. We normally ran PT in the mornings, but the time we were scheduled to go for uniforms was too early to do it first. Staff Sergeant Louis and Sergeant Black were both on duty today, but Staff Sergeant Louis could have already left for the day. He probably wanted to get in some PT for himself, was how I figured it.

The next day was full of training. We ran the obstacle course, ran PT, drilled and cleaned uniforms and gear. It was a hectic day with a discernable nervousness in the air, as we were preparing for Phase II of our training. That evening we were instructed on how to properly fold our clothing and pack it in our sea bags so as not to wrinkle them. Another reason for packing was that we would be going to the Rifle Range the next day and would spend two weeks in a barrack there.

We prepared our field marching packs, but would wait until the next morning to pack our sheets and blanket into our shelter half, where we would roll them up and secure them to our packs. There was electricity in the air. Sneaking quick glances, I could see the excitement in every recruit evidenced in how they moved about securing their gear. After all of my gear was secured in my sea bag and pack, I decided to answer the letters I received from my mother and sister over the past week.

5 December 1969

Dear Mom and Girls:
Hi. Here I am on the day before we move out to the Rifle Range and since we don't have time later tonight to write letters, we are doing them earlier in the day. We packed up our sea bags and other trash, including our new Marine Corps uniforms, which we were issued yesterday, and alot of it. We received two green dress coats, two trousers, three khaki trousers, six shirts and a long overcoat plus many more items. Our graduation uniform will be dress greens. The uniforms are being tailored now. Thanks for your letter, and yours too Sarah. Your question about me catching up with my old platoon,--no, because they are already close

to graduating and will be getting home for Christmas. I still have five weeks before I go to ITR (Infantry Training Regiment) at Camp LeJeune, NC. Send me Janet's picture and a few other nice pictures of any girls I have at home, but nothing ugly. We will have a "Hog Board" for the prettiest girl contest, while we are at the Range. Our Platoon won their first 'flag ribbon'. It is a white cloth streamer. (Our platoon flag is not the American Flag). This award was for having 100% of the recruits passing the 1st phase test. If we are the best at the rifle range, we will get a red streamer and we also change from a yellow flag with red numbers, to a red flag with yellow numbers. There are streamers awarded for different parts of training. The reason we were told to write is to request Christmas presents be sent here. Send one if you want to, but only a few things. (Enough in the package to divide amongst 70-80 recruits). A bag or two of candy should be enough. We made a PX call yesterday and bought a lot of junk we needed. I'm sending you $10.00 to help you a little in buying a gift. Well, I hope you can manage your needs, have a nice time, don't rush into things like you did before please, because that's what causes sorrow. I hope you can manage your bills by yourself. Use the $10.00 for bills instead, if you need to. If you do send me anything, don't make a package with a lot of junk. They'll only throw it out after they throw it in my face. Send Christmas candy only, because they said they will allow some candy. Send enough for the platoon. A bag has about sixty pieces. That should be enough to share, but two bags would do well and I might even get a piece or two from it. Write back soon and mail the package if you can afford it, if not, don't even try, okay Mom, it's not that important. But mail soon if you want it to get here in time. Hi girls, have fun and take care of the house for Mom.

Love Always,
Jack

I decided to hold on to the letter until we had relocated to our new barrack at the range and write about the way our new place looked and so added the following the next evening. When I mentioned not to send a lot of junk, I thought of writing about the day our Polish immigrant recruit Walski got a big package of salamis and other 'old country' meats from home and the DIs made him eat it until he turned green and puked. But then I decided Mom would not understand and get funny ideas.

The next morning we had chow at the 3rd Battalion mess hall and saddled up for our march over to the Rifle Range. Our sea bags were piled on the back of a truck and would be waiting for us when we arrived there. We formed up and started off on the march and Sergeant Wyeth was apparently feeling very Marine today. He had us sing every verse of the Marine Corps hymn and count cadence all the way there. It was not really that far from our battalion area, perhaps a mile and a quarter. It was a beautiful march, because to me, we looked like what Marines should look like according to the many pictures I had seen since joining the Marine Corps. We were wearing packs and helmets, with our rifle slung over our shoulders and we could have just as likely been marching to our ships for transport to the war. This scene was enhanced by the other three platoons in our series, which added mass to the overall picture.

As we neared the new barracks we passed by a wooden sign built with four by four posts in an A shape. The top of the A was not pointy and was topped with triple stack of longer boards projecting about two feet from the frame. This was originally cut with the center of the top board cut in a vee and the ends cut about four inches in from the one above it. It was an Oriental design and it was painted bright red. There were three wooden signs hanging off of it. The smaller top signs were suspended from under the triple boards and in yellow block letters stated:

WEAPONS
TRAINING
BATTALION

From under that was a narrow sign displaying the name and rank of the Weapons Training Battalion commander. There was a center four by four beam running through both support posts and projecting about ten inches out further. These were also cut on two sides leaving the ends in a vertical indentation. This beam supported a much larger lower sign which stated proudly:

**WE TRAIN THE
WORLDS BEST
MARKSMEN**

I knew this sign well, because while I had been a long-time resident at the range area, I was assigned the job of repainting this sign. Using a large brush, I painted the open red surfaces and using a very small brush wandered into the small areas between the block print and along the many straight areas of the letters. I did not smudge any of the lettering and it was apparent.

We moved on and into a barrack on the far left side of the complex. This huge barrack was red brick and constructed in a three story E. The long side of the E faced the road between it and the rifle range. Our barrack was on the second floor at the lower portion of the E as one observes that letter. Sergeant Wyeth began barking orders to get our trash squared away and get ready for inspection. We spent the day getting squared away in our barrack and ran PT. During the evening free-time I finished my letter home.

> *PS: I got your nice letter yesterday. I also had time to read it. We are in the range barracks now. They are big and have two platoons in the squad bay, because they are so big. I can see the other platoon and their drill instructors from my bunk area. They are placing wall lockers between our platoons right now. We will have two hard weeks ahead of us now. The drill instructors say it will be painful on our bodies, snapping-in and firing using muscles differently. I am also in the same barn that my old platoon was in. Same side too*
>
> *Love,*
> *Jack*

"Lights out!" Wyeth ordered as taps ended and his froggy voice permeated the darkness promising a hard day tomarrow.

CHAPTER 8
RIFLE RANGE

ONE

We had become disconsolate due to the psychological silence, which was becoming unbearable. Since arriving on the Island, there was no talking and there were no personal sounds allowed. The only sounds we were allowed to make fell into group noises. Banging a razor on the sink was proscribed, but swishing it in water was acceptable. Likewise, nobody ever farted within my hearing. Thank God, because if one recruit farted the drill instructor would expect the whole platoon to produce the same noise. Working on rifles and the subsequent clatter of metal on metal was acceptable, however if a stray sound was heard by a drill instructor, such as dropping a component of the rifle, all hell would break out. Once, when a recruit dropped a trigger assembly on the deck during a rifle cleaning period, we spent an hour in punishment PT, outside in the sand flea ridden sand, under the harsh drill of Sergeant Wyeth. Our environment was best described as hostile, demanding and cheerless.

The never-ending silence created a feeling not unlike being covered with a heavy blanket. We could never talk amongst ourselves. We were becoming a solid cohesive team now. But it was strange that such a team effort could be achieved by people who, because of the silence here, could never really get to know each other. In order to build a team, one must trust the other. At present, we had seventy-five recruits who individually had to trust the other seventy-four. What method was achieved in bestowing this trust? Was it freely given by each of us, or was it earned by the demonstrated efforts and achievements of each of us? It had to be earned.

Perhaps it was simply because we were all in the same room in hell and equally feared the drill instructors. We had developed a common bond. It was possible that we would have bonded and exhibited the same awareness of distance between us and our captors, had we been prisoners of war. Sensing this distinction I recited Article IV in my mind.

If I become a prisoner of war, I will keep faith with my fellow prisoners. I will give no information, nor take part in any action, which might be harmful to my comrades. If I am Senior, I will take command. If not, I will obey the lawful orders of those appointed over me and will back them up in every way. The problem here was that the DIs were the enemy to us and since they were also our seniors we were caught in a dilemma regarding the Article's intent that we obey them. Taking no part in harming my peers was also a dilemma, since any one of us could cause harm to each other through our screw-ups and the resulting punishment PT. If I screw-up and they get punished, I have to back up the DIs in their decision to punish the recruits. Also, have we not aided our enemy when a DI orders us to stop one of our peers, who is mentally fed-up and attempting to jump ship by trying to run out of the mad-house of our barrack and we obediently stomp him into a blood-puddle.

Christ, it would be easier to do what the article implies if we really were prisoners. I decided.

The only way to know another recruit was to watch his actions, note his features and remember what fuck-ups he had amassed. Each recruit had a story. He had come from a small town, suburb or city and had any sort of background imaginable. We all came here with individual personalities and with an appearance to match it. Now we were all bald young men wrapped in wash worn utilities of the same color.

Many times I had sensed an aura throughout our barrack, as if we were in a spirit world. These hallucinations occurred when we were slamming our bodies hard into the deck for long periods of punishment PT. A fuzzy bubble seemed to form surrounding the entire squad bay and the recruits would move in slow motion with the sounds of recruits counting off and the DIs screaming all garbled and drawn out in a distant muffled-sounding delivery.

Sergeant Wyeth was the king of punishments. He would use up

valuable training time in order to show us the error of our ways. Maybe we weren't the best platoon in marching, but we could kick everyone else's ass in PT.

When his periods of disgust were exceptionally long and painful, my mind would spin off and often experience this hallucination for a few seconds. The amount of punishment we received had noticeably increased each week. Sergeant Wyeth was always pissed off at us. His vocabulary was growing richer with fouler language.

When he berated a recruit, it was always accompanied by a knuckle in the solar plexus, a bop on the forehead with the brim of his campaign hat, or a punch in the gut. Sometimes the unlucky guy would get all three. We were here and could go nowhere else. The only way to endure this was to go straight through it and take the pain. It was also evident that the attacks were far more prevalent when the other two drill instructors were not on duty.

We recruits had a code of honor. It was not told to us, but it had evolved in us. This code was to never willingly tell on a drill instructor; not to the other drill instructors, the officers, the doctors or the corpsmen. That meant Wyeth could keep it up until we either died, or graduated, and thus he would not fear retribution from his seniors.

Over the past week we had four more recruits drop out of our platoon. One of them went crazy and the other three were injured. The incidents where these injuries occurred were memorable. It had occurred during four separate training days back at 3rd Battalion, each one sending a shock through the platoon.

Hyde, our guide's brother, had been doing his best to screw-up and Sergeant Wyeth was finally fed up with him. Hyde had not shaved that day. When the duty drill instructor, who was Wyeth on that day, had walked down the squad bay, he caught Hyde lying on his bunk. His voice bellowed out like a raging animal, "What the fuck do ya thank yer ah doin'?___Ah cain't beleeve,___ah doan beleeve this!___Awe sheeit!____Drag it out fuck-head!"

Hyde refused to move and this provoked Wyeth into rushing in on him. Wyeth grabbed him by the shirt collar and his belt and pulled him from the lower bunk and dropped his ass hard on the deck.

"Ah said,___git yer fuckin' maggoty pusillanimous ass outta the bunk,___asshole!" he shouted while planting his boot into Hyde's ribs.

"Git yer ass up to the duty desk now?___Ya lazy mutha fucka!" Hyde clumsily got to his feet and stumbled drunkenly towards the end of the squad bay, towards the head, and stopped. Sergeant Wyeth was right on his heels with body stooped, arms spread out with palms facing up, waving them up and down as he both herded him and emphasized his words. He verbally worked Hyde over. Suddenly he stopped and stuck his head close to Hyde's face. "What the fuck is this,___numb-nuts?" he grimaced in full disgust, "Why didn't you shave today scumbag?" There was a mumbled answer heard, but nothing loud and clear. This of course further enraged Wyeth.

"Ya haven't learned enythang here!___Have ya,___hog?___Ya haven't learned ta shave, ta stay outta the rack, or ta answer yer drill instructor propally!___Why is that puke?" Once again Hyde was vague and got a shot in the gut for it.

"Git yer bucket an' yer razor,___ya son-of-a-bitch!___Now!"

Hyde ran faster this time, obviously showing signs that he was getting back with the program. He was exhibiting fear and had dropped his bucket because of it. Picking it up amidst the clanging sounds it made as it repeatedly bounced, he ran back up to Sergeant Wyeth.

"Where's yer razor___ya dumb fuck?" Again, he ran and noisily rifled through his foot locker for the razor. Sergeant Wyeth ordered him to stand in front of the full length mirror provided to each barrack. It was on the left wall next to the hallway to the head and DI shack.

"Put yer bucket over yer hed and begin side straddle hops.___ Ready begin!" he growled slowly. "Shave yer fuckin' face and yell yer crazy with each jump.___Do it!___Shit-fer-brains."

Hyde started jumping, which caused the bucket to bounce up and down bruising his shoulders and pounding his collar bones. The bouncing subsided somewhat when he had struck his hand and razor under the bucket. He scratched at his beard and started crying as he sounded off, "I'm crazy!" *Jump, jump* "I'm crazy!" *Jump, jump.* This went on for at least five minutes, while during the time Sergeant Wyeth had walked over to Hyde's foot locker.

"Yer foot locker is open maggot and not properly aligned to the bunk.___Holy shit!___The contents are not squared-away atoll!" he stated, snapping-out the last two words 'at all' into a single word-sound only those from the same holler in the back-woods valley he was from, would understand. He then spilled out the foot lockers contents onto the deck. This action could be heard by Hyde and must have snapped something in his mind.

Sergeant Wyeth was busying himself peering into every nook and cranny of the squad bay and closely at recruits apparently seeking out a new game to play. While he was scanning the squad bay like a submarine captain behind a periscope, a loud clang, followed by lesser clangs echoed through the barn. Hyde had thrown the bucket down and started running toward the exit hatch at the end of the squad bay.

"Stop that fucka now!" he screamed suddenly, "Doan let em out!"

The poor guy was running for his life, past all of his peers however, it was more like he was running through a gauntlet of his enemies. His face was twisted and his eyes were red as he ran down the squad bay like a berserker. What happened next was disappointing to me. Like crazed animals, the recruits nearest Hyde pounced on top of him and flattened him to the deck, hard. The crunch and sounds of meat and bone being slapped resounded throughout the squad bay and it definitely appeared that the eagerness to hurt Hyde was revenge for all the punishment PT he had caused. The participating recruits also hurt themselves by banging heads together and getting their arms and legs tangled in the melee. But Hyde was stopped, he was down, and he was broken. There he lay, not moving, not crying and not caring. He simply stopped functioning. Sergeant Wyeth ran up to him and shouted more outrageous threats to stop bleeding, stand up and get squared-away. But they fell on deaf ears. He then went to the DI shack and called for the corpsmen.

A short time later, corpsmen had taken Hyde away on a stretcher. He had cracked up, gone bonkers, and lay still on the deck until the corpsmen arrived. It had been less than a week before this incident, that corpsmen had grabbed his ankles and dragged him-with his head bouncing-across the deck of our Morse code classroom to attend to him, when he supposedly passed out during our training session. That recruit had serious issues. We never saw him again. *Na Na Hey Hey....*

I wondered what our guide, his brother, was going through, while this went down. *He must be very disciplined to have endured this and to not have acted out in protest. Or maybe he was that scared.* I considered, feeling very concerned about all of it. *Hell, being scared here is a damned sight different then being scared in a situation outside of here. There is the need to stay out of trouble here, in order to just graduate, while outside you can attack and be damned about a graduation. Brig time maybe, but fuck that!* I reckoned.

Over the next three days, two of those recruits involved in the squad bay smash-up to stop Hyde, were dropped due to injuries. One of them had severely twisted his ankle and the other had a severely bruised head. The third one must have received a knee in the crotch, which turned black and blue over the next several days and was so swollen the guy couldn't walk normal. That recruit had also been injured in the tackle to stop Hyde. The fact that he was injured is a plain fact, however many things happen here that none of us see. He also had to go.

We were going even further away from Regimental Headquarters, from our own battalion and from the officers. This was terra null, no-mans land, and anything could happen here. It was an unspoken fact that being assigned to the 3rd Battalion meant a very rough place to be, so the normal ass-kicking we received there would naturally increase at the range.

TWO

It was Sunday, December 7, the day the Japanese launched the surprise attack on Pearl Harbor twenty-eight years earlier. The guys at Pearl Harbor got to sleep in on that day, because it was Sunday. Well it was Sunday here and we did not get to sleep in and the Japanese did not attack either. It was our second day at the range and we weren't going to waste any time, while here.

Staff Sergeant Louis had already made it clear that he wanted this platoon to win the Red Streamer, which was awarded to the top shooting platoon of the series. We had already been issued our shooting jackets and leather shooting gloves the day before. Whatever was involved for us to qualify, seemed to make Louis nervous. Over the next two weeks we were going to find out why Marines are considered the best infantry marksmen in the world.

We woke up to a stereo presentation of our usual noisy morning ordeal. Since there were two platoons in the squad bay, the other platoon's drill instructors were competing with ours for best, loudest and most original wake-up call. Shit cans, shit can lids and foot lockers flew down the squad bay and desks scraped back and forth with froggy voices echoing throughout.

I think these wake up noises all sounded the same and they all copied each other.___So who was the original?___I take that back, Wyeth was the king of original tortures here, only he did them when nobody else was around.___The crazy fucking hillbilly! I considered, while we were counting off.

"Get your tired asses out of the rack!" he shouted, and then continued, "Girls,___it's time to learn how to shoot.___You got ten minutes to square away this barn and yourselves," he warned, while looking around with a gaze that stated clearly that we shouldn't screw with him today. "Do it!"

"Sir, aye-aye Sir!" we bellowed and got to it. With anticipation and eagerness to see what the rest of the day at the range promised, we dashed through the head, made up our bunks, dressed and policed the squad bay before the allotted time for these tasks was up.

Staff Sergeant Louis was hounding us all the while. Outside it was cold and foggy. The morning darkness was total, due to the overcast sky. Staff Sergeant Louis was eager to get us running. The platoon was formed up and waiting for his command. While I stood there I took in the dark morning. It was invigorating being outside breathing in this crisp, moist air. Once we started running, we warmed up quickly. This would be our first three-mile run. Physical Training would also increase now, creating a new level of stress as we challenged this added weight. It seemed that the run would go on forever this morning. As our boots struck pavement, creating a rhythm, which resounded through the darkness my mind started to go numb due to that repetition of sound. I was just going through the motions, keeping up in my place in forth squad. If anybody had dropped out so far, I had no idea.

We started running songs to help with the rythem.
"Mama and Papa were layin' in bed,
Mama rolled over--this is what she said!
Ah give me some__PT
Good for you!
Good for me!
Umm good – PT!
Step__step__step__step__step__step__step__step__step__step__step__step....
Up in the morning to the rising sun,

Gonna run all day till the day is done!
PT um good___gimmy some__PT!"

It was well into our third mile when I noticed the heavy drag in our platoon. We were all feeling exhausted. After all it was our first day going one third further than before. But surprisingly, we did it with only two recruits falling out.

The mess hall was a familiar place for me. Seeing it reminded me that I had been on the Island for a very long time compared to the other guys in 3074. I thought about the recruits we lost who must now be over at the Medical Platoon or watching us march past them as they hobbled about their day.

Wish I could have told them about the Medical Platoon and what to expect there. I thought with regret. *Bet they were real down when they got word they were being sent there. I would have told them they would get back into training real soon and not to worry.* I contemplated.

Morning church services felt different here. That is, we had a different priest and he was almost as good at telling stories as our regular priest back at 3rd Battalion. Same story, different approach, but his way was not keeping our total interest. After church, more training was expected. We were not getting free time to square-away our gear or write letters.

Staff Sergeant Louis started with snap-in demonstrations.

"You will go through a series of snap-in instructions while here. There will be sitting, kneeling, standing and prone positions you will be required to master. This instruction is necessary for your bodies to adapt to contortions you have never imagined before," he explained as he stood in the center of the circle we had formed around him. Next he ordered us to spread out making enough room to begin the movements. We held our rifles at port arms and waited for the first position.

"For the prone position you will drop to your knees, while still at port arms.___Next you will place your right hand and the butt of your rifle forward and pivot down to your right side___placing your left elbow to the right side and forward, so that it will be directly under your rifle.___Your legs will be spread wide.___Ready.___Assume the prone position.___Huah!" he ordered.

Our first attempt was klutzy and Staff Sergeant Louis wouldn't have any of it. We attempted the initial drop four more times before he would accept it. The next movements resulted in his individually inspecting each of us. He pushed arms, pulling the rifle closer to the recruit's body and poking the right elbow far up and back, kicked legs further apart by tapping boots with the toe of his boot, and pushed left elbows until they were properly under the rifles.

We lay there with legs spread far apart, feet flattened down and our upper bodies twisted sideways with our left elbows awkwardly wrenched over to our right side, our right hands pushing down on the rifle's butt, while we lifted our arms high. We had got it this time.

"Push the butt of your rifle into your shoulder.___You should now be ready to fire your weapon." Satisfied, he went on. "Next you will assume the kneeling position.___Get on your feet.___When I give the order, drop your right knee to the ground pulling your lower leg inward to the left while placing your right hand on the butt of your rifle.___You then drop your ass and sit on your foot while pulling the butt up and into your shoulder.___Assume the kneeling position,___huah!"

This time we caught on fast and he had little meat to sink his teeth into.

"Okay girls,___you think you got it,___huh?" he snorted with a slight laugh in his words. "Well let's see how you handle the sitting position."

The sitting position required that we cross our left leg over our right, while in a standing position. We dropped to the ground using our right hand to break the fall. Next we placed our upper left arm inside the left knee, while still sitting cross legged, and pulled the butt into our shoulder, while resting our right elbow inside of our right knee area. There was some ass chewing going on now. Some of the recruits were left handed and struggled with this awkward reversal of what seemed normal to them. Soon Staff Sergeant Louis settled the problem by simply telling all left handed recruits to train on that side by reversing the position procedures.

"The Marine Corps wanted marksmen.___They do not care which shoulder you fire from as long as you hit the target," he explained.

Each position we got into presented its own new pains. We were pulling our muscles in ways that were not normally done before this. Our muscles were also larger and tighter from all of the training we had undergone here on the Island. Therefore, they resisted more. Later, Staff Sergeant Louis ran us at a brisk pace, over to the range area and showed us the entire layout. He seemed in high spirits and eager for our range baptism to begin. We concluded our sightseeing tour running through the streets of the entire building complexes of the Weapons Training Battalion. I had seen it all before, but this time, thank God, I was seeing it as a trainee and not one of the sick, lame or lazy.

The eighth of December was our first day at the range. We had been introduced to Sergeant Utter, our Primary Marksmanship Instructor, called a PMI. He was a tall man with a huge head bulging out from under his campaign hat. His facial features were fleshy and appeared like miniature muscles. Those features reminded me of American Indians. His cheekbones were high and flat and his jaw was long. He had a flat Slavic nose, which appeared pushed in, creating a squashed effect. His ears were small and thick like sausages. With beady brown eyes, he glared at each of us for a full minute. Then he spoke.

"My name is Sergeant Utter,___I am your PMI.___Don't think you can slack off around me, because I would love nothing less then to have you perform feats of physical impossibilities if you do slack off and I'm not talking about the anguish of snapping in.___Here you will know you are in the Corps," he stated, paused and looked around again to see if his first words exacted any observable fear from us. I don't know about the rest of these guys, but I got the 'oh shits' from it.

Then he said. "You will learn to be a marksman here.___The world's finest.___You cannot become a Marine if you fail at marksmanship.___There is no place for you here.___I don't believe there is a person who, if properly trained, cannot become a capable shooter.___Snapping-in proper position is only part of it,___but first you will learn how and you will conduct dry firing exercises until you might be ready to fire live rounds.___Do you understand me?"

"Sir, yes Sir!" we answered in unison. Sergeant Black, our duty DI for today, had wandered off toward the firing line and left us in the hands of Sergeant Utter. His first lesson was, of course, the snap-in procedures. We spent longer periods in each position with Sergeant Utter's clock then Staff Sergeant Louis had us spend. However, he had covered every position we were to do today and we felt grateful that he gave us a heads up for what this torture was all about. Sergeant Utter could not fault our platoon today, because we were good, damn good. I glanced up at our platoon numbers fluttering in the breeze and felt proud of the numbers on the guidon telling all on-lookers who this squared-away platoon was.

So that's why Louis had us out yesterday, he didn't want us to look bad out here today, because it would have embarrassed him. I concluded.

However, nothing lasts forever. One of our gang had screwed-up by getting into position a second faster then Utter had ordered and it pissed him off.

"Get over here, shit-head!___Pull back your bolt," he said sharply and told the recruit to put his right thumb into the chamber area and slowly released the bolt. Once the bolt was firmly squashing his thumb against the firing pin he had to hold the heavy rifle straight out. The rifle's weight was around nine pounds, supported only by his thumb now. "Let me introduce you to your new discipline program girls," he sneered,___"who's next?".

It wasn't long before we found out another trick from his bag of new ideas for punishment. We learned how to watch television, his version. This variation involved assuming the push-up position, basically. But this time we supported our body off the ground by using our toes and elbows. Periodically, he would order for us to change channels, which involved sticking one arm straight ahead to imitate turning a knob. The result of this was that we had to balance our bodies on three points now. This procedure pulled at the stomach muscles. After holding the three point position for a length of time, a wobbly effect resulted along our bodies, due to the increased stress on the stomach muscles, while the sand fleas bit into our hides. He kept this up, until the majority of us crashed into the dust.

My new song for this crazy bullshit will be Grazing In The Grass. Who made the song? Ah yes, it was the Friends of Distinction. I had decided when shards of the song started sparking in my head and then became decernable parts of its lyrics.

Throughout the day, we continued learning how to place the rifle sling on our arms. This involved positioning the strap behind our left elbow for steadiness during firing and dry-firing. Dry-firing was accomplished by sighting in on black dots painted at various locations of a white 55 gallon drum. Sergeant Utter explained how we should align the sight assembly in the center of the bull's eye to attain our sight picture. Finally, Sergeant Black returned and literally rescued us from this maniac.

After running and completing our physical training requirements for the day, Sergeant Black finally led us to chow for a welcome break. The evening continued with rifle cleaning, inspection and the cleaning of our personal gear. Once our brass was polished and our boots were cleaned and shined, we were informed that we could ready our clothing for laundry pick-up. Each of us had a small mesh bag and a large safety pin. The safety pin was about six inches long with a number stamped on the flat metal area, where the pin is held secure. We stuffed our white skivvies and towels into that bag and threw them into a pile where several detailed recruits stuffed them into fart sacks. Our utilities had been properly marked with an indelible ink and those were piled up on the deck, then scooped and also crammed into fart sacks, as well.

"Starboard side, make a head call!___Move it!" Sergeant Black ordered. It was now apparent that he was taking the night duty for Sergeant Wyeth, because he would have been long gone by now. The platoon finished head calls and stood on the white line awaiting orders.

Well I guess tomorrow will be a gaint shit sandwich with Wyeth all day long. I fumed in disgust.

"Hit the racks girls," Sergeant Black said in a low froggy voice.

"Sir, aye-aye Sir," we thundered our loud acknowledgment and we stepped off the white line and turned to stand by our bunks, the upper bunk recruits all placed both arms on their mattress.

"Prepare to mount,___mount!" Black barked and everyone dove into their bunks. The upper bunk recruits stepped on the lower mattress for their boost and swung up and the lower bunk recruits just bent low and virtually rolled into their bunks.

THREE

Well, good morning to you too Sergeant Wyeth. I thought groggily, while standing on the white line. Sergeant Wyeth always put a lot of effort into his wake-up technique. However, this morning was noticeably different in that he seemed to be enraged about something. He stormed down the squad bay screaming at a recruit here and there. It was much sharper this time, than his normal slow sarcastic southern drawl.

"What da fucks' yer problem,___ya fuck-head?" he bellowed at a black recruit. "Why da fucks' yer tal hangin' crookid on yer rack

Jack Shipman

maggot?" he asked when he had spotted Saunders towel hanging askew. Normally, he would have gotten into the offender's face and growled froggily that he should straighten it and give a gift of fifty push-ups. But, today, the ninth of December, Sergeant Wyeth was on some sort of war path. Before we moved from the white line for head call, there were about fifteen recruits cranking out push-ups. Sergeant Wyeth was livid now and threw his clipboard on the deck causing papers to fly all over the squad bay. In the other part of our barn, recruits were sounding off for port side to make a head call. Their drill instructor simply said for them to get it done. On our side of the barn, it had become hot. We were all ordered down on the deck. After a full fifteen minutes of bends and mother-fuckers, we were given our sentence.

"Because you stupid turds cain't seem ta git yer act tagetha,___y'all will def'nitly learn taday what tha Coah an Ah require of ya'll___an not evah fergit it.___I doan know if Ah'm gettin' through ta enyone o'ya,___but fer startas there will be no head calls, an' no chow!___Ya'll will have duck fer breakfast,___duck fer lunch,___an duck fer supper!___Duck in!___Duck out!___Don't eat!____Cause,___y'all doan deserve eny!" he concluded his malicious pronouncement and ordered us into utilities and then straight out the hatch to form-up outside. The platoon was in formation when he marched out to us. I had just then remembered that we hadn't done our usual count-off this morning, let alone a head call.

Boy he must be pissed off about something. I had thought and visualized Hueston's rampaging. *I have to piss like a race horse. What the hell is he trying to prove. I know everyone else is hurting to take a leak,___or more. When will we get to go, while we're out here?* My mind was becoming unclear, because I was concentrating on holding my bladder.

Sergeant Wyeth double-timed us toward the mess hall and reiterated his no-chow order. We fell in line asshole-to-belly button and proceeded down the serving line. Only this time we kept our trays vertical in front of our faces as we side stepped along the way. We piled our clean trays in the dirty tray rack and ran back outside to form up. The serving line recruits never blinked an eye. They had seen other platoons go through like this and possibly they had also done it. Sergeant Wyeth had signed in Platoon 3074 for morning chow and that's all that counts. The officer-of-the-day will review the sign-in log during his rounds and only see that we had been there.

Since we had time to kill as a result of our meal time not being utilized, Sergeant Wyeth decided we should do some close order drill. We returned to the barrack to grab our rifles and then returned outside. Still there was no head call. I noticed that as long as I was moving, my bladder did not feel so bad for now. The fact that I was holding it in by contracting my stomach and groin muscles only made me feel clumsy. I could see there was a similar problem for the rest of the platoon. Sergeant Wyeth also knew we had it bad, but he was determined to make us suffer. We drilled on as the last ink spot of the night yielded to the morning sun, as it sent its shafts of light between the buildings and other structures. It was warming up quickly, promising a very hot sand flea infested day.

"You girls doan know what pain is yet.___Ya take it fer granted that ya have a right ta make a hed call when ya feel like it," he stated froggily, "don't cha?"

"Sir, no Sir!" we replied in a high pitched, solid, unanimous, negatory.

"Wo-ho!___Hells bells, ladies.___Ya'll no doubt jes' challenged me.___Well let me tell ya somptin'!____In the Nam we layed in ambushes fer hours.___Hell,___all damn day long mostly.___We could'nt jes take a swig from our canteens when we was thirsty,___get up ta make a head call when we had ta go,___or eat chow when we was hungry.____no, not ever in the A Shau Valley we could'nt,___no siree!" he told us in a pissed-off tone. "So consider this as trainin'___hogs!___Ya'll will definitely always remember me maggots and this might save yer miserable lives someday."

While he talked, we marched and it was not our best by far. Nobody was relaxed, at least not yet. The recruit in front of me had developed a strange hop in his step and then I noticed piss running off his boot. He kept his pace as if nothing had happened, but his jerky movements were gone now. He at least was feeling relaxed. I wondered if he also wore a broad shit-eating grin, because he no longer had to fight to hold it in?

After having marched over to the range for more snapping in, I noticed many recruits had wet trousers. Sergeant Wyeth had to have seen this, but did nothing about it.

Tough shit! I sniffed the air to make sure I wasn't mistaken the smell. *Sure as shit, it was!___This is getting out of hand now.___What does*

Sergeant Utter think of this? I considered bitterly. The PMI was obviously aware of our dilemma, but continued his training lessons without a hint of concern. It was getting more and more difficult to concentrate on the lesson. When we started to drop onto our knees, the jolt sent a stabbing pain through my bladder.

Ah shit! My mind shouted. And then we assumed the sitting position, which caused immediate shock waves through my gut from the pressure. *Should I just let it go like the others?___We're definitly going to have to scrub our utilities this evening.* I thought with absolute conviction.

As the snapping-in progressed, I suddenly realized that I didn't feel I had to take a piss. It had somehow subsided. There was a new fear now. How much more will it hurt? When will I feel it again? I had to tell myself not to think about it. My mind was able to focus on the work at hand now, so I had better not remind myself any more about it.

Sergeant Wyeth had not walked around the range as Sergeant Black had done. He stayed right next to us and worked over any recruit who looked the wrong way. Sergeant Utter acted unconcerned when recruits were dragged from his training by Sergeant Wyeth to run laps with rifles over their heads, holding their rifle by the thumb in the bolt or doing assorted physical training, as Wyeth usually did. If one person had screwed-up, Sergeant Utter would have been pissed.

Sergeant Utter stood in front of the rest of us with his shoulders hunched forward making his upper body appear to stoop. He was at least six foot four and while stooped he was still taller then Wyeth. His mouth had a permanent grin, which made his flat face look like a mischievous boy.

Grazing In The Grass!

Noon chow was a repeat of the morning trip. We were getting thirsty, but he did not allow us to drink. Anyway, it would only complicate our bladder's ability to hold our night piss. It really didn't matter a short time later, because I had joined the ever-growing number of recruits with wet utility trousers. It felt good to release the pressure, but it soon caused a rash from the rubbing of my trousers.

At least I didn't have to take a crap yet. I thought with gratitude. I had tried so hard to hold it and when the rush of urine was spilling down my utility trouser legs, I felt a combination of fear, relief and humility all at once. This was immediately replaced with shame, helplessness and anger.

That bastard!____Look what he made us do to ourselves.____I hate his fucking guts! I complained mentally with gritted teeth and bile filling my mouth.

The air around me was getting thick with the smell of shit. We continued our free time, that is, the dead time we had once again earned from our chow time. Sergeant Wyeth decided to run us at port arms through a vast area of soft sand. Since we had to dig in to get a grip with each step, we soon tired and developed a hearty thirst and I wondered how those who shit in their trousers were faring with all this running. I'm sure it was extremely uncomfortable as my piss rash was tearing me up.

I literally prayed for Wyeth to take us back to the barrack for a head call, a drink of water, a shower and a change of clothing. It was not to be. However, we did eventually get back to the barn after our afternoon training at the range. A head call was finally granted and many recruits went about removing body waste from their skivvies and depositing it into the toilet. There was little more to do except wash our hands and return to the white lines.

Sergeant Wyeth spoke: "The Marine Corps requires that ah ensure ya take yer salt tablets.____You will file up to receive yer pill.____Do it!" We received our yellow salt tablet and got back to the white line. "Choke em down girls!____Ya doan deserve watcha git,____so git em down!"

Bull shit, if I swallow this without water! I rebelled, and pretended to put it in my mouth. Sergeant Wyeth smacked several recruits, nearest to him, hard on their backs as he observed them coughing and trying not to dribble the frothy spittle collecting in their mouths. He then ordered us to fall out for chow. As soon as we were outside, Wyeth ordered us to double-time and we ran over the grassy areas, which had sandy soil. The sandy soil made it more tiring to run in. At the first sign of grass during our run I let the pill drop onto the grass, where many more lay, but not seventy more.

The dumb shits took their pill, what did they expect? I observed with rage against this day's idiocy. *I'd like to give that bastard a free proctological tonsillectomy for what he is doing to us.* I considered with boiling contempt.

Our arrival at the mess hall proved to be just as dietary as the other two meals. Our platoon literally dashed sideways through the chow line leaving the digusting smell of an open shitter in our wake, and formed up outside where Sergeant Wyeth was already waiting for us. The smell of one recruit who accidentally shit himself could also smell up the mess hall, Wyeth must have gambled – so what. We returned to our squad bay, after that charade, and earned another attack from Wyeth.

"Git yer buckets shit-heads,___an fill em half way up.___Port side first.___Do it!" he ordered. When all of our buckets contained water he ordered us to dump them in front of us. *Splash*! The squad bay was suddenly transformed into a shallow lake.

"Hit tha deck,___cock-suckas!" he ordered, and we splashed onto the deck. After push-ups we were ordered to lay flat on the deck, roll over and stick our arms and legs in the air and then wiggle them. "Let me hear dying South-Cackalaki cockroaches maggots!"

"Sir, we are dying South Cackalaki cockroaches," we complied with much resentment. Next, he ordered us to grab our rifles and we began conducting close order drill, while lying on the deck.

"About___huah!" we splashed sideways and flopped onto our stomachs. "Rait___huah!" he barked next. Each turn soaked up more water. After tiring from watching this show, he ordered us to strip and run these wet utilities into the head to be quickly wrung out. Recruits ran all about, many with with large brown stains covering the seat of their skivvies. The mopping-up party ensued, and it was nasty. There was a strong scent of Pine-sol all over the damp squad bay deck. Finally, we were ordered to take our long desired showers, however this time we were ordered to put on fresh utility trousers and combat boots afterwards. Normally, after evening showers, we started our free-time, while wearing skivees and shower shoes.

"Ya got a half hour ta scrub-out yer skivees and utilities,___ya filthy critters!" Sergeant Wyeth ordered with a haughty sneer in his tone. "When ya finish that, ya'll start cleanin' yer rifles.___There will be a rifle inspection one hour from now!" he croaked froggily.

Apparently, even he could no longer stand our pungent smells. Once this extremely nasty and distasteful ordeal was completed outside at the wash racks and our clothing hung over the fronts and backs of our racks to dry, we cleaned our rifles and were back on the line awaiting Sergeant Wyeth's next game plan. At least we had on clean dry utilities. Instead of our rifle inspection we were introduced to his next game for the day.

Sergeant Wyeth was sitting behind the duty desk at the end of the squad bay. While he tilted back on the back two legs of his chair he held a long ruler in his hand. Tapping it on the desk and then slapping it in the open palm of his left hand, he stared down the squad bay at us. "Ah doan think you turds have learned enythang taday.___An' 'cause ya have been such a disappointment ta me pers'nally,___ah thank ya'll need moah motivatin." Suddenly, we were running from our positions along the white lines in an oval around the squad bay. When we were sufficiently mixed up and at some distance from our racks, he slammed down the ruler and yelled. "Git back in front of yer racks." We ran into a chaotic wall of green as we pushed and shoved each other trying to get back.

"Not good enough hogs!___Ah want cha back in three seconds!___Ya heah?" he croaked loudly. We continued this madness for almost an hour. In between, we did push-ups and bends and thrusts until we were grimacing from the built up anxiety. I saw glazed eyes starring towards me from the recruits on the starboard side. Sweat poured down our faces and we were going mad from this crazy ordeal.

Was this really motivating us? I thought while gasping air.

"Again!" *Slap!* His ruler smacked down hard on the desk top. He had been pounding the ruler for each PT movement and for each time we were to stop running around the squad bay and return to our racks.

Slap! We dashed through our fellow recruits, bumping hard into each other, as Wyeth had most definitely intended. It was sheer chaos and our tempers were now at explosive levels. I ran hard and careened into Cassavetti by accident. His boiling point had reached its zenith and within a split second's time he threw a round house punch which struck me hard between the eyes. *Thwack!* The blow, sounding like a slab of meat thrown hard against a wall, was heard by everybody and they froze.

"Git back on line.___Now!" Sergeant Wyeth said hesitantly and ran toward me. I stood there bleeding copious amounts of blood that was dripping all over the deck. My shirt and trousers were soaked with blood and the two recruits on each side of me had been splattered as well. I stood there in shock, but I did not feel any pain yet.

"Why the fuck er you bleedin' all over ma M'rine Coah deck,___ numb-nuts?" he blasted me in the face with spittle. This was followed by a punch to the gut and a shove toward the head. "Git inta tha hed and wash that shit offa yer silly face,___asshole!"

"Sir, yes Sir!" I shouted and ran towards the head dripping more blood all over the deck. There were a few groups of recruits from the other platoon sitting on the deck in the head, cleaning their rifles. When they saw me, their faces literally turned white and their eyes bulged wide. I looked into the mirror as blood dripped into the sink. The contrast of the bright lights, white tiles and white porcelain against deep red got to me. I felt the pain now and I was scared.

Holy shit!___Look at the mess.___No!___Christ what happened? My face was covered with blood and a steady stream was running freely down from between my eyes past my nose and dripped off my mouth. My forehead was swelling outward. There were no offers from the other recruits to help me. In fact they had quickly disappeared and headed back to their platoon area. All I could do was wash my face and hands, but to no avail, they got bloody again. So I held my head with my right palm pressing hard. Blood squirted from between my fingers. It did not help. My white tee shirt was crimson, as was the front of my utility trousers and boots. Perhaps fifteen minutes had passed and I was still bleeding. A fair sized drip pattern had formed around my boots. Nobody had come in from my platoon, or from the other platoon, to check out the situation, not even Sergeant Wyeth.

Finally, several corpsmen came into the head. They made me lie down on the tiled floor and put a compress bandage over the wound. One corpsman ran out to grab a stretcher. They poked and prodded my forehead and then put me on the stretcher and proceeded to carry me out the back hatch of the barrack.

Why not parade me through my platoon?___The psychological impact would make them all shit on themselves, again, and Wyeth, the malefic prick, could gloat at me.___What happens now?___Shit, shit ...shit! I gritted my teeth as my mind spun with wild thoughts of this situation. *No way will I go back to that fucking Medical Platoon!* I swore angrily. I would have attacked Wyeth, if he was near me at this moment.

The ambulance spun out of the parking lot and made its way to the main hospital in the Regimental Headquarters area. I was holding a blood drenched surgical gauze against my forehead. It was the forth one the corpsmen applied since assisting me. They carried me into a room and deposited me on an examination table. Very soon, after the corpsmen had exited the room, a doctor came into the room and looked down at me.

"My name is Commander Steiniger.___What seems to have happened here?" he asked a little bit too sternly. "What's your platoon number?"

He seems pissed off.___Is it at me?___Am I interfering with your peaceful evening?___Fuck you asshole! I thought bitterly and then I replied.

"Sir, Platoon 3074,___Sir!" my words came out loud and strong.

"Not so loud private.___I can hear you fine, if you just answer normally.___Okay?___What platoon?___Did you say 3074 recruit?" he asked, his voice was calmer now, and I regretted my angered prejudgment of this man.

"Let's see.___Ahuh.___Okay,___clean break.___What's your name?___I forgot to ask you.___Ahuh.___Needs stitches," he mumbled all the way, obviously totally engrossed in his work.

"Sir, Recruit Shipman Sir!" I answered sharply, but not so loud this time.

"Shipman,___huh.___Should have joined the Navy with that name___and you could have avoided mishaps like this.____I'm sure of that," he said with a tone of sarcasm, and proceeded to pour hydrogen peroxide over the wound and dabbed at it. He got up and grabbed for some items in a drawer in a medical cabinet located by the hatch. Returning, he placed a blue cloth over my face. It was the kind with a tennis ball sized hole cut out and the holes edges were stitched around.

As I lay there, I could feel a warm sticky pool of blood filling both of my eye sockets. I had yet to see the face of the doctor. Before he started to stitch me up, he had numbed the area. Suddenly, I heard another voice in the room. It was addressing me.

"My name is Lieutenant Gholson.____I'm the Regimental OD tonight.___Give me your name and platoon number," he spoke seriously, as if he were interrogating me. I answered from under the cloth and felt blood spill down my cheeks from the movement. The blood pools in my eye sockets must have been disturbed by my facial movements. I had made a jerking attempt to get up. After all, he was a Marine Officer and that's how I was trained to respond to one. The doctor's hand pushed me back, but not roughly.

"Exactly,___as it happened.___Tell me," he continued. As the doctor tugged the stitches, I thought for a moment.

What happens now, if I tell him what we were doing in the barn?___He'll probably tell the drill instructors and I'll be called a snitch. I thought distrustfully.

"Sir, the recruit slipped in his shower shoes and hit his head on a rack, sir!" I stated immediately as my un-rehearsed explanation. It was odd for me to have come out with that answer without having thought about it beforehand. But, it would do fine, I thought.

"Nothing else to say?" he asked and hearing my negative reply, departed from the room. The doctor did not say anything about my answer as he worked and not even when he finished. All he said was that I should try to keep the dressing dry and clean. He told me to go the range dispensary every other day so they could observe the healing process and change bandages.

"Sir, aye-aye Sir!" I rasp. What else could I say? The fact that he said go to the range dispensary did not mean I was going back to my platoon, because the Medical Platoon was also there.

A PFC, who was my driver, came into the room to fetch me and drove me back to my barrack. For some odd reason I was overwhelmingly happy it was not the Medical Platoon. He handed me some paperwork as I climbed out.

"The doctor instructed me to give these papers to you.___You give them to your DI," he said plainly, "Got it?"

"Sir, yes Sir!" I barked, and watched a wry smile work itself onto his face. "Hey,___it hasn't been that long since I was in there.___Just hang in there.___Now get moving," he said in a quiet voice as he pointed at the barracks. I moved quickly up the stairwell and entered my squad bay. The entire platoon was already in their bunks. Saunders had fire watch tonight. He came up to me and breaking all rules not to speak, whispered.

"Christ!___What the fuck happened man?___You okay?___Everything went dead in the platoon after it happened.___Wyeth never did anything else to us and he just went into the shack until Black relieved him.___Man!___How many stitches ya got man?" he whispered fast and excitedly in the dark. A few recruits stirred nearby, propping themselves up on elbows and trying to listen in on our conversation. A conversation while in training was very rare. Nobody risked talking, because of the punishment we would all surely get. This incident had apparently out-weighed any such fears.

Hesitantly I whispered. "Told em I slipped in my shower shoes and hit my head on a rack.___I don't know how many stitches.___They never told me."

"Does it hurt, man?___From the blood all over the deck and in the head we had to police up,___you must a' been half dead!" he asked and stated all at the same time, obviously wanting every scrap of information on this episode. "It got really spooky here for the rest of the evening."

"Pounds a little.___The Novocain is still working." I was walking toward the DI shack as I said this, with Saunders following to my side. Bunks squeaked all over the squad bay as I passed by. As I positioned myself by the wall to begin pounding the requisite three times, Saunders acted up. Patting his index finger to his lips, he waved the other hand with palm outward, indicating for me not to rouse the drill instructor and squad bay. What he really meant was not to do it loudly and maybe not at all.

Fire watches could rap gently on the door during night hours for important reports and so Saunders proceeded, evidently having decided this was important enough. A few moments later Sergeant Black opened the door. He was in his skivees with his campaign cover on and stood there with wide eyes looking at the visage I presented. I handed him the paperwork.

"Hit the rack, you'll live!" Was his only response and without reading the paperwork, shut the door and apparently went right back to sleep. This had obviously disappointed Saunders as he surely hoped he could glean more dope on this incident if the drill instructor read the paperwork and spoke to me. I raggedly climbed into my bunk with a sigh and starred at the ceiling, thinking about how happy I was not to have been dropped again and then I thought about more days like today with Wyeth. Which was better? My eyes slowly shut and the pain and misery of the day slowly ebbed away with cleansing sleep.

FOUR

There was not so much noise in the morning when Sergeant Black had the night duty. Sure he barked and clanged shit-can lids together, but he did not kick them or roll them down the squad bay as Wyeth liked to do. As I stood there with my head covered in a wraparound gauze I noticed the wide-eyed recruits across from me starring directly at my head. As we moved around to get our head gear, I stole a glance at Cassavetti. He had also been looking at me. There was a sort of bewildered look in his face. Perhaps he was wondering what the hell happened as much as I had. I know I never did anything to him to warrant any hostility. He had never been subjected to any punishment PT on my account and I had never been near enough to him to form any close contact resentments. As far as I was concerned, I had no feeling what-so-ever about the fact that he had struck me.

After we had put on our utilities, we stood on the white line and waited to be ordered out to chow. Staff Sergeant Louis marched into the squad bay. His campaign hat was tilted forward at a very sharp angle, which always indicated he was extremely pissed off about something. He continued down the lines of recruits heading directly toward me, stopped and eyed my head while he spoke.

"What the fuck happened to you sweet-pea?" he croaked lowly, sounding perturbed with the last word sounding a bit high pitched.

"Sir, the recruit slipped in his shower shoes and hit his head on a rack, sir." I answered loudly. This gave the whole platoon the answer they were all eager to hear. I'm sure Saunders had already gotten the word out to most. They wanted to know if I had squealed on Cassavetti and Wyeth.

"Bull shit!___Get your ass in my shack.___Now!" he boomed.

"Sir, aye-aye Sir!" I replied and ran to the shack and waited for Louis to enter and then started to smack the wall.

"Just get in here!" he snapped and closed the door. He paused by the only window in the small drill instructor's office and looked out toward the mess hall. A full minute must have passed before he finally turned and faced me.

"I want to know exactly what happened to you last evening and what Sergeant Wyeth was doing at the time you got injured," he asked in a surprisingly calm voice. It was as if we were standing in a garage working on a car together and having a casual conversation. This was unprecedented, because recruits in this platoon had never just talked with him.

"Sir, the recruit slipped..." I started to reply, and he held up a hand to stop me.

"Think hard about your answers to this incident,___we are going to drive over to 3rd Battalion Headquarters in a few minutes and you will first see Master Sergeant Rite, the Chief drill instructor for our series," he said and paused for a moment and then explained further.

"Lieutenants Lindseay and Gains will speak with you afterwards.___ Grab your cover and fall out by my car and wait for me there!" he concluded.

"Sir, aye-aye Sir!" I shouted loudly. I made an about face, opened the door and ran out into the squad bay, where I watched the other recruits fall out for chow.

Lucky guys, I'm going to miss chow again and that means I haven't had chow since the day before yesterday. I thought in disgust and then another more important problem entered my mind. *What the hell is going on here?___I might be in trouble for saying I slipped in my shower shoes and now I'll be accused of lying and get dropped from the platoon. Oh shit!___How did I get into this mess?* I thought in despair.

Several minutes went by and suddenly Staff Sergeant Louis came walking up. He simply said for me to get in the car. I obeyed, but my body was unnerved. Once I had closed the car door I did not know how to act in this situation. I was sitting next to my senior drill instructor, a man who made all of us cringe with fear. He started the car, a white 1967 Polaris, and backed out of his parking space. As we started to move off, he spoke to me in that normal voice again.

"I want you to know something.___You joined the Marine Corps to become a Marine just like everybody else in the platoon.___It is my job,___our job,___to provide the best training we possibly can while you are here.___The boot camp training program requires a lot from you recruits and also from us drill instructors.___We are hard on you, because of this.___That is,___you must be disciplined in order to learn how to become a Marine.___This requires occasional ass-kicking from us during the short time you are here," he explained and then stopped talking for a few seconds, turned toward me and continued.

I wonder what his definition of a short time is?___I feel like I have been here all my life. I thought with droll humor while he caught his breath to continue. *His choice of cars is the same as that son-of-a-bitch Hueston,___ great.* I thought, while assuming that all of the staff sergeants in the military must think the same, act the same, and therefore, purchase the same type of car.

"What I'm trying to say is that we drill instructors have a lot of pressure on us to perform a miracle,___to put you all through twelve weeks worth of training in eight weeks. This pressure is hard for many drill instructors and can cause some of them to be heavy handed. But you are not supposed to go without chow, water, head calls or scheduled training.___That is not the mission of boot camp!" he concluded, and spoke no more about it.

Jesus, what's he mean.___I can't believe he just sat there and spoke to me about all of this.___He knows about yesterday and all the other days Wyeth skipped those things.___But he didn't say anything about all the punishment PT, because he gave his share as well.___That must be why he said we must be disciplined.___Am I going to Battalion Headquarters___to be disciplined?___What did he say about recruits going without chow?___I have been going without chow right now! My mind buzzed with anxiety. I was beginning to think I was being kicked out of the Corps. Why else is he talking to me like that, as if it didn't matter anymore, because I was out, a non-recruit.

He turned his car into the 3rd Battalion parking lot. Staff Sergeant Louis then told me to get out and follow him. We walked down a concrete sidewalk, which had metal spikes running along both edges. These spikes supported a string, set at six inches above the ground, which clearly indicated for personnel not to walk on the grass. There was a large red sign, about three by four feet, with yellow lettering, next to the sidewalk. It had large letters denoting H and Co. at the top and a drill instructor Campaign hat between those letters. Underneath that, in the middle line, was 3RD R.T.BN and on the bottom was the letters CO on the left and CDI on the right. 1st Lieutenant Gains' name hung on a sign, by hooks, suspended under the large sign. Master Sergeant Rite's name hung on another plaque to the right.

"Wait by the door." Staff Sergeant Louis stated, and pointed where I was to stand. "When I call for you,___you will report properly.___Got it?"

"Sir, aye-aye Sir," was my only required response. Staff Sergeant Louis entered the door and almost immediately poked his head back out and grunted for me to enter. I marched in, stopped several feet from a desk and shouted the proper response for reporting.

"Sir, Recruit Shipman reporting to the chief drill instructor as ordered Sir!" I caught a glimpse of him as I passed through the hatchway. He had a swarthy complexion and looked literally like a bulldog. His dark brown eyes were wide spaced on his oval hard muscled face. They were pulled into a hard scowl, which made his forehead crinkle between two bushy eyebrows. There was a heavy fold of skin running over the top of his small nose, which connected with his eyebrows. The outward ends of his eyebrows arched up a little and then curved down slightly. This made him look pissed and surprised at the same time. His mouth was hard set and his thin lips were closed tightly, making a slit. A large muscular cleft chin jutted out from under that slit. There were several deep creases on each side of his face that ran downward at a slant. On his chest were ten ribbons. He had been to Vietnam. The top was the Presidential Unit Citation and aside from the campaign and service ribbons for Vietnam, his Good Conduct Ribbon and the National Defense Ribbon, I had no idea what the others were. There was a studied pause before he spoke. It seemed to me that all of these drill instructors did this before laying into you.

"Staff Sergeant Louis informs me that you maintain that you slipped in your shower shoes and hit your head on a metal rack.___Is that what happened?"

"Sir, yes Sir!___That is what the recruit stated sir." I answered hoping that, saying it like this, wasn't actually saying it was true.

"Are you satisfied with that answer?" he growled in his gravelly voice. I couldn't tell what his question implied, so I answered with an affirmative.

"Sir, yes Sir!" I barked.

"Staff Sergeant Louis,___there isn't any reason for this recruit to see anyone else.___Return him to the barn and put him back in with the herd.

Staff Sergeant Louis told me to wait by his car and stayed in Master Sergeant Rite's office for a few minutes longer. During the drive back, he only spoke once, where he informed me to get out to the range and to continue snapping-in at the School Range. I ran into the barrack, grabbed my rifle and ran at double-time over to the range and reported to Sergeant Utter and Sergeant Black.

"Snap-in,____over there!" Sergeant Utter said and pointed to an unoccupied space by other recruits already aiming in on a white barrel, with small painted target symbols, from the kneeling position.

Grazing In The Grass! I sang a few lines of the song in my mind.

Half way through snapping-in, Staff Sergeant Louis arrived and relieved Sergeant Black. There were no thumbs-in-the-bolts and there was no punishment PT, or other such special attention today. Apparently, we were doing just fine or they were not in the mood. Sergeant Utter had us form a half circle around him with space enough between us to get into positions and we began a new lesson on firing positions.

"The steadiest position for firing is the prone position, and it is used for rapid firing when targets are closer than 300 yards. For targets up to 500 yards away, slow fire is preferred," he explained.

"We will practice the prone position, making sure you have learned the proper preparation procedure," he said, and then ordered us to insert a magazine, inspect the chamber and place the piece on safe and counted each movement of the exercise as we prepared.

Holding my rifle at port arms, I dropped to my knees, pointing my right knee toward an imaginary target. Then I thrust my right arm forward, while letting the butt hit the ground, forward of my body. Next, I let my upper body fall forward to the ground, placing my weight on my left elbow, while I spread my legs into a wide vee. As soon as I had assumed the position, I forced the butt into my right shoulder and waited for Sergeant Utter's next command.

Sergeant Utter and Staff Sergeant Louis moved between each of us checking to see if our leading hand was up to the upper sling swivel, with the rifle resting in the vee of our thumb and forefinger. They checked to see if our slings were high on our left arm and that our elbow was well under the receiver as far as possible, without putting any pressure on the magazine. Here and there, they pushed a butt closer to a recruits' neck, into the hollow of the shoulder, or pressed backs to get shoulders level to the ground and cheeks firmly pressed to the rifle stock or thumb.

"You will spot weld your cheek in the position most suitable for your control of the weapon, there will be daylight between your trigger and stock.____The positioning of your body should be adjusted so that you absorb the kick or recoil when firing.____When you fire, you will apply steady pressure straight to the rear of your trigger.___Do not jerk your finger." Sergeant Utter explained over the sound of shooting from the firing line nearby. "You will learn how to obtain the natural point-of-aim by shifting your body until the sight rests naturally on the target at center mast.___You will close your eyes, count to ten and when you open your shooting eye, observe which way your sight has drifted.___Using this technique you can obtain your natural point of aim.___When adjustments are required, pivot on your left elbow until you acquire the proper sight," he instructed while he moved his gaze from left to right, to ensure we understood him. "When you breath and see the sights moving from center mast to twelve o'clock, you are well balanced and dead on target," he finished.

Staff Sergeant Louis took up the explanation by discussing breathing while firing. "Listen up hogs!___While firing, your breathing will affect your aim.___Therefore, start practicing holding your breath for a few seconds, while you aim and fire.___To do this properly,___you will take a breath, hold it for three seconds,___let out half of it and hold in the rest until the round is fired.____If you feel tension, breath normally for ten seconds before continuing.____I don't want you girl scouts to lose the high shooter streamer!____Got it?"

"Sir, yes, Sir!" we screamed with motivation.

When we entered the mess hall for noon chow, I was feeling dizzy. I knew this was from not having had any food for almost two days. Anyway, I figured I'd feel better once I got some chow. The chow was hearty today. We had meatloaf, mashed potatoes, corn and hot biscuits. I washed all of it down with a straight drain of my milk. Within a few minutes, I began to regenerate my strength. This food was damn overdue, because I had begun to fear falling-out during the PT run. I started thinking about Wyeth.

That malefic son-of-a-bitch, I bet he's having a beer right now and telling his buddies how he pushed us hard yesterday, yeah___what a laugh.___Can a locomotive keep running without coal and water? I thought with heated contempt.

Our next training period was at the pistol range. We ran over the soft soil of the range field and halted near a smaller range. The distance of the target from the firing line was not very far compared to those on the rifle range. There were four Marines waiting by the firing line. They all wore earphones and shooting jackets. However, these

Marines wore utility covers, instead of the campaign hats the drill instructors and PMIs wore. They were a mix of corporals and sergeants. We were formed into a semicircle and listened to one of the instructors, a sergeant, as he gave us a lecture on the .45 caliber pistol. He was a true city-boy from New York City or Jersey, judging from his accent, and a scrapper, judging from his nose.

"Yous are here to familiarize yourselves with da pistol, caliber .45, 1911A1._Yous will fire live rounds in an effort ta unnerstand da feel an' function ah da weapon._A little background ah da weapon._ Back during da first decade ah this century,_U.S. Military forces were engaged in suppressin' a native rebellion in da Philippines._Da natives would attack after dey had drugged demselves up an' tied cords tight around der legs an' uppa ahms._Dis cut da circulation an' if dey was hit by a round, dey would not feel it much, on top of being doped up._Our military used a .38 caliber pistol against dem at dat time._Dose rounds was not powerful enough ta stop da natives an' after bein' hit da wounded natives would keep comin' until dey could hack da shooters with der machetes," he paused, and looked at us. He spoke very rapidly, with hardly a pause between sentences.

Seeing he had our attention real good now, he continued, "Dey complained to Congress dat we needed a more powerful pistol ta drop dese guys.___Da natives._So,_in 1911,__da military accepted da new .45 caliber pistol from Colt, which did not only stop da enemy,___but buried em as well._Da pistol has ah maximum range of approximately 1500 meetahs an' a minimum effective range of 50 meetahs.__Dat means,__don't waste your ammunition shootin' at ah target past 50 meetahs.__Use your rifle for dat.__Da approximate length is eight an' five eights inches an' da triggah has a pull of five ta six an' a half pounds.__Da pistol weighs approximately three pounds.__Da magazine capacity is seven rounds an' da muzzle velocity is eight hunnert an thurty feet per second."

He was holding a .45 in his hand showing it to us during his lecture. When he finished talking about the background of the weapon, he pointed at different parts of the weapon. "Der ehr three safety devices.__Da grip safety, which blocks da rear ah da triggah yoke preventin' movement.__Da safety lock is a stud,__which blocks da shouldah ah da sear,___preventin' any movement ah da sear out ah da full-cock notch ah da hammer, an' half-cock notch,__which is ah notch right over the full-cock notch ah da hammer.__Da device has a lip projectin' off da cockin' notch,__which prevents movement ah da sear from dat lip, when pressure is applied to da triggah."

He sounded like a New York City cabbie, as he droned on and on in a monotone of poor English. The final demonstration was testing the position of the half-cock notch to see if it was working properly. The instructor pulled the hammer part way to the rear. We heard metal click, which he explained was the sear engaging the half-cock notch. Then he pulled the trigger and nothing happened. The hammer did not fall. He pulled the hammer all the way back nearly to the cock position and released it before the sear engaged. The hammer only fell part way and stopped at the half-cock position.

Next, several of the other instructors demonstrated how to hold the pistol and they fired several rounds down range. We had worn our M-14 rifles over our backs with the sling running from the right side of our neck down to our left hip. Staff Sergeant Louis decided to give us some working room and had us stack our rifles in groups of four. We were placed in our squad formations and at the head of each squad was one of the instructors. They decided to move some recruits from the rear of each squad and form a fifth line of recruits. Staff Sergeant Louis would act as the instructor for the new line. After all, Staff Sergeant Louis wore a Pistol Expert Badge on his chest, next to his Rifle Expert Badge. I would have thought all of the Drill Instructors would be or would have to be an expert at firing, but this was not the case. There were many drill instructors with Sharpshooter Crosses and a few with the Toilet Bowl or Marksman Badge.

When my turn came to fire, I marveled at the size and weight of the .45. I really liked the feel of it and felt comfortable with firing it. As I gripped the handle, I felt the grip safety depress and *blam!* We cropped the base of the pistol grip with our left hand for stability. There was the kick of a mule in this pistol. Damn! It was great. *Blam! Blam!* I fired again and again. Even though we used two hands, the pistol wanted to escape upward and away with each round fired. We were allotted twenty-five rounds apiece.

As we left the pistol range, I was suppressing a smile. This had been a singular event, the best I had so far on the Island. My head hurt somewhat where the stitches were, but I attributed that to the combined pressure of the days PT and firing the pistol.

That evening after squaring away our gear, Sergeant Black informed us of the Field Meet we would have tomorrow. He informed us that we could practice the events.

"Take about fifteen minutes to write a letter or whatever you have to do and we will start practicing," he said and then selected groups out of the platoon for specific tasks and told us that was what we would practice. "Go ahead now,___get your other shit done," he said loud enough to be heard down the squad bay. No sooner had he finished, when the duty Drill Instructor from a neighboring platoon yelled over to him not to waste our time practicing, because his hogs will whop us good on the field tomorrow. "Who's going to take the Field Meet and get the streamer Platoon?" Sergeant Black questioned.

"Sir, Platoon 3074 Sir!____*Ahhoorraah!*"

We nearly shattered the windows. I was surprised to hear how motivated we sounded. Yesterday and many days before that, when Sergeant Wyeth had the duty, we never seemed to achieve the same high level of motivation with him. Sergeant Wyeth was preoccupied with making us squirm, resulting in diminishing our desire to achieve. More often, our desire to just get through the training event or a physical event was all there was. There was no inner spark, no zeal and no motivation to do better. There was only the desire to get through it.

It was not because he occasionally punched us, hell most drill instructors did that. But, what Wyeth did was more like digging his heel into our backs after we were down, not being satisfied with just getting our face down on the deck. I grabbed my writing gear and started a letter to my mother. Before I had started, I looked at a letter I had received from my father a few days earlier. He had sent me a check for twenty dollars. After considering the check, I had decided I could not cash it here and, therefore, what use would it be to me? So I signed the back and decided to send it to my mother.

10 December 1969

Dear Mom and Girls,
   Hi, I only have a few minutes to write you, because I am part of a team, which is going to set up a tent after running fifty yards. We will wear a field

marching pack, which we have to take apart quickly and start erecting a tent. The event is called a Field Meet and what my team and the other teams will do is represent one of the platoons in our 3rd Battalion series against the series at the same stage in training from the 1st and 2nd Battalions. A trophy is awarded to the winners. We are going to train in a few minutes, so I have to hurry. Here's a check. I hope you can cash it. It came from Dad, but don't let him know I gave it to you, because I told him I needed it, okay.

We have been doing lousy on our snapping-in, prior to live firing. But, there's hope, because we are showing some signs of improvement. The .45 caliber pistol was today's subject. I fired 25 rounds, did okay.

Yesterday I had an accident and tore my forehead open and I got five or six stitches. The cut was about a half inch deep if you count the swelling in with the depth and is about an inch and a half long. The slit was between my eyebrows a quarter inch over more to the right eye side. Everything is okay, I'm alive, so don't go and worry.

Right now all I'm worried about is qualifying on the rifle range. I really don't have much else to say except my injury's part of training. You know it's rough here.

If you see my recruiters Master Sergeant Herbert and Sergeant Jim Warner, tell them I'll kick their asses when I get out of here. No, I'm joking, tell them hi.

Love always,
Jack

To write a letter or receive one was always a reality check to ensure that we were alive and not dead, even though we were in a bad-dream-place in the sub-basement of hell.

The evening ended with confidence. We had done well, according to Sergeant Black. My team, which was the house mouse and I, whipped through the pack within seconds and, although we could not hammer tent pegs into the concrete deck, we allowed so many seconds for that task. Overall, he gave us a nod of satisfaction and then suggested that we don't fuck it up tomorrow. He moved on to the other teams and critiqued their work. Taps echoed in the darkness of our new home. It was time to secure for the day.

CHAPTER 9
QUALIFYING

ONE

Staff Sergeant Louis appeared agitated this morning. It was becoming easier to figure out his personality prior to every event on this Island. He was the worrisome type, like a fat hen clucking around its' nest fearing its' eggs would be taken, and they very often were. Today's Field Meet was Staff Sergeant Louis' eggs and whatever happens will do just that-happen. The only part we contribute in these events is the effort. If we try very hard, perhaps our efforts will be just a little bit better than those of the other eager and motivated platoons. Maybe this time his eggs will hatch.

"Come on girls.___Move it!___I want you to shit-and-get this morning.___You have fifteen minutes!____Port side first.____Hit it!" he croaked harshly. His voice had that extra hard edge of someone who had been drinking whiskey until the wee hours of the morning and had little sleep.

"Sir, port side make a head call,____aye-aye Sir!" we boomed in unison and made a dash for the head. It had become almost comical to see how a large group of males could descend on a small room and perform all the necessities of the morning in such a short time. Those who were first into the head always grabbed the lines of shitters and the others grabbed sinks. Brushing our teeth and shaving almost at the same time had become a practiced habit. As soon as we got the zipper on our toilet-bag open, the shaving cream came out and went straight onto our face. As the cream soaked in, the tooth brush went to work with a regulated amount of brush strokes, then spit and grab the razor. Nobody rinsed their mouth out until they finished shaving. The mouth and face were rinsed in one big double-handed splash. Then dry and run to an unoccupied shitter. *Flush!* Drop our towel and make a quick sprint into the showers.

The head echoed a very noisy wet sound of running water, razors swishing in water, brushing scratches and toilets flushing all at one time continuously. As the last port side recruit cleared the hatch-way of the head, he barked the requisite report.

"Sir, port side clear Sir!" To which the DIs would follow with the go-ahead for starboard side. This system worked so well we were noticeably knocking off seconds with each day. If boot camp lasted six months we should be able to do all of this in one second.

When starboard side was back on line and our last squad bay clean-up efforts were accomplished, it had all taken only thirteen minutes.

Staff Sergeant Louis walked down the squad bay with Sergeant Black inspecting each of us for shaving, appearance and any other forgotten thing. Forgotten things fell into the category of buttons left undone, bootlaces improperly tied, trouser blousings uneven, red books missing from rear pockets, unclean utilities or tarnished brass.

"Today is the Regimental Field Meet.____We will be going to the Circuit Course and take on 1st and 2nd Battalions," he stated loudly. "And do what?"

"Sir, kick ass, Sir!" we screamed back in our warrior voice. This warrior voice was not something we could have accomplished during our first weeks on the Island. It was achieved slowly and evolved as part of our new inner confidence. We had moved up a notch, in Staff Sergeant Louis' assessment of us, when he heard our confidence.

"Great!____You know there is only one thing to do today.____ Right?"

"Sir, yes Sir!"

"What is it 3074?"

"Sir, to win Sir!____*Ahoorraah!*" we bellowed.

"Saddle up!"

"Sir, aye-aye Sir!"

We grabbed our field marching packs, cartridge belts, helmets, and rifles and fell out into formation. I could hear the sound of drums beating in my mind, they were beating us to quarters. I had heard the drums in the movies of old British Navy stories with Lord Nelson and thought this was missing in the Marine Corps, as it was very motivating. This was a moment to remember. Looking at this large assembly bedecked in combat gear, I felt we were finally looking like Marines, the way I had always imagined infantrymen appeared.

Our platoon merged with the other three platoons of our series and the image I had first imagined swelled four-fold. There were now over two hundred eighty recruits on the march from our series alone, toward the Circuit Course. The 1st and 2nd Battalion recruits, who were also at the rifle range at this time, were also moving toward the Field Meet marshaling area.

The march was much longer than the mile to the Circuit Course. The DIs first led us around the Weapons Battalion area streets toward Ballast Creek. After traversing all of the Rifle Range area, we finally struck out for the main road toward 3rd Battalion and the Circuit Course.

The march was not tiring at all, perhaps because of the exhilarating feeling of the real Marine image we projected within ourselves. Our footfalls were heavy and our cadence strong as we neared the event.

We had called out cadence counts and heard the other platoons in our train follow with their own. The sky was cloudless and the day promised to be warm. We were wearing our field jackets, but they were not necessary as evidenced by the sweat we were manufacturing. The temperature was sixty-three degrees.

Staff Sergeant Louis ordered column right and we entered the grassy area of the field. The gravel running road, on which we ran so often, was congested with many platoons from the 1st and 2nd Battalions. My earlier appraisal of our numerical mass had now been dwarfed by this massive green ocean of recruits kicking up dust clouds as far as I could see.

The columns were moving in slow motion it seemed, from the angle I was observing. There were shouts in the distance from their DIs and from the responses of their platoons. Guidons were fluttering in the slight breeze. It was magnificent to watch, this morning. I began to imagine the way it must have appeared during the Civil War, the Napoleonic Wars or in the days of the Roman Legions.

This spectacle of strength was very motivating and I have no doubt that I had adopted a new faith in our country's ability to crush any enemy. To see over a thousand combat-dressed Marine recruits on the same field, was to date, the largest congregation of boots I had ever experienced, while on the Island.

Come Together! By the Beatles, was the first thought I had seeing this broiling mass of green.

"Stack rifles over there." Sergeant Black ordered and we complied eagerly. He then had us place our packs, helmets, and web gear in rows in front of our feet.

All about the field other platoons were doing the same thing. The assigned areas for each platoon left the field empty in large areas for the events. In a few minutes all of the recruits were wearing utility covers and waited for the contest to begin.

"Shipman and Davids!___You two are competing in the tent event.___Grab your field marching packs and the rest of your gear,___except rifles___and get over there." Sergeant Black said and pointed to a part of the field where we were to go and get ready for the competition.

We formed along a line of recruits. There were twenty-two other recruits on that line when everyone was present. Several sergeants were walking around with clipboards and whistles. They were the judges for the day's events.

"You will run fifty yards to the area marked, disassemble your field marching packs, and erect your shelter halves to make a tent.___When I blow the whistle.___Ready?" The shrill blast of his whistle rent the air.

Shit and get,___was what Staff Sergeant Louis had said this morning and that's what I'm doing now.___Beat these other hogs. I thought in lightning speed and in the same split second Davids and I streaked across the field. The other recruits were almost neck and neck with the others, but we were a few feet ahead of them and every second counted.

The markings were clear at the fifty yard point and as if we had telepathic communication both of us slid to our knees, while pulling our packs off at the same time. This action saved valuable time, because we were already unbuckling our straps as the others were struggling to get their packs off their backs after they had arrived.

We pulled our shelter halves out and flung our pegs and entrenching tools (E-tool) and guy lines across the ground where we would work.

The seconds were ticking away as we frantically snapped the canvas halves together across the top and nodded toward each other to grab the tent pegs next and then grab our E-tools in preparation to pound the pegs starting from the front. This way, we would not waste seconds, by going to opposite ends and then trying to realign ourselves as some other teams must have done.

Once we plugged our three tent pole pieces together we inserted them loosely into the metal eyelets located at each end of the tent, called grommets, and attached a guy-line to the front metal peak of the tent pole protruding out the top. I pounded a tent peg into the ground, while Davids held the tent pole in a vertical position. I pulled the guy-line up to the peak of the pole. We each pounded a peg into the ground at each side of the front corners of the tent. I tightened the guy line, which pulled the front pole up straight, and from there, we moved toward the back of the tent. Davids pulled the flaps over in front, which would be secured to the center pegs when we got to that point.

We raised the rear of the tent the same way as the front had been done. The rear guy line was affixed to the rear corners of the tent and was secured into the ground with pegs. Once I tightened the rear guy line, the tent was up and tight, leaving only the side pegs to be securely pounded into the deck. We did this. Davids ensured the rear guy-line was secure, and then, when the side pegs were secured, we stood up and waited.

We were very lucky to have had our tent react the way it did. There was no need to reposition any pegs to dress the tent or to make it straight and tight.

The judges saw us stand and, holy shit, we were the first. I was so dizzy from the fast pace, I hadn't even tried to sneak a peak at the other twenty-two recruits. But there we were, with our chests puffed-out with pride. Back on the side-lines, Staff Sergeant Louis and Sergeant Black were pounding their knees with joyous delight.

The judges pulled and prodded our shelter and concurred with the decision that it made the grade. We disassembled our tent, remade our packs and ran back to our platoon. Our DIs did not make further overtures; they only left us alone. The next events were beginning and their concentration was on who they sent out. This was a lot like football, where the strategy was on the mix of players for the next assault.

Staff Sergeant Louis ordered several recruits to join in the push-up contest. These were perhaps our best men, who never seemed to tire, when we were doing PT. One was Richards, a small wiry black recruit and the other was a strong, large square-jawed white recruit, named Kieffer. The fireman's-carry event was next. Lerhman and Pikeman were picked for this event. Lerhman, a strong large white recruit, was another who always endured in PT and Pikeman, a short stout black recruit, was his equal.

The next event was the relay-run where four of our fastest runners were picked and several more fast runners were placed in the Dizzy Izzy event. The Dizzy Izzy event involved running to a baseball bat, picking up the hilt and placing their forehead on the hilt of the bat, while rotating around it several times, and if capable, and not too dizzy and disoriented, running back to the starting point.

The sounds of screaming recruits echoed all about the field, as the platoons cheered their best recruits on. Even the drill instructors joined in the fray. Lerhman and Pikeman each ran with the heavy burden of a recruit over their shoulders and it appeared neck and neck for the most part. The other recruits faltered, stumbled or dropped their burdens, leaving only our recruits to cross the line first. The other events went just as well and Staff Sergeant Louis was beside himself grinning at his peers, as they returned his cockiness with sneers and rolled eyes. He had taken the field with Platoon 3074 and he was in high spirits. We had won the coveted streamer and trophy. He got the privilege of bragging, because we were his hogs and he had trained us.

Many marching songs were sung during our trek back to the barracks. Our new streamer fluttered in the breeze and our hearts were pounding with pride. The smoking lamp was lit. It was the first cigarette we were allowed, since I had arrived on the Island. The entire platoon stood around the wash racks at attention raising right arms in unison, to take a drag.

The next three days of snapping-in were the same as Monday and Tuesday had been, with the exception that we had finally got it together and there were no personal punishments. By Saturday, all of the recruits in our platoon had finally passed Sergeant Utter's course, with the ability to demonstrate competence.

The priest's choice for a biblical story was rendered just as dully during this Sunday's church service however, it was still a reprieve from training, to attend services.

TWO

The next morning we got up at 0430 hours, ran for a half-hour and were rushed over to chow. By 0630 hours, it was on to the Rifle Range, where we were divided into groups for the relays on the range firing line. Today we would fire our rifles for the first time.

Normally, Sergeant Wyeth would be on duty according to the routine schedule we had up to this point. However, he did not show up this morning, and nothing was said about why he had not been on duty. Instead of Sergeant Wyeth taking us to the range we were introduced to a new DI who completed this task.

"My name is Sergeant Hodson!" he began his introduction. "I am your new assistant drill instructor, and I expect a hundred percent from you hogs in every thing you do!___Got it?" he concluded.

"Sir, yes Sir!" we blasted back in stern unison.

Sergeant Hodson was a short Marine, of about five foot five inches. He had doughy features. His nose was small and shaped like a button, with small slits for nostrils, and his eyes were sad, with the lashes pointing at steep angles downward to the left and right side. His cheeks were puffy and enclosed a smallish mouth, which had additional puffiness around the down turned ends. He was a chain smoker, we would learn, evidenced by a lit cigarette he held almost constantly. Overall, he appeared to resemble a small boxer dog and we would soon learn he had a bite to go with the look.

We had been formed into groups for the relays. Some of us were to fire during the morning hours and the others were to go to the pits. I was on pit-duty during the first half of the day. Our group marched down range to the target area and there we were assigned to target positions.

The pits were interesting in their design. A mound of dirt was built up into a high berm, which on the back side had a roof extending out a few feet overhead. The targets were constructed on a pulley system that allowed the huge square paper target to be hauled up or down to us in the pit. The rounds fired would either hit the target or continue into the impact area, or impact into the berm. The Marine Corps called these constructions hard houses.

My turn to fire would come later, but for now, the job at hand, was to spot the shooter's hits. I did just that and found it interesting. The first hour of firing indicated poor shooting by our platoon. There were many hits outside the rings of the target. That is, they did not come close to the rings, or missed them entirely, and thus resulted in Maggie's drawers. Maggie's drawers, we were informed, is a term used by the Corps to denote a complete miss. A red flag attached to a pole was waved back and forth over the exposed target to notify the coaches and recruits.

During this time my head started to hurt with a dull ache. The wound was feeling tight and itchy. I found myself concentrating on that, instead of the work at hand. This distraction did not last long, as I forced myself to concentrate on the work at hand, instead of the throb, but it still throbbed.

Our platoon would be firing from the B line today. The range is divided by A through E lines. Since we had been conducting our snapping-in training behind the B line over the past week and had observed another platoon firing from behind that section of the range, it seems the powers that be had decided to keep us in the same area.

We would be firing ten rounds sitting, five rounds kneeling and then five rounds off-hand (standing), from the 200 yard line. Next would be five rounds sitting and five rounds kneeling, from the 300 yard line, all slow-fire. After that, we were to fire ten rounds in prone rapid-fire from the 300 yard line, and then ten rounds prone slow-fire from the 500 yard line would follow.

Sergeant Hodson informed us that an Expert qualification would require 220 points minimum, out of a total possible maximum of 250 points. A Sharpshooter needs between 210 to 219 points and a Marksman 190 to 209 points. If any recruit fired below 190 they are unqualified, referred to as UNK.

According to our PMI, we could achieve 100 points or 40% of the 250 points from the prone position in both slow and rapid firing. Overall the slow fire positions can net 150 out of the 250 point maximum. This includes the slow firing sitting and kneeling positions from the 200 and 300 yard lines. We would fire five rounds at a time, for a possible 25 points.

From a loud speaker centered on each firing line, we heard the metallic voice of the Line Boss start the show. "Firing line!___On the 200 yard line, you will be firing in the sitting position.___Coaches!___ Ready your shooters.___Keep your weapons pointed down range.___ Coaches!___Load that first round.___Is the firing line ready on the right?___Is the firing line ready on the left?___Firing line ready?___ Commence firing!"

There was a sound, much like a string of firecrackers, exploding in the distance. I could hear the impacts of the rounds tearing the paper targets. When the first volley was fired we were ordered by the Pitt Boss to lower the targets, locate the hole, if any, and plug it with a round disk, in black or white, with a stick attached, approximately two inches long, which fit neatly in the holes, and then raise the targets. If the shot had missed, we held up a pole with a red flag. The red flag was for a miss and received the Maggie's-drawers wave back and forth. Marking was done for any adjustments required by the shooters on their windage and elevation. We then patched the holes with black or white paper patches.

They fired their next volley and we marked the targets once more. My target required a white disk marker two rings further into the target, right next to the bull's eye. The first round impacted at seven o'clock on the edge of the outer ring, while the second impacted closer to six o'clock right under the bull's eye. The third round hit the bull's eye.

This guy was getting his shit together. I thought with respectful appreciation.

The morning ebbed away and noon chow time was announced. We had been provided brown-bag lunches today, and informed that, while physically on the range, this would be how we will be eating all week. They also set up water cans, which we had to use our canteen cups to drink from. The food, which consisted of two bologna-with-mustard-on-white-bread sandwiches, yellow with an apple, had sat in the sun all day. The sandwiches tasted like stale shit. However, the apples were crisp and juicy.

Staff Sergeant Louis arrived at the pits to give us a pep talk during chow, while we choked on the sandwiches. He had already told those who had fired, that they had better be paying attention to their errors and adjustments. He promised he would collect their data books to review entries for completeness. He finished by warning the rest of us to do better after chow, and to make damn sure we entered all firing data in our data books correctly.

Following chow, we made a head call at the range and readied ourselves along the 200 yard line. As promised, Staff Sergeant Louis did pick up the data books from those who fired earlier. He would review each book later and deal with those who did not properly fill out their data and those who were bad shots.

The firing lines were marked-off at distances of 200, 300, and 500 yards. These lines were referred to as known distance or KD. There were sandy pits all along these lines from the thousands of recruits and Marines who had fired from the same spots. The grass had been worn away revealing the natural sandy-soil underneath.

Staff Sergeant Louis ordered the recruits, who had already fired, to follow Sergeant Black to the pits. Sergeant Hodson went off-duty after chow, because he would take the evening duty. The rest of us stayed at the 200 yard line and divided up evenly behind the firing positions. After the first relay fired, the next relay would assume the sandy niches and so on, until each relay had fired that distance.

Sergeant Utter started his list of do's and don'ts: "You will be firing twenty rounds at slow fire.___The target is our A target, which means there is a constant factor from the center of the bulls eye to its edge and to its succeeding ring.___The bull's eye is eighteen inches in diameter.___You will adjust your sights to true-zero for 200 yards. There is no wind today.___Make sure your windage knobs start from mechanical zero.___If any of you has a rifle, which shows the long line of your receiver or fixed base not lining up, raise your hand in the air.___Make sure your elevation knob is tight and all the way down.___Remember, on the KD range the maximum elevation is usually 25 to 30 clicks.___After each round fired, you will lock your weapon in the safe position and enter the results in your data book.___Remember your breathing and trigger control techniques.___First string on the firing line.___Get ready to assume the sitting position."

I was in the second relay, and felt this gave me an advantage when my turn came, by being able to watch these guys. There were about twenty-five range NCOs, called coaches, along the line assisting Louis and Utter. There were two recruits assigned to one line coach. The coaches issued ten rounds of ammunition to each recruit. There were five rounds in each clip, which were pushed down into the magazine.

The recruits were busy adjusting their slings and sights. When the order came to assume the ready position, each recruit chambered a round and faced the target executing a half right face and crossed their left leg over their right. They placed the web of their leading hand out to the upper swing swivel. I observed Davids, the House Mouse, and several other short recruits place their hands back slightly toward the balance of their rifles, because they could not reach the upper swing swivel. They all sat down when the order came and moved their backs around to achieve their desired position while keeping their ankles crossed. After placing the upper portion of the leading arm inside their leading knee they raised their rifle butts up and into their shoulders with their right hands on the butt plate, and then slid them to the small of the stock. Next they lowered their right arm inside their right leg and obtained a spot-weld.

Ensuring everybody had been sitting properly and was locked and loaded, Utter gave the Line Boss a signal. A moment later a loudspeaker mounted on a telephone pole behind the Line Boss box boomed and the order to commence fire was given.

There was a staggered explosion all along the firing line followed by the sulfur smell of gun smoke. Due to the absence of wind the smoke hung horizontally for some time, before it wafted slowly skyward and shredded into nothingness. There were a few hands sticking up through the layered haze getting the attention of the armorers. A PMI was adjusting one recruit's elevation knob with a tool. The other two recruits had not fired yet and it became clear that due to nervousness they had not chambered their round. Another recruit was unable to fire, because he could not achieve a sight line-up on his target in the allotted time.

Their ass chewing drifted down the firing line and dissipated with the smoke. The remaining nineteen rounds were fired and after several more pops were heard from the far left end of the firing line, the order to cease firing was heard from the Line Boss over the PA system.

"Cease fire,___cease fire!___Unload clear and lock.___Release the magazine.___Pull the bolt to the rear and lock it to the rear.___Insert a magazine clip into the magazine guide.___Let the bolt go forward.___Put your piece on safe.___Is the firing line safe?___Firing line safe on the right?___Firing line safe on the left?___Coaches remove your shooters.___Make sure the weapon is in the up-end position.___Lead them back and report scores.___Bring your next shooters on line."

The first relay string rocked forward and stood up with their legs still crossed. The coaches checked their weapons to ensure they were safe and the recruits moved to start writing their scores in their books after the targets went back up. There were five Maggie's drawers followed by Staff Sergeant Louis promising to stop their ability to bear any offspring and future potential of fucking-up his Marine Corps.

After the first relay had fired their ten rounds of slow fire in the sitting position, five rounds slow fire in the kneeling position and five rounds slow fire in the off-hand position with ever improving results, for the most part, they withdrew from the firing line. It was now my turn and I was both eager and scared. My fear was not of firing, but it was of screwing-up. I opened my data book, wrote in the date and entered True Zero in the upper left corner, decided on 16-2R and entered it. Next I turned my windage knob sixteen clicks to the left and then the elevation up two clicks. Once we were in our standing position, I started to concentrate on my breathing and remembered not to jerk the trigger. There was a chalk bucket on the line that I had used to rub on the windage knob and that made the lines stand out more. As the Line Boss called out the standard safety statement for the position to be firing from, we dropped into the sitting position and waited until he gave clearance to commence firing. I inserted a 5-round clip into my magazine, inserted the magazine, and chambered one of the 7.62 mm rounds.

Here goes,___breathe steady,___don't jerk the trigger,___sight,___let out a little breath,___squeeze. Bra-rooom! The rifle kicked hard to the rear and jerked up toward the left and just as suddenly my sight fell right back into proper alignment with the target. *Hot damn___this is great!___Jesus!___Great!___Aahhoorraah!___Too bad we have to do it so slow.* I thought excitedly.

Next, we stood and waited for the butts to mark. A group of black disks appeared just to the left of the bull's eye, even with it. While I marked my data book, I had decided that, if the rounds struck even with the bull's eye, it would not need elevation. My decision was to go down one click on windage. After the first round had been fired, we experienced the same ass-chewing as the first string had received. A few of my group had missed their targets. None of these mistakes would go unpunished, but that was to be done later, as the Line Boss would not tolerate anything except firing on his range.

I fired five more slow shots from the sitting position and had found my proper dope. Three were bull's eyes, the second, forth and fifth. I figured I had jerked my trigger slightly, just enough to miss hitting a bull's eye on the first and third shot. When we fired five rounds from the kneeling position, I hit the target almost in the same places that I had during the last five shots from the sitting position, but in a tighter group.

Sergeant Utter came up to me, clicked his tongue and said, "You ain't Sergeant York___yet,___but you are not doing bad at all.___Work on control.___when you fall back into position after each squeeze don't relax a bit.___You did.___Hold until finished and see what happens," he offered and then moved onto the next recruit. During firing I had absolutely no time to scan the line and snoop out what the others had done, but I felt I did alright on the 200 yard line.

After the third relay had fired, we moved back to the 300 yard line and started firing five rounds from the sitting position and five rounds from the kneeling position. We would also fire ten rounds in rapid fire from the prone position. The first relay did a fair job and everyone fired this time. That is nobody stalled or forgot to release the safety or forgot to load.

Ass-chewing abounded after the first string had fired from the prone position. Some shooters were accused of being hurried and forgetting to follow-through during rapid fire. They had squeezed their trigger until they expected the hammer to fall and relaxed their concentration. Even if they had good sight alignment before they snapped one off, the snap in lieu of a squeeze moved their sight off the previous picture. Sergeant Utter was yelling something about a baseball batter not following through with the bat only gets a bunt.

"Natural relaxation,___natural relaxation!___That, plus a good body alignment lets the rifle fall back into the same position for the next shot," he said loudly through the smoke. "Next relay,___get on line."

My relay moved onto the 300 yard line. I fired better this time, giving credit to Sergeant Utter for his advice. This kneeling position definitely felt more difficult, since we had to rest our arm on our knee, which could slip if not spot-welded properly. I fired five more slow fire rounds from the sitting position. Next, for the rapid fire prone position, the coach handed me ten rounds for my two magazines, to load with five rounds each. The order to fire was given and I fired five bull's eyes. I was amazed at this feat. Hell, I was so amazed and impressed that I forgot to change magazines. This was ass-kicking fun to me and I wanted to fire all day long. There was a problem developing, and it was of no fault of the firing. My head started to pound with an itchy ache between my eyes. I reached up to touch it and brought my fingers down in front of my eyes. They were covered with a sticky mixture of puss and blood. Apparently the pressure from constant tightening of my facial muscles and the furrowing of my forehead had squeezed the eyebrows together causing the wound to discharge down along my nose. I had the stitches removed the day before and the doctor felt the wound had sealed properly and did not notice any inflammation. I did feel a slight swell forming this morning when I touched it through my bandage, but paid no attention to it.

Sergeant Utter started chewing my ass for forgetting to insert my second magazine, when he suddenly exclaimed, "Jesus fucking Christ boy!___What the hell?___You been shot or something?___Staff Sergeant Louis could you come here a moment?" he asked, and motioned him over. Staff Sergeant Louis came over and examined my head visually and then looked at me saying, "You having trouble firing?"

"Sir, no Sir!" I replied. He said okay and walked away. Sergeant Utter waited for him to leave and said, "If you bleed more and it gets into your eyes, you stop firing and let me know.___I'll see that you go to sick bay.___Got it?"

"Sir, aye-aye Sir!" I answered. After the third relay had fired we moved to the next area and I continued firing from the 500 yard line. My scores were average and I felt more like shit with each passing minute. What I needed was a hot compress to reduce the swelling, clean the wound and ease the pounding. The itch was due to healing, I figured, and assumed the puss was resulting from dirt and sweat accumulated during training. Staff Sergeant Louis did not seem concerned, so why should I?

As I was starting to enter my results into my data book one of the coaches walked over to me. He reviewed my 500 yard results and then my 200 and 300 yard results and after a moment of consideration said, "You had good dope,___but you should check your windage,___after looking at your data book for the other distances, it appears you did alright there.___Try clicking to 20-1R," he said and handed back the book. "Don't forget to insert your second five rounds tomorrow," he finished with a wry smile. I entered 20-1R in my book for the Tuesday prone firing. The Range Boss blared the safety notification over the range and ordered us off the firing line.

THREE

As soon as we had returned to our barracks complex, our very first concern was to thoroughly clean our weapons on the racks located outside, next to the buildings. The smell of rifle cleaning fluid permeated the air and was accompanied by the sounds of many small brushes working at the carbon buildup on many rifles. This was totally different cleaning than we had been experiencing prior to firing.

Once we got our weapons in order, Staff Sergeant Louis held an inspection. He and Sergeant Black each worked down a squad. They snatched our rifles hard out of our hands while we held our weapon at port arms. They inspected every inch of each weapon and waited for any opportunity to visit death on the non-conformists who failed to meet the strict standards of Marine Corps rifle maintenance. Since this was our first opportunity to foul-up the rifle with the day's firing, it was also the DIs' first chance to instill the terror awaiting the recruit or Marine who fails to uphold this one non-negotiable standard.

"You call this piece clean numb-nuts?___*Jeez*___what did you do,___drive a mud ball through it?" or "This piece has cleaning fluid squirting out all over the place," or "The trigger housing group needs cleaning too, ass-hole,___not just the bore." On and on, the DIs found fault and verbally castrated the offenders. "You have fifteen minutes to get these weapons in ship-shape condition maggots.___Do it!" Staff Sergeant Louis bellowed.

"Sir, aye-aye Sir!" our motley crew responded and hit the cleaning racks again. Since I was called on the amount of cleaning fluid still glistening on the outside of my rifle, I decided to wipe more off, rather than apply more. We fell back into formation and the DIs resumed their inspection. Surprising me, they only criticized two recruits this time, but promised us our rewards for the entire day's fuck-ups and these two recruits crowning effect on top of it all.

"Place your rifles in stacks and fall back into formation," Staff

Sergeant Louis ordered harshly. We complied and were soon in spaced ranks. This formation allowed for punishment PT and we immediately received our reward. After fifty push-ups, plus fifty bends and motherfuckers, Staff Sergeant Louis ordered us to grab our rifles and duck-walked us all around the field, while we held our rifles over our heads. We quacked away for another ten minutes.

Having run out of time for putting the pressure on us, Staff Sergeant Louis ran us over to the barrack to secure our rifles and double-timed us over to evening chow. Sticky from our exertions, we lined up and received the heavy meal. Our day had exhausted us and our exertions had developed a hearty appetite. The meal consisted of Salisbury steaks, mashed potatoes with gravy, corn and a bun. We were ravenous and attacked our trays of chow heedless of the loud offensive sounds of moist mastication.

After returning to our barrack, Staff Sergeant Louis had ordered us to square away our gear while he did paperwork, reviewed our range data books, and prepared the next day's schedule.

Sergeant Hodson relieved Staff Sergeant Louis to assume the night duty and allowed us the remaining few minutes to continue our work. Apparently, he had no bone to pick with us and left us alone before lights out. We had some time to write letters home, so I took advantage and began one to Mom.

15 Dec 1969

Dear Mom,
Hi, today was another fast day gone by. First we got up, ate, ran out and divided into relay groups at the range firing line. I got up to the firing line in the afternoon group. This means I will be firing afternoons, and during the mornings I raise and lower the targets in the pits for the morning shooters. The pits are really something. We stand behind a dirt berm while the recruits on the other side fire at them. We lower the targets, mark the holes, and raise them up again. If they miss, we poke up a red flag and wave it. That is called Maggie's drawers. It is safe in the pits, because it looks like this (see the drawing below-that's how

looks). They call the pits hard houses and we really had to work hard in them. I did alright today, for the first day that is, but I messed up a lot. I still got a bunch of bull's eyes. Now I have to qualify Friday and shoot a high score at that.

A funny thing happened today. I fired five shots rapid fire and all five were in the bull's eye. Then I forgot to change my magazine with five new rounds (bullets) and fire again. Maybe I could have shot ten bull's eyes. Yeh, in my dreams. All I got was a royal ass chewing.

My head is still infected. The stitches were taken out yesterday, but pus keeps coming out.

This week should go by fast, then comes Mess and Maintenance week and the hard physical training with a PFT (Physical Fitness Test) for strength and then graduation week (on 12 January 1970). Well I have to close Mom. Please take care and say hello from me to the girls. Tell them to pray hard for me to make it. Write soon.

Love from your son,
Jack

I drew a cross section of the pits and placed small figures standing under the targets to give a scale of how big the pits and targets were. I addressed an envelope, sealed the letter and made my way up to the DI desk to deposit it in the outgoing mailbox. Sergeant Hodson did not make any comment, nor did he act aggressive. He just sat there and stared down the squad bay with a vigilant eye hoping to spot a recruit performing some kind of stupidity.

When I returned to my rack I decided to square away my footlocker, which had become disarrayed while I worked on my gear and wrote the letter. I could now stand any inspection and pass.

We finally hit the rack and as I lay there waiting the very short time it always took me to fall asleep, I thought of the week ahead with the excitement of firing our rifles each day and how that action was for me the very heart of being a Marine.

FOUR

Sergeant Black and Sergeant Hodson got us out of our racks in a fairly civilized manner this morning, which meant no shit-cans had careened down the squad bay. There was, however, a fair amount of loud provocative shouting and recruits voices acknowledging their personal encounters with a DI. Within seconds we were on line and counting-off in a more noticeably eager voice than we had over the past weeks. I knew the firing bug had to be in all of us. It was 0430 hours.

After eating a hearty breakfast we were once again organized at the range. I was even eager to pull and spot targets this morning, because it was all part of the firing process.

Staff Sergeant Louis had arrived at the range a few minutes after we marched in. He spoke to us, or rather made a forceful pep talk of it, and reiterated that he wanted to take the trophy.

That feat would require practically all of us to fire expert. I thought dryly.

When the morning firing commenced, the shooter I had been marking for required more use of the red flag than the spotter disks.

Christ, if this is how they're shooting now, how the hell are we supposed to win the damn trophy? I imagined Louis screaming mad. *Louis is probably kicking this recruit in the ribs right this second.* I thought and visualized Staff Sergeant Louis kicking a recruit and screaming while waving his arms around in frustration. I was much too busy with marking my target to eyeball any of the others in the pits, but I did catch a few other Maggie's drawers being flagged. I decided to try observing the pits on both sides between the lull moments of my target being fired at.

What was making this morning's firing so disappointing to our instructors is that it was not windy, not foggy and not raining. It was totally perfect shooting weather and the reason for not hitting bull's eyes was simply that the recruits were jerking their triggers and not adjusting their windage and elevation according to the results of each round fired.

There it was again, a Maggie's drawers to each side of me and as I stole a glance down each side of the pits I noticed a fair number of them this time. What I could not discern was the hits on the targets. I could not tell how well the recruits were hitting bull's eyes or outer rings, because when they were marked, they could not be seen from my angle of observation. The red flags being waved from side to side were easy to catch. So, what I was hoping for, was that the average for the morning firing group was better than I imagined it was. After all, we had to qualify and Staff Sergeant Louis expected us to win a goddamn trophy along with it.

It was a warm morning with a bright sun and a scattered pattern of cumulus clouds floating slowly across the sky. The smell of cordite permeated the air and the sounds of gunfire had been going on for so long that it had to be listened for to hear it. The morning hours wore away fast, because we had been so busy pulling and marking targets, we did not notice the time rapidly passing. My shooter had not demonstrated an aptitude for shooting, as his rounds had been all over the place.

Sergeant Black walked through the pits and motioned for us to fall out for chow and as he did so, we could hear the Line Boss on the PA system ordering a cease-fire and securing from the firing line.

After a sun-hot shit sandwich and an opportunity for a second, plus a hot bruised apple this time, which tasted like wet cardboard, we drank tepid water from the water dispenser and moved to the 200 yard line to get ready to fire. We were very eager to start. There was a real feeling of power and accomplishment when firing the M-14. It was exhilarating. The power behind this rifle was truly awesome. Sergeant Black ordered the morning firing team to fall out and reform ranks. He then marched them off to the pits.

"Alright,___listen up.___The weather is perfect for firing,___ don't forget what you have learned and you should hit the target every time,___in other words don't fuck-up like the morning team.____I swear I can't understand how they did it, but they fired like girl scouts." Staff Sergeant Louis lectured us in a strange fatigued voice. What he was not saying was that at this point there was very little he could do.

The snap-in training was over and what you could do to teach a recruit how to handle his rifle and how to fire was also over. While on the real firing phase of training, the DI just brings his recruits to the range and prays they learned how to fire. The only thing a DI can do while they fired was assist in adjusting windage and elevation, plus chew ass if the recruit doesn't breath right or jerks the trigger. However, he cannot do any of this for all of the recruits at the same time all of the time. They should have learned while the training was provided. Of course, there was the shed work available, if needed, each evening, but that was time needed elsewhere and the subjects should have been covered and learned during snap-in week. If there is enough stress demanding all available help, Staff Sergeant Louis would go for the evening shed work, but for now he seemed to feel the fear of God would get us in shape.

The afternoon passed by with mixed speeds. It felt like everything was done slow or that we all moved in slow motion, while during the same time the hours of shooting were over in an eye blink. During our firing shift, Staff Sergeant Louis behaved, compared to his normal moods, as he moved between recruits and adjusted slings, calmed breathing, adjusted sights, checked range data books and urged the good shooters on. However, Staff Sergeant Louis would have had justification in kicking the shit out of most of us for our dismal display of marksmanship and normally would have done just that. Maybe he did not wish to shake any recruits up at this time.

I know that I was part of a team, and because that was a fact, I felt angry that our team was not firing at top capability. Even if some of us were firing high points, the majority was not, and that diluted the high points. We were all there together during snapping-in week, while Sergeant Utter drilled and drilled us. What went wrong here today, I couldn't begin to guess. My spirit was at low tide as I sat on the bench behind the firing line. It was a simple two-by-ten board nailed to round telephone posts stumps sticking out of the ground about one and a half feet. These bench sections ran the entire length of the firing lines. My eyes took in the scene playing out in front. We were on the 500 yard line now and I was firing from marker eleven right. The range had one through fifty left and one through fifty right, marked by wood plaques, six by six inches, painted white and lettered in black. The control tower was centered directly behind each firing line. The recruits from our platoon fired along the right side, while platoon 3073, from our series, fired from the left fifty.

Our evening would be interesting. That was the only thought I had as we marched back to the rifle cleaning racks to clean the carbon out of the rifles that had so seemingly betrayed so many this day. Whatever the gods had against us was kept in the scrolls secreted away in their lofty archives. We would never know their reason for playing such a trick on our platoon. It had to be them, of that analysis we would all confidently confess.

There was no way we could have personally fucked-up so much and by so many. I personally fired like a girl scout today and I could not figure out how I had dropped from 208 to 200 in just a day. I resolved that tomorrow, Wednesday, I would concentrate on my instructions during training and not let the results of others influence me if their results proved to be less than qualifying. I'm not sure, but I think the platoon is going through a depression of some kind. It was a feeling like heavy air. We, or at least I, felt the thrill of firing the M-14, but there was a lethargic mood, which has been increasingly evident, since Sergeant Wyeth had his big day all by himself.

Did Staff Sergeant Louis get his ass in a sling because he wasn't on duty that day? Was he supposed to be on duty, but arranged with Sergeant Wyeth to be elsewhere? Did Staff Sergeant Louis even know what Sergeant Wyeth did with us when he or Sergeant Black were not around?

Whatever the answers to these fleeting thoughts were, we would not find them this evening. Staff Sergeant Louis was in a very shitty mood and the games were about to begin. I was very surprised that we were able to actually eat evening chow. Staff Sergeant Louis did not knock off for the evening and turn the platoon over to Sergeant Hodson. He stayed for rifle inspection, gave a very interesting performance of punishment PT, all before evening chow. But he stayed longer than he usually did. He was studying our data books, which he always collected now, and kept making notes. Sergeant Hodson was busy doing the regular routine with the platoon, but our senior DI was acting very busy and quiet. At 2000 hours, Staff Sergeant Louis walked out the back exit of our squad bay.

The rest of our evening was used for polishing brass and boots and general clean up of our gear and barrack. We finally got the green light to hit the rack and with a sigh of relief we melted into our mattresses. The lights were turned off and the weight of sleep settled over the platoon. The only sound was the soft footsteps of the fire-watch walking by wearing sneakers.

The glare of the lights shocked our systems, because it was 0200 hours and we were not used to waking up that early unless for fire-watch, but not as a platoon. Just as suddenly, the lights went out.

"Get yer sorry asses outta da rack ya sorry pieces of shit___I'ma gonna fix yer asses, but good.___Move it!___Get dressed and fall out!" Staff Sergeant Louis whisper-barked. We obeyed his orders, and knew he was very upset, so we seemed to have moved faster than we had ever done before. We crashed through the dark hatch and sailed down the stairwell and slid on the wet grass trying to form up in a miracle moment, rather faster than ever before. We were scared and knew our senior DI was very pissed at us.

"Platoon,___aah ten huat!" he whisper-bawled at us and we became statues. "You probably wonner what is up.___Well ya miserable shits!___I'ma gonna tell ya whatcha got commin to ya!" he slurred his words nastily. He was very drunk and I for one got very scared because, I knew from experience what could happen when one of these military types got this shit-faced. Should I fight him or should I just wait and see what he does next? That was what was spinning wildly through my mind. I was sure I had the ability to become violent at this moment. I was indeed in hell. It had to be, where else could such insanity be displayed day in and day out with nobody stopping it? I decided to wait and see.

"Git on yer fuckin' faces pukes!___Now!___Do it now!"

"Sir, aye aye Sir!" we also whisper-replied and he put his finger to his lips and said *"Sssshhhh!"* in a wet spittle slurring blast of breath.

"Haf at it assholes!___Do it!___Up, down,___up, down!___Not good enough!___Stah ovah!___One, two, three, foah, why da fuck did cha join my Corps?___One, two, three, foah,___why da fuck can't cha score?___One, two, three, foah,___there ain't much time no more!___One, two, three, four,___it's shits like you that I deplore!" he whisper-talked-sang each verse, as if he had just invented it tonight, while sitting in some nearby bar.

We kept pumping off push-ups and he went on slurring his personal ugliness. Sergeant Hodson was off to the side, now fully dressed and looking very nervous. He neither interfered, nor did he say anything, but if he were approached by a superior, he would hopefully be able to step aside and defer to his superior to answer for this past midnight ordeal.

Staff Sergeant Louis kept saying the word score, but it came out sounding like scoah. We knew the reason for his irate disposition. It was the range, plain and simple. He wanted the General's Trophy and our platoon couldn't even achieve a passing prequalification score today. He felt he was running out of time and we were personally screwing-off.

"Haf you evah heard of Staff Sergeant McKeon?___Nooo?___Well he was my drill instructa' in April 1956,___when I was a recruit here on da island.___Do you remema where Ribbon Creek is girls?___Well guess what happened there in 1956?___McKeon woke us all up like I did you maggots ta'night.___An' he ran our asses inta the dark an' on into Ribbon Creek an' drowned six of my fellow recruits.___Yeh shit heads,___did ya know about that?___Well, I would like ta run yer asses inta that Creek.___What I would like from you pukes is ta get yer goddamn shit tagetha' an shoot nuthin' but bull's eyes.___What's so damned hard 'bout that?___Huh?___Ya all got da same trainin',___ya got da same rifles,___same distances,___but ya can't all do a good job tagethaah.___Why is thaat?___You all train as a team,___a single moving unit.___So why can't you shoot as one unit an' all fire espert?" he finished in a really slurred voice with the last word definitely sounding like espurt.

He was really drunk and it seemed he was determined to run us into the butts, which was the swampy area behind the rifle range. The proper term for the area was the tidal marshes. The area was about a thousand yards from the main road running between the rifle range and us.

How would he get us passed the sentries guarding the entrances of the roads going back there? I considered nervously.

Whether his real point was to seriously do this thing or just try to scare the shit out of us, we would never know. He did scare the shit out of us and that was a certainty. So what was left was would he now run us into the dark waters of Ribbon Creek.

Sergeant Hodson went over to Staff Sergeant Louis and gently led him further away from our formation. Any sentries walking by were mere recruits and would probably not make any attempt to question two DIs. We waited for several more minutes and Sergeant Hodson came over to us and told us to fall out and get ready to hit the rack for the second time this night. It was 0300 hours and we had to get up at 0430 hours. Staff Sergeant Louis did not come back into the barrack and Sergeant Hodson did not say a word beyond ordering us into our bunks.

It seemed like I had just fallen asleep when the lights were turned on again and we were standing on the white line. Sergeants Hodson and Black did not say anything this morning beyond the morning orders to,___Move it,___move it!" Urging we normally would hear along with the shit-can band playing. We moved like molasses and the DIs knew why. Nevertheless, Sergeant Black got us through chow and onto the range.

Surprising all of us, we saw Staff Sergeant Louis come walking up, although a bit shakily. His skin was pale white with an ashen hue and his stare was hostile.

"You think you can improve your scores today girls?___Do you think I won't cash in on my threat to take you on a swim?___Just try me!___Fuck-up today and it's a done deal!" he croaked in perhaps the meanest frog croak we had heard on the Island yet.

"Sir, yes Sir!" we bawled out, and not at all surprised, heard him say he couldn't hear us.

"Sir, yes Sir!" Platoon 3074 exploded with a throat tearing scream as if it came from maniacs and I for one tried hard not to cough from the fanatic effort of the reply.

"Just show me.___Don't talk about it and don't say anything." he said in a dejected froggy voice. It was very clear he expected us to do better, but I thought, as did perhaps all of us, that he wanted a miracle. He walked over to the benches and poured a hot cup of coffee from a thermos he brought along this morning.

Hang-over Louis?___Don't try your drunken shit any more and we'll do our job.___Alright! I thought angrily. I really hated drunks. As the morning wore on, the targets revealed an improvement in ability by the morning firing group. Once again we ate those stale-outer and soggy-inner sandwiches and savored the succulent dryness of an apple and hoped we did not choke before drinking the tepid water in an urgent attempt to wash it all down.

Ahh,___chow at the range.___What a meal to wait for. I goofed mentally.

When we were sure we had survived lunch we lined up on the 200 yard line and gave our best shot as they say. By the time I was firing from the prone position at the 500 yard line, I was very pleased and fully aware that I had fired 216 points, and felt the platoon had done much better. However, by the time the Guide had tallied the platoon's total, Staff Sergeant Louis was in a rage. We had improved from the dismal average of 194 yesterday to 203 today and he was not content.

"Get your asses back to the barn!___Get your asses moving!___ Now!___Sergeant Black,___I want these sorry excuses for recruits ready for inspection by 1600 hours and ready for Sergeant Utter and me to see them individually by 1630 hours!" Staff Sergeant Louis ordered speaking fast and angrily.

Sergeant Black moved us out and double-timed us at port arms all the way back to our barracks complex. We cleaned our rifles and Sergeant Black conducted the inspection alone. Therefore, in order to get us into the barrack to see the senior DI and PMI by 1630 hours he did a spot inspection. That meant he only randomly checked rifles.

When we had lined up in front of our bunks, Sergeant Black had ordered us to pull out our red books and study, while we waited to be called by the senior DI. Meanwhile, Sergeant Utter and Staff Sergeant Louis had arranged a bench in the center of the shower and called one recruit in at a time.

They reviewed the data book of the recruit as he stood in the shower. The bench held the pile of data books and Sergeant Utter, standing with one boot on top of the bench, read it and gave a quick evaluation of the recruits firing habits and capabilities.

Staff Sergeant Louis, wearing right and left shooting gloves, stood in front of the recruit summoned, and depending on what he heard Utter say, worked the recruit over accordingly. When my turn came I reported properly and listened to my review. My review sounded like a court sentencing a prisoner. Sergeant Utter stated that, in general, I had fired very well, but I seem to lack consistency and proper improvement motivation.

What the bastard was saying, was that I can do much better and don't care to try. I understood immediately. *And that means some type motivational punishment.*

"What's your excuse?___Goddamn it!___I want an answer!" he growled and jabbed me in the stomach. My normal reaction to the sudden hard punch was to bend at the waist. "Who told you that you could move at the position of attention,___numb-nuts?" he barked with a mock disgusted surprised look on his face and sent a sharp jab to my chin. That made me jerk up straight again and my eyes got glassy. I feared he would see the pain I registered and send a round house to my cheek. Instead he simply looked at me and inquired whether I would shoot my best for the next two days, to which my mind responded. *Positively!___You're goddamn right I will.* But it came out differently.

"Sir, yes Sir!___The recruit will fire better Sir!" I screamed affirmatively.

"Good.___Now get out of here," Staff Sergeant Louis ordered in that ultra froggy voice of his, "and send in the next scum-bag!"

As I ran out the next recruit ran in. I got back to my bunk and stared straight ahead. The pain on my face registered fear on the recruits across from me. They had been watching all of the faces lined up on my side as we returned. Some faces were nearly in tears, as those recruits had obviously suffered more punches than I had. I could not really look at them to see if they were bleeding or showed bruises. However, when the recruits across from me were finally called and returned, I saw what they saw when we came out. He was tightening up each recruit with expectations that each of us would shoot better tomorrow. We had to 'goddammit', because he had personally tightened us up, so the only logical outcome for him is that we will do better now.

The storm is threatening my very life today,___whoa children,___it's just one shot away.... I started thinking of that Rolling Stones song and felt it was appropriate to this situation. *That one shot could be the qualifying shot or if a miss,___the disqualifying shot on the range.___I would be in a world of hurt if this little shower room pep talk is an indication of what Staff Sergeant Louis would do if I did not qualify.* I thought, and felt very uneasy.

I could see four to six recruits directly across from me without moving my eyes. Even though we were supposed to be reading our red books I could simply look over the top, of my book, to scope out the front view. What I saw was bad. Several recruits had a hard time standing straight and there were obvious red areas on their faces. All of those recruits had wet eyes. It was not that any of us were crying, that was too easy to do. What happened here was the sting of pain caused moist eyes and the shame of being treated like this added to the reaction. What really made me think was that the guys across on starboard side had watched all of us return and exhibit this same appearance. We on the port side did not have to see it before going in. So, starboard recruits had developed more anxiety, because of it.

Sergeant Utter and Staff Sergeant Louis left by the rear hatch and

Sergeant Black came out of the DI shack for the first time since he had come in from rifle inspection. Sergeant Hodson had also conveniently arrived a few minutes later and came down the squad bay from the front hatch and relieved Sergeant Black.

He must have waited for Staff Sergeant Louis and Sergeant Utter to drive away before he came up. I thought with loathing. It is very evident in situations like this that even those recruits who were still fairly invisible got caught up in a personal one-on-one introduction with the top DI.

Sergeant Hodson went into the shack and was obviously briefed on the recent events. He came out and ordered us to fall out for chow. The evening was an anticlimax as we simply just worked at squaring away our gear and counted down the clock for lights out. It had been a trying day and we were dead from lack of sleep and sore from their twisted perception of what should motivate us. Mail-call was even dreary, and I notice many who had received mail only shoved it, unopened, into their foot lockers. Sergeant Hodson told us to mount our bunks and that was the last I remembered hearing, as I must have fallen asleep immediately.

FIVE

Thursday morning exploded into our eyes and ears as the ever-expectant Staff Sergeant Louis hit the lights and clanged shit-can lids like giant cymbals and chorused our wake up ritual along with Sergeants Black and Hodson. The other side of the barn was experiencing the same type of wake-up and this made everything sound like stereo.

"Wake up girls!___*Clang-bang!*___Wake up hogs!___*Clang-clang-bang!*___Move it!___It's a new day on the island and you will impress me with what you can really do with all that training you got.___Right 3074?" Staff Sergeant Louis shouted, sounding energetic and cheery.

It must be his new tactic to motivate us and still warn us that he was very eager to win best training scores today. I figured, while I wondered what he would do to us tonight, if our average was unacceptable to him today.

"Sir, yes Sir!" we screamed with thick tongued voices. Our mouths were full of morning scum and our minds were like a cold car engine trying to warm up. We counted off and hit the head. Within minutes we were standing in the mess hall entrance. Staff Sergeant Louis took us over to the range this morning, and was so eager, he ran us there at port arms.

It was the best day this week, as the sun was very warm and the deep blue sky was devoid of clouds. There was not even a breeze. The pits were busy marking hits and as far as I could discern no Maggie's drawers were waved neither in my view, nor by me, when I was in the pits.

After an extra bad shit-sandwich lunch, my group got on line and surprised the shit out of both Sergeant Utter and Staff Sergeant Louis. I myself did something that amazed even me. While I was firing off-hand from the 200 yard line, I had hit five bull's eyes. Both Louis and Utter came up to me and expressed their delight like purring cats.

"Holy Jesus!___Do that again!___Don't move!___Just repeat it,___please!" Sergeant Utter purred. His please sounded out in a long drawn-out comical way, while he put on a toothy grin.

"Don't spook him now.___I'm talking about this being what I'm trying to get from this herd.___Keep it up!___Don't stop now!___Let's see much more of this," Staff Sergeant Louis spoke in a strange voice. It was a voice you hear when someone let's you into his club. He was acting like; "If you impress me and meet my expectations,___you are in."

They actually stood next to me for the next five rounds in the kneeling position. I got nervous about their proximity, but surprised myself and hit five more bull's eyes.

"Jesus!" Was all they said and went around in circles looking down the line. Suddenly Staff Sergeant Louis yelled at the line. "Come on 3074!___Get some!___You are all capable.___So show me.___Let's kick ass today!" And, as if we really listened to them and their private ass-whipping had done it, we fired a 207 Platoon average. I fired a 226, Private Waulker fired a 240, Private Delahey, our guide, fired 230 and there were five more who fired Expert between 220 and 225. Nineteen qualified as Sharp Shooters and forty-three qualified as Marksmen. Only one failed to qualify. However, this was all pre-qualification. What we fired tomorrow is what counts.

Staff Sergeant Louis was definitely born again. He strutted around like a new father and called cadence in a high clear voice. We were ordered to clean rifles and informed that after the inspection we would be receiving a reward for our outstanding efforts on the rifle range.

Our inspection was conducted with very few calls and after securing our rifles we were marched over to chow. Instead of going back to the barrack after chow, Staff Sergeant Louis marched us over to the Weapons Battalion area theater.

"Because you hogs did so well at the range today___and I'm sure you will do even better tomorrow.___You will be allowed to watch a movie.___Have you ever seen *The Sands of Iwo Jima* with John Wayne?"

"Sir, no Sir!" we relpied in what sounded like the most popular response. I thought I heard a few affirmative responses mixed in there.

Bull shit!___He has to take us to see the flick and all that head bashing probably did not make us shoot any better then we personally really wanted to, without the physical denting he gave us, along with that smirky shithead Utter sneering at us, as though we had willingly ignored his training, before these reminders. I fumed, thinking the worst about Louis.

He marched us in, had us fill the rows one after the other, and ordered us to sit. After minutes went by in the total silence of the theater, I thought that I had never heard such silence in a civilian theater. The lights dimmed and the projection displayed 'A Republic Production, Herbert J. Yates presents, *Sands of Iwo Jima*, starring John Wayne, John Agar and Forrest Tucker, directed by Allan Dwan' and then a black and white World War filled the screen.

At first I was confused as to how Marines, who had already been through boot camp, could be so clumsy, sloppy and individualistic. One Marine couldn't run without tripping and was totally unable to use a bayonet.

He must have been on sick call, while his platoon was on the bayonet course, and his DI must have been his brother, to allow him to make it through boot camp. I mused with a deep inward laugh. *Did any of his bunch even go to boot camp?* I wondered.

As the movie progressed, we watched the iron fists of Sergeant Stryker, the no-nonsense professional Marine, pound his motley squad of Neanderthals into lean mean fighting Marines. Sergeant Stryker was acting more like a DI in boot camp, than a squad leader in the regular Corps, as he personally bashed in faces with his rifle butt and fists. His misfit bunch had soon shed their innocence at Tarawa, where we learned that we should not skate while our buddies are relying on us, because it could get someone killed. Although Stryker tried to be friendly and fair to each man in his squad, some of them worked hard at open rebellion and fanned the flames of dissent with their buddies. As the reality of combat sets in, these individuals begin to respect Sergeant Stryker, understanding that all his efforts were for them.

There were absolutely no sounds made by the audience during the viewing of this movie, but I'm sure all of us were shocked by the graphic scenes depicting Marines getting killed and awed by the metal of Marines holding the line or storming the enemy's defenses. The final lesson of this movie was that Marines fight to win, some die, regardless of their professionalism, and surviving Marines carry on the traditions of the Corps and sergeants are always mean and will kick your ass.

My personal thoughts on an additional lesson I had already learned, and this movie had emphasized, was that good Marines don't squeal or rat on their fellow Marines. I was thinking about how the Officer of the Day had asked me how my head got injured and I stated that I had slipped in my shower shoes and hit my head on a rack. In the movie, when Sergeant Stryker and Private First Class Thompson had been fist fighting, the Officer who caught them was given the story by Thompson that they were training in judo. Sergeant Stryker displayed a new respect toward Thompson for his loyalty and maturity.

The lights were turned on and Staff Sergeant Louis ordered us to fall out and form up. When we were marching toward our barrack in the dark it was impossible not to notice a change in the platoon. The sounds of our boots striking the asphalt thundered louder then usual and with such precision that only one footfall could be heard. If I could have looked, I'm absolutely sure that everyone had puffed out their chests and held it. I know I did.

"Yer leht, hiat, leht, hida, leht." Staff Sergeant Louis was calling cadence and Sergeant Hodson was marching at the rear only observing us, as the platoon was totally marching by the book. "Callum riat,___ huah!___Leht,___leht, yer leht, hiat, leht,___count cadence, delayed cadence, count cadence,___count!"

"One, *step step step*, two, *step step step*, three, *step step step*, four, *step step step* one, *step step,* two, *step step*, three, *step step*, four, *step, step,* one, *step,* two, *step,* three, *step,* four, *step,* one, two, three, four,

United States Marine Corps.____*Ahhoorraah!*" We stomped onward, nearing our barrack, but I was dreading that soon we would have to stop marching.

When we hit the racks that evening our collective thoughts had to be of how perfect our day had been in all respects and could we possibly repeat it tomorrow. Only fate along with the weather would tell.

SIX

The urgency of our wake up call was not so much the normal rude invasion of sounds and light into our brains as the urgency to get out there to the range and qualify.

Swiftly and with near total silence we dressed, hit the head and dashed off for a hearty breakfast and rapidly made our way onto the range. As the first relay of the morning team was leaving the 200 yard line and the second relay prepared to fire, the black ball was spotted on the flagpole and the Line Boss announced over the PA system to cease all activities and stand-by.

Perhaps an hour had passed and scuttlebutt increased. I overheard some coaches talking to Sergeant Black about a couple of UA first phase recruits who had taken off from their barrack last night and have not been found yet. They said that it was possible they made their way into the impact area behind the targets. There were many sand bars and rotting trees in that area. After about another half hour, word came that the search party located the recruits in the impact area and found them, behind a rotten tree on a sand bar, riddled by 7.62 MM rounds. The black flag came down, but a new problem started to develop. A wind was slowly building up and blowing from the left side of the range, across the shooters, at 22 miles per hour. The rest of the day would be windy at variable speeds, and the maximum was 25 mph before cease-fire would be called.

The Line Boss broke the silence as he ordered the continuation of qualification firing. "Firing line.___On the 200 yard line you will be firing in the sitting position.___Coaches,___ready your shooters,___keep your weapons down range.___Coaches,___load that first round.___Is the firing line ready on the right?___Is the firing line ready on the left?____Firing line ready?____Commence firing." Immediately there was a long crackling sound as the line exploded.

My shooter had not done well in the sitting position. Where I plugged the target the fine holes were in three different areas. One was at two o'clock, two at five o'clock, and two at four o'clock and all were barely inside the outer most ring.

This guy is not doing well at all.___I hope he does better at the kneeling position. I rooted for him.

Sure enough, the shooter got better firing from the kneeling position. He got a tight group of five rounds right next to the black, but at five o'clock. The wind was really blowing now and the Line Boss could barely be heard. His next five off-hand rounds were in the four o'clock area of the outer ring.

My second relay shooter ended with disaster. When he fired from the sitting position, I had to wave Maggie's drawers for two out of five and score the other three about four o'clock, five o'clock and two o'clock near the edge of the outer-most ring.

Christ, what's he using,___a shotgun? I wondered.

His second five rounds from the sitting position and five rounds from the kneeling position were not much better, resulting in three more Maggies drawers and scattered results all around four, five and six o'clock, near the outer ring.

The horn blasted on the firing line, which meant the Line Boss was getting ready to let the third string fire. Each firing lasted five minutes for five shots. We could hear the PA system give the order to commence firing and once again my shooter was hitting all over the target

What the hell's the matter? I wondered. *This is a completely different shooter, but he's having a hard time.___Is it the wind?___I thought we were trained in firing on windy days, so why are they having problems?___The Line Boss wouldn't let us fire if it were too bad.* I concluded rationally, but still feared that I might fuck-up because of the wind. The results of the shooters on my target also added to my feeling of inevitable bad results later when I fired.

The morning wore away, each minute a leaf blown by a fall wind. We were ordered to eat lunch and I found the bologna sandwiches even more soggy and drab tasting than usual, if that was possible. My throat was parched from the cordite and wind. While we ate our lunch, Staff Sergeant Louis came up to us and glowered. He did not say anything for some time, but judging his mannerism, he was past expecting a good shooting day due to the wind.

"The wind is strong.___Remember your training,___you have been shown how to compensate.___Do so,__and fire a high score." Staff Sergeant Louis said in a dull, barely convincing tone. He figured it was a pep-talk and we figured he felt helpless. He knew it was too late to achieve the scores necessary for the General's Trophy, but now he was numb with realization that one half of the platoon had fired for qualification and did poorly as a whole. However, at this time none of us knew this. If anything, we knew only that the recruit we individually pulled the target for, did lousy, and since we didn't talk, nobody shared and compared results.

The PA system blared suddenly and my anxiety level rose a few degrees.

This is it!___Oh God, please don't let me fuck this up. It was my only thought.

"Firing line.___On the 200 yard line you will be firing in the sitting position.___Coaches,___ready your shooters.___Keep your weapons down range.___Coaches,__load that first round.___Is the firing line ready on the right?___Is the firing line ready on the left?___Firing line ready?___Commence firing!"

All along the firing line we dropped from the standing position to the sitting position in our sandy shooting boxes. We scooted our asses around for a more comfortable position and loaded our clip of five rounds, chambered that first round, breathed shallowly, while adjusting our rifle strap for the proper position and waited for the word to commence firing.

All of this last second body adjusting had taken place while the Line Boss was announcing. By the time the words commence firing had been said, we were a trigger squeeze away from compliance.

"*Bbaaruumm!*" The rolling sound was of rifles fired in volley, like musketry on a battlefield in previous wars. I had stuffed cotton into my ears to absorb some of the sounds, but it was still loud. There were ten minutes allotted to fire ten rounds and I tried hard to concentrate on breathing, sight picture, sight alignment and time consumed before squeezing that trigger. *Blam, blam, blam, blam, blam.* I did not rush my shots.

The wind was blowing steadily against my left side and I had the urge to look at the spotter's comments of the target to my right.

I bet that is my hit and the guy to my left is on my target, with this damn cross-wind. I thought with a bit of sarcastic humor. When my first round was marked, I was very pleased, and continued my smile when the following five sitting shots were spotted. Be assured that my smile was only mental.

Next came five rounds from the kneeling position, so I adjusted to that position after the Line Boss announced the orders and cranked off five rounds for a welcome score. I was seeing Maggie's drawers all around and felt sorry for those guys, but hey, I was not being rattled. I felt the force of the wind much more in this position and forced myself to pull the rifle back against the wind and freeze. Whether that did the trick or was a placebo move, I could not say, but I fired three bull's eyes and two entered on the edge of the black at three o'clock. The rounds were in a tight group.

All along the firing line, we recruits stood in our shooting boxes waiting to fire five rounds from the off-hand position and loaded our clip of five rounds into the magazine, chambered the first round, breathed shallowly and waited for the order to fire.

Bbaarruumm! I popped each round with confidence and was rewarded, for trusting what these crazy Marines had taught me, with bull's eyes and near bull's eyes, in the midst of what felt like a range hurricane.

The PA system invaded the bubble of concentration we had each developed around ourselves during the shooting.

"Cease fire!___Cease fire!___Unload, clear and lock!___Release the magazine, pull the bolt to the rear!___Lock it to the rear!___Insert a magazine clip into the magazine guide!___Let the bolt go forward!___Put your piece on safe!___Is the firing line safe?___Firing line safe on the right?___Firing line safe on the left?___Coaches,___remove your shooters.___Make sure the weapon is in the up-end position.___Lead them back and report scores."

Staff Sergeant Louis was studying the results as the scribe wrote them on the chalkboard. I watched as the results were written and noticed Louis go hot and cold as each number was entered. Wilken fired highest at the 200 yard line, but there were very good results for Willam, Davids the House Mouse, Delehey the Guide and me. Staff Sergeant Louis was silent and I think it was because we still had two firing lines to go and his sarcasm could only serve to disrupt an already extremely fragile day. Instead, he just glared and walked away. There

Yellow Footprints

was still one more relay from the 200 yard line and maybe they will fire really well. But when Louis saw the results of the third string, he was not pleased. Except for McFallory, Lamond and Holderman, who fired very high, the scores were dismal.

The Line Boss announced for the firing relays to move back to the 300 yard line. We formed up into ranks and marched at right shoulder arms up the one hundred yards and waited to spread out along the line. Staff Sergeant Louis decided to give us another pep-talk and called for our attention.

"Go ahead and grab seats if you can,___the rest of you pull in a little closer." Staff Sergeant Louis said in a more energetic voice than before. We were standing next to the Line Boss stand, a wooden construction about ten or eleven feet high, eight feet wide and four feet deep, with a wooden ladder in the rear to access the box. There was a flag sticking out of the top left corner and a big white letter B painted on the rear wall next to the ladder.

"Pay attention to each shot.___Remember what you have been taught here, goddamnit!___You guys, for the most part, are letting this little breeze get you.___Forget that shit!___If it was the Chinese at Chosin you'd be overrun by now.___Your rounds would have blown to the fucking right of the whole gook horde.___But I tell you this is not a reason to shoot like boy scouts.___Do you see those targets?" he asked and pointed toward the pits. We looked as instructed. There they were, up over a huge berm, with an even larger square below each target in alternating black and white, with huge numbers, in sequence, running down the entire range. "You can see how large those targets are.____ What is so hard about putting a round through the fucking bull's eye every time,___huh?" he asked with that surprised look a person makes when they are bewildered, but he added a comical overacting feature to his look.

Staff Sergeant Louis just stood there in his crisp utilities with his hands balled and resting on his hips, his head jutting forward past a normal setting and his cheek muscles taut with anger.

"Just do your jobs here.___Don't give up!___Shoot better than you ever have.___Show the Corps what Platoon 3074 can do,___got it?" he finished his speech with boiling expectation emanating from his body.

"Sir, yes Sir!" we screamed with renewed motivation.

"Let me hear your warrior cry!"

"Ahhoorraah!" our young cordite-choked throats bellowed in one shrill voice.

"Let's do it!___Spread out and take your positions by your assigned target area."

"Sir, aye-aye Sir!" we responded and fanned out to the numbered shooting areas we were assigned. Since I was on the second relay I sat on the benches along with the third relay team and together we watched the first relay team fire. If we paid attention we could learn a lot from the mistakes or correct moves of those ahead of us. I made many mental notes myself. The coaches were constantly talking to us. That alone was worth a higher score, because all we needed to do, was do what they said. So the only reason for not scoring well was the recruit himself not performing the routine he was taught by the PMI, because the coach couldn't fire for the recruit.

Like Louis said, the targets are hugh and how could anybody miss one?___Ha!___They are hugh, but the bull's eye is only eighteen inches in diameter, centered inside that huge sucker, which is less then the average man's chest is wide.___At a distance it is a fucking coffee mug ring stain in the middle of a large bed sheet.

Suddenly, the PA system crackled and the Line Boss ordered the cease-fire and clearing from the firing line of the first relay. We all eagerly watched the Scribe note the scores. Each chalkboard had seven lines for seven names and recruits entered the progress of the shooters whose names were on those boards. The Scribe wrote that information down on a master ledger that kept cumulative scores and it was that information we eagerly waited to hear. But that was not to be, because the PA system squelched and with the lost time earlier, he was moving fast now.

"Second relay on the firing line.___Firing line!___On the 300 yard line you will be firing in the sitting position!___Coaches!___Ready your shooters!___Keep your weapons down range!___Coaches!___Load that first round!___Is the firing line ready on the right?___Is the firing line ready on the left?___Firing line ready?___Commence firing!" The Line Boss finished his barrage of slow exact and spaced sentences and we responded with a volley of fire.

The wind had started to wane, but now it suddenly picked up. My first round went too far to the right of the bull's eye at about five o'clock.

The coach asked if I needed to adjust my windage, but I declined and sighted again. Once I acquired the sight picture, held my breath, let a little out, I slowly squeezed the trigger and son-of-a-bitch, I put the round further out to the right.

"Think you better do some clicking now?" The coach asked with a humorous voice. He knew I did my best and I guess he had been a recruit doing this same stuff not too long ago and he hadn't forgotten it. He also knew the wind was fluctuating right now, which screwed with any previous adjustments for what it had been blowing a moment before. If it was steadily blowing, our clicks would have had better results, as they were doing up to this firing sequence. So I clicked one click to the left, and sighted in and fired. Bingo, a bull's eye.

"Good for you!" the coach said, and turned to check on the other recruit in his care, who was Martinelli. Martinelli had a similar problem in that his first rounds were hitting at nine o'clock and further out from the black then he cared for. I heard our coach repeat his question about clicks and waited for the results. Sure enough, Martinelli cranked off a bull's eye and I felt we were now in business.

We only had five minutes per five rounds, so dicking around with windage and elevation can eat up valuable time. The consequence of not taking the time can result in poor point accumulation. However, if one uses time to adjust, the pressure to fire well, in less time, can be nerve racking.

We fired five more rounds from the kneeling position. I did a fairly good job but cursed the wind, because I felt it robbed me of a better result. Next we fired ten rounds of rapid fire from the prone position. This had to be the most nervous moment for any recruit today, because of the lack of time. We only had sixty seconds to fire the ten rounds.

Firing ten rounds at rapid fire also had its positive side. First, it doesn't allow you to think a lot, so you tighten up your grip without even thinking about it. Second, because the body is tighter, the rifle falls back into its proper sight picture after each round fired, thus reducing scattered hits and promoting a tighter group. This is great, as long as you have a tight group in the black, and not in Bumfuck Egypt. And lastly, it is a hell of a blast to fire ten rounds rapidly with an M-14 rifle.

Okay, the deed is done, a screw-up here costs fifty points, and for some the wind is still carrying their shots somewhere into South

Carolina. As always, I marked my score and pertinent information in my data book between shooting positions. I was thinking positive thoughts now, because I knew my sights were hitting the bull's eye. But, did the wind change the picture? Targets were marked all over the place and sadly some were greeted with Maggie's drawers. Martinelli got his score and he scooped a total of forty-three points.

Great shooting Martinelli. God, I hope I did alright. I thought glancing at him. He was having facial spasms, or rather he wanted to shout with joy, but suppressed it. The coach was watching for my results. Suddenly, the target rose up and the anticipated results were greater than I had imagined. I had two very tight groups. One was completely inside the bull's eye and the second was partly inside the black and spilled out just a little at three o'clock. I was doing the same thing Martinelli had been doing with his face when the coach said something.

"Good shooting guys,____damn good shooting!" he stated, and then looked over for Staff Sergeant Louis to see what he was up to.

"Seems your DI is smiling widely boys, but don't let em know I told ya.___Got it?" he finished with a friendly grin on his face and we both smiled back and nodded affirmative. "It's a windy day,___wonder how you two woulda done?___Wait now.___I remember yesterday.___Ya both shot higher,___but still___that was a dead calm shoot," he concluded his comment just as the Line Boss began squelching over the PA system.

"Cease fire!___Cease fire!___Unload, clear and lock!____Release the magazine!____Pull the bolt to the rear!___Lock it to the rear!___ Insert a magazine clip into the magazine guide!___Let the bolt go forward!___Put your piece on safe!____Is the firing line safe?___Firing line safe on the left?____Firing line safe on the right?____Coaches!____ Remove your shooters from the firing line!____Make sure the weapons are in the up-end position.___Lead them back and report scores.___ Bring your next shooters on line."

Once again the same recruits as before came up with the higher scores. The third firing relay began their firing and we sat and watched as the wind blew sand into our faces. The only thought I had for now was how no sand fleas had been biting today.

The minutes rolled away like dried leaves and the wind kept gusting from our left in swirls, updrafts and in steady side blows. I watched wondering what an updraft did to the rounds the recruits fired at that given moment and concluded it was naturally the opposite of what a down draft did. Both cause a Maggie's drawers. I suddenly felt a reminder of our lunch for that day. It was just as shitty tasting as the rest of the week, but because of the importance of the day I for one did not even remember it until now, because it was churning in my stomach like a concrete mixer. The wind rapidly dried our throats as did the cordite, however for the entire week we had been allowed to drink water when the urge hit us. They did not fuck around on the range in the Marine Corps.

The PA system boomed and the words to cease-fire bounced around in the wind causing some words to be loud and clear and others to be low and almost inaudible. The order then came for us to relocate to the 500 yard line, so in rapid order we formed up and marched the two hundred yards. There was one more pep-talk, but Staff Sergeant Louis apparently already knew the score and figured that those who couldn't hit the target from the closer distances would only be pissing into the wind from 500 yards.

The first relay had done fair and their mood was evident when they withdrew from the firing line. A good many of them had not qualified. They had scored below 190. Some had earned the Marksman Badge, referred to as the Toilet Bowl, and yesterday those who were today's UNKS had the Toilet Bowl and those with it today had earned the silver cross of the Sharp Shooter yesterday and today those who had earned the Expert's Badge yesterday were Sharpshooters today. Whatever today's results, these recruits were good shooters, who would in battle tear the ass off the enemy, as long as it wasn't windy.

The Line Boss promptly got the second relay on line and ordered for us to commence firing. We had ten rounds of slow fire from the prone position. From a distance of 500 yards the targets had become smaller than a postage stamp with tiny black dots for bull's eyes. This was only possible, because we could lay flat on the ground and if we paid attention during snap-in, we could hold the rifle secure enough and adjust our sights properly enough to hit that target. I cranked off the rounds and waited for the score. Martinelli fired his last round a few seconds later. The coach mumbled something that sounded like a good luck. Then the targets rose up. First up was Martinelli's, he had a tight grouping for forty two points and then my target rose for forty three points.

"Good shooting guys,__real good.__And good luck for the remainder of your training."

"Sir, thank you Sir!" we both replied and saw him grin and shake his head slowly from left to right and back again. Apparently, he was not going to chew our asses out for saying the word 'you'.

The Line Boss shouted the final words of cease fire and ordered us off the firing line. The third relay was then ordered out to conclude the qualification firing of Platoon 3074. There was no decrease in the wind and the sand blowing into their eyes was no less than the rest of us got all day long, but the third relay must have blinked more. When their scores were tallied there were many who fired thirty five points or lower and a hand full between thirty-five and forty points.

The smoke drifted up slowly throughout the week, but today it didn't drift upwards, but instead blew sideways into our mouths. The shooters were disappointed for the most part, because they knew what their scores were. Staff Sergeant Louis was silent and ordered us to form up. Sergeant Black was moving the rest of the platoon up to the 500 yard line from the pits.

We marched in silence up to the road and crossed it. Staff Sergeant Louis suddenly said "Shit!" and ordered us to port arms and ran us all up and down the Weapons Battalion area. When we were finally allowed to go into our barrack, he let his true feelings for the day's results flow out like hot lava.

"I will read off a list of names and those recruits will fall out to the wash racks for a smoke.___Wilken, who fired Expert,___Willam, Delahey, McFallory, Jackson, Martinelli, Shipman, Lamond and Holderman,___who fired Sharp Shooter,___fall out.___The rest of you hogs hit the goddamn deck.___Push-ups!___Ready begin," he snarled.

Meanwhile, we whose names were called, were obliged to get the hell out of Dodge, before he changed his mind. We first had to open our footlockers to get that stale smoke and questionable matches. My hands fumbled at the combination lock, because I was nervous. It was a very strange feeling to be doing something else, that is not a punishment, while the rest of the platoon was shouting push-up counts all around me. The reason I said stale cigarettes, was because we had only had two cigarettes on the Island so far, and like me, the others were not stupid enough to do push-ups instead of having that smoke. Actually mine were a month staler and Gunnery Sergeant Bishop did not allow any during my time under his tutelage, nor did the Medical Platoon DIs.

We stood around the wash rack at attention and waited for orders. Staff Sergeant Louis opened a window and looked down to us.

"Sir, the smoking lamp is lit for one cigarette and one cigarette only,___even though we know that smoking is hazardous to our health we don't give a damn Sir!___*Ahhoorraah!*" we screamed with youthful joy." I had a *Marlboro*.

"Light em up!" he croaked, and from the window spilled out the PT cries of our Platoon.

We lit our smokes and stood there at attention and in unison pulled our arms up, took a drag, dropped our arms, held, exhaled, and repeated the procedures until the cigarettes were only filter butts. I didn't really smoke normally, but on this Island I took what I earned and enjoyed it. This however, was the first time we split our platoon like this, and I'm sure Staff Sergeant Louis was driving a point home for the others education. We heard that point when we went back upstairs.

"It is my opinion that those recruits who fired Expert and Sharpshooter,___in the fucking heavy wind mind you,___had learned the fundamentals of a Marine Corps rifleman,___those of you who fired Marksmen did qualify, but you could have done much better.___How many was that?___Twenty nine.___Which left thirty three unqualified!___That is fucking unsatisfactory.___If you had shown the same learning skills as the nine who fired well, then you too would have qualified today and those with toilet bowls would have had Sharp Shooter badges instead.___Do you think there are no windy days in war?" he croaked in a froggy voice and after saying the last, never spoke about it again. "Tomorrow we move back to the Battalion area and Mess and Maintenance week begins."

That evening Sergeant Hodson had the duty and gave us time to write letters home after we got our gear ready for our march back to 3rd Battalion in the morning. I decided I should write a letter home and let the family know what I had accomplished today.

19 Dec 1969

Dear Mom and girls,
How is everybody doing? I hope you are comfortable and have enough money to get by on. I have some great news. Today I fired on the rifle range for qualification and fired a high Sharp Shooter. I got a 218 score. So your praying helped. A Sharp Shooter badge looks like a German Cross (I drew a picture of it here) and it is silver. Only one recruit fired Expert, the highest, and seven others got the Sharp Shooter badge. A few of these fired higher than I did (219), but so what, they got the same medal. Our whole platoon together, did badly, because a lot of them didn't care according to SSgt. Louis. It was a very windy day.
Thanks for your letter Anna and also yours Mom. We start Mess and Maintenance duty tomorrow (lunch room work) and will march back to our regular battalion area in the morning with packs, helmets and rifles. Mess and Maintenance will last until next Saturday.
We saw a movie last night. John Wayne starred in it and it was called Sands of Iwo Jima. It was about Marines fighting the Japanese in World War II. It was very good, but bloody (a true story). Iwo Jima was where the Marines raised the flag (look at the bottom left corner of this letter-see the flag-raising)-that battle.
My head is almost healed now and I feel a lot better. I also hope that Sarah has a better time with Aunt Gretchen.
Love,
Jack

We secured for the evening and hit the rack. As sleep settled in, I felt great for my accomplishments, sad for the platoon, and wondered what the following week would bring.

CHAPTER 10
MESS AND MAINTENANCE

ONE

On the morning of Saturday December 20, 1969 we marched back to our 3rd Battalion barrack. There were mixed feelings in our ranks, due mainly to our dismal qualification average on the range. Normally, the recruits who failed to qualify would have to be set back and attend a marksmanship training course and re-qualify before they could be Marines.

It was probably due to the war and the need for quick training and prompt replacement in Vietnam, where along the way they would certainly be re-qualified on some range.__Another reason for this apparent anomaly, could be that due to the extreme high wind and the decision to go ahead and fire, knowing that the average round would not seek its intended target, platoon 3074 had to get moving to meet training schedule deadlines.__It was only reasonable that the other three platoons, along with the 1st and 2nd Battalions, who also fired at the same time, would also been granted exemptions, due to the severe wind conditions.__The recruits who had fired dismally would certainly have fired better in more reasonable weather conditions.__These recruits also would so certainly have fired much better if the wind had not been blowing with such a fierce velocity. I thought long and hard about all of this and this is what I figured has to be the answer.

We would have to wait until after we graduated to know the real reason.

During the last days at the range, we had also observed staff non commissioned officers and officers visiting our barrack in the evenings. Recruits had been ordered into their vehicles to be driven away. Anything that had occurred on the Island was known only to the drill instructors and never disclosed to us recruits. We stomped along in good order sounding-off to the drum beat cadence of Sergeant Black. Our gear rattled and clanged in a hushed mixture of metal and canvas rubbing together.

For whatever other reason, I felt the subdued manner of our overall attitude was very noticeable and Sergeant Black probably knew full well the reasons and perhaps sympathized. It was odd to us to see an assistant DI be suddenly removed as Sergeant Wyeth had been, with no explanation given to us recruits. We thought they were gods, impervious to any external powers observing their domain. They could do to us whatever they desired and we would comply. We were nothing less then maggots, shit-birds, pukes, and pusillanimous pieces of grabastic amphibious shit, deserving nothing beyond reacting to the whim of these DIs.

Sergeant Wyeth had no problem considering us all as putrid. He had often informed us that we would never pack the gear to be Marines. He told us often that while in Vietnam he and his unit would lay mute in ambush all day long in the stink and heat of the A Shau Valley, with no movement to drink water, eat, shit or piss. He had extolled how his unit were hard-assed, gook-killing, baby-eating green-machine Marines in Vietnam. Perhaps he had a point, we were soft and innocent little shits who had absolutely no idea of the hardships of combat. He was making a platoon of recruits learn early-on what lay ahead and we would be ready when those situations presented the need to adapt.

Left, right, left, right we stomped along the road and never once missed a step, a reply or a turn. When the time came to execute a movement we were obedient and precise. Sergeant Black called for us to halt and enter our old barracks. We ran inside and I felt that feeling one gets when returning home from a vacation. The familiar bunks, bulkheads and head were comforting in a very bizarre way. We had shed copious amounts of sweat and blood on this deck and had to endure muscle-wrenching agony performing the regimen of exercises that produced that sweat. The blood had been shed for both compliance and non-compliance.

"Secure your gear!___Fall out in PT gear!___You have ten minutes.___Do it!" Sergeant Black barked.

"Sir, aye-aye Sir!" we thundered back and scurried to unpack our field marching packs and our sea bags, along with our ditty bags, which were inside the sea bags. Our sea bags were waiting in trucks outside of our barrack and we grabbed them on our way up. Our packs were crammed with an extra set of utilities, socks and skivvies. Once we had unrolled our shelter halves and ponchos, extricated the E-tool and straps from the packs, we were quick to secure the gear and fall out.

Sergeant Black ran us over to the Circuit Course and engaged a three-mile run once our feet hit the gravel track. Afterwards, we formed up in front of a training stand and were grimly welcomed by our old PT instructor.

"Okay hogs.___Now that you have been fattened up at the range,___my job is to sweat that pork off your flabby bodies!___Bends and thrusts!___Ready begin!" he barked.

We hit the deck, rose and hit the deck for what seemed like an eternity, although it was only twenty minutes. Next came the push-ups, squat and twists with hands over the head, sit-ups and finally over to the ropes. We climbed up the ropes at least five times and returned to our barrack for a head call and showers. Then Sergeant Black ordered us to fall out for drill. After noon chow he held an inspection of our footlockers, rifles and bunks.

The afternoon wore on in slow motion as we engaged questions and answers in Military History, General Orders, Code of Conduct and weapon nomenclature. Sergeant Black was very to the point and ordered push-ups for stupidity. He had rapidly developed into a hard-ass over the past week and Sergeant Hodson was mellow now, compared to him.

Had we pissed him off somewhere, over the past week? I wondered and I was sure this was what everyone was thinking. He had no patience at all anymore.

As evening approached, Sergeant Hodson entered the barrack and went straight to the DI shack where he stayed until he relieved Sergeant Black for the evening and night duty. Apparently he had familiarized himself with the duty rosters, personnel files and any other duties germane to the platoon's training before taking over the duty. That evening I had noticed my head was no longer swollen and the area, around where the stitches had been, appeared red. It had healed and I no longer thought about the injury and its cause was now past history to me.

Sergeant Hodson ordered us to fall out to the wash racks and scrub our utilities and skivvies. Otherwise, for the remaining part of the evening, he only held mail call and left us to do whatever we needed to get ourselves squared away. He sat at the duty desk at the head of the squad bay and observed our doings without a hint of expression on his face. One thing I had learned since arriving on this Island was that if the DI doesn't say anything he is not necessarily content, because he may be formulating a scheme to hatch on us later or he may simply be content with our doings and go on to his own work. Therefore, nobody was ever relaxed, since we could not predict the reaction, if we did something to goad him.

I had decided to shine my brass and boots and fiddle with my footlocker to add an extra touch of military neatness, if that were possible here. After shining all my gear I had a hard time figuring out how to fold my socks any neater or fold my skivvies any better. We were in a funk and it was becoming apparent.

TWO

Sunday morning was equally dissmal. We fell out for chow and attended mass. The priest delivered a strong mass, delivered with story-telling action, and I paid attention, but felt sleepy for some reason. When mass ended I was approached by a DI. To be stopped by a DI was a shock at first, but it was even more of a shock when he spoke. It was Staff Sergeant Rogers from Platoon 3063, my old DI.

"How are you doing, Shipman?" he inquired with a slight smile.

"Sir, fine Sir!" I answered in an unusually calm manner. I was also surprised he had remembered my name or me in particular.

"Things alright back home?" he continued with genuine interest.

"Sir, yes Sir, as far as the recruit's mother's letters have informed,___ they appear to be, Sir!" I answered directly, but had a hard time not looking directly at his face. He apparently sensed my uneasiness, but continued his comments.

"I'm pleased to see you back in training.___I know it was hard to drop out, but you are going to make it.___You were a capable recruit in 3063 and you'll do fine with your new platoon."

Holy Shit, he's speaking to me in a normal way and he isn't even upset that I looked right at him. He's even giving me a compliment, which is like getting a medal here. I am confused as hell now. Staff Sergeant Louis spoke to me this way the day after I hurt my head and now Staff Sergeant Rogers is doing the same thing. I thought they were not allowed to do this, only chew our asses, constantly.___But he actually seems to care, and showed an interest in my welfare. My mind flashed these thoughts with much uneasiness.

"Sir, thanks Sir!" I answered, consciously omitting the you, while he concluded by shocking me even more.

"If you need anything, or need to talk to me, let me know, just request it from your drill instructors.___Good luck while completing your training."

"Sir, aye-aye Sir!" I responded and followed the remnants of my platoon through the door.

Well, he thinks I'll do alright! Hot damn! That's a good thing to know. I thought I was barely holding on. I chuckled to myself and headed for the barn feeling extremely motivated. Maybe he just had a kid or was feeling 'churchy' to be in a good enough spirit to be nice to a recruit.

Staff Sergeant Louis had the duty today, and that was very much an unusual event.

That's odd, since he usually had Sundays off, but what the hell, maybe he and his wife aren't getting along and he wants to spend as much time as possible away from the old War Department. I thought, hoping it didn't mean we were going to have a bad day. Guess again. I swallowed hard at what I was seeing.

He wasn't here alone. A full colonel, a major, and a captain came down the squad bay. We froze at attention in solid lines along starboard and port sides. If DIs were gods then these guys were Emperors of gods. They wore dress greens bedecked with many rows of ribbons. All three had been to Vietnam and, judging from their looks, were in no good mood to be here on a Sunday. Staff Sergeant Louis called out three names and those recruits were ordered to follow the officers to the H Company offices.

After about two hours, three more recruits were summoned.

Apparently, they wanted to work on a Sunday to reduce the time recruits would be pulled from a training day. For us Sundays were no less a training day as far as PT, studies, inspections, and so on, the only thing different with this day and others is that we did not attend any classroom lectures, field instruction or run the Circuit Course. With each recruit going out, Staff Sergeant Louis looked noticeably more and more with a grimace. His face reflected a 'What-in-hell is going on!' look.

It became noticeable that the regularity of DI punching, slapping and pushing incidents within our platoon had seemingly come to a halt. Staff Sergeant Louis was never shy about doing those things. Sergeant Wyeth however, was prone to do them more often, with mean inventiveness and with alacrity. Sergeant Black had only pushed us with harsh punishment PT when he became exasperated, and Sergeant Hodson, except for PT, had not touched any of us yet.

This was an IG investigation and such things were an anomaly for a training series. We did not understand this in its true form, but sensed that it was causing a change in our entire platoon and our DIs behaviors. Specifically, no discussions were filtering around about it. The entire situation was about as indiscernible as ghosts spiriting about our platoon. We recruits, who were not talked to, were definitely uninformed and were clueless about it all.

What the hell is going on here? I wondered. *Is it because our platoon fired lousy during qualification day?___Or was it a snitch writing his goddamned Congressman?___The DIs warned us to keep our mouths shut and tell them if a problem arises, but never tell a Senator or a Congressman.___Hell, they even told us to shut our mouths if we were ever questioning by officers, other then when we were asked about military subjects.* I considered. *I wonder if these recruits are answering the officers' questions or clamming-up.___What are they going to say or bitch about anyway?* My mind went on and on with many questions, but no concrete answers were forthcoming. Hell, I didn't even know enough about what might be going on to base my conclusions on.

Sunday wore on, but earlier a group of names from the platoon were called upon to report to the battalion supply building. I was one of the names called. By evening the IG group had ceased requesting recruits, and Staff Sergeant Louis seemed to have decided to hang around the barrack until later. Sergeant Black had already assumed the duty for the evening and night and had no readable look about him. He projected his usual mask, which was a deeply reclusive facial expression.

The familiar ass-chewing sessions did not dissipate. Those recruits who warranted one got their full issue. The overall ending of the day involved the standard questions on the basic military subjects to see if we were learning and retaining what we were taught. I had been stewing for the best part of the day over an incident that had occurred during the morning hours. After Staff Sergeant Louis had requested three recruits to follow the IG officers, he had assigned fifteen of us to report to the battalion supply building across the drill field from our barrack.

I had stood amongst the entire group with a look on my face no different than the rest. I was simply awaiting my instructions. We stood on the gravel drive next to a loading dock located on the side of the supply building. The open port had a railroad tie running horizontally along the wall as an apparent bumper guard for trucks backing up while loading or unloading. A beefy redheaded corporal was standing in the open port. He had orange hair, pink splotchy skin, pale blue eyes and fat lips. He addressed our group demonstrating his glee to have authority over lowly recruits.

"You will be sweeping down the entire supply office floor area and the warehouse, then police the entire area around the building. I will also assign some of you to clean the head, wash the windows, stack boxes, un-load vehicles and anything else I think of later," he spoke thickly and with an air of snobbery. Suddenly he jumped off the loading dock and pushed his way through our group over to me and started screaming.

"What's your problem shit-head, you don't like what I'm saying or you don't want to work here asshole?" he finished by poking his chubby finger into my chest. I stood there staring at his chest and didn't say a word, but I thought.

What's your problem you fat ugly mother-fucker, I didn't look at you funny or otherwise, nor did I look like I didn't want to work.___What the hell do you think you're doing messing with me! My mind screamed and raced with obscenities against him. This was somebody who I would have liked to kick in the balls, because I hated self-important pricks like this. He wants to act like a DI and fuck with the recruits and he apparently chose me out of all of us. I had such a hot flash of anger that I knew steam had to be rising from my body. *This sorry sack-of-shit should never have been allowed to graduate from boot camp.* I rationalized. *Because he is a fat, no, grossly overweight for the Corps poor example of what my image of a Marine and his behavior should be, after watching lean Drill Instructors.___Don't they have a Pork Chop Platoon for active duty Marines?___In this case , the Corps had already decided he lacked the look, the discipline and the intelligence to be a DI.___Hell, I bet this puke-faced sack-of-shit was slipped into the Corps by a Recruiter with a sick sense of humor or who was getting revenge.*

He turned and walked away, not caring for my response, because he had his fun and had shown his ass. He must have felt he could get away wih this, because he knew we would never tell our DIs.

Only chicken-shit assholes and smug cowards hide behind their badges or rank. I fumed in my body and mind.

Yes, I was hot and extremely pissed-off at this joker. He had trashed my day, because he was no DI and had no right to try to act like one and I was not authorized to tear into his smarmy ass. I don't know how the rest of the recruits in 3074 felt when a regular Marine was addressing them. Perhaps with fear no less than around a DI. Since I had been on the Island longer than the rest and taken so many bus rides, dealt with bus drivers, corpsmen, doctors, and the Medical Platoons' assortment of Marines, I had learned who to fear and who was not important. I did know one thing. I feared DIs and would never get salty around one of them.

Bet your ass boy!___What I would love to have done would be to take on this prick with pugil sticks. I fumed on. *Bet you'd look real funny with a pugil stick shoved up your ass, fatso!*

The pecker-headed corporal assigned me to sweeping out the office area. While working in that area, I saw a tall master gunnery sergeant, with an uncountable stack of ribbons, walk by me and enter one of the smaller offices. What shocked me were not the vast decorations he wore, nor the seemingly endless strips that his rank warranted, but the loose sleeve of his left arm. There was no arm there, only an empty sleeve.

How in the hell did a one-armed man stay in the Corps? I wondered and kept snatching glances at him when I could. When I left that building I pondered the question for hours. I was not aware of this part of the Corps yet. The Corps was not turning its back on one of their deserving brothers, who had lost his arm in combat, but still had time to go before retiring and was not without capabilities desired by his Corps. *It had to have happened in Vietnam, of that I am certain.* I decided.

That evening Staff Sergeant Louis announced that tomorrow was the beginning of Mess and Maintenance Week. We stood on line with eagerness this evening awaiting the assignments. Tomorrow we would be the old salty recruits who would have the chance to load up the trays of the wide-eyed FNGs who ventured down our serving lines. We would have our revenge in the traditional way. Staff Sergeant Louis read off our duty assignments for a few more minutes. The majority were assigned to mess hall duty. I wanted to get on that list, but alas it was not to be. Some poor recruits got assigned to battalion supply and would suffer for a week under that fat-pig red-headed corporal.

"Shipman!" Staff Sergeant Louis barked. "You report to the bakery.___It's way over past 4th Battalion,___the split-trail battalion." he laughed. "It's quite a hump by foot.___Report to me for your pass and a map after I finish reading off these assignments."

"Sir, aye-aye Sir!" I answered and wondered what I did wrong to get bakery duty. I really wanted to sling hash. I wanted to see the FNGs squirm and watch to see how they got rid of their mountains of chow. Others, perhaps equally disappointed, were assigned to various other duties. When I reported for my paperwork, Louis was grinning as if he knew I was disappointed.

"Look at it this way," he said, "you would hate the mess hall after one day and the bakery smells better and has a fringe benefit you will soon discover,___numb-nuts," he said, while handing me the paperwork and told me to be ready to get there at 0400 hours the rest of the week. He had issued a list of piss-calls for the fire watch to ensure we all got up and out for our tasks. I was the only one on bakery duty from our platoon.

THREE

At 0300 hours the fire watch shook me awake and continued to roughly shake a couple of other recruits further down the squad bay.

Oh God, I feel tired. I can't believe we have to get up this early. It's pure torture. I grumbled to myself and moved quickly to the head. I'm sure we all felt unsure of ourselves to be in the head through our own decision to get there without a DI. A few minutes later we felt like old-timer Gyrenes aware of this trust, this privilege, to be able to get around without our ever-present guardians. We knew the mess hall boys would be blasted out of their bunks and stampeded into the head by the DIs as we used to be, at 0330 hours, but that's what they get for getting that duty.

When I got outside, the combination of the extreme darkness and the shockingly cold morning, along with my new-found independence, felt exhilarating. I walked swiftly down Boulevard de France, past the Iwo Jima Monument by the huge meat grinder, crossed over the road and headed toward the regimental headquarters buildings. I had to stop under street lamps to study the map Staff Sergeant Louis had prepared for me. Soon, I was passing barracks and read a sign, stating this was the 4th Battalion Women Marine training area. I thought of Louis' remark and smiled. He had referred to them as BAMs. My directions were good and my path correct, but the time was early so I would not see any girls. They were still in their racks.

Do they get extra sleep,___like beauty sleep. I pondered stupidly. *That's what I had always heard before, about girls needing that extra sleep time.*

A few minutes later I saw a sign declaring the bakery and stopped to contemplate how I would report to the senior Marine. I decided that banging on the hatch would not work like it did on the DI hatch. If I simply stood out here they may be waiting for me inside and consider me UA, but then I thought that if I walked right in all they would do is chew my ass out. This of course would create a bad blood between us from the start. As I stood there trying to analyze this dilemma, I wondered where the other recruits were. I couldn't be the only one here when hundreds were sent to the mess hall. Surely, it would take more than one helper to work a bakery.

Suddenly the hatch opened and a gunnery sergeant walked out, or rather exploded out. He was of medium height, powerfully built and had a face of chiseled rock that reminded me of the Bizzaro people from Earths parallel world in the Superman comics.

"Hey, there you are.___Just get here?___What's your name kid?" he asked in a staccato way, but really in a kind voice. There should be a couple more showing up as well.___What battalion are you from?" he asked further, before I could respond to the first question.

"Sir, Recruit Shipman, 3rd Battalion, Hotel Company, Platoon 3074 reporting as ordered Sir!" I barked smartly.

"Very commendable kid!___Nice reporting skills,___but can you bake?" he said with a wry smile.

"Sir, the recruit had never been given the opportunity to determine that skill sir!" I answered with less feeling of confidence than the answer sounded.

"Ha!___You won't have to anyway, kid.___Just wanted to know if you ever did," he chuckled and took my paperwork. As he was reading it under the porch light there were three other recruits walking over to us.

"Get on your faces!" he snarled suddenly. "Push-up position!___Ready.___Not you Shipman,___you get up.___The rest start counting four counts.___Start!" As the familiar scene of recruits doing punishment PT got underway, I felt strange being an observer rather than a participant. I also had a feeling that this gunnery sergeant was quick tempered and although he appeared amicable, he could be cruel.

"You ass-holes move this slow in my bakery or show up late again, I'll have your asses.___Jesus, I can't believe you made it this far in training!" he said in a DI type voice. I wondered if he had been a DI at one time, because he sure had the skill and voice. But then I felt ashamed to be singled out in front of these guys to watch and not be involved. This causes attitudes to develop and these guys may resent me for his actions. We'll see.

"All right,___get on your feet!" he snapped after they pumped out twenty. "I don't want any more of this laziness.___You got me?___Unlike in your training,___I punish individually for mistakes," he said as a harsch warning.

"Sir, yes Sir!" we all answered and followed him into the building. The smells of fresh baked bread and rolls wafted through my nostrils. I immediately thought of the Children's Home and the fresh baked goods the sisters had placed out on the racks in the hall by the church entrance very early each morning. It was always a pleasing smell and then I thought of the guys working in the greasy mess hall and felt that it was better to be here even though I would still have liked to be a line server and see the faces of the new recruits getting their first meals.

"My name is Gunnery Sergeant Whetzel and I run this bakery.___

You will find working here to be a memorable experience.___You are expected to keep the area in working condition,___which means as soon as a bowl is finished being used,___wash it!___Trucks bring supplies daily.___They must be unloaded and all items must be placed in their proper storage areas.___Much of what a bakery uses is perishable and must go into the freezer or refrigerator.___When I,___or that is, any of the baking staff,___yell out for any items they need,___you hustle double-time and get it.___Got it?"

"Sir, yes Sir!" our small group replied as loudly as possible. Judging from our new leader's look, we had appeased him with the proper display of discipline and motivation.

"You can get chow at the headquarters mess hall, which will still be open for breakfast when you get there.___For the rest of the week,___I suggest you leave here to get there by 0600 hours each morning and hustle back over here as soon as you are finished with chow___Do not be late,___ever!" he warned, making the word 'ever' sound deadly.

"Sir, yes Sir!" we acknowledged.

"You will march to the mess hall as a group, when going from here.___You may walk individually to this building in the mornings, since you are from different areas,___but always have your pass on you," he finished and walked away to oversee the mornings baking work. We sounded off and stood awaiting our assignments. The wait was only mere seconds before Marine bakers gabbed us for their tasks.

FOUR

After morning chow the four of us practically ran back to the bakery, eager to do well at our first jobs in the Corps. We were also eager not to piss off the Gunny. We had seen his disciplinary side from the start and would see more over the week. He did not need a campaign hat, because he could deal out his punishment, wearing his Pillsbury dough boy hat, with no diminishing effects. The bakery was kept spotless, based on our first view of it this morning. I wondered if the other three in our team felt the same as I did, in thinking this would be a cinch job.

However, within an hour of our return from chow, the entire working area was trashed. There was butter all over the deck that caused everybody to slide about. Bits and pieces of crusts, nuts, candied fruits and assorted spices, lay stuck to the floor. On top of all the tables and floor was a fine coating of flour with several areas displaying enough flour in piles to bake entire loaves of bread. There were large bowls mounted on electrically driven turntables, each with a huge paddle running down the center, to knead the dough. There were many other large bowls of various sizes, for various uses. Each of these bowls had to be scrubbed out and readied for the next use throughout the day. When evening wore away sufficiently to cause the Gunny to remember us and the fact that our mentors would soon be looking for us, he gave instructions for our arrival time and duties for Tuesday and dismissed us.

It was already dark outside as the days now had shorter daylight hours and the evening temperature had dropped significantly from the forty-five degrees of noontime. This evening promised to be at least in the low thirties. I was amazed at how absolutely still everything was around regimental headquarters. There were no significantly lighted areas, no vehicles on the roads and no Marines walking about. However, by the time I got to the 3rd Battalion area I could hear hundreds of voices muffled by the closed windows shouting in timed responses. The loudest noises came from the most recent arrival platoons. The more confident and *ahoorraah* sounds came from our section of platoons.

Standing alone outside of a training barrack hatch on the Island is not only in a category of rare to never, but an event that will create axiety. The rare occasions fall into reporting-in from the Medical Platoon for example or the return from an individual visit to sickbay. In this case an individual return from bakery duty. Whatever the reason, any recruit finding himself standing outside of such a hatch has had the same thought. That thought is,'I know that when I open this hatch I will re-enter the sub-basement of hell and therefore, I should run the other direction'.

I entered my squad bay and wasn't sure at first what shocking thing I might encounter. Over the past weeks bodies would be slamming into the deck along with cries of pain, grunts imitating count-offs and DIs screaming oaths of vengeance on our heads and our offspring. This evening everybody was busy at their footlockers cleaning gear. There was no sound at all inside our barrack, so all those sounds must have been from the other platoons in our series. I was feeling disappointment, as I had felt pride listening to what I thought was my platoon's confident sounds at our training level. Sergeant Hodson had the night duty and several seconds after I had entered the squad bay he suddenly shouted out.

"Where did the Marine Corps earn the sobriquet 'Devil Dogs'?"

"Sir, Belleau Woods Sir!" the platoon answered loudly.

"Where is that?"

"Sir, France Sir!" the platoon followed with a confident reply.

"What do you think of that?"

"Ahhoorraah!" the platoon thundered.

Well, it was my platoon after all and also some of the other platoons in our series, and they all sounded great. I thought proudly.

"Well if it isn't Frosty the Snowman," Sergeant Hodson said as I made my way to report in. "you're supposed to work at the bakery not wear their supplies," he continued and chuckled. "You are a mess!___ It's 2015 hours now,___so hold out for showers and use the time to square away your gear.___Perhaps you should concentrate on your boots Recruit Snowman," he chuckled dryly from behind me, as I returned to my bunk. My boots were caked with so much dough crud that I had to ask permission to go to the mop sink to wash them before I could polish them.

Sergeant Hodson was agreeable, since he apparently knew this was necessary and all of the other recruits who had worked in the kitchen areas at the mess hall had grease and slime they needed to wash off, prior to polishing.

Wow!___I feel like I just ran the Obstacle Coarse three times in a row. I sighed silently. My muscles were aching in places I hadn't known there were any. *I thought nothing on this island could do that anymore to muscle groups, after getting in shape during all the previous weeks.*

"What Marine division landed on Tarawa?" Sergeant Hodson continued his history lesson.

"Sir, the 2nd Marine Division Sir!" we bellowed a positive response.

"What Marine division landed on Guadalcanal?"

"Sir, the 1st Marine Division Sir!"

"What Marine divisions are in Vietnam?"

"Sir, the 1st and 3rd Marine Divisions Sir!"

"Who do I consider one of the bravest Marines of 1969,____and when, where and what unit?

"Sir, Lieutenant Wesley Fox,___February 1969,___A Shau Valley,___1st Battalion, 9th Marine Regiment Sir!"
"What did he do?"
"Sir, immediately recovered from a sudden enemy attack,____ engaged the enemy,____destroyed the enemy,____saved his company from destuction and was awarded the medal of honor____Sir."

Sergeant Hodson continued his question and answer period with more lore about Lieutenant Wesley Fox. On several occasions, since arriving on board, Hodson had told us the story about Lieutenant Fox and his company's heroic stand last February.

"On 22 February 1969", he proudly started his recital, "Alpha Company, 1st Battalion, 9th Marines, commanded by 1st Lieutenant Wesley L. Fox, had fought a skirmish in the A Shau Valley, involving the 1st Platoon, with an NVA squad dug into a hillside.___When the shooting was over, 1st Lieutenant Fox sent a detail of twenty Marines with canteens to a nearby creek to replenish the company's water.___The detail came under intense enemy fire as soon as they had reached the creek.___Mortar and machine gun fire raked the area while Lieutenant Fox ordered the detail back and sent the 1st Platoon forward in an attack.___The jungle was extremely thick and the enemy fire was very intense, coming only a short distance in front of the Marines from a reinforced NVA company occupying well fortified, mutually supporting bunkers.___Lieutenant Fox knew he could not use air or artillery support due to the distance between his Marines and the bunkers.___ He led his remaining platoons in an assault on the bunkers.___While attacking, an enemy mortar devastated his command group, leaving only 2nd Lieutenant Lee R. Herron, his executive officer, who instantly took command of the 2nd Platoon.___The Marines fought a close quarter assault involving hand-to-hand contests.___Lieutenant Herron was killed in the assault and Lieutenant Fox, initially wounded by the mortar, was twice more wounded while he personally destroyed two enemy positions.___This action was the last major engagement of Operation Dewey Canyon, which resulted in the loss of eleven Marines killed, seventy-two wounded, and one hundred five NVA dead.___A large cache of automatic weapons was seized. Lieutenant Fox was recommended to receive the Medal of Honor and Lieutenant Herron to receive a posthumous award of the Navy Cross!" Sergeant Hodson concluded his heart-felt speech.

Wow!___That was a hell of a fight. I thought, with a long moment of imagination on how it must have been for them.

Sergeant Hodson, finished with his history questions, ordered us to secure all gear and write letters or take care of personal matters with the time left that evening.

"Shipman!___Front and center!" Sergeant Hodson barked suddenly.

I scrambled to my feet and nearly tripped over my footlocker as I bolted toward the duty desk. Sergeant Hodson was busily going through a pile of paperwork consisting of a variety of memos, reports, schedules, and battalion notices.

"Sir, Recruit Shipman reporting as ordered Sir!" I bellowed while standing like a statue.

What the hell is wrong?___What did I forget to do,___or what did I do? My mind raced trying to come up with some clue so I wouldn't feel the bite of a DI so badly.

"Here's your chit to report to the dentist at 1000 hours tomorrow.___ Be there on time," he said snapping off the end.

"Sir, aye-aye Sir!" I replied and took the chit. I made a proper about face and retreated back to my bunk.

They know they are screwing with us when they call our name out like that.___Son-of-a-bitch!___And only for a fuckin' dental appointment! I muttered mentally to myself.

Overall the evening was about as good as the day was, and on the Island nobody complained, if they had a non-eventful day, because they were as rare as a warm day in Canada in January. We hit the rack and I felt like this was perhaps the most perfect day I had on the Island so far, excepting while with the Medical Platoon.

FIVE

At 0245 hours Staff Sergeant Louis woke us by kicking shit cans down the squad bay. As we hit the white line we could see he was not smiling and we felt his mood through the wee hours PT. He had us on our faces as soon as the lights registered in our brains. In a surrealistic voice he counted off the cadence of our rhythm. Even though we only spent fifteen minutes grinding our bodies into the concrete deck, we felt like it was three times that long. Staff Sergeant Louis was in a sour mood.

It was extremely evident. What the reason was for this totally harsh and spiteful displacement of anger was not explained to us. We bore the brunt of it nevertheless, and he was inclined to be reticent about it. In addition, it was now 0300 hours.

He had wanted to punish us without interfering with any of our schedules. Knowing full well we recruits had to be on duty at specific times this week, he decided to drop the showers for the 0300 crew in exchange for PT time.

"Get your miserable asses in the head and do everything except showers.___Port side,___hit it!" he growled.

I shot through the head, bolted out of the barrack, and virtually ran towards the bakery. I didn't want the Gunny taking a big bite out of my ass, after having made a good first impression. This mornings' bad PT ordeal wasted valuable time and could certainly wreck everything with the Gunny by making me late.

What the hell was the matter with Staff Sergeant Louis?___He does get pissed off___sure,___but this morning was scary as hell.___I wonder why? My mind turned these questions over and over, as I hurried to get to my duties and as far away from Louis as possible.

Gunnery Sergeant Whetzel was already shouting at the first recruit to arrive. He couldn't have been there but a few seconds, because I could barely see him ahead of me as I was making my way to the bakery.

What could he have done in a second___and are we on time? I wondered.

"Don't you dare leave here before you check your area and make damn sure it is clean.___Do you hear me?" he said in a harsch DI voice.

"Sir, yes Sir!" the recruit barked back.

What was his name?___I think it was Croft. I thought. He was a medium sized white kid with sad eyes, ripe pimples, and scarred acne cheeks. From what I had observed, he was not a skater, because I had observed his eagerness to work yesterday. The Gunny would have checked him then, if he thought he was a yard-bird.

I reported to Gunnery Sergeant Whetzel and handed him the note from Sergeant Hodson stating I had a dental appointment at 1000 hours. He read it, grunted acknowledgment and commented.

"Don't waste any time there.___I need you here, because we have a shit-load of work to do."

"Sir, aye-aye Sir!" I answered and went to my work area.

The other Marines who worked in the bakery were quiet and not inclined to pretend they were DIs. I thought of that red-headed fat asshole over at battalion supply, who did pull that shit. These guys would just tell us what they wanted us to do and get on with their own work. Only Whetzel pulled hard-ass around here and not really constantly, but when it seemed to be warranted, according to his judgment. For the most part, he was easy-going. I noticed Croft was scrubbing out a large dough-mixing machine. Apparently, that was what he failed to do yesterday. My work area was the loading bay, walk-in freezer and refrigerator area. I spent my day off-loading trucks full of bakery supplies, or loading delivery trucks with fresh baked goods for distribution to mess halls throughout the Island. Towards the end of the day I worked with the other three recruits in the main bakery area, cleaning-up the daily disaster.

While I also pulled stock and brought it to the bakery work area, I spent a lot of time in the walk-in freezer and refrigerator. Inside of the refrigerator were large containers of nuts, candied fruits, dried fruits and an assortment of other delicious items required for cakes, muffins, and breads. Tomorrow was Christmas Eve and today fruitcakes, cookies and other seasonal baked goods were being made.

No wonder the Gunny was on edge.___The workload has tripled from what we did only yesterday, with this Christmas baking. I observed.

This morning kept me busy pulling candied fruits and nuts for the fruitcakes being baked. The containers were very large, like the size of five-gallon liquid containers. Several were loosely capped and so, what the hell, I looked in on the contents. God, they appeared appetizing and especially so, because I had been on this damned Island since Christ was a corporal, and going for so long without sweet food. I looked left and I looked right. Nobody was around to see me grab a few handfuls of the contents. I chewed fast and only regretted not being able to enjoy the flavor longer, while it became a paste in my mouth. Instead, I had barely chewed it and greedily swallowed the evidence, lest I be caught red-handed.

Wow!___Jesus take me now!___I've had my reward.____Man this is good! I almost dove into the canister, but instead grabbed another handful of the addictive stuff.

At 0945 hours Gunnery Sergeant Whetzel informed me I should

head over to the dentist. I hustled toward the Regimental Headquarters and was soon passing the 4th Battalion barracks and this time saw the area ripe with screaming females. They were marching, dropping to do PT and running in formation. Very little difference was evident in their training from ours except the intensity. One platoon was positioned close to the sidewalk I was on. The female DI was screaming, in a shrilly voice, at them about something, but I was not able to hear all of the words clearly until I was closer.

".....can't march worth a shit!......waste my time!.....no good flighty-headed whores!" Is what I heard as I neared their formation. Their DI was not looking at me, as she had her back to me the entire time.

Several of the female recruits' faces, which came into my line of sight were grinning at me and one licked her lips, I swear, and their DI catching this anomaly in her formation wheeled around only to see this blushing recruit passing by. Instead, of saying anything to me, because I was rightfully using the sidewalk and not trying to make any type of contact, she turned to her platoon and screamed.

"Quit eye-fucking that male recruit and get on your backs.___That's what's on your sleazy minds anyway.___So start bicycle peddling.___ Do it.___Count off!" she barked in satisfaction. "There's over forty miles of cock on this island and you sorry cunts ain't gettin' an inch of it!" she screeched with evident delight.

My face and neck were crimson by now and I moved faster to get the hell away from that loony-tune episode. I was thinking how everything the females talked about was sexual in nature and in our barracks there was only the Suzy-rotten-crotch songs, while we ran. As I was entering the door at the Dental Office a corpsman noticed my face and asked if I was feeling all right. I had no idea I had a very red splotchy blush lingering on my face, neck, and chest. Less then a minute passed in the waiting room and to my surprise I was called and led to a dental room down the hall.

There were several young Navy officers or dentists in the room and one of them asked me to get into the chair. The other immediately placed a bib on a chain around my neck and asked me how I was doing.

"Sir, the recruit is doing fine Sir!" I barked and saw the smiles on their candy-assed faces. *These two little sadistic shits were delighted to push buttons on Marine recruits to watch our robotic responses.*___I thought with some anger.__Man, *I've really been getting short tempered at everybody who gets on my nerves since I've arrived on this island,__It has definitely got something to do with all this pressure and abuse.* I decided. *And I'm damn sure I've developed a total unacceptance of anyone who screws-up, doesn't think first, acts over-authoratative or purposefully hurts others.*

I suppose my sudden anger blush, perpetuated by the residual first blush really caused my face to redden.

"Open wide," asked one of the candy-asses. "My!__What have we got here?"

He must be a faggot. I figured with instant discomfort.

"Have you been sneaking sweets private?" he asked in a voice that suggested that he'll tell on me!

What the hell was he talking about? I wondered and was getting angry again. *Oh shit! __The nuts and candied fruits were stuck between my teeth.__That's it,__Shit!__I'm busted!*

"Where have you been to get something to eat like this?" the fag pushed the question and got his asshole buddy to have a look as well.

"I absolutely hate fruitcake," the other said. "Where are they serving fruitcake around here?" he asked me in a musically sounding voice.

"Sir, they will be tomorrow Sir!" I answered crisply.

Well, if that's true,__where did you get yours first, and how does a recruit know what the menu will be for the next day?" he said jokingly, and opened his mouth and eyes wide, as he looked at the other dentist for approval of his lame humor.

"So, where did you get some,__private?" he persisted.

"Sir, the recruit did not eat fruitcake,__Sir!" I stated and thought how these two were fruitcakes.

"But you have the residue of the makings!" he protested almost doggedly. "Don't you think so John?__Take a look again." The other looked and said. "I think he has been eating something that looks awfully like fruitcake,_after all, where do you see candied fruit elsewhere?" he finished.

After a few more minutes of their corny humor, they finally fit me with a plate and a tooth that filled the gap left on the right side of my two front teeth. It looked great and I was very pleased. Hell, I was so pleased that I actually didn't mind these two faggots' humor.

Let them ramble on, I got me a new look.__Hot damn! I smiled inwardly.

As I walked back toward the bakery, I wondered if the irritating feeling of having the plastic plate and the wire that secured the plate, attached to the tooth immediately behind the opening filled by the new tooth, would go away. The longer I wore the plate, the more I noticed I had it. By the time I got to work, it was bothering me. Dr. John had told me it would be a while before I became accustomed to it and I should be patient. Above all, he said don't take it out until you hit the rack, that way you will get the time in where it will stop being a foreign object. It's like a wrist watch when you first wear one or after a long time of not wearing one and you feel it for awhile.

Of course Gunnery Sergeant Whetzel busted my ass over the new look.

"Hey Shipman,___with that Hollywood grin you got there now,___you didn't by any chance stop by the BAM barracks and get a piece before you came back?___Did ya?"

"Sir, no Sir!" I replied with a blush.

"Christ!___Look at you blushing.___I bet the BAMs attacked you and dragged you off to have their way.___Huh?"

"Sir, no Sir!" I answered half wishing he'd shut the hell up and half wondering if had I smiled going by the BAMs would that have happened. It would have been nice, but with my luck, which had not been great so far, I'd be busted by that nasty-mouthed female DI that I saw earlier. Whetzel had other things to do and walked away apparently thinking he was funny and left me alone for the rest of the day.

Around 1500 hours I tried a scoop of nuts and fruits and found I had made a serious mistake. When I started chewing the pieces got under and around the edges of the plate and boy it hurt. I grabbed the plate and pulled it out. The feeling of the sharp pain subsided and I finished the mouthful, went to the water fountain and rinsed my mouth free of the residual nuts. That was the last time I had any of that stuff. At noon chow I did not have any food, which was that crunchy, so I never expected the same results I got eating the contraband this time.

Sergeant Hodson had apparently swapped duty with Sergeant Black, because he was there this evening. Sergeant Hodson was not in his history teaching mood tonight. I entered the squad bay and reported. He jerked his thumb over his shoulder towards the big sink wordlessly telling me to clean off my boots. But this time there was a line of recruits still formed there, waiting to wash-off their boots.

Perhaps 3rd Battalion had a particularly greasy menu today. I surmised.

Working in the bakery had really worn me out today and I am sure we were all beat, regardless of duties assigned. Therefore, we were all very surprised when Sergeant Hodson ordered us to assume the push-up position.

"Ready!__Four-count!__Begin!" he growled in the froggy voice of 3rd Battalion DIs.

"One__two__three__four.__United States Marine Corps.__One,__two,__three,__four __we love the Marine Corps.__One,__two,__three,__four,__let's do this some more." On and on for a half hour more we did a variety of indoor PT. We finished with the hated bends and mother-fuckers. With sweat pouring from our heads, we were allowed to start working on our rifles and other gear before showers.

Sergeant Hodson was not at all in a bad mood and he wasn't even pissed off at us for an infraction of his harmony. He just plain didn't want any of us to grow soft during Mess and Maintenance week and decided the jolt of the PT would remind us of why we were here. After showers we were given time to read or write letters. I decided to read and pulled out my big green book on Military subjects and began to study. I felt that the Command Inspection week, which was twelve days away, would be pure hell for any recruit not fully prepared to answer any questions on any subject queried on. It seemed that every time I read the Guidbook For Marines there was always something I either missed before or had apparently forgotten. This was no time to be slacking, because they tolerated nothing short of perfection. I had developed a pace to ensure that I re-read each chapter at least twice, before the inspection day arrived. The only fear I could not shake was interference with my time to study, as it was not unlikely here.

SIX

Staff Sergeant Louis was not as loud this morning as he and Sergeant Hodson shouted and rattled shit cans, but none were thrown and no racks were spilled during this wake up call. It was 0300 hours.

"Listen up!" Staff Sergeant Louis shouted down the squad bay. "The following names will report to the Series Commanding Officer today." he stated and continued to read off six names and ordered each one up to him for paperwork authorizing the absence from work details and giving the time and place to report.

Recruits Davids, the House Mouse and Haught, the Scribe and Walczak, the Polish kid, were among those called. I was not aware of what was going on, because no recruit was allowed to talk and especially not about the reasons for these recruits being called away.

I made my way hurriedly to the bakery and found the other three recruits had converged within seconds of each other. Gunnery Sergeant Whetzel had not yet opened the hatch, as was his custom. Therefore, we had a moment to say hello for the first time. Until this day I only heard the name Croft, who was the slim, sad-eyed, acne-scared, pimple-faced kid. Hirta was short and stocky, with a dark complexion that made him appear mean. However, when he talked he sounded kind and even shy. Ruppel was tall and willowy with red hair. Hell, it was orange and his complexion appeared washed out. When he spoke his arms moved around like they were wind blown and when the imaginary wind stopped they would float down rather than drop. I wondered if he gave his DIs daily fits moving like that.

From my observations, all three of these recruits were hard workers. Except for Croft getting his ass eaten out for not properly cleaning a batter mixing machine the other day, no other incidents had occurred. We each introduced ourselves to the others and shared short quiet laughs over how hard it was here to do something as simple and as civil as say hello. I could not even imagine sneaking a conversation back at platoon 3074. Two seconds after we had stopped shaking hands, the hatch opened loudly and Gunnery Sergeant Whetzel came out.

"Well recruits,__you're on time!__Learning the system I see.__ Let's get to work,__because we will be cranking out one hell of a lot of baked goods today.__Lord,__you have no idea!" he said with a wide grin. He was in a festive mood it seemed, and it became evident as the day wore on. Not once did he chew ass and often one could hear him humming a cheery Christmas tune. He was a man of his word, because by the end of the day, as promised, there was an exceedingly larger array of baked goods than were produced on an average day. There were rolls, loaves of bread, cookies, cupcakes and, not forgotten, fruitcakes.

Later in the day, while we four recruits were marching over to noon chow, an incident occurred. As required, when we were all going to chow at the same time, we formed in two ranks of two and marched in step. The recruit in the front right position called the movements. This position alternated through the week so we could each learn and today Hirta was in charge.

We never talked during these unsupervised periods, because we were conducting a military procedure. The only voice would be our guide saying, 'Column left!___Huah!', for instance. As we were nearing the mess hall by the Regimental Headquarters, a woman's voice called out to us.

"Excuse me!___Hello!___Hey,___uh___excuse me!" the woman kept saying in a desperate-sounding voice. She was definitely determined to talk to us, however, we kept on, eyes front, marching. The woman and another girl, maybe her daughter, started running alongside of us trying to repeat the question.

"Excuse me!___One of you,___would you please.... ," she gave up exasperated. "Why won't they answer?" she asked the girl in a shrill voice.

"Maybe they aren't allowed to, while they are marching," the girl said.

Go to the head of the class. I thought amused.

We kept on our course down the street. The woman was probably lost and here to visit her son or daughter during Christmas.

Good luck Lady. I mused over her dilemma and then forgot her.

As for why we did not answer, that was due to fear, confusion and confidence. We were afraid to talk and afraid to casually stop and chat with these females. Our handbook did not cover such an incident and due to our confusion we, or really Hirta, decided to err on caution and not speak. As for the rest of us, we automatically deferred to Hirta as our leader for that moment and what the leader of a group of Marines does, is what goes. We were also confident we were correct and would not suffer any ass chewing over this situation.

They were all dressed in green,___no hair,___black boots___and oh yes,___two of them wore black rimmed glasses___and they all had hats on. I thought with a mental laugh and visualized what the complaining, frustrated woman would have stated.

That evening nothing was said about our encounter with the lost females and I was convinced that, with thousands of recruits on this Island, they would have had a really impossible time giving a description of one of us.

We did PT before hitting the showers. Sergeant Black had the duty and he was also in a festive mood since, after all, it was Christmas Eve. He seemed to have had fun during mail call. Apparently, all packages received during the last week or so were held in the DI shack. The receipt of cookies, chocolates, candies or the like was strictly forbidden and considered contraband and referred to as pogey bait. However, the Marine Corps relaxed this law for Christmas. I received a small parcel of candy and a letter from Mom and a letter from my brother in Germany.

"You will not eat anything this evening.___Put it in your footlockers until tomorrow!" Sergeant Black ordered.

"Sir, aye-aye Sir!" we answered, and with salivating mouths and silent oaths, put the legal contraband away.

Wow!___Another PI contradiction, but what the hell,___who's complaining.___We can now officially eat sweets.___However, the day after and forever more-none! Ha, ha! I laughed in a silent gut giggler. The only sad part about this shit, is that I won't be celebrating on Christmas Eve with my family.___It was a Bavarian custom, and I felt the loss of this, but what the hell should I be bothered about,___we actually get to participate with Christmas festivities in the sub-basement of hell! The only thing I knew for certain was that the day after Christmas we will pay the DIs back for this moment of festivity.

SEVEN

Crash, bang! The metallic noise resounded throughout the squad bay.

"Merry Christmas turds!___Get your lazy asses out of the racks!___Move it!"

We hit the white line and waited for what came next. It was 0300 hours. Staff Sergeant Louis did not explain why he had decided to wake everybody up at the earliest hour even though only a few of us were supposed to get up earlier than the rest. It was the third time he had done it this week.

"It is Christmas morning, girls.___Merry Christmas!" Staff Sergeant Louis barked.

"Sir, Merry Christmas Sir!" we chorused back as cheerily as 0300 hours steam permitted.

"On the island there will be no time off for recruits.___So make the best of your day.___*Aahoorrah!*" he growled the Marine Corps warrior grunt.

"Sir, aye-aye Sir!____*Aahoorrraah!*" we responded equally as tired as before.

"You had better sound off like you got a pair,__girls,__let's hear your war cry!" he boomed in exasperation at our lackluster tone.

"Sir, aye-aye Sir!____*Aahoorraah!*" our voices reached far down into our guts and nearly popped the glass out of the windows.

"Damn!___*Sniff*!___You couldn't have given me a better present," he feigned a touching moment and just as fast screamed out. "Now get your asses into the head!___Port side!___Hit it!" he finished, sounding satisfied.

He was right about working today, because we all did the same routine and went out to our various duty stations, only we worked harder.

There were no colored lights celebrating Christmas on the Island. There were no wreaths or garlands hanging about hatches, bushes or trees, no mistletoe and no Christmas cards decorating hatches and bulkheads. The Island was the same today as always, with steam jets shooting off from the above ground pipe system and morning fog lingering over the grounds and obscuring the brightness of street lamps. The heavy Spanish moss hanging from every tree was as close to a Christmas tree decoration as we would see today.

When I arrived at the bakery, Croft and Hirta were just ahead of me. Ruppel was nowhere in sight. I was feeling a bit of anxiety for Ruppel, knowing he would get his ass in a sling if he was late and Gunnery Sergeant Whetzel may not care if it was Christmas Day. If he got mad at us, it could very well ruin the day for us all.

Gunnery Sergeant Whetzel opened the door and greeted us. "Well, boys,___I see you're all here.___So Merry Christmas!___Now get to work!___Its going to be another very busy day," he sounded cheery and calm.

I believe all three of us were perplexed about the greeting. Where was Ruppel? However, Ruppel walked around the corner of the building at the moment we turned to look at Whetzel, and so, he saw four faces as he came out.

Gunnery Sergeant Whetzel was again true to his word. We busted our asses getting supplies from storage to the bakers and they cranked out rolls, breads, cookies and yes, more fruitcake. I knew these baked goods tasted fine, because we had our chance to eat them at the mess hall. There was no tolerance for eating the baked products at the bakery. Gunnery Sergeant Whetzel was firm on that order. He was so positive of his baking skills that he wouldn't eat his own product to test it. His philosophy was that if the commanding general did not complain about his baking, then all was well. By the end of this day at the bakery we had cleaned, scrubbed, polished and chipped every square inch of the building and its contents three times. We looked like doughboys as we walked shakily out through the main hatch.

"Merry Christmas recruits!" Gunnery Sergeant Whetzel and his staff all called out to us while maintaining straight faces. That is, no smiles.

"Sirs, Merry Christmas Sir!" we turned toward them and stated solemnly. I know some of us said plain Sir without the plural however, this was another anomaly. How does a recruit respond to many Marines at once?"

When I entered my barrack, all was quiet, and that worried me. I figured that Sergeant Hodson, who had the evening duty, would be asking history questions, talking about Vietnam or military subjects. It really didn't matter if it was Christmas, because there were no lights, trees or songs anywhere on the Island where recruits were and the lack of decoration ruined the mood anyway. After I had cleaned up, returned to my bunk and started working on my boots I had realized that I was the last recruit to finish getting squared away and Sergeant Hodson did not make any wry comment to me about it.

"Everybody knows how many baked goods are made during Christmas,__your utilities suggested how trashed-up the bakery was.___So we decided to give you time to square away before we celebrated Christmas," Sergeant Hodson explained in a kindly voice. He definitely had the Christmas spirit.

I was stunned to hear one of our DIs give a shit and realized at the same time that what we had been doing on this Island all along was teamwork. Therefore, to wait on a member of the team was being a team. They knew I wasn't screwing around wasting time so I wasn't about to feel embarrassed for having the misfortune of being the last one done, hell I was even the first one out as well.

"What I suggest is that we open our packages from home and read whatever personal mail they contain.___Bring up the contents and pile them here on the desk.___I will make individual piles for each recruit and you will then come up and take your present.___Do you understand me?" he stated in a faily mild voice.

"Sir, yes Sir!" we answered very eagerly and very loudly.

"Okay platoon 3074, prepare to celebrate,___celebrate!" he stated in that froggy Third Herd voice.

"Sir, aye-aye Sir!" we boomed eagerly and got to work on our mail.

Some recruits had no mail and no packages. Perhaps their families were poor or they had no family, but that's why we would be sharing, because we were their family now. I had received several bags of German chocolates and was happy to see there would be enough for everyone to have a piece. I had been wondering about how come we got some more mail on Christmas day and figured that with so many recruits on this Island it would take quite a while to sort out everybody's mail on the day it arrived on the Island and so they worked overtime to get it to us. As for packages arriving over the past week being delivered to us for mail call on the day it arrived in the barrack, it didn't matter, because the DIs had held them.

We formed up on the white lines and each side filed up to the DI desk and scooped their pile of Christmas cheer into their utility covers. Sergeant Hodson just watched and said nothing. Once everybody was back on line he spoke.

"Merry Christmas recruits!"

"Sir, Merry Christmas Sir!" we shouted back with a hint of joy amplifying our voices.

"Enjoy the pogy-bait,__because__one, it will be your last here, and__two, you'll be running it off next Monday.__That's a promise!__ Ready eat!" he concluded his lecture and we attacked our small hoard of sweets. There was enough for about ten pieces of assorted chocolates, candies and cookies per recruit. Within a half hour it was history and we were all once again standing on line and reading our red books looking no different this evening than we had any other evening before today.

Mess and Maintenance week came to its inevitable end for me on Saturday and I regretted to have to stop working at the bakery. Gunnery Sergeant Whetzel wished each of us good luck in our training and even stated we were a good crew, especially for our performance on the busiest week of the year, and then mumbled something about having to go and train a new crew all over again, as he turned and went inside the front door of his bakery. We recruits said our militarily correct goodbyes and headed to our respective battalions.

Saturday evening at the barracks was no picnic. Staff Sergeant Louis was on duty and not at all in a good mood.

"You girls are getting fat, sloppy and lazy while you have been out playing around food all week.___Well tonight I'm going to give you a sample of what I promised will be the taste of standard fare starting Monday. Do you hear me,___maggots?" he croaked in a froggy voice with a hint of old-time First Phase malice.

We stood rigid and waited for the games to begin. It had been nice for the most part during this week, but we had not been receiving our old familiar ass-kicking sessions on a daily routine, except for the early morning samplers, and I for one thought things had improved, for a short time. Regardless of our mentor's hammer coming down, signifying the closing the holiday season, I had thought how the last days were stabilizing our platoon's sense of accomplishment and our feeling of being closer to becoming Marines. Our mentor didn't agree and was doing his best to impress upon us that we were far from achieving the eagle, globe and anchor. We ended the PT session with just enough time to hit the showers. We had banged into the hard concrete deck for over an hour. Staff Sergeant Louis had us duck walking, watching TV and performing the entire manual-of-arms between push-ups, squats, side-straddle-hops, mountain-climbers and bends and mother-fuckers.

When lights were finally turned out and we jumped into our bunks, I swear we all passed out immediately.

Sunday morning was not met with clanging shit-cans or even severe shouts and threats. Sergeant Black had the duty and was content to get us up, washed, dressed, fed and off to church services. When we had returned from church, we squared away the barrack and attended to personal requirements such as washing utilities. A larger portion of our platoon was still working at the mess halls, as they were not yet finished for the week as those of us who were assigned to bakery, warehouse, supply and other maintenance related duties, had been.

Late in the afternoon, Sergeant Hodson relieved Sergeant Black of the duty and had us until Monday morning, when Staff Sergeant Louis would greet us with his sadistic promise. That evening, at the suggestion of Sergeant Hodson, I began a long overdue letter home.

28 Dec 69

Dear Mom and girls,
Hi Mom, hope you and Annie are feeling better about Sarah leaving to stay with Aunt Gretchen. I'm sure you both miss her.
I guess I won't be seeing her when I come home from training. Send me her new address please and I'll write her. In the mean time tell her hi from me when you write next. Tell her what's new here as she'll want to know. What I'm doing today is spit-shining my new dress shoes, getting ready for graduation and Command Inspection. We are all able to talk with our DI right now and he has been telling us about Vietnam and our basic training at the Infantry Training Regiment (ITR) at Camp Lejeune. Actually at a place called Camp Geiger, which is next to Camp Lejeune. I went to church today, had communion and prayed a little. When we got back to our barrack, Sergeant Hodson told the few of us here to write a fast letter home.
The rest of the platoon are working serving chow at the mess hall, we others don't work today. This next week will be the testing week for becoming a Marine. It will be a hard week. I starched both of my covers (hats) and made them stiff. Then I formed it to make a fancy dip in the crown. There are only fourteen days left in our training and I pray to graduate.
We switch to our red guidon flag tomorrow and get rid of the yellow flag we had up 'till now. The red flag means we are in the Third Phase of training. Just think, I would have graduated and been out of here a long time ago, had it not been for the bad luck during that tug-a-war that broke my foot. We are supposed to get our hair cut tomorrow, where the barber leaves

the hair on the top alone so it grows out and only cuts the sides to the skin. This depends on our Senior DI and how he feels about us earning this privilege. When others see us they know we are advanced trainees. I was told that I could get twenty-one days of training at ITR or depending on my MOS (Military Occupational Specialty) I could have eight more weeks. That means if I become a permanent Infantryman it will be eight more weeks.

I'll hear what my MOS will be before I leave this jerky island. Hey, I almost forgot. Remember the tooth I lost, you know next to my two front teeth, well I got a new one and I think it looks nice. Well, its night time and I got yelled at twice, big deal, it's not my night. Both times were for something like trying to help someone in the platoon from getting themselves in trouble. So I get yelled at for helping, but it's not anything to worry about.

That's all except to ask you all to keep praying like you did while I was at the Rifle Range. I'll need it just as much to graduate from this place.

Happy New Year.

Love,
Jack

P.S. Today isn't my day. Maybe it will be better tomorrow, while we will get our dress uniforms fixed up again, and sewed where needed, to get a better fit.

As I was sealing the envelope, I thought about what I said in the postscript about it being better tomorrow. What was I thinking? Staff Sergeant Louis has been promising us a giant shit-sandwich for each day next week.

CHAPTER 11
ENDURANCE

ONE

A solemn occasion is supposed to be some memorable day where formations of men stood in stiff ranks, while the band played and the flags fluttered in the wind. This may even be the standard procedure in the regular Marine Corps but, this is the Island. Today marked the beginning of Third Phase and our Platoon was eligible to put away our yellow guidon flag and take on the red guidon flag. It was a symbol of seniority on the Island, and we had seen many red guidon flags over the First and Second Phase weeks of training, and had envied those recruits. But now our day had come and there were no formations, no bands and no ceremonies.

"Delehey grab the guidon and get up here!" Staff Sergeant Louis growled.

Delehey ran up to the DI shack, reported and entered. When he came out he had the red flag attached with 3074 blazing in bright yellow.

"Don't get too used to it girls!" Staff Sergeant Louis shouted. "Because if you fuck-up just once during testing and inspections you'll get the yellow guidon back.___Oh,___before I forget.___Laundry detail, get all the laundry bagged and ready for pick up by the base laundry.___Also, within an hour you will receive haircuts and then off to pugil stick training.___You'll love it!___Because, it's going to be near seventy degrees today.___But I'll love it, because it'll give you a chance to beat the shit out of each other," he said, finishing his froggy presentation and grinned in his devious way.

While we were standing in line to get our haircut, I noticed those recruits, who were in before me, running back outside with broad grins on their faces. That grin must mean we got our Third Phase haircuts. They left the hair on top alone, so it can start to grow out again and they only cut the sides. What we now had was called a high and tight haircut. A Third Phase hair cut was another badge of seniority on the Island, a rite of passage. We felt proud as we marched with our red guidon toward the Confidence Course, where we would begin pugil stick training. It was a warm day, so we were able to leave our field jackets in the barrack. Staff Sergeant Louis felt good today, which we could tell by his voice and his style of cadence.

"Platoon!___Count cadence,___delayed cadence,___count cadence,___count!" he bellowed in his croaky voice and we complied eagerly.

"One, *step, step, step,* two, *step, step, step,* three, *step, step, step,* four, *step, step, step,* one, *step, step,* two, *step, step,* three, *step, step,* four, *step, step,* one, *step,* two, *step,* three, *step* four, *step,* one, two, three, four, United States Marine Corps.___*Ahoorraah!*" we finished with a hearty growl.

When we reached the area where we would practice with pugil sticks, there was a green official car parked with several officers standing by it. Staff Sergeant Louis saluted and spoke with them for a moment, then turned and called several names from the platoon. Those, whose names were called, were ordered into the vehicle and driven off. Nothing was said to the rest of us, but some knew why and where they were going and others, like me, didn't have a clue.

Pugil sticks are simulated rifles with two round pads, one at each end of a stick. The stick is approximately three and a half feet long with one pad for the rifle butt and the other for a bayonet. We were provided helmets and a plastic cup jockstrap for safety reasons, but nobody wore armor against an extra strong recruit's crushing blows. The jock strap was worn over the utility trousers and looked like a diaper.

We started the events pitted against members of the other platoons in our series. The DIs, in high spirits, were yelling, swearing, laughing and taunting the other platoons, prophesying their defeat. This event was so popular amongst the drill instructors that even those who had last nights' duty were out here. They were carrying on like wild men at a cockfight and we were their roosters. Part of this training involved fighting the opponent with only two gloves, while he had a pugil stick. That was to be part of tomorrows training session.

As the morning wore on, the frenzy of these events grew louder, and the recruits were allowed to jeer, shout, cheer and laugh along with the DIs. This was evidently a right of passage into the senior recruit ranks of the Third Phase. We stood in line along a barrier constructed with seven inch diameter by eight foot long branches, inserted between fence posts, all of which only came to our knees in height.

Sergeant Black and Sergeant Hodson were conferring with Staff Sergeant Louis, like kids placing bets. Suddenly they would run over to our next gladiator as he came from behind the barrier and give pep talks to motivate the recruit more than he might already have been.

"Holderman!___You see that skinny turd 3072 has sent out to fight you?___Well, don't sweat it.___He's a wimp.___Kill him!___*Ha!*___ Kill his skinny ass!___Go, go, go!" They each seemed to be yelling the same thing at the same time and the DIs from 3072 were saying the exact same thing to their recruits.

There was an instructor assigned to oversee these proceedings and offer training critiques. He was a sharp featured blond haired sergeant who wore stiff creased utility trousers, a red sweatshirt and a starched utility cover. A whistle hung around his neck. Judging from the long lines of our respective platoons, this would be a long day. The instructor blew his whistle and the first two recruits ran towards each other to do battle. They literally crashed into each other with their pugil sticks moving like helicopter blades. They were blindly whacking each other as hard and as fast as they could, while going in circles. This bashing event went on for sixty seconds or until one recruit fell down. When they both remained standing, the DIs judged the winner by the highest number of deadly body contact counts.

Over the next twenty to thirty bouts, I saw no difference in style and ferocity. All of the recruits yelled loudly as they attacked. Most fell, some remained standing, some were clear victors and a very few got their asses soundly beaten. While I watched the events I thought how this would be if it were done more structured, like fencing. When we were on the bayonet course we used the rifle like a tool to thrust, jab, butt stroke and parry. The feeling I got there was that the only way to fight, or defend, was to watch our opponents moves, and then counter. Here, with the helicopter or canoe paddle approach swinging a lighter stick with pads, I felt something was missed in what could have been great training. I just could not visualize two men with heavy rifles swinging at each other that fast and that blindly. I do know that it could knock the enemy down, but the exchange would result in being totally drained of energy, while there were other enemy soldiers to deal with. One would be wise to conserve energy here and therefore make every move count toward a very fast and efficient kill.

The drill instructors were still running around in a fast frenzy. They seemed to never tire of the sport here. Grinning and conspiring, they prepared each recruit like a gladiator to be pushed into the arena. Helmets flew off some of the recruits' heads, often resulting from hard butt stroke blows, which caught the rim in an upward surge. Most recruits who had lost their helmet ended up sprawled in the sand absorbing sand fleas. Davids, our house mouse, was up next. The senior DI of 3072 heard Staff Sergeant Louis call him the mouse and promptly called for his house mouse to be the challenger. Their mouse was a black recruit with small features except for thick lips. His eyes were intense and flitted nervously from side to side, as if he was looking for an escape. He was about the same overall size as Davids.

The whistle blew and they crashed into each other. Both being small and nimble enabled them to move faster than the others had previously demonstrated. Davids gained an edge by repeatedly coming down on his opponents head. In seconds, his vicious blows drove the other mouse into flight and, as he tried to break and run, Davids pursued and slashed. The whistle blew and our DIs ran over and slapped Davids' back and made such a general fuss over him I wondered why they didn't pick him up and carry him around as a hero. We recruits were very pleased with Davids' victory and knew it wasn't his fault how the DIs acted.

Soon it was my turn and while I suited up, I stole glances at my challenger. He was a stocky recruit with short legs. He had a round rosy-cheeked face with platinum bristles for hair. He also had a sneer on his thin lips.

Okay, if you want it that way, asshole, we'll see if you keep it when we're through. I thought with a cold smile on my face. The whistle blasted and *wham,* I felt a hard impact on my helmet while I was connecting with a thrust into his stomach. He pissed me off now and caused me to stop concentrating on tactics. No wonder none of the others were able to fence as they were also immediately swept into the viciousness of the attack. *Umph!* I caught a hard punch in the gut, while at the same moment I swung hard and connected with his helmet. In addition to these notable impacts, were dozens of minor punches, jabs and glancing blows delivered between us. My head throbbed, my stomach ached, my arms felt like lead weights, my legs became rubber and my ass hurt from the fall. My opponent was undoubtedly a baseball player. And then the whistle blew and it was over. I scrambled to my feet and caught Staff Sergeant Louis looking at me.

What the hell you want from me? I thought angrily. Because, I gave it my best and damn-it, if this were real perhaps I would have already killed the other guy before he rallied later for the knockdown punch. *That jab in the gut, in the first seconds, should have given him something to worry about, while I looked for my head on the battlefield.*

The other recruits were of two minds. Those who had already fought looked at me with understanding, while those who were still waiting looked at me thinking they would win. Good, they should be positive in their thoughts, but when the other guy rearranges those thoughts they'll understand the difficulty and luck combination here.

Later, when my turn came again, I felt my second bout was going to be different. They matched me up with a big black recruit who would have normally intimidated me simply due to his height and weight. The whistle blew and we struck sticks at the same time. After about fifteen contacts I had given and received a like number, I suddenly shoved my stick upwards and caught him under the chin with it, knocking him backwards and on his ass. The whistle concluded the bout and I felt better for it.

As I watched the remaining recruits complete their bouts, I realized why the DIs appeared so excited about the competitors. It suddenly occurred to me that we were no longer dropping recruits and those of us remaining were all hardened and aggressive. We were on our way to being finally honed killing machines. Our energy, aggressive spirit and determination to win was like a stew at boiling point and as the DIs watched us bubble and pop they extracted pleasure in their workings as they watched us do battle. Any disappointment over a loss was brief, because they knew the difference between real life and training, the mismatch of sizes and weights and knew the losing recruit could come back and kill his next opponent.

As if a lull appeared in a battle we formed up and limped off to noon chow. I noticed a headache developing and a throb over my left shoulder slowly beating to our cadence. All of us were sore from the events of the morning.

Chow was good today and very welcome. We had really worked up an appetite and knew we would work our full stomachs off in the remaining hours of the day. The serving line recruits, upon seeing our Third Phase hair cuts, knew better then to try screwing with us. The truth is however, if they had dumped double portions, like we got on our first meal, we would more then gladly have eaten it all now.

TWO

Sure as hell, the Obstacle Course had remained exactly as we had left it weeks back. The obstacles were still formidable and we would soon find out again, how difficult they were to engage. Our lines formed up for the Dirty Name obstacle. There it was before us, large, rough, hard and impartial as to whether we made it over, or not. There is a trick to getting over it. First, nobody could just walk up to it and expect to get over the middle log. They would have to run and gain enough speed to jump onto the lower log, which was two feet off the ground and vault up to the higher middle log. The middle log was about eight or nine feet off the ground and had a girth larger then a telephone pole, as were all of the horizontal logs. These logs were placed over more massive logs, at least three times the girth of the horizontal logs, with metal straps looped over them holding them secure with large bolts. The vertical logs were spaced approximately four feet apart and there was a two by twelve board nailed slanted to the center log near the top and to the tallest rear log at the ground level.

The rush to get over the obstacle was underway and some recruits had to repeat the Dirty Name, having failed to get over the middle or last log. There were a few accidents already, where recruits fell and hit the two by twelve boards, severely bruising legs, arms and ribs. Luckily, no one had hit their head yet. When it was my turn, I ran as fast as I felt I needed speed for the first vault up. My left food struck the first log and my knee bent and snapped straight for the spring upward. My right leg came alongside my left and my stomach slammed into the middle log. *Umph!* I made it this far, and moved my left leg over to obtain purchase enough to pull my body over on top, and then stood up. There was another recruit to my right.

Two at a time attacked this obstacle, and while we were struggling over the middle log, the two recruits before us were just falling over the third log. The smell of creosote was everywhere on this course and it got worse further in. While standing on the middle log, I had a second to assess the third log, which was approximately five feet higher up, and spring just enough to slam into that log. *Umph!* I hit it hard and did not slide backwards and fall like so many had done before. I got my left leg over and slid over the top. The goddamned metal strap securing the log pinched the shit out of my hand. I had placed my hand just where the meat could crunch under the metal a fraction, due to my body weight pressing down, while I slid over the top. There was a long drop now, of about twelve feet into the sand below. *Splat!* I hit the ground, jumped up to my feet, and immediately ran to the next obstacle.

Green River, how did it go?___Green river da da da... . For whatever reason, my mind suddenly locked on to Credence Clearwater Revival's song *Green River*. I couldn't shake that song for the rest of the course. *It's the perfect song for the rhythm of the course.* I reasoned.

Just as I got to my feet, two more recruits were flying through the air to impact in the same place I vacated a second before. There was only momentum on the obstacle course, with no room for delays. The next obstacle was an immense double ladder built on a sharp angle with metal pipes for rungs. It was twelve feet wide, the rungs were two feet apart and there were eight rungs. The obstacle was about eighteen to twenty feet high and we had to go up one side and down the slanted back side. We then grabbed ropes and swung over a water pit, pulled our bodies over double pull-up bars, hand walked, while hanging under horizontal ladders, crawled through drainage pipes and came out to face a very large structure with all sorts of fun things to break our ass, smash our balls or turn us into a midget, if we fell.

This contraption was all telephone poles and rope. It appeared as a rectangle sitting high up on poles approximately twenty or so feet off the ground with two poles running east to west on front and back, supporting three poles north to south resting on those. Above the three rear butts of the north to south poles was a fence of three more poles spaced a foot apart. Tied to the top fence pole were two ropes. At the front or east to west pole were two frames projecting even farther upward and also made of poles with rungs between. These frames were about twelve feet high and rested on a larger pole hanging across the top and were supported by two telephone poles at least fifty feet off the ground. These poles, built in an A structure, had two ropes, one at each end, suspended from the very top, which reached to the ground.

Shit! I mumbled. *No one could forget how much fun this one is.___ The Dirty Name bruised and this one blistered.* I gulped air as I prepared to engage it. I was muddy, bruised and bleeding from scrapes and burns acquired so far on the course. But now the blisters had to be added.

"Move your lazy asses!___Move it!___Faster goddam it!" Staff Sergeant Louis yelled. The other DIs were doing the same thing at other points along the course, and the instructors for each obstacle urged us on as well.

I grabbed the rope and shimmied up to the log fence, which had to be grabbed the same as the Dirty Name logs were, by both hands over it, gut resting on top, hike a leg over, then slide our body up over the top. *Whew!*

Next I spread my arms for balance and negotiated one of the precarious logs suspended from north to south, and scrambled up the A frame. Once at the very top, I reached outwards several more feet and grabbed the rope, and then slid down to the ground. Blisters? You bet your ass and splinters too. We eventually came to the Ladder. It was a giant structure seemingly reaching up into the clouds, appearing like the biblical Tower of Babble, with telephone poles for steps spaced two feet apart. What was required to engage this monster, was to wrap our arm around each wooden rung while lifting the opposite leg high to the rung below the arm-wrapped rung and slowly surge upwards. It was more like a crawl to get over the top log and then go back down the other side.

Stupid! I mumbled. *Why not just go around it?* I laughed in my mind at my corny wit. I knew I was getting punch drunk from the whole ordeal so far. I had grass in my mouth along with the crunch on my teeth from grit and sand. I had sand in my eyes, ears, and nose and down the crack of my ass accompanied by an army of sand fleas. *Go around it!___Ha!*

But there sat Staff Sergeant Louis, straddling the very top rung, waiting to give each recruit his blessing, or curse. When I was next, I gritted my teeth and attacked the first pole and reached up to the fourth pole. What I looked like was one foot on the bottom pole, the second foot stepping on the second pole, my right hand on the third pole and my left hand reaching for the fourth pole. With each step all the positions reversed and eventually we got to visit the Senior DI. What joy. He was busy shouting at the House Mouse when I pulled over the top, so nothing was said to me, and I was happy. The mouse, being short, had a harder time on this obstacle.

Our last obstacle was the Slide-For-Life and it was always last for several reasons. It was over thirty feet high with the three ropes running about one hundred feet down over water to poles protruding only four feet off the ground. We climbed up a rope to get to the top, straddled a second rope, while facing forward at a downward slant, and placed our right foot instep backwards and on top of the rope, with our left leg dangling down for ballast. Our left arm was straight out, with our hand grasping the rope. With the right hand behind the left, we started downward, hand over hand, inching our way forward. A third of the way down, we switched position, by rolling under the rope and with our head pointing down-hill and our legs crossed over the rope pointing up-hill, we continued another third of the way. The last third required dropping our feet, leaving us hanging by our hands and swinging our legs forward to gain purchase on the rope. If the right leg gets high enough to get, first one heel of our boot over the rope, and then the other, all is well. If one fails, he gets wet. When the foot does grab rope, we keep going, hand over hand, pulling our crossed legs forward, to the drop off point.

While I was enduring the slide, I smelled the pungent odor of the pool, which was green with algae slime, full of frogs and along with many unseen aquatic critters, had a very muddy bottom. The trees here were extra heavy with Spanish Moss and the overall feeling one got about this sand flea pit was to be anywhere but here.

The DIs took revenge at this point, on any recruits who had performed poorly, or lacked confidence, during the run-through. Their names were called out while they slid down, and as trained to do, they snapped to attention and splashed into the mud and water. In general, those recruits who were not yet at the proper conditioning level to complete this obstacle, would betray that inability, and fall anyway.

Alas there was an end here, confirmed by the order to form up. I was sore, bleeding, bruised, tired, thirsty, blistered, splintered, but most of all I was dry. I had nothing to bitch about, only sweat had created a little dampness. I made the course, I was not dunked, I got no ass-chewing and I was on my way to becoming a Marine.

Our herd stomped and squished back to the barn at double-time, and crashed through the barrack hatch, showered and fell out once again. This trip was very welcome. We were going to the tailor shops to try on our dress uniform issue, have the tailors adjust any fit problems and ready ourselves for the Command Inspection next week. In two weeks we would graduate, but that seemed a thousand miles and a hundred years to go, on the Island.

It was a strange sensation to wear the dress uniform of a Marine. We knew we were still recruits and still capable of failing to meet the requirements. Our ordeal on the Island was nearing the end and we would then know if we had made the grade and earned the right to wear this uniform. We tried on dress greens, khakis, tropical dress, and dress green overcoats, which always reminded me of soldiers in the war movies from all armies, on all sides, who had worn the same type of coat in different colors. Nevertheless, I felt the dress green overcoat wore exceptionally well and I liked it very much.

The cotton khakis were of a rougher cotton material. We were issued three short-sleeved shirts, and three trousers, made of this fabric. The tropical uniforms were of excellent light-weight material in a khaki color. The trousers held a knife-sharp crease, much better than the cotton khakis did. This uniform was referred to as 'Trops'. There were three long-sleeved tropical shirts with a light-green nylon material sewn around the inside neck area. This shirt was to be worn with the dress greens and dress tropicals and it held rigid and sharp crease lines. There were two creases running vertically from the shoulders through the pocket buttons down to the tails and in back a horizontal crease across the area below the shoulder blades with three vertical creases running down to the tails.

From the time I first arrived here and saw the tropical uniform shirt worn by Marines around Parris Island, I thought they appeared very sharp. However, after looking at the dress greens, there was never any question in my mind of that uniform being the true cut for a Marine. The color and cut of the uniform, matched with the khaki colored tropical long-sleeved shirt and khaki tie, was perfect. When the red and green chevrons and hash marks were worn, the uniform was unchallenged by any other military branches.

Of course the dress blues have always been envied by all other U.S. military branches and foreign armies and navies. So that uniform was the ultimate status symbol of a United States Marine. Nevertheless, my favorite was the dress greens. We were issued khaki and green barrack covers and fore-and-aft-caps, which of course were aptly called piss-cutters. To complete the uniform issue, we were sized for dress shoes and provided dress socks and lastly ties that the Corps calls field scarves. The time involved in processing an entire platoon through the stages of dress uniform issue was a surprise. It took us three hours. One noticeable thing about the Marine Corps is that they have a lot of different uniforms and they will go to great lengths to properly fit each one. If any Marine fails to continuously wear their uniform exactly the way he was taught, he would be in a serious hurt-locker.

We marched directly to evening chow and spent the remaining part of the training day cleaning the barrack, our rifles and squaring away our gear. Sergeant Hodson called for an inspection of gear and rifles, and later we wrote letters or studied for Command Inspection week. With aching muscles and darkening bruises, we finally hit the rack.

THREE

Our new day started with the general routine duties, such as squaring away the barrack, which always involved swabbing the deck and scouring the head. After morning chow we headed for the Confidence Course and were immediately introduced to the Naked Stranglehold. This particular hold was simply a killing maneuver designed to take out the enemy with our bare hands. All three of our drill instructors were present.

The drill instructors ordered us to form into two lines of thirty five recruits. One recruit stood behind the other recruit and the only recruit, out of the current seventy-one platoon count, without a second person was immediately snatched by Staff Sergeant Louis to become his training aid.

"Listen up!___This is not a training event where you can afford to fuck-up in any way.___The purpose of this technique is to enable a

Marine to kill his enemy in approximately fifteen seconds by utilizing bare hands.___So,___when you demonstrate this maneuver on each other, I do not want to find out you just killed your fellow platoon member.___Pay strict attention here!" he stated, as he walked up and down the front of our formation.

He then moved behind his shaking training aid, placed his right arm around the front of the recruit's throat, reached up to the top of the aid's left shoulder with his left hand and grasp his own right hand in a four finger inside the other four finger's lock. He did not place his fingers individually between the other fingers like a Baptist praying. He raised his left knee and swiftly rammed it into the aid's lower back as he simultaneously pulled the aid's body backward as his own body went backwards and dropped to the right knee. The recruit was now in a sitting position with his head buried in the crook of Staff Sergeant Louis' right arm, with the DI's hand gripped vise-like and choking his throat tightly. The aid's legs were initially flat on the ground, pointing forward from his attacker, but immediately started kicking violently. With frantic, spasmodic, bent-knee kicks, the recruit's resistance ebbed into futility. He released his grip and ordered the shaken, gasping, red-faced recruit to stand up.

"Alright,___listen up!___When I give the word you recruits standing in the back row will place your arms around the throats of the recruit in front of you.___You will repeat what I have demonstrated and when you do it you will do it for real!___You will pull inward to choke your target.___Those being choked must hold on for the appropriate amount of seconds to pass before you start to black out.___You will clap your hands together at that point and your attacker will release his hold.___Do understand your instructions?"

"Sir, yes Sir!" we bellowed.

"Do not let me catch anyone clapping early,___because I know how long it takes, and if you panic I'll know.___If I catch any of you pulling that crap___I'll give you a personal lesson.___Do you read me?" he said with sinister grin, translating to 'please do it, so that I can legally choke your little scum-bag ass!'.

"Sir, yes Sir!"

The first group had several recruits start coughing severely, but overall the lesson was going as instructed. The three DIs were extremely attentive to every action we undertook in this physical lesson. I was alarmed at how close I came to blacking-out, only to be released as I clapped my hands, and with a huge intake of oxygen, rebounded.

When I demonstrated the naked stranglehold on my designated enemy soldier, I was amazed at how powerless he was to escape my vise-like grip around his neck. The poor recruit thrashed about like a fish out of the water.

"When you do this in a combat situation,__remember not to let go until the target is dead.___You will know he is dead, because he forgot to clap," Staff Sergeant Louis said with a hugh grin on his face. "If he does clap,__you might be choking one of your own Marines in the dark,__but don't stop until he's dead, just in case you do have an enemy soldier,___because the Marine you let go will definitely kill your sorry ass for what you almost did!" he stated while wearing that sarcastic grin again.

We spent the next hour at close-order drill and then double-timed back to the Confidence Course. Once more we stood behind the small barrier surrounding the pugil stick combat arena, only today it would be a different training problem. One opponent would have a pugil stick, while the other would only wear padded gloves, much like a boxer would wear. While we prepared to train, a vehicle arrived and several recruits were called out of training and rode off in it. An undertow of sorts had noticeably developed in the personality of our platoon due to these disturbing interruptions in our training. It was also apparent in the personal attitudes of some of the recruits who had already been called out.

Undaunted by the interruption, the DIs were really punchy this morning. Staff Sergeant Louis was running around like he had bet a month of his pay on the results of our recruits against Platoon 3073. Platoon 3072 had pretty much tied with us yesterday and 3073 had trounced 3071. So today Platoon 3073 felt like king of the hill, but they weren't as pissed-off as we were. We were hungry and when Staff Sergeant Louis came over and told us what the DIs and recruits of 3073 had said about our platoon and our mothers we were ready to kill them.

"Let the games begin," the Instructor shouted loudly. He was a sharp-featured white Marine, who looked like he was a weight lifter. "Send out the first two," he finished.

Staff Sergeant Louis had Kellerman suit-up first, probably because he had been so ferocious yesterday. We would challenge the turds from 3073 with pugil sticks first and then with gloves later. Kellerman was matched with a kid who was almost his twin, but there were no brotherly feelings here. Kellerman came out swinging his stick and his opponent, also very aggressive, came straight in and punched upwards as hard as he could, but Kellerman beat him down and backwards. The recruit came back again and wrestled Kellerman in a head-lock that yanked his helmet off. No whistle blew, even though his protective gear was off, and Kellerman obviously pissed-off, punched down with the lower end, or butt, of the pugil stick, and really drilled it into his opponents' guts. The kid fell, the whistle blew, and Staff Sergeant Louis and Sergeants Hodson and Black ran over to congratulate him. What a switch. We were allowed to shout out, jeer and hoot and grin and laugh. It was a real change in how we had been acting and feeling, up to this training exercise.

Even yesterday, when we were initially letting out our feelings of cheer, we had been much more subdued and reluctant to earn a punishment PT session for over-stepping our learned boundaries of discipline. The cheering was loud and I was reminded of crowds at football games. There were broad grins on the faces of recruits whom I had never seen smiling before, nor thought they could. I looked down the line and saw our scribe Haught shouting very loudly at one of our recruits who was battling. Sergeant Hodson stood nearby and ignored the outburst. Looking further, I saw Pikeman grinning broadly, while the House Mouse looked at him with an agreeing grin. The ever shy-looking Esculla held a slight grin and Zeigger, next to him, was staring with a very serious face. Green had a broad toothy smile, which contrasted with his dark complexion and it reminded me, for that split second, of the Cheshire Cat smile in *Alice in Wonderland.*

Kilroy, with his ever-present black glasses, had a concentration thing going, while he smiled here and there. He was apparently learning moves for his moment out there. Saunders was out there now, drilling his victim. He had a natural killer instinct and always held a calm efficient expression on his face. The whistle blew, and he added a final hard jab into his opponent's side, for sheer joy. I felt he was destined to become a good Marine, maybe even a DI.

It was becoming so comical to me, that I suddenly started thinking of appropriate songs for the actions of these recruits. I thought of

Tennessee Earnie Ford's song *Sixteen Tons*, 'If ya see me coming, better step aside,___a lot of men didn't, and a lot of men died.___One fist of iron and the other one steel,___if the right on don't get cha, then the left one will.'

My turn came, and my opponent was a white recruit about my size with a real academic face. The whistle blew, and to give the other guy credit, he came out with a plan. He started moving straight at me. I stepped to the right and turned side ways to thrust downward. He suddenly jumped hard to my left side and was trying to run around me to start punching my back. But I countered, by continuing my turn completely toward the right. Turning around like that caught him in the back with a beautiful straight in stab that propelled him forward. I kept after him and smashed down over and over, forcing him to fall flat into the dusty sand. The whistle blew and Sergeant Black came over to grab my gear. He simply looked at me and smiled.

Staff Sergeant Louis was busy heckling the senior DI of our enemy. Sergeant Hodson was busy suiting up our next gladiator. I think I heard cheering from my platoon. I'm sure the other platoon was totally silent. As we ended the first round of challenge with pugil sticks and readied ourselves to start with gloves, that green car drove up again and stopped. The two recruits who were borrowed earlier, and a captain, got out and Staff Sergeant Louis walked towards them. He saluted the captain, ordered the two recruits back into the pugil stick line and called out two more names. This time it was our House Mouse and Scribe.

What-ever this is all about, they are working overtime today. I pondered deeply. Because, up until now, they rarely talked with more than two recruits in a day.___I did have my own suspicions about what was going on.___Sergeant Wyeth was replaced suddenly with Sergeant Hodson.___Staff Sergeant Louis talking with me about my injury and driving me over to 3rd Battalion to talk with the Chief Drill Instructor.___ There were no recruits driven away before the DI replacement, but now they have talked with over half of the Platoon.___Our training was still hard and rough.___The DIs were still kicking ass when one recruit or all of us did something to warrant their ire.___The only change was that we were given three meals a day now and regular head-calls.___In addition, we now always had a drink of water at intervals.___Staff Sergeant Louis had denied head-calls, on occasion, during training periods because we had *fucked-up something.___But he never had denied them from lights out the evening before and all the next day, as Sergeant Wyeth had done.*

While I was daydreaming, we had already started our second match with Platoon 3073. We had kicked their asses with the pugil stick. Now they wanted revenge and we only had gloves with which to hang onto our bravado. The shrilly rings of the whistle blew often and even became nerve racking. These uneven matches tended to be much shorter than those where both recruits are armed with pugil sticks. Well placed and powerful punches were what we needed to beat the pugil stick. Most recruits were not boxers and many were held at bay by a swinging stick. If they were held back, they lost. If they failed to hit in the right places, they lost. A very few had over-powered their stick wielding opponents, because of their weight and height advantage. They literally swallowed the smaller recruit and spit him out, pugil stick and all.

Inevitably my turn came, and while the DIs placed my gloves on and secured them, I looked over to observe my opponent. He was over six feet tall, very black and very muscular. I could see his bright white eyes move and the coal black irises settle on me.

Shit! Let's get this over with. My mind had no other thought. Was this a taste of what going into battle would be like. We see an enemy, who appears very intimidating and we know we must fight. The option to run is not there and the instinct for survival not being fulfilled by flight must be fulfilled by combat. Fear will become a tool for our own defeat, if we let it overpower us, and our opponent will simply claim his victory. Fear can also be that catalyst to victory, because your adrenalin makes you stronger. If you keep a clear head about what you are required to do to win, the victory can be yours.

The whistle blew and my enemy advanced towards me holding his pugil stick at port arms. I had also advanced, but once there I had to contemplate what to do next. All of this thought process took a millionth of a second. Suddenly, he slashed down at me and I was barely able to jump back. As he slashed down, I jumped forward toward him and landed several punches. One connected with his helmet and the other on his shoulder. Instinct told me to jump back and as I did, he jabbed upward where I had been.

What the hell. I thought as he lunged upward. *Why not hit him in the gut.*

While he was raising his arms and exposing his stomach, I slammed two punches into that area. Reality was different from planning. One punch connected with his right elbow and the other hit his left rib cage and part of his gut. My attack cost me a butt stroke in the shoulder. While he was thrusting upward, and I was moving in to hit, he had the butt of his stick in position to kick it out and then swing it down for another slash, but I charged in. I hit him repeatedly on the back, the head and the sides. The whistle blew and I was suddenly numb with exhaustion. As the DIs took off the gloves I stood there happy that it was over. I thought about my fist-fight outside of my High School Biology classroom, and the one against the cop 'Tank', and how I was glad when they were over with, back then.

Everybody had his own luck or misfortune during their bouts. If their opponent didn't trip, then that meant they usually lost, because the stick was far more formidable. Some recruits were much bigger and stronger than their opponent and they could win by simply grabbing the stick and the recruit in one big squeeze and throw them on the ground. That was acceptable.

The DIs never lost their overt excitement. They let each bout be its own situation. If the recruit lost, the DIs on the losing side would kick dust, sneer, grumble, and in the same moment light up their eyes when they looked over at the next recruit to go out. Once seeing him, they waved and pointed to their next recruit and boasted on how he would kill the other DIs' next recruit. Meanwhile, the ADIs would suit-up those recruits and give them a pep talk. This training did take out its pound of flesh, because the pain from the punches and scrapes from the stick and pads, plus the gloves, slowly started to ache. Bruises were to appear later, but these things were no more than minor inconveniences. As the last recruits fought their bouts, it was apparent that it was a proven fact, since the first tribes of Homo sapiens, that those who used weapons always beat those with none. We left the field with a score of one to one and headed for noon chow. Staff Sergeant Louis was in a fairly good mood and started calling fancy cadence.

The chow was excellent. Because we were so beat, a pile of dog shit on a board would have been welcome. Once we had been fed, and returned to our barrack for a head call, we changed into PT gear and headed to the Circuit Course. We ran three miles and completed the full regimen of exercises. Sergeant Black ran us back over to our barrack.

As we entered the meat grinder between the 3rd Battalion barracks, I noticed three DIs, approximately five steps behind each other, chasing a recruit. The recruit ran like a scared rabbit. I watched this, as we marched towards it, so the scene was on my side, fourth squad, and I didn't have to turn my head to see the show. The recruit suddenly tripped on the rope barriers staked into the grass running along the sidewalks to keep people from walking on it. The recruit skidded face first into the grass and a split second later each DI hurled into the air and crashed into the kid's back. He was a blood puddle. His shit was stomped flat and the DIs were seen to reach arms into the air from their kneeling positions and those arms held tight fists that repeatedly rained down on the prone recruit.

He must have been a real fuck-up recruit, who ran out of his barrack, or swung on one of his DIs, that's the only thing I can think of that would piss them off that much. I figured as we marched on. *He shouldn't have joined the Corps, if he was that much of a pussy.*

FOUR

"Reveille,____reveille!____Get the hell on your feet!____Move it!" rasp the froggy voice of Staff Sergeant Louis. "Drown-proofing training is today, sweet-peas.___Going to learn the second lesson, of what being a Marine is all about."

We shit, showered and shaved in record time this morning and bolted out to form up. The morning was foggy and cool, with overcast skies. Right after eating chow the sky displayed deep charcoal-gray in some areas with light-gray clouds floating away from a deep blue sky trying hard to win the heavens this morning. By the time we had marched to the indoor swimming pool building, the sky had changed into a deep azure-blue and the fog had totally dissipated. The temperature had risen significantly and the field jackets we wore had become hot and extremely uncomfortable. When we finally reached the building, Sergeant Black ordered us to file into the door by squads and to take off our field jackets, when we got inside. Good thing he said that, because it was so damp and warm inside we would have passed-out if we were ordered to stand in here for any length of time.

"Good morning recruits!" a strong voice boomed suddenly.

"Sir, good morning sir!" we shouted back with a bit of thunder and heard an echo inside the massive pool room.

"Listen up recruits.___My name is Sergeant Neidig.___My assistants are Corporal Getz and Lance Corporal Decker.___We are your instructors in drown-proofing training.___As you are aware, the United States Marine Corps is an amphibious combat force, and as such, you are going to be in the water more than most sailors would be.___Amphibious landings are often the only way for Marines to enter onto hostile land masses.___Sometimes the ships or landing craft you are assigned to are hit by torpedoes, aircraft attacks or Moby Dick and can sink.___As such, you will suddenly find yourselves in the ocean with combat gear on and,___if not properly trained not to panic,___you will drown.___I guarantee it.___Our job is to train you in the proper procedures to remain alive for long periods of time, while in the ocean waters with no life preserver on,___waiting for possible rescue.___While you are in the initial phase of losing the deck under your feet, you should first try not to panic, and second, get out of all of your gear and boots immediately.___This training will demonstrate how you will remain afloat once you have prepared yourselves for the long period of endurance.___In other words, we will let you start with your boots, belts and socks off.___It is much easier to take them off while on dry land than to try taking them off in the water.___Believe me."

Man___this looks like a real challenge. I thought with much apprehension.

"For those of you who have lost so much weight, while here on the island, that your trousers will fall off without your belt, there are sections of rope available for you skinny-asses to secure your trousers.___If you pay attention to my instructions there will be no accidents.___If you don't pay attention,___or if you pull a stupid panic episode,___you may be an accident waiting for my big foot to kick your stupid ass.___If you cannot swim raise your hand now.___No fucking around if you can't swim,___or if you are a poor swimmer,___raise your hand," he finished his speech and looked around for the response.

There were six hands in the air and Lance Corporal Decker called them out of formation. They were led over to another area to start a swimming training session. They would receive their instruction, while we participated in classroom instruction by the pool.

"You pay attention recruits.___Our first period of instruction will be artificial respiration and after that you will learn other life-saving methods and techniques.___Before you engage the actual survival swimming, you will be given a swimming test to see if there are more than six recruits who can't swim.___Got it?" he croaked and eyed us with a knowing look that there were more then six.

"Sir, yes sir," we bellowed and I realized that these two were real DIs. No sooner had I realized that when I saw their gear hanging on pegs with campaign hats over the uniforms.

Sergeant Neidig was a tall muscular white man with a close-cut Third Phase style hair cut. His hair was black and his features were rock-like. His facial features appeared to have been chiseled from rock, displaying sharp angles and deep crevices. Corporal Getz was a shorter man of about five foot seven and he had a wrestler's build. His face was Germanic and his hair was blond and also cut in a Third Phase style cut. Lance Corporal Decker was a slim, medium height youthful Marine with a calm face under brown hair, slightly longer than the other two. He reminded me of the studious type I used to see in High School. He was not a DI, but he was a Swimming Instructor.

Maybe I appeared to others as one of those studious types myself. I figured and started thinking about my mother, the girls and wondered if that cock-sucker Houston had been bothering them. Suddenly, I felt a dark cloud in my mind and how much I would like to be home to protect them. *I'd like to kill that bastard if I ever saw him again.* I envisioned, as Sergeant Neidig spoke about artificial respiration. I became very angry and it grew worse. I felt like leaving and getting home. My mind would not leave the subject. This thought was always in a subconscious holding pattern, but today it rankled me so bad that I felt I had to do something about it. I started wondering where Staff Sergeant Rogers was and if I could talk to him. Just as suddenly as this anger cloud passed through my brain, I dropped it and the absurd idea of Staff Sergeant Rogers helping me now. I started paying attention to Sergeant Neidigs' instructions. I knew I could not do anything at all to help my family. *Fuck it!___*I thought bitterly. *Sir, this recruit is all fucked-up in the head sir!* I admonished myself big time, because I knew I would end up in a hurt-locker if I even started to try to do something now. It was better to stick with my program here and see if I can find a way out of this sub-basement in hell.

We endured a simulation of artificial respiration and thank God we didn't have to practice on each other. I figured a guy had better really be croaking before I got any motivation to help him that way.

Staff Sergeant Louis, Sergeant Black and Sergeant Hodson were now in swimming trunks and sweatshirts like the other instructors. The instructors, like every teacher on the Island to date, had a whistle hanging around their necks. The building was part cinder block and part corrugated metal. The pool, extremely large, had a white painted rim with a step, approximately eight inches below the concrete deck area. Life preserver rings had been placed at intervals along this white step.

Along the cinder block wall was a small metal table with a metal folding chair. Here and there along the walls were a few more folding chairs. The corrugated metal wall had translucent panels between the two by four frame structures, which allowed light through, but blocked direct sunlight. Unlike stud walls with two by fours every sixteen inches, this wall was probably twenty feet high with the boards spaced six feet apart with a section three feet apart and another six foot space, a three-foot space and another six-foot space, a three-foot space and so on, along the wall. At the level of six feet off the ground, between the six-foot sections, were the translucent four by six foot corrugated plastic sheets. These also ran all along the wall separated by the three-foot solid spaces. Along the pool at one end were various metal pole or pipe structures and a diving board several feet off the deck. The pipe structures were ten to twelve feet or higher. What the purpose for those structures was, I never would find out.

Sergeant Neidig waited for us to line up in three rows. We were wearing utilities and had taken off our shoes, socks, belts and covers. This was our swim test and as he blew his whistle three recruits would dive into the water and swim across the pool. I found this to be more difficult than I had expected. The utilities were bulky and acted to drag our bodies back a ways, while we strived to go forward.

Across on the other side of the vast pool were the first six recruits, who had stated they could not swim, learning how to swim. As our group went through this initial test, the group on the other side was increased by four more. Next we were given instructions on how to remain afloat for long periods without a life preserver. This required taking a deep breath and putting our head into the water, which made our backs float up to the surface leaving the lower torso and legs hanging straight down. Our arms were stretched straight out to our side like wings. Our body will float in this position, the instructor guaranteed us. When our need for oxygen gets to be alarming, we were instructed to calmly pull in our arms bringing our hands to the front of our chest, while at the same time raising the right knee up towards our chest. Once this procedure was completed, kick down with the raised leg, release the last air in the lungs, spread the arms out straight to the side and raise our head out of the water for a large gulp of air and then put our head back underwater.

"This process is repeated for as long as your energy or endurance holds out.___Hopefully,___you will be rescued before your strength ebbs," Sergeant Neidig explained and followed with how this procedure is not supposed to exert the body rapidly and thus reserve strength.

Sergeant Neidig gave this instruction on the concrete deck of the pool. He demonstrated the body position including leg and arm positions and told us to enter the water without forgetting what he said or else he would let our stupid asses drown if we did.

Okay,___that's a pretty simple thing to do,___according to Neidig. I pursed my lips skeptically.

The water was really very warm, so entering it was not a shock. The fact is that a person who has a soaking wet set of clothes on and is told to jump back into cold water is going to have a near heart attack if not actually have one. But this water was so warm it was like a hot bath.

Nothing went smooth from the moment we were in the water. Immediately, the instructors went crazy blowing their whistles yelling and pointing. Soon Staff Sergeant Louis, Sergeant Black, Sergeant Hodson got into the act. Their froggy reprimands and threats against our cluster-fuck display were building up like a kettle boiling. To their eyes we must have appeared as a bunch of bobbing heads in a screwed-up mass, while what they were trying to achieve was a neat formation of bobbing heads in rows with enough space to stretch our arms out sideways and have clearance for the drown-proofing movements.

"Get over!___Get…!___Hey fuck-head!___Pay attention!___Not you numb-nuts,___I'm talking to fuck-head!___Keep moving the way you were going.___Ah hell!___Stop!___Stop swimming around and freeze in place!" Staff Sergeant Louis yelled at the top of his voice. "Now watch for who is pointing for you specifically to go in a specific direction.___Everyone else will remain where you are until directed to move.___Do it!"

"Sir, yes Sir," we yelled in unison amidst the very loud sounds of water splashing.

"That's it.___Go that way.___Hello!___You should know your left by now.___Stop there!" Sergeant Neidig was heard shouting at some recruits. During this wet fiasco I was not exempt from the confusion. I had started to swim out to the far side of the pool thinking I should fall into approximately where I stood in the forth squad. The only problem was, which direction the front and how many other recruits were thinking the same way.

"Shipman!___Get yer ass back over here!" Sergeant Black ordered loudly.

I guess I was going the wrong way after all. I frowned in thought and swam back toward the cluster-fuck of recruits.

By the time we were in the proper positions we were worn out from all the swimming around trying to get organized. I was really pissed now, because I got yelled at for being where I am now. In other words, I was really in the right place at first.

Whistles blew and Sergeant Neidig yelled for our attention.

"You will now take a deep breath.___Assume the proper position and maintain a motionless posture for as long as you possibly can.___ Do not panic.___When your air is gone, follow the procedures to kick up and re-fill your lungs.___Then resume the floating position. Should you start to sink, repeat the procedure and get more air.___If this does not work, leave the pool or we will assist you if there is any problem.___Try not to panic."

With nearly seventy recruits in the pool, six sets of eyes should be able to spot any body in trouble,___or because nearly seventy recruits were in the pool, it would be hard to see any recruits in trouble. I thought with sarcasm.

Wet clothing weighs a person down to begin with, but to have to float in the water like a cork, while being weighed down, was definitely an experience. It was difficult at first to simply trust your body's ability to be buoyant. The first time I kicked down for air, I felt I was too far underwater to raise my head for a gulp of air, without getting a mouthful of water. Surprising me totally, I easily cleared the water, replenished my oxygen and settled back in the water to float like a cork. I continued this procedure for the next hour. As the time went by there were the occasional recruits who, no longer able to endure this, swam to the edge of the pool.

I imagine this is how it is in real life, where those guys who swam away to get out would have been the first to drown. I thought grimly and kicked for another gulp of air.

This was a very relaxing exercise. There was no fatigue here and I felt I could do this for a long time. The brain is the biggest problem it would seem, because humans tend to panic in an alien environment. The brain knows there is a very real threat of drowning and panic usually wins the coin toss against calm logic. Logic, in this case, would mean remembering our training, trusting there are rescue operations underway and survival is dependent on our ability to stay afloat long enough to allow them time to get to us.

It would be a damn shame to hang in there for hours and no hope of rescue was there. Maybe those who drowned first were lucky. Those of us who tried to survive would only die tired. But if I hang in there, maybe a miracle rescue would be my reward, so I think I'd keep trying. My mind floated in and out of many such ponderous and noble thoughts as I bobbed up and down in that pool. While I had my head underwater it was peaceful with the whistles and other surface noises so subdued as to be unrecognizable white sounds.

I recalled reading about the USS Indianapolis being torpedoed by a Japanese submarine during World War II. The survivors of that ship had floated for days, but they had life vests. More tragically was that hundreds of them had been eaten by sharks. *At least we don't have sharks,___so that balances it between us and them.* I decided lamely.

When Sergeant Neidig prepared us for this training activity, he had presented us a lecture on drowning. As my body floated and the noise was filtered, there was little else to do except think. Since the featured event was drown-proofing, my thoughts kept going back to drowning. I imagined how it would be and filled in the book language of Sergeant Neidig.

Our transport ship got torpedoed and many of our unit were suddenly blasted overboard. While the ship listed, the rest of us jumped into the water and we were the lucky ones, because those blown overboard were *mostly severely injured or drowned while in shock. After hours of floating with no life preserver vest and using the technique we were taught today, many began to tire and sink. The water temperature was about fifty-two degrees and we lasted approximately four hours.___It was at least a valiant effort to survive.___In the end, we only died tired.* I chewed on this bit of futility and continued listening to the contorted underwater sounds of thrashing recruits.

The crash of the above surface noise hit my ears like an artillery barrage as I raised my head for oxygen and just as abruptly the silence resumed when I submerged my head again. *My insides started to feel like I was in a vise, with my sternum and spinal column exploding in unimaginable pain. I wanted to gulp air and my chest heaved and jerked in spasms as I fought to keep my remaining air and not drink in the water. My chest pains started to disappear as I fell into unconsciousness and then I became fish food.* I resumed my morbid scenario and picked up where I started to descend into the depths.

Either way, according to Sergeant Neidig, a Marine will drown. His lecture kept floating around in my brain just as I floated around in his pool. He further explained that if we fell into unconsciousness before our lungs filled with water, it was due to something called a laryngo spasm, which blocks the airway from water getting in and flooding the lungs. If that happened and you were underwater, you would die from oxygen deprivation. If water did get into the lungs, it would wash away something called alveolar, a fine hair like substance coating the inside of the lungs, which traps oxygen that is absorbed into the bloodstream. If water washes away this surfactant and the pulmonary artery, which moves blood from the heart to the lungs, begins to constrict, ventricular fibrillation results. This causes the heart to function irregularly, moving no oxygen, because the lungs aren't getting oxygen to the heart, everything starts to shut down, leaving only the brain alive. The central nervous system doesn't know what's happening to the body, but does know that sufficient oxygen is not reaching the brain. The central nervous system signals breathe, breathe, breathe, but the response by the body does not get the oxygen, the brain's electrical activity dies and ceases to function and you become food for the fish. He was certainly being lugubrious about our potential deaths by drowning, as he lectured.

FIVE

It had been a more strenuous day than any on the Island so far. My legs felt rubbery and my arms felt like heavy useless weights hanging, or rather dangling, by my side. If I felt like this, I know the rest of the platoon also felt like wet rag dolls. It was also strange how hunger was overwhelmingly the winner of the many pains I now felt from the unusually high drain of strength I endured today. My stomach felt empty and growled. I could hear lots of growling stomachs, while we stood in formation, waiting for one of our DIs to show up and just get us to a mess hall.

It is always when something is not desired or welcomed on this Island that we get it in full force. Sergeant Black, daily becoming a real hard-ass DI, decided to run our wet asses back to our barrack. It was December and even on Parris Island it was not very warm. Even with our field jackets on, we were shivering. I know that if we had marched all the way back to 3rd Battalion we would have been stiff and moving like the robots in the Buck Rogers movies.

The run was pure torture, but it did two things. It kept us warmer and got us inside the barrack faster. The rashes from our wet utilities had taken their toll. Some recruits returned from the quick shower, we were allowed, walking like saddle-sore-cowboys.

"You who have rashes,___put powder on the affected areas and clean up the mess on the deck afterwards.___Got it!" Staff Sergeant Louis said in a concerned voice. There were many of us in obvious pain from rashes.

"Sir, aye-aye Sir," we bellowed the response gratefully. Grateful, because we knew we would make a great mess, if we used our foot powder without the approval of our DI, and would suffer mightily for it. We would have made such a mess he would have probably skipped chow, only to square away our squad bay. His permission to mess up the deck did allow us to squelch our burning pain and offer relief. So we doused powder all over our raw flesh and tried hard not to spill it all over the deck.

Foot powder is still powder and my inner thighs were chafed raw from the rubbing action of wet trousers against the skin as we ran, so I'm damn glad he let us do this. I thought as we applied the powder. Otherwise, had we marched back, we would be rash-free, but blue with cold.

There was quite a mess on the deck now anyway, from what

looked like every recruit needing relief. We had an interesting clean-up ahead.

"Come on girls!___Move yer asses!___Enough powdering already.___You maggots seem to be a tad delicate for recruits close to graduation.___I can arrange something to toughen you up.___Now get yer asses out into formation.___Move it!" Sergeant Black hollered from the entrance of the passageway next to the DI shack.

He was aggravated about something, but it was not due to our platoon performance or any individual screw-up today. In the past Sergeant Black's forbearance was the opposite of Sergeant Wyeth's amorphous hate of stupid recruits. Sergeant Wyeth had been obtuse when recruits were being injured around him or when we suffered through one of his meaner days and had large numbers of recruits dropping to the dirt in total exhaustion. Sergeant Wyeth's respect for the Marine Corps uniform, tradition and flag was one thing and the choler in his heart was something else. His ability to be a totally competent DI was marred by his irascible behavior. We did not miss him, but now Sergeant Black was starting to stick the knife into our hides, more and more each day, since Sergeant Hodson had arrived.

Sergeant Hodson shared no similarities with Staff Sergeant Rogers, from Platoon 3063, as the good DI. We noticed quickly how Sergeant Hodson liked to nail us individually and not so much as a total platoon. Staff Sergeant Louis liked to get us as a platoon by ordering mass bouts of punishment PT. I could never just walk up and talk to any one of these DIs, because they might just ignore my concerns and punish me. Staff Sergeant Rogers listened to a recruit. He would judge the problem, weigh it and issue orders to help, or not. But we would still bust our asses for him and we still feared and respected his authority.

These DIs did not do that. Instead they punched through the problems around them and demanded full compliance from us recruits. No whiners, no problems is how they liked it. Perhaps platoons that allowed the recruits to talk about a problem showed weaknesses according to that line of thinking. While Sergeant Wyeth was around, there had developed an enmity between him and the recruits, but on the Island there is no escape possible for recruits.

We were warm in our field jacket and dry utilities, as we stood in formation on this unusually cold day for this Island. The temperature had dropped very suddenly. It was in the forties now, with a gusting wind. We had a good chance to compare our condition, since a short time ago we were out here soaking wet. We were not going to stay this comfortable for much longer than a few minutes after chow. The chow was devoured and we all really wanted more this time. We could have been served pure dog shit with a side order of buzzard guts and we would have fought for a second helping. Sergeant Black came out with Sergeant Hodson and gave us a wry smile as he spoke.

"Promises sweet-peas,___promises!___I haven't forgotten my promise to give you girls something to toughen up yer hides.___ Well,___I think a run through the bayonet course and a three-mile run after that might just start to meet that need.___What do you say 3074?"

"Sir, yes Sir," we screamed the lie loudly. Maybe we were dressed warm and dry and maybe we had a hot meal, but our bodies were still sore lumps of rubber.

We marched over to our barrack, ran in, grabbed our rifles and bayonets and fell out to the constant yells of the DIs. Staff Sergeant Louis had now joined in the fray. In the eagerness of the trio of DIs to get over to the course, we ran double time at port arms.

They told us that the effective use of the bayonet in combat depends ninety percent on sheer aggressiveness. They also promoted how this training engenders an aggressive spirit of power and confidence in each one of us warriors. Most of all, we were taught to be exceedingly aggressive, while developing an ever-advancing fighting style. In other words attack, attack, attack, kill, kill, kill and keep going forward until you arrive back where you started, or until there are no enemy soldiers left alive.

The course had a series of four by four posts set up. One set was a single post with a rear support beam and a forward angled two by four with a padded end jutting up to our elbow height. The angled post was set up with pivot ability and there was also a padded head on top of the main post. This soldier was to be attacked by several approaches. One method was to block the upward angled post with the butt of the rifle and then slash down on the head. The other was to shove the angled post to the left with our upper thigh, while butt-stroking the head from right to left.

Another row of four by four posts were set up about a man's height with the posts approximately two feet apart with two back slanted support posts, holding it firm. There was a car tire mounted at the top of each of these, between the two posts. This enemy soldier was aggressively slashed and butt stroked with direct butt bashing or upward butt strokes. The direct butt stroke was simply holding the butt straight out next to our head and driving it forward to strike the enemies head very hard.

The next obstacle was constructed from metal pipes in the shape of a T with slanted two-foot support pipes welded between the post pipe and top pipe on each side for support. These posts stood twelve feet high and the top bar projected out ten feet to each side, from which hung a rope supporting a stuffed canvas sea bag. The bag had another rope running from the bottom to an anchor peg in the ground so the bag had very little play. The bottom of the bag was even with the sternum of a recruit on some bags and on other bags lower, around the crotch. There were five such poles supporting ten bags. We formed up into two lines in front of the first two bags and waited to attack. The other soldiers we attacked were struck by our M-14 rifles. However, for this attack, we were provided pugil sticks to avoid the ripping damage our rifles would give the canvas bags.

"You will run through this obstacle of five enemy soldiers and aggressively jab, slash, butt-stroke and smash the shit out of them!___ Got it turds?" one of the instructors croaked from behind our lines. The whistle blew and the first two recruits attacked.

Aahhhooorrraah!___Aahoorrah!___Ahoorrah!___Puff___puff,___ ahorah,___puff. Was all I could hear for the next half hour, as we further abused our very tired and already extremely hammered muscles.

As Sergeant Black had promised, we concluded our training day with a three-mile run in formation, at port arms. Where we got the energy to accomplish that feat, was a mystery to us. My mind was numb by the time we approached the two-mile mark. Each footfall was made out of habit and not through any mental order. My arms were locked in the half-cocked position of carrying the M-14 at port arms, with my hands glued tightly around the piece. The sounds of seventy-one recruits' footfalls pounding on the sand and gravel of the running track, was all that my mind heard. It had become very loud and the rhythm was what drove my feet to keep going forward. Sergeant Black had initiated running songs as we ran, but I don't remember what they were a few minutes before, as I concentrated on the one he was starting now.

"One mile____no good," he croaked.
"One mile____no good," we repeated weakly.
"Two mile____no good," he shouted louder.
"Two mile____no good," we responded louder.
"Three mile____um good," he shot back.
"Three mile____um good," we lied loudly.
"Here we go____all the way," he continued.
"Here we go____all the way," we shouted with a feeling of 'let's just get this shit over with and get to our bunks'. That was all my mind could think.

We had adjusted to being here on the Island and had even gotten used to being driven by the drill instructors, but what we thought was physically hard before was nothing compared to now. They had cranked up training ten more notches and it felt like being on a merry-go-round spinning at a hundred miles an hour. If you couldn't hang on during the spin, you'd whip off and drop in a heap on the ground. If a recruit dropped out here, he would resemble a sweaty, dirty, smelly, disheveled, broken heap.

Step,____step,____step,____"I know a girl who lives in the hills,____she won't do it but her sister will." *Step,____step,____step.*

"Ah-aah-men,____ah-aah-men,____amen,____amen.____Let me hear you now!" he boomed.

"Ah-aah-men,____ah-aah-men,____amen,____amen." Over and over we sang these songs and stomped along.

What's that? I wondered as I saw a couple of cars pull over and park next to the Circuit Course. *Those are a bunch of civilians.____Yeh.____Two women, three teenaged girls and three small boys.____What the hell are they doing out here on a cold day?* I decided that I did not really give a shit.

At that moment I felt I had developed a second wind. It was probably a feeling of not letting the platoon down. From my spot in the middle of the fourth squad I could stare straight ahead and see the cars and people. Sergeant Black was well aware of them. Look alive, 3074.____Tighten up the formation.____Get those rifles aligned," he growled.

"I don"t know,____but I been told," he started.
"I don't know,____but I been told," we repeated.

"Eskimo pussy is mighty cold," he continued.

"Eskimo pussy is mighty cold," we obliged and he dived right into another song.

"If I die on the Russian front," Black boomed louder than usual.

"If I die on the Russian front," we shouted equally loud.

"Box me up with some Russian cunt," Black continued with a smile.

"Box me up with some Russian cunt," we followed knowing full well the absolute shock it made on the two women and the humor it provided the three teenaged girls.

The three boys were confused about what we said, but showed great big wide eyes while watching our massive green train go chugging by. The other three platoons in our series were also pounding down the running track and what choice songs they sang as they passed the visitors was only a humorous guess for me. The two women were probably trying to get as far away as possible, while the six children were begging to stay and watch.

I had always guessed that the DIs did not enjoy civilians and officers in the training area. Both invariably proved to be bad news. Sergeant Black and the other DIs knew that the civilian women would not report any wrong doings, because they might have to repeat what they heard and they would probably defer to the vulgarity and not repeat it, even if they remembered how the song went.

Only due to the sure passing of time, the training regimen for this day had finally reached a required pause. Our rag-tired platoon finally returned to our barrack, grateful for a good hot meal and the nearing hour to hit the rack. We had wiped ourselves out. We were rubber recruits, merely walking by instinct and making our way through the remaining evening time by habit. There was no conscious effort on my part to do more than clean my rifle, clean my brass, shine my boots, square away my footlocker and bunk area.

Mail call resulted in a rich catch for me. I received a letter from my brother in Germany, my brother in Maryland and my mother. The trouble was that I was too tired to read and yet dying to read them. However, what all of us seemed more intent on accomplishing was to turn our raw, pore-pitted leather boots, garrison cap visor and dress shoes into mirrors. This was accomplished through tedious periods of spit shinning. We were allowed to light the shoe polish, which after a few seconds would melt and then we doused it by placing the lid over the flame. Next we took a tee shirt, worn out during training, which could now be used as a rag, and twisted it tightly around our index finger. The shoe polish lid was filled with water and we opened our bottle of alcohol and placed the cloth-wrapped finger over the open bottle and tilted it enough to wet the cloth. We then dipped our cloth-wrapped finger into the water and then the melted shoe polish, and began a vigorous series of small rotations over and over, until the pores filled and the leather took on a smooth mirror-like shine. This was very time consuming, so reading our mail would have to wait.

I ended up placing the letters in my footlocker for a blind-grab tomorrow evening. That way I would not be playing favorites and I would enjoy the mail much more, but only if I have enough energy tomorrow and a moment of free time to read then.

As it turned out, the rest of our week was heaped with more of the same madness and I barely had energy left for anything beyond preparation for the next day. There were no more drop-outs in our platoon and we drilled and marched and performed as a well-oiled machine.

Each night, when lights were secured, not a soul had a problem falling asleep. Those poor guys who drew fire watch duty would have to sleep harder then the rest of us to equal the required rest for the following days' demands. The sound of taps echoed across the night sky of Parris Island and we of Platoon 3074 knew we had earned the right to rest and not even a DI could deprive us of what we sweat and bled so hard to receive. They got their pound of flesh and were content to go away and let us be, for a few hours at least.

CHAPTER 12
REWARDS

ONE

It's Monday, January 5th, 1970. I thought in amazement, while I stood on the white line in front of my bunk. My mind was sharp and clear, even though Sergeant Black had hit the lights only a few seconds ago to wake us up. *Here it is, a new year, and last Wednesday night we had made absolutely no mention of it being New Year's Eve or Thursday as New Year's day.___Shit, shit, shit!___I could have graduated a long time ago if it weren't for my damned foot.___But today is better than New Year's day.___It's the first day of our last week on this fucking island.* My mind flashed these angry and good thoughts simultaneously.

"Congratulations girls!___You have made it this far___and if you don't fuck-up,___you might even graduate next Monday.___This is command Inspection week___and it will be loaded with all kinds of new experiences and shit like that," Sergeant Black announced in a comical voice. "Port side, make a head call!" he ordered, while heading into the DI shack.

A very short time later we were dressed in PT gear and marching to chow. All we really had to do was put on our sweat shirts. It was very dark and very cold this morning since the temperature had dropped to 27 degrees during the night, but we were motivated to play any new games to get this show on the road. Arriving at the mess hall with bloused trousers, spit-shinned boots, starched utility covers, third phase hair cuts and displaying a red guidon, we had forever dispensed with the ass-hole-to-belly-button line-up and like a robot, step through the mess hall serving line. Our tray was still placed in front of our faces vertically until arriving at the beginning of the chow serving line, where we dropped our trays, and as the servers piled on chow we side-stepped. The only difference now was that we stared into the eyes of the recruits serving instead of straight ahead as was previously mandatory. We intimidated them this way and dared them to play any games with us, like double portioning a mess sergeant's particularly foul meal-special.

When we formed up again after morning chow, I was pleased with the appearance of our platoon in formation as I approached it. We were tanned and muscular with the faded well washed or 'salty' utilities and topped-off with starched covers. Delahey stood there with our red guidon flapping and I now saw our platoon as that platoon I saw so long ago, which had marched by my first platoon over by the supply buildings, as we were being issued our 7-82 gear. We all stood within our bubbles of fear watching that salty professional-looking formation of senior recruits march by. We thought two things at once. One was that we were not even close to being like that platoon and may never make it that far and the other thought was that is where we will be someday, if we pay attention and keep up.

The other important hurdle to jump was our ability to make it through the unimaginable psychological obstacle course the DIs liked to place before us. Those of us still standing in the formation of Platoon 3074 had met that physical and psychological challenge and with the exception of some unforeseen mishap, would graduate next Monday.

The faces before me no longer showed the shocked, glazed-eyed expressions we wore for so many weeks after these DIs literally ripped the civilian soul out of each of us and replaced it with a never-say-die, cocky, strict, warrior who knows that blood makes the grass grow green and his mission is to kill, kill, kill. We had nevertheless evolved from whatever our pasts were, into members of an elite culture. We did not think of ourselves as mindless robots. Our new values were honor, commitment and courage. A robot had no heart and sole and therefore could not live those values. The Marine Corps was accused of being military-minded robots by the liberal civilians and Jane Fonda was their reigning Queen of mindless rhetoric.

The sun was rising, revealing a blue sky promising a warm day. It will be in the lower fifties today, warm enough to enjoy a good workout on the Confidence Course. That is exactly what we were going to do and Sergeant Black was eagerly getting us underway.

"Platoon,___aah___ten,___huat!___Riat,___huah!___Foart,___huah!" Sergeant Black barked in a very crisp voice. We snapped to attention, made the right face and stepped off. Apparently, we were in such good formation that he didn't even want to have us dress right. But, as soon as we stepped off toward the parade deck, he ordered us to double-time, making it even more unnecessary to be in perfect formation. As a rule, we kept a tight platoon formation when we ran, but some recruits had longer legs and some had shorter legs, so there was an ever so slight wavering in the formation as a result.

"Road guards,___out!" Sergeant Black boomed.

We crossed the road still without stopping and entered the Circuit Course running track. The din of noises sounded like someone was slowly turning up the radio volume as we neared the first and second phase platoons as they ran or were spread across the grass engaged in exercising.

"Amen,___Delahey!" Sergeant Black ordered.

Our guide started the running song and we chorused back. As we sounded off, another platoon came near our platoon singing about a girl who wouldn't do it, but her sister will, while our song interjected the word amen at exactly the right moment. This was too much and everybody had smiles or unrestrained guffaws over it, even the DIs.

We broke away from our three-mile-run and scattered across the grass to begin exercising. Staff Sergeant Louis and Sergeant Hodson appeared as we began doing side-straddle-hops. After a while, our Physical Training Instructor ordered us to start doing bends and thrusts. At that moment I saw our three DIs walk away a distance and stop to confer about something. Each time I came up to a standing position to start a new bend and thrust, I could see them still in conversation and also what was happening beyond them.

It was painfully obvious that the platoon I was observing beyond them was in their First Phase and perhaps in their first days on the Island. They were spread out doing PT, but a hand full of them were not up to speed and one of their DIs was exploding on them with vengeful indignation. It was like looking at snap shots, because each time I came up from the ground position to the standing position I saw that DI doing so many different things, but I did not see him complete the total movements. What I observed, while I did bends and thrusts, looked more like: He had kicked one recruit in the ass *drop,___ thrust,___up,* screamed in the face of another with his campaign hat touching the recruits forehead *drop,___thrust,___up,* that recruit was bent over clutching his stomach *drop,___thrust,___up,* he grabbed another recruit and slammed him into the ground by kicking his feet out from under his body, while grabbing him by the sweatshirt neck and back of the trouser belt and pulling him sideways in an arc over and down *drop,___thrust,___up,* our drill instructors were ignoring the scene *drop,___thrust,___up,* another platoon from that series was running by and several recruits fell out *drop,___thrust,___up,* their DI was bending over one pointing his arm straight out toward the passing platoon, with the first finger extended *drop,___thrust,___up,* he kicked the other prone recruit in the side *drop,___thrust,___up,* that recruit in the fetal position, the other running toward his platoon a distance ahead, and judging from his speed, he had more of the juice he tried to tell his DI he didn't have.

I had absolutely no feeling in my heart, nor any thought in my mind, for the things I was seeing. This was Parris Island and that was normal training. We in Platoon 3074 had endured that when we thought we couldn't make it. Once a DI got a hold on our lazy, civilian, candy-asses, we proved to ourselves that we could make it. So what was the fuss? As long as they didn't kill you, there was a good chance you would make it.

Those recruits will go through their culling process and eventually get their head and ass wired together. I concluded and promptly forgot about them.

TWO

It had been 23 degrees last night and this morning welcomed us with an icy cold temperature, hard cold rain pouring down on our ponchos making drum-beating sounds. The sun would not come out today. It was 0600 hours. We had just finished morning chow, and due to the weather, nobody appeared to be in a good mood. Staff Sergeant Louis had ordered us to get our rifles and bayonets, because we would be tested indoors today on our various rifle skills and stand a junk on the bunk inspection by the battalion brass. Since it was raining so hard we slung our rifle barrels down with the sling over our shoulders and dropped our ponchos over them.

We marched over to one of the support buildings, which surrounded the 3rd Battalion parade deck, and entered, dripping puddles of water on the deck.

"You three!___Grab mops and buckets from the storage closet and swab the deck dry!" Sergeant Hodson ordered three recruits from the first squad, who had entered first. It would be much better to have a dry deck to work from than a sloppy, slick, wet deck. He had ordered the rest of us to take off our ponchos and shake them to dislodge the majority of water onto the deck and then fold and secure our ponchos. Since the deck was being swabbed, it seemed the best way about it. A short time later we stood with dry utilities and held our dry rifles with the butt on the deck and the barrel along the seam of our trousers.

"Platoon!___Aah___ten___huat!" bellowed Staff Sergeant Louis as a group of officers entered the room. They had been in an inner room waiting for our arrival. There was a lieutenant colonel, a major, two lieutenants and a major general.

"Fall into a tight group!___Those in front sit down," the general said. "Good morning,___I am Major General Oscar F. Peatross and I command this Recruit Depot." He had thinning hair on top of a round face supporting eye-glasses, which did not hide serious piercing eyes. He had a straight mouth and jowls beginning to form on his fifty three year old jaw. There were six rows of ribbons on his blouse. "I am here to meet you young recruits and have a chat about your tour of duty in the Marine Corps."

"Sir, good morning Sir!" we shouted in a strong unified clipped voice and moved into a crescent formation around him.

"You recruits are about to graduate from boot camp in a few days.___ You have demonstrated that you have the necessary tenacity and skill to become a member of the United States Marine Corps.___Furthermore, you have demonstrated the proper loyalty and motivation to claim that title.___Your training here has tested you for those skills and traits and you have endured the most difficult and the most demanding physical and mental challenges that a military establishment of the United States can demand.___As for that,___this is the hardest damn training in the world,___and you recruits have earned the right to wear the eagle, globe and anchor of the Corps.___Good work recruits.___ Although this is a few days early,___I have to say it now,___because you have earned it and sometimes schedules preclude me from being where I wish to be on a given day.___What I mean, is that I will be out of the area on your graduation day," he said, speaking softly, yet with a hard edge in his voice, as he stared at each of us with those warrior eyes. He had been around, and he was speaking to us like a proud father would have, as he continued. "When you men graduate, you will be sent to ITR,___which is the Infantry Training Regiment, located at Camp Geiger, North Carolina.___That is right next door to the Second Marine Division at Camp Lejeune,___the east coast Marine Corps Amphibious Base.___Upon completion of ITR some of you will be sent to a variety of different schools for further training in that particular work.___Many more of you will be transferred to the School of Infantry and will have extended training in that skill at Camp Geiger, before you are transferred to the Fleet.___There is still a bitter war being fought in Vietnam and some of you will be sent there.___It is my hope and my expectation that the drill instructors here and the training NCOs at Camp Geiger will provide only the best training, so that you men can come home from Vietnam once your tours of duty have been completed.___Once again, let me congratulate you on a fine showing as a team.___Good day recruits," he concluded.

"Sir, good day Sir!" our voices, now charged with pride, bellowed louder then ever before. However, my mind couldn't help but think about what he said about Vietnam.

It seems to me that no matter how skilled we are, or our training has made us, as a fighting man we can get killed by snipers, mortars, hand grenades, booby traps or massive infantry fire.___So what the General was really saying was that for a sounder mind and self assurance, due to our feeling of how well we were trained, we can go to war and survive everything else that could happen to us except the above.___But, I think he was just not saying all of that, because it was negative stuff to say in a pep-talk. I thought soberly.

The General walked back into the room he had come from, put on his raincoat and yelled 'good luck' to us as he went out the front door. We thanked him courteously and started to form up along port and starboard sides.

I had been thinking about what the General had said. *Would I be* *infantry and would I go to Vietnam?__How many of us would end up in jobs that were needed in Vietnam by the 1st and 3rd Marine Divisions?__ What we were doing here had now a sudden reality to it.__There was a war and we could go there and we could get wounded or killed.__This possibility was so real now that attention to our lessons, what we had been trained to do so far, had increased by epic proportions.__It had become survival food and I felt I could eat a lot more of it right now.___Going into a country at war was scary shit.__So once we graduate from this sub-basement in hell called Parris Island, we land in the fires of another hell called Vietnam.__ What a deal!__But, I joined the Marine Corps to be a warrior and that would be expected of us.__It would be a real drag to be a warrior with no war to go to.__Becoming a Marine and serving, in case needed for a war, but never having to go to one, is just as honorable.__Earning the title of Marine is really what counts.*

The remaining group of officers, along with a master sergeant and a gunnery sergeant, divided us into two teams and worked their way down our ranks shouting orders and asking questions.

"Right shoulder,___huah!"

"What's you fifth General Order?"

"Butt-stroke and slash,___huah!"

"Who is the Commandant of the Marine Corps?"

"Where was the U.S. Marine Corps created?"

"Port,___harms!"

"What first aid treatment is used for a compound fracture?"

"What's your serial number?"

"Where does the dress blue red trouser strip come from?____What battle and why?"

"What happened at the Chosin Reservoir?"

"Where is Mount Suribachi?"

"What's the weight of the M-14 rifle?"

"What is the mission of the Corps?"

"What is your first General Order?"

"What is the Officer sword called and why was it adopted by the Corps?"

"Rifle salute,___huah!"

"Present,___harms!"

"Bayonet jab,___huah!"

"Inspection,___harms!"

"What's your eighth General Order?"
"What do you do for a puncture wound?"

They had asked their questions or ordered a maneuver with the rifle and we responded with the proper answers and movements. They were content to declare our platoon ready in all these respects and Staff Sergeant Louis and his assistants were beaming with pride. Hell, they were so happy with these results that we were ordered to go back to our barrack and prepare field marching packs. With feverish speed we constructed our packs, rolled our blankets into our shelter halves and as soon as the last strap had been fastened we formed up to await the drill instructors.

Our platoon looked like we were ready for disembarkation from a transport ship, where you go over the side on the cargo nets, down to the landing crafts. We wore helmets, packs, and web gear and held our rifles along our right legs. Our web gear included a full canteen, first aid pouch, two M-14 magazine pouches with magazines and a bayonet. We also wore a field jacket and combat boots. There would be no lightening of loads today. Today we could only wish we were allowed to wear sweat shirts and sneakers. There had been many runs on this Island with boots, rifles and helmets, but those runs were without this added gear on. Today we wore everything and we would be observed for grading this time. This was the Physical Readiness Test.

"Platoon!___Aah___ten___huat!" Staff Sergeant Louis growled. "Riat shoulder,___harms!___Riat___huah!___Foart,___huah!___Let,___riat,___let,___riatah,___let.___Pooart,___harms!___Double time,___huah!___Let,___let,___let.___Column let,___huah!" he croaked and our platoon swerved left behind the barracks and headed over to the Confidence Course.

The track was muddy and the rain continued to pour down heavily. We literally plowed through the slush and each foot fall created an explosive geyser of slurry to splash up and onto our legs. We looked and sounded like a train careening through a storm chugging along on its tracks oblivious to the conditions around it.

Splash,___splash,___splash,___humph,___aah,___humph,___splash___umph___splash. Our individual sounds of effort, much muffled by the weather, were none-the-less heard by our tightly packed group. This was a different feeling in strain today. We had run with our rifles before, but not with full packs, web gear and helmets. The water absorbed by our field jackets and 7-82 gear had added significant weight to our bodies and the rain added misery to our breathing. Each gasp for air inhaled a spray of water.

Nobody dropped out of this run. We were all determined now that we were in reach of that coveted title of Marine. We would leave our DIs behind us on this day. All three of our instructors were in this run, albeit not with all the gear we carried. They opted not to wear their campaign hats in this rainy weather. Staff Sergeant Louis was in his glory this morning. His entire attitude flashed like a neon sign.

"You turds want to be Marines?___Well show me what you got!" he shouted, combining the weather and his personal hard-assed approach to this run. Whatever was ahead was still a mystery.

After we passed the two-mile marker things shifted into a questionable state. Most of our tight formation had unraveled to some degree. Efforts were constantly underway to shore up the ranks, which ended up causing accordion-like surges in each squad. These surges were not military in their execution. An observer would think we were pushing and pulling at each other to get ahead of the recruit ahead of each of us. Once someone lagged behind for even a footfall the others behind him had to adjust their stride to compensate. It was the exact same effect observed on a highway when a car suddenly slows down or drives slower than the rest of the vehicles around it.

"Keep the ranks even.___Don't slack up ladies.___You're falling into your old civilian habits girls.___Let's get the old head-and-ass wired together and do this right!" Staff Sergeant Louis screamed over the sounds of mud and water being pounded by over three score of recruits along with the clanking of our gear and occasional muttered oaths. He was really only shouting to personally feel that he was still in charge.

The morning was very dark with so much mist and fog, that it seemed like nighttime. The shapes of Sergeants Hodson, Louis and Black appeared like ghosts in the mist. They moved like wraiths herding our formation as if on a cattle drive in hell. They were the head demons with whips and cat-o-nine tails sneering with great broad grins as they lashed out at us with hatred and loathing. However, in reality they were probably happy as clams about our performance as a platoon, but they very rarely showed their true feelings towards us. If there were a chance to get into our shit, they would choose that over a compliment. Even the two days of merriment during Pugil Sticks training, where we were not chastised for shouting and jeering, had been snipped immediately afterwards. We went right back to the platoon silence we had trained in through-out boot camp.

The three-mile-run finally ended, and we continued at route step over to the ropes. We had climbed the ropes so many times we wore calluses from those ropes. This time we had to ascend to the top with the weight of our rifles slung over our backs along with our packs, deuce gear and helmets. It promised to be an ugly ordeal. These were straight ropes, without knots, and they were wet.

"Get yer asses up there!" Was the most often heard order during this hell-morning. Many times our hands gripped and slid lower, due to the extreme wetness of the ropes. Our feet were constantly grasping for a better locking hold, but the damn rain made the ropes feel as slippery as ice. We slid down a foot for every two feet gained.

I grasped the rope high up to get my normal start so I could lock on with my feet faster. My hands slid down right away, but I tried again and the weight kept pulling me down faster than I had expected. The DI voices were blasting away with obscenities in the wet foggy mist, which only fell on already determined ears. We would have been trying just as hard without their added insults, or their presence.

"Damn it!___Get your asses up the fucking ropes!___Do it again!___Stop fucking around and get up the ropes!___Stop slacking and start climbing!___Move!___Move!___Move it girls,___we don't have all day!___So get your lazy asses up the fucking ropes!" They each bellowed repeatedly.

We didn't care what they said at this point. All we personally really wanted to do was beat the fucking ropes. The DIs could go to hell, for what it was worth, because we wanted to win. Our training had brought us to this level of will-power. We would have attempted this climb in this weather without any DI within miles.

On my third jump up to grab higher I got a purchase and scrambled to get my feet locked onto the rope. I did it and immediately with angry will-power, clawed my way up to the top. The awkwardness and weight of the gear was nearly overwhelming. There were rope climbing towers around the area with knots every few feet, which would have made it easy to climb, but according to the general, our leaders would not think of denying us the finest training available.

"That's it girls.___You can do it!___Great!___Keep it up!___No slacking!" Staff Sergeant Louis boomed in the downpour. The platoon was knocking the crap out of this obstacle now and I wondered what the next one would be. The next one was not long in waiting.

Orders to form up, followed by a mad-dash across the road and onto the Obstacle Course where they introduced us to an exceptionally difficult obstacle. Looking down from above onto this ball-crusher, it appeared like an ugly metal and wood picket fence lying at a slanted horizontal angle. The construction of this obstacle started at the high end, about ten feet high, with three big telephone poles spaced approximately fifteen feet apart, which supported a metal pipe layed across that thirty-foot span. There were sixteen-foot long metal pipes spaced at five-foot intervals, secured over that metal support pipe, at ninety-degree angles, that ran downward horizontally, toward a lower center wooden support rack. The center wood rack was about eight-feet off the ground. From the center support area, going downward the same design as the metal pipes, was a series of sixteen-inch in diameter, by sixteen-feet long, tree poles. These tree poles rested, at the end, over a third support frame about five-feet off the ground. Three-feet forward of the end support rack were three more large telephone poles sticking out of the ground, approximately ten-feet high. Over the top of that structure was a ten-inch in diameter wooden pole, secured to it. Shorter copies of these structures followed at intervals, sicking out of the ground about four-feet, were constructed as hurdles.

The object of this challenge was to step up onto a low one foot high support pole or step, and then spring upwards to grasp the metal pipes. Once a pipe was firmly grasp, we had to swing our body upwards and lock our feet around the pipe and, while upside-down, crawl downward and maneuver our bodies to get on top of the pipe, before we tried to stand upright at the wooden center frame. Next, we side-stepped down the wooden poles with our arms stretched out like birds for stability, toward the lower wooden end frame. If you waiver here, even slightly, on the second half of this obstacle, you will hopefully fall between the wooden poles and crash hard into the ground below. If not, a trip to sickbay will be your next stop, while you talk like a girl explaining what happened. Once we were standing on the lower end support frame, we jumped high and forward to catch our stomach on top of the ten-foot tall structure, with the ten-inch in diameter horizontal pole, and slid over it to hang for a split-second with our hands, facing backwards, holding on to the pole, and dropped to the ground. The series of hurtles were next.

This damned rain was a curse on this obstacle. It was a ball-busting bitch on a dry day and a difficult obstacle to engage normally. But today, in this heavy downpour, we suffered with the added weight of our gear, wet uniforms, wet metal pipes, slippery-wet smoothly-worn wood poles and the foggy darkness.

Figuring out how to best negotiate this obstacle was one part of the equation. The wrath of a DI was the other part of that equation. This required loosening the rifle strap and slinging it over the back of the pack with the strap running from the left side of our neck down under our right arm pit the same way we did over at the ropes. The rain kept coming down in torrents, creating frustration, but we kept going up in angry determination, not letting it stop us.

After that exhilarating ordeal ended, we engaged the hurdles. This obstacle was a long series of horizontal waist high telephone poles placed on top of shorter support poles. We battered our guts and hips as we slammed into each pole and climbed over them. Our helmets slipped around our heads to some degree and our rifles slammed into our heads, as we negotiated the obstacles. Staff Sergeant Louis had us run straight over to the ladder, the tallest obstacle on the Island, and go up and over it.

Thank God we have helmets on, or we would surely knock ourselves out. I fumed as the back of my helmet was banged again and again.

The Ladder was next. Sergeant Black stated that if anyone failed to make it over the top we would all climb it again. Sergeant Hodson waited on the other side and shouted encouraging slander at each of us as we descended. Staff Sergeant Louis, as always, straddled the top and screamed at us for the sake of screaming, while rain cascaded off of his body.

We engaged many more of the obstacles and surprisingly, none of us failed to meet our challenges this day, and also no recruit had to go to sickbay either.

Bloodied, muddied, bruised, blistered and soaked to the bone, our herd formed up and headed for the barn. A shower and change into dry utilities was helpful, but not a cure for what ailed us today. The rash we had started on our drown-proofing day was nothing compared to our raw flesh now and powder hardly helped at all today. Endure it. The very first order, after showers, was to start cleaning our rifles. A quick rifle inspection followed, and then we marched off for chow. The food was hardy and very welcome, after such a physically demanding morning. It was fried chicken, corn, mashed potatoes with gravy and two buttered rolls.

THREE

After chow, we were told to get our junk on the bunk and await an inspection. Junk on the bunk required laying out all of our 7-82 gear on our bunks in a specified arrangement. This particular arrangement included our M-14 rifle along with the rest.

We started our task and it really took some thinking. The spacing between each item was not approximate, but specific and a ruler was required. At the foot of the bunk we placed the haversack to the right and pack to the left. Across from these we laid the cartridge belt straps, called doggie straps. Next we placed the ponchos, folded into a rectangle slightly larger than a 10 x 12 notebook, to the left and to its side was the shelter half, folded to equal size. Across these we placed the cartridge belt, all scrubbed with toothpaste and the eyelets and holders freshly painted with EmNu. After that, centered in the middle of the bunk, from left to right, came the canteen cup, knife, spoon, fork, mess tin and canteen. Behind that toward the head of the bunk we prepared the canteen canvas cover, five tent pegs, three tent poles, one tent line and the bayonet. There are much more elaborate junk on the bunk preparations, which even have dress uniforms laid out. Thank God we didn't have to do that one. The picture in the Manual looked very complicated. Besides, we did not have dress uniforms yet anyway.

Staff Sergeant Louis and Sergeant's Black and Hodson conducted a precise preliminary inspection and were not shy about cursing at any offenders. At least nothing was said about our still-wet 7-82 gear. It was showing signs of drying though.

"You son of a bitch!___What are you trying to do,___huh?___Are you a Communist insurgent trying to sabotage this platoon?___Are you tired and want some rest before you can perform properly?___ Huh sweet-pea?___Now do it right___shit-for-brains!" Sergeant Black boomed from some bunk area close to the other end of our squad bay.

Just as he finished his words, he tore that bunk apart. "You have five fucking minutes to get this bunk squared away numb-nuts!___So if your squad leader wants to keep his job he should help you get it squared away.___Squad leader!___Get your ass over here.___Now!" Sergeant Black was very annoyed for some reason, because he had very rarely gone this deep into a corrective action. Perhaps it was only inspection jitters.

There were other minor eruptions throughout the squad bay from the other two drill instructors, which more or less confirmed they were only nervous about our forthcoming inspection. And, as if the time we were using-up, to get it perfect, were precious grains of sand slipping between the two spheres of the hourglass, our time was now up. The hatch opened and a group of officers and NCOs came into the squad bay. We were called to attention immediately by Sergeant Hodson.

"Platoon!___Aah___ten___huat!" he screamed loudly.

The squad bay lapsed into immediate silence and our drill instructors assumed a strange stance. They were proud and displayed a type of daring posture. They were saying, come and look, but all you will see is finely honed Marines here and I dare you to say otherwise.

The inspection team walked up to Staff Sergeant Louis and exchanged a few silent words. There were six of them and one of our drill instructors accompanied each two of the team members during the inspection. They disbursed and at one end of the squad bay on the starboard side Sergeant Black walked down the rank with a 1st lieutenant and a staff sergeant. On the port side Staff Sergeant Louis was with a lieutenant colonel and a master sergeant. Sergeant Hodson went with a 2nd lieutenant and a gunnery sergeant. This team waited for the starboard side inspection team to move along a bit before they started inspecting the junk on the bunk. The other two teams looked behind the recruits as they approached, but were more attentive to our persons. We were checked for posture or military bearing, boots and brass maintenance, utilities, shaving and overall rack appearance. They looked at the uniformity of our towels, rifle, and clothing bag arrangement.

The inspection was a success. There were no comments, no eruptive displays such as those before the inspection and the team started for the hatch. The lieutenant colonel turned and stated to Staff Sergeant Louis for our hearing.

"Outstanding preparedness and appearance,___Staff Sergeant Louis," he complimented, turned and left. Our instructors were quietly absorbing this compliment just as they had done this morning and when we kicked-ass on our full combat gear run through the Obstacle Course and ropes during the Physical Readiness Test.

As if the moment had been a light switched on, it was immediately switched off. Two officers walked into the squad bay. They must have passed the others on the stairwell. Staff Sergeant Louis turned a shade of gray. From my position I could catch the scene in the outer picture of my peripheral vision. The major spoke to him and a few moments later four recruit names were called and those four were ordered to go with the officers. The scribe, the mouse, Cassavetti, and Delahey were the ones called.

With a surly mask worn on his face, Staff Sergeant Louis marched out of the barrack and was seen no more this day. Sergeant Hodson had also departed and would return for the night duty. Sergeant Black was showing signs of being content with the fact that after two inspections, both being a test as well, and a full combat gear Physical Readiness Test having been completed today and having passed with flyer colors, there was absolutely nothing more to demand this day. He ordered us to secure our 7-82 gear and prepare our dress shoes and brass for the final inspection in dress greens.

We eagerly engaged in this ritual of graduation preparedness, which was part of every graduating platoon's tradition going all the way back to the first U.S. Marine Corps training. In addition to the dress shoes, we had the barracks cover brim to shine. Both of these items of our uniform had been issued as raw leather.

There was a serious effort to learn how to tie our field scarves. We stood along the white lines and practiced as a platoon.

The dress green uniform belt had a rectangle brass buckle, which like all the other brass, had that damned protective lacquer coating applied at the factory. That coating seemed to have been contracted by the Marine Corps to take the entire time in boot camp to remove. Our mission was to remove every bit of this stubborn material and then polish the brass underneath to a brilliant shine using up our entire tin of Brasso coated cotton balls to accomplish this tedious task.

While we were engaged in this work, Sergeant Black mellowed and sat at the desk placed at the end of the squad bay in front of the passageway. The passageway divided the DI shack to the left and the head to the right. There was also a storage room further up to the left, which is where we stowed all cleaning gear and additional training items.

Sergeant Black barked one of the most welcome orders we had heard on the Island to date. "Listen up!___I want you to fall into single file and line up in front of my desk." At that moment the four recruits who had been called away earlier, had returned. "Get in line!" Sergeant Black told them with no malice in his voice.

We were each provided our National Defense Ribbon box and our Shooting Badges. There were some who only got a Shooting Badge. Because they were on Reserve Duty they were not authorized to wear the ribbon. Some who had not qualified at the range only received the ribbon.

Christ, if any reservist was unqualified at the range he would get nothing for his uniform.___Hell, Louis would have thrown a scum-bag like that outta the Corps. I thought with a humorous grin.

When I returned to my bunk I was eager to look at what I had received. I first admired the intricate design of the Sharp Shooter Badge, which displayed the eagle, globe and anchor on the center of the cross. The Sharp Shooter Badge had a design similar to the old German Cross. Supporting the cross by a chain link at each end was a silver bar stating the words 'Sharp Shooter'.

The blue box, Sergeant Black gave us, contained a ribbon and a medal. He told us that the ribbon is used to denote the wearing of a medal without the actual metal disk being displayed. In other words, the ribbon indicates that the wearer was awarded that medal. In some cases there is no medal for a ribbon award, such as a Meritorious Unit Citation ribbon. If the medal is worn, it also has a large ribbon attached to it. This ribbon is a long piece of material exactly like the bar shaped ribbon. Anyone can look at a Serviceman's ribbons and know which medals they were awarded.

I sat on my foot locker and examined my blue box. It was cardboard, approximately four and one half inches long, two inches wide and a half-inch thick. A white label displayed Medal Set, National Defense Service, Regular Size, along with a Federal Stock Number. The ribbon was all red with a quarter inch strip of the yellow down the center and to each side of the yellow were thin lines in red, white, blue, white, and then the broad outer red bands. The medal was colored gold with the words National Defense over the top and an American eagle perched atop or rather grasping a sword by its talons. The eagle looked just like the one on a quarter. The backside displayed a large shield in the flag bars running north to south, but the area where stars would normally be was void. There was a Romanesque wreath running around the bottom half of the medal. It was beautiful to us recruits, because it was a symbol of the military that we were hoping would soon welcome us into its ranks. The reservists were of two minds. There were a few who probably regretted not going active, but personal events warranted it and there were the others who thought we could have all the medals and glory. As for them, 'No thank you, I'm staying out of this war, as long as I'm not part of the 26th or 27th Marines, along with their artillery and support elements, who did go to Vietnam'.

Whatever their reasons, it was their own business. They had run the gauntlet in this sub-basement of hell like the rest of us and could damned well do what they wished to do with their title of Marine.

FOUR

It had rained all throughTuesday and Wednesday, creating cold days, but the nights had suddenly gotten wickedly cold. The night temperatures had steadily declined from 27 degrees last Sunday to 16 degrees on Thursday. The days were also colder with 39 degrees on Thursday. Today, Friday, 9 January 1970, it is 33 degrees outside and our leaders had decided to hold our final inspection inside the barrack. Since we were wearing dress greens it would be too cold to stand around without also wearing our horse blankets. Then that would cover our greens and all they could inspect would be the coats and black buttons.

We had started this final training morning eagerly rushing to chow and back to the barn to start preparing our uniforms for inspection. This moment held a rush of emotion for each of us, because if a recruit is doing this, he knows he is graduating and finally leaving the Island. The proverbial light at the end of the long dark tunnel of training is finally visible.

Our pressed uniforms had arrived yesterday evening and this morning we were putting our uniform on in its entirety for the first time. We had practiced tying our field scarves all week when we had a spare fifteen minutes here and there. There is a prescribed knot for the field scarf and a Windsor knot is not one of them. The length of the field scarf had to be just so, right above the belt, but not touching it. Over the past week we tied and re-tied the damned thing until it was something we could do in the dark.

"Platoon!____Aah____ten____huat!" Staff Sergeant Louis called for our attention. We scrambled to the white lines and stood at attention. "Starting with port side, you will each file by my desk.___Ready,___ huah!" he finished, and we started filing up to him. He handed each of us a plastic covered cardboard square which held three lapel-sized and one garrison cover-sized black Marine Corps emblem. It was our moment of achievement. Once he had handed us that emblem we knew we were finally Marines. The only man in our platoon to receive a second plastic covered set, which was in gold for dress blues, was Waulker. Waulker was a very mature and slightly older recruit, who had quietly pulled his own ass through training and somehow achieved the highest score on the rifle range, thus receiving the only Expert Marksman Badge in the platoon. Because of that day of sheer anger, on the part of Staff Sergeant Louis, he was eager to recognize those who pulled off high scores, so Waulker made Private First Class. A total of six were awarded PFC and it goes as practically a Marine Corps standing order that the guide and squad leaders make the promotion, but there are always exceptions to that rule.

"You are no longer hogs, turds, maggots, shit-heads, pukes, scumbags, or girls.____As of this moment you have earned the title of Marine.___Congratulations___Marines!" Staff Sergeant Louis shouted in a deep froggy voice and we responded with a simple grunt.
"Aahhooorrraah!" we chorused. It was singularly the most emotional response we had ever yelled on the Island.

"You will hear the brass welcome you to the Corps and proclaiming that you are Marines next Monday___but,___as your Senior Drill Instructor,__I feel it is only proper for me to say it first.___Also,___in case some of you are wondering why we did not go to Elliot's Beach,___it was due to the weather mostly,___but you were given a hearty workout in full combat gear on the day of the Skills Assessment Inspection and Physical Readyness Test.____The only part about Elliot's Beach you missed, was the long walk there in full combat gear and a chance to sleep in a tent.___Over the past days you were marched all over the

Jack Shipman

Regimental area.___That was added to the daily training to give you the average march workout for the distance to the beach," he finished his explanation. We were not used to hearing him simply talk to us and to offer any type of general explanations. Perhaps I alone had heard him come close to that, on that day he drove me to 3rd Battalion. It was interesting to know why we did not go to Elliot's Beach and the rest, but it was even more interesting to be talked to by this, or any Marine, in a normal voice. It was more, than any other thing, a sense of acceptance and an admission into the Corps' brotherhood, of course except for the rank differences.

"Let's get squared away for the final inspection.___It is scheduled in fifteen minutes." Staff Sergeant Louis said with no sense of worry. We were all dressed anyway. The longest one thing I had to do, involving any amout of time, was to properly place my ribbon and Sharp Shooter Badge over the left pocket of my dress greens and attaching the Marine Corps emblems. That took a total of three minutes. Tying my field scarf went surprisingly easy. We were all standing on the white line holding our M-14 rifles along our right legs and waited.

Right on schedule the hatch opened and the command to stand at attention was barked by Sergeant Black. A lieutenant colonel, a major, a gunnery sergeant, and three drill instructors entered. All four men were over six feet tall and all wore three or more rows of ribbons denoting tours of duty in Vietnam. The officer and the gunnery sergeant each wore piss cutters, which they continued to wear, but they were not wearing a cartridge belt. They were not under arms. The two DIs and our DIs wore cartridge belts and the rest of us held M-14 rifles, so we were all under arms. I supposed it looked better to keep their covers on, while the rest of us had them on at the same time. Besides, if this were outdoors, as originally planned, it would be required for them to be covered. Some of these hard-faced Marines had inspected us the other day, during junk on the bunk, and earlier on skills demonstrations.

The lieutenant colonel was named Johnson, our Battalion Commander. He had intelligent eyes, which always looked like he was assessing someone or something. His face was a no-nonsense display of straight eyebrows, large straight nose and a natural smile surrounded by a large strong jaw and chin. His smile projected confidence and self-assurance. He could easily confuse anyone stupid enough to think he was being friendly, when he was really evaluating what he observed. The major had a hawkish face with sharp features and deep-set penetrating eyes. The gunnery sergeant, wearing the piss cutter, was round-faced with high cheekbones and held his mouth in a pursed-lip decision mode, while he read a Military ID card or a dog tag from a recruit. He really reminded me of the Russian or German soldiers we often saw in movies checking the papers of civilians. There was another gunnery sergeant with the pair of DIs who had entered with the team.

The DI gunnery sergeant wore glasses and appeared more like a High School principal with a pissed-off outlook. One of the two DI sergeants was white and his head and face looked like a skull. His face was skin pulled over bone, with lips pulled tightly in thin strips. He had deeply sunken eyes and a small upturned nose. He scared the hell out of anyone dealing with him, there was no doubt. The black DI sergeant was small-featured and very intense-looking, with a small body build, and who was obviously the hard-assed DI in his platoon.

Staff Sergeant Louis walked with the colonel and the skull-faced DI sergeant. Sergeant Black walked with the piss cutter gunnery sergeant and the black DI sergeant. Sergeant Hodson walked with the major and the DI gunnery sergeant. These three teams started at different spots in our formation of port and starboard side. One of the visiting inspectors in each team, the junior one, maintained a clipboard to mark any infractions during the inspection.

They checked the length of our trousers and blouse sleeves, our piss cutter fit and distance from the bridge of our nose, which should be two fingers wide. Our ribbon and marksman badges were measured for proper placement. Brass and leather was checked for perfect shine and that absolutely no preservative varnish was left on our brass blouse buckle. We held out our military identification card and dog tags for review. Of course, our M-14 rifle was also thoroughly inspected. Faces were checked for proper shaves. They rubbed our ID cards, in reverse of our facial hair growth pattern, along our chin or cheek. They did not forget to check our field scarves, which were observed for proper knotting and length.

Since the inspection was very lengthy, we were allowed to stand at parade rest and snapped to attention when we were approached. The ever expected military history, military procedure, General Order, or Code of Conduct questions were popped at us like a machine gun, as the inspection teams moved down our ranks.

These Marines all wore very hard faces as they eye-balled us, scrutinized our appearance and tested our knowledge of their beloved Marine Corps. They acted almost like a last line of defense to stop the hoards of civilian scum-bags from entering their Corps and contaminating its ranks. If these Marines say it is all right to cross the line and join the brotherhood, then you are in body and soul, for life. Once a Marine, always a Marine, becomes a reality and is proven, over and over, many years after the uniform is finally hung, covered or protected in plastic, in the closet for eternity and the inactive or former Marine goes on reacting to all things in life as if still an active Marine.

On Monday, we tadpoles will evolve to the next level and crawl out of the primordial Parris Island tidal marshes as amphibious creatures called Marines. That is where our trip through life as Marines begins and will only change once or twice thereafter. One change will be death in combat or on active duty and the other two-stage change will be when we hang up that uniform and die later. Either way we will always be Marines until death. A lot had happened since taking our first step away from those yellow footprints.

This inspection, must have been extremely important, judging by how intense Staff Sergeant Louis' face appeared as he nervously looked over his shoulders at the other two teams and observed the colonel next to him. It was the colonel who had come to inspect me. I snapped to rigid-attention and presented port arms. He snatched my rifle out of my hands, pulled back the bolt and looked into the chamber. He looked down the barrel and inserted his thumbnail into the chamber to achieve a reflection that allowed him to see down the barrel. Any dirt, oil or lint would show right up.

Apparently, satisfied with my rifle he threw it back. I grasped it firmly by both hands and returned it to the deck along side of my right leg. He checked my ID card, and scrapped my cheek. He almost grinned, obviously knowing that peach fuzz shaves smooth every time. Next he asked a history question.

"What units wear the French Fourragere and why, where and when was it awarded?"

"Sir, the 5th and 6th Marine Regiments were awarded the French Fourragere by the French Government for bravery in action in the Belleau Woods area of France during World War I,___Sir," I cranked out in rapid-fire response. However, I did not know that Marines call them pogey ropes.

"Why did you choose the Marine Corps, son?"

My mind immediately processed the reasons into something resembling a bowl of spaghetti. I wanted to get away from home, because it had been a mixed-up shit-sandwich. I wanted to be a warrior since early childhood, but did not want to enlist in the Army or Air Force, because of the two men who had been in those branches and who were involved with my mother and fucked-up all of our lives. I wanted the Navy, because I love the ocean and ships, but they were too slow in their recruiting process, so I joined the Corps, because Master Sergeant Frank Herbert told me I'd go to the Island and get three square meals a day, lots of sun and exercise and a great looking set of uniforms, plus deployments on ships. I thought that sounded great, but the ability to leave in two weeks was the real selling point. I was in a hurry to go to hell Sir. So I gave him my response. "Sir, to be part of the world's most elite military organization___Sir!" I stated proudly."

Chew on that answer,___Sir! I thought with amusement.

Apparently he was content with me and my bull-shit answer, because I saw no entries being written by the scull-faced DI sergeant and they both moved on. Staff Sergeant Louis gave me a funny look, as if he read my mind's real answer, and then he moved on.

We passed the inspection with a handful of findings. They found mostly Irish Pennants, but overall, we were presentable enough to be called a Marine platoon.

I swear, those Irish Pennants must actually grow, 'cause every time you think you have cut them all off, they jest poke out again. I surmised with absolute belief.

We were told to fall out. All three DIs were also present. We marched over to a grassy training area next to 3rd Battalion where bleachers for training had been built. We were arranged on the bleachers by height and a photographer took our platoon picture. All three of our mentors stood in front with Delahey and the guidon. The order to get back into utilities was given and, after a head call, we fell out for chow.

After chow another memorable moment was about to get underway.

"Prepare your buckets and 7-82 gear for return to the supply shack.___Get it done now!" Staff Sergeant Louis growled.

It was another confirmation that we were finally done here on the Island. The act of packing and shedding our equipment was like a shaft of sunlight being discovered on a storm cloud day.

"Sir, aye-aye Sir," we screamed in a very loud voice. All of the guys felt the same way I did, judging by that response. Within fifteen minutes we were marching toward the Supply Building. Our footfalls were as one, our faces and chins pointed straight out. We were also turning in our beloved rifles and our formation appeared heavily laden, with all of our gear, to be marching so accurately.

A series of recruits in their first days of training were at attention along the road by the Supply Building. They watched our platoon march by in awe.

I heard one of their drill instructors growl, "Do you pusillanimous pieces of shit see that platoon?___Well they had what it takes to become Marines.___They graduate on Monday girls.___Look hard!___That is a reality one million miles ahead of you undeserving momma's boys," he stated sternly in a froggy voice.

I smiled inwardly and we all heard that praise and puffed out our chests just a little more and stepped with firmer stomps. The DIs all noticed it and they also smiled with pride, because they had achieved another miracle, the transformation of globs of civilian shit into Marines.

It left me feeling strange when I turned over my rifle. Somehow the bonding between the recruit and his rifle became both a physical and spiritual thing during boot camp. Our feelings on that subject must have been known by our drill instructors.

"Don't worry.___In a few days you will all be issued an M-16 rifle and you'll learn how to use the fucking Mickey Mouse *Mattie Mattel* piece of shit!" Staff Sergeant Louis said with disgust. "When Marines were assaulting up hill 888 in Nam,___their brand new M-16s kept jamming.___There was no cover,___as it had all been blown away.___While the Marines tried to deal with their stoppages,___Charlie was busy wasting them.___So be dammed careful with the M-16," he finished his warning comment with a baleful look on his face.

I felt it was odd for him to condem a rifle we would use and possibly use in Vietnam. Maybe I would learn why someday.

Our march back to the barrack left us really light-footed and we showed off our stuff. Staff Sergeant Louis called every marching

Yellow Footprints

command he could remember and we performed all of them with perfect skill. Pavlov would have been proud.

"Why couldn't you people do this while we had drill competition?" he croaked.

I'm sure each of us wanted to yell back, 'Because you screwed-up, not us, and forgot to close ranks, while we passed in review'. I remembered the moment with a mental grin. But he knew all of that, because he too was grinning, while he stood by the road as we marched past him. *Yeh, we had marched so damned well that cold windy day and had he given the order to close ranks, before we passed in review, I'm positive we would have won the Drill Compitition Streamer.*

Even though we were near graduation it was still boot camp and still the Marine Corps. We changed into PT gear and headed for the Circuit Course for an invigorating session of exercises.

Later, when we had showered and evening chow call had been completed, we stood along the white lines reading our Red Guide Books on General Military Subjects, the same way we had been doing it from the first day on the Island, when we got the word.

"Listen up!___I want you all to form-up in front of me.___Sit on the deck.___You are about to hear your MOS," Staff Sergeant Louis said in an exceptionally calm and friendly manner. He started calling out Motor Transportation to at least ten recruits, with another ten for Artillery. A few were going to Tanks and some to Amtracks. Next, he called a handful for Administration and Supply.

Suddenly, he called my name and I perked up. Shipman!___0311,___ infantry,___you're going to be a grunt!___Goin' to the Nam!___Gonna' die!" I was shocked at how he announced it. He was being sarcastic about how the infantry was being used as bait in Vietnam to get the enemy to hit them so that artillery and air strikes could blow Charlie away. I did not know all of this yet. All I knew was that he said I was Infantry and I was going to die. I was the first 0311 he had called out. He started calling out about thirty more names and told them they were all Infantry and that they were going to Vietnam and were going to die. Suddenly, I felt the shock of what he had said to me begin to fade. I no longer felt privileged to be the only one, but the reality of Louis' omen was still there for all of us. Perhaps Staff Sergeant Louis had done the math and knew that regardless of what a U.S. serviceman stationed in Vietnam did, they had statistically a one-in-seven chance of getting killed or wounded. Since it was an infantryman's war, he felt positive that infantrymen were going there in far greater numbers than the other occupations and they had a one-in-three chance.

I now had much to think about over the weekend. My mind tried to conjure up images of me in the infantry and how I would fare. Invariably, I did not like what I saw most of the time, but just as often I reminded myself that I was doing the main job of the Marine Corps by being a grunt. I should consider myself lucky that I get to be a member of the Fleet Marines. All Marines were trained infantrymen and those who went to other skills schools are often required to become instant grunts during conflicts. The benefit of actually being a full-time grunt is that we are trained constantly, and thus, even more capable in that job.

We spent Saturday outside on the meat grinder marching, or on the Circuit Course running, and then more PT. It was another cold day, with temperatures only warming to 36 degrees. The temperature had dropped to 11 and 12 degrees during the past two nights, which left the sandy soil of Parris Island hard as a rock. The bright side was that the sand fleas had retreated and we suffered a slight degree less without their bites. Instead, we bruised our bodies, inflicting more pain than the sand fleas could deliver, while smashing our bodies on the frozen earth.

FIVE

It had started to warm up some on Sunday, with the temperature reaching 40 degrees, however the clouds grouped together and a gray overcast, which threatened a downpour, remained all day and night. This Sunday morning was to be our last Sunday on the Island. We attended church services and were acknowledged during the mass as the graduating Marines. The priest gave us a special blessing and wished us luck. A special prayer was given for those who may have to go to Vietnam.

Back at the barn, we were able to spend our entire day preparing our gear. Our graduation dress uniform was squared away and hung on our racks. We polished our shoes, boots and brass and started packing our sea bags. It was amazing how much gear we had accumulated on the Island. There was a prescribed procedure for folding and stuffing the many uniforms, skivvies, towels and any other gear we owned, into our sea bags. One set of utilities and boots were also kept out.

The rest of Sunday was relaxed, to allow for letter writing, and any other quiet pursuit of interest. Sergeant Hodson had the duty and spent time talking about the different occupations members of our platoon had received. He told us where some of their training schools should be. When he mentioned the grunts, half of our platoon stopped what we were doing and we listened very intently.

"All of you new Marines will be going to Camp Geiger, North Carolina where you will go through the Basic Infantry Training School.___They call it ITR, for Infantry Training Regiment.___Camp Lejeune is right next to Geiger and that is the largest Amphibious Fleet Marine Corps base on the East Coast.___And, the other one for the West Coast is Camp Pendleton,___near Los Angeles California.___ Anyway,___all of you will go through Basic Infantry Training at Camp Geiger, but those of you with infantry MOSs will continue training there in all sorts of tactical training.___Youre next stage in training will be the Advanced Infantry Training School. There's even a Viet Cong village mock-up for search and destroy training,___while those of you, with other types of MOSs, will depart for other schools around the country.___But believe me,___those of you with a grunt MOS will know you're in the Corps when you get there!" Sergeant Hodson said and concluded his remarks on Camp Geiger. He started talking about Motor Transportation, which was his MOS, Embassy and Sea Duty and a variety of other interesting tidbits of Marine lore, duty stations and liberty ports. I kept wondering why he emphasized the word 'know' when he mentioned us grunts.

The day went by like some surrealistic nightmare. We had suffered physical trials, endured psychological trauma, survived beatings and were denied food and water at times. Our bodies were now tight springs, very tense and always anticipating a reaction to a barked order or a sudden challenge. However, all day long there was no punishment PT, no yelling and no intimidation. We went to sleep eagerly, knowing that this would speed up the time to our final goal on this Island. I was assigned to fire watch from 0400 to 0500 and found myself eagerly counting down the last minutes to lights-on.

SIX

Monday morning wake-up call came into the conscious mind of the sleeping platoon without the familiar clatter of shit-can lids, barking orders, racks being pushed and individuals being personally singled out for special haranguing. Instead a simple order was given.

"Hit it!" Sergeant Black said in a clipped, but not unkindly voice.

We counted off, ran the course through the head and fell out to a very wet morning. The temperature was climbing out of a freezing night temperature of 18 degrees to reach 51 degrees later today. The forecast called for rain through the entire day. We trudged off to chow knowing our big day was not to be as we had dreamed it would be. All recruits go through boot camp being told about their graduation day in formation on the big parade deck with the band playing, the flags fluttering in the wind and the graduate's families watching them perform their marching skills.

Sergeant Black had already informed us we would march over to the base theater for an indoor graduation ceremony. Regardless of the disappointment of an outdoor ceremony, the excitement was building up inside each of us, with a concentration of explosive force equivalent to a bomb. However, the training we had endured had produced a Marine so complete that to the observer we were sullen-faced and the entire squad bay was only rustles and scuffs, and nothing more, upon hearing the news.

We busied ourselves with final spit-shine touch-ups and started putting on our graduation dress uniforms. When all of us were finished dressing we stood on line and Sergeant Hodson and Sergeant Black inspected us for any, God forbid, Irish pennants or other numb-nut goofs.

Staff Sergeant Louis entered the squad bay with a slight grin on his lips. He walked slowly down the squad bay and looked at each of us in turn. He was taking his last real look, I guess, to see us as products of his labor. When he got to Waulker, he smiled broadly at the new Private First Class. Waulker was looking splendid in his dress blues, with his gold and red chevrons on each arm and his expert marksman badge with its wreath and crossed rifles, gleaming on the dark blue blouse background.

We stood along the white line, at attention, awaiting our orders. Our facial expression had definitely transformed from the earlier training days. The faces across from me were no longer displaying shock, fear, uncertainty, or sadness, as they had so many times before. All of these faces appeared that way, to each of us, during training. Nonetheless, our new facial expression shone with relief, fatigue, joy and impatience. We wanted to get to our next step in the Marine Corps.

The rain had stopped for now and the clouds threatened more at any time. The decision had been made to march. We would not bring raincoats, so it was get over there fast. We formed up outside and snapped to attention, while impatiently waiting for our trio of DIs. Staff Sergeant Louis shouted the commands.

"Dress riat___dress!___Ready,___huah!___Riat,___huah!___Foart,___huah!" We executed all of these moves with precision making only one sound. Near us, we heard the sounds of the other three platoons in our series. They looked sharp and as a series we stepped off. All the guides moved over to the front of the forth squads of their platoons, their guidons and streamers fluttering, displaying the trophies of each platoon's victories. Each platoon's drill instructors shouted commands and it sounded like music to my ears. All the training we had undergone accumulated to produce this moment. My only regret was not continuing this fine moment by marching on the parade deck. We had held that dream all through training, but regrettably any graduation will suffice, to conclude this ordeal.

"Let,___let,___yer let, riat, let.___Road guards out!" Our commands sounded out loud in the morning chill. "Let,___let,___let, riat, let.___road guards out!" The sounds of the other DIs were heard. And the sounds continued further back in our train of graduates. "Let,___let,___let, hiat, let." I heard these froggy sounds continuously all through the series, and with varying pronunciations, as we neared the theater. When we passed through the 2nd Battalion area there were platoons along the road in formation. They wore running gear on their feet and sweatshirts. They were preparing for PT. Their eyes were wide as they watched our formations march past. I knew their thoughts, because I remember how I felt when I saw such things. These sights always inspired recruits to make it all the way. They couldn't wait until they wore the dress uniform and marched to their graduation ceremony.

If a recruit was a fuck-up, who had no balls to stick it out, but could have, they would not feel any of this motivation or be inspired to have it for themselves. They would get a Bad Conduct, General or

Dishonorable Discharge and brag to everyone out there, who would listen, that the Crotch sucked, the Corps is no good, etcetera. Also, over the years, some would tell stories in some bar, that they had been in the Corps and hit their DI or say other such pure bull-shit! If you didn't graduate and got kicked out, you were never in the Corps. Of course, years later, when they finally matured, if at all, they would regret not sticking it out and participating in the brotherhood of Marines. They would forever be non-hackers and continue to be that way in everything they did in life. I had met recruits like that from the Casual Platoon, when I was in the Medical platoon.

Those who did not have the physical strength and those who had a medical problem and were discharged were not non-hackers and they too would long to be a part of this Corps, which had been elusive to them, but at least they tried.

The base theater was in the Regimental Headquarters area and it took quite a lot of marching to get there from the 3rd Battalion area. It had been a real gamble to get to the theater between cloudbursts. No sooner had we entered the doors, there came a downpour. Dress greens were made of wool and smelled awful when wet. The creases disappear, leaving stove pipes for trouser legs and blouse sleeves. Our beautiful crisply creased uniforms would turn into Joe-Shit-the-rag-man outfits and there was no way in hell a Marine battalion would graduate looking like that. Our DIs were probably thanking God at this moment, for not screwing-up our uniforms and the graduation ceremonies.

We were ushered to our seating area inside the theater. Our platoon was seated to the left side facing the stage. The front two rows of the right side of the theater were reserved for the dress blue and all other private first class recipients. A few officers were also seated there. Our Private First Class, Waulker, was the only one of the four dress blue graduates who had a Rifle Expert Badge. Three of the private first class recipients in dress greens, from the sister platoons, also had one. The other three dress blue winners had rifle sharp shooter badges.

Apparently the award of expert shooter isn't the main reason for winning the dress blues. I considered, as we passed these rows, heading toward our seats.

There was an area toward the rear of the theater for parents, wives, and other family members and I observed their nervous excitement by their mannerisms.

Yellow Footprints

Wow, normally these people would have been seated on bleachers located on the drill field with a band marching and playing various military and national tunes, and of course the Marine Corps Hymn, while we marched and they watched. I thought with regret for all of us.

I did not have any visitors, nor had I expected to have any. It seems a hollow achievement, to go through the ordeal of boot camp, and not have a parent or relative smile at you on the parade field as you marched by. That smile, stating you have surprised everyone and pulled it off, and had endured a difficult task, without quitting. But, this morning there was no parade and the visitors could only listen to the officer on the stage tell us we were finished here.

The drill instructors and officers of the entire series assembled in front of the stage. There were sixteen of them. Lieutenant Colonel Johnson, our Battalion Commander, was the main speaker. The theater was full and silent. The visitors and graduating recruits exuded an air of anxiety. We sat with serious faces and numbed minds, which reflected on the ordeal we had just come through to finally arrive at this moment.

The ceremony continued with the dress blue recipients and the other private first class awardees being called up one at a time. Their respective senior drill instructor was also called up to stand, with the colonel, to hand out the certificates. These certificates expressed the pleasure of the Corps in presenting the recruit the promotion and gave a mention of outstanding performance, while undergoing recruit training. The senior DI, and the colonel, then shook their hands and the proud, sullen-faced recruits went back to their seats.

The senior DI from each platoon in our series had been up on the stage to express courtesies toward his favorite hogs and the speech portion of the ceremony was about to begin. Lieutenant Colonel Johnson, stepped up to the lectern to give the graduation speech.

"Good morning ladies and gentlemen.___On behalf of the Commanding General of the Marine Corps Recruit Depot,___welcome to Parris Island and today's graduation ceremony. I am Lieutenant Colonel Johnson and I am the Battalion Commander of these fine new Marines, of H Company, 3rd Battalion.___We are conducting the ceremony indoors for obvious reasons.___Normally, it would have been conducted on the main parade field.___Today these young men have completed a very psychologically and physically demanding training regimen,___one of the world's most difficult.___I sincerely hope each of you is enjoying your visit and I am confident that you have noticed a remarkable change in the young man you sent us months ago.___These young men are now proud Marines. The pride comes from the fact that they have earned the title Marine and now proudly wear the coveted eagle, globe, and anchor,___the symbol of the United States Marine corps."

Applause.

"It has been said,___ladies and gentlemen,___that the true test of a person is not what they do in times of comfort and convenience,___it's what they do in times of challenge and controversy.___These new Marines have passed that test,___but they have done so with the help of many dedicated people,___mentors,___who have encouraged and instructed them on the road that ultimately led them to this day."

Applause.

"As you well know, these young men came to us from cities, towns and farms across this great Nation where you,___their parents, family members, and loved ones, helped instill in them the character that allowed them to become United States Marines.___You laid a foundation, and in so doing, you provided us the basic metal to make Marines out of your sons."

Applause.

"Those hometown Marine Corps recruiters recognized the foundation you laid and challenged these young men to become United States Marines.___Their personal examples of honor, courage and commitment helped ignite a desire in these Marines that ultimately led them to Parris Island.___Parris Island,___ladies and gentlemen,___is a destination that tells its story in three simple words.___We make Marines.___It was here where these young men met their drill instructors,___the people who are directly responsible for transforming them into Marines.___These new Marines will never forget their drill instructors and teachers, who trained them here at Parris Island,___and in fact,___they will make reference to them for the rest of their lives.___You see,___ladies and gentlemen,___every day these drill instructors,___the Marines wearing the campaign covers,___shoulder the awesome responsibility of exemplifying extremely demanding standards,___qualities your young Marines will strive to emulate throughout the rest of their lives.___These young

Marines know that every moment of every day, their drill instructors were absolutely committed to ensuring they earned the right to become Marines___and it is that commitment of the drill instructor to the recruit, and the recruit to the drill instructor,___as well as the recruit to the recruit,___that ultimately transforms young Americans into United States Marines.___That shared commitment, ladies and gentlemen, is the essence of life as a Marine.___And so,___I ask that you all join me in a round of applause for all those very dedicated people who helped these young men earn the title of Marine."

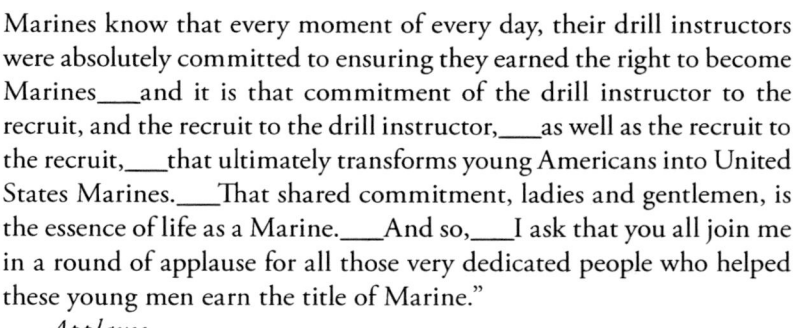

Applause.

"And now,___ladies and gentlemen,___I would like to take a moment to address your Marines.___Good morning,___Marines!" he said while emphasizing the word Marines!

"Good morning Sir!" we sounded off like a frigate firing a broadside.

I welcome you as new members of our historic military organization.___What is ahead is unknown.___Your contribution to the needs of our nation___during any crisis,___will make new history and build on the proud tradition of the Corps.___Marines,___success in life takes teamwork___and as you have all heard time and again,___there is no I in team.___Team effort got you here,___team effort trained you,___and it was a team effort that allowed you to successfully complete your gauntlet through Parris Island.___You are now very important members of a team that has earned a proud legacy by demonstrating valor, fidelity and courage.___Protecting that proud heritage demands that you,___as a member of our team,___remain semper fidelis,___always faithful.___Faithful to your God,___faithful to your family,___faithful to your country,___faithful to your Corps,___and faithful to our Corps values of honor, courage and commitment.___As you depart today,___strong in mind, body and spirit,___I challenge each of you to live up to the words of the late President John F. Kennedy.___Very simply,___President Kennedy said,___From those who have much, much is expected.___Good luck and Godspeed,___Marines.___Ladies and gentlemen,___it is my privilege to introduce to you our newest United States Marines."

Applause.

He completed his speech and we sat there feeling a sense of weight being lifted from our shoulders. The Marine Hymn was playing over the speaker system now and the song now belonged to us. We had earned the title of United States Marine.

The Colonel exited the stage, we stood up at attention and the visitors poured toward their targeted Marine like the surge of a wave rushing onto a beach. Camera flash bulbs popped and voices in all stages of excitement exploded in the theater. Some cries were from mothers, which were more like wails. Perhaps these women had built up worry during their son's time here and now let it all out in one big exhalation.

Fathers and brothers were not as loud, but their common contribution to the event was exhibited by a lot of backslapping and handshaking. The brothers often looked with awe at their Marine brother's uniform and perhaps thought about joining themselves. Their desire to join would increase when their Marine brother got home and told them how hard boot camp was. It becomes a desire to achieve the difficult. Some brothers, who were already Marines, proudly congratulated their newly forged Marine family member.

Sisters, girlfriends and young wives presented a different picture. The graduate's sisters looked at every new Marine they could, like a child in a candy store with many selections. The graduate's girlfriends were jumping up and down like pogo sticks, and dove at their green targets, once they had definitely identified the graduate as theirs. The young wives were a mix between the pogo stick and the wailer and some ran toward their target with one or more tots carried, trailing or being dragged by the arm, resembling quail families.

The fathers started seeking out their son's drill instructors to speak with them. The drill instructors endured the barrage of questions, compliments, handshakes and war stories from those who were veterans. I heard numerous, "Well back in my day... .", or "In the old days!",or "Buildings!___Shit, we had tents!".

Soon we gravitated to the street and the drill instructors tried to politely extract their Marines out of this new cluster-fuck of grabastic civilian mass. When the order to fall-in was heard, the family members gasped to see their Marines disengage the reunion and swiftly gravitate to their formation spot. Those Marines who had visitors would be able to go back out later. But first we had to follow orders and it was time for noon chow anyway. Even the heavens were smiling at us, because it had stopped raining.

SEVEN

Our meal tasted fine, but the appetite had ebbed and the urgency to store up energy and shovel the shit down the hatch was gone. Marines with family waiting had picked at their chow more than the rest of us. Eventually, we ate what was served, dropped our tray off and fell out.

Sergeant Hodson came out of the mess hall and marched us back to our barrack. Once inside Staff Sergeant Louis told those with visitors to remain in dress greens and the rest of us to change into utilities. Several minutes after we had changed into utilities he shouted for us to form up around him. Even though we were graduates now, our platoon still remained silent. There was absolutely no small-talk or whispering.

"Sir, yes Sir!" we chorused.

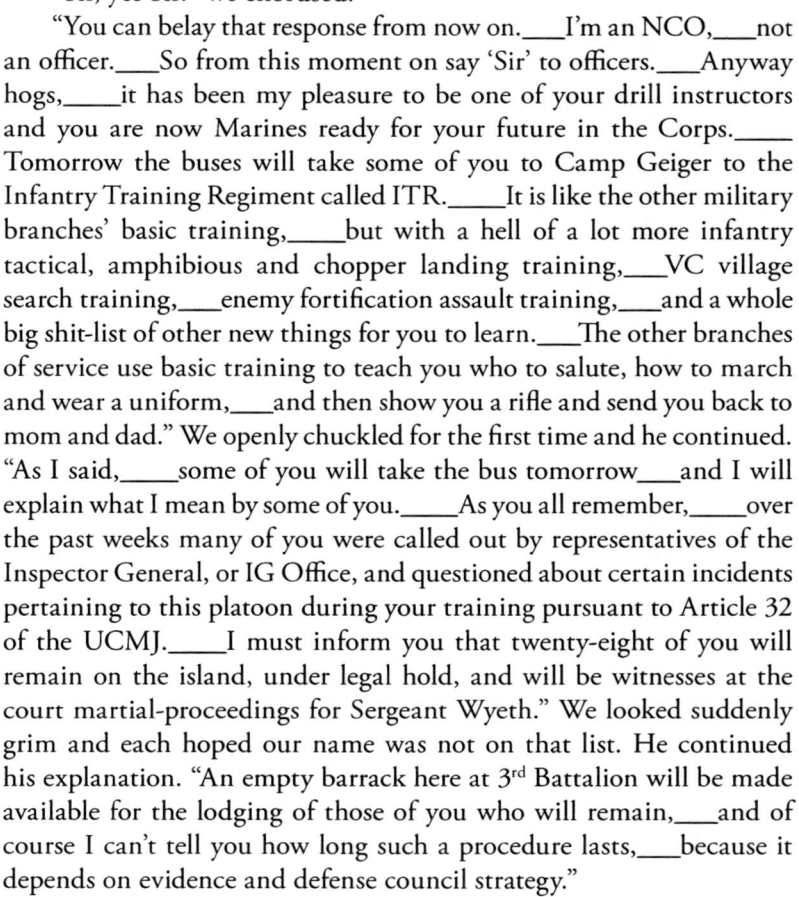

"You can belay that response from now on.___I'm an NCO,___not an officer.___So from this moment on say 'Sir' to officers.___Anyway hogs,___it has been my pleasure to be one of your drill instructors and you are now Marines ready for your future in the Corps.___ Tomorrow the buses will take some of you to Camp Geiger to the Infantry Training Regiment called ITR.___It is like the other military branches' basic training,___but with a hell of a lot more infantry tactical, amphibious and chopper landing training,___VC village search training,___enemy fortification assault training,___and a whole big shit-list of other new things for you to learn.___The other branches of service use basic training to teach you who to salute, how to march and wear a uniform,___and then show you a rifle and send you back to mom and dad." We openly chuckled for the first time and he continued. "As I said,___some of you will take the bus tomorrow___and I will explain what I mean by some of you.___As you all remember,___over the past weeks many of you were called out by representatives of the Inspector General, or IG Office, and questioned about certain incidents pertaining to this platoon during your training pursuant to Article 32 of the UCMJ.___I must inform you that twenty-eight of you will remain on the island, under legal hold, and will be witnesses at the court martial-proceedings for Sergeant Wyeth." We looked suddenly grim and each hoped our name was not on that list. He continued his explanation. "An empty barrack here at 3rd Battalion will be made available for the lodging of those of you who will remain,___and of course I can't tell you how long such a procedure lasts,___because it depends on evidence and defense council strategy."

Oh shit, now I know why so many recruits were taken from training over the past weeks. I wasn't talked to, so perhaps I won't have to stay.___ Why did Louis say it depended on evidence the way he did?___God, I just want to get off this island and get on with whatever is out there waiting for me with the Fleet Marines.___I know Sergeant Wyeth had been harsh towards us, but I thought he was allowed to be and he did it in response to our lack of discipline or to put a fire under our asses when we slacked-off from expected proper motivation. My mind rummaged through its box of recollections and reason and sprinkled the thought with fear and panic. These guys may know, yet I don't. They can't talk about it and I can't ask.

"Alright,___listen up for your names to be called." After he had called out about twenty names I began to relax and began to feel real safe by the twenty-fifth name. Suddenly, I heard my name and instantly went white with shock. I had no interest in staying on this fucking Island one more day than I had to. That is, I had really expected to leave tomorrow morning. I looked around and noticed more wide-eyed faces on those whose names were called.

"You will move over to the empty barrack in the morning.___I am instructed to tell you not to discuss any thing related to Sergeant Wyeth or what will be covered during the next days of the court-martial," he concluded sternly.

All was tensely silent around those of us whos names had been called. The rest of the platoon was equally silent, however in the usual manner, as we all emptied our footlockers and finished packing our sea bags. We kept out our toilet kits and towels for morning head call. We would turn in our sheets and blankets in the morning and fold our mattresses in half on the racks.

This night I slept in interrupted bouts of wakefulness, drowsy eye-openings with periodic moments of true sleep. Because I had been so prepared to leave, I now felt betrayed. I even wondered if I had indeed died and went to hell and this was one more disappointing frustration to really leave the Island as if it was a loop in hell, where everything is designed to reach a certain point and then just as I am ready to move on, I get snagged and put back into the sub-basement. By morning I was tired and in low spirits, as we returned from chow to watch the other forty-three put on their utilities and march off to the buses to actually leave the Island.

When we twenty-eight had settled into our new lodgings we found bedding had been supplied for us and left in stacks. We quickly made our bunks and then the only thing left to do was to stare at the bare walls. It was odd for so few men to be in a room furnished for over a hundred recruits. The other odd feeling was due to the sudden disappearance of drill instructors. We had no NCOs in with us.

There was also a dull silence in the squad bay. Our training had been successful for the Corps, due to our DIs, because even without senior leaders present, we shut our mouths. There was no small-talk, no laughter and no horsing-around. We were like knick-knacks on the shelves in a home, gathering dust, as we either stood by our bunks or sat on a footlocker and did not move.

Eventually we were remembered, when a corporal from Headquarters and Supply (H&S) Company came by to take us to noon chow. He suddenly stopped, as he entered, and looked at us strangely, because he sensed there was something odd about our behavior. We were marched over to the mess hall. The corporal ate over at the NCO section and we sat silently in the main section and slowly consumed our chow. Our appetites were gone, judging by how everyone picked at their trays and only ate small amounts. When we got up, our trays held uneaten food. This reminded me of how our trays looked on the first day on the Island. There was no DI now, to tell us to eat it all or suffer eating it out of our trays, without silverware.

Our behavior remained glum and silent for the rest of the day and when the same corporal returned to take us to evening chow he had remarked.

"You know you guys can talk now and I'll tell you about the Enlisted Club and base theater hours after chow."

His word was good, as he told us about base facilities and theater hours.

"The only thing you can't do is go to the Enlisted Club,___I was informed, because you are still in training status," he said with a shrug. We still had to go to ITR after this trial and that meant training status.

None of us went out that evening. To complain to somebody or anybody about the unfairness of having to stay behind, would be the same as pissing into the wind. We stayed in the barrack and remained silent.

CHAPTER 13
COURT-MARTIAL

ONE

It was Wednesday, 12 January 1970, two days after graduation, and it was no longer raining. The temperature was heading into the low 50s. Morning chow was just as numb an event as yesterday's slop-feast was. A different corporal had apparently been assigned to perform oversight duties for us. He was a young lean Latino, about five feet seven inches, with light olive skin, black hair and coals for eyes.

The corporal shook his head and said, "Yous guys can relax, ya know.__Yous don't have ta be so uptight, ya know.__It's ovah, an' da big bad wolves are gone." But, his rank was corporal and therefore, he was an NCO, who by definition was like a DI to us. However, this guy was no DI in his demeanor, because he was so unmilitary and easy going, and obviously trying to sell his no-sweat approach to us, for all things from now on.

Perhaps all Marines don't act like the DIs, but I hope they aren't all as fucked-up as this guy.__I wonder why they had let him into the Corps anyway? I thought and scrunched my forehead. We had nothing to gauge the various personalities of Marines at this time. Our general perception, to date, had been that they all ate nails and hated everybody who wasn't exactly like them.

Every time we went to chow, while going through boot camp, it was in formation, and to do otherwise would be out of character. Therefore, when the corporal showed up to march us to chow, it was normal. As if the corporal was our new leader, we followed him obediently to chow.

If he had ordered us to attack one of the boot platoons in training, we would have massacred them. Even though we had no rifles and bayonets we would have improvised with sticks, hands, or anything else to fight with, until we got the rifles and bayonets from the untrained recruits. But, our new leader only wanted us to eat chow.

What the fuck is wrong with us? I complained mentally.

The answer was still elusive and the day was long, therefore the question only nagged at me more and longer. The only words I had heard from our group were from Saunders.

"Ah man,___this is shit!" Saunders moaned.

At 1300 hours, after another dismal meal, the corporal formed us up outside the mess hall and marched us over to the Regimental Headquarters area. We arrived at a building with signs indicating the Judge Advocate General or JAG offices. The corporal ordered us to enter the building and led us down a hallway. The hallway was decorated with pictures of unknown generals, war scenes and military aircraft. We were told to enter a room and seat ourselves.

The room had been arranged with the judge's bench at the front, which faced two tables, each with chairs facing the judges bench, and a lectern between them. A jury box was to the left of the judge, along the wall between his bench and the prosecuting lawyers' table. The defense lawyers' table was to the right of the judge. Behind the attorneys' tables was the general courtroom seating area. There was also a court stenographer table and chair set up to the left side of the judge's bench.

After several minutes the room imploded with about fifty Marines coming in through the front doors accessing the room's general seating area. Not more than five minutes passed and two groups of officers and NCOs entered. The first group was comprised of a major, a captain, and a first sergeant. The second group was comprised of a major, a 1st lieutenant, a gunnery sergeant and Sergeant Wyeth. Therefore, the first team had to be the prosecuting team and the second team was definitely the defense team.

The collective features of the prosecuting team appeared, coincidentally, all hawkish. Their eyes shone like hot emeralds. They appeared as sentinels of justice and it made one feel that regardless of the guilt or innocence of the poor defendant wretches who were brought before them, the verdict would always be guilty.

We twenty-eight sat at rigid attention while we waited. Since we had only been told that this was a court-martial for Sergeant Wyeth and no officers or NCOs had spoken to our group, nor had any conversation erupted amongst us, we were so brand new and so disciplined, that we could not do otherwise. Now, without any command, we shot straight up and stood at attention when the officers were sighted.

"Remain seated.___You only have to rise when the judge arrives.____Relax and pay attention to these proceedings." The major on the prosecuting team had walked over and spoke in a semi-whisper so as not to embarrass us or not to yell loudly in the courtroom. We did not care which, as we had been yelled at for so long one more time would not have mattered.

Several minutes passed, and another officer entered through a rear door. He was a tall silver-haired full colonel with a ruddy complexion. He was fierce looking in demeanor and his uniform only served to accentuate that image. His collection of ribbons was stacked six rows high. Some were even hidden behind his dress green lapel and he looked like he didn't give a shit if anyone ever saw them.

The entire assembly of Marines in the courtroom sprang to attention. Sergeant Wyeth never looked behind to our group. He sat sullen faced, wearing his dress greens. His blouse displayed three rows of ribbons. His personal achievements were diluted here in this room, where most all of the others wore their own array of salad.

The defense major was short and muscular. His salt and pepper hair bristled like a porcupine. He had dark penetrating eyes and he too was a veteran of Vietnam. He wore three and two-thirds rows of ribbons. The bullet headed 1st Lieutenant was of medium height with platinum colored hair, cut in a high and tight, and sported a smashed nose, much like a boxer. The gunnery sergeant was a big gangly red-head, with a thin red face. He wore five rows of ribbons and he looked like a rattlesnake would slither away from him. His mouth was a slit with a sharp angled dip at the left side, which promised a very dangerous person, if provoked. If appearances could predict an outcome then the defense team would win hands down.

After observing many Marines since arriving here, and counting my recruiters, it appears that the Marine Corps doesn't hand out many ribbons in general and no bull-shit ribbons specifically. I mused respectfully. *That's why Marines always have less fruit salad then the other branches of service,* *even if a Marine had been all over the world and also in combat,___like these guys.*

"Be seated.___This proceeding will now come to order,___this is the Special Court Martial of the United States versus Sergeant Wyeth, Richard A.,___formerly an Assistant Drill Instructor attached to Hotel Company, 3rd Recruit Training Battalion here at Parris Island.___He is charged with numerous violations of Article 93,___Cruelty and Maltreatment,___and Article 128,___Assault and Battery under the Uniform Code of Military Justice... .

Jeez!___They really get right to the point here.___And the charges,___ holy shit!___Is he ever in trouble.___All these charges sound bad,___but what does it all mean? I was now aware of the whole thing, that is, I was now at least let in on the big secret. The entire hoopla that had been going on around our platoon for the last weeks was all about this. *Sergeant Wyeth was in trouble for how he did his job.___Did he do something wrong compared to all the hell other DIs gave us?* I concluded my initial thoughts and waited to see what was going to happen next. Since my first day on the Island, it had always been my opinion that drill instructors were gods and they answered to no man for their deeds.

The two opposing teams looked at each other with cool calculating expressions.

Looks like the way we squared off on the pugil stick competitions. I smiled inwardly with this thought. *They are about to beat each other's brains out___and I find it odd that this makes me feel like the Marine Corps is performing some weird kind of cannibalistic rite.* My mind wandered all over the place now.___*What exactly was it that got Sergeant Wyeth in trouble.___Was it my injury?___It seems so, because he left our platoon the next day and was replaced by Sergeant Hodson.___So now, what had caused his departure makes sense.*

"Major Savage,___how does the accused plead?" the colonel asked.

"Colonel Lasher,___the accused,___Sergeant Wyeth,___pleads not guilty to all charges," Major Savage replied. He bent over the desk and said, "Lieutenant McIntyre and Gunnery Sergeant Ashton pull out the preliminary drafts regarding the separate charges.___I'll need those to remind me of the dates Sergeant Wyeth was supposed to have committed these offenses,___when I discuss any dates at length, go ahead and pull out the file on the counter arguments and be ready.___ Okay?" They both nodded. Gunnery Sergeant Ashton looked like he had just bit a nail in two.

Wow!___If he looks like that when he's just acknowledging a question, then I wonder how he would look when he's mad? I was amazed. *Did any of the other guys in my platoon see him that way or think the same?* I wondered.

The nameplate in front of the judge indicated his name was Colonel Lasher and he began to settle in for the proceedings.

"Major Pouscher,___would you begin the proceedings?" Colonel Lasher asked.

"Sergeant Wyeth is charged with multiple violations of the Uniform Code of Military Justice.___Specific charges are Maltreatment and Cruelty of a Subordinate and Assault and Battery.___The specifications of the charges are as follows," he stated and read off the charges:

Charge I: Violation of Article 93 UCMJ, Maltreatment and Cruelty of a Subordinate.

Charge II: Violation of Article 128 UCMJ, Assault and Battery.

"Major Pouscher, would the Prosecution please provide opening remarks?" Colonel Lasher asked.

"The United States is prepared to corroborate and demonstrate that these charges are true.___Through evidence obtained during a lengthy Inspector General investigation,___with a significant number of recruits from Platoon 3074 having provided testimony___individually and with no ability to collude their statements,___due to talking being prohibited in training.___Each testimony was either collectively accurate to incidents witnessed directly or heard by witnesses in proximity to the incidents.___Each recruit was advised,___as a further IG precaution,___not to discuss their interviews with drill instructors, other Marines or their fellow recruits.___Further evidence will be presented through expert medical personnel___and through incident reports of Maltreatment, Cruelty and Assault of a Subordinate."

"Thank you Major Pouscher.___Major Savage, would the defense please provide opening remarks," Colonel Lasher said.

"The defense for Sergeant Richard A. Wyeth will provide testimony from former recruits, from base personnel such as drill instructors, rifle range instructors and in addition, from officers of the day,___who had the duty on the dates of alleged incidents," Major Savage stated and sat down.

"Thank you Major Savage," Colonel Lasher said.

"If it pleases the court,___we will begin introducing the witnesses," Major Pouscher stated.

"You may proceed," Colonel Lasher said.

"Commander,___please approach the witness chair," Major Pouscher called out. A tall naval officer rose from the benches and walked over to the witness chair. He wore the dark blue 'suit' Navy uniform, which had the gold piping or rings around the jacket sleeves down by the wrists. He too had been to Vietnam and he had four rows of ribbons to declare what he did and where he was. He was a doctor.

I wonder if any of those ribbons were given for every one hundred Marines he put back together again. I thought in a mixture of awe and general curiosity on how ribbons are given beyond those awarded for bravery, because he was in the medical field, in a hospital. I had learned about the white and green Vietnam Service and the yellow, red and green Vietnam Campaign ribbons. This was mainly due to repetition, as nearly every Marine I saw on the Island had them and they said they had been there. That is, the drill instructors had said so, and therefore, all others with the same ribbons naturally had to have been there as well. Suddenly, I recognized and remembered him as the doctor who had stitched up my head.

"Please raise your right hand Sir.___Do you swear to tell the truth,___nothing but the truth,___so help you God?" Major Pouscher asked while both he and the doctor held up their right hands with palms facing forward.

"I do," the commander answered in a serious tone.

"Please state your rank and name," Major Pouscher continued.

"Commander Steiniger," he replied in a hard voice, "Where are you assigned?"

"At the Naval Hospital here on Parris Island."

"Did you have any association with recruits from Platoon 3074?"

"Yes,___my records indicated numerous sick calls by recruits from Platoon 3074."

"What,___if any,___incidents are of particular memory,___or could be considered suspect?"

"Objection!" Major Savage cut in. "Council is drawing a conclusion for the witness!___He is insinuating premeditated action by the accused."

"Overruled," Colonel Lasher said blandly.

"I'll repeat my question.___What if any___incidents are of particular memory or could be considered suspect?"

"Starting back, as early as the eleventh of November, I have treated recruits from Platoon 3074 for what I would classify as normal training injuries.___There were numerous bumps and bruises on the lower part of the legs and on the arms,___or scratches and scraps in the same general areas___however,___my first suspicious observation was a recruit___on the same date stated,___who had a severe contusion,___a bruise,___on his solar plexus.___Several days later I treated a facial contusion,___left cheek area.___Another two toward the middle and end of November,___who had several contusions around the ribs and one had a black eye.___On the fifteenth of November, a recruit was treated for severe contusions of the left side of his rib cage,___the other had a left eye contusion.___The eye was so swollen it was shut for several days.___On December forth, two recruits had been treated for a twisted ankle and one had a severe contusion to the head. The next day one recruit had swollen testicles___and it was during this time that I suspected there was a pattern of maltreatment and maltreatment risk going on in Platoon 3074!" The commander stopped when Major Savage interrupted again.

"Objection,___none of these injuries were reported as attacks on the recruits,___by the recruits!"

"Sustained.___Answer that question Commander," Colonel Lasher said.

"No.__And when I inquired,___as I always do as a standard practice,___the answer was always either 'no' or 'it was an accident'."

"Were you left with a feeling the injuries were not due to accidents?"

"The solar plexus, eye, crotch and rib injuries were very suspicious to me."

"Were there any additional incidents of suspicious injuries?"

"Yes,___as I had stated before,___there were the steady scrapes, rope burns, blisters, etcetera,___which diminished in numbers as the training weeks increased___and especially since Platoon 3074 had reached the point of training where they went to the range.__Normally recruits are more-capable and their boots more broken-in as the weeks of training build up.___In other words, their ability to run the punishing obstacle course without receiving injuries or running in boots,___well broken-in,___reduced blisters, burns or scrapes.___However, on the late evening of nine December, a recruit was rushed to the infirmary by two corpsmen.___The recruit was from Platoon 3074__and billeted at the rifle range for training."

"What was exceptional about that recruit?" Major Pouscher asked.

"Well,___first, as I had previously stated,___he was undergoing rifle range training, which reduces the chances of a lot of injuries normally seen in other phases of training.___Second, it was a head injury,___which usually occurs as a result of falling or contact by or with another person."

"Elaborate please."

"Their training was not involving high obstacles, nor pugil sticks, at that time.___So I asked the question.___How then,___in plain language,___does a recruit get his head split open?___When blood is drawn on recruits, I automatically get very suspicious and that is why I submitted my file of injuries to Regimental Headquarters and requested an investigation."

"Did the recruit tell you how he was injured?"

"Yes, he did give an answer,___he stated an answer to me and the Officer of the Day.___I had called for the OD, while I was working on suturing the recruit.___He stated that he had slipped in his shower shoes and hit his head on a rack."

"Why was his explanation not acceptable?" Major Pouscher asked with a sense of tell me more. Once more Colonel Lasher appeared just as curious.

"If he had hit an object, there would have been a different look to his injury.___Perhaps a deeper cut,___heavier bruising,___perhaps a dent.___But,___his injury appeared to be a laceration resulting from a softer object,___such as a fist,___which could also have twisted slightly upon impact causing the tear in the skin,___especially where there is bone, without much cushion,___such as the head."

"Objection!" Major Savage cried out loudly. "That is speculation!"

"Sustained," Colonel Lasher responded.

"What is speculation?___The fact that a recruit was injured and required sutures or the fact that a professional surgeon made a professional diagnosis of how an injury was sustained?" Major Pouscher responded with vigor.

Colonel Lasher was attentive to this question and waited patiently for Major Savage's reply.

"Once again,___the statement of a fist being the tool or object used to cause the recruit's injury is speculation."

"That point is to be debated," Major Pouscher replied.

"Sustained," Colonel Lasher's decision sounded like he wanted to hear more.

I hope this doesn't mean I'm in trouble.___Oh shit!___Am I in trouble?___No, because I never squealed on Sergeant Wyeth.___No way can the Corps give me the boot. I was envisioning thoughts like Dominoes falling. This scared me, because it was something involving me and I didn't ask for it. I tried to keep an even-keel through training and graduate and that's all I wanted. We were warned by our DIs not to squeal on our DIs.

"Do you wish to cross-examine at this time Major Savage?" Colonel Lasher asked.

"Not at this time, Sir."

The prosecution had a group of IG personnel up on the stand and their testimony basically corroborated what Commander Steiniger said. However, one major new development was introduced into the trial. The incidents where recruits had cracked-up, and had been processed through psychiatrists, had not been part of the commander's testimony.

I wonder why they left out some of our more interesting episodes? I thought questioally. *Maybe it will be addressed later.* I decided.

TWO

First Sergeant Sanchez walked up to the witness stand and seated himself. He looked like a man who would kill anything in his path however, when he spoke, an entirely different man appeared in the mind's eye. His manner of speech was educated, calm and articulate. Major Pouscher administered the oath and then asked him to discuss the findings concerning two incidents where recruits of Platoon 3074 had suffered nervous breakdowns and what actions by Sergeant Wyeth had contributed to the incidents, if any.

"On 26 November,___Recruit Ditz of Platoon 3074 was verbally punished for his alleged inability to pull his weight in training.___He had caused,___through his alleged inabilities,___the entire platoon to perform numerous sessions of punishment PT.___Due to his small build and apparently under-developed muscles, Recruit Ditz was not capable of performing some exercises and negotiating some obstacles.___The date I had referred to was the date Recruit Ditz was punished in front of the platoon while the platoon was doing bends and thrusts and other punishment PT because of him,___while shouting 'Ditz–shits!'.___He tried to run out of the squad bay,___and the platoon was ordered to stop him.___Some of his platoon members had successfully detained Recruit Ditz by tackling him.___One note in the investigation was that the mere order to stop the recruit put many other recruits at risk of unnecessary injury and in fact several recruits had suffered bruises, and one a bloody nose, as a result of striking other recruits while jumping to stop Recruit Ditz.___Lieutenant Commander Cohen,___the senior psychiatrist on Parris Island, had performed the evaluation of Recruit Ditz and his findings were that the recruit had suffered a severe nervous breakdown and recommended a Medical Discharge.___Recruit Ditz received three weeks of therapy and is being evaluated for a Medical Discharge.___According to Doctor Cohen, Recruit Ditz will most likely be referred to a Veteran's Hospital for indefinite follow-on treatment after his discharge."

"Objection!" Major Savage shouted. "On the date mentioned where Recruit Ditz was punished in front of the platoon and suffered a collapse,___all three drill instructors were engaged in shouting at Recruit Ditz for his failings.___Therefore, if what you are alleging, all three DIs should then be part of the reason for Recruit Ditz's having had a mental collapse.___I mean to say his breakdown was the result of pressure building up due to his own failings and the strain of training,___not due to Sergeant Wyeth's personal attacks."

"Sustained."

"Please continue first sergeant," Major Pouscher said. "Also,___answer who shouted the order to stop Recruit Ditz."

"The investigation did not determine who actually shouted that order.___It was determined that such incidents would automatically cause a DI to shout stop.___On the third of December,__Wednesday,___a second incident occurred where a recruit, named Delahey, had also suffered a nervous breakdown. When Sergeant Wyeth discovered the recruit laying in his bunk,____which is proscribed during day hours,____ he noticed the recruit had also failed to shave.___Delahey was ordered to get his razor and bucket and stand before the squad bay wall mirror and shout over and over that he was crazy,___while wearing the bucket over his head.___He was ordered to perform side-straddle-hops with one arm, while dry shaving with the other.___Recruit Delahey threw the bucket down and bolted for the main hatch.___Whereby Sergeant Wyeth ordered the platoon,___who were standing on-line, reading their red books at the time,___to stop Recruit Delahey.___They tackled him and,__once again,__several recruits were injured with bruises and could have suffered more serious injuries.___Sergeant Wyeth had the duty alone that day."

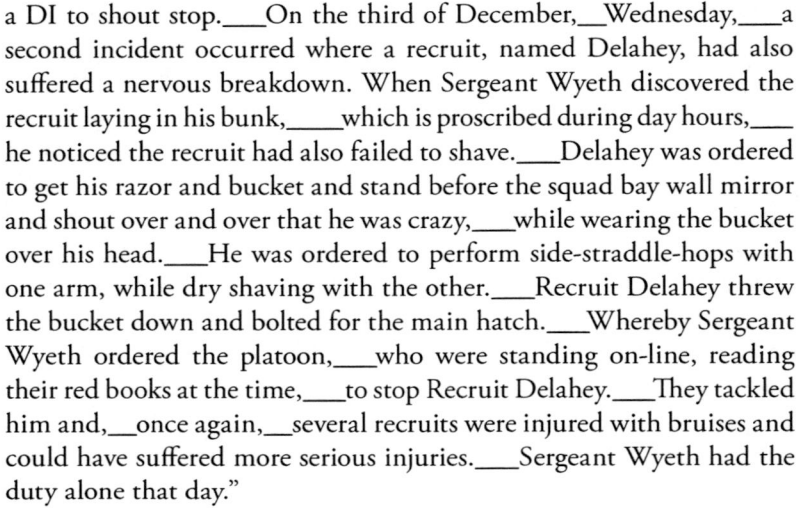

"Objection!___That's speculation!" Major Savage interjected.

"Overruled.__It is very clear to me that additional injuries could occur in such a situation." Colonel Lasher stated while displaying a sour face to the major as he spoke.

"It also seems evident that Sergeant Wyeth had started the Ditz punishment alone,___that is, before Staff Sergeant Louis and Sergeant Black were present.___Which suggests that Sergeant Wyeth has a propensity for putting recruits in dangerous situations."

"Objection!" Major Savage boomed. "That is inflammatory!___ He's assuming... ."

"Overruled.___I am starting to see Major Pouscher's point!" Colonel Lasher said coldly, cutting him off.

Sergeant Wyeth sat and stared straight ahead, with no facial emotions, as if he were ignoring the proceedings and could care less about what the Corps was doing to him. The statement being given by First Sergeant Sanchez continued.

"Private Delahey was bruised by the incident and had numerous facial cuts from the dry shaving.___He was referred to psychiatric counseling and is currently undergoing evaluation for a possible Medical Discharged from the Marine Corps,___with probable therapy at the Veterans Hospital being required,___depending on the medical evaluation," First Sergeant Sanchez concluded.

"Do you wish to cross examine,___Major Savage?" Colonel Lasher asked.

"Not at this time Sir," he answered.

A Navy Lieutenant Commander, named Cohen, was called to the witness stand. Major Pouscher administered the oath and immediately started asking technical questions and inquired how the two recruits had come to suffer their nervous breakdowns.

"Repeated mental trauma,___mixed with low self-esteem.___The low self-esteem is the main objective of the drill instructor's training program.___That is, to create the low self-esteem and rebuild the recruits with positive reinforcement,___the recruits who had adapted to this rebuild program flourish and become hardened competent Marines.___While those who fail to start the rebuild basically flounder in the initial stage.___In other words,___their mind accepted the abusive comments by their DIs challenging their capabilities and accepted their comments as holy writ.___The environment created by the very dominating DIs further reinforced the recruits' withdrawal and stifled their ability to believe they could realize victory and make the grade,___compete and achieve success,___and become that competent capable recruit their DIs desired.___In a sense these recruits may have suffered some of the beginnings of this syndrome in civilian life.___However, there were avenues of escape there and none what-so-ever here.___So their failure was drilled into their minds by abusive parents, teachers, and playmates___and these fears of being failures were driven home permanently by their DIs and branded into their psyche.___These two recruits were classic cases," he explained and took a drink of water before he continued. "Recruit Delahey had numerous scars in his scalp, possibly from some traumatic incident or incidents in his life.___He was scarred emotionally and physically and apparently not very successful in life.___His twin brother,___the Platoon Guide of 3074, was apparently unscarred, both emotionally and physically, and totally successful.___What direction had the scarred brother taken, which resulted in the vast personality differences between the two, would require further research.___However, it is a valid point of observation."

"Could these two recruits have made it through training if they had not been singled out as they were?" Major Pouscher asked.

"There are so many abused persons going through life,___therefore, there are a proportionate amount going through boot camp.___The drill instruction and physical and mental training everybody receives here cannot be accepted by all.___There are those who are totally incapable of accepting any orders,___accepting control___or in some cases accepting failure. I believe these two recruits could not accept failure and because they were unable to accept this fact in civilian life they broke down here when it became fact to them.____Furthermore, Recruit Delahey was unable to accept authority.___Therefore, both would have failed to make it through boot camp if their instructors saw these same things and could not correct them.___If recruits are able to keep up and also have serious mental problems, but remain undetected and graduate,___they either fail while serving with a Regiment in the States, or worse, while in combat.____And,___if they survive, they end up discharged._____At that point, often with a less than honorable discharge."

"I have no further questions," Major Pouscher stated.

"Major Savage,___your witness," Colonel Lasher said.

"Commander,___would you say that in order to,__*ah*__let's say, weed out undesirable recruits,___the drill instructors are performing part of their mission for the Corps?" Major Savage asked with the last word sounding higher pitched and trailed off.

"Yes!"

"Would you say that in an effort to achieve this weeding out process, the Corps has devised the shock and hazing treatments to bring these behavior problems to the surface, while at the same time testing all recruits for endurance?"

"Yes,___I would agree."

"So if the drill instructors note such a behavior in a recruit, their job is to expedite the conclusion,__*er*__force the issue earlier___and drop those recruits to be discharged?" Major Savage concluded slyly.

"Well,___I'm not sure what you mean by expedite or force the conclusion?" Lieutenant Commander Cohen asked.

"Do you agree that aside from training recruits in the art of military ways, history and skills,___the drill instructor must instill discipline and push the recruits to their breaking point.___In that process the recruits who can handle the constant hazing and physical hardships are becoming ideal Marines through discipline?"

"Yes,___I would agree."

"But,__any recruit who lacks discipline and also lacks one or more of the categories of military ways, and exhibits inability to achieve the physical requirements or respect for authority,___then those recruits should be pushed harder to either get motivated and comply,___or throw up their hands and quit."

"Yes,___I agree that the drill instructor has that task___however, the methods used to push those recruits who are lacking abilities,___to their breaking point,___is questionable," Commander Cohen stated.

"What precisely would you categorize as methods?_Are you implying the drill instructor can read minds__and can identify a problem recruit and just walk up and tell them to pack up their gear and leave?__No,__I believe they must rely on pushing the situation to the point a response occurs,__positive or negative,___so the rest of the platoon does not get pulled down by a weak member.___What do you say to that?" Major Savage drove the point in like a nail.

"It is difficult to identify and cull the problem recruits.___I agree."

"Thank you Commander___that's all," Major Savage stated.

I was keenly interested in what was being said. It was so clinical, in a sense. Because we were part of that experiment hearing the procedure and goal of training being expressed this way was chilling. Anyone of us was a target to be culled or kept. Not just us, but every recruit who went through boot camp.

The members sat there and dutifully observed the proceedings, while showing neither shock nor surprise.

I glanced over at Saunders and Shelby who were transfixed on the drama before them. It would take a snap of the fingers to pull them out. The rest of our group had to be experiencing the same effect.

We were there when Ditz and Delahey cracked up.___We saw that recruit jump out of the third floor window at 3rd Battalion___There were the wrist cutters and the frozen bodies.___The frozen bodies were the recruits who just literally froze in place and no amount of yelling by a DI could get through to them.___That recruit on the bayonet course was a frozen body.___When I was in the Medical Platoon I witnessed many additional mental and physical problems amongst the recruits there.___We were the broken and busted bodies on the island___Many of us healed and got picked back up in the training cycle, but those with internal breaks, better known as mentally impaired recruits, never got picked up.___There were also those fat-bodies and no-bodies out at Weapons Battalion, those

Jack Shipman

marshmallow recruits who looked like a platoon of behemoths with a bunch of skeletons rattling behind them when they marched by.___I wonder what psychological shit was rolling around inside their minds? I was suddenly lost in thought remembering all of those incidents and those recruits who were involved in them.

As I sat there in mute witness of the drama unfolding in front of me, I started thinking about how none of us has yet sat down and compared notes on our training. We had no idea as to how to compare our training to other platoons. Was there some part or parts of our routine, which were not part of the other platoons' training? Saunders was prone to be vocal, but even he remained silent. Shelby was prone to be impulsive; yet he remained stoic. The rest of our group was no different, and I followed their example.

"Do you have any further questions Major Pouscher?" Colonel Lasher asked.

"Yes sir,___I do," he responded and moved toward the witness.

"You had just made the statement that in your opinion it is justified to weed out,___or cull,___recruits who lack the proper,___or desirable,___ingredients to be a Marine."

"Yes,__that is correct!"

"Over the past several months there have been incidents where recruits who were culled,___were also killed or died as a result of actions by their drill instructors.___How could that happen?"

The Commander was suddenly exhibiting a cautious face. The jury perked up and we blinked and stared with shock and interest at what was just said. He blinked several times apparently composing his thoughts and then continued.

"A former colleague of mine,___Doctor Waldo Lyon,___who served at Parris Island as a Navy and Marine Corps clinical psychologist from 1961 to 1968, had publicly stated that brutality is normal in Marine training.___He had asserted that brutality and other maltreatment are so ingrained in the Marine Corps, that the Corps may [serve as a laboratory for the study of institutionalized violence] *sic*.___He was speaking to the American Orthopsychiatric Association during a convention last year,___where he was a mental health coordinator.___ The convention was held at the New York Hilton Hotel.___In the <u>New York Times</u> article published last April, Doctor Lyon stated the Marine Corps [satisfies the needs] *sic* of youth for order, self-control, pride and accomplishment.___He did question whether the end justifies the means."

"What exactly do you mean by your last comment?" Major Pouscher queried.

"Doctor Lyon questioned whether we must rely on a brutal anachronistic organization to give the youth that vital feeling of competence and maturity."

What-ever that word 'anachrontic' or whatever he said, means, I don't care, but if he means did we feel competent and mature?___Hell yes!___We needed to get thumped a little to get that, and it got us all in line as a team.___It made us get our heads and asses wired together.

I thought and believed it worked.

"Doctor,___I'm still waiting to hear from you___how,___if the nature of training is normally as tough as your statements attest,___how do recruits end up dying?___Would those incidents be the exception,___ and consequently,___the responsible drill instructors prosecuted.___Or because an occasional accidental death may occur,___prosecute all drill instructors who bark loud and swat at errant recruits?___Which is it,___Doctor?" Major Pouscher asked with challenge in his voice.

"Well naturally the training is exceedingly rough and the recruits have to achieve a preset goal to become Marines,___therefore,___if so many recruits go through boot camp and only an occasional accident occurs,___it is unfortunate,___but not entirely avoidable.___So it is the exception."

"Thank you Doctor."

"Objection!" Major Savage slammed down the word. "That is not in evidence here!___The deaths of recruits in other platoons have nothing to do with Sergeant Wyeth's case?___He did not cause any recruits to die.___Therefore,___the statement alludes to Sergeant Wyeth's alleged actions as part of that exception the doctor refers to!" Major Savage finished with a red face displaying his anger at the prosecuting counsels' attempt to make that similarity.

"Sustained!" Colonel Lasher stated with hardness in his voice.

"Major Pouscher,___what is the point here?" Colonel Lasher asked.

"Sir,___if I may continue,___my reasons will become clear."

"Objection overruled Major Savage.___Then proceed Major

Pouscher___and please demonstrate to all of us what exactly your point is," Colonel Lasher stated with a hint of impatience.

"I have only one final question for now,___Sir," he stated to the Judge and then looked at Lieutenant Commander Cohen. "The maltreatment of recruits is explicitly forbidden and is officially condemned by the United States Marine Corps.___However, you maintain that it is a fact of life here on the island," he said while glancing around the room slowly and then suddenly plunged right back into his attack. "Last summer,___in less than six weeks, two teen-aged trainees died after having accused their drill instructors of beating them.___The charges were unsubstantiated.___A short time ago an eighteen-year-old recruit named Melsen was allegedly beaten by his drill instructor,___dragged out of the barrack by Military Police___and placed in the hospital in Charleston.___He died there."

Major Savage started to stand up, but sat down again and Major Pouscher continued.

"These are not just accidents that occurred here once every twenty years.___They are frequent and happen almost monthly.___Several months ago, recruit Jose T. Conception's body was found near Ballast Creek.___His face was badly mangled.___The Marine Corps attributed that to shrimps, crabs and perhaps sharks.___They listed the cause of death may have resulted from accidental drowning.___Conception was a Puerto Rican from the Bronx in New York City.___His Congressman,___Mario Biaggi, ordered an investigation and asserted Conception was a good swimmer.___The Marine Corps officially thinks Conception got fed up,___ran away from his barrack and tried to swim to the mainland.___His wife had received a letter where he stated the following," he pulled out a piece of paper and read, "All I want to do is get the hell out of here.___I'm not going to let them hit me like I was an animal or something and I don't like nobody putting their hands on me.___So, me and my senior drill instructor had it out."

"Objection!" Major Savage shot out.

"What is your point in this Major Pouscher?" the colonel asked.

"To make a correlation between brutality, maltreatment and inhumane treatment and these deaths,___which in each case has either been proven or is suspected to have resulted from such things,___Sir," he responded, with great annoyance in his voice.

"Objection overruled.___Major, you may proceed."

"The autopsy resulted in a possibility that Conception had been severely beaten.

"Objection!" Major Savage yelled in disgust. "What does the death of Conception,___who was in another platoon,___have to do with Sergeant Wyeth's charges?"

"What is your point Major Savage?" Colonel Lasher asked.

"Sir,___records state clearly that the doctor who performed the autopsy admitted it was a perfunctory autopsy and that he did not examine the skull and therefore, there is no real proof that the recruit died of beatings!" Major Savage stated in one breath.

"Objection overruled!" the colonel replied. "Go on Major Pouscher."

"There was no examination made to say that Conception drowned.___He was reported to have been an excellent swimmer,___ yet he wore combat boots when his body was found.___All of which suggests his senior DI beat him to death and threw his corpse into the creek."

"Speculation!" Major Savage barked.

"Sustained!" the colonel agreed.

"Where exactly are you going with all of this Major?" the colonel inquired.

"Sir,___Sergeant Wyeth is accused of Maltreatment, Cruelty of a Subordinate and Assault and Battery.___What I am doing is describing incidents, which occurred on this island over the past several months, that are similar in that drill instructors were charged with the same violations of the UCMJ and where recruits were injured and some died as a result of such treatment.___In the cases,___such as the boots on the feet of Conception, and the letter stating his Senior DI was beating him,___I have no problem visualizing him being beaten to death and his body being dumped in the creek.___Melson's alleged beatings by his DI before he died,___another case.___Commander Steiniger stated the series of unusual injuries to recruits in Platoon 3074,___which occurred over several weeks,___which may have or could have,___ended in the death of recruits," Major Pouscher stated looking at Colonel Lasher as if daring him to disapprove his point.

"Objection!" Major Savage was irritated now and squirming to get at the stand and counter attack.

"What is your objection?"

"Sir,___that Sergeant Wyeth could have caused the death of recruits," Major Savage said with vinegar in his words, "That is all pure speculation."

"Overruled," Colonel Lasher said acidly. "I want to hear the rest of Major Pouscher's point,___before I am willing to consider granting your point."

Major Savage sat down and glared like a vulture with his shoulders arched high and his head pulled down low between his shoulder peaks. Sergeant Wyeth sat stiffly and stared in that cold way we in Platoon 3074 knew so well, yet could never read his mood.

"Continue, Major Pouscher," the colonel said lazily.

"There has been occasion to document the types of incidents which led to recruits' injuries or deaths in the past,___that is,___when drill instructors have engaged in heavy-handed tactics to discipline their platoons___there has,___almost universally,___been a series of small incidents including multiple bruises, cuts or heat exhaustion cases.___ As recruits drop their performance during hot days, where they received no water,___were deprived chow, and head calls as well as being denied breaks between PT,___the weaker recruits start to really display their inabilities and literally ignite their drill instructors anger.___The result is more intense mass punishment where the weaker recruits are the brunt of the punishment or the individual recruits are beaten by their drill instructor either on the spot or later more severely when there are no witnesses,___and at times by their fellow recruits in a blanket party," Major Pouscher paused, looked around at the members, and continued.

"Platoon 3074 had been deprived in all of the above and had suffered beatings at the hands of Sergeant Wyeth or,___due to his actions,___were injured.___My point in discussing the other incidents, which occurred on the island over the past months, was to show that drill instructors,___like Sergeant Wyeth,___create conditions, which often result in severe injuries or death of recruits.___Over the past forty-five months___fifty-eight drill instructors have been court-martialed on charges of maltreatment,___with thirty-four convicted.___ Approximately one-third of those occurred this year.___The New York Times even reported this high number of drill instructor incidents.___It must be stopped, or soon all drill instructors may resort to these tactics if they see so many of their fellow instructors going unpunished.___It's just a matter of not getting caught."

Major Pouscher concluded his speech and sat slowly, as if to allow more time for his point to sink in before the defense started countering.

Holy shit!___I can't believe all this___They actually do control these drill instructors and catch a lot of them doing much like Sergeant Wyeth.___Man, this is all too weird, because I thought the DIs was totally untouchable. I exclaimed silently, while displaying the wide-eyed face of one suddenly realizing there was a normal rational world beyond boot camp.

"Major Savage,___do you have any further questions? Colonel Lasher asked.

"Sir,___I wish to review what has been said first before commenting."

"This court is recessed until 1330 Hours," Colonel Lasher announced, as he rose and left the courtroom. All personnel had risen to attention and now began exiting the room.

THREE

We were met by our faithful corporal, who promptly marched us over to the mess hall. Between counting cadence he asked questions.

"Left___left, yah left, riat, left.___Hey, how's it goin' in der?___Riat, left.___Dey nail da dude?___Riat, left.___Eny ah yous been up on da stand yet?___Left, riat, left,___column riat, hut!___Left,left, yah left, riat, left," he quietly mumbled the cadence and seemed unperturbed that we remained mute.

We entered the mess hall and with Pavlovian precision held our trays high and vertical in front of our faces. Moving mechanically, we lowered our trays to the horizontal position as we arrived in front of the first menu item. The recruits on mess duty were perplexed, because they did not see sloppy un-starched utilities to go along with our very boot tray handling and they also observed PFC chevrons amongst our group. So they decided to err on the side of caution. We all performed like boots, as if telepathic, because we were all somewhere between pissed-off, betrayed, confused and uncertain.

The trial kept replaying in my mind while I attempted to eat. I saw

Sergeant Wyeth's cold staring eyes locked on a fixture or something across the room and stay glued there throughout the proceedings. His face was a frozen mask. He was never going to be the same Marine after this trial, regardless of the verdict. I knew this without reservation. Did I feel contempt toward him? I had no definable feelings, only numbness. To me he was just a hard-assed DI. I was often pissed-off at him and thought he had an evil streak in him. But then, considering the messed-up childhood and upbringing I lived through, could I judge him against ass-holes like Hueston.

Saunders looked over both of his shoulders and then lowered his head over his tray. "Man,___I heard some shit in my life,___but this shit is way-out shit.____I never thought they killed any recruits here___and now, thinking back, Sergeant Wyeth's games could have gotten outta hand, ya know.___What do you guys think?" he said in a hushed conspiratorial voice. Aside from his speech breaking our silence spell and proving we could talk without having a DI break our bodies, his comment hit home. Some nodded in agreement, but not without additional comment.

"Yeah,___maybe so,___but none of us croaked,___so why make a big deal?" Woodly said. It was the first time we heard him speak as an individual. As for that, except for some of us speaking to the prompt of a DI, none of us had spoken as individuals. I heard Saunders speak to me the night I got back from getting the stitches in my head. Now Saunders was a PFC, which does not surprise me, because he does have the ability to take risks and had always been assertive.

"Apparently, the Corps frowns on DIs denying recruits head calls, water and food___hell, they even forbid thumping recruits.___Why, I can't see how they could make a herd of hogs into Marines without thumping heads to achieve it," Kellerman said and many of us grunted in agreement, including me.

"Hey Delahey,___what's with that nosy corporal?___Do you think he's trying to make us talk,___you know,___did they send him to test us?" Saunders asked.

"Yeah,___I wondered about that too.___Watch it guys,___we won't give him one word!___Got it?" Delahey said sounding charged-up.

The meal break went by fast and shortly we were met in front of the mess hall by the corporal. He ran his mouth between cadence, as before, and as before, we did not speak.

"Boy,___yous guys are an odd lot of FNGs.___Man,___no wonder deys bringin' up charges on dat guy.___Look what he's done to yous."

What's an FNG? This guy is calling us something, but I don't get his meaning. I thought as I plodded along with the others on the neverending asphalt of Parris Island.

Once again I found myself day dreaming, or just plain in some type of daze, while I sat in the courtroom. It was inevitable to fall into this numb gawking mode, because there had been so much said here this morning, with more to come. What had been said so far today was shocking to all of us in general, and what the shrinks related about recruit training brutality and how it was used directly during Platoon 3074's training, specifically. What would be said this afternoon that had not been said already? What more could be said? What would they do to Sergeant Wyeth. Would they kick him into a jail cell and throw away the key?

"All rise." The order came from an MP and Colonel Lasher entered regally.

"Be seated.___Major Pouscher do you have more to add to your presentation?" the colonel asked.

"Not at this time,___Sir," Major Pouscher replied.

"Major Savage,___you may have the floor," the colonel said.

"Everything said by Major Pouscher earlier in the morning seemed to relate to drill instructors running around beating recruits unchecked by their superiors.___Why should they do this when they have alternatives?___The Commanding Officer of the Recruit Training Regiment at Parris Island,___Colonel Perrich,___made a public statement for the Marine Corps to the New York Times last October, that a drill instructor doesn't have to resort to physical abuse if he has problems with a recruit, because he can simply send him over to the Special Training Battalion,___referred to as STB,___and let them handle it," Major Savage rationalized, and stopped talking for a moment, to let this nugget lay there, to be considered.

"If STB can't handle the problem," he continued, "the recruit is discharged.___There is absolutely no reason for maltreatment,___it does nothing towards making a better Marine out of anybody, according to Colonel Perrich," Major Savage stated and then waited to let this sink in as well, then continued his attempt to put the apple skin back on Major Pouscher's peeled apple.

"Drill instructors use all sorts of scare tactics as part of their bag of tricks to completely break down the recruit ego,___and as we all know,___the recruits are then slowly motivated and built back up into what the Corps desires them to be."

Boy, it wasn't a bag of tricks to me.___I never thought of it as 'find the pea under which nut shell,' and I don't think any DI, who was super pissed-off, was going to send a recruit to STB only because the recruit wasn't hacking it.___Hell, any DI with pride would want to keep as many of his herd as possible to show he trained them, transformed a glob of grabastic civilian shit into Marines and that means he would thump the wayward turd long before he sent him to STB.___If I know drill instructors, and by now I should, then I know they would be so frustrated and pissed-off at a failing recruit that such recruits would be delivered to STB in pieces, before they let another sergeant show them up. I mused as I listened to this on-going bullshit.

"I would now call Private Delahey to the stand," Major Savage announced.

Delahey was visibly surprised to hear his name called and we all suddenly felt pulled directly into the trial. We had felt more like spectators up to this moment. He stood up and walked stifly over to the witness chair and raised his hand.

"Do you swear that everything you say here will be the truth, the whole truth, and nothing but the truth?"

"Sir,___I do Sir!" Delahey said sounding every bit the boot that each of us still was, with the only exception being that he referred to himself in the first person

FOUR

"Private Delahey,___you joined the Marine Corps with your brother and both of you were in the same platoon,___3074.___Is that correct?"

"Sir, yes Sir!"

"A simple 'yes Sir' would suffice,___private," Major Savage said not unkindly.

"Yes Sir!"

"Objection!" Major Pouscher barked suddenly.

"What is it Major?" Colonel Lasher said.

"Could the defense counsel please correctly refer to the rank of his witness.__After all, __it was hard won recently," he finished, sounding deadly serious.

"My apologies,___Private First Class Delahey____and for expedience I'll use PFC," he corrected himself and continued. "Your brother was admitted to a Navy psychiatric ward for treatment after suffering a nervous breakdown while undergoing a punishment ordeal.___Is that correct?" Major Savage said.

"Yes Sir, I had been so informed during the investigation."

"Was your brother ever roughly handled by any drill instructors?"

"Yes Sir!"

"When and for what reasons?"

"There were numerous occasions where he and many other recruits were corrected.__They called it thumping, and there are thumpers in every platoon on this island.___I'm not complaining."

"Thank you, PFC Delahey.___I'm sure you are not complaining.___ But,__were you beaten?"

"No Sir!___I was only personally tightened-up once___but, I also did a whole hell of a lot of punishment PT and other types of punishment.___That's what made me tougher,___Sir."

"Was your brother beaten?"

"No Sir!__He was hit, not beaten!"

"So you were also___hit___then?" Major Savage asked turning his face sideways offering a serious squinting eye, which bored into Delahey's eyes.

"Yes Sir!"

"Why and how was your brother___hit?"

"He was cuffed on the back of his head for several things he did stupidly and ordered to dry shave with a bucket over his head, while doing side-straddle-hops, on the day he suffered his breakdown."

"Why were you hit?"

"Sir,__while at the Rifle Range,___we were all called into the head and asked about our level of motivation to fire a high score the next day,___qualification day."

"Were you hit?"

"No Sir!___I was corrected."

"How do you mean___corrected?"

"A jab here and there,___nothing really harmful,___or painful Sir!"

"Who did this?"

"Sir,___I don't recall."

"Was it Sergeant Wyeth?" Major Savage asked.

"No Sir!"

"I am finished with this witness," Major Savage stated to Colonel Lasher.

"Does the prosecution have any questions?" Colonel Lasher asked Major Pouscher.

"Yes Sir," Major Pouscher said.

Way to go, Delahey___don't tell on Louis and Utter.___They don't need to get into trouble as well. I thought with surprising support for our senior drill instructor and for our platoon. I suddenly felt we were all on trial now. *Wow, a real can of worms___They know that Wyeth was gone by the time we were firing on the range___and I think they decided to drop this line of questioning, because it opens up new charges against other DIs and they don't want more drill instructors dropped from the field.* I surmised, apparently correctly, because no further questions were asked on that motivational visit to the showers.

"Did Sergeant Wyeth routinely strike recruits during your training period?"

"Sir,___Sergeant Wyeth was a stern DI who came down hard when we were slacking-off or lacked motivation."

"Did he routinely strike recruits?"

"No Sir,___he had thumped a few turds,___*ah er*,___excuse me Sir,___recruits in our platoon, who really dragged their butts, however I can't say he beat us as much as he punished us."

"How did he punish your platoon?"

"Sir,___if we slouched or lacked spirit,___for example,___he would tell us we were going to have duck for chow.___Which meant duck-in,___duck-out,___don't-eat."

"Were there any other types of punishment?" Major Pouscher asked.

"Sir, if we really irritated him, we would drop and do punishment PT, no head calls were authorized and no water breaks___and once in a while a recruit would get a jab or punch to tighten them up."

"Which means if you had no chow all day,___then no water in between chow time slots,___you did not drink liquids all day.___ Correct?"

"Sir, that is correct."

"What did you think about this treatment?"

"Sir, I was angry when it happened,___but I figured it was part of training and it was expected to be hard here on the island,___so we all got an idea of how it would or could be in a war,___where there could be days without food and water due to situations created by the enemy."

"That's very astute, PFC Delahey,___unfortunately your awareness of real world and the rules of training are not equal.___You are to be trained hard here, but not while being beaten or subjected to maltreatment."

Well hell!___It's a little late to be hearing that bit of enlightened news.___We all doubt the drill instructors share your view,___major.___Where were you trained?___No hitting there? I thought with sarcasm.

"Objection!" Major Savage shouted, sounding like a mortar round exploding in the midst of this seemingly personal dialogue Pouscher and Delahey had going. "Counsel is drawing a conclusion for the witness!___You are telling the witness what he thinks,___when you should be satisfied to hear his answers to your questions!"

"Sustained!" Colonel Lasher had decided.

"I am finished with this witness." Major Pouscher said suddenly. He displayed a sour look on his face.

And so it went for the next two hours. One after the other of our group had been called to the witness stand and asked pretty much the same questions. The only exception was the question which would have exposed Staff Sergeant Louis and Sergeant Utter's day in the shower with Louis wearing right and left shooting gloves and Utter interpreting our range data books, pronouncing sentences.

Some were cross-examined by Major Savage and no one questioned had spilled more information than they had been asked. I was never called to the stand and wondered why. I would have stated the same thing I said to the doctor, Staff Sergeant Louis and the 3rd Battalion chain of command. *"Sir, the recruit slipped in his shower shoes and hit his head on a rack, Sir!"*

The defense counsel had tried to weave-in strong objections

whenever any answers were given, which were followed by a comment on why Sergeant Wyeth had done it. These objections were all overruled. Colonel Lasher apparently did not find answers like: "The platoon was punished all day long. We had constant PT, including watching TV and no chow, no water, no breaks all day, because Sergeant Wyeth didn't like the time it took for the platoon to get up and out that morning," to be sustainable when Major Savage objected or lacked relevance when Major Pouscher elicited the answer.

"Major Savage,___do you have any witnesses to testify on behalf of Sergeant Wyeth?" Colonel Lasher asked.

"Yes Sir,___I would like to call on Second Lieutenant Osbourne."

"Please proceed."

Major Savage called the officer to the stand, administered the oath and began asking questions. Lieutenant Osbourne was skinny, blond and of medium height, wearing only a National Defense ribbon.

"Lieutenant Osbourne please state your unit and duties," Major Savage asked.

"I'm assigned to the Weapons Battalion at the rifle range___and I am an armorer officer."

"Have you ever been assigned the duties of Officer of the Day?"

"Yes Sir."

"Were you on such duty on the ninth of December 1969?"

"Yes Sir."

"Do you recall if any platoons failed to make it to the mess hall that day?"

"There were no missing platoons that day?" Lieutenant Osbourne stated matter-of-factly.

Would you know for sure that all platoons were at chow that day?" Major Savage asked with a smile forming.

"The drill instructors are required to sign in their platoon number and time of arrival."

"So you are positive Platoon 3074 arrived for morning,___noon___ and evening chow?"

"I do not recall any day that I had the OD duty,___that any platoon failed to have chow!" the lieutenant stated and smiled.

The lieutenant appeared very pleased with that important accomplishment. I thought sourly. *I know what we did that day and it sure as hell didn't involve eating anything.*

"If you discovered any platoon did not sign in___wouldn't it be reportable?" Major Savage asked affecting a more serious face then the usual look he carried.

"Definitely.___That is a serious violation."

"Did any such violation get reported during your OD duty assignments at all during the period of the sixth through the twentieth of December 1969?"

"Never!" the lieutenant stated confidently.

"Thank you.___No further questions."

"Do you have any questions Major Pouscher?" Colonel Lasher asked.

"Yes Sir,___I do," he said as he walked up to the witness. "Do you stay at the mess hall all day lieutenant?"

"No Sir!"

"Why not?"

"I have to make my rounds Sir," the lieutenant stated and looked at the Major oddly, as if wondering why this major didn't understand the duty requirements of an OD.

"Okay,___then how would you know that the recruits actually sit down to eat, even if their DI had signed them in?" Major Pouscher asked slyly.

"Well,___ah___I can't know that if I am required to be all over the Weapons Battalion area during my duty hours and not sitting for that entire time in the mess hall," the lieutenant stated what he deemed as the obvious answer to such a dumb question and seemed to relax after saying that.

"Aren't you aware of the practice by drill instructors to order 'duck' for chow?"

"I am sure the recruits would be noticed passing through the chow line and then not eating."

Major Pouscher looked at the lieutenant as though he was the village idiot. "They do walk by the serving line and hold their tray vertically in front of their faces and stack their empty trays at the door and fall out.___That is how it is done.___So you did not see that,___ nor suspect that,___nor inquire of that?___I can guarantee the mess NCOs never noticed such things either."

"Objection!" Major Savage growled. "That's an assumption and an unproven statement of fact.

"Sustained!___Major Pouscher please keep your personal comments to yourself and stick to proper questioning," Colonel Lasher said unamused.

"That's all I have for this witness," Major Pouscher said.

The lieutenant left the stand and Colonel Lasher asked if any more witnesses for the defense were to be called.

"Yes Sir.___I wish to call Sergeant Utter to the stand," Major Savage said. The sergeant went to the stand and the oath was administered. He was wearing his dress uniform for the first time we had ever seen and he had three and two thirds rows of ribbons. A two tour Vietnam Marine.

"Please state your unit and duties."

"I am assigned to the Weapons Battalion as a primary marksmanship instructor,___Sir."

"Did you ever notice any unusual incidents or observe anything which could be considered a violation of the UCMJ when dealing with Platoon 3074 while Sergeant Wyeth had the platoon alone?"

"I can't say that I did,___Sir."

"Do you recall any instances where Sergeant Wyeth punished recruits while they were performing snapping-in exercises?" Major Savage asked.

"No Sir!___I never did!"

"So you recall that Sergeant Wyeth performed his duties in a proper manner for a Marine drill instructor,___at all times,___while he was in your work area?"

"Yes Sir!"

Son-of-a-bitch!___That lying bastard!___He knows damned well we smelled like a turned over shit-wagon and Wyeth loved to thump us hard during our snapping-in lessons. I fumed while starring angrily at Utter.

"That's all sergeant.___Thank you," Major Savage said.

"Do you wish to cross examine Major Pouscher?" Colonel Lasher asked.

"Yes Sir!" he replied.

"How's the air on the range sergeant?"

"It can really get foul,___Sir."

"So I bet you look forward to the snapping-in training,___to clear the old sinuses so to say."

"Yes Sir!"

"I would think working on the range develops a sensitive sense of smell," Major Pouscher smiled as if to make the sergeant feel his understanding. "How's your sense of smell now,___after working there?___Sensitive,__huh?"

"I can smell the faintest odors since working there," he smiled feeling relaxed now.

"Really sergeant,___I thought you couldn't smell shit!" Major Pouscher said suddenly in an angry tone.

"Sir?"

"A whole platoon crap in their utilities and sit in front of you for hours___and you can't smell them.__Why is that,__when they all admitted they had shit in their trousers on the ninth of December and sat in front of you?"

"Sir, what are you asking?" Sergeant Utter asked with a confused expression on his face.

"Your stated that Sergeant Wyeth had never done anything in an unmilitary manner while in your presence.___What do you call seventy plus recruits all smelling of feces and urine,___if not unmilitary?___A drill instructor is required to give his recruits the opportunity to vacate their wastes during periodic head calls.___So what do you say now?___Or have you also performed in a non-military manner sergeant?" Major Pouscher looked at him threateningly.

He's referring to his little episode in the showers with Staff Sergeant Louis thumping us. I know for sure. I thought expecting the sergeant to admit it now. I wonder why they left out some of the more interesting episodes?

"Yes Sir,___I knew it was due to that when the platoon arrived and I smelled them all day."

"Then why did you just say nothing done by Sergeant Wyeth was unmilitary or openly evident to be so?" Major Pouscher asked with dry disdain in his voice and facial expression.

"I did not see how it was his fault what a recruit did in such a case Sir!"

"Huh?___What?___I do not have a clue what you meant by that response sergeant.___You had better state more plainly what you mean."

"Crap in their utilities.___How is another responsible for a recruit doing that___Sir?" Sergeant Utter said looking smug.

"One recruit maybe.___But you said you smelled___them___all day.___So you are saying that it was not due to any external reasons for an entire platoon to have vacated their wastes in an area other then their barrack head.___In plain language they were forbidden to make their morning head call and any head call during that day, what-so-ever, by Sergeant Wyeth."

"I have no answer as to the reasons and I did not feel it was my business,___at the time,___to interfere with a DI and his platoon___ Sir!"

"You may step down sergeant," Major Pouscher said.

"Does the defense have further witnesses to call?" the colonel asked.

"Not at this time Sir," Major Savage responded.

"Does the prosecution have witnesses to call?" the colonel asked.

"Yes Sir!" he followed by requesting another witness. "The prosecution wishes to call Staff Sergeant Robbins to the stand."

Staff Sergeant Robbins was sworn in. He had a dark complexion, a natural tan with dark brown hair. He was tall, about six feet two inches and had broad shoulders and a slim waist. There were three rows of ribbons attesting to Vietnam service. He was a poster Marine.

"State your name and unit and duties."

"Staff Sergeant Robbins,___Senior Drill Instructor of Platoon 3073,___Sir," he answered in a calm gravelly voice.

"While you were at the range,___were you billeted in the same barrack as platoon 3074?

"Yes Sir!"

"Could you see the recruits of platoon 3074 normally or easily?"

"No Sir!___There was a full divider of wall lockers separating our areas."

"Could you hear them and their drill instructors?"

"Sure,___at times___Sir."

"Why only at times?"

"Because we made our own noise and my instructors and I were very busy running our own platoon to pay any attention to their training noise,__Sir!"

"Did you ever hear noises that were either evident of irregular treatment of the platoon or after training hours were secure,___meaning specifically after lights out?"

Yellow Footprints

"Yes Sir,___on the night of the ninth of December and again on the night of the eighteenth of December.___When I had the evening and night duty."

"Would you elaborate on what you heard?"

"On the evening of the ninth,___starting with Commanders Time up to around the wind-up hour, when recruits normally write letters, clean rifles and square-away their gear,___I heard a series of loud noises,___like something being slammed down on another object at intervals,___Sir."

"Did you look?___Was there anything peculiar to you?"

"Well,___no Sir.___I had my own platoon to handle,___so I did not even consider looking in to that drill instructor's area of responsibility.___However,___I thought they were doing a lot of PT,___running and that slapping noise was always going on for well over an hour."

"Nothing else caught your attention?" Major Pouscher asked with a tone of incredulity.

"Uh___yes Sir,___I was able to hear some recruit being chewed-out for something and the slapping noise also ceased just about at that time.___I heard their DI yelling at a recruit and then their noises suddenly stopped for the rest of the night until lights out." Staff Sergeant Robbins was looking straight ahead now as if thinking about something.

"What else Staff Sergeant Robbins?___What aren't you telling me?___What did the recruit get yelled at for?"

"Sir,___he was yelled at for bleeding on the deck without permission and told to get into the head an wash it off."

"What happened on the eighteenth of December?"

"It was reported to me by my fire watch,___as it was approximately 0230 hours and I was asleep,___that there was much shouting and movement in Platoon 3074.___The entire platoon fell into formation outside and their drill instructors were apparently tightening them up,___Sir!"

"What do you mean by tightening them up?___Hitting them?" Major Pouscher was moving in on this as if he felt he was getting more trash on the drill instructors of Platoon 3074.

"Objection!___That is not in evidence here!___The prosecution is well beyond the parameter of the purpose of these proceedings and

457

Sergeant Wyeth was not involved," Major Savage shouted as if his words were a Gatling gun firing.

"Sustained!" Colonel Lasher said quickly.

Holy shit!___There they go again trying to squelch anything done by the other DIs. I thought in amazement. *And that night didn't involve any hitting, but it was scary as hell.*

"I have no further questions for Staff Sergeant Robbins," Major Pouscher stated.

"Do you have any questions for this witness Major Savage?" Colonel Lasher asked.

"Yes Sir!"

"Staff Sergeant Robbins,___do you know Sergeant Wyeth personally?

"Yes Sir!"

What do you think of his abilities as a drill instructor and how he had handled his platoon during periods you could observe him?"

"He could drill a platoon fine___Sir!"

"That's all you can say about him is that he can drill recruits fine.___Come on sergeant, let me hear what a fine drill instructor he is," Major Savage demanded, apparently feeling certain that based on his cautious testimony, when Major Pouscher questioned him, he was defending a friend and this was a chance to make Sergeant Wyeth appear a diligent hard working drill instructor.

"I did not like him personally and felt he was cold and unnecessarily harsh toward his recruits and during evening hours deprived them valuable time to get squared away, study military subjects and for personal stability and motivation,___use some of that time for them to write their families."

"No more questions.___You can step down," Major Savage said quickly and with a facial expression and voice that advertised he was kicking a dead horse. "I wish to call the accused to the stand."

"Proceed," Colonel Lasher said.

"Sergeant Wyeth,___please approach the bench.

Sergeant Wyeth snapped out of what appeared to be a trance and focused on the Major for a few seconds. He registered the order and rose slowly and walked equally slowly to the witness chair. He stood there slightly leaning forward and held his right hand up as he was sworn in. As he spoke the response words, his face remained emotionless yet projected an eerie cold picture.

"State your name, rank and duty station," Major Savage asked.

"Wyeth, Richard A.,___Sergeant,___Assistant Drill Instructor,___ assigned to Hotel Company,___3rd Recruit Training Battalion,___Sir," he responded sullenly.

He was asked to describe what type of training techniques he felt worked for him and those were compared to other DI tactics. Additional questions dealt with his relationship with Staff Sergeant Louis and Sergeant Black. All questions and responses were of the utmost futility.

Damn it!___Let's get this bull shit moving outta here! I fumed, thinking how tired this was making me. *I want off this fucking island and this is nothing to me but an anchor.*

Finally Major Savage came to a similar conclusion and said.

"I have no further questions."

"Does the prosecution have any questions?" Colonel Lasher asked sounding equally tired.

"Yes Sir!"

"You may proceed.

"Sergeant Wyeth," Major Pouscher said.

Sergeant Wyeth appeared to be thousands of miles away and took several long moments to focus on Major Pouscher.

"Sergeant Wyeth,___PFC Delahey mentioned that you would tighten up recruits by jabbing or punching them.___Is this statement correct?"

"When recruits slacked-off or needed additional motivation to get them back on the ball,___I pushed them harder___Sir!" he replied with virtually no hint of his awful southern accent. He did still have a southern drawl, but he pronounced his words correctly here in the courtroom.

"What exactly do you mean by that sergeant?___Specifically,___ how did you achieve the desired results?___Give me examples," Major Pouscher raised his voice to a higher pitch at the last part demanding examples.

"I'd run them harder___Sir!" he mumbled.

"Bull,___sergeant!___Try again."

"I'd PT them more___Sir!"

"Bull crap!___You are trying to give me a phony story of how you only worked them harder.___Try again!___And this time remember you are under oath and that we have the results of an IG investigation with corroborating statements from over three quarters of the Platoon 3074 recruits.___Got it now,___sergeant?" Major Pouscher asked the last question with true condescension.

"I'd keep them from a meal here and there to motivate them."

"Try again!___Last chance before I start bringing up each former recruit,___each doctor, and each psychiatrist.___All of whom would have a wealth of information, including facts and proof,___corroborated proof, that you have maltreated and beaten your recruits on numerous occasions.___So which is it Sergeant Wyeth?___Are you going to play games, which will bring out the witnesses,___or are you going to save everybody's time and admit to these charges?___Then we can bring all of this___to closure," Major Pouscher nearly whispered the last two words sounding like an understanding friend.

Major Savage stood up shaking his head, his face red and obviously deciding not to shout out the objection he had nearly screamed and apparently finding that he did not really have one, sat back down.

"I did not injure every recruit you state was injured by me.___I didn't twist anybody's ankles.___I didn't bust any recruit's head open___Sir!" Sergeant Wyeth stated with hostile defiance.

"Well the court,___the Marine Corps,___and the witnesses beg to differ on your perception of these charges and specifications," Major Pouscher waited a moment and suddenly blasted out. "I'm tired of your games Wyeth!___Call my threat,___or start talking.___Now!"

"I___*uh*___may have gotten carried away at times.___Goddamnit!___The stress of training these no-brained, clumsy civilians is too much at times.___The only way to get through to them is to kick ass,___their ass___and maybe a drill instructor can finally produce a decent semblance of a Marine capable of fighting in, and surviving, Vietnam in the short time we get to accomplish this fucking miracle.___All you officers want to see is the perfect Marine at the end of training,___but you don't want to know what we have to do to give you that during the training period,___with no break, most of the time, between picking up a new platoon.___So only when somebody calls foul or orders an investigation, we drill instructors wind up getting sacrificed by our superiors.___If mothers and Congressmen kept their noses out of it,___then there would be a hell of a lot less problems, and if mama's boys, punks and weaklings would not get accepted by the recruiters, we could do much, much better," he blurted and seemed to be out of breath from the storm of words and feelings he had obviously stored up inside for a very long time.

"Is that all you want to say sergeant?"

"Hell yes!___I kicked asses where needed.___I busted heads,___ pushed and pushed those shit-asses until I felt they had reached my plateau of what a combat Marine needs to have.___If recruits got hurt when I'd PT them,___tough!___Marines get hurt when we attack as a unit in combat,___so why does it bother you people when recruits get hurt in training situations.___Hell,___I considered my actions as being necessary to achieve what the Corps expects and what I know from experience."

"What exactly are your perceptions of adding your experience to the current training regimen, Sergeant Wyeth?" Major Pouscher asked questionably.

"We set up ambushes in the A Shau valley before daylight, and lay in that position all damned day long, waiting for the enemy.___Charlie didn't give us a copy of his daily work schedule.___We did not move at all,___to eat, drink, make a head call or whatever.___If we had to make a head call, we did it in our utilities.___That's what I was trying to teach these civilians who were soon to go there, and not be prepared for what it would be like," Wyeth stated with conviction.

"Whatever hardships you may have personally experienced during your tour of duty in Vietnam is of couse to be commended Sergeant Wyeth, however it is not your decision to deviate from the prescribed Marine Corps training regimen,___period," Major Pouscher said, while heaving a sigh, as his voice trailed off. Sergeant Wyeth clenched his jowls tightly and stared straight ahead.

"Did you strike the recruits in the face, solar plexus, stomach, groin, eyes or other parts of their bodies?"

"Yes Sir!"

"Did you force recruit Delahey to place a bucket on his head and to dry-shave while doing side-straddle-hops and screaming that he was crazy, and then order the platoon to stop him, when he ran towards the exit hatch?"

"Yes Sir!"

"Did you refuse head calls for an entire day and refuse chow for an entire day, or at other times refuse any meals during a training day?"

"Yes Sir!"

"Did you also refuse to allow your recruits to drink water for entire training days?"

"Yes Sir!___A few times."

"Sergeant,___are you aware that the less water one receives the thicker their blood becomes.___The thicker blood causes the heart to pump faster,___which causes dizziness, clumsiness and faster fatigue," Major Pouscher stated sternly.

"No Sir!___I am not aware of that."

"That is also why your recruits failed to meet your expectations.___ How could they, without food and water, and with unrelieved body functions.

"As I had said Sir,____I did not know."

"After dousing the deck with buckets of water, did you also have your recruits perform bizarre rifle exercises and PT in that water?"

"Yes sir!"

"Did you then run your platoon in circles after they swabbed the deck, which caused a recruit to sustain a head injury?"

"Yes Sir!"

"Did you strike that recruit in the stomach after he had been struck by another recruit, who had caused the head injury?"

"Yes Sir!"

"Did you strike that recruit for 'bleeding on your Marine Corps deck without permission'?"

"Yes Sir!"

"Why did you ignore his injuries and refuse to assist him, while he was in the head?" Major Pouscher asked with incredulity.

"Objection!" Major Savage shouted and just as he was about to state what he objected to, Colonel Lasher boomed his response.

"Overruled!__I want to know why he didn't help,__as well."

"That's what corpsmen are for,___isn't it?___At least that is what I was taught in boot camp and that is what we did in Vietnam.___ Remember, we were trained to move on.___Don't let the enemy put more men out of action,__move on and let the corpsmen handle the wounded," Sergeant Wyeth said with disdain.

"That's correct sergeant,___in combat,___not in training.___

Perhaps you are confused on what your roles are," Major Pouscher said with a sense of understanding as if he realized the drill instructor was a product of the same indoctrination, culture and system he is being accused of being in violation with. "I am finished questioning the accused," he finished, sounding out the word accused as ak-cused.

"You may step down," Major Savage said, obviously no longer floating this case.

"Alright,___let's convene this court again tomorrow at 0900 hours to hear the sentencing," Colonel Lasher stated, rose, walked to the door, and exited.

"All rise," the senior MP called out as the colonel was getting up.

We stood and soon started filing out behind the others. Our faithful new shepherd stood by a tree with a cigarette in his hand. He saw us, dropped his smoke and crushed it under his foot. As we approached, I noticed at least eight butts in a scattered circle.

So he has been waiting out here for quite some time. I observed. *And he didn't police up his own butts!___What a shit-bird!*

"Well, well, I never thought this would take so long," he stated, confirming my observation. "I figured it to be a real cut-and-dry case.___Ba-da-bing,___ba-da-boom,___yous guilty!" he chuckled at his own wit and then said. "Okay,___yous hungry?___Well fall in an I'll take yous to a terrific restaurant I know over at Thoid Battalion," he snorted. We didn't.

Our evening was uneasy. None of our group wanted to go out and see a movie or go to the various, but few, other areas the Island offered as a service to shop, call home or play pool. We were more moody than ever before. No comments were made about the trial. There was still no offer to analyze our former drill instructor, nor what may happen to him based on anything we could have analyzed. No, our group was as quiet as a first week batch of recruits.

I watched the guys fidget with writing gear, shoes, uniforms and other seemingly necessary things we learned in boot camp. However, nobody seemed to do any of these things with intent. I was trying to judge the distance of my footlocker to the edge of my bunk. Who really gave a shit right now, whether I was an eighth or a quarter of an inch off?

Delahey hit the lights when we heard taps. He had been elected our leader simply because he had been our platoon guide and we followed him everywhere he went, even though he in turn followed our drill instructors. Plus, he was a private first class now. Only three of our newly promoted graduates were among us now and the other two looked to Delahey as our leader the same as the rest of us lowly privates did.

The sound of taps permeated through the window panes and floated across the squad bay mournfully reminding us of the sacrifices our predecessors had made. I remained awake for sometime after the last note had evaporated in the darkness of our squad bay. I kept my eyes open for as long as it took for sleep to win the tug of war.

Yeah, the tug of war.___If it hadn't been for that screwy competition I'd have been long graduated and gone from here in 1969.___I thought with a surge of mixed anger and regret.___What would it have been like if I'd been in 3063 the whole time with Staff Sergeant Rogers and Gunnery Sergeant Bishop.___But then they had Sergeant Kranz__that lovable twin brother to Wyeth.___Judging by their personalities, those two really hated people it seemed,___or they loved to hurt people with a sense of protection the Corps would offer them. I was wandering in and out of memories about the two platoons, the Medical Platoon and the other training platoons I had observed during training. *Hell, all the platoons had a least one wacko sergeant or corporal in them, now that I think about it.___ Shit!___It seems that I and the rest of the platoon had been so busy training and dodging all of the ongoing hell of our platoon during training, we forgot to really see or observe the other platoons during their training.___Maybe there would be equal hardship or less in the others.___If more, then that would be where the DIs killed their recruits.*

FIVE

The new day did not explode in my ears, yet we arose on time at 0500 hours, just the same. It is not that the noise during wake up, while in training, was unnecessary, because it helped recruits get used to shock sounds and stress.

Damned if it wasn't pleasant to rise to reveille, instead of being blasted awake by Sergeant Wyeth, or Staff Sergeant Louis. I thought with a yawn._*I'll take a bugle over a loud mouth any day.* I considered with a grin and busied myself with getting ready for the day.

While we were squaring away our squad bay, we had a visitor.

"Where's your NCO?" the corporal asked in a quizzical voice, "I'm Corporal Burk from H and S Company."

"PFC Delahey's in charge," PFC Saunders told the corporal. Apparently, that did not really surprise the corporal, because he just asked to get him. I went to the head and saw Delahey shaving at a sink.

"There's a corporal in the squad bay.___Says he wants to see you," I said in a matter-of-fact tone.

"Oh yeah?___Wonder what he wants?___Where's our corporal at anyway?___He's late," he responded in an equally as matter-of-fact tone and while wiping his face on a towel, started walking out to see the corporal.

"You Delahey?" the corporal asked, not unkindly.

"Yes corporal,___I'm Delahey.___What do you need?" he asked somewhat hesitantly.

"Colonel Lasher's office,___at JAG,___called the commanding officer of 3rd Battalion to inform you there will be a delay of at least two days before the Court Martial will convene again.___You will be getting orders today, which will assign members of this group to duties during that waiting period.___The battalion sergeant major sent word he has a list of details he could use people for.___You will be given those details after chow.___Any questions?"

"No.___Sounds like we will be busy for a few days," PFC Delahey concluded, in a voice that sounded relieved to hear such general everyday information. He was no different than any one of us regarding fear of unexpected events. Our platoon had been involved in a harsher training than most and our naturally apprehensive personalities could be recognized by any outsiders. The corporal, a runner from the 3rd Battalion Headquarters and Supply (H&S) Company, departed with no further words.

Five minutes later Corporal Bronx, as I decided to call him, came into our squad bay.

"Goo' mornin' mah new Mahrines.___It's goink to be a bootiful dey toodey.___Goink to be fifty-fuckin'-six degrees guys,___ahkordink to da weddermahn.___An' tomarrow,___wow!___It's gonna be sixty-fuckin'-foah degrees.___Can yous fuckin' believe dat!___huh?___Da sand fleas are bitin' big time. Anyway, I got da woid dat yous will be gettin' woik to keep yous busy a few deys, while da judge decides to fry dat guy or not.____Okay,____let's eat.____Fall out!" he finally shut up and we fell out.

The mess hall was one big clatter of mess gear banging together this morning. The menu was the reason. Whenever there were pancakes and sausages, the forks smacked the metal trays with glee. The orange juice was extra cold this time and the batch of pancakes must have just been dumped into the serving tray from the skillet, because they were so hot the butter soaked into the moist steaming stack immediately. When I took that first bite of buttery maple syrup drenching a fork full of hot pancake, I recalled those days back in Little Rock, Arkansas, having brteakfast in that grease-pit restaurant with my father. Even though I got sick of pancakes after eating so many breakfasts of that one thing, I felt close to a parent this morning because of it. Besides, it had been a very long time since I had a good pancake breakfast.

With a hot delicious breakfast in our stomachs to get our day going, our group of taciturn enlisted men once again formed up to be led away by our new, though odd, leader.

"Okay!____Lissen up yous guys,____an I'll tell yous wotcha gonna do tadey.____Okay,____Delahey,____you can count off ten ah your guys.____ Dey go ovah ta Thoid Battalion Supply for further instructions.____ Got it?" he said, looking directly at Delahey with a weird smile.

"Got it corporal," Delahey responded equally with a smirk.

"Okay," he looked strangely at Delahey and then continued, "PFC Saunders____you take da rest o'er ta da Regimental Supply builden' an' report to da Gunny in charge.____His name is Hill.____You can tell who he is 'cause he got plenty tattoos.____Okay?____Now, eny questions?" he concluded, while staring at Delahey with a challenging, open mouthed glare.

"Yes corporal.____I know where it is," Saunders said with a little sarcasm.

Apparently Saunders was just as ticked at this uncouth corporal. I chuckled inwardly. Hell, we don't even talk and we communicate fine.

When Saunders got us formed up and ordered us to snap to attention, I was very pleased to see our old platoon spirit, still there, ignited by the soul Saunders projected.

"Pla____toon!____Aah____ten____huat!" he bawled so loudly the other personnel and drill instructors in the area stopped, looked and

466

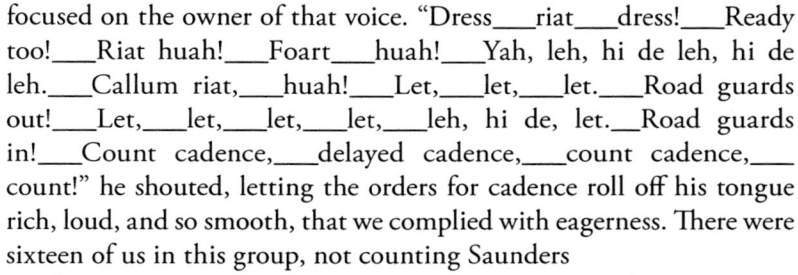

focused on the owner of that voice. "Dress___riat___dress!___Ready too!___Riat huah!___Foart___huah!___Yah, leh, hi de leh, hi de leh.___Callum riat,___huah!___Let,___let,___let.___Road guards out!___Let,___let,___let,___let,___leh, hi de, let.___Road guards in!___Count cadence,___delayed cadence,___count cadence,___count!" he shouted, letting the orders for cadence roll off his tongue rich, loud, and so smooth, that we complied with eagerness. There were sixteen of us in this group, not counting Saunders

"One, *step, step, step, step,* two, *step, step, step, step,* three, *step, step, step, step,* four, *step, step, step, step, one, step, step, step,* two, *step, step, step,* three, *step, step, step,* four, *step, step,* one, *step, step,* two, *step, step,* three, *step, step,* four, *step, step,* one, *step,* two, *step,* three, *step,* four, *step,* one, two, three, four, United States Marine Corps.___Aahoorrah!!"

Our cadence was perfect. We stomped along Boulevard de France, past the Iwo Jima monument and main meat grinder, toward the PX. When other Marines spotted our small unit, they stopped and observed our passing. PFC Saunders was in his glory.

Suddenly we were before our goal and ordered to halt. Gunnery Sergeant Hill had even come outside to see what all the commotion was about as PFC Saunders was unabashedly screaming cadence like an old British drill sergeant in the movies.

"Platoon halt!" Saunders shouted.

"Christ!___What ya got here?___A real live group of Marines?" Gunny Hill said gruffly, but not chidingly.

"Sir,___PFC Saunders and a detail of sixteen Marines reporting as ordered,___Sir," Saunders spit his report out with equal pride for his remarkable drill achievements.

"At ease,___I'm Gunnery Sergeant Hill.___Okay leathernecks,___since ya got so much vinegar and piss,___I got just the thing for you to sink your eagerness into.___Follow me." Gunny Hill said with a chuckle and we followed inside in an orderly group. Gunny Hill was totally white-haired and with his pink skin he appeared as a bright blue-eyed Santa Claus without a beard. He had a massive frame, but by Corps standards he was still fit. "Okay, listen'up.___The 7-82 gear in this building needs to be sorted, eye-balled for damage, counted and repacked neatly inside the buckets.___There is a current IG inspection and they want us to have a proper inventory.___So how you do it is okay,___as long as it is accurate,___and the buckets look perfect with all their gear, and I look good to the colonel.___Got it?"

"Sir, yes Sir," we boomed like true boots.

"Gawd!___I'd love to be a DI,___*ha*___but you know you never have to do that shit again to an enlisted man, NCO, or a Staff NCO.____Got it?"

"Sir,___*ah*___yes,____*ah*____we got it Gunnery Sergeant Hill!" we finally came to a decision on a response, which really sounded like a train wreck.

"Better.___Now get to it.___I'll get you to noon chow when it's time.___Here are paper, clip boards, pencils, and there's the gear," he pointed in a zig-zag with his finger indicating the whole building and its contents and then walked away.

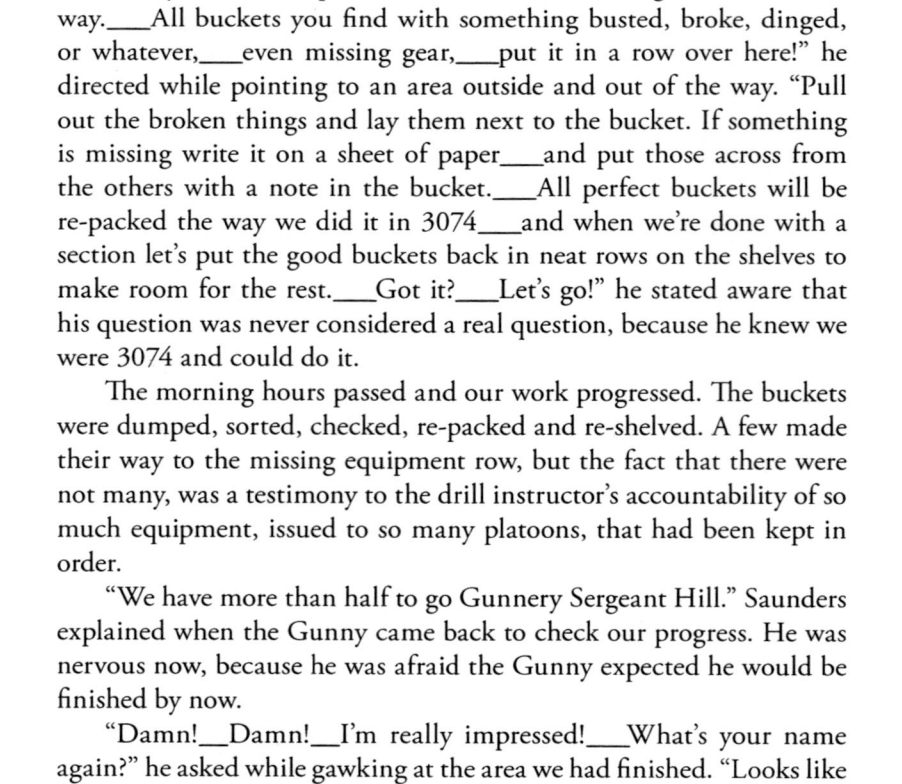

"Okay,___listen up!" Saunders said. "We are gonna do it this way.___All buckets you find with something busted, broke, dinged, or whatever,___even missing gear,___put it in a row over here!" he directed while pointing to an area outside and out of the way. "Pull out the broken things and lay them next to the bucket. If something is missing write it on a sheet of paper___and put those across from the others with a note in the bucket.___All perfect buckets will be re-packed the way we did it in 3074___and when we're done with a section let's put the good buckets back in neat rows on the shelves to make room for the rest.___Got it?___Let's go!" he stated aware that his question was never considered a real question, because he knew we were 3074 and could do it.

The morning hours passed and our work progressed. The buckets were dumped, sorted, checked, re-packed and re-shelved. A few made their way to the missing equipment row, but the fact that there were not many, was a testimony to the drill instructor's accountability of so much equipment, issued to so many platoons, that had been kept in order.

"We have more than half to go Gunnery Sergeant Hill." Saunders explained when the Gunny came back to check our progress. He was nervous now, because he was afraid the Gunny expected he would be finished by now.

"Damn!__Damn!__I'm really impressed!___What's your name again?" he asked while gawking at the area we had finished. "Looks like you guys really have your shit together.___Really.___You boys should all be in Supply.___I'm really impressed.___Keep it up,___you have two days.___So slow down.___Get my meaning?___Huh?"

"*Er___ah___yes,*" Saunders replied.

The Gunny told us we did good, but slow down, why?___Oh,___because we would finish here too fast and probably get a real shit-detail somewhere else later. Saunders must have thought that also,___due to his response. I decided.

"Oh, yes___Gunnery Sergeant Hill," he spit out hastily.

Unless Colonel Lasher wants Sergeant Wyeth back earlier, we now know how our afternoon and all day tomorrow will be spent. I laughed to myself. The work was not difficult and it was something we had learned to do in our sleep. Saunders' method of keeping track was brilliant and all credit should go to him.

"Okay.___Take your men to chow and be back here by 1300 hours to continue.___Don't look for me,___just get to work.___You are going to eat at the mess hall over by the Enlisted Club and Depot Headquarters.___Here's a chit to get you in," he explained while handing the piece of paper to Saunders and then left the area.

The chow was good, but not like a recruit mess hall at all. We did not feel fed and our stomachs complained at that insult to our training diet expectations, because that appetite was back. The afternoon was slower at work, as expected, and Saunders was apparently as pooped as the rest of us on the return, because he did not bellow as loudly. However, he did put an effort into the many drill commands.

Once back from evening chow, and the usual evening silence had settled in, we jumped into our bunks and Woodly, the appointed fire watch, flicked off the lights as the soft echoing of the notes of taps danced through our dark squad bay. Our return to the barrack, and the boot-silence of our mind-set, ending with the sounds of taps, had reminded me of a past sensation I had experienced once. I recalled entering a very large, extremely cold, utterly empty barn on a snowy winter day, where there too, such a silence had danced with the sounds of old creaking wood and the soft icy wind.

"*Psst!*___Delahey!" a voice whispered in the darkness.

"What?" Delahey answered blandly.

"What do you think about what they are doing about Sergeant Wyeth and how does it affect us?" the voice in the darkness asked betraying eagerness to hear an answer.

"Yeh!" another voice from further back chimed in and then more piped up to the querying going on. Suddenly our entire group got involved in a conversation.

"My feeling is that the DIs have some kind of unwritten code where a DI is safe if he thumps a recruit, but if he makes them bleed, he's on his own.___Shipman got his head busted open like a melon,___but even though it was not done directly by Wyeth,___he still caused the action that resulted in it.___From the testimony neither Shipman nor any one else squealed on Wyeth directly,___and Shipman never was pulled off by the IG.___So he never said squat," Delahey started to really explain this whole mess in a clean logical way.

"Said he slipped and dinged his head." *Haw, haw!* Someone chimed in. "That's rich."

"Least he was true to the platoon," another voice said in the blackness of the squad bay.

"Hey___Shipman!___What are your thoughts on this?"

"I wanted to graduate and get the hell outta this place.___And nothing they did would make me get into a situation they could drop me for.___But, I didn't figure on any court-martial to keep us here," I stated with true conviction.

"Hit his head! *Ha, ha, ha!* On a rack! *Ha!* The voice of Saunders boomed in the squad bay. "At least he proved he can take their shit and more," he said as a true friend, with pride. I mentally thanked him for his friendship and understanding.

The two who got dropped for busted ankles and the one with blue balls were discussed and for a long time nothing was brought up about Hyde and Ditz. Perhaps nobody wanted to upset Delahey.

"When Wyeth did what he did to trash my brother, I really got pissed," Delahey said suddenly. While he spoke we all shut up and listened, because we were so surprised he would even talk about it. "I almost ran over and punched that cocksucker out, but I'd only get arrested,___so I held back.___But it must be God's doing that that swine got his after all.___I can feel like a Marine now,___instead of a pissed-off brother wearing a green suit waiting to bust that crud up bad some day and get myself court-martialed.___I really wanted to do it before he did the same to some other recruits during their training.___ Now I can be a brother to my brother and still wear the uniform with pride,___because I'm sure Wyeth is going down," he choked a little, but got his voice back. "As for Ditz,___well, his father is a DI.___I'm also sure he has heard about this court-martial and definitely knows what happened to his boy.___DI or not, and don't forget what he said about Ditz that day,__that's still got to affect him."

"Hell yes!___It's a Special Court-Martial he's in,___an' that means he's goin' down!" one of the Marines, somewhere in the darkness, contributed.

"How did that shit-head ever get to be a DI?___I mean,___I woulda done all the crap they dished out without his added crap,___ya know," another voice stated.

"Well if you want my opinion,___or not,___so what,___fuck-you!___I would rather have a tough-as-nails DI than a take-the-easy-road type, to stroke me.___I want to be a professional hard-ass like the Corps always showed themselves to be.___You can't get that with a pretty-please, guys." the voice finished gruffly and many probably wondered who said that, because I know it was how I felt and from all the grunts and *ah ha's*, I heard, the majority did as well.

"Fuckin' eh!___That's what I'm sayin'.___But do you all agree he had to prove it by starving us, denying water and making us crap and piss ourselves?" another voice commented, which had sounded familiar, but I couldn't be sure exactly who it was.

Our discussions continued until sleep claimed the last round. We had exploded as a group. Our silence was shattered and we were human once again, to some degree. Since the damn had burst, we would never be silent again.

Reveille came too early, because we had talked away sleeping hours. Hours we were not used to expending. Groggily, we rose and, while scratching our asses, stumbled toward the showers. That at least invigorated us into wakefulness.

"Goo' mornin'.___Guess wot we're doin' tadey guys?___We're gonna run for a while.___Do some PT and den have chow." Our beloved Bronx corporal, wearing PT gear, announced in an unpleasant voice. Perhaps he finally sensed our hostility toward him and now he is paying us back. "Fall out in PT gear!___Sweatshirts, utility trousers an' boots___an' don't forget yer covahs," he finished and chuckled.

Outside, he barked more seriously. "Platoon!___Ah___ten___hut!___Riat huah!___Fo'art huah!___Quick step march!___Fast pace,___run!___Like it fellas?" he sneered and then ran us five miles and made us complete a full PT workout. When we hit the mess hall we were starving as much as we had during boot camp. "Enjoy,___yous guys.___ When yous are done,___you can repeat yestardey's assignments.___I'm outta heah," he finished in his awful Bronx drawl.

After a quick meal, mindful of the time, we formed up into our two groups. This time I heard PFC Delahey march his group off and was proud to hear my platoon as an observer. They sounded good, very good. But, Delahey only had a hundred yards to scream to the heavens, while Saunders had a mile, or more.

Gunnery Sergeant Hill, ever the comedian, was dumbfounded when he saw how Saunders had finalized the bucket deficiencies. He had not told us how to do it, but there it was, done right and done the Marine Corps way. Saunders had cannibalized each bucket's contents for the missing parts until only ten buckets were left with missing components of 7-82 gear for which there was no item to be scrounged from elsewhere. He did a jig like a country-boy from West Virginia to state how happy he was.

"Hell, Saunders,___I'd cut your orders this minute to stay here and be my Informal Account Clerk,___but I know you would rather slit your wrists and take a hot bath than stay on this here island.___ Right?___You gotta see the world for a few years first.___Get shot at and all that crap,___and then you'll be calling me up begging for a desk here.____Okay, you did damn good and I thank you,___the colonel thanks you and the IG people will hate you.___But that's life.___Take your people and go Moses.___*Ha!*___Really,___take them to chow and then go back to your barracks.

It was early in the afternoon. We had chow and now after loudly marching back to our barrack, we sat around, talking this time, and wondered what would be our next orders. We waited for four hours until evening chow and then our Bronx corporal showed up. PFC Delahey and his detail were not so lucky and obviously had to work all day, but then again, they did not have to experience the Bronx corporal, as we did.

"Okay,___yous guys.___Hadda lazy dey,___huh?___Lots ah people woiken on da island an yous jus' sit on yer asses,___huh?___Why does dat s'prize me!___Huh?___Guess yous are special,___huh?___Wait 'till mornin' and I'll give ya a good wake-up call!___Right?___Yous'll like dat,___huh?" the greasy slime-ball blabbered on and we kept wondering what we did to piss him off so much or whether this is a gradual realization, on his part, that he had new power over twenty-eight newly forged Marines. Something a puke like him, evidently never had before he was assigned to shepherd us.

Delahey entered the squad bay and heard the last comments the slime ball had said.

"Well,___heah come da leedah ah dis pack.___Delahey!___*Hey-hey.___Get it___scuz?*" the corporal sneered.

"Corporal,___if you are drunk,___get your ass out of here.___If not,___then I think I have enough witnesses to swear you are slandering me and harassing the entire group of platoon 3074.___Do you wish for me to express our concerns to Colonel Lasher?" he stated coldly, and there was no answer from the Bronx clown. "I thought so.___I'll take the platoon to chow and you go away.___Sleep it off some place,___but go.___We will take this up in the morning,___depending on your personality," Delahey concluded in his best intimidating voice. The corporal left without a word. Maybe he was just sober enough to realize his dilemma.

"Way to go Delahey," we cheered in unison.

"Now yous can git us ovah to da mess hall.___Huh?" one of our group said goofing on the Bronx corporal's pronunciations.

When PFC Delahey got us formed up in front of the mess hall hatch he was stopped and asked for his authorization to bring a group of Marines to this facility. The staff sergeant was new to us, so it was not really a surprise.

"You have a chit?" he asked almost with no care one way or the other.

"No!" Delahey said, showing only slight aggravation.

"Well you can't come in then," the staff sergeant stated without even looking at Delahey or our group. There was only the same non-feeling attitude in his words.

"The corporal who is normally in charge of our group is___*ah*___sick___and a few minutes ago left suddenly,___leaving me in charge.___Apparently he forgot to give me a chit in his hurry to leave.___I have twenty-seven Marines to feed and we have been eating in this mess hall for months," Delahey said sternly.

"Sign in!___Put your unit and name and head count.___Next

time bring a chit," the staff sergeant said with only a little more life in his voice.

Delahey signed us in and we all moved through the chow line trying our utmost best to suppress outright laughter. If that had happened, it would have been the second time for Platoon 3074 and the third time for me, since being bunked with the Three Stooges in the Medical Platoon days. Platoon 3074 laughed during pugil stick competition and if they laughed anytime before that I would not have known it, but gauging Sergeant Wyeth's personality, I doubt it. Sergeant Hodson had replaced him by the time we were in pugil stick training. As for me, I had only really laughed two times on this Island. We must have really learned restraint, because what could have been a belly-busting roar of laughter was swallowed and reduced to silent grins and smirks. But, I felt like I had baking powder and water bubbling in my throat.

The recruits serving us were so wide-eyed and intent on doing their jobs well that they gave no indication they saw us smirking and choking back laughter. Our meal was really good tonight. We had fried chicken, mashed potatoes, corn and a chunk of cornbread. I lucked out by getting a large chicken breast.

Back in our barrack the laughter exploded as individuals replayed Delahey's moments with that staff sergeant.

"Why didn't you just tell him the corporal was drunk.___Hell!"

"Man!___You were cold,___and in his face.___Dead-eye Delahey!"

"Whatcha do when the man says no, Delahey?"

"Yeh.___We all get sent to bed without supper?"

"Christ man,___that shit-for-brains corporal really had some nerve showing up the way he did,___man."

"The chicken was *sooo* good,___I'd have kicked that corporal's ass if he had cost us that meal."

And so, on-and-on it went, between laughter, for the remainder of the night. Delahey just shook his head, grinned, acknowledged with up-and-down head shaking and generally accepted our banter. Reluctantly, he hit the light switch as the first notes of taps sounded. We stopped our talking as though that switch had also turned us off. The bugle was given full passage through our hearts and minds, evoking emotions and contemplations.

SIX

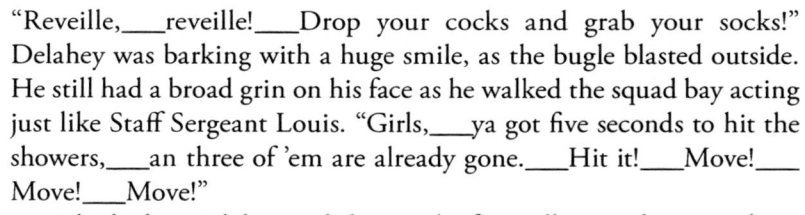

"Reveille,___reveille!___Drop your cocks and grab your socks!" Delahey was barking with a huge smile, as the bugle blasted outside. He still had a broad grin on his face as he walked the squad bay acting just like Staff Sergeant Louis. "Girls,___ya got five seconds to hit the showers,___an three of 'em are already gone.___Hit it!___Move!___ Move!___Move!"

I looked at Delahey and then at the faces all around just gawking at Delahey. Saunders chuckled and offered his input.

"Looks like old Delahey wants to be a DI and stay on this island forever.___Fuck that man!"

"Jealous Saunders?___You don't have what it takes to be crude, rude and destitute," Delahey chided back.

"Destitute?___What's that?" came a voice from the group.

"Lacks a fucking personality,__you idiots.__Not really.___It means poor,___got nothing to do with rude or crude,___just rhymed," Delahey answered with a bright smile, "I feel like today is our last day here.___Got me a gut feeling,___and I feel the court martial will end today as well."

"Think so Delahey?___This is the crotch and they like to screw with you.___So don't get your hopes up," a voice in the crowd commented.

"Yeh!___But let's pretend he's right and enjoy a day around here," another voice stated cheerfully.

"Expect the worst.___It's the rule here," Woodly said gloomily.

"You guys want the good old days back?___From the way you're talking___you miss ol' Wyeth and his yard stick___*thump-thump-thump*," Kellerman mimicked the yard stick crashing down.

"I gotta get off this island!" I said quietly, while shaking my head left to right in disgust. I had been suspicious for some time now, that something was always cropping-up to keep me on the Island and I would never go home. Maybe I did die and this was hell.

"If we stay any longer they'll promote Delahey to Sergeant and make him our new drill instructor and we'll never leave this island," Saunders protested with a grin, "How long have you been on the island?" he asked me. I looked at him as if he had just read my mind, and when I told him, he exploded.

"Holy shit!__You been here that long?__Christ, no wonder you seem pissed to be staying even longer for this trial." Saunders said, now shaking his head left to right.

"I want to see what's next in the Corps.___So I hope today is it," I stated, with real belief that it had to be over today.

"Yeh!___Let's hope," Saunders said solemnly.

After we showered and decided to go ahead and put on our utilities, because the Bronx corporal was late and we did not expect PT if he was late and chow was not going to wait either. So it turned out we waited for a long time.

The hatch opened and Corporal Burk from H&S Company marched in.

"PFC Delahey!___The rest of you go on and fall out for chow," he said in a calm voice.

When the chow word is heard no man waits. Just like all those times in boot camp, our feet pounded the stairwell and stiff arms smashed open the double hatch doors to eject bodies eager to hit that pavement and salivate awaiting chow.

Delahey came out with the corporal and we fell into formation. Corporal Burk marched us over to the mess hall and left after signing us in.

After we were seated, many eyes kept trying to get Delahey's attention, but he remained silent about what went down this morning.

As our group finally formed up outside the mess hall, Delahey called us to attention.

"Listen up!___Corporal Bronx was not available this morning.___So I was informed of our schedule and here it is.___At 0900 hours we go back to the courtroom.___If there is a final decision before noon chow, then we have duties after chow.___Those duties will be explained at that time.___" "Ah___ten___huat!" he growled and got us moving toward the courtroom.

Once seated in the courtroom, we watched the other personnel involved in this matter come in randomly and find their seats. Approximately fifteen minutes after we had arrived Sergeant Wyeth and his counsel team entered. Sergeant Wyeth looked more bent and gaunt then usual. He neither smiled nor looked about. He definitely never looked over at 3074 filling a good portion of the benches.

Major Pouscher and his team entered and each team nodded

pleasantries toward each other. The jury filed in and five seconds later the chamber hatch swung open and Colonel Lasher stormed in.

"All rise!" the court clerk boomed.

The rustle of uniforms rubbing material between arms and sides, chairs scrapping, pens dropping to paper tablets, short coughs, shoes hitting wooden bench legs and chair legs all resonated through the room at the same time.

"Colonel Lasher,___residing judge over The Case of United States versus Sergeant Wyeth, 3rd Recruit Training Battalion,___3rd Recruit Training Regiment,___for charges of Maltreatment and Cruelty of a Subordinate and Assault and Battery.___Be seated."

Again the same noises were heard echoing throughout the austere room.

"Counsels for the defense and prosecution please approach the bench," Colonel Lasher stated.

They walked up to the front of the judge's bench and all three were in whispered conference. A head bobbed here and there and then the huddle broke up and the counsels returned to their seats.

"The clerk may now take the verdict. Mr. Foreman, would you please stand.___Mr. Foreman have the members reached a verdict?"

"Yes Sir,___they have," the Foreman said.

"Mr. Foreman,___how do the members find on the charge of maltreatment and Cruelty of a Subordinate?____Guilty or not guilty?"

"Guilty Sir!"

"So say all the members?"

"Yes Sir!."

"Mr. Foreman,___how do the members find on the charge of Assault and Battery?___Guilty or not guilty?"

"Guilty Sir!"

"So say the members?"

"Yes Sir!"

There was little reaction on Sergeant Wyeth's face and his team showed absolutely no emotion.

I felt a numb feeling take hold of my mind and felt sure it was the feelings shared by our entire group.

"I wish to thank the members for their attendance and also state that their service is now complete.___You are hereby excused."

Colonel Lasher stated and the MPs escorted the members from the courtroom.

"Sergeant Wyeth,___the jury has found you guilty of all charges for which the court imposes the following penalties.___You are to be reduced one pay grade,___to corporal,___thirty days restriction,___ and to forfeit one hundred dollars per month for three months.___ Furthermore,___I am personally pleased to inform you that you are no longer eligible to serve as a drill instructor.___You have very likely evaded charges for similar violations of the UCMJ,___recruit training procedures SOP,___and rights of recruits in the past months you have been on the drill field.___I find that your methods of training and your interpretation of what should be added to the established Marine Corps training regimen have done little toward producing a better, more capable recruit,___and has instead succeeded in demoralizing, injuring, and disrupting the spirit, health, and progress of those in your charge," he stated sternly, and then rose and started toward the hatch.

"All rise,___This court is in recess," the court clerk stated.

Corporal Wyeth never looked at any of us as he left the room with slow deliberate steps. His counsel group walked a few paces behind him. The prosecuting team was busy packing their briefcases and they too left without even a look towards our group. When the aisle was clear we exited as well. Outside we saw a bright blue sky and felt the warmth of the 62 degree day with an equally warm breeze blowing against our faces. No talking was heard and no faces exhibited joy. Not one Marine involved in the court-martial ever spoke to us again. It was as if our group was on a raft cut adrift by those in power to sentence.

Corporal Burk came over to our group and called us to formation. He then marched us back to our barrack with little cadence being called. It was a solemn sounding march back and our minds were still numb. The corporal had handed a stack of papers to Delahey and left. We started to like that corporal. He was white, with a small build, seemingly efficient and easy to talk to.

Delahey read off our assignments for the remaining part of the day. I got brig-chaser duty. So after noon chow I was to report to the Regimental Area and locate the brig.

Chow was quiet, with only a few words here and there about the duty assignments pulled after eating. Outside, Delahey gave us leave to get where we had to be. The assignments really fragmented our group this time.

With my orders in hand, I started walking rapidly back towards the area we had been that morning. I had an odd thought that I might have to deal with Wyeth, but then I remembered he was not in the brig. When I reported in, a gunnery sergeant gave me my first assignment. He issued me an M-14, ammunition and cartridge belt with a canteen and nightstick and the name of my charge.

I saddled up and waited for Recruit Schlass. The kid was a first week recruit from 3rd Battalion and I was supposed to run him over to his platoon's barrack, see his DI and have him pack his gear and then return him, with his sea bag, to the brig.

Schlass turned out to be a skinny, five foot five white lad with platinum stubs. He had blood-shot blue eyes and they were saucer wide with fear.

"Sir, Recruit Schlass reporting as ordered Sir!"

Schlass screamed into my ear. I was shocked to be addressed as a drill instructor would be and at the second the kid did it, I felt power.

Well that's the reason the DIs eat this shit up and ask for seconds.___It is also why they look for errors to punish us and hear our desperate responses. I mused and had a chill run through my body. *Hell, I don't feel the same as them though.___The power is undeserved on my part.___I'll just treat him as a prisoner,___and do my job.* I concluded, knowing this is now my job as a Marine.

"Fall out!___We're taking a walk to get your gear," I said in a normal voice.

"Sir, yes Sir!" he boomed.

As he walked in front of me, I followed with my M-14 at port arms as instructed. We entered his barrack and moved to the DI shack. The platoon was out training, but one of his DI's was in his office doing paperwork.

The hatch was open, so I stood in front of it and made my presence known.

"Private Shipman, with a party of one prisoner, reporting as ordered." I stated, and even looked right into the eyes of the DI, and the second I stopped talking, I realized it was the Skull. The sergeant was one of the team on our Final Inspection Day.

"Schlass!___You scum-bag piece of shit!___Get your trash

packed___now,___and get the hell out of my Marine Corps!" he bawled with a grimace, which made his skull-image more pronounced. The recruit ran to his former bunk and got to it. I looked at the DI and he was grinning at me. His face appeared very normal now.

"How they hanging, Shipman.___You doin okay?___I remember you from the inspection primarily, but Staff Sergeant Rogers told me about you,___says he wishes you luck.___He mentioned your bad luck on the tug of war, which landed you in the Medical Platoon and then,___Christ,___Sergeant Wyeth's hell hole.___Don't believe all drill instructors share in the same methods of training."

"Thank you for the information.___I wondered about Staff Sergeant Rogers and how Platoon 3063 fared."

"Yeh,___3063 did really well,___took the most streamers,___highest shooters,___a real good batch of recruits,___now good Marines.___I was going to pay your group a visit anyway, before you leave and I would have passed Staff Sergeant Rogers' best wishes along then," he spoke in the calmest voice one could imagine and I did not even feel I was talking with a DI.

"The gang is doing fine___and the court martial is over."

"Yeh,__I already heard.__Hey!__Get yer ass moving scumbag!__ You don't have all day.___What?" he switched voices to bawl out Schlass and got his response and continued in his normal voice to me. "Well good to hear all came out the way it did.___You get this piece-of-shit outta here for me.___Okay?___Take it easy," he finished, offered his hand and went into his office.

Schlass labored hard for the long walk between 3rd Battalion and Regiment. He kept switching his sea bag between shoulders. When we reached the Iwo Jima Monument, by the main parade deck, I let him rest for a few minutes. He kept looking straight ahead scared shitless to speak or look at me.

When I had my charge safely turned over to his new care-takers I could not even try to imagine what fate he had ahead of him. I was able to sit in the duty shack, to wait for any other orders. There were postcards of Parris Island in a stack, a large stack, lying on top of a bookcase near the door. The picture was an orange or mauve colored evening sunset with the main bridge or causeway over Archer Creek, between the Island and Beaufort. I decided to utilize one of these cards and write home. The first thing I needed was an ink pen. I scrounged around the duty shack until I found one and quickly told Mom the whole story in the space available on the card.

16 Jan 70

Dear Mom,
Hi. I have waited to tell you that 28 of my platoon had to stay for a week to attend our former DI's court-martial for stuff he did against the rules. Well tomorrow I get to leave across this bridge. I get to leave the island finally and go to Camp Lejeune, N.C. The trial ended today and he got busted to corporal, 30 days restriction and $100 a month fine (light fine) out of pay and no longer a DI. I am guarding a prisoner right now and watching T.V. too. (He's not!) I hope you and the girls are fine. So now I say goodbye Parris Island.
Love,
Jack

I read the card over again and smiled at how I wrote I was guarding a prisoner right now. But, I figured it was a way of telling her what I'm doing today on the small three-by-three inch white writing area. As for the TV, I had to get up a nerve to turn it on. But, I finally did. *I Love Lucy* came on in fuzzy black and white. After several hours I had chased a few more prisoners and finally got the word I could knock off. I literally ran back to my barrack to make chow-time. I made it with just a few minutes to spare. Most of the others had been waiting in the squad bay.

After chow we were visited by the Skull. His presence did unnerve a few of our group at first, but after he spoke and wished us all luck, they relaxed. He especially encouraged us to get into our dress greens and go out to enjoy a movie or something.

I got dressed and opted for a movie. I did not care if anyone else was going and I did not wait around. I dug out a six-cent stamp and pasted it on the postcard. Having spotted a mailbox earlier, I was bound towards that area to mail it. I also wanted to ensure I saw a movie and was not too late.

The theater was not packed and the lights went out earlier than the beginning of the flick. Because it was dark I did not identify any 3074 guys who may have decided to see a flick as well. Hell, I hadn't even looked to see what was playing, but then the movie credits announced *Father Goose*, staring Cary Grant and Leslie Caron. The film originally came out in 1964, but who cared, it was a flick and a good one to boot. I had never seen it before.

After the movie ended, I was just starting to cross the street when my eye caught movement off to port side, next to a bank of phone booths. I looked over to see a pretty girl in a Woman-Marine uniform. I slowly walked over and she just watched me. There was no fear on her face and I felt more comfortable when I noticed that she was also a private.

About five minutes had passed while I was trying to get into a really comfortable conversation. My hands crept up and into my dress green pockets and I was suddenly kicking invisible dirt clods or something, with my shoes desperately poking air in that *aw-shucks* way.

Just then a car screeched to a halt behind me. It startled me enough to turn my head around to catch what was making the sudden interruption in what had been a quiet and peaceful night, only to catch a loud voice boom from the rolled down window.

"Get your hands out of your pockets Marine!___You should know better than that!"

It turned to see Colonel Parrish glaring at me.

Oh shit!

"Aye-aye Sir!" I shouted, while we both snapped to stiff attention and saluted him.

He drove off and the young woman Marine, showing no reaction, said she had to get back to her quarters.

I walked back to 3rd Battalion in an angry mood. I was angry with myself for screwing-up on what I was supposed to have learned on the Island and on possibly getting a date. But, then I vowed to keep my mind on proper military procedures from here on and felt foolish for even thinking about getting a date on the Island, when I'd be leaving."

When I got into the squad bay, I saw at least five guys there. They had also seen the flick and had just returned.

We changed into utility trousers and tee-shirts and sat on our footlockers to shoot the breeze.

"What do you think about the outcome of the trial?" was the first inquiring question voiced out loud. It was Kellerman.

"Crap!__Pure crap!__He shoulda been shot," quipped Shelton in his usual nervous voice.

"He's off the drill field,__that's what matters," Woodly said slowly and apparently with more thought behind his statement then he voiced.

"They should have caught him a long time ago," Saunders said making sense. However, we could not answer why he had never been in trouble for this stuff before, or if he had been.

"Yeh man!__He shoulda been busted a long time ago," Jackman offered.

"I was sure we would have eventually had a fatality if that guy kept it up," Woodly said."

"Getting through boot camp with a guy like that as your DI can seriously narrow a guy's chances," I said seriously.

"Hell, Shipman, you eat this Marine stuff up.__You can hack it and you proved it.__I think you will have fun in the Corps," Kellerman said equally as serious.

"Saunders is another one, a grunt who eats it up," Shelton said and Jackman gave a big grin and an affirmative shake of his head.

We hit the rack early, deciding that we'd have a big day tomorrow. The others trickled in over the next hour in two's, three's, alone or in bunches. What they found to do on this Island was a mystery to me.

Lights were finally switched off and taps was especially moving tonight. Perhaps a different bugler, but it was noticeably well played.

I slept soundly, due to the outside temperature, and a window being left open, while a cold rain fell all night. In fact, I slept so soundly, that I had to be shook awake by Kellerman to wake me.

"Get up!__Jeez!__How can you do that,__just sleep right through all the noise?" he grinned broadly.

"Corporal Burk just came in and told us to grab chow and get back here to saddle up.__We're leaving the island today."

EPILOGUE

Jesus had a last supper and we had a last breakfast, but it was just as much symbolic of the end of an ordeal. Corporal Burk marched us over to the mess hall and told us to get back with PFC Delahey and pack our gear. We would then march over to the Receiving Barracks and wait to board a Greyhound bus, which will then take us to Camp Geiger North Carolina.

Our breakfast tasted better then any meal we had since arriving on the Island and we were grinning like we got away with a prank. Perhaps our grins were more an expression of pride in our accomplishments, joy in our departure and eagerness to explore our new occupations in the Marine Corps. We were neophytes ready to take on the world.

This morning I thought a lot about our next stage of training at the Infantry Training Regiment (ITR) which would be basic training in Infantry skills and then each of those Marines would go off to their specific school for their military occupation skill (MOS). My MOS was Infantry and I knew that meant I would continue my Advanced Infantry Training and then be transferred to an Infantry Battalion with the Fleet, in one of the three Marine Corps divisions, where they did nothing less then constant training in the skills of a professional infantryman.

Our conversations this morning were eager and as usual very quietly spoken. Each spoke about their MOS and where their schools were or where they might be transferred as a first duty station. Several comments were in response to a question about what the ITR training would be like. The big question was how we would be treated by the instructors, since we were now graduate Marines. Would they use the same shock and punishment tactics used here on the Island, or would they just tell us what they wanted and let us demonstrate our grasp and execution? No absolute answer was arrived at. We finished chow and fell out to make the short march over to the barrack.

As we marched, I could not help but note that as long as I had been on the Island, I had never seen any personnel in the training areas, in groups of two people or more, ever just walk around. Other then the DIs, everybody marched about their business.

Once inside our barrack our mood had somehow changed to one of urgency, as if at any moment an order would come to us delaying our departure. So we packed our sea bags in record time and fell out into formation. There we stood, wearing crisply starched utilities and covers, with our sea bags in perfect orderly position to our right leg, sitting on the deck.

I wish Staff Sergeant Louis, Sergeant Black or Sergeant Hodson would suddenly appear and march us to the Receiving Barracks.___That would be fitting as the proper conclusion to our training.___The rest of our platoon was marched to the buses by them when we graduated.___Ah well,___I guess we are already forgotten by now and they won't show up.___Maybe they are busy at the moment screaming at a new batch of civilian turds. I thought morosely.

Instead Corporal Burk showed up long enough to inform Delahey he would have to march us over to the buses.

What the hell!___At least one of our leaders has the honor and not a H&S corporal to herd us off the island. I figured. *We deserved to be marched to the buses by a real DI,___because we earned that right!* I decided somewhat miffed.

"Plaa___toon!___Ah___ten___huat!" PFC Delahey barked loudly. "Sea bags to the left shoulder,___huah!" We reached down, grabbing the shoulder straps of the bags and in a very orderly manner hefted upwards and swung the bags toward our left shoulder, while our left hand grasp the straps to complete the swing over our shoulder. "Riat,___huah!___Foart,___huah!" he bellowed the orders from deep in his gut, and in a froggy voice, marched us the long way to our bus.

We marched across the main parade deck passing the Iwo Jima monument and I remembered my first day and the chaotic madness during our cattle drive across this monstrous meat grinder to our first barrack. I moved my eyes to port, to catch a last glimpse of our old white wooden World War II barracks. As I looked, I saw hundreds of recruits marching in the first weeks of training and knew their DIs didn't miss the opportunity to point us out as something their pusillanimous hogs would never aspire to become. I had to grin, knowing that many would, in the capable hands of their drill instructors.

The long march, like all things, had come to an end and there waiting before us, was a big shinny Greyhound bus. As soon as our driver saw us he walked over to a DI sergeant who apparently was on recruit receiving duty today and spoke to him, while jerking his head toward us.

PFC Delahey ordered us to a halt and to execute a perfect maneuver to lower our sea bags.

I hope that DI liked Delahey's work. I thought with a mental smile.

"Go ahead and stow yer gear under the bus and get on board," the DI sergeant said, not unkindly.

It was the best order I had been given on the Island, with only two others close to it and they were to march to our graduation ceremony and to leave the Medical Platoon and return to training.

I boarded the bus and found a seat. I did not care one bit about the stench of hair oil, vomit, diesel, baby powder or the overall mustiness of the bus. It smelled like heaven now. Saunders climbed aboard wearing a big grin and found a seat. Since there were only twenty eight of us and many more seats everyone figured to stretch out. However it was not to be. A few minutes after we were comfortably sitting in our roomy seats seven more buses drove up and an entire graduating series came marching over to get on board.

Shit!___There goes my nice elbow room. I thought sourly as a graduate recruit, looking like a country boy, plopped into the seat beside me.

Hell, it would have been nicer to have Saunders or Kellerman or any of our group to make the long trip as a seat-neighbor. But it was too late, as no sooner had they sat down, the driver hopped aboard and fired up the diesel engine. I heard the other diesels idling and then the *swoosh* of the doors closing A moment later another sharp blast of air, mixed with what sounded like a yelp, came from the brakes being released. A low rumble accompanied by a slight vibration indicated that we were underway. Our convoy was slowly passing the hatches of the Receiving Barracks, the Big White Elephant, as the DIs had called it, and I looked out at the sign over the door, which proudly proclaimed that through this portal pass prospects for the world's finest fighting force and in larger letters under that was written United States Marine Corps.

Suddenly, as if my mind had become a meteor, it shot through the entire bulk of my training trails and tribulations, much like when one fast-forwards a film. As the bus moved forward, the last image of the Receiving Area my eyes settled on, were the yellow footprints.

I swear I heard the sound of many breaths being exhaled as we passed the MP shack at the front gate of Parris Island. My reaction was exhalation and an inner exhilaration causing a great weight to slough-off of my body. I was now genuinely ready for what the Corps had in mind for me. I did not ever feel that way while still in the mental quagmire of the Island.

The buses rolled over the causeway and then meandered through the streets of Beaufort. While our driver negotiated the city streets, I gazed hungrily at the long forgotten images of an every-day town. It was hard to imagine people going freely about their way without a DI in charge. Once free of the magnet of Beaufort, our convoy rolled onto Route 17, where it broke free and shot forward for the entire trip of approximately two hundred seventy miles to Camp Geiger. Camp Geiger was a training base next to Jacksonville, North Carolina and near the giant Marine Corps Amphibious Base, Camp LeJeune, and home of the famed Second Marine Division Fleet Marines.

The trip was long and I was content to stare out the window and look at the passing sights, but I asked the guy next to me for his name, if he had graduated today and what his platoon number was. He sounded both tired and eager at the same time, I thought, as he answered in a southern drawl.

"My name's Williams,__Johnny.__An' we was in Platoon 2081,___ which,___thank God, finally graduated yesterday," he answered with a broad smile, "Come from Newport, Kentucky.__Where you from?" he said, sounding proud of his town and state.

"Glen Burnie, Maryland," I answered. We both agreed we had never heard of each others home, so he said Cincinnati, Ohio was across the river and I said Baltimore was up the road. We spoke off-and-on between dozing here-and-there, due to the bus vibrations and the long drive. As the miles passed by, my thoughts went over my ordeal in boot camp, and I found myself thinking about Sergeant Wyeth.

Was he really our enemy? No, I figured he really was convinced that he was training us harder and better then the Corps allowed for other recruits going through Parris Island or San Diego. He had been to a war and whatever hardships he and the Marines there were enduring would leave a man to learn something from it. Sergeant Wyeth had stated as much during his court-martial. And now where would he go in the Corps? Maybe he would rather go back to Vietnam, where his upside-down version of the world was learned and still would make since to him. I knew that the harsh training had to have a value attached, and perhaps what we learned to endure, would enable us to live through some future hardships. The men at the Chosin Reservoir in Korea or on the islands in the Pacific Ocean and numerous other tests of endurance had to be glad to have been offered the hardest training their DIs and boot camp could offer. Perhaps they also had tough DIs who busted their asses on the sly.

The more I thought about it I felt proud to have been able to endue that gauntlet, and knowing it was as rough as it was, I would consider myself lucky to claim that achievement. I do not agree with beating recruits to death, but I do agree with tightening-up wayward turds. So maybe the DI code has merit when they say: 'You can beat your turds, but don't make them bleed!'. The DI who makes a recruit bleed is shunned by the others and testified against, so it figures that the DIs know what is required for proper training more so then the Marine Corps Public Relations people who cater to vote-seeking elected officials and worried mothers. Perhaps mothers want to see their boys in splendid uniforms, but don't do anything to them during their training that might hurt them.

Ah___fuck it! I suddenly fumed at myself for even thinking I knew a damned thing about anything and sat silently staring out at a lot of nowhere and nothing.

The buses eventually came to a loud stop full of the hissing and belching of air, as before. The door *swooshed* open and a gunnery sergeant in starched utilities came aboard.

"Welcome to Camp Geiger Infantry Training Regiment.___Now get your tired asses off the fuckin' bus and form up in the parking lot!___Move it!" he barked nastily.

We did as he ordered and as fast as possible. There were no yellow footprints for the dummies. They expected us to know instinctively how to form up.

"Ahh___ten___huat!___Dress___riat,___dress!___Ready,___to!___Second squad one step backwards,___third squad two steps backwards,___fourth squad three steps backwards,___huah!" the gunnery sergeant bawled so loud the buses must have shook, "Push-up positions,___four-count!__Get on your faces!___Hit it!___Now!" he growled like a nasty junk-yard dog.

A very tall Marine stood in front of me. I did not know where any of the 3074 bunch were, amidst the nearly three hundred newly arrived Marines. At the instant we slammed into the deck, I watched in slow motion as the heel, of the Marine in front of me, came up as he dove down and punched me in the jaw, causing me to bite hard into my lip. With a mouth full of blood, I cranked out as many push-ups as that sadistic gunnery sergeant demanded of us.

Welcome to the Marine Corps! We don't promise you a rose garden!

AFTERWORD

The reason I decided to write this book, was due to a persistent mental nagging that kept at me to do it for years. In fact, my decision to actually start resulted on the 10th of January 1996, when I woke to find a winter storm had dropped several feet of snow over the Virginia countryside. I remember thinking that morning about what I can do on such a day, stuck in the house, and then I thought about being caught in a situation where a man has to answer to his on promises. My decision was to start writing and stop promising.

I owned and worked at my own construction business and found myself working steady seven day work weeks. This hectic schedule can seriously limit the time available to write a book. It was a debilitating on-the-job injury, during the winter of 2009 – 2010 (and again during a series of rare heavy snow storms), that finally forced me to take a lengthy break from my business and get back to the book. So I dug out my manuscript, which had all the chapters already written, dusted it off, and while recovering, finished editing my book. My personal motivation to write this account was to share what I had always wanted to say about my gauntlet through Parris Island, South Carolina.

Former DI, Staff Sergeant Rowland had remarked in Thomas E. Ricks book *Making The Corps* in 1997 "One reason today's DIs display such an edgy determination to keep standards high, is that most remember the bad old days when Marines came close to being a broken family. It isn't just the drill instructors who carry this feeling." And in the same book General Krulak, who was the commandant of Marines during the 1990s, remarked about that nadir, "The people who are now generals, at my level, and what we went through,...the late sixty-nine and seventies experience would say, 'if you can get through that, you carry in your heart and soul: Never again. Never again'."

I met with Dr. Keith Flemming during the late 1990s and discussed my project. Dr. Flemming, who had endured Parris Island and later served as a rifle company commander in Vietnam, had published the book *The U.S. Marine Corps In Crisis* about the Ribbon Creek incident, and recruit training. He presented a study on why boot camp training was not only tough, but extremely brutal as well. The following are excerpts of his writings mixed with my comments on some statements from his book, which I felt were germane to my book.

After World War II and Korea, where the Marines had won so many battles, the Cold War became the new threat, which meant combat could be possible at any time. The decision to maintain the harsh training the Corps was known for, was the concensus of Marine Corps advocates, that poorly trained, poorly disciplined troops do not win battles and that a change to the training format, used by the other branches of service, would decrease the Corps combat readiness. However, the 1956 Ribbon Creek incident, which cried for a congressional investigation, would become detrimental to the Marine Corps' ability to maintain their record of victory in battle, if they were forced to change. Therefore, the Corps proposed to congress, in response to the Ribbon Creek tragedy, which resulted in the drowning of six recruits, that they would change their training procedure and set their own house in order to avoid the investigation.

That change proposed adding several weeks to the training and introducing a new emphasis on physical training, which pleased the Corps' combat arm, the Fleet Marine Force, which demanded more physical capabilities from reporting recruits for the rigors that advanced infantry training demands. Additionally, more officers were sent to the recruit depots to provide more supervision of the drill instructors. A 'social program' for the overweight, weak or unmotivated recruits was created to take the pressure of these problem catagories from the DIs.

These extensive reforms, which were mostly administrative, did not touch the 'shock treatment' that formed the fundamental element of Marine Corps training. The concensus of the shock treatment and harsh disciplinarian training is to try to break the recruit before they end up in a combat situation where a man's breakdown will result in the deaths and injuries of others, or if enough fail to handle the stress of combat, the battle will be lost.

The terms 'hazing' and 'maltreatment' are difficult to define in recruit training context and, in Marine jargon. Maltreatment usually covers both terms. The official definition (varied with time) include: official restrictions on DIs to use profanity (tends to degrade the recruit), 'duck walking', hiking with packs filled with sand, dry shaving while doing a physical exsercise with a metal bucket over the recruit's head, using foot lockers as rifles or barbells, watching television (body supported off the deck on four points using only toes and elbows). The list of prohibited hazing contained twenty-two items. The maltreatment list contained twenty-nine items, including punching recruits in the stomach, burning recruits with cigarettes, forcing recruits to eat cigarettes, stacking recruits in trash bins, refusing recruits the use of insect repellant, making recruits run the 'belt line' (a gauntlet of fellow recruits swinging belts). The basic Marine Corps definition of maltreatment is any practice which degrades the individual or causes them pain or injury. The introduction of the Uniform Code of Military Justice (UCMJ) served only to create a high level of frustration amongst the drill instructors and other NCOs in the Corps.

DIs believed that a swift kick in a recruit's ass will motivate them, or any other form of required or appropriate corporal punishment to get the desired results, were aids in teaching proper discipline. In the process, they narrowed the group definition down to any practices that did not 'make the recruit bleed or require hospitalization'. DIs vigorously protected each other as long as this rule was not violated.

DIs believed that success in combat was directly related to discipline. The collective Marine NCO thinking was to use the autonomy of the DIs for two purposes. One was a tool to ensure the desired high level of recruit discipline and the other to shore-up the groups diminished authority and prestige. These two trends combined at Parris Island to create a pressure cooker situation and fostered the brutal treatment of recruits. In this environment, the level of brutality reached unprecedented levels. Never before had recruits suffered so much. After all, Parris Island has been defined as the equivilant of a tribal puberty rite. (End of Dr. Flemming's contribution).

The reason I felt so strongly about telling this story, was that I felt it did reflect the experience of the end of the nineteen sixties, a decade of drastic change in our American way of life. That decade moved from Camelot to the jungles of Vietnam and left our military hardened with the reality of possible defeat and a portion of our society in fear and doubt of our political leaders' resolve to finish what they started, while the other part of our society slapped themselves on the back, praised their political leaders and condemned those who served in Vietnam.

This reminds me of the Revolutionary War, during which one third of the population fought the British, one third were pro British Crown--called Tories, while one third just watched and either bad-mouthed one or the other thirds, or both, and reaped the benefits of the end results.

Although the subject matter of this event does not make the Marine Corps, my Corps, exactly shine with duty, honor, country within the character of some of those who trained us, it never-the-less displays the intent by the majority of instructors, regular Marines and recruits, to still participate in the meaning of esprit de corps, honor and love of country. During the time of my training many Marines had already died in Vietnam and our drill instructors were mostly all war veterans and all were perpetually hard men, who were often cruel, and always demanding of us recruits. Simply put, it was the Corps' meritocracy of that time, the ethos of the Drill Instructors was the wall we recruits had to conquer, before they would let us take over the future of their Marine Corps and ensure eternal victory.

I have often felt that the Marine Corps is looked upon by the general public, not unlike a professional football team, that once having won the Super Bowl, it is 'expected' to win forever afterwards (eternal victory). But no hitting! The government and the public want the glory of the results, without wanting to know the details of the way there. Of course, once a scandal germinates, the whole news media feasts on it like ravenous piranha, caring not about the damage being inflicted to the body.

This story about my training was never intended as a 'complaint' or 'slam' against the Marine Corps. My feeling is that many more recruits had rough physical and mental training without the violence, abuse and injury that some in my platoon, and in some others, had suffered.

I had changed all the names of recruits, drill instructors and junior officers from the battalion level down. Senior officers, from regimental level and higher, were named correctly. Violations of the Uniform Code of Military Justice (UCMJ) were handled professionally and promptly by those senior officers once violations were discovered. Congressmen and other politicians are also named correctly. The deaths of recruits mentioned in the court martial are actual incidents and correct names of all involved are provided. The Marine Corps and public knows that these events had happened, so I was not divulging information being kept from the general public.

Some sad news came to me while I served a year in Vietnam. My former company commander of H Company at Parris Island had also been assigned there and had informed me that Staff Sergeant Louis (not his correct name) had been killed several weeks after our platoon had graduated. He was involved in a car accident in Beaufort, South Carolina. In 1995, I had met a retired Marine Colonel, (his name has now escaped me) who had told me that as a 1st Lieutenant assigned to Parris Island and who had relieved the company commander I had at that time (and as a Captain in Vietnam), that Staff Sergeant Louis had been killed in an automobile accident, shortly after he assumed command of H Company 3rd Recruit Training Battalion. He even showed me a Cruise Book from Parris Island, which displayed Staff Sergeant Louis' picture. Not to doubt my old company commander, I am only stating that when one hears the same story years apart and by different officers, it has to stand as correct, as I have never been able to personally research it further.

During my conversation with the captain, I had asked him why I had to stay at Parris Island for the court martial, since they never called on me to testify. He informed me that the defense counsel wanted to and had slated me to get on the stand, but the prosecuting counsel talked them out of it. Their reasoning was that because the IG investigation had already determined how each recruit, in our platoon, had been injured. Therefore, that had made it clear how I was actually injured, while I was still holding to having 'slipped in my shower shoes and hitting my head on a rack'. There was enough evidence without my testifying, as I would have perjured myself with the 'rack' story anyway. He asked me why I persisted with my statement. I told him that I simply did not trust the Corps enough at that time to 'squeal' on a DI and feared doing so, because DIs had warned us never to open our mouths, they would discharge me as a 'non-hacker'. He laughed at that notion and I grew to agree over time, while I was serving in the Corps.

If I have stated any event incorrectly, I apologize now, as I tried to recall all events as best memory served. My mother had kept all of my letters from boot camp and they have been placed in their correct sequence of training, along with any misspelled words and bad grammer as I had written them as a very young man during my ordeal in training in those 1969 3rd Battalion barracks. Those letters served to enable a very significant recall of training events.

My feelings about what we recruits had to endure have changed over the years, because the mind of my youth, is not the mind of this older man now. My feelings about the Parris Island gauntlet were practically nonexistent while I was on active duty. It had changed over the years, due to my ability to reflect back and compare it with the new Marine Corps training regimen. Books like that of Thomas E. Ricks *Making The Corps*, obviously state that vast differences in the treatment of recruits, and the language used on them by their drill instructors, have been made since my time on the island. I had visited my old barracks in 2007, and was given a chance to observe the training. I thought the volumn had been turned down, while the training actions were still the same.

A 1969 New York Times article written by James T. Wooten on Parris Island stated: "The maltreatment of recruits is explicitly forbidden and officially condemned by the United States Marine Corps. It is also a fact of life and a source of continuing problems here on this sprawling training base. In the past 45 months, for example, 58 Parris Island drill instructors have been court-martialed on charges of maltreatment. Thirty-four have been convicted. Nearly one-third of those trails (18) and one-fourth of the guilty verdicts (8) have occurred since the beginning of this calendar year (1969)."

I am confident in believing that Lieutenant General Chesty Puller would have smiled at the rough training Platoon 3074 had to endure. However, even he would have drawn a line at those violations for which Sergeant Wyeth had been court-martialed.

A note of interest: In 1970 Chesty Puller and his son had trooped-the-line of my battalion during a pre-deployment courtesy inspection. I was appropriately awed when he stood a few feet in front of me with his bull dog face and barrel chest still popping his buttons. His son was in a wheelchair, having lost his legs while serving in Vietnam, as a Marine officer.

As for Hueston, I never saw him, nor heard from, or about him, again. My Father died in October 1987, and my mother in October 2001. My uncle Max died in 1973 from complication of the illness he developed as a prisoner-of-war. His wife Lotte is currently living in a nursing home in Weilheim, Germany. Anna, Ian and I went back to Kinderheim Sanct Josef in April 2008. It no longer serves as a children's home and is a home for the mentally ill with the nuns now attending their needs. One of the nuns dragged out an old photo album titled 'The American Children' and we were privaliged to see they kept quiet a few momentos of our stay there. Lucious is a scientist and resides with his wife in Virginia. Ian stayed in Germany, now retired, and lives in Munich where he raises horses. Anna received her degree in Jounalism, is married with two children and resides in New Hampshire. Sarah, an avid reader of romance novels and frequent letter writer, had three children and resides in the state of Washington.

ACKNOWLEDGMENTS

I wish to thank my wife Shelly, my youngest sister (Anna in the story) and her husband, for their assistance with computer problems, typing some of the chapters and getting this book into print. I wrote this book in long hand and found that even though this approach kept my flow of thought, without the two finger typing bottleneck, the need to have it typed was even more than Shelly could attend to. So I found several friends to take this book to completion. I thank Ms. Barbara Hunt, of Spingfield, Virginia and Mrs. Susan Guadagno of Fredericksburg, Virginia for their tireless assistance typing the many pages.

In addition, I wish to thank Major McGill, USMC, 3rd Battalion Parris Island (1996), for sending me training schedules and Marine Corps Manuals during the first weeks of this effort. I wish to thank Major Joseph Guadagno, USMC, for researching a variety of information related to Marine Corps policy and procedure and Attorney Major Quincy Ward, USMC, both stationed at Quantico Marine Corps Base, Virginia. Major Ward was especially helpful with the court-martial proceedings, ensuring the proper format of presentation.

My life long friend Manfred "Eddie" Jahn of Weilheim, Germany (Bavaria), deserves a medal for not only reading this book in English, with so many Americanisms, military/Marine Corps terms, acronyms, idioms, jargon and slang, but for fully understanding the story. His comments were very helpful during the editing.

Special thanks to Mr. Al Wallace of the National Climatic Service

(1996), who researched and provided the daily weather information for each day I was at Parris Island.

One of the more difficult chapters to write about was the Rifle Range. I was grateful to get a complete overview from my old Marine buddy and great friend, former Sergeant John R. Williams of Newport, Kentucky, who was a Primary Marksmanship Instructor at Parris Island during 1972 and 1973.

I must also thank those people who read my manuscript and encouraged me to get published. Thank you all for your help and motivation along the way.

APPENDIX: FAMILY HISTORY

ONE

My father, a retired Master Sergeant, had made the U.S. Air Force his career. He had entered the U.S. Army Air Corps through Little Rock, Arkansas in 1939. He met my mother during the allied occupation of Germany. He was born and raised in the small town of Red Flint, Arkansas. She was born in Schloss Paehl (the castle Paehl), which crowned the mountain over-looking the town of Paehl and she grew up in Weilheim, both neighboring towns near Munich, in the German state of Bavaria. My life began in Texas, and had moved through England, Arkansas and Kansas by the time I was eight years old.

My father, who went by JT, retired from the U.S. Air Force in 1960. After failing to get a job around Wichita, Kansas, he made arrangements to go to Arkansas.

I had two older brothers, Ian and Lucious and two younger sisters, Sarah and Annie. We were living in Wichita until Papa took all of us kids, except Ian, to Red Flint, Arkansas in 1960. Our mother and Ian stayed in an apartment in Wichita. An arrangement necessitated by marital difficulties.

We had rented-out our house on South Glen Street in Wichita, and our household belongings were packed in huge wooden boxes for long term storage and trucked away in a Kansas warehouse, while we where in Arkansas. After a few months our mother decided to reconcile her marriage and joined us in Red Flint.

After many attempts to find meaningful employment, it became apparent that no worthwhile work was to be found in Arkansas, so Papa moved us all back into our recently vacated house in Wichita Kansas. During this time our household items had remained in storage.

My father, still unable to find decent work, had told us that he figured it would be easier to find work with the American government at a U.S. military base near Munich, Germany. So we made arrangements for our household goods to be shipped to Germany and boarded a train to New York at the beginning of February 1962. He planned to start looking for work once in Germany and kept that plan to himself.

We arrived late at night at Grand Central Station in New York, and Papa decided we all stay there the rest of the night. In the morning we took a taxi to the city docks. After many more uncomfortable hours processing paperwork, we were finally boarded. Our ship was the ocean liner SS America, a huge luxury passenger ship of the United States Line.

By the time we had sailed halfway across the Atlantic Ocean our father had managed to squander all of our family money, what little there was, in ill-advised card games. He eventually had to send a telegram to my mother's family in Germany to arrange funds for us at our docking port city. Otherwise, we couldn't have purchased train tickets toward our destination. Mama remained in a constant state of anger throwing hateful accusations at Papa, whenever an opportunity opened.

The ship docked at Bremerhaven, a German port city on the North Sea, in the German state of Niedersachsen, (Lower Saxony). Our nerves were settled when Mom managed the receipt of money wired from her brother.

Our family continued the journey by train, from Bremerhaven through the heart of Germany, stopping at Bremen, Hannover, Goettingen, Kassel, Wuerzburg, Augsburg, and many smaller towns, all the way down through Munich, towards Weilheim, our destination. It was a fascinating long journey taking an entire day.

We arrived near midnight at the Weilheim Bahnhof, (train station) and were received by our Onkel (Uncle) Max and Tante (Aunt) Lotte and taken to our Oma's (Grandmother's) home. Onkel Max, her son, lived on the first floor of the three floor house, which had a full kitchen, two bathrooms, a living room and one bedroom.

Upstairs was Oma's living quarters, which included a small kitchen-dining room, and two bedrooms. At the top of the stairs there was also a small landing area. This landing area was about eight feet by five feet, enclosed on two sides by rails. Along the wall of the landing was a large wooden cabinet in which Oma stored all canned food, cheeses, coffee, wursts (salami, sausage and other such preserved meats), dry peas and beans, flour, bread and noodles and many other nonperishable other food items. Cream and milk were set along the inside of the large single pane kitchen window where the winter cold transferred through the glass keeping it as well as a refrigerator could.

To celebrate the occasion, Tante Lotte and Oma had spent considerable time preparing a very-rich and unfortunately very-late traditional German meal, which included Weiss wurst (white pork sausage). It is a custom in Bavaria that no weiss wurst be prepared and served after twelve noon, but since this was technically very early in the morning there was no violation of traditions. However, I did not appreciate the cultural feast and promptly vomited the excellent meal onto the floor. This earned a well aimed slap across the back of my head from my Onkel Max. Max was a strict, but fair, man who had earned his veteran status serving the Third Reich in their Luftwaffe (German Air Force). He had been a navigator with a crew of three in a Junkers JU 52 nicknamed the 'Tante JU' (sounding as U), which was the work-horse of the German Luftwaffe.

On rare occasions, over the years to come, Onkel Max would tell me about what he did during the war. One especially memorable story took place during the last days of World War II.

At the beginning of April 1945, as a result of the Luftwaffe having no more airplanes, he was transferred to the Panzergrenadieres. These were tank destroyer teams that used anti-tank weapons called Panzerfausts and were part of the German Army (Wehrmacht). He was defending an area of the front lines in the southwestern part of the state of Brandenburg against Soviet Army attacks. At that time the front lines were changing daily. The American and British armies were massing to the east, up to the Elbe river, and the Soviet army was driving west, into Berlin. The German army was being squeezed.

His unit, exhausted from battle, was put into a reserve capacity on the west bank of the river Elbe in the state of Sachsen-Anhalt, around the 20th of April 1945. Many soldiers were already voicing their acknowledgment that continued fighting was senseless and the units had already begun fragmenting as officers and men just started walking away towards safer areas or if possible towards home.

Onkel Max listened to a large group of men from his unit argue about which way to go. The majority wanted to head towards the southeast into the state of Sachsen. Onkel Max told his buddies that he did not agree that it was a good plan and started walking southwest towards the state of Thueringen, hoping to avoid capture by the Soviets. He felt positive that the others would run right into the Soviets.

The problem with the Soviets was that they took no prisoners, preferring to simply shoot Germans where they were caught. This preference to kill all Germans was fueled by the exhortations of the Russian journalist Ilya Ehrenburg to extract from the German's two eyes for an eye and a pool of blood for every drop of blood. When the first Americans arrived, they were not in sufficient force to accept the many Germans who, upon sighting them, often surrendered immediately. Unfortunately, those prisoners taken by any of the few and only advance units who had ventured across the river Elbe, were simply turned over to the Soviets, who were assumed to be better able to handle them.

"All continued fighting was senseless to me and my fellow soldiers," Max would say, "Because, the reason was gone, leaving an empty sensation in our hearts." Shortly after he had departed, his friends came running after him suddenly in agreement with his plan. There were only a hand full of them in the group and they were able to move along at night evading harm.

Early one morning at the end of April 1945, while around Erfurt, in the state of Thueringen, Onkel Max and the others were washing their faces at the bottom of a steep bank along the Gera River, when they heard the bolt action of an M-1 rifle chambering a round, from the top of the bank. A young red-headed GI, a Texan, pointed his rifle at Onkel Max and his friends and while chewing gum drawled, "Y'all jes' hold it rat there an' put yer hands up now!___Slowly like!___Ya hear!"

At least it was the Americans who had caught them. This unit was placing all captured Germans in retention and sent him to a concentration camp in Sinsheim near the Rhein river. Sinsheim was in the state of Baden-Wuerttemberg between Karlsruhe and Heidelberg. After half a year had past and his background had been sufficiently investigated he was allowed his freedom. He had never been a Nazi party member.

My Onkel Max was a well read man and told me how the conditions in that camp were as wretched as the historical accounts of the Civil War prison camp Andersonville, in the south. He had also been subjected to living under a tattered shelter half, propped up by sticks over a hole dug into the ground. He survived a very harsh winter in those conditions truly owing his life to a few friendships he had earned while there.

One friend, an architect, had spent many hours redrawing, over and over, Onkel Max's mothers' house in Weilheim. He died there. Max said he was a war-tired man who had wanted to die. His other two friends were a couple of survivors. One was a genius at making things and the other was a genius at scrounging things.

Years later, in 1974, my Onkel Max would die from medical complications of a stomach disease he had contracted in that horrible prison camp.

That night, however, I knew nothing of my Onkel, except that he was my Onkel and his hand hurt my head.

The next morning, excited and eager to explore our new surroundings, my brothers and I passed through the front gate of Oma's house and started walking down Nordendstrasse (street), toward Muenchener Strasse, the main street, which would take us to downtown Weilheim.

TWO

The morning air was cold and crisp. The sun was shining brightly through an azure sky, its' beams reflecting off the snow covered landscape. Our feet crunched through the frozen crust of the brilliant white snow and our breath formed clouds of vapor. As we rounded the corner from Nordendstrasse onto the main street, we observed our father walking very unsteadily up the street, on the other side. He picked his unsure steps, while starring straight ahead and having said nothing to us, not even a wave of recognition, he continued on towards Oma's house. We continued towards town.

We had rarely seen our father over the years as it was, his being off in Turkey or some other unaccompanied one year tour of duty, which he often extended. Therefore, his behavior that morning was as normal as his famous Sunday morning appearances back home, when he was transferred back from over seas duty or on leave from there.

He would suddenly appear at the front door of our home in Wichita Kansas, early in the morning, holding a bag of hamburgers, which always reeked strongly of pickles. That would normally have been a nice treat, if it were not for fact that he always purchased the hamburgers the previous evening, and his propensity for sitting on them in the car, thus smashing them and causing their contents to squish out.

That view of my father walking unsteadily up the street was to be the last time I saw him, until 1968. He had come back to Germany to return our mother to her family, to rid himself of his responsibilities and to return to those bottomless barrels of famous tasty German beer he remembered, and dearly missed over the years since, while stationed here.

My life's odyssey was to take a severe turn that crisp winter morning. Since my mother had been taken back to her hometown and literally dumped on the proverbial doorstep, along with five young children, she was forced to develop a survival plan. Unfortunately, she never developed any plan. Her brother Max did. Was it a better plan? Since she had none, it prevailed.

Being dumped there also provided negative ammunition for many of her relatives, especially her older sister, Lotte Hager, (the other Lotte) who were, from the onset, all very opposed to her marriage to an Amerikaner. In other words, her marriage went over like a lead balloon, given the very German and military background of her family.

Her father had fought the French as a cavalryman during World War I and later had joined the SA (Sturmabteilung), better known as the Brown Shirts. He was a German patriot. He spent his remaining life as a gardener. She had a brother-in-law who served in the Wehrmachts' (Regular German Army) Seventh Army, defending the Siegfried Line, who had been severely wounded by a British hand grenade, near the Seine river, during the allied operation Market Garden. Her brother Max served with the Luftwaffe (Air Force), and many other relatives also served in the German forces during World War II.

For several wintry months, after our arrival in Germany, my brothers and I got up each weekday morning at 4 a.m., munched down a fast breakfast and bolted from Oma's house. We would walk to the Weilheim Bahnhof (train station), crunching through the frozen snow for fifteen minutes, to catch the 5 a.m. train to Murnau. The train would arrive in Murnau in about forty minutes and we would then have to walk to Kimbro Kaserne, a U.S. Army Engineer base. The walk took around fifteen minutes and, once there, we would have to wait until 6:30 a.m. for a U.S. Army bus to pick us up and drive us to Garmish-Partenkirchen. The bus ride took another hour, making three stops to pick up children, and would arrive at 8 a.m. in time for the classes to start.

The reason for the choice of wake-up time was explainable. We had to take the only train available to enable us to connect with the only early morning bus to Garmish-Partenkirchen. Since we did not live in an American neighborhood on a U.S. military base, we had to set aside a lot of time each day for transportation in order to make it to and from school each day. They hardly ever cancelled school for snow, as this was Bavaria, snow country and we had walked through enough of the white stuff to last a lifetime. However, if they did cancel, we would not know about it until we were at Kimbrough Kassern.

Our school was literally at the foot of the mountain Zugspitz. At 2963 meters, it is the highest mountain in the German Alpine range and sits on the border between Germany and Austria.

We returned the same way, arriving home late each evening, long after it was dark. After several months, the cost of the train fare had begun to concern Onkel Max, as he had been footing all the costs thus far and at that time was trying to save every penny to build his own house. Our father had not sent any money and our mother was still unable to find a job. We definitely had no fat bank account to draw from in dire times.

Up to this point, we boys had been living in the cellar. It was in a portion that was used as a storage room, until we had invaded Oma's house. The room had two windows, situated high up, one on each white plastered wall of the back corner of the house. The windows were one by two feet in size within two foot thick walls. The bottom portion of each window opening in the wall slopped at a forty five degree angle, which allowed more sun-light into the room. The room was about eight by ten feet. Our single beds were arranged along three of the walls with a small table and radio situated between my older brothers' beds.

There was no electric heater, no central heating system and no wood stove. It was very cold in that room. However, we did have very warm comforters and pillows stuffed with goose down. The comforters were so large that they billowed several feet high over our bodies, while the pillows enveloped our heads, leaving us virtually hidden from view.

Only when we had to get up to piss did the Winter Hawk take a large chunk out of our frozen little asses. The nearest bathroom was on the first floor, a long way to have to go if you were freezing, and that room was an icebox anyway. Later we decided to stop the nonsense and got a large can to piss in. It was a foot tall with about the same circular opening size. It had formerly been a pickle container. This was more convenient and through necessity more than our eagerness to work, we cleaned it every day. If we did not want to freeze unnecessarily longer during the night, we soon learned to do any other body functions during the day.

We would listen to the Voice of America radio broadcast on Friday and Saturday nights, while the lights were out. There were mystery episodes, The Green Hornet, The Shadow, Sherlock Holmes and many other memorable episodes. Onkel Max and Tante Lotte would bring down platters of snacks for us to enjoy, while we listened to our programs. The snack tray would always contain fresh squeezed orange juice, tangerines, chocolates, pastries, assorted *wursts* on buttered German bread slices and candies. Tante Lottie worked for a grocery store called Tengelmann and was never without a horde of great food.

I do not wish to give the impression that Onkle Max and Tante Lotte were wealthy. To be truthful, they were barely making it through each month, while also helping us and attempting to save a little towards building their own house on Oma's land. After World War II, Germans were not eating well for the first decade. It was not until after 1955 that many were starting to move into a little comfort. Food had become more available and affordable, however, until then food was hoarded, when obtained, for fear there would be none again for some time to come. That is also why so many Europeans tended to have gained so much weight in those days. Furthermore, Tante Lotte was able to bring home fruits and vegetables and meats that were starting to go bad and after cutting off the spoiled portions, prepared us those great meals.

In a larger room, just off to the left when exiting from our bedroom, was the washroom. There was a large round tub in that room that required a fire to be built underneath it and maintained, in order to wash clothes. The fire was set in a safe circular metal containment device, designed with a vented door and latch. There was also a bathtub in there, which was stored against a wall. It looked ancient, like a mummy's coffin without the lid. When we wished to take a bath, we had to heat our own water and as it cooled a periodic recharge was required, using a tea kettle full of boiling water. After each use of the tea kettle, the kettle had to be refilled and placed over the fire. The fire also needed constant attendance.

If the tub accumulated too much water we had to dip out the overage amount. The conclusion, when taking a bath in Oma's house, was that it was always a comical ordeal. The best part about this room however, was the many rows of bottles containing apple cider. This apple cider was homemade and over time had fermented. We boys would sneak a bottle here and there and get happily smashed.

A third room, located across from our bed room, was the coal room. This room offered no fun, as we boys each had to shovel coal into the large furnace, which heated the floors up-stairs and never heated our room.

As spring was nearing, things were forced to change. Our mother was given a firm warning by her brother Max. He told her that she could no longer put her children through the crazy daily routine of traveling so far and losing so much sleep in order to accomplish this. The girls were not yet attending school, however Sarah was due to start in the fall.

Onkel Max told her to find a job so that she could start absorbing some of the costs and to accept that her husband was not going to help, nor return. This was more true than not, as we had heard how our mother had greeted dear ol' Papa at the front door that first morning and severely dented his head with an iron frying pan. He left shouting drunken curses and sought out a clinic to get stitched up. If the local newspaper had heard about this fight, their head-line would surely have had to read *'Amerikanischer Luftwaffe Soldat suffered injuries during attack by local resistance fighter'*.

Max had patiently endured the costs and waiting period for Mom to find a job and putting his foot down finally told our mother that the time had come to teach all of us children the German language and start getting us accustomed to the German culture. It was in September when the day came to engage the plan, we boys had still been unaware of the impending changes afoot. Onkel Max had been packing the Volkswagen for about thirty minutes. Lucious had noticed he was acting nervous. Onkel Max suddenly called for Lucious and me, as he headed down into the cellar.

Lucious sensed the threat and quickly hid under his bed, from which Onkel Max had to pull him out by both feet. He was crying and kicking his legs wildly. I recall how he violently opposed being forced to leave Weilheim, our mother, Oma, Tante Lotte, Onkel Max. We had just started to make new friends and our new and best friend was Manfred Jahn, or as he preferred to be called 'Eddie', a nickname he adopted from one of the gangster characters *Bomber Eddie* in the Walt Disney *Scrooge McDuck* adventure comics. He was also referred to as Bomber Eddie when others spoke of his frequent successful home made explosives going off in the neighborhood fields or nearby forests. His command of English was good and he learned to speak it practically fluently in an American accent the more we hung around with him.

Eddie was six years older than I was. He loved all things military and on occasion would sadly talk about his father and his grandfather. He told us that his grandfather had served in the Wehrmacht and was killed in action on the Russian Front, during World War II. His grandfather was stationed in the Ukraine and was buried in a boarder town at the Ukrainian-Hungarian boarder. In 1946 his father went into the Russian occupied zone to try to evacuate his parents and became a missing person.

Ian, Lucious and I taught Eddie and several other neighborhood boys how to play baseball, which gave us a link to America and the German boys a strange new game to play. Eddie was always finding munitions on American maneuver grounds and bullets disposed of by the retreating German Army, which were thrown into a local pond called Blasl Weiher. The word 'Weiher' means pond and the term Blasl means bubbling. So it is a bubbling pond. We boys often dove into that pond to retrieve the plentiful booty. On camping nights Eddie led the raids on local farms to dig out potatoes or nab a chicken. We would then shove the potatoes into the fire coals of our camp fire and roast the chicken over it. Eddie struck me as an above average boy when it came to intelligence. His ability to make things and make them function at the age he was, seemed incredible.

Our last great adventure involved Eddie and I planting an explosive device in a mound of dirt. He had taken an American training hand grenade and rebuilt it. After packing wads of paper and gun powder neatly around a homemade fuse running down into the hollow chamber, he then sealed the grenade and ensured that it was airtight. We climbed up a moderately steep highway embankment across from the Eselberg, a hill next to his home, on which most of our gatherings for play had occurred. Eselberg was also a gathering place during the Middle Ages, where criminals were executed. The old hill just appeared as if it grew out of the flat field on its own, resembling a giant wart. Once we reached the top of the embankment, we could see a large field on which were many piles of dirt deposited by dump trucks.

Eddie secured the grenade in one of those dirt piles. He hollowed out an area on the side of the pile and packed it down leaving enough space for the fuse to stick out. He lit it and we ran like rabbits. There was an explosion so loud that the lights of the neighborhood, some distance away, went on as if one switch had lit them all. The police had also heard it and with the shock of *da-di-dah-da-dah* piercing the night, they sped toward our location and our fun came to an abrupt end.

I didn't know which direction Eddie chose to run, but I ran towards the highway bridge and hid in the high weeds growing in abundance there. I wore leather shorts and squatted there for about an hour. I could smell the sulfur in the air. When I finally sneaked home, I was aware of my mistake. I had hundreds of small itchy water blisters all over my legs, arms and face. The weeds were called 'Brenesel' and skin contact with the plant always resulted in the tiny, itchy blisters. We had successfully eluded the police.

By the end of the week I had recovered, but the day I had recovered had also become a memorable day. It was a day of anger and anguish, a day that would remain imprinted in our minds. It was 23 September 1962.

Most of all that terrible day, and until this moment unknown to Lucious and me, we were to also leave Ian and the girls, for a long time. I was too young to really understand the gravity of the whole situation at that moment, but in a few hours I too was feeling like the world had suddenly turned over on top of me. As soon as Lucious heard what was going on he bolted down to our bedroom and trying to escape, dove under his bed. I was very upset watching Uncle Max literally dragging

Lucious from under his bed, while he was wildly kicking with both legs.

Onkel Max had a very tough time getting him into the car. We drove up Nordendstrasse in his Volkswagen. The trip lasted for several long hours as Max headed toward Ramsau, a very small dorf (village) near Haag, the nearest larger town. We arrived at a strange place atop a hill with extremely high stone walls surrounding, or as we would find out very soon, containing the buildings within.

As Onkel Max drove up the dirt road to the gate, a huge arched-top mediaeval wooden two door affair, over which were the metal letters announcing Kinderheim Sankt Josef, (Children Home Saint Joseph).

The huge doors were swung open by two Catholic Nuns who motioned for Onkel Max to drive into the court yard. He got out and spoke to the Nuns pointing at us boys, as we hunched low in the seats and peered through the car windows at these strange looking creatures dressed in black robes from head to toe.

There was a large white square starched thing covering their upper chest extending from the neck, a white scarf-like article of apparel wrapped around their face with another white three or four inch stiff object, which sat on their head covering their forehead. From the top of their heads was a black drape which fell on three sides to their waists. They each had a string of black beads around their waists, with another foot of it hanging down their right side on which hung a cross, a crucifix, which pointed toward their severe looking black shoes. All we could see of a human appearance was their pinched faces, which appeared to pop out of the tightly bound wrappings.

"Wow,___lookit' that!" Lucious said slowly, while he was still starring at those aliens outside, "I can't believe Onkel Max will leave us here!" he exclaimed.

I just sat there wondering where our mother was, while this was going on.

Onkel Max opened the car doors and ordered us out, not unkindly. The Nuns stood there, with no visible hands, faces devoid of smiles or frowns, and looked at us. Onkel Max unloaded the car and told us to pick up everything and follow the Nuns.

At this time we did not speak very much German and Onkel Max did alright in his broken English. He hardly spoke the entire trip up to this place.

Onkel Max called after us to say goodbye as we were herded into a doorway. The Nuns did not speak English.

We were motioned to put all of our belongings on a table. The Nuns opened everything and put things in several piles. We noticed that we had chocolates in our bags, put there by either Tante Lotte or our mother, but the Nuns put that in the pile along with any toys, books, sweets or American clothing they deemed unnecessary for our indefinite stay.

The Nuns led us into a large room up on the second floor and marched us before the occupants. There were many German boys between the ages of eight and twelve, sitting at the many tables in that room. They looked at us curiously for a moment and then continued on with their work. It was quiet in that room as they worked at a variety of things, including school work and crafts.

After about an hour of nobody talking to us, though by now some were intently staring at us, the doors opened and several Nuns entered. One carried a very large pot with a lid over it, while the other pushed a rolling cart loaded with smaller pots, a tray of plain bread rolls and a pitcher of water. On the bottom of the cart were the stacked dishes.

A Nun clapped her hands and the German boys quickly put away their things and moved the tables into two rows of four tables each. They then moved benches from along the walls or from where they were used with the tables where they had been situated a moment before and positioned them along the tables. Each bench accommodated six children.

The boys moved between the tables and benches and stood waiting. As they stood, several other boys had brought dishes and silverware to the tables and stacked them at the head of each table. The Nuns promptly started ladling boiled potatoes, boiled purple cabbage, and what looked like boiled pork, onto each plate. The full plates were passed down the line, followed by a freshly baked roll, until both tables were served.

Since Lucious and I were not familiar with these proceedings, we stood off to the side and waited until we were shown what to do. It was evident that the benches were all filled with the German boys, which obviously left no room for us.

Soon a Nun moved a small round table over to us, after clearing it of craft materials and placed two wicker-seat wooden chairs at the table. Another Nun placed two plates of food on the table and returned again with rolls and two glasses of water.

One of the Nuns started a prayer, which immediately caused the German boys to bow their heads and place their hands flat against each other with fingers pointing towards the ceiling.

Lucious and I, being sound non-practicing Southern Baptists, just stood there gawking at what was our first encounter with such a strange scene.

Finally, a Nun said Amen and the German boys sat down, as one, and silently began eating. Lucious and I also sat and began to eat. Lucious did not eat much, because he was still angry and scared, but I was hungry and in order to get those elusive pieces of food onto my fork I used my left thumb to assist by pushing the food onto the fork.

Ssslapp, slap, slap, was heard throughout the room as one of the Nuns, after having enough of watching an uncultured heathen, such as I, eat the way I did, landed open handed blows across the side of my face from behind. I was literally knocked onto the floor and received several more nasty slaps across my cheeks.

The Nun was furious and grabbing me by the hair, jerked me toward a corner in the room and left me there for the remaining part of the evening. I remember feeling betrayed by my mother that night, a feeling I would never forget. My head hurt and I was mentally crying and wondering what terrible thing I had done to deserve the punishment. Also, my thoughts were 'How can they treat us this way?'

THREE

Months had past since Lucious and I had arrived at the Children's Home. We had by then learned to speak the German language and fell into the pattern of daily routines. Even the religious aspects of this place had become part of our indoctrination.

Before we left the United States, we had worshiped in the Baptist church, the church of our fathers' family. When we did attend, which was mostly only while living a short time in Red Flint Arkansas, where his family and relatives lived. The Preacher there would really tear into sinners, tell stories from the Bible while speaking in low voice and then suddenly in a loud shout with arms raised high and fists shaking. This had to be the church for us since, dear ol' Papa, following the ways of his family had us children all baptized as Baptists. Sunday school there had involved making gifts for our parents by painting molded plaster shapes of cherries, peaches or dozens of other similar designs. We even expected these ugly, oversized, poorly painted things, to be proudly hung on the walls of the recipient's homes, and they always were.

Now Roman Catholicism at the Children's Home was another matter, very mystical to us, as it was spoken only in the German and Latin languages during mass. We learned about how it was directly descended from the church founded by the apostle Peter, and is headed by the Holy Pope in Rome. We were to blindly accept the gospel of Jesus Christ and the teachings of the Bible.

Masses consisted of a low mumbling of prayer or songs in equally low key. The seven sacraments were conveyed through God's grace. This was especially celebrated at mass during the Eucharist or communion. We even got our second baptism here along with our confirmation, two more of the seven sacraments, which also included penance, holy orders, anointing of the sick and matrimony.

Of course the nuns made damn sure we never forgot that redemption through Jesus Christ was the sole method of obtaining salvation, without which you were not going to be allowed into heaven. Furthermore, in accordance with the religious thinker Soren Kierkegaard, who held that truth is subjectivity, therefore man's relationship to God requires suffering. The nuns were devoutly intent on carrying out Kierkegaard's beliefs.

Ramsau, was the name of the very small gathering of farms here in Bavaria Germany and other varied structures which surrounded a small church of white plastered walls, high narrow vaulted stained glass windows and a steep conical roofed steeple. The church was surrounded by an ancient graveyard which was still in use. Next to the graveyard, was a very small grammar school, a 'gymnasium', attended by children over nine years of age. There was a gravel and dirt road, about a quarter mile long, which led from the main gate of the walled-in children's home at the top of the hill down to the church and school house.

There was also a church inside the Children's Home, not very old, nor as ornately decorated as the one in Ramsau. It had been built up to one of the high walls with an entrance cut through the wall. The Children's Home was several hundred years old and the original chapel did not offer enough space, as they took in more and more children.

Inside the walls were also a series of classrooms, for children between kindergarten and eight years of age. Discipline was always harsh and all of the nuns were prone to be strict. Any mistakes in lessons being taught, we would be ordered to walk to the front of the class, extend our hands open palm up, whereupon the nun would strike a switch, made from a fresh thin tree limb, across each palm, five or more times depending on the severity of the infraction. This form of punishment was called 'tatzens' in German. An infraction could be more severe, if you were ever caught talking, or not paying attention in class. Those punishments would warrant severe slaps across our face, accompanied by our ears being twisted and our hair being pulled.

On a sunny and warm spring day I was sitting in my second-floor classroom, adjacent to the church graveyard. I had been observing a grave-digger at work, not more than thirty five feet from me. He was digging a fresh grave into an old grave. His shovels of rich black earth flew up into the air and formed an ever increasing mound. The grave digger stood inside the hole and his head poked out of the hole with each scoop thrust upwards, placing his head at about the middle of the old moss and lichen covered grave stone of the original occupant.

The nun was writing on the chalk board, preparing a lesson on the Hundred Years War, while we were supposed to be reading about Gottfried Wilhelm Leibniz, a master mathematician and philosopher, who held that the entire universe is one large system expressing God's plan.

There were several long whitish items lying across the mound of soil and several others protruding out of the soil. I focused my eyes on the objects and they began to reveal themselves for what they were. In Germany, there is no embalming and the coffin along with the corpse rots rapidly, allowing the reuse of a grave for another family member, or if no claim on the grave by relatives, reuse for others.

At first I was horrified at what I saw, then, as my mind accepted the scene unfolding in front of my eyes, I became transfixed on the grave. The grave-digger stooped real low in the grave for a moment and then slowly stood up straight, holding a human skull in his palm. He held the yellowish dirt-stained skull with its dirt filled eyes facing his own face and appeared to be staring at it for a long while.

It reminded me of a similar singular event that happened several years earlier in Red Flint Arkansas, when I was about six years old. I had been watching my Uncle Bob Barnes, who was Red Flint's only cab driver, and also a part time Undertaker, pull a gurney from the back of his hearse at Koffman's Funeral home, which was literally across from the backyard of our house.

The body on the gurney had been a local farmer. He was just laying there on that gurney, with a completely crushed head. The bone was visible where the skin and muscles were torn from the crushed skull looking much like a peeled orange, with a little bit of the only piece of eyeball remaining, peeping out from under bone and flesh fragments with a lifeless cloudy stare. The farmer had been crushed under his own tractor. It had rolled over on top of him, while he was plowing on a steep graded slope, Uncle Bob had informed me.

"Jakob!" screamed Schwester (sister) Maria Theresa who, after trying to say Jackie (Tchackie), which always sounded brutal the way she pronounced it, had resulted in their using its origin name.

My head was jerked upward from my desk as Schwester Maria Theresa grabbed my ear with a fanatical twist, and as she had me half way up, slapped me back down into my seat. She pulled me up again, this time by my hair, towards the front of the room and ordered me to put out my hands, palms up. After she had delivered approximately fourteen tatzens, my hands were so sore and puffed up, I was relieved to stand in a corner in the front of the room for an hour, instead of sitting down where Schwester Maria Theresa's lessons would require constant writing with my sore hands.

I stood with my hands hanging down at my sides, which did not help the constant pounding, as they throbbed with pain. Having my hands hang downward seemed to cause the pounding in the hands to hurt more.

I started thinking about Gunther, a classmate, who once said that if you smear butter into your palms, the tatzens would leave severe blisters. Yeah, that would teach the nuns not to do it again. But then I thought about it again and realized Gunther's plan did not take into account that we never had the time to obtain any butter, as the nuns struck immediately. The blisters would hurt us even more than the throbbing alone and besides, the nuns would probably find delight in the blisters they had conjured up. Oh, how glad was I when the day had ended.

The pain remained for several days, apparently by design, to keep offenders honest for at least that long. This would not be the last time I would endure the Children's Home Standard Operating Procedures.

FOUR

During our stay at Kinderheim Sankt Josef, we were introduced to the sport of soccer. We had never heard about this sport in America. I was a defensive guard and we actually played against other German schools in the surrounding dorfs. Haag was the bigger town in the area where playoff games, along with other competitive physical capability events being held there. We went on many very long walks away from the Children's Home. These walks started very early in the morning and lasted until very late in the evening and were often around twenty miles during the summer months. The walks during the snow melt at the end of winter, with crocuses blooming and patches of lush green grass peeking out from areas of melted snow here and there, would always thereafter, remain my favorite time for walks.

Once, we had walked all the way to Altoetting, not far from the Austrian border. Altoetting was famous for miraculous healings, with a chapel in the town that displayed hundreds of crutches, numerous old wheelchairs and other testimony to faith healing miracles having occurred there. We saw no miracles during our visit.

There were many trips into the surrounding pine forests to hunt for mushrooms. We had learned to identify many types and could easily discern the poisonous from the edible variety. Those mushroom hunts were also to remain amongst some of my most treasured memories. Other memories, though not treasured, included the death of Pope John XXIII, on the third of June 1963. His real name had been Angelo Giuseppe Roncalli.

I thought he was a kindly looking man who, because of my daily association with the Catholic Church, I felt was saintly. The nuns wailed their grief away in silent prayers until on the twenty first of June 1963, Giovanni Battista Montini was elected Pope Paul VI, and the nun's world was back in order.

It was the evening of 22 November 1963, when Schwesters Maria Theodolinda and Maria Theresa announced that President John F. Kennedy had been assassinated in Dallas, Texas. They spent as much time mourning his death as they did Pope John XXIII. I recalled the arguments, when we lived in Wichita, between my father, who had voted for Richard M. Nixon and my mother, who thought Kennedy was so handsome, which subsequently earned him her vote.

That was a funny time, because my father, along with his family in Arkansas, were hard-line Democrats, but our father had ignored all that at the polls on Election Day. His feeling was that Kennedy would not be a strong supporter of the Armed Forces and to hell with good looks. He felt that the outright granting of the party-line vote would create a disaster. My mother felt a 'party' was something that handsome Kennedy was going to have after he was elected President of the United States of America.

My sisters, Annie and Sarah, were eventually also sent to the Children's Home during the winter of 1962 and placed under the care of sister Maria Luvitica. Annie would end up staying until the summer of 1963 and Sarah stayed until Lucious and I left. They were placed on the other side of the courtyard from us and we occasionally saw them from a distance. The policy of Kinderheim St. Josef was to restrict interaction between the boys and girls.

The Children's Home was constructed of four buildings attached to form a square, with a large courtyard in the center. There were three floors to each side. From a distance, the place rose from the top of a prominent hill appearing to have very high sheer walls, as though it were a castle. In one wing, opposite the courtyard from the main gate, was the office of the Mother Superior, various functionary areas including the bakery and the living quarters for the nuns. Jutting off from that wing, at the far right outside wall, as one would see from an aerial view of the place, was the church surrounded by a rose garden, vegetable garden and the beehives.

Our mother visited, along with Ian, when they brought the girls. Ian had been undergoing an apprenticeship program with a German firm at the same time we were in the Children's Home. While Ian and I had been waiting in a stairway landing for our mother and Onkel Max to finish with the Mother Superior, he had noticed a nun's floor length hooded cloak hanging on the back of a heavy wood and iron door.

Obviously trying to provide me some entertainment, he donned the cloak and acted like a vampire. He had only succeeded in making me homesick. I would have preferred goofing around with all of my family present, back in either Weilheim or Wichita. Our mother visited us as time off from her work allowed and transportation could be begged. She made it to our Holy Communions, which where a big event for Catholics and a proud event for our mother.

During our time at the home, Lucious and I were to become altar boys. We were required to learn the prayers in Latin and would practice with each other, one reciting the Priest's words and the other the altar boy's response. For instance, as we would study the Stufengebet, Lucious, stating the priests part, would recite "In nomine + Patris et Filii et Spiritus Sancti.___Amen.___Introibo ad altare Dei," (the symbol + indicates the priest raises his hand and makes the sign of the cross). My response would then be, "Ad Deum qui laetificat juventutem meam". All of this fancy talk was only usable around the church here.

Lucious was even talking about becoming a priest himself, although I could not even begin to understand his motives. Our abilities as altar boys improved along with our abilities reading, writing and speaking German and not only reading and writing regular German, but also the old German method of writing. The old method appeared to be comprised of many sharp angles amidst an assortment of curly loops.

I had become very ill one day, without any early warning signs of an oncoming sickness. The nuns had placed me in a small one bed sick room on the third floor of their wing. My fever was well up to 104 degrees, and I had started suffering strange dreams all the time I was sick. One such dream, which reoccurred most often, involved a feeling throughout my body of being microscopic in size with the immensity of the earth and the heavens weighing heavily upon me while, as I looked up with my minds eye, buildings and trees appeared a mile high all around me. I often awoke weak and soaked with sweat. After lying, in what I thought was the death room, for nearly two weeks, I had improved and was eventually allowed outside. I kept bleeding from my gums for several more days, until that also had ended, and I was finally on the mend.

The winter of 1963-64, was to be the last time we were to see one of our classmates and Sarah one of theirs. We had been skiing about a mile from the home, jumping over a homemade ski jump, and having a great time. Fritz Kastner had been a local farm boy who attended my classes, and his family owned a farm next to the Home. That day, he had taken a terrible fall after attempting a ski jump we had constructed. He had struck the ground hard, hitting his right temple on a rock hidden under the snow. Feeling woozy and refusing any of our offers to help, Fritz had almost made it all the way to his home, when he suddenly fell to the side of the road and died. A day later, one of the girls at the Home had fallen backwards from her chair, striking her head, and consequently died.

The Head Priest for the Home, Pfarrer (Father) Ernst Eisenschmid performed the Mass. I was numbed with thoughts of how easy one could die and of that grave-digger, at the church, that kept appearing in my mind. The Mass was held at the old church in Ramsau, since the boy Fritz had attended mass there and, as a courtesy from the priest of that church, the Pfarrer combined both children's funerals there. It was the first time I had been to that church and I had been amazed to find shelves in a room, off from the main area, where many human skulls and assorted bones, mostly thigh and arm, were neatly arranged in rows and on display for everyone to see behind chicken wire.

So this is where you were put. I mused, thinking of the skull that grave digger had unearthed last spring.

It was around five in the morning on 5 June 1964, when Schwester Maria Theresa had shaken me awake. The air was damp, but warm, as I walked outside to Onkel Max's Volkswagon. Sarah was already there, waiting, and soon Lucious joined us. What little personal belongings we possessed, had been pre-packed by the nuns and Onkel Max was busily arranging them into the front storage trunk of the car.

Schwester Maria Theodolinda made sure we had our Bibles and gave each of us a Rosary with crucifix and beads hand carved from wood. The nuns said their goodbyes and Onkel Max drove out of the gate. Thus we had come to the end of our time at Kinderheim St. Josef.

Onkel Max drove us to the Haupt Bahnhof, (main train station), in Muenchen (Munich). During the drive he explained that the man our mother had befriended several years earlier, an American Army Staff Sergeant had completed his tour of duty and was being transferred back to duty in the United States. We understood how that worked, because of our father's military travel. He had arranged to have us all stay with him in America, all except our brother Ian, who would stay in Germany with Onkel Max and Tante Lotte and work for the firm where he was completing his apprenticship.

Our mother and Annie were already waiting for us at the Bahnhof, and after giving us a hello hug and kiss, said goodbye to her brother Max, who was looking at her and us with a mixed emotions and wearing an apprehensive facial expression. I never forgot that look on his face, which appeared to ask our mother if this was the right thing to do? He gave us all a big hug and kiss and walked us to the train's access steps.

There was a metallic sound as all the metal train couplings where pulled taut, causing at the same instant, the train to lurch forward. At first very slowly, then with speed increasing gradually, the train moved out of the station. Onkel Max waived goodbye from the loading platform, a stony expression on his face.

We never even had a chance to say goodbye to Ian, Oma, Tante Lotte, Eddie or any other relatives. I had thought with confusion about the whole affair.

The trip was over late that evening, when we had arrived in Bremerhaven. A taxi ride followed from the Bahnhof to the pier area and shortly we were processed through customs and walked up the gang plank of the German Ocean Liner MS Berlin.

During the voyage, I found that I was often the only person eating at our assigned table in the dining hall, since the others were prone to chronic sea sickness. I appeared the model child, sitting with my back ramrod straight in the dining chair, knife in the left hand and fork in the right hand, bringing my food up to my mouth, instead of bringing my mouth down to my food.

Schwester Theresa, you should see me now! I thought, and then I thought of the nuns, wondering who was getting their head worked-over in my place, now that I had been freed from Kinderheim Sankt Josef.

The ocean voyage was spectacular, a virtual thrill a minute. I felt that I could have stayed on the ocean for the rest of my life. As often as I could, I would spend hours as far forward of the bow as the ships crew and safety allowed, and just watch. A never-ending series of monster waves swelled to unimaginable heights culminating with white crests exploding into vaporous mists at the moment of climax, while between these titanic creations equally magnificent troughs and caverns were formed. Over the bow of the MS Berlin came wave upon wave crashing down onto the deck as though trying to sink her as she plunged precariously downward into the deep troughs. Then suddenly, as she shot her bow out of the depths, the waves simultaneously exploded off both sides of the ship in spectacular white mists, seemingly throwing her higher into the air. That had been perhaps the most exciting experience of my life up to that point.

When we reached landfall, we passed by the Statue of Liberty, while being towed by tug boats, which eventually steered the MS Berlin safely into her berthing area at the Manhattan ship docks. We disembarked and were met by Staff Sergeant Charlie Hueston, whom our mother always called Karl for some damned reason. He was in civilian clothes. However, we knew his rank after having had to hear about him unendingly, perhaps because our mother wanted to make us like her trip-ticket back to the States.

He welcomed our mother with a quick hug and virtually ignored us four kids.

FIVE

Charlie Hueston drove us to his sisters' house on Long Island, where he was staying while on leave from the Army. He had been in the Army since World War II, where 'he stated' he was in the Normandy Invasion on Omaha beach on the 6th of June 1944. 'He also stated' that he was in the Korean War. He did not seem to make much rank in all those years, as he was currently only a Staff Sergeant, an E-6.

His sister lived in a run-down single home, with dirty walls, un-swept cruddy floors and a single bathroom with mildewed grout between filthy tiles, which they probably hadn't bothered cleaning since they had moved in years before. The bathtub and sink had been so filthy you could have planted seeds and they would have rooted.

We were introduced to her and her children, all wearing dirty clothes. There were two early teenage girls and a boy about my age. After we had been there about an hour, food was prepared and served in the back yard. We sat on an old half-rotted picnic table. However, there were also a few metal porch chairs available. These were severely rusted-out and appeared to be of questionable support. I was perplexed as to why they had not been thrown into a landfill long ago, since they obviously were no longer safely usable.

We ate bologna sandwiches with sliced American cheese on Wonder Bread. Ketchup and a large pitcher, which was really a reused pickle jar, of strawberry Kool-Aid sat on the table along with an assortment of former small jelly and pickle jars as substitutes for drinking glasses.

After we tried to eat that strange meal, which was so distasteful after the high life on board the Bremen, Hueston told me and his nephew to walk to the store and get him a pack of Winston cigarettes. He gave me a five dollar bill and off we went down a dirt trail, which served as a short-cut to the back of a strip of small stores.

While inside a Rexall Drug Store, I saw a plastic bag of toy U.S. Army soldiers. They cost ninety nine cents and I was enraptured by them, mainly since playing with toys, especially toy soldiers, had been strictly forbidden in the Home and I had sorely missed playing with toy soldiers.

I paid the Rexall clerk for the cigarettes and the soldiers and we walked back to the house. As I gave Hueston the cigarettes and change, I had a huge smile of childhood pleasure as I told him that I couldn't resist buying the soldiers as well. Charlie Hueston glared at me, grabbed the soldiers out of my hand and at the same instant slapped me across the face, while calling me a lying, sneak.

He threw the soldiers in the trash and told me to get out of his sight. My mother said nothing, obviously because she was used to European fathers behaving harshly toward children and therefore, this to her was nothing. Mostly, she did not want to start an argument with her boyfriend so soon. I was hurt and severely confused about the incident.

That night I had to share the same bed with Hueston's nephew. It was a single bed with unwashed sheets, gray with filth. The bed was arranged in a corner with one side up against the wall. I lay awake all that night, scrunched up as close to that dirty wall as was possible, repulsed by this strange house, the filth, the weird kid next to me and that son-of-a-bitch Charlie Hueston.

The next day we started driving toward Fort Belvoir, Virginia. Every time we stopped for gas and a short break, Hueston would tell me to get out of his sight and call me a sneak. I would go around the building and wait for the car to load up and then come back and get in. Hueston did not talk to Lucious much either, but he constantly doted over the girls. Traveling along with us was a young German Shepard named Milda. Hueston had purchased her from a breeder in Bavaria,

Germany and brought her over with him a few weeks before we had left Germany.

We moved on base, into a single story yellow-painted cinder block structure with rusty metal single-pane window frames, concrete floors and water-stained ceilings, from numerous roof leaks. This was the best Base Housing had available. There were four homes built side-by-side, making a long narrow rectangle structure. Outside, there were no bushes, no flowers, not even grass, just stark naked, ugly Virginia red clay. The pale yellow paint was peeling or had already worn away in many places.

We endured a Spartan life there, with little furniture. All of our beds were stolen U. S. Army cots and our bedroom furniture was one wooden Army footlocker. Our own household goods were never released to us, while we were in Germany, since it required our father's signature and certain transportation and storage costs to be paid first. Therefore, our household goods stayed at a U.S. military base in Germany and would stay there until the 1980s.

As the months passed, Hueston daily demonstrated his ability to consume large quantities of Seagram Seven Crown whisky in High-Ball mixes. As he got drunk, which he always did, he would, sure as shit, turn mean and start talking about our real father, calling him a 'clown' and how he had once punched our father, while over in Germany, when our mother had him up for divorce court at the U.S. Army base in Murnau.

It became a ritual each night, first with his abusive comments towards our mother about how he had saved her and her brats from Germany, while he was stationed in Murnau, at the U.S. Army Engineering Base. Then he started about our father, always calling him the clown, followed by attacking me about being a liar and sneak. Each time he did this, I would believe more and more, that he was correct in everything he said, especially about me.

My mother, deciding that since I had been in a German school and that I should be set back a year in an American school, had never thought to asked me what I wanted. She did not discuss this with me, nor did she realize that, being in a German school, I was already at a higher level of learning achievements then my American peers. This situation was to become a life-long bitterness for me. She did not do this to Lucious.

I started to develop a low self-esteem, but I also seemed to work harder in school and in any other work assignments, apparently trying to make Hueston praise me and accept me and stop referring to me in derogatory ways. I was not alone in the abuse, as he would eventually attack all of us in the course of an evening. For instance, he would yell at Annie for simply sitting and crossing her legs, with a 'Who the hell do you think you are!___Huh?'.

Base Housing finally authorized our move into a modern red-brick duplex, during the summer of 1965. It was luxury, compared to the dreary rust and concrete box we lived in up to this point. There were many bushes and we had a lush green lawn. After having suffered through the months in that cold, austere concrete rat hole, the move was celebrated by us kids. We were there hardly a month when we had to move again, this time off of the base.

We moved to Woodbridge Virginia, which was outside of Fort Belvoir. I believe Hueston's alcoholic episodes had pissed-off the neighbors. Consequently, the U.S. Army demanded that he find lodging off-base, since he disrupted our neighbor's rights to enjoy peace and harmony.

I was in the sixth grade during all this disruption and relocation. I should have been in the seventh grade.

Life in Woodbridge had been a twilight zone of unreal situations and his treatment of our family was only to get worse over time. Our furniture never improved and if we obtained something, in addition to our other motley collection, it was equally bad. To make my point, our dining room required a table, so Hueston placed one side of a six foot in diameter wooden cable spool on top of a wooden crate to make a table with an assortment of wooden boxes for chairs. We children were never allowed to open the refrigerator and eat a snack or get a drink. Lucious and I were forbidden to 'hang around the house'. This was the beginning of my 'long walk days', where I would visit school friends who lived many miles away from Hueston's house. They could never figure me out, because they had never walked very far to do anything in their young lives and I had often walked twenty miles or more, in Germany, just to pick mushrooms.

SIX

During 1966, Hueston was transferred to Fort Meade Maryland and a couple of months later we moved into a pink painted, single story, ranch-style house in Suburbia, a housing development, which was part of Glen Burnie, Maryland.

Shortly after we had moved in there, Lucious and I were suddenly sent off to live with our Grandmother in Red Flint, Arkansas. Our Grandmother, owned a small country grocery store, creatively called 'Shipman's Grocery', which was situated between her house and her other son's house. There were probably fifteen feet between his house and its respective wall to one corner side of the store and six feet from the other corner side of the store to the side of her house.

The entire store, approximately twenty-six by seventy-five feet, extended to the road from the front corners of their houses. The store only had two small windows on the front, the rest was comprised of rough wooden floors, white wood siding, a tin roof and a faded four by six Coca Cola sign announcing it simply as 'Shipman's Grocery'. In other words, it was a regular old country store. Our Grandmother also sold grave stones in her yard, with a motto that she served the citizens of Red Flint during and after life.

My uncle in Red Flint was several years older than our father. However, he was very much different than his brother. He had stayed in Red Flint, and was married to an American woman, who bore him six children. He did not serve in the military, did not drink alcohol and overall, was a very taciturn and conservative man.

While in Red Flint, I started boxing and playing football on the school team. I seemed to pick up boxing very well and was fair at football, where I played in a line-backer position.

As time went on, I started spending much of my time doing things alone, such as drawing ships and reading novels. My brother Lucious was equally into silent personal pursuits, as he would often be in the same room and study or read his books for hours, without ever saying a word to me. This was not due to sibling issues, as we got along.

In 1967, after a year and several months since arriving in Arkansas, I went back to Glen Burnie, Maryland. Lucious stayed in Red Flint. I was received coldly by Hueston, who had, for some contradiction of personality, decided to give me a Mandolin as a gift. It was a pear-shaped instrument with a pattern of seashell pieces decorating the body and had a fretted neck utilizing the same material. It was a nice looking hand made instrument, which Hueston had brought back from Vietnam.

I was unaware that Hueston had even been in Vietnam during the time that I had been in Arkansas, as letters from our mother were scarce and information deprived, when it came to her personal affairs. If he was gone, then why did Lucious and I have to be away from our family? This was another unsolved burr in my ass.

I started attending school in Glen Burnie and made new friends. One friend, who's name was Arthur, had a very difficult father as well. One Saturday, Arthur and I were headed toward a K-Mart store where he had wanted to purchase a BB gun. There had been a very authentic looking Winchester model at the store, which Arthur had been visiting for months. He had mowed lawns and done other odd-jobs around the neighborhood to earn the money.

That day, he decided, was to be the day he would finally buy that BB gun. Arthur was in high spirits and I was happy for him. He displayed extreme pride when he paid the clerk all by himself and then scurried out of the store so fast I almost had to run to keep up. Once outside, he ran up the hill towards the woods behind the store tearing the box apart as he ran. His smile was a combination of teeth flashing and lips twitching at the same time, as he held the BB gun over his head victoriously.

He loaded the gun and taking turns we shot at everything in sight. As it got late in the evening, his smile vanished and he nervously asked me if I could take the gun home. He explained that he was expressly forbidden to buy the gun. So, feeling sorry for him and understanding why he could not take the gun home with him, I took the gun home instead and placed it in the utility closet in back of our house. The utility closet was at that time used to house Milda, Hueston's German shepherd. Hueston was apparently too lazy or incapable of building a dog house.

Later that same evening, after I had taken a shower and started doing some left over homework, there was a loud knock at our front door. It was Arthur and his father. Arthur was crying and his bullying father was telling Hueston about how: "Those boys had sneaked over to the store and bought the gun and were hiding it here." He wanted the gun that very minute. Hueston walked over to me and lashed out his hand slapping me in the face so hard I fell backwards. He shouted the order to get the gun and I did so.

Why don't you make your new buddy a drink and tell him all about me being a liar and a sneak. Hell, he will surely agree that his boy was just like that too, by God! Ha, ha! Make me another drink___ol' buddy! I thought with lava-hot hatred.

Arthur's father was leering at me, obviously enjoying how Hueston mistreated me. They left, and Hueston, against my mother's attempts to pacify him, started to beat me. He pushed me into the utility shed and locked the door. I spent the night with Milda, in that cold, dark utility room, which reeked strongly of dog stench. The smells were not the dogs fault. It was natural for some of the odors however, that bastard Hueston did not try to clean up daily. I knew Milda was my buddy and she really hated Houston. I went over the events during that day, thinking how Hueston was now really going to call me a sneak, thief and liar even though all I felt that I had done was help my friend during a difficult time. As I sat in the dark, Milda placed her paw on my lap.

He opened the door late the next morning and simply said to get the hell out and to not hang around the house, as was his usual comment.

Hueston had strange attitudes about children, as he denied us freedoms such as the simple ability to open the refrigerator to get a drink or snack. We boys were never allowed to hang around the house and were therefore always doing homework late in the evening, since it was after dark and we had to be home by then. However, he did allow the girls to stay home, but they were also restricted all the other things we boys were.

In 1967, Hueston was discharged from the U.S. Army and suddenly moved us all out of the house in suburbia. We relocated in an apartment on the exact opposite side of Glen Burnie. Hueston found a security guard job at Westinghouse and arranged for me to start working at a place owned by people he had acquainted himself with while working there. The company was called Wagon Wheel Diners.

Wagon Wheel Diners was located in Glen Burnie and was owned by an old Greek and run by his two sons. The old Greek had apoplexy, after having suffered a stroke the year before I had started working there, which resulted in his left side remaining paralyzed. This type of business served coffee and food from the sides and backs of their smaller trucks at area construction sites and used their only panel truck to service Westinghouse workers.

The panel truck had a large window on both sides of the 'box' as we referred to it. We served coffee from two big coffee urns situated against the wall of the box facing the front of the truck and sandwiches, donuts and pastries on a table that ran along the inside of the right side window. A wire tray hooked to the window and hung off the truck at a slant, offering the early morning work shift easy selection of their breakfast sandwich preference.

An old man, named Bill, and I worked the box. He was a tall skinny man of about sixty years of age. He had short blond hair, which was turning white and a face traversed with red capillaries. Bill served the window and I poured the coffee. It was a hectic pace each morning. Upon return, I had to scrub the urns and stainless steel interior of the box before school started. At the end of each morning, I felt so exhausted that school was becoming an undesirable follow-up to the job however, I endured.

I woke at 3:30 a.m. each morning, ran to Ritchie highway, the main road next to our apartment, and waited for Johnnie Alexis, the younger of the owner's sons, to pick me up. Upon arrival at the office there was immediate activity to start the day, with a dozen men and women already stocking their trucks and making the coffee in their urns. Steam wafted everywhere through the shafts of lights, which glistened off the wet concrete of the dark truck yard.

Everywhere one could hear the metallic drumming sound the water hoses made while spraying into empty pots, as the workers rinsed-out things, filled coffee urns or sprayed their trucks clean. There was always the smell in the air of brewing coffee, fresh coffee pastries and donuts as the baker unloaded dozens of trays from his truck each morning, six days a week.

My first task would be to start grabbing the donut and pastry trays and placing them on the panel truck. Bill would already be there every morning, sorting things out, arranging the sandwiches and other items, in preparation for the Westinghouse morning-shift horde.

Next, I would start making the coffee and make sure to fill the water tank between the two coffee urns, which was used for dispensing hot water for tea orders. Finally, I would make sure we had stocked-up with enough small, medium and large paper cups for coffee and tea, along with enough plastic lids and arranged them for quick access. For once serving had started, I would go through these things at such a rapid pace, that to run out, would be disastrous, and to delay, while digging around for cups and lids, would piss-off the customers.

Then off we would go, with me holding on to the stainless steel shelving in the box, swaying back and forth, while up front, in the only seat, Bill drove as fast as he could toward the job site.

During the summer of 1967, while I waited along Ritchie highway for Johnnie to pick me up, I had begun taking along a Sony transistor radio and was starting to really get into the current music. During that summer my favorite song was *'Groovin'* by the Rascals and all my mind ever did was repeat the rhythmic sounded words *'Groovin' On A Sunday Afternoon'*. That beat would be my pace-tune during work.

The work was hardest during the school year and seemed to be less demanding during the summer. I was earning a good paycheck for my age however, what little money I did earn, was mostly taken by Hueston. He maintained that I should pay rent, if I was staying in his house.

We moved once again, later in the summer of 1967, to a fairly upscale housing complex called Glen Burnie Park. It was even closer to were I worked. This was probably due to Hueston's retirement checks, his raises at Westinghouse and my monetary input and Moms nagging. The house was a nice split-level, in a nice neighborhood.

Lucious, who had returned from Red Flint shortly after we moved into the house, was working at a carwash and contributing his hard earned income as well. He and I had decided to buy some new bedroom furniture and settled on two unfinished night stands, a double dresser with mirror and an upright dresser. Hueston said fine, because if we put it in his house, it would belong to him anyway. What the hell, we thought, as we were tired of the Spartan shit we were using. We stained the wood ourselves, a mahogany stain and then varnished everything, which in our young eyes, when finished, appeared as good as any professional could have done.

My relationship at home, with Charlie Hueston, was as always, in a constant state of hostility. He was getting meaner as his drunkenness reached entire fifths of Seagram Seven Crown whisky each night. My mother, practically a non-drinker, was always trying to get his attention onto other subjects when he started lashing out at us kids. He seemed to especially attack me which, even though I virtually never spoke at all around him, perplexed me greatly.

So, each night, it always seemed he got onto talking about the clown. He'd bitch about how the clown doesn't pay the child support money and finally, how I was just like my father: a liar and a sneak. I always heard his screaming from my room, which was where I stayed, in seclusion or rather solitary, most all of the time.

But it was always the same each night as he rooted me out, wherever I would be. He would come into the room in a drunken rush, pointing his finger at me, while at the same time screaming the same accusations like in a television show re-run. Each time, my mother would be next to him trying to get his attention off of me, and each time, ignoring her, he would shove or push my mother out of his way and continue his barrage of hurtful insults.

Up to that point, I had not provided that son-of-a-bitch any reason to accuse me as he did. That repetition of hate and persecution had spawned the first day I had arrived in the country, in Long Island, when I bought those toy soldiers and told him right then and there I did. Mom could have or should have told him to shut-up and then given him the dollar back.

During the summer of 1968, during the extremely rare days when Hueston was out of the house, I could catch the news on TV and enjoy reading any *Life* magazines lying around the living room. The news was always covering the war in Vietnam as did the *Life* magazine company. There was one picture of many wounded soldiers holding on to each other while precariously riding on some sort of tracked vehicle. One soldier appeared to have an octopus-looking thing attached to his helmet. I think it was a bandage he had opened and stuck there for quicker use.

I remained very confused and extremely bitter, and towards the end of the summer of 1968 it came to a head when I had asked to be sent to Little Rock, Arkansas, to stay with my father. Hueston, in his hurry to get rid of me, did not ask the type of questions a responsible adult and supposed guardian should. My mother only thought he was the man of the house and therefore, knew what was best. His answer was, "Sure kid,__what evah ya wan't!__Ya wan't me ta drive ya to da airport right now?" he said in his New York accent, with an oily smile. He sent me outright to my father, a man who, after not having seen any of his children since February 1962, was not going to deny himself the ability to get at least one child, regardless of his inability to properly care for one.

The problem was that he made little money, had his meager U.S. Air Force master sergeant's retirement check and lived in a run down boarding house on that. The small wage he did earn came from carrying a pole on a road surveying crew. I always believed my father thought the word 'retired' from the military was synonymous with 'old age can't work no more' retirement. So he simply worked to earn cigarette money.

SEVEN

My father picked me up at the Trailways bus station in Little Rock. It was September 1968, the temperature was in the high eighties and my father had no car.

"*Great!*" I thought, thinking at the same time that my stay here, with dear ol' Papa, was going to be less than comfortable, at best. There he stood, wearing worn blue jean overalls and a stained and yellowed tee-shirt. Protruding out from the piled up excess length of his overalls were scuffed blood-red clay covered construction boots. His head and arms were deeply tanned and his hair was all cut off in a fuzzy burr-cut.

"Hello Jackie," he said, sounding the name as 'Jekey'. He simply stood there with a crooked pursed-lip smile. He was obviously not sure how I felt about him and waited for me to make the first move.

"Hi Papa," I finally greeted stiffly, while I simply stood there waiting for him to tell me what to do next. It was a very intense and awkward moment.

"Are ya hungry?___Do ya want some catfish?___When did ya last eat?___Do ya have eny bags?" Papa tried to brake the icy moment the best he could. It was very clear that while he had waited for my bus, he had mulled over and decided on every question he would ask me, and while deliberating, he had apparently developed a hankering for catfish.

We walked many blocks under the hot Arkansas sun, toward North Little Rock, until we finally reached a very spare, but typical, southern-style cafe and went inside.

As I put my only travel bag down and slid it under my chair with my heel, I glanced around the cafe. It had a big picture window with a couple of small clay potted plants, which were dried to a crispy texture, after having died years ago. Next to the dead plants was a severely chipped plaster figure of a man sitting on a log with a fishing pole extended from his lap. There were also dozens of dead flies lying randomly on the window sill.

The furnishings were made of rounded chrome legged tables and chairs. The table tops had red and white flaked patterns in a hard laminated board with a three inch ridged chrome boarder running around it. The chairs had round red vinyl cushions each with a split, revealing the white stuffing inside. The walls were painted a light mint green color. Overhead, hanging from sagging square black ornately patterned ceiling tiles were several cobweb and dust coated four bladed fans lazily rotating in slow revolutions, moving around the hot air inside, but not really cooling anyone.

A fat, red-faced waitress came over to us, set down two scuffed plastic glasses of ice water and took our order.

Within fifteen minutes, we were served large servings of crisp deep-fried catfish, with balls of hush puppies, cornbread and a serving of black-eyed peas. For drinks, we drank from our scuffed plastic water glasses, which due to the ice inside, and the heat in the room, appeared to sweat as much water onto the table as was inside the glasses.

Our conversation, if it could be called one, was an occasional comment on the taste of the food. I had to admit that it was all good and I had been very hungry. However, I was still slightly nauseous from the long bus ride and that awful smell of vomit, hair oil, sweat, booze, cigarettes, farts, baby shit and a variety of other nondescript odors, which seemed to permeate every bus. We hardly talked at all during our meal. When we finished, we just looked at each other for a moment until Papa quickly snatched the bill off the table and stood up.

We left the cafe and Papa's generous fifteen cent tip and walked five or six more blocks to a weather-worn, clapboard-sided, white house.

There were two floors in this house, a kitchen, living room, bedroom and bathroom on the first floor and three bedrooms and a bathroom on the second floor.

Mrs. Nelson, the proprietor, lived on the first floor. Except for the entrance foyer, which had a locked door to her living area, the only time anyone was on the first floor was to gain access to the stairs off the foyer and leading up to the second floor.

Papa had rented a bedroom here, approximately sixteen by sixteen feet, two sides of which had windows. There were two single beds with a small night stand between them. On another wall, an inside wall without doors or windows, was positioned a small one by three foot table on top of which was placed a two-coil electric hot-plate. A small closet, the width of the door and only two feet deep, led off the wall were the exit door was located. The wallpaper was old and peeling in many spots. That wasn't as bad as the color, which was a combination of tight little patterns of brown and yellow. The bare wood-strip floor was darkly stained, appearing nearly black. The room was dark, dingy and dirty.

The entire effect was enhanced by the single electric cord and a bare light bulb dangling from it. Off in one corner was a yellow coil of sticky fly paper, laden with dead and recently captured flies, that buzzed and wriggled, trying vainly to escape their inevitable slow death.

The bathroom was located across the hall. It contained an old claw-footed bathtub, a sink and a toilet. The floor was finished in a black and yellow checkered ceramic tile and illustrated the usage effects of three single men who were not fastidious. Obviously, Mrs. Nelson did not clean the upstairs area either. The hall area was equally bleak with its dark stained wood doors, door frames, floors, trim and dark nondescript wall paper. It was so dark in that windowless hallway that I was unable to determine the design, nor color of that wallpaper.

Once back in the room I noticed there was only one coffee mug sitting next to a small glass jar of instant Maxwell House coffee, restaurant sugar packets, powdered creamer and a couple of unclean plastic picnic spoons on the hotplate table. That was the only furniture other than two single beds. Other than that, there was only a sheet, pillow and blanket, which were scattered on top of his unmade bed.

"Didn't think I'd show up?" I asked Papa.

"Thought Ah'd wait in' see what cha needed first," he replied lamely. He hadn't said much at all since I arrived, except talk about our relatives in Red Flint and what types of businesses were in Little Rock.

Enough of this awkwardness! I thought and asked to have a talk. Within a minute we sat opposite from one another on the edge of the beds and started into a discussion, which shortly got around to his explanation for never sending any support money to my mother. He rationalized this decision by stating that as long as our mother did not let him see us children and lived with that son-of-a-bitch Hueston, he was never going to send any child support money.

I did not argue with his perception. However, when Lucious and I had lived in Red Flint, he was not exactly a model father who came rushing to see his boys. Where was he then?

The discussion gradually involved those things I would be needing immediately to get situated and where I would go to school. We made up a short list of items such as sheets, pillow and case, blanket and towels, coffee cup, glasses, silverware, etcetera and then we headed towards the stores.

Papa led the way up and down residential and small business streets and eventually we spotted a discount store. Inside the bleak store were four rows of folding tables supporting scores of cardboard boxes, which contained a large variety of household necessities. There were plates, glasses, cups, table cloths, dish rags, soap dishes, brushes, silverware, can openers and there were also sheets, pillows and blankets. The prices were very reasonable, because much of the merchandise was either second-hand or had factory defects.

We purchased the basic necessities we agreed on earlier and nothing else. As we walked back to the house, Papa had explained where he kept some groceries in the room. When we reached the door, he said he had to run some other errands and unlocked the front door for me. He handed me the room key and said he'll only be gone a short while and turned away. I entered the room and immediately sensed the long-time accumulative smells, which permeate the walls, floor and furniture. It was a musty combination of years of nicotine saturation, added to by the more recent odors of sweaty, damp laundry, and oily fish.

The first thing I did was prepare my bed. The mattress was old and heavily stained with rings of overlapping half-inch wide dark boarders surrounding the lighter colored basketball sized stains within. Smelling the mattress and curling my lip in disgust at the foul stench of old sweat and urine, I flipped the mattress over and studied that side for a moment. Thank god the previous owners didn't rotate the mattress regularly. I found there was hardly any stain damage there and proceeded to make my bed.

Still feeling exhausted from the long bus ride, I decided to lay down for awhile. At first, I just lay there, without any thoughts and stared at the old yellowed ceiling and then focused on the simple electric cord dangling from its center supporting the clear low wattage light bulb. The room was silent except for the *tick-tock* of his alarm clock. My attention was lazily drawn to one of the fly paper strips, perhaps subconsciously attracted by the drone of the struggling flies.

The ominous sticky yellow strip dangled from the ceiling with several curls luring the flies to their death with a delicious scent, which to me smelled vile. I watched as several flies landed on the strip and agonized as their attempts to fly were frustrated. They struggled until a wing got stuck, then their body, as they slowly sank into immobility and awaited death. My eyes closed at some point during this unemotional observation and I fell into a deep sleep.

It was dark outside when I awoke. I had to concentrate for a moment to determine where I was. I got up and went to one of the windows and peered out onto the dark street. There was really nothing to see, because there were no street lamps and no light reflecting from other buildings.

Actually there were only a couple of structures neighboring the house. This house was on a corner lot with a large front yard and equally large side yards. There was a run-down house directly across the street, which I had noticed earlier, was almost obscured by weed tree and larger tree growths. Diagonally across the street was a vacant lot and across the street, looking to the right, as one would exit the house, was another house set deep into their lot. Looking to the left side of that house I could see the long weathered back walls of an abandoned factory or warehouse, which were very old and in decline.

Papa was still not home. I looked over at his round faced alarm clock, which displayed 10:15 p.m., I could see he had been gone for hours. Feeling very hungry, I walked over to his side of the bed and pulled the box of food out from under it. There was an assortment of canned and dried foods in it, including two pots and one pot lid. There were cans of sardines, beans, corn, stew and boxes of noodles, macaroni and cheese, salted crackers and rice. A bottle of Tabasco sauce, shakers of salt and pepper and a jar of Jalapeno peppers were crammed in the survival box as well.

Now I know where that oily fish smell comes from. I mused and looked into the small trash can next to the small table verifying that an empty sardine can was indeed the culprit.

I made a run to the bathroom, filled a pot with water, took a piss and returned to the room. I turned the ancient hotplate on and boiled water for a cup of instant coffee. After digging around in the box I found a can opener and opened a can of stew. I poured the chunky contents into the second pot and placed it on the burner and within minutes the room smelled of meat and gravy.

The hot plate cooked faster than I had expected as the stew bubbled and popped. I found a large spoon and stirred the stew so it wouldn't stick to the pot, but the hotplate got far too hot too fast and still burned the food, causing it to stick to the pot.

I ate my simple meal and washed it down with the cup of instant coffee. The instant coffee, my first, had tasted like shit. After having worked at Wagon Wheel Diners and drinking coffee made of fresh ground coffee beans, I was shocked at the poor quality of instant coffee. However, not to complain, this was here, not there, so adjust to it. Well, at least there was no refrigerator to be restricted from and I could stay inside this flop-house all damned day long, if I wanted to.

Papa entered the room around 3:00 a.m.. I listened as he noisily prepared himself for bed, keeping the light off and apparently thinking I was sleeping through all of his racket. I smelled beer and knew he was drunk. I rolled over and went to sleep.

The next morning the alarm clock woke me at 6:30 a.m. as Papa dragged himself out of bed and left the room. A half hour later, wearing boxer shorts and a tee-shirt he returned from the bathroom. He apparently took a bath, because he now smelled of soap and shaving cream instead of piss, beer and stale farts. He lit a Lucky Strike cigarette and sat on the side of his bed and began pulling on socks and overalls.

"Mornin'!" I managed, attempting to be polite.

Papa said the same, in a hoarse voice. His first words, I remembered, had always been that way. He turned to look at me, saying nothing about where he was yesterday.

"See ya made somethin' ta eat," he said nodding toward the empty stew can in the garbage and the pot with water that had been soaking over night to loosen the burned stew, which had stuck fast to the bottom. He then fixed himself a cup of coffee, having heated my remaining water in the other pot.

He got up and pulled his wallet from his pocket and dug out a twenty dollar bill.

"Here," he said, with his arm stretched out stiffly, holding the bill, "Ah think twenty dollars a week should be enough for you ta live on here."

I accepted the money saying thanks, however I had no idea what it was going to cost nor what he meant by his comment.

"Papa," I said. "Are you saying that I should take care of myself,___and buy my own food and all,___while you do the same for yourself?"

"No!___Ah'll buy you meals and stock up the room when Ah get a ride to the commissary at the Little Rock Air Base.___You can spend that money on whatever you want," he said.

From that day on, we would usually eat at a restaurant down the hill from us, which was across the street from the old Main Railroad Station. I generally had greasy pancakes and Papa habitually had bacon strips and greasy eggs sunny side up, which were always speckled with bacon bits. Then he went off to work at some surveying company he never named, where he held the rod all day under the hot Arkansas sun, and I went off to school.

I attended Little Rock Central High School, a huge school, which had gained notoriety in 1959 when the Arkansas National Guard had been called out by the Governor to enforce the desegregation order and protect the black students from attacks by angry whites. Central High was considered the finest high school in the south.

I talked Papa into the idea of getting an apartment and then I spent most of my free time looking. I would try to drag Papa to the few I had considered as acceptable and he would make all manner of excuses about them. It was really simply a matter of money that we never moved.

As time passed, I was increasingly withdrawing into a personal world. Embarrassed about our lodging, I made no friends at school and there were no boys my age living near these run-down boarding houses. I took walks and discovered a few shops. One of these sold used records and the other used books. Papa had recently brought home an old record player so I figured I'd buy a couple of records. The only two records I ever bought while there, were 45 RPMs. One was a classical instrumental with *'Interlude-Instrumental'* and *'The Interlude Triangle'* conducted by Georges Delerue and the other was *'Sixteen Tons'* and *'Mule Train'* by Tennessee Ernie Ford.

EIGHT

I started reading *Nick Carter* pulp fiction secret agent books. There were so many of them, that I fell into the world of cloak and dagger and dreamed of becoming a secret agent one day. I would lay on my bed all day long on weekends and read the Killmaster Nick Carters' adventures, while playing the now-scratchy Interlude record over and over. I really liked the books, but often wondered why there was no author listed. Papa was hardly ever home, and when he was, he would beg to borrow back the twenty dollars allowance he had given me only a day or two before. He did this so often I had to ask him to either stop giving me an allowance or stop asking for it back. He chose to stop the allowance.

I would get so angry at his nightly trips to the restaurant across from the train station, which is where we ate during the day and where he drank at night. I would walk around outside in the dark and watch him through the window just sit there and pour beer down, one after the other, until I always felt like throwing a rock through the window at him.

One night, after he had particularly pissed me off, I became so angry I stomped off down the road still clutching the rock I had picked up by the restaurant. My mind was so anguished that I suddenly and randomly threw that rock into the glass door of a business and heard the glass break. I felt lost and helpless and just walked on, back to that miserable hole we lived in.

There was a man who lived in one of the other two rooms in our building. One day he knocked on our door. Papa was actually home that day. We did not really know him, except to say hello when very rarely passing him in the hall, so a visit was unusual. He asked if he could come in and talk for a while. His eyes were bloodshot and watery.

Oh hell! I thought. *Another drunk!*

He stared at me a long moment and then, looking toward Papa, said, "They jes' came by,___the Army,___and tol' me mah boy was ded, that he was kilt in action o'er in Vietnam!"

He started to cry so hard his body shuddered. Papa told him to sit down and did not say anything until the man had gained composure again.

"Ah'm sorry,___is there enythin' Ah kin do?" Papa asked him.

"No,___thanks fer lisnin',___ah don't have nobody else, now, ta talk to,___he was all Ah had,___Ah hoped he'd carry tha name an' do better than Ah did,___but he didn't have no kids___an' no luck,___jus' like me."

He got up looking very tired and sad, apologized, looked at me a long moment and then excused himself from our room.

We never learned about any funeral and the old man became even more reclusive then he already had been.

Days alone came and went and spring was nearing. School at Little Rock Central High was boring me now. I still had not tried to make friends at my school. However, I did meet a girl my age, in the neighborhood. We hung around together, taking walks and exploring the area around North Little Rock.

Her name was Paula and her parents ran the restaurant located across the street from the old train station and adjacent to the run-down restaurant where Papa and I usually ate. Their restaurant, which was equally run down, was on the first floor of an old civil war era hotel.

Always alone in my 'hole-in-the-wall' room, I would see Papa when he came home from work, wearing the same overalls and construction boots, which were always covered with that very red Arkansas clay. He would only stay long enough to clean-up, change clothes and then go out again, to his beer joint.

During my stay in Little Rock, Papa had never ensured that I received a balanced diet. Consequently, I started getting sick often and would break out with boils on my forehead and cheeks. These painful boils would keep me in bed for days. With no proper food supply in my room and no refrigerator to keep fresh milk, cheese, eggs and other essential nutritious food stuffs, I could not properly fight illness. I had also refrained from eating at the train station restaurant as I imagined it was that greasy shit-hole that made me sick to begin with.

Thanksgiving, Christmas, New Year's Eve, New Year's Day, then Easter and Valentine's Day had come and gone, with no mention of the day, no symbols of the event and no residual tangible item to remind me of their existence in later days.

Papa rarely spoke about anything relating to why he had left us in Germany or why he and Mom split up. However, during melancholy periods he would volunteer how sad he was and how he still loved my mother. He stated that she was the reason he had left us in Germany, never really explaining what had been behind the separation.

It was during the month of April 1969 when I had announced that I had enough of this shit and wanted to return to Maryland, even though I had equally despised that place, with Hueston there. Nevertheless, Mom and the girls were there and for no other reason, it seemed preferable.

Papa paid for a plane ticket this time, which surprised me, knowing he always opted to use buses. A friend of his gave us a ride to the Little Rock airport. As we were pulling away from the house, I saw Paula from the rear window. Paula, the only person I had truly befriended while there, was walking towards the boarding house door to visit me. When she saw me looking at her from the car window I put my hand up and held it still. She blushed, put her head down, turned and started walking in the opposite direction, perhaps sensing I was leaving for good. I was sad for her and a little angry that she picked this day to make her first visit to the house, as that could have proved interesting. What was I to do? I learned something that day. It was that when it comes to my personal survival, a female would never win over my decision. In this case – get the hell out of Little Rock!

NINE

When I arrived at Friendship airport, I phoned the house hoping to get Mom, but got Hueston instead. I told him that I was at the airport. After a very long pause, he growled "Why!" I told him I wanted to come home. I had not really thought about it up to that point, but I was making my first independent decisions concerning my life.

Surprisingly, he came and picked me up. We did not talk much and when we arrived at home I only saw my fourteen year old sister Sarah. I had to ask where my mother and Annie were. She informed me that they were in Germany visiting our brother and relatives. This news came as a shock to me, as I knew I would not get along with Hueston.

I would be guaranteed a rough time and would really hate life. This realization was driven home when Sarah told me they had been gone for weeks and would probably stay for a long time.

My brother Lucious was away in college, working to pay his own way, so he would not be around all through the summer. Why should he come by? He felt the same as I did regarding Hueston and the home life here.

I started working at Wagon Wheel Diners again, and as before, what money I made, Hueston would take almost all of it. Consequently, I came to hate working for no money and figured I needed to earn more in order to keep a little more for myself. The only plus in this was I got out of the house and away from that bastard.

I developed a plan to work for a drug store at the local shopping mall in the evenings. I could walk there directly after school was out and this gave me even more distance from Hueston. This job involved merchandising the isles and maintaining the stockroom. The store closed at 9:30 p.m. and after sweeping the floors and straightening out merchandise, I usually left at 10:00 p.m. Once at the house, I did my homework and went straight to bed because I had to get up at 3:30 a.m. Regardless of this routine, I maintained an A-B academic course average at school.

On the days I did not go to these jobs I would find something to do around the yard and then at night, try to read in my room. Sarah was always very distant towards me and had been acting strange ever since I came back from Little Rock. When I tried to talk to her, Hueston would chase me away while screaming, "leave her alone!___Don't bother her.___You two don't get along,___so stop talking to her___and quit hanging around the house!"

I could not figure out why he was always keeping us apart and why Sarah was acting so weird. I did know that he did not ever allow me in the house until late at night where I had only time to do my homework.

As the school year was nearing summer break, I had a strange encounter in my Biology class. There were several really tough guys in my school and fortunately they were friends of mine. One had already developed extremely heavy facial hair and even though he would shave daily, it looked like a black patch covered his face. His name was Steve and sporting an Elvis style hair cut, completed his look by wearing a black leather jacket, white tee-shirt, blue jeans and motor cycle boots.

Steve was so tough looking, that everyone who did not know him would prefer to stay clear of him on the assumption he was mean and would kick their ass if he were bothered.

On several occasions Steve would shake his head side to side and ask me how I did it? How could I always be working and still maintain high grades. He was a poor student who preferred motorcycles and chasing girls. He was a taciturn guy, making few acquaintances, but we seemed to hit it off.

My best friend was Barry. He and I had attended Marley Junior High School together. Marley Maryland, a real rough red neck suburb of Glen Burnie, bred the kind of kids who extorted student's lunch money so they could eat, and would later beat the shit out the victim, if they didn't like the lunch.

I started to spend all of my free time at Barry's house during my wait for my mother and sister to return from Germany. I still had no idea how long they were staying there and there were no letters that I knew of, hence I had no address to write her and explain what was going on here.

There was this very pretty girl, named Heather, in my Biology class. We had those two-seat lab tables and she had been assigned to the other seat at my table. One day, near the end of the school year, while Biology class was settling down to begin and the teacher had not yet entered the classroom, a student named Chuck walked over to our table. He was followed by several of his cronies and they represented one of the self-appointed tough-guy clicks at the school. Chuck was very tall, with long shaggy muddy-blond hair and brown eyes, set in a plain blunt-nosed face. Until that day, I had never had any run-ins with this group and they did not know me at all.

Chuck, with self-righteous indignation, began to harangue me about Heather talking with me. He was even insinuating that we were dating. He obviously envied me and desired to date her himself, a situation I could not even envision. He was too stupid to try asking her out when class was over, at any time, during the school year. Any chance he may have had was totally lost here this day and the idea of caveman-logic to win the female in mortal combat was not quite the accepted custom anymore.

Yellow Footprints

"Hey asshole!" Chuck began brilliantly. "Who do you think you are,___huh?" Sounding like that bastard in my life, Hueston. "Do you think you're man enough for her?___I want to kick your ass!___So meet me in the Shop Class parking lot after school pussy and I'll carve you a new asshole!" he snickered and was chorused by *yeh-yeas* from his cronies. He had apparently heard someplace that one had to carve the thing.

Heather appeared frozen in shock, as she said nothing at all. I replied with, "What are you talking about?"___"I haven't done anything to cause you to challenge me.___Why don't you just go away?___I don't intend to meet you anywhere,___Chuck!" I pronounced his name in a forced manner, as I had not been afraid of him, but was somewhat surprised by his bravado.

"Chicken,___*bawk, bawk, baa_ba_bawkk!*" Chuck and his mimicking cronies chided. "We'll get you anyway!"

Ah hell,___not the chicken clucking, fight-demanding, baiting, comment. I pursed my lips and shook my head side to side wondering who this hillbilly bone-head was and where did he come from? Worse, why did it take his slow wit so long to discover that Heather was even in the class room? After all, the school year was nealy over. The dolt must have forgotten we were assigned our seating at the beginning of the school year.

Barry, hearing this from his table in another part of the classroom, had told Steve about it later that day. After school let out that day, I did not go to the Shop Class parking lot to meet Chuck and his friends. Instead I went to Barry's home with Steve tagging along. Steve wanted to know what I was going to do about this crazy challenge.

Once we were at Barry's house, his older brother Dave, who was also a close friend to me, offered his services along with his friend Greg. Greg, standing six foot six weighing a solid two hundred fifty pounds was a high school dropout. He was also legendary in the area as the tallest, strongest and unequaled meanest bad guy around. Before the evening ended I had a virtual army of the toughest dudes around at my disposal. All of these guys were willing to beat the living shit out of Chuck's gang. However, I was not asking for their help, while I listened to their plans to do this and that to Chuck and company.

The next day, upon Biology class ending, the teacher called my name and instructed me to pick up lesson papers from all the desks, while the class emptied out. I placed the papers on his desk, while he went to put chemicals away in his storage closet, and left the classroom.

Outside the classroom the hall was jammed with students standing and waiting to see what was happening. While I was picking up the papers Chuck had been bragging in the hallway about how he would get me. When I stepped into the hallway he suddenly sucker punched me in the face, causing me to drop my books and stumble backwards a few steps. Bad move on his part.

Something inside me had apparently been building up over the years, because I retaliated instantly and with such ferocity, that Chuck's cronies and the students gaped, as I pounded Chuck in the face, kidneys and stomach with rapid blows, causing him to literally drop to the floor and cower with hands covering his head.

The Biology teacher heard the commotion and ran into the hallway to break up the fight. Naturally, we were sent to the principal's office for our punishment. Surprising both of us, there was only the standard stern warning not to repeat the infraction. Chuck, accused by the teacher as the instigator, was given the guilty-as-charged notice that he would be suspended if it ever happened again. I did not offer any comments and only agreed not to start any fights.

When we exited the principals office Chuck turned to me and smiled.

"You got a mean left hook guy!" Chuck laughed and shook my hand. We never had any differences after that day.

You'll never know how lucky you are Chuck, because a bunch of guys were really looking forward to rearranging your life and 'carve' you a new asshole. I thought and figured the boy was too slow-minded to even comprehend his own stupid actions.

When I finally made it to my next class, Steve sat at the back of the room beaming a broad smile at me. Apparently word had flashed through the entire school in the short time I had been in the principal's office. I had been elevated to that group no student would mess with. Heather moved to Florida two weeks later.

I began drinking beer, wine and even whiskey when I could get it. My life was sliding into a limbo world. Not wanting to go home and not wanting to stay with other people, I was starting to hang out in the Marley neighborhood until it was two or three o'clock in the morning. I was angry at everything and waited for my mother to return from

Germany, thinking that this alone would stabilize my situation. This amorphous hate was so great that I didn't even want to hang around my friends. I was still able to focus on work and school subjects and found that this allowed the time to fly by disabling my mind from dwelling on my home-life situation.

Barry, Dave and Greg were into drinking, so through their connections with older friends, we could obtain booze without difficulty. Regardless of a variety of choices, we mostly drank *Carling Black Label* beer, which was brewed up the road near Baltimore. I would find a table at the library each evening to do my homework and then go to the drug store to work. After work I met up with Barry and the others and would start drinking. The feeling of being drunk numbed me enough to forget the shitty feeling I dragged around through the day.

I decided to go home and check the status of my situation there. Hueston did not question where I was all the time, nor did he indicate that he gave a shit. He really only wanted me away from the house. I was really trying to slow down the drinking and hanging out all the time. If Hueston would leave me alone, maybe I could survive the hostilities and spend time in my own room.

Only a few days had passed since I had attempted to stay at home again. It was around ten in the evening, with a violent thunder storm raging about the area. While I was lying on top of my bed with my knees bent, reading a book, my bedroom door suddenly burst open with a loud crash. After he had sat upstairs long enough, while seething about me between drinks, a very drunk Hueston charged into my room waving a German Luger pistol. He pointed it at me and screamed about me talking with my sister Sarah that day, after he had warned me to stay away from her. Next there came his old list of verbal abuse calling me a liar, cheat, sneak and finishing with an order to get the fuck out of his house.

I had left my top dresser drawer half way open and Hueston was weaving around in front of it. Hearing his verbal barrage and reacting to the threat of the pistol, I instinctively kicked out with my right leg from my bent-knee position. My foot connected with his stomach and sent him crashing into the open top drawer, smashing it.

Hueston fell to the floor with the wood fragments and clothes around him. The clothes apparently confused him as he had trouble locating the pistol he had dropped during the fall. I jumped out of bed and started kicking him and throwing punches trying to keep him down. However, he was much bigger then I was at sixteen, and retaliated. He was punching at me trying to get up. One hand grabbed my throat gouging a furrow into my skin. I raged back into him with my knees, feet and fists until he fell flat on the floor.

I seized that moment to run from the room and out the front door into the storm. All I was wearing was blue jeans and a tee-shirt, now torn. I was being drenched and looking rapidly about trying to figure out my next move. Across the street I caught the break lights of a neighbors car as it backed out of their drive way. Splashing barefoot through the sheet of water covering the cul-de-sac, I ran to the drivers' window and pounded. The startled driver hit the breaks, causing the car to lurch backwards then forwards, followed by the window being lowered a few inches. The man inside was staring at me with a hint of fright on his face. Seeing that I was only a kid he noticeably relaxed, but asked quickly what I wanted, as the rain splattered into his car.

"I need a ride!" I bellowed through the heavy rain.

"What!__Why,__what's wrong?" he queried. Apparently, he had not really recognized me with my flattened rain-soaked hair and blood running down my neck creating a pink stain on my tee-shirt.

"I live there!" I said pointing toward the house. "I had a very bad fight with my mothers boyfriend and she's out of the country.__I need a ride over to a friends house,__now!" I looked like a drowning cat at this point. "He's going to come after me again!__He's crazy and drunk!"

"Get in!" he snapped, obviously feeling he'd regret getting mixed up in our family disputes.

As I told him where I wanted to go, I also told him I'd keep him out of this by not mentioning his help driving me. As I related the story, I purposely kept the pistol out of the picture thinking the cops getting involved would be more harm right now, then help.

Barry's mother and dad were very nice. When I showed up they simply said that I should stay there as long as I needed to.

"When everybody goes to sleep you can crash here, on the couch." Barry said as he threw me a pillow.

The next day Barry's Dad went to the mall to buy me sneakers, socks and a shirt. He bought them with my promise that I would pay him back when I was paid next. I knew he would not have asked for the money back had I not insisted. They were a poor family of six children and his wife could not work, as she suffered from some kind of chronic fatigue. He worked as an engineer at Westinghouse, the same place I served coffee every morning during the week.

For the next weeks I stayed completely away from Hueston. I did worry about Sarah, but figured that as protective of her as Hueston was, she would be alright. After all Mama had thought it safe to leave her with him while she was visiting West Germany.

TEN

A week after the incident with Hueston I started to feel better and struck out along Ritchie Highway for the Armed Forces Recruiting office in Glen Burnie. I did not care if I had to quit school. I just wanted to get the hell out of here.

Once there, knowing full well I didn't want the Air Force, because of my father, and didn't want the Army, because of Hueston, I went into the Navy office. The Navy recruiter showed me all sorts of pictures and discussed the whole program finishing by informing me I would receive basic training at Great Lakes, Michigan. I tried to get a confirmed time to go to AFEES (Armed Forces Entrance Examination Station) for my entrance physical, but the recruiter simply told me to come back after I turned seventeen along with parental consent. Damn, I was mad. Where was my mother and Annie.

Not deterred, I went back to the Recruiting office a week before my seventeenth birthday to look at the Navy posters and talk with the recruiters. While visiting, I had questioned the recruiter about the submarine service. He told me it would be six months before I could start basic training, where upon completion, I would be in line with that training program. The big let down was when he said I needed a least a High School diploma.

Holy shit! I was thinking, this was not the way I had envisioned my bold entry into the military would be. This bit of news prompted me to do something that was to be one of the most major decisions and have one of the largest impacts in my life.

"Who is that?" I asked the Navy recruiter, while I pointed through the glass partition to another recruiter in the adjoining office. The Navy recruiter, following my finger, saw I was pointing at a man wearing a khaki shirt and tie and blue trousers with red stripes running down the seams to a pair of beautifully spit shined shoes.

"That's a Marine!" the Navy recruiter said with obvious respect.

"What's a Marine?" I asked innocently. I told him that growing up in Germany and around Air Force bases, I had never seen the uniform before and couldn't remember anyone discussing them before. I simply did not know anything about them and that man was not in his office the first time I was there.

"They're the infantry of the Navy," the Navy recruiter said respectfully.

"Can I talk to him?" I asked.

"Sure,__why not," he replied.

I went next door and the Marine stood up, walked over to me, extending his right hand.

"How ya doing?___My name is Master Sergeant Herbert.___What can I do for you?" he said smoothly. He was very tall and square-jawed, with sharp features and wore the most immaculate uniform I had ever seen. He wore so many ribbons on his chest that they obscured the left part of his shirt.

We talked about the Marine Corps for about a half hour and he gave me several brochures to take home. I looked at the posters on his office walls of Marines running through an obstacle course, in parade formations, in jungle attire, all looking tough as hell. Yes sir, this was for me.

"I want to join the Marine Corps!" I announced suddenly, while thinking 'fuck going in the Navy!' "Would there be any problem getting the paperwork from the Navy recruiter?" I asked.

"No problem," Master Sergeant Herbert said with a smile.

In 1969 there was no such thing as a hard time for recruiters, except for the Marines. A war was raging in Vietnam, the draft was in full swing and many volunteered for their preferred branch rather than being drafted into the Army, so why should there have been any problems for the other branches. Even with those who volunteered for their own branch, many chose the Air Force or Navy. The Marine Corps was not a branch of service one chose idly.

I left his office day-dreaming about being a Marine all the way back to Barry's house. I couldn't wait to tell Barry and all of my friends. In the end they were appropriately awed, but then came the torrent of questions.

"Are you crazy?___The Marines!___They're way too tough!___You'll hate it!___Why quit school?" my friends shouted with incredulity, but they didn't have the home situation with limited options I had.

I had been drinking beer with Barry, Dave and a half dozen neighborhood friends. We would usually sit along an old crumbling four foot high brick wall at the entrance to the development.

These were Marley boys, tough red-necks who at a young age started hating anybody not from Marley. Now that we were out of Marley Junior High and going to Glen Burnie High School, we picked on those from other High Schools and only accepted those from our school area.

An example of this rivalry happened on this night, as we sat drinking and talking about current events in our lives. A car load of boys from a competitor school drove into our neighborhood. Their car was blocked and after a lot of tough bravado had been exchanged, Dave came out of the dark wielding a long truck crow bar. He just walked up and smashed in their windshield. Naturally a fist fight ensued and after enough energy had been expended the losing side jumped into their newly air conditioned car, and with promises of revenge, sped away. Who cared, we were done playing around with them anyway and wanted some new action.

It didn't take long to find something new. We felt great after the scuffle and what we found was perfect. We located a truck parked next to a submarine sandwich shop, which also served Maryland Blue crabs. The back doors of the truck were padlocked. Dave, still carrying the crow bar pried the lock. Inside, there was a half a dozen bushels of live crabs in baskets covered with ice.

Since we didn't feel like messing with cooking these crabs, we decided to free them. So we dragged all the baskets out and emptied the crabs all over the parking lot. This stupidity accomplished, we looked around saying nothing and sensing there was no more mischief in us, we all headed for home. Barry's house was only five houses down the street from the back of the shop.

The next day, feeling hungry, Barry and I went to get a sub. We ordered a crab-sub and got the expected 'sorry we don't have any crabs today'. While waiting inside the shop for our hamburger-sub, the humidity inside the place was creating a sticky sweat box. One of the workers went over to prop the front door open and let some fresh air inside. Seconds later, a crab came through the door with pinchers high snapping the air. We burst out laughing so hard we had to run outside. The owner came out with our subs and eyed us suspiciously.

"We thought you said you didn't have any crabs.___Yes you do,___ theres one." Barry said and we laughed again. Wearing wry smiles on our faces, we walked down the street while munching our hamburger-subs.

A few nights later, I had been at the beer again. After several hours of driving around looking for girls, which we were always unable to find, I asked Dave to drop me off at Wagon Wheel Diners. It was about 2:30 a.m. and I was supposed to start work at 4:30 a.m. Therefore, I decided that I would get more sleep in the two hours I had, if I stayed here instead of wasting more time going to Barry's house, and then make a return trip to work

I was very tired when I climbed over the chain link gate. It was about eight feet high with an additional three strands of barbed wire deterrent along the top. I walked over to the unlocked panel truck Bill drove and climbed aboard. I crawled into to passenger side where there was no seat, but where we stored boxes of cups and lids. I moved a few boxes and went to sleep. Bill would wake me up when he arrived.

Unfortunately, a woman in a house next door, who was up late washing her dishes, had called the police, upon seeing me jump the fence.

I was suddenly jerked from the truck and out of a deep sleep. A police officer had pulled me out by my hair. The pain of this action had made me so mad that I started punching at whoever it was who had me by the hair, not yet aware it was a cop. I purchased flesh as my fist caught the cop several times solidly in the jaw. I was a handy scrapper at seventeen, having started boxing while in Red Flint, Arkansas.

As the cop and I were going at it, another cop had dropped over the fence and the two of them had pinned me to the ground and pummeled me with their night sticks.

Handcuffed, I was now focusing on the entire scene before me. There were three squad cars with their lights dancing in the night, reflecting eerily off the walls of Wagon Wheel Diners and the back wall of the drug store next door.

"Don't fuck with a Marine!" I said proudly or foolishly, but more due to anger. I had imagined that the mere act of deciding to become a Marine was grounds enough to state it. However, that fallacy would be fully realized in the near future.

The police officer looked at me, and with a snort smiled, while slowly shaking his head from side to side.

A Volkswagen drove into the parking lot and parked. Johnnie Alexis got out, went over to unlock the office entrance and walked inside. Several minutes later I was driven to the police station. I was told to stand in the corner of the office, while still wearing cuffs.

A police officer, the one I fought, came over and unlocked my cuffs. He told me that Mr. Alexis wasn't pressing any charges, as he was content that I didn't break in or damage anything. He agreed that all I did was jump the fence to wait for the morning shift to start, as I had stated earlier to the arresting officer.

They let me go. There was no official arrest and the officer even admitted that if he were grabbed and dragged up while asleep, he would have started swinging at whoever had done it. Why shouldn't I have the same reaction? Since he was aware that I was trying to join the Marine Corps, he probably didn't want to place a police record in my path to manhood, which could have hindered my enlistment.

Johnnie Alexis drove me to work. He wasn't mad at me at all, rather amused as was indicated by his chuckling and head shaking.

"I'm surprised you fought that particular officer," he chided. "He's called the 'Tank'.___You're lucky he didn't break you in half!"

I did not speak at all, nor even smile at his attempts to cheer me up.

"Look, I'm aware of your problems at home.___I ran into your friend's father over at Westinghouse and that's why I understand what you did. But next time try to come in at a normal hour.___Okay?" Johnnie said, not unkindly.

"Okay Johnnie." I promised with a tired smile. I worked that morning tired and sore, appreciating my luck. Everyone at work had heard about my adventure that morning. Old Bill was joking about it as were all the others with comments like 'Watch out America, there goes a real mean Marine!' or, 'The take no shit kid!'.

Several days later, while Barry and I were trying to find a way to obtain some beer, we saw a guy wearing a military uniform standing next to his car in the liquor store parking lot. We walked over to him and started a conversation. He told us his name was Mack and that he was a Marine PFC, home from ITR and was thinking about getting some beer, but didn't want to go to any bars that night. He explained that he was from Salisbury, Maryland and had swooped home with a buddy in the Corps. The buddy was out on a date with his girl that evening. He was bored and thought a few beers were a start, before he figured out what was next.

"I'm trying to do a lot of partying before I ship out to Vietnam," Mack said. He had a real matter-of-fact voice when he spoke. It was a cool, low pitch sound with a confidence about it. We decided we liked this Marine and invited him over to Barry's house for some drinking.

"Mack, why not come over to the house where you can kick back and have some beers___and stay as long as you feel like it," I offered.

"Sounds better than standing here.___You got booze?" Mack replied with the question.

"Er,___no not yet," we both stammered awkwardly. "But we got the cash!" I stated hopefully.

"Okay guys, I thought that was your reason for stopping me.___No sweat!___Give me the money and I'll get the beer," Mack chuckled, while stooping to tuck the money in the top part of his sock.

We both eyed this strange maneuver.

"Marines don't stick things in their pockets.___Bulges ya know.___Very unmilitary," Mack said smoothly and matter-of-factly, knowing full well that we were gawking.

Mack returned with a case of Rolling Rock beer and a bottle of Jack Daniels Bourbon. We had never had any Rolling Rock beer before and figured beggars can't be choosers. We drove over to Barry's house and introduced Mack to some of the other guys in the neighborhood.

Mack was the first and only Marine that I had actually met and befriended before leaving for boot camp. He would come over with beer every evening before he shipped out.

Several days later, Barry's dad told me my mother had called and that she and Annie were home. He drove me home. It was a drive of about five miles, which I had walked very often.

I had mixed feelings about being home and about seeing Mom. However, I was happy to see Annie. Hueston was out getting drunk somewhere. So I told Mom why I had been at Barry's these past weeks and how I was angry with her for not telling me she had gone to Germany, for how long, and of my disappointment in not receiving a letter once in a while to say when they would return. I also told her of my desire to join the Marines. Mama apparently thought I was just being angry and threatening to join the Marines. Hueston made no mention of our fight and I did not go near him.

"But, I did send letters," she said confused. "I sent letters here to be forwarded to Little Rock, but maybe you had already left." Hueston refused to comment on Mom's letters when she asked.

A few days after Mama and Annie's return, something terrible happened. I had been downstairs in my room when I heard Sarah screaming as she ran downstairs past my room and on into the recreation room. I heard Hueston yelling at my Mother, but I heard her screaming back at him in her German accented English much louder then I have ever heard her before.

I looked out of my room and heard Sarah sobbing in the recreation room and Mom clearly leading the shouting upstairs. Suddenly, Hueston stormed downstairs shouting, "Jackie did it!___I didn't!___Jackie did it!" He had nearly ripped the front door off the hinges as he careened outside to his Polaris. Tires squealed, as he backed out and burned rubber all the way out of the cul-de-sac and raced out of the Glen Burnie Park subdivision.

A few seconds later Mom was flying down the steps towards Sarah, who was in the recreation room. Mom came out of the recreation room dragging Sarah while slapping her and berating her. She pushed her out the front door with Annie following. Annie wore a look of utter confusion. A few minutes later a Maryland State Trooper car pulled fast into our drive way. Mom, Sarah and Annie piled into the police vehicle and it pulled away.

"What the hell?" I wondered aloud. I had absolutely no idea what just happened. Why did that son-of-a-bitch keep yelling, 'Jackie did it'? *Did what?*" I wondered. I sat in the house as several hours passed and I did not move. I was experiencing a numb fear that could not be described as the clock ticked away. I started conjuring up all sorts of ominous thoughts of Hueston killing all of us, shooting us, cutting us up and hiding our bodies. He portrayed the type, a wholly evil creature who had threatened us continuously. For myself, I recalled him threatening to kill me, on numerous occasions, if I didn't watch out.

"You watch yourself you sneak, ___ or I'll kill you!" That had been one of his favorite verbal attacks against me.

Later that night mom returned with the girls. Hueston was still away.

Her face was twisted in rage, as she came into the house. Sarah quickly ran off into some room in the house and hid. Annie, still looking scared and confused, shadowed Mom.

"What happened, Mama?" I implored her for the answer, not really wanting to hear it, fearing I would hate the answer.

"Dat son-of-a-bitch Arschloch (asshole)!" she cried suddenly, and then told me all of it. During her trip to the police department she had demanded Sarah be checked at the hospital and take a lie detecting test at the police barracks. What had happened was that when Mom opened the bathroom door upstairs, earlier that day, she had witnessed Sarah inserting a tampon and immediately slapped her, screaming that she was a slut and wanted to know why a virgin was using an insert device for her period. Mama, being old fashioned, was absolutely confident that her fifteen year old daughter was nothing less than a virgin. Therefore, she attributed this type of sanitary napkin to be used only by non-virgins and only a pad being used by virgins. She had so shaken Sarah with her verbal and physical barrage, that Sarah spilled her story like vomit spewing out.

Since Sarah was thirteen, when we had lived in the apartments, Hueston had been having regular intercourse with her. Sarah had been told by Hueston that he would kill all of us if she ever said anything. The police were preparing paperwork for Mom to arrest Hueston and take him to court. He had tried to tell Mom that I had done this to my own sister, not him. Obviously, that was so much bull shit. Sarah stated that only he had done these things to her and she was finally able to say it. That was why he feared seeing me around Sarah. He was afraid she would tell me.

"Holy Mother of God!" I said when she finished and then shouted, "I'll kill that fucking filthy piece-of-shit!" I stated and fully meant it. I ran upstairs to find the pistol he had threatened me with on that rainy night.

I could not find it, suddenly fearing that he would appear later brandishing the thing at all of us. However, while searching in a crawlspace between the wall of the master bedroom and the attic over the lower roof of the living room, I found a stash of his filth.

I had pulled out at least twenty nudist magazines, an 8 MM projector with a half dozen X-rated films. There were sexual devices and many pictures of Sarah in various sexual positions. Sarah looked like a victim of long abuse, showing eyes with a distant expression, and of being drunk.

These were all turned over to the police and we waited. Apparently, the police had not found him yet, because he drove up later the next morning and came into our house and sat at the kitchen table as if nothing had happened.

I looked at him with outright loathing, while tensing my muscles preparing to attack him.

"Get my whiskey!" he demanded, pointing at the cupboard. "I want a drink!"

I turned stiffly and opened the cupboard, saw the full bottle of Seagram Seven and pulled it out. I looked right at him and began a precis of everything I loathed about him as I began pouring his whiskey down the kitchen sink drain.

"You are a fucking liar, thief and a sneak!" I began, "You are a filthy piece of shit!___You are a pedophile!" I could not stop. The loudness of my voice attracted my mother and Annie. They ran into the kitchen and Mama joined in the attack on him as well. He hadn't been in the house for three minutes when all of us were glaring at him and screaming at him. Even Sarah could be heard from the bedroom sending down her shrilly contempt.

Apparently he was very hung-over and scared as well, because he cowered, instead of his countering with his usual aggressive lunging. He looked pitiful, however no pity was offered by any of us, only loathing.

"Get the hell out of this house and stay away from us!" I screamed at him shaking with years of pent up rage.

Hueston did leave immediately that morning and we began our first day of freedom from that oppressive pedophile, psycho son-of-a-bitch. Mom called the State Police to tell them he had come back and had left again.

By mid September, my Mother finally signed my papers to enlist without anymore arguments. I couldn't wait to get them to Master Sergeant Herbert and get through AFEES.

Sure enough, not long afterwards, I found myself at AFEES in the long lines of young men going through for various reasons. Some of the men had been drafted, some were joining a preferred branch of service simply to get it over with, rather than getting drafted into the Army. Aside from my having a high blood pressure reading and being told to sit for a period of time before they gave me another try, which I passed, there were no major incidents other than what an occasional potential draft-dodger did. There were a few who would try to act gay or sickly, or had eaten or drank something in the hope they would foul-up their physical.

Back at the recruiting office, Master Sergeant Herbert was congratulating me for passing the physical and we talked some more about the Marine Corps.

"So when can I go?" I asked excitedly.

"You have to be sworn in first.___That's the day you become inducted into the Marine Corps.___You'll be inducted on September 30.___Then you'll ship out for boot camp on October 15.____That's two weeks after induction and you'll be at Parris Island in the sun and fun with three square meals a day and plenty of exercise that I promised you, son.___Yeh,___you'll enjoy it kid."

My brother Lucious visited a few days later. When I told him, he actually became distraught. He drove me to school and encouraged me to go inside to enroll and get back to my classes. I argued and refused to get out of the car. He finally accepted my points of argument. I told him what he already knew.

"If Mama had put me in the correct grade, I'd be in the 11th grade now and if I was, I'd stay and finish one more year of high school.___ But not two!___I've had enough bull shit with male figures who come into my life, screw my head up and piss on me whenever the urge hits them!___I want to get away and start my own life.___I will get a GED in the Marine Corps as soon as I can do it."

I showed up on schedule and was inducted into the United States Marine Corps on September 30, 1969.

"I do solemnly swear to defend my country against all enemies foreign or domestic...!" we chorused with our right hands held up while staring at the American flag behind the Officer presiding over the induction ceremony.

I felt the moment. It was a feeling of being an adult, with responsibility, a patriot, with a role in our country, our way of life. I was exhilarated.

After the next two weeks passed by, I prepared for my departure, said my goodbyes and reported to the Recruiting Office at five in the morning. Several other inductees were there as well.

We drove in Herbert's Marine Corps vehicle to AFEES and then from there we would ride in an Army bus to Friendship Airport.

Master Sergeant Herbert shook hands with each of us and said to me as he was leaving, "Good luck,___you'll do fine.___Come back a PFC."

As we drove toward the Airport I watched the cars on the highway pass our bus. I swear I saw that son-of-a-bitch drive by in his Polaris. The sight of that Polaris chilled me and started a pang of fear in my gut. It had renewed my worries for the girls and Mama. What if he bothers them, with me unable to help? Why is he free to go around anywhere he wants to go? Because of the personal embarrassment to herself and the severe mental anguish Sarah would endure, Mama had dropped the charges. I was informed of this much later.

The DC-8 lifted off the runway at Friendship Airport and started its journey to Charleston, South Carolina. The flight was very crowded and the stewardesses appeared noticeably stressed trying to get all the meals and refreshments served in the prescribed time.

Staring out dazedly through my window into billowing structures of cumulus clouds, I reconfirmed my decision to do this and wondered what tomorrow would be like.

USMC RANK STRUCTURE

E-1 Recruit and/or Private

E-2 Private First Class – PFC.

E-3 Lance Corporal – L/CPL.

E-4 Corporal – CPL. (NCO)

E-5 Sergeant – SGT. (NCO)

E-6 Staff Sergeant – SSGT. (Staff NCO)

E-7 Gunnery Sergeant – GySGT. (Staff NCO) "Gunny"

E-8 Master Sergeant – M/SGT. (Staff NCO) > see * for next rank

E-8 First Sergeant – 1st SGT. (Staff NCO) Administration > see ** for next rank

E-9 Master Gunnery Sergeant * MGySGT. (Staff NCO)

E-9 Sergeant Major **– SGT.MAJ. (Staff NCO) Administration

WO-1 Warrant Officer One

WO-2 Warrant Officer Two – Chief (CWO-2)

WO-3 Warrant Officer Three – Chief (CWO-3)

WO-4 Warrant Officer Four – Chief (CWO-4)

01--Second Lieutenant – 2nd Lt. (Gold bar)

02--First Lieutenant-1st Lt. (Silver bar)

03 – Captain – Capt. (Two silver bars)

04 – Major – Maj. (Gold oak leaf)
05 – Lieutenant Colonel – LtCol. (Silver oak leaf)
06 – Colonel – Col. (Silver Eagle)
07 – Brigadier General – BGen. (One silver star)
08 – Major General – MajGen. (Two silver stars)
09 – Lieutenant General – LtGen. (Three silver stars)
10 – General – Gen. (Four silver stars)

WORD GLOSSARY

7-82 Gear – Metal bucket, tent w/pegs and spikes, web gear and all other field equipment.

Ahoorrah – Warrior cry (*ah-oo-rah*) pulled up from the gut (modern Marines use oorah).

ADI – Assistant Drill Instructor.

Armorer – One that makes, repairs, assembles or test fires weapons.

Arrivees – Term used for first day arriving recruits.

ARVN – Army of the Republic of Vietnam.

Asshole-to-bellybutton – Recruits in a line with their chins on the other recruits head-*no space.*

Barn – The barrack building.

Barrack – A building housing multiple squad bays for quartering military personnel.

BCD – Bad Conduct Discharge.

Blanket party – Revenge or reprisal against a foul-up recruit at night, by fellow recruits.

Blouse – The dress uniform jacket. Blousing trouser legs over the boots with elastic fasteners.

Bulkhead – A wall.

Bunky – One of the two recruits to a bunk bed (rack).

Cartridge belt – A belt with eyelet holes to attach various field equipment – canteen, bayonet etc.

CCP – Correctional Custody Platoon.

Charlie – Viet Cong guerrilla fighter.

Chevron – Stripes and rockers denoting rank.

Chit – A piece of paper authorizing the bearer to pass and/or receive something.

Chow – Food.

Chowing Down – Eating.

Chow hound – Person who loves to eat.

Corpsman – Enlisted Navy medical personnel attached to the Marine Corps – paramedics.

Cover – Head gear. Helmet or any cloth item worn on a Marines head, (also a hand will do).

Deck – The floor.

Deuce gear – 7-82 gear

Dite bag – A *ditty* bag used to store small personal items and clothing.

DI – Drill Instructor.

DI house – The room at the end of a barrack used as an office and night duty DI sleeping quarters.

DI shack – Same as DI house.

Diddle-bopping – When a recruit's head bounces up and down while marching – not flowing. Often pronounced as ditty bopping.

Dizzy-izzy – Sport event. Run to a baseball bat and spin around with forehead on bat hilt.

Doggie straps – Canvas suspenders clipped onto the cartridge belt to support the weight of gear.

Duck for chow – Duck-in and Duck-out of the mess hall – Don't Eat.

Duck walk – a squat walk, like a duck.

EmNu – A black paint with a small brush attached to the cap, used to paint metal chevrons, cartridge belt eyelets etc.... .

Fat-body – A recruit who is too overweight to meet to physical demands of training.

Field scarf – A khaki-colored dress uniform tie.

Fire watch – Night guard duty in the barrack assigned in shifts through the night.

FNG – Fuckin' new guy.

Free-time – The last period of a training day, where gear is squared away and letters are written.

Froggy – A patois. 'The froggy voice of Drill Instructors', unique to 3rd Battalion – *raspy*.

Fruit salad – Term used to describe the array of ribbons worn by those in the military service

GEAR – Government Equipment Army Rejected. Or 'Goddamned Excess Army Rejects'.

General orders – Permanent instructions issued in order form that apply to entire command.

Grinder – Also called Meat Grinder. A large asphalted area used to perform military drill.

Grunt – Nickname for infantrymen.

Guide – The person who carries the platoon guidon.

Guidon – Small flag carried by a military unit as a marker to guide on.

Gung ho – Derived from the Chinese meaning *all strive together*. Also, a hard-charging Marine.

Hash marks – Strips worn diagonally on the lower sleeve, each denoting four years of service.

Hatch – A door.

Head – Bathroom.

Head and Ass Wired Together – One who functions as a properly trained whole warrior.

Head-call – Going to the bathroom.

Herd – Reference for a recruit platoon.

Hogs – Reference for recruits.

Hump – Walking, often with a heavy load.

Hurt locker – DI term meaning *you can't run or hide* and you will suffer heavy PT to motivate.

In country – Serving *in* Vietnam.

Irish Pennant – Threads, left from tailoring, hanging loosly from uniforms requiring snipping.

ITR – Infantry Training Regiment. Where recruits go after boot camp for infantry skills training.

Joe-Shit-The-Rag-Man – A recruit who fails to wear their uniform properly, or is dirty.

Lifer – A Marine who acts too gung ho or a Marine making the Corps their career.

Little Red Monster – A pocket-sized red book containing general orders and USMC subjects.

M-14 Rifle – 7.62-mm magazine fed, air cooled, gas operated semiautomatic shoulder weapon.

Maggies drawers – A total miss of the target at the rifle range.

Maggot – A stage in the metamorphosis of a fly and similarly of a recruit to become a Marine.

Meritocracy – Leadership by the talented. Advancement goes to the best.

Motivation – Possessing the desire to achieve.

Motivation platoon – Punishment platoon for slackers and shit-birds.

MP – Military Police.

Neophyte – A new convert. A beginner. Green or novice.

Non-hacker – A recruit who does not pack the gear. Is not motivated.

Numb-nuts – A recruit who, no matter how many times he is verbally kicked there, learns nothing.

NVA – North Vietnamese Army.

Oblique – 45 degree angle of march, as in *To the right oblique,__march*.

OD – Officer of the day. Or olive drab, as in OD green.

Office hours – UCMJ none judicial punishment.

Overhead – The ceiling.

Patois – The characteristic special language and jargon of an occupational group – ie., *froggy*.

PCP – Physical Conditioning Platoon.

PFC – Private First Class (E-2).

P. I. – Parris Island.

PMI – Primary Marksmanship Instructor.

Pisser – A urinal, from the French word pissoir.

Piss cutter – Fore and aft cover which is flat when not worn.

Pork Chop Platoon – PCP for fat and skinny bodies.

Port – An opening in a ships side to admit light or air. A window.

Port arms – Position of the rifle held diagonally in front of the chest with the muzzle to left.

Port side – The left side.

PT – Physical training and also punishment *training* exercises.

Puke – Endearing term for a recruit. Someone a drill instructor feels ill toward.

Pusillanimous – Very small, lacking courage and resolution, timid and contemptible.

PX – Post Exchange.

Red Monster, The Little – General Military Subjects booklet carried in the left back pocket at all times.

REMF – Rear echelon mother-fucker.

R&R – Rest and Relaxation. A break from action or stress. Referred to during the Vietnam war years as 'rape and reproduction'.

Rockers – The U shaped chevrons denoting rank beyond a sergeant E-5* (*see rank structures).

Round – A bullet of any caliber.

Salty – A long time Marine. A Marine who has been around. Well worn utilities.

Sand flea – Special added punishment San Diego Recruits don't endure. Indigenous to Parris Island.

Scum-bag – Term used by DIs to express their interpretation of difficult recruit.

Sea bag – A large cylinder shaped closable canvas bag with a carry handle & shoulder strap.

Semper Fi – Slang for Semper Fidelis (latin for *Always Faithful*).

Scarfing-up – To eat very fast or hungrily. Also, to grab up things, like ammunition.

SDI – Senior Drill Instructor.

Servus – Bavarian greeting for hello or goodbye. Origins from Latin meaning *to serve*.

Shit-bird – Totally unkempt recruit. Failing to dress in a military manner. Sloppy bearing.

Shit-can – Large galvanized garbage can.

Shitter – A commode or toilet.

Skate – To skate out of a work assignment. *He is a skater, or he always get's to skate.*

Skinny-body – A recruit too underweight to endure PT, or only needs to bulk up more.

Skivees – Underwear.

Skuzz-ball – A filthy recruit.

Slime-ball – A filthy recruit or Marine failing to keep themselves squared away.

Snapping-in – Learning the various rifle firing positions and sighting-in on target techniques.

Spit shine – To rub shoe polish onto shoes with a damp cotton cloth, rubbing alcohol and *effort*.

Squad bay – Platoon sleeping quarters in a barrack.

Squared away – In it's place. Proper or correct military behavior.

Squaring away – To put into proper order. To properly fold and tuck sheet and blanket on rack.

Starboard side – The right side.

STB – Special Training Branch.

Stove-piping – Wearing utility trousers loose over combat boots without elastic holders.

Sub-basement of hell – A nasty neather region of hell reserved for the pleasure of the DIs.

Swoop – To catch a ride home from base with a group in one Marines car and return.

Swoop-circle – Base location where ride-seekers go to catch a swoop home.

Toilet bowl – Term used for the Rifle Marksman device as it is a square design.

Trops – Short for the tropical khaki full summer dress uniform (shirt & trousers with field scarf).

UA – Unauthorized Absense. Also AWOL – Absent Without Leave.

UCMJ – Uniform Code of Military Justice.

UD – Undesirable Discharge.

UNK – Unqualified on the rifle range.

Utilities – Every day work clothes also worn in the field for training and combat.

VC – Victor Charlie radio call sign for Viet Cong.

Wash rack – Long concrete structures with spaced water spigots, used to scrub clothing.

WTP – Weapons Training Battalion.

Zero-in (rifle) – Clicking the elevation & windage knobs from mechanical zero to battle sight.

BIBLIOGRAPHY

I – BOOKS

Flemming, Keith. *The U.S. Marine Corps In Crises: Ribbon Creek and Recruit Training.* University of South Carolina Press 1990.

Olson, James, (ed.) *Dictionary Of The Vietnam War.* Peter Bedrick Books, New York,,1987.

Murphy, Edward F. *Semper Fi Vietnam: From Da Nang to The DMZ, Marine Corps Campaigns, 1965-1975.* Presidio Press, 1997.

Ricks, Thomas E. *Making The Corps.* Simon and Shuster Inc. 1997.

Davis, Burke. *Marine! The Life of Chesty Puller.* Little, Brown & Company (Canada), 1962.

Dunnigan, James F., and Nofi, Albert A. *Dirty Little Secrets Of The Vietnam War,* St.Martin's Press, New York, 1999.

Melson, Charles D. *The War That Would Not End: U.S. Marines In Vietnam 1971-1973.*

Hellgate Press 1998.

Nofi, Albert A., *Marine Corps Book Of Lists: A Definitive Compendium of Marine Corps Facts, Feats, and Traditions.* Combined Publishing 1997.

Pfeifer, Vellag J., *Holy Bible*: German print 1950, Muenchen (Munich) Bavaria, Germany.

II – MANUALS

Marine Battle Skills Training Handbook, Book 2 PVT-LCPL, Individual Combat Basic Tasks. Marine Corps Institute, January 1993.

Guidebook For Marines, Sixteenth Revised Edition. Published by the Marine Corps Association, Quantico, Virginia, July 1990.

III – CRUISE BOOK

Marine Corps Recruit Depot Parris Island South Carolina, Platoon 3074, 1969. Published by Albert Love Enterprises, Inc.

IV – NEWSPAPERS

Leo, John, *Psychologist Charges Brutality Is 'Normal' in Marine Training.* The New York Times, Tuesday, April 1, 1969

Wooten, James T., *Recruit Maltreatment Persisting In Marines Despite Official Ban,* , Special to The New York Times. The New York Times, October 13, 1969.

Wooten, James T., *Autopsy On Marine Recruit Is Sought, Re: Private Jose T. Cocepcion.* The New York Times, October 1, 1969.

(No Reporter Given), *Beating Alleged, Marine 18 Dead, Re: Private Stephen E. Melson.* Special To The New York Times, The New York Times, Monday, September 22, 1969.

(No Reporter Given), *Marines Deny Recruit's Death Was Caused by Drill Instructor, Re: Private Stephen E. Melson.* Special To The New York Times, The New York Times, Tuesday, September 23, 1969.

V – MAGAZINES

Winter, Rolf and Hoepker, *Die Killer-Schule der Ledernacken,* (The Killer School of the Leathernecks). German, Stern Magazine, 15/1970.